58-IN-MIND

58-IN-MIND

Multilingual Teaching Strategies for Diverse Deaf Students

Edited by
Debbie Golos
Marlon Kuntze
Kimberly Wolbers
Chris Kurz

Gallaudet University Press | Washington, DC

Gallaudet University Press is located on the traditional territories of Nacotchtank and Piscataway.

© 2023 by Gallaudet University
All rights reserved. Published 2023
Printed in the United States of America

ISBN 978-1-954622-20-3 (paperback)

ISBN 978-1-954622-21-0 (ebook)

Library of Congress Cataloging-in-Publication Data

Names: Golos, Debbie, author. | Kuntze, Lon, author. | Wolbers, Kimberly, author. | Kurz, Chris (Professor), author.
Title: 58-IN-MIND : multilingual teaching strategies for diverse deaf students / Debbie Golos, Marlon Kuntze, Kimberly Wolbers and Chris Kurz.
Other titles: Fifty-eight-in-mind
Description: Washington, DC : Gallaudet University Press, 2023. | Includes bibliographical references and index. | Summary: "This book describes and demonstrates theoretically-driven, research-based, and classroom-tested best practices for using American Sign Language and English in instruction across the curriculum"—Provided by publisher.
Identifiers: LCCN 2023030810 (print) | LCCN 2023030811 (ebook) | ISBN 9781954622203 (paperback : acid-free paper) | ISBN 9781954622210 (ebook)
Subjects: LCSH: Multilingual education—United States. | Multicultural education—United States. | Deaf—Education—United States. | American Sign Language. | English language—Study and teaching—United States. | Language arts—Correlation with content subjects. | Special education teachers—Training of.
Classification: LCC LC3731 .G628 2023 (print) | LCC LC3731 (ebook) | DDC 370.117/50973—dc23/eng/20230913
LC record available at https://lccn.loc.gov/2023030810
LC ebook record available at https://lccn.loc.gov/2023030811

∞ This paper meets the requirements of ANSI/NISO Z39.48–1992 (Permanence of Paper).

Cover description: White cover with an illustration of three children and their teacher sitting on a rug. The teacher is signing "WHAT" at the end of a question she is asking the class. Before she finishes, a boy is already responding by raising his hand. Under the graphic art in large colorful text, reads "58-In-Mind". Left of the cover has black boxes in a vertical line. At the top left of the cover, large black text reads, "Multilingual Teaching Strategies for Diverse Deaf Students". Underneath in a blue circle, small white text reads, "Spans early childhood education through high school and beyond." At the bottom, small text reads, "Edited by Debbie Golos, Marlon Kuntze, Kimberly Wolbers, and Chris Kurz."

Cover design by Joy Chu. Cover art by Malvana Ramborger. Interior design by click! Publishing Services. Icon design by Laura Perez.

While the authors have made every effort to provide accurate internet addresses and other contact information at the time of publication, neither the publisher nor the authors assume any responsibility for errors or changes that occur after publication. Further, the publisher does not have any control over and does not assume any responsibility for third-party websites or their content.

How you language is beautiful. Don't let anyone tell you
your languaging is wrong. Your languaging is the story of your life.

—*Dr. Jon Henner*

One child, one teacher, one book, and one pen can change the world.

—*Malala Yousafza*

CONTENTS

Contributors   ix
Acknowledgments   xi

1 Introduction   1
Marlon Kuntze, Debbie Golos, Chris Kurz, and Kimberly Wolbers

2 Early Childhood Instruction (Ages 3–5)   14
Leala Holcomb, Debbie Golos, Courtney Hipskind, and April Rivera

3 ASL Language Arts and ASL in Content Areas   41
Barbara Motylinski, Chris Kurz, and Julie Stewart

4 Writing   69
Kimberly Wolbers and Sarah Jerger McGaughey

5 Writing in the Content Areas   97
Hannah Dostal and Shannon Graham

6 Reading   118
Marlon Kuntze, Jessica Scott, and Stacey Katz Shapiro

7 Reading in Content Areas   144
Debbie Golos, Susan Outlaw, and Sarah Jerger McGaughey

8 Deaf Identities and Social/Cultural Perspectives   171
Marlon Kuntze, Chris Kurz, and Debbie Golos

9 Social Studies   199
David H. Smith and Kathleen K. Mockus

10 Mathematics   229
Samantha Braidi, Brenda Call, and Chris Kurz

11 Science   256
Elizabeth Henderson, Scott Cohen, and Chris Kurz

12 Incorporating the Arts Across the Curriculum   283
Fred Michael Beam, Scott Gentzke, Debbie Golos, and Chris Kurz

13 ASL Immersion I and II   314
Petra M. Horn-Marsh and Kester Horn-Marsh

14 Transition   336
Carrie Lou Bloom and Kristin Ryan

15 Conclusion and Next Steps   363
Marlon Kuntze, Debbie Golos, Kimberly Wolbers, and Chris Kurz

References   367
Index   377

CONTRIBUTORS

Fred Michael Beam
Performing/Visual Artist
National Technical Institute for the Deaf
Rochester, New York

Carrie Lou Bloom
Co-Director, National Deaf Center on Postsecondary
　　Outcomes
Assistant Professor of Educational Leadership and Policy
University of Texas
Austin, Texas

Samantha Braidi
High School Mathematics Teacher
California School for the Deaf
Fremont, California

Brenda Call
Mathematics K–12 Teacher Specialist
California School for the Deaf
Fremont, California

Scott Cohen
Doctoral Student
Georgia State University
Atlanta, Georgia

Hannah Dostal
Professor of Literacy Education
University of Connecticut
Mansfield, Connecticut

Scott Gentzke
Visiting Assistant Professor
National Technical Institute for the Deaf
Rochester Institute of Technology
Rochester, New York

Debbie Golos
Associate Professor and Coordinator of Deaf Education
　　Teacher Preparation Program
University of Minnesota
Minneapolis, Minnesota

Shannon Graham
Curriculum and Assessment Coordinator
Washington School for the Deaf
Vancouver, Washington

Elizabeth Henderson
Middle School Science Teacher
California School for the Deaf in Riverside
Riverside, California

Courtney Hipskind
DHH Infant/Itinerant Teacher
Yolo County Office of Education
Woodland, California

Leala Holcomb
Researcher in Deaf Education
University of Tennessee
Knoxville, Tennessee

Kester Horn-Marsh
ASL/English Bilingual Specialist
Kansas School for the Deaf
Olathe, Kansas

Petra M. Horn-Marsh
Associate Professor of ASL and Deaf Studies
University of Kansas
Overland, Kansas

Marlon Kuntze
Professor Emeritus
Gallaudet University
Washington, D.C.

Chris Kurz
Professor
Rochester Institute of Technology
Rochester, New York

Susan Outlaw
Executive Director
Metro Deaf School
Saint Paul, Minnesota

Sarah Jerger McGaughey
Elementary Principal
The Learning Center for the Deaf
Framingham, Massachusetts

Kathleen K. Mockus
Content Area Curriculum Teacher Specialist
California School for the Deaf
Fremont, California

Barbara Motylinski
ASL/English Bilingual Specialist
New York School for the Deaf
White Plains, New York

April Rivera
Early Childhood Education Teacher
The Learning Center for the Deaf
Framingham, Massachusetts

Kristin Ryan
Transition Coordinator
Metro Deaf School
St. Paul, Minnesota

Jessica Scott
Associate Professor and Coordinator, Programs in Deaf Education
Georgia State University
Atlanta, Georgia

Stacey Katz Shapiro
Director of Online Programs
American School for the Deaf
Hartford, Connecticut

David H. Smith
Research Professor
University of Tennessee
Knoxville, Tennessee

Julie Stewart
ASL Specialist
Ohio School for the Deaf
Columbus, Ohio

Kimberly Wolbers
Professor and Coordinator of Deaf Education
University of Tennessee
Knoxville, Tennessee

ACKNOWLEDGMENTS

We would like to take this opportunity to express our gratitude to two Deaf illustrators whose creative work made this book more engaging and visually appealing. First, we'd like to thank Malvana Ramborger for creating the cover art. Malvana was born and raised in Seattle and is a third-generation member of an artistic Deaf family. She graduated with a bachelor of fine arts degree in illustration from the Rochester Institute of Technology.

Second, our thanks go to Laura Sanchez, who created the Intentional 8 and legend icons you find throughout the book's interior. Laura was born in Michoacan, Mexico, and raised in Michigan. She studied illustration at the Rochester Institute of Technology and currently works as a freelance illustrator.

Finally, we would like to thank all current and future teachers for their continued dedication and commitment to teaching and for inspiring Deaf, Hard of Hearing, DeafBlind, and DeafDisabled students to grow, be empowered, thrive, and feel positive about who they are. These students are our future teachers, leaders, and creators! Remember also to take care of yourselves and your own well-being. We value and appreciate you and all that you do every day.

Introduction

Marlon Kuntze
Debbie Golos
Chris Kurz
Kimberly Wolbers

A watershed moment in the education of Deaf students happened in 1989 with the publication of *Unlocking the Curriculum* (Johnson et al., 1989). The publication jump-started the nationwide dialogue about bringing American Sign Language (ASL) into the classroom as a natural and essential language in the education of Deaf children. As the title reflects, ASL is viewed as the "key" to unlocking the floodgate of curricular learning. Deaf children's access to ASL in school has significantly expanded over the years. The dialogue related to access to learning has continued to broaden, and even though it still emphasizes the classroom as a space where ASL is seen as integral to Deaf students' education, the classroom has more recently been increasingly seen as a place where students' home languages and cultures should also be recognized and honored. In this book, we seek to inform teachers how to center Deaf students' multiple and intersecting identities in education and how they can broaden Deaf students' access to the curriculum through multilingual, multicultural, multimodal, anti-bias, and antiracist approaches to teaching and learning.

Substantial progress has been made in the past few decades to help make the timing now right for moving the field in this new direction. We are seeing a growth of literature recognizing Deaf epistemology as a research method and the indigenous knowledge related to teaching that Deaf teachers bring to the classroom (e.g., Cue et al., 2019; Holcomb, 2010; Reagan et al., 2021). We are also now looking more closely at how the lack of access to language impacts many Deaf children and their development (e.g., Gulati, 2018). This has led to new theories being explored (e.g., Kuntze et al., 2020) and multiple research studies examining effective practices in Deaf education (e.g., Wolbers et al., 2022). The drive to make learning for Deaf students as equitable as possible has sparked innovative teaching and curricular transformations (Derman-Sparks et al., 2020). Further, some textbooks on teaching methods for Deaf education are no longer in print. Those still in circulation are becoming less current and, in our view, do not represent the changes that are happening or need to happen in the field.

In addition, certification for Deaf education licensure is often granted for birth–21 for all content areas. Yet, not all programs include methods courses to address content areas across all age spans. For example, programs rarely include teaching methods on early childhood, ASL, or Deaf studies. The same applies to STEAM (science, technology, engineering, arts, and mathematics) content. The omission of teaching methods in these content areas in teaching preparation programs represents the extent to which many of these programs are out of step with the changes that either are happening or need to happen in the field. This book seeks to provide foundational knowledge for all subject areas that teachers should have regardless of the student age or content they teach.

To the best of our knowledge, there are no methods books in Deaf education that address multilingual and multimodal practices in any content areas across the preschool through Grade 12 (P–12). In addition, not one of them has tapped the expertise of Deaf professionals at the same level as this book. We believe the time has come to highlight the critical foundational knowledge that this important but overlooked group of professionals has and to share it with others. This book represents the first time that innovative multilingual practices used in public schools across the United States have meshed with the use of ASL across the curriculum. Twenty Deaf coauthors out of 27 authors from coast to coast share their expertise as researchers or classroom teachers, with 12 out of 15 of the chapters having a Deaf lead author.

This new methods book incorporates recent research, emerging evidence of what works in the classroom (ecological validity), and the drive to make education as equitable as possible for each child. Our intention here is to provide a methods book that is engaging to read as well as practical. We need a book that recognizes the diversity of Deaf students and strives to align the field with best practices that are embedded in social-emotional, cultural, linguistic, and intellectually sustainable approaches to learning. The book aims to help both current and future teachers provide meaningful education for Deaf students from early education through high school. Although each chapter can be read independently, it is our hope that instructors in teacher preparation programs will require the reading of all the chapters. We also encourage teachers already working in the field to review as many chapters as possible because there are strategies in varying subject areas, even those outside their content areas, they may be able to tap into in their teaching.

Ideas and perspectives shared in the book also have the potential to offer general education teachers innovative tools for reaching a diverse body of students. We believe that teachers who teach hearing children can benefit from the methodologies discussed in this book. Children in general are diverse, and all teachers may struggle with meeting the needs of individual students. Learning that is visually based and builds on students' strengths, backgrounds, languages and cultures can benefit many students, whether or not they are Deaf.

In preparing this book, the coeditors drew from their experiences both as kindergarten through Grade 12 teachers and college educators. Debbie Golos taught middle school reading and writing. As a professor, she has devoted her time to training teachers and engaging in research and curriculum development for early childhood education and the use of multimedia to support language, literacy, and identity development, as well as well-being practices for students and teachers. Marlon Kuntze taught high school English and, since becoming a professor, has been working on the role of bilingualism in supporting literacy development. Kimberly Wolbers taught language arts/English, mathematics, science, and government at elementary and secondary levels. As a college professor, she has been working on a model of writing instruction designed for Deaf students. Chris Kurz taught secondary mathematics and science, and as a professor, he has worked on methodologies for making science and math accessible and using technology to support language and literacy development through stories for younger children. This book is a product of professional relationships that the coeditors forged with one another over the years in their respective roles as teacher trainers.

Each chapter is coauthored by at least one researcher and one P–12 teacher, with at least one of the authors being Deaf. We felt it was of the utmost importance that Deaf perspectives were reflected in every chapter. The authors combine experience, time-tested practice, and research into each chapter to produce a book that shares perspectives, examples of lessons, and real stories from those working in the field from preschool through age 21 (and transition ages). Although the targeted readers are preservice teacher candidates, in-service teachers, and faculty and instructors who teach methods courses, we also believe that educational researchers, school administrators, content coaches, specialists, and others can also benefit from this book.

In creating the title of the book, we drew on an ASL sign that reflects the goal of the book, which is for teachers to use the practices discussed across the chapters to positively impact their students' learning. The number 58, because of the way it is signed, is a playful way to transcribe the ASL sign STICK. The phrase "58-IN-MIND" in the title refers to the version of the sign STICK that is made on the forehead, which is equivalent to the English idiom "stick in one's mind." In short, when learning is delivered in a culturally responsive manner, it is more likely to stick. The sign 58-IN-MIND also alludes indirectly to the collective aspirations of the chapter authors that the practices discussed in the book will also stick in the readers' minds and have a transformative impact on the way we collectively teach Deaf students.

One theme that recurs throughout all chapters echoes the need for teachers to create an environment that ensures high-quality communication in the classroom. A language that is fully accessible is a necessary condition for making communication high quality. It is one of the reasons why it is important to make ASL available for Deaf children. A vast majority of Deaf children come to school with limited ASL skills. Teachers need to meet each child where they are when they arrive in their classroom. It is not only how they can best support Deaf children's language development but also how they can ensure that communication is happening. High-quality communication between teachers and their students is mandatory in order for the teachers to learn what their students already know, the nature of how they have come to understand the content, what it is about the content that is still not clear to them, and how to engage each student in learning. This will also help teachers decide what to pull from their toolbox of multilingual and multimodal strategies discussed within and across chapters of the book and determine how to best use them to deliver instruction.

Ultimately, when you build on the foundation of Deaf-centered instruction, as conveyed by this book in ways that connect with the full spectrum of diverse Deaf identities, you will provide education that is not only equitable but will result in learning that sticks for *all* students.

As editors, we recognize that we are all white. Although we did our best to seek out chapter authors who represent the diverse and varying communities within the field, we also recognize that most of the authors are white. We want to acknowledge the contributions of the Black, Indigenous, and People of Color (BIPOC) members of Deaf communities for providing teacher tales and/or feedback to ensure that we would present a perspective that aligns with a multilingual, multicultural, and multimodal perspective and honors home/heritage languages, cultures, race, gender, abilities, and other multiple and intersecting identities. We are grateful for their input and contributions. This includes terminology regarding antiracist and anti-bias education; varying perspectives on terms for social justice, transformative justice, and restorative justice; and terms of identity including *Deaf, deaf, Hard of Hearing, DeafDisabled, DeafBlind, Lesbian, Gay, Bisexual, Transgender, Queer or Questioning, Intersex, Asexual, and more (LGBTQIA+)*, and so forth. In addition, we wanted to recognize the ongoing discussions and perspectives that are in a continual process of change. These changes will continue, and we hope that this book will, in a small measure, contribute to a dialogue that will help generate new perspectives and further work to make education more equitable and just for as many Deaf students as possible and that this will create a welcoming and equitable space for all teachers from diverse backgrounds as well. With all this in mind, we feel it is important to also acknowledge our awareness of our own bias and privilege. We welcome continued and ongoing conversations and invite you to join us on this journey.

Philosophical and Epistemological Foundation of the Book

The practices discussed in this book align with the content proposed in *Guidelines for Multilingual Deaf Education Teacher Preparation Programs* (Kurz et al., 2021). As discussed in the *Guidelines,* we have changed the term from *bilingual* to *multilingual* to address all languages that students bring to the classroom. In addition, although the previous definition of bilingual Deaf education included the word *bicultural* (i.e., bilingual/bicultural), it is now recognized that culture is already embedded in language and refers to more than just Deaf culture. So, when we talk about ASL or other sign languages, we also talk about the cultures of Deaf communities. That helps resolve the tension that came into being when the term *multiculturalism* became current and inadvertently competed with the word *biculturalism* and created a situation that forced educators to choose one term over the other. The term *biculturalism,* as in *bilingual/bicultural,* for the lack of a better term, was understood to refer to ways of being that reflect the views of those who live in the Deaf World as being distinct from those that reflect the Hearing World. The term *multiculturalism,* as it is currently understood in education in general, is important to embrace in Deaf education and is also now recognized as a key component of multilingual education. For that reason, we have chosen to use *multilingual Deaf education* as a comprehensive term to include all languages and cultures. However, the reader needs to keep in mind that in Deaf education, the term

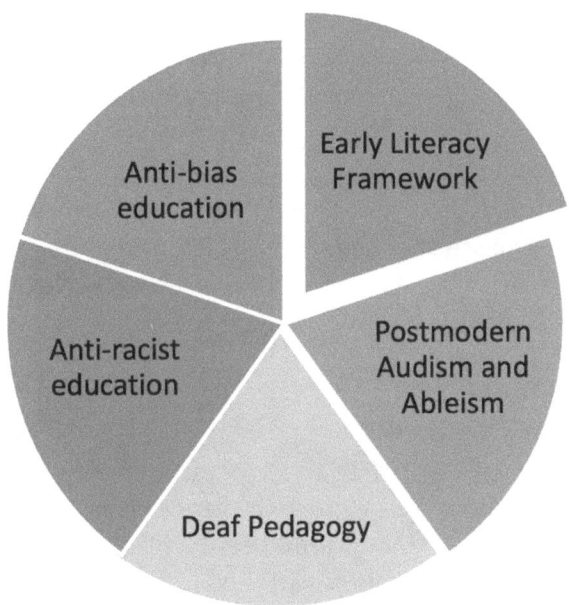

Figure 1.1. Multilingual Theoretical Framework.

multiculturalism includes the concepts embedded in the prior definition of biculturalism.

One of the foundational frameworks presented in the *Guidelines* emphasizes the importance of children having access to communication in a fully accessible language from birth. A paper on early literacy (Kuntze & Golos, 2021) introduced and discussed a framework in depth, and a graph of the framework is shown on page 16 in Chapter 2 of this book and in *Guidelines for Multilingual Deaf Education Teacher Preparation Programs* (Kurz et al., 2021). This framework aligns both with the whole-child approach (Slade & Griffith, 2013) and with what we currently know about the impacts of **language deprivation** (Hall et al., 2017). We believe it is important for all teachers to understand that the key to success in academics, and specifically literacy, is through communication in a language that is fully accessible and that accessible communication from birth onward is what ultimately impacts language, literacy, and identity development.

Many chapter authors in this book are mindful of the challenges of teaching Deaf students who are language deprived, and the needs of these students are brought up and addressed in multiple ways throughout the book. The strategies discussed in different chapters will provide the readers with a broadened perspective on working with students who have language delays or have experienced language deprivation in all content areas from preschool through Grade 12.

In taking into account the whole child (e.g., their languages, cultures, gender, identities, abilities, race, ways of learning and knowing), we are taking into account languages; current perspectives and pedagogy in Deaf education; and anti-audist, anti-bias, and antiracist education (see Figure 1.1; Kurz et al., 2021).

We need to embed the four goals of anti-bias and antiracist education: identity, diversity, justice, and activism throughout instruction (see Derman-Sparks et al., 2020). These goals thread into teaching strategies, interactions, and communication across the P–12 grade span and involve the following principles:

- "building and drawing upon intergroup awareness, understanding and skills creating classroom environments that reflect diversity, equity and justice.
- engaging families and communities in ways that are meaningful and culturally competent encouraging students to speak out against bias and injustice.
- making the implementation of anti-bias curriculum part of larger individual, school and community action.

Key Vocabulary

Language deprivation is the result of a child not having access to meaningful communicative interactions with adults on a consistent basis during the critical period of language acquisition at home and in school, and it has a profound impact on language, literacy, and social-emotional development.

- supporting students' identities and making it safe for them to fully be themselves.
- using instructional strategies that support diverse learning styles and allow for the development of critical thinking skills." (Southern Poverty Law Center, n.d.)

We also need to contemplate how we can work to expand the curriculum to incorporate Deaf experiences related to audism, linguistic oppression, sharing narratives and coping strategies, interest convergence, and intersectionality. We use the acronym *ABAR* throughout the book in reference to anti-bias, antiracist approaches (see Terms Used Throughout the Book for definitions).

Your Road Map: How to Use This Book

We asked the authors to follow a similar structure for each chapter. Our intention for this structure is to help you as a reader not only navigate the book but also know what to expect from the chapters. The authors were also asked to write in a personable way, such as using a second-person reference (i.e., *you*) to communicate directly with you as a reader. Each chapter begins with the authors introducing themselves and then explaining the focus of the chapter and how it contributes to multilingual Deaf education. Note that theoretical perspectives or concepts, such as the implications for mitigating language deprivation as well as other "Intentional 8" components, are threaded throughout the book and are applicable to each chapter. As you are reading, we encourage you to return to this chapter as needed to review key terms.

After the authors introduce themselves, they share **Deaf Experiences/Perspectives** related to the area of learning covered in the chapter. The purpose of this is to provide background or contextual information to illuminate Deaf-specific needs related to the content covered in the chapter. This section of the chapter closes with a list of core recommendations for the instruction of the targeted content for teachers and teacher candidates, which the next section, titled **Effective Practices**, expands on. This section is the heart of the chapter, and it is where the authors give examples of how to apply each core recommendation using multilingual practices. As always, there are additional considerations not covered in the core recommendations that the authors may wish to mention. You will find these additional considerations, applications, or extensions in the next section, appropriately titled **Additional Things to Consider**.

The following two sections are where the authors attempt to help you visualize how ideas related to the core recommendations may be actualized in lesson or unit plans. In the **Bringing It All Together** section, authors share an example unit or lesson plan to give you an idea of how they may be fashioned to reflect the core recommendations. The section titled **Your Turn to Practice** is structured as an assignment for you to develop a lesson that incorporates the core recommendations of the chapter and to teach the lesson. Then, you are to reflect on how the lesson turned out. If you are already a teacher, we hope you will apply the lesson in your own classroom. If you are a teacher candidate and do not have access to students, we recommend that you practice developing and teaching a lesson in a mock setting or field placement experience. The crucial part is for you to reflect on the lesson you taught and consider what went well and what you would do differently if you were to teach it again.

The remaining sections are for winding up the chapter and bringing it to a close. **Recommended Readings/Viewings** lists materials separately for teachers to review and for teachers to use with students. The particular emphasis on selecting the materials is that they include Deaf people and/or align with an ABAR curriculum. The conclusion is short, a one- to two-paragraph summary of the key concepts covered in the chapter. This is followed by bulleted **Sticking Points**, which allow you to quickly revisit the key points of the core recommendations.

In a nutshell, the brief structure of the chapter is as follows:

1. Introduction
2. Deaf Experiences, Perspectives, and Core Recommendations
3. Effective Practices
4. Additional Things to Consider
5. Bringing It All Together
6. Your Turn to Practice!
7. Recommended Readings/Viewings
8. Conclusion
9. Sticking Points

The Intentional 8

We asked the chapter authors to intentionally incorporate content across specified areas to align with our previously mentioned frameworks. We call it the "Intentional 8" also as a play on words with the number 8 from "58 IN MIND." The eight areas are listed next. The authors were asked to incorporate at least five of these areas within each chapter. The first three in the list were required, and they are incorporated in all chapters. Each area has a code that the authors were asked to use to indicate where they incorporate different areas of the Intentional 8. You will find these areas to the left of some of the headers and subheaders in each chapter, and you will see them integrated in various ways—as a core recommendation or central focus or as an example of effective practice. Each of the Intentional 8 areas, briefly listed here, is expanded on in the later section of this chapter (see **Terms Used Throughout the Book**).

1. (MM) Multilingual and multimodal strategies (ASL and additional languages, Deaf and additional cultures, and modalities)
2. (ABAR) Anti-bias/antiracist approaches or curricula
3. (DI) Differentiated instruction for diverse learners (Deaf with disabilities, culture, race, languages, and so forth)
4. (PI) Fostering a positive sense of self/identity development
5. (SEL) Social-emotional learning
6. (CM) Classroom management
7. (ES) Considerations for varying educational settings
8. (MT) Educational media/technology (which also includes distance learning)

Legend Items

Last, each chapter is stocked with inserts to help you as the reader easily identify useful additional information, pictures, examples, or illustrations. Here, we provide the icons and definitions for each of our legend items, some playing playing off the concept of "stick" in "stick-in-mind" (i.e., stick it into action, chew on this, handstamp).

 Key Vocabulary is provided in bold, along with a definition.

 Key Strategy is a name and description of a particular strategy that the chapter authors wanted to highlight and draw attention to.

❝❝ **Quotes** are added to convey a thought/perspective/statement/experience from one of the authors or a teacher or others that the authors want to share.

 Handstamp Sample is a sample of student work. You will find it framed in a box within a page.

 Chew on This! begins with the statement "Did you know that...?" and is followed by key points highlighted by key research, statistics, facts, or interesting information. You will find it boxed in the text or in the margin.

 Stick It Into Action! is where the authors provide readers an example or step-by-step guide of what they can do or how to apply something to their own teaching.

 Teacher Tales are teachers' stories of something that happened in the classroom that illuminates a core recommendation, concept, or key strategy (e.g., "One week we were studying farm animals and . . .") or shares a classroom dialogue or interaction. You will find them framed on a page.

Terms Used Throughout the Book

Identities: In many programs in Deaf education, Deaf studies is not sufficiently infused across the curriculum, and when it is done, it is often not taught through a multicultural lens. The goal of this book is to make instruction transformative and more inclusive of the multiple identities (e.g., race, gender, culture, disability) that can intersect with one's Deaf identity (Bayley et al., 2019; McCaskill et al., 2011). These are all important considerations to make in lesson planning. Teachers should know how to identify goals and objectives to target key standards of Deaf studies and integrate these concepts throughout the curriculum to ensure they are fostering equitable education. As such, rather than having a specific chapter called Deaf studies, we have a chapter called "Deaf Identities and Social/Cultural Perspective," and Deaf studies content is integrated into each chapter and includes the following:

- The history of Deaf people and ASL within general history (e.g., Deaf people in the U.S. Civil War, segregated schools for the Deaf, and Black ASL)
- Deaf gain, Deafhood, Deaf epistemologies
- Deaf communities are represented by individuals of diverse ethnic, racial, geographic, and gender-based backgrounds. There are organizations such as National Black Deaf Advocates, The Intertribal Deaf Council, and Council de Manos that represent Deaf communities.
- Deaf people in science, mathematics, history, literature, and other disciplines
- Understanding and awareness of Deaf space
- Deaf poetry, storytelling, theater (language arts, literature, history)
- International and federal disability-related laws
- Deaf artists and filmmaking, photography, newscasting, Deaf View Image Arts (De'VIA)
- Languages and cultures of Deaf people around the world

Classroom management (CM): There are many techniques that teachers use to ensure that time in the classroom is well spent. In this book, we try to focus on specific techniques that consider social-emotional development and that are conceived from multilingual, anti-bias, and antiracist perspectives. The goal is to help ensure that teachers are able to facilitate active engagement for individual students and groups of students to enhance learning.

Deaf: All Deaf and Hard of Hearing people who use ASL (or other sign languages) and/or English (or other languages), including DeafBlind (Larsen & Damen, 2014), Deaf-Disabled (Burke, 2014), and late-deafened people, regardless of varying hearing levels, signing levels, cultures, race, identities, and home language usage. Note that we use this term to be all-encompassing when used as a collective term (e.g., Deaf students, Deaf teachers) but recognize that individuals may choose different terms to reflect their own identities.

Deaf culture: The set of core values that inform the belief and behaviors of members of Deaf communities (Holcomb, 2013). It is something that cuts across the diversity within the Deaf communities while allowing for variations within Deaf communities. Some examples of these core values include full access to communication, the value of information sharing, an opportunity to develop healthy self-identities, and the right to self-determination. In the United States and parts of Canada, the use of ASL and other variations (e.g., Black ASL) is a core value for many. In this way, Deaf culture encompasses both the common and unique shared experiences of diverse Deaf people.

Differentiated instruction (DI): This occurs when teachers tailor instruction or adapt lessons to match individual student needs, interests, and strengths (e.g., Taylor, 2015). Students vary in different dimensions, and their knowledge of content may depend on the extent to which they have access to communication with others in their lives, both in the classroom and in the community at home. With DI, teachers should consider the extent of prior knowledge students have, their language and literacy abilities, and their cognitive development. When teachers modify lessons and activities to account for these individual needs, they are in effect applying DI. Doing so allows students to demonstrate their knowledge and skills with regard to the content and through varying processes and products.

Educational settings (ES): When we refer to educational settings, we are referring to activities that could take place in varied types of classroom settings for children. One-to-one or paired activities, for example, could take place in a classroom setting, itinerant setting, or resource room setting. While many of the activities we describe throughout the book could be used in any of these settings, we use the term *educational settings (ES)* when we describe how activities can be modified for more than one setting and/or when we are describing how to set up the environment to foster learning.

Educational media and technology (MT): This encompasses strategies for effectively including technology in the classroom and within lesson plans. MT includes media in ASL, apps/tablets, internet, vlogs, and so forth, as well as online learning.

Heritage language/heritage language learner: In a given social environment, any minority language, whether signed or spoken, that is connected to a community is a heritage language (Ortega, 2020). Immigrant, Indigenous, and minority community speakers learn their heritage languages at home, in their communities, or at school. Deaf and hearing children of Deaf adults (Codas) who learn ASL at home are considered heritage language speakers (Compton & Compton, 2014; Pichler et al., 2019). While Deaf children who have hearing parents may have additional home languages, they can be heritage language learners of ASL only if they learn it at home with older Deaf siblings, in the signing communities, or at school (Isakson, 2018). It is important that multilingual Deaf education provides cultural and linguistic role models and considers ASL a heritage language; this includes inviting Deaf role models from diverse backgrounds into the P–12 classroom.

Multiculturalism: The practice in which two or more cultures—one of them being Deaf culture (Leigh et al., 2020)—are acknowledged and respected within the educational instruction and curriculum. This includes embedding and teaching aspects of Deaf culture throughout P–12 education (e.g., identity development, Deaf epistemologies, understanding and acceptance of self and others). We believe that within multicultural education, we must also integrate anti-audist, anti-bias, antiracist, anti-sexist, and anti-ableist education. This includes addressing injustices throughout the P–12 curriculum related to race, sex/gender, disability, power and privilege, and other minority groups (Christensen, 2017; English et al., 2018).

Multilingual Deaf education: The practice of using two or more languages for the teaching of academic content (Valdés et al., 2015), at least one of which is the sign languages of the Deaf community. Increasingly, we see Deaf students from homes representing multiple ethnic and racial cultures (e.g., Black, Latinx, Indigenous, immigrant) and multiple spoken and signed languages (Cannon et al., 2016; Gallaudet Research Institute, 2013; Gárate-Estes et al., 2021; Musyoka & Adeoye, 2020). We also recognize intersectionality and multiple identities and abilities of Deaf students (Dunn & Anderson, 2019; García-Fernández, 2020; Leigh et al., 2020; Pichler et al., 2019). It is critical to consider these factors when redefining what bilingual Deaf education means in the 21st century. In the United States and parts of Canada, although multilingual Deaf education settings use both ASL and English as the primary languages of curriculum, instruction, and assessment, they also strive to serve Deaf children from homes using languages other than ASL and English (e.g., immigrant Deaf children from families who use Spanish, Lengua de Señas Mexicana [LSM], Navajo, Somali, or Arabic). To the extent that it is possible, they aim to honor students' use of their home and heritage languages (Musyoka & Adeoye, 2020).

Multilingual strategies: This term is an expanded version of the previously used term *bilingual strategies,* largely by taking into consideration the multiple languages and cultures students bring to the classroom. We define multilingual strategies as strategies that support Deaf children's diverse cultures and linguistic repertoires (e.g., ASL, English, and other signed and written languages). However, we also recognize that teachers themselves are often not multilingual. Although we encourage them to learn and use home and heritage languages (in addition to ASL and English) as much as possible, we also recognize that teachers are not typically fluent in all of the home languages used by their students. However, they can support vocabulary development in a Deaf student who moved to the United States after having gone to a signing school in a place like Colombia by learning and incorporating Lengua de Señas Colombiana (Colombian Sign Language or LSC) into lessons as a bridge to ASL and English. For example, the teacher can create pictures of LSC words, ASL words, and printed English words. They can connect to student's cultures by learning about students and their families and tapping into this knowledge in the classroom (See Multiculturalism). There is limited research specific to multilingual teaching strategies for deaf students in the United States and Canada. Even if the focus is mainly bilingual, reflecting research-based best practices for connecting ASL and English in the classroom, we choose to call those strategies *multilingual* because we strive to consider additional languages and cultures as well.

Multimodal strategies: Modalities are the channels by which communication happens. These channels can be visual/manual (signed languages), auditory/oral (spoken languages), print (written languages), and tactile (Protactile sign languages), among others. Here, we support the concept of a semiotic repertoire, as explained by Kusters et al. (2017), wherein people combine multiple modalities for the purpose of ensuring positive communication environments with a variety of language-support partners. We want to emphasize that multimodal strategies should be tailored to enhance Deaf students' abilities/needs for learning, not the teachers' preferences or abilities. Deaf students who do not benefit from using auditory input for learning, for example, should be provided with multiple modalities that optimize their learning channels (e.g., visual/manual, tactile, kinesthetic). Teachers need to advocate for their Deaf students, such as stating on a student's individual education program that the student's instruction is carried out in the most accessible modality/modalities.

Positive sense of self/identity (PI): The identity/well-being of teachers, as well as the well-being of Deaf students, are often overlooked in Deaf education. Current and future teachers should have an understanding of the implications and impact that language deprivation has on Deaf children's identity development and social-emotional well-being. Because children's sense of self and others begins at birth, they may internalize whatever positive or negative messages they learn from an early age. In order for teachers to be able to skillfully facilitate their student's identity development, they first must have a good awareness of their own identity: who they are, their privilege, their values, and who they want to be as a teacher. They then need to understand the complexities of multiple and intersecting identities, as well as how to facilitate identity development in their current/future students. It is important for teachers to take this into consideration before engaging in these discussions and activities. These suggested activities are integrated throughout various chapters:

- Incorporate activities in the classroom that facilitate identity development (e.g., art, drama, storytelling, multimedia in sign language, and/or include Deaf individuals).
- Promote the importance of identity acceptance and a sense of belonging.
- Invite Deaf role models from diverse backgrounds into the classroom.
- Include children's books and media (e.g., videos, apps) that include diverse Deaf characters and are in ASL.
- Discuss messages conveyed regarding portrayals of Deaf people in media and literature (with consideration to potential bias and stereotypes).

Social-emotional learning (SEL): Here, we focus on the social-emotional well-being of children. In doing so, it is also important that teachers are familiar with trauma-informed approaches/curricula and examine societal ignorance, assumptions, and definitions of proper behaviors. There are many instances of behavioral issues being mislabeled due to mistaken assumptions about Deaf students. Teachers should be aware of how to recognize potential cultural conflicts, communication breakdowns and frustrations, and cultural behaviors. Teachers should also be aware of the lasting impacts of language deprivation on communication and behaviors (Glickman & Hall, 2018; Gulati, 2018).

Mindfulness practices can provide strategies for dealing with challenging emotions and difficult situations and conversations (e.g., Schonert-Reichl et al., 2015). Teachers can benefit along with their students by engaging in these practices (e.g., Neff & Germer, 2013). We have included some suggestions for mindfulness and self–awareness activities within varying chapters.

We also recommend incorporating self-care and mindfulness practices into teacher training methods courses so that teacher candidates begin to develop practices early on and have them in place in their classrooms before their first year of teaching. These foundational skills may help prevent teacher burnout (e.g., Roeser et al., 2013; Taylor et al, 2021). Some recommendations for how to do this are as follows:

- Begin and end your class sessions with a short mindfulness activity. Have students take turns leading the activity.
- Integrate a self-care assignment into one or more of your courses. Ask the students to do some sort of self-care and reflect on their experience.
- Invite Deaf presenters who are certified in yoga and/or mindfulness to demonstrate techniques in the classroom.
- Have students develop their own mindfulness videos in ASL (and additional languages), which you can try to incorporate into your classrooms.

Translanguaging: Drawing upon one's full linguistic repertoire helps optimize communication and learning (De Meulder et al., 2019; García & Lin, 2017; Swanwick, 2017). Deaf children's linguistic repertoires may include elements of various spoken or written languages, sign languages, language variations, initial communication systems (e.g., home sign, gesture), or alternative communication systems (e.g., augmentative and alternative communication [AAC]). For example, Black Deaf students in the United States may activate ASL, Black ASL, and spoken English language resources to communicate ideas; Hmong Deaf students may use what they know of ASL and Ho

Chi Minh Sign Language to explain their ideas (Kurz & Kurz, 2021). Translanguaging practices in the classroom with Deaf children seek to validate the linguistic resources students bring, encourage students' full use of their communicative repertoire for negotiating meaning, and expand students' linguistic resources for greater communicative flexibility (Wolbers et al., 2023). One's current linguistic resources serve as a bridge for learning new elements of target languages and expressing ideas the way they understand.

Conclusion

We truly hope that you will have a positive experience engaging with this book! Come back and revisit it again and again. Remember that even activities recommended for a classroom-based setting can be modified for any type of setting in which you teach—classroom, resource room, or itinerant. Also, no matter what age or subject you teach, you will find something within each chapter that will fit or that you can modify to meet the diverse needs of your students. It is our hope that each of our recommended practices stick with you and your current/future students throughout your teaching career.

—Your Editors

Early Childhood Instruction (Ages 3–5)

Leala Holcomb
Debbie Golos
Courtney Hipskind
April Rivera

We believe early childhood education is the most significant time to build a foundation in language, literacy, and identity development that will last for life! In this chapter, we provide varied examples of multilingual approaches that you can use to foster positive growth in Deaf children. Regardless of what age you teach, information on early childhood development is beneficial for all teachers, as what happens during these critical years impacts later learning. Plus, in many states, licenses for teaching Deaf students cover Birth–21. You may at some point find yourself placed in an early childhood setting, and you might just love it!

Who Are We?

We are a mix of Deaf and hearing educators and researchers working in early childhood classrooms or universities. We all have one thing in common—our passion for early childhood education. I (Leala) come from a multigenerational Deaf family and was an early childhood educator. Currently, I work at the University of Tennessee, Knoxville, and enjoy researching approaches to language and literacy instruction. I (Debbie) am an associate professor of Deaf education at the University of Minnesota. I teach and conduct research on emergent literacy, language, educational media, well-being, and identity development. We (Courtney and April) are early childhood educators with years of experience working with Deaf preschoolers. Drawing on our research and teaching experiences, we could write a book that goes in-depth about

Chew on This!

Did you know that . . . ?

- A foundation of language from birth is critical for Deaf children's language, literacy, numeracy, and social-emotional development (Hall, 2017).
- Approximately 85% of the brain develops by the age of 3 years (Kuhl, 2010), but some people still believe that children are not "ready to learn" until they are 5 years old or even older. Can you imagine?

different aspects of early childhood education for Deaf children! Our hope with this chapter is to get you started in thinking about what you can do to educate young multilingual Deaf children in ways that honor their identities, languages, cultures, and communities.

Deaf Experiences, Perspectives, and Core Recommendations

Deaf Children's Experiences Before Preschool

The first few years of life are the most impactful on toddlers' developing brains and will shape the rest of their lives. Toddlers are innately dependent on human interactions to nurture language, cognitive, and social-emotional development. This means that socialization needs to happen long before age 3, which is when many enter the early childhood classroom. Toddlers instinctively (and brilliantly) figure out ways to communicate that they are hungry, need a nap, or have soiled diapers. Families that are responsive to toddlers' early bids for communication stimulate and propel development in all domains, especially in the area of language. Language milestones during the first few years of development involve maintaining eye contact, babbling, gesturing, following simple requests, and producing one- and two-word utterances that lead to simple sentences. When toddlers reach preschool with abundant prior experiences using language in meaningful social interactions, they are primed for emergent literacy development and begin to connect language to print. However, this does not happen for many Deaf children due to insufficient access to language during their early years.

Indeed, many Deaf children do not have enough access to language (i.e., language deprivation; see **Introduction** for more information) during their first few years of life, which in turn negatively impacts their development (e.g., Hall, 2017). As a teacher, you will see these implications firsthand regardless of the grade you teach. Once you become (if you are not already) a teacher of Deaf children, you will find that the creation of an environment rich in accessible language such as American Sign Language (ASL) is crucial, and this chapter is stocked with tools, strategies, and resources to get you started.

Recognizing the importance of ASL for Deaf children's development in the United States does not mean other languages have to be excluded. Children's connections to their home languages should also be nurtured and strengthened as much as possible. Unfortunately, many professionals believe Deaf children cannot handle multiple language learning. Consequently, some Deaf adults have lamented that they were not provided with an opportunity to learn the language of their family.

You may encounter common misconceptions that stem from monolingual bias, such as that Deaf children have limited language learning capacity or that learning non-English languages such as ASL and Spanish will disrupt their English development (e.g., Grosjean, 1989). However, as seen in Kuntze and Golos's framework for early literacy (2021), language acquisition is not specific to English. Rather, it is full access to any language that is the requisite building block for becoming literate and gaining opportunities to connect with communities that children are part of. Thus, you will want to be mindful of Deaf children's access to signed language and also be inclusive

> "My parents' primary language is Spanish. When I was enrolled at a school for the deaf, my teacher told my parents to not use Spanish with me and that it would be better if they used English only. My teacher believed that if my parents used Spanish, it would confuse my lipreading skills in English.
> —Carla García-Fernández

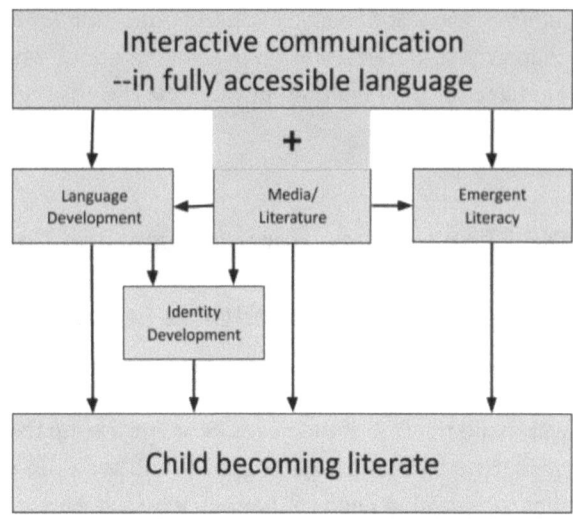

Framework for early literacy (Kuntze & Golos, 2021).

of their home languages as much as possible. Their home languages could be another signed language (e.g., Mexican Sign Language), spoken language (e.g., Mandarin), and/or written language (e.g., French), or they could also be variations of ASL, such as Black ASL or Protactile (largely used by DeafBlind communities).

As children are acquiring foundational language skills at home and in your classroom, you will find that they also simultaneously develop emergent literacy skills such as awareness of print in the environment. Language and **emergent literacy** are interconnected and are among the most important components of early childhood education along with social-emotional learning (SEL) and positive identity development.

Core Recommendations

Our core recommendations for early childhood educators of Deaf students are as follows:

1. Create a language- and literacy-rich environment.
2. Engage in language and emergent literacy activities.
3. Foster a positive sense of self and well-being.

Effective Multilingual Practices for Deaf Learners in Early Childhood Classrooms

You can start by purposefully providing children with multiple opportunities to interact with ASL, home languages, and print inside and outside your classroom. In this section, we provide suggestions on how to integrate each of the core recommendations in your classroom. Examples from Courtney and April's teaching unit based on a farm theme are presented throughout the chapter.

Key Vocabulary

Emergent literacy involves children learning about print prior to formally learning to read and write (e.g., Sulzby & Teale, 1989). This includes becoming aware that print carries meaning as well as starting to connect fingerspelling to letters and signed words to written words. There's no need to wait; when children are acquiring language, they can simultaneously gain emergent literacy skills!

(MM) (PI) (ABAR) Core Recommendation 1: Create a Language- and Literacy-Rich Environment

Visualize your classroom. Do you see how you can integrate ASL, home languages, and print in each corner of your classroom? Think about different ways to add print around the room. What kind of books and other reading materials do you provide? What kind of writing materials do you have? What kind of filming and viewing materials can you add? Consider how these materials will reinforce children's language and literacy development through reading, viewing, writing, and signing.

(ES) Environmental Print

Let's start with the print around your classroom. For children to benefit from environmental print, the text should be at the children's eye level (e.g., Bennett-Armistead et al, 2005). Keep in mind that you can include environmental print in multiple languages. For example, you can have both printed images of ASL words and/or fingerspelled words and written labels of English and home languages on tables, chairs, and walls. Some environmental print can remain throughout the year (e.g., daily schedule and labels around the room), whereas print related to themes, decorations, and exploration centers should be changed regularly. It is important to frequently call attention to print during interactions.

> " Our goal is to create a classroom where all students can learn, thrive, and explore through intentional play in a hands-on, language-/print-rich environment. Not only will language flourish but all areas of development will blossom as we support the whole child.
> —April Rivera

(ES) (PI) Reading Area

The reading area may have different names. Some call it the "book nook" or "classroom library." Regardless of the label, it is important that you have one! It should be designed as a comfortable, attractive space that is furnished with sofas, chairs, and beanbags to draw children in. Because children love seeing photos of themselves and their loved ones in the classroom, you will want to put up photos in this area of your students and the adults in their lives reading books. It would be good to have at least 5–10 books per child that are changed regularly to align with the changing themes of your learning activities (e.g., Bennett-Armistead et al., 2005). Children should be able to access the books easily through an organized bookshelf that is reachable. It is important to ensure that the books are inclusive of various genres; include both fiction and informational texts; and portray diversity in languages, cultures, families, racial identities, gender identities, and abilities. Unfortunately, many books with Deaf characters are not written by Deaf people themselves and often portray deficit, rather than cultural, perspectives. You will want to include books with diverse Deaf characters and review all books and materials beforehand for potential stereotypes or biases. At the end of this chapter, we provide recommended readings to guide you through the process of reviewing and selecting books for your classroom.

Schedule of the day in ASL and English. Other home languages should be added next to the English label.

ASL Viewing Area

The viewing area could be called the "ASL nook" or simply the "viewing area." The purpose of the viewing area is similar to the reading area, but the focus is on ASL literature and other media in ASL, such as videos of books translated into ASL. It should be set up like the book nook that warmly invites children to view ASL and other signed languages on videos or educational apps. See **Recommended Viewings** for popular

Books in the book nook.

ASL videos and apps at the end of this chapter. Through the viewing area, children are exposed to various language models, which also expands their linguistic repertoire. Be sure that the signers in the videos are diverse in their gender, race, body differences, and disabilities. If a child uses a signed language at home that is different from ASL, you will also want to include videos in which their home language is used. To create a viewing area, you will need to have at least one of the following: a smart board, laptop, tablet, or any other screen with videos played in a loop. Do not be surprised if you find children gravitating to the viewing area and spontaneously imitating content from the videos or asking questions about the stories in the videos. We see that happen often, and this is a great kind of incidental learning.

(ES) (MT) Exploration Centers

There are multiple types of exploration centers you can have in your classroom, including but not limited to dramatic play, art, science, writing, signing, and math. These centers should be modified regularly to align with learning themes that change every few weeks and incorporate various forms of print. Let's say, for example, that you have a dramatic play center with a structure representing a barn. You can add written labels of the word *barn* in multiple languages (ASL, English, and home languages). In addition, you can put copies of pictures with printed words for farm animals in a center dedicated to role-playing or matching games. You can even set up a grocery store related to your farm theme with labels in multiple languages beneath each food item and on recipe books, shopping lists, and toy phones. These literacy tools provide children options such as writing shopping lists or making "mock" video calls to their families to ask what food they want to add to their list. You can further enrich students' literacy experiences by making informational books and stories related to your theme available in the exploration centers as well. For example, books can be put inside the barn and in the grocery store where children can grab them and sit down to read. Remember that books can be part of daily activities, and they do not need to be limited to the book nook.

EARLY CHILDHOOD INSTRUCTION (AGES 3–5)

(MM) (DI) (ABAR) (PI) Core Recommendation 2: Engage in Language and Emergent Literacy Activities

Once your environment is rich with multilingual labels and literacy tools, you are ready to think about the activities you can provide for your students. You will want to be intentional about creating meaningful interactions with language and literacy and provide opportunities to have them in multiple contexts. We also encourage you to affirm students' home languages in the classroom, both in teacher-led activities and during informal social interactions. Here, we will highlight how you can embed language and literacy strategies throughout the day.

ASL Time

We increasingly understand how important it is to build children's foundations in ASL. You will want to allocate time in your daily schedule to focus on ASL acquisition. Planned language activities such as language play through rhyme, rhythm, and stories are an excellent way to foster metalinguistic awareness and literacy skills in ASL (Holcomb et al., 2022). In addition to engaging children in language play, you should also use this time to expose children to various genres of ASL literature (e.g., poetry, narrative, informational, persuasive, and folktales). We will share some ideas for activities that you can use during ASL time.

(MM) **ASL Rhyme and Rhythm** You can capitalize on children's fascination with linguistic patterns by engaging them with ASL rhyme and rhythm. One way of producing rhyming patterns in signing is by pairing two signs with a similar visual pattern. For example, in ASL the following two signs—RED and WORM—share the same handshape (X), and the following two signs—HAT and CHAIR—share the same movement (down and up). Rhythm is the patterned beat that children see through the movement of the signer's hands and body. They can also feel the vibrations of drums when you include them. Rhythmic signing is visually pleasing and often captures children's attention as well as lifts their mood. Just as hearing children are captivated by nursery rhymes, Deaf children are also enthralled by ASL rhyme and rhythm. You can engage children in renditions of ASL rhyme and rhythm or encourage participation in call and response. There are many creative ways to make language fun, and even funny, through rhyming and rhythmic activities like the following example connected to the farm theme:

Teacher	SILLY—COW (Y-handshape)
Students sign	PLAY—PLAY—PLAY (Y-handshape)
Teacher	FUNNY—HORSE (3-handshape with unspread fingers)
Students sign	HAHA—HAHA—HAHA (3-handshape with unspread fingers)
Teacher	SMELLY—DONKEY (5-handshape with unspread fingers)
Students sign	GO AWAY—GO AWAY—GO AWAY (5-handshape with unspread fingers)

Stick It Into Action!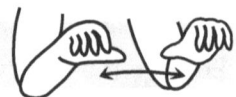

ASL Rhyme and Rhythm

- Rhythmically bang on the table or clap or sway your heads to the right and left. Choose a handshape (e.g., Y) and ask children to come up with signed words that have the Y handshape. Children may come up with something similar to these words:

  "YELLOW, SILLY, WHALE, BULL, STAY"

- Rearrange the words into a fun song and ask the children to sing along.

  "YELLOW, WHALE—STAY, STAY, STAY

  YELLOW, BULL—SILLY, SILLY, SILLY"

- Encourage each child to take a turn reciting the ASL rhyme and rhythm, and cheer them on when they finish!
- Leave videos of ASL rhyme and rhythm on a loop in the viewing center and let children naturally come and watch the songs. Do not be surprised if you catch children singing along by themselves!

Key Vocabulary

ASL phonological awareness means knowing how signs can be broken down into small units and how to manipulate the small units to create words. In signed language, "small units" mean handshape, movement, location, palm orientation, and nonmanual markers (Holcomb et al., 2022).

ASL rhyme and rhythm, along with language activities similar to the recent example with the Y handshape, is one way to build **ASL phonological awareness** skills. ASL phonological awareness falls under the umbrella of metalinguistic awareness, which is known to reap multiple benefits in language and literacy development. Through ASL phonological awareness activities, children learn to recognize and manipulate parts of signed language, such as handshape, movement, location, palm orientation, and nonmanual markers (Holcomb et al., 2021). Because the most important factor in literacy development is having a strong foundation in language, you will want to enrich your students' language experiences with varied types of input.

Stick It Into Action!

ASL Phonological Awareness: Sabotage

Teacher	Sing the ASL rhyme and rhythm:
	YELLOW, WHALE—STAY, STAY, STAY
	YELLOW, BULL—SILLY, SILLY, SILLY.
Teacher	"Sabotage" the song by using a sign with a different handshape:
	YELLOW, DONKEY—STAY, STAY, STAY.
Teacher	Pause and wait for children to notice and correct.
Children	DONKEY IS WRONG!
Teacher	Confirm. YES. WHY? WE WANT Y HANDSHAPE (on dominant hand), NOT B HANDSHAPE (on nondominant hand). DONKEY, B HANDSHAPE. WHICH WORD HAS THE Y HANDSHAPE?
Children	WHALE!

(MM) ***ASL Folklore and Stories***   ASL folklore involves stories and humor about Deaf experiences that have been passed from one generation to the next (e.g., conduct an internet search for "The Deaf Tree"). Although folklore and stories exist in all languages and cultures, genres like ABC, number, and handshape stories are specific to ASL and Deaf culture. ABC stories involve signed words with specific handshapes that follow the alphabetic sequence (e.g., A = game, B = soccer, C = ball). Number stories include handshapes that follow the numerical order (e.g., 1 = mouse, 2 = raccoon, 3 = rooster). Handshape stories mean telling stories with a limited number of handshapes (e.g., 1 handshape, A handshape, and Claw handshape), making an artistic rendition. You can share ASL folklore or stories as an introduction or a follow-up activity related to your theme while also building ASL phonological awareness skills. Here is what teacher–student interactions can look like in early childhood:

1. First, tell the story and then ask an open-ended question to check for comprehension, such as, "What happened in the story?" Make sure you have confirmed the children's understanding of the story before moving on to the next step.
2. Second, say, "My story has manual alphabet letters (or numbers)! Which alphabet handshapes (or numbers) did you see?" (Wait for response, student signs "B.") "Yes, my story has a B handshape." Do you see any other objects in the room that has the same B handshape when you sign the words?" (student signs, "door"). "Yes, door is also signed with a B handshape.
3. Third, tell the story a second time. Give each child a handshape to look for. Ask each child to raise their hand when they see their specific handshape or number in the story, elevating their metalinguistic awareness.
4. Finally, ask children to try retelling the story themselves or have everyone take a turn telling the story one sentence at a time. If this is too challenging, have them sign the story along with you.
5. As an alternative or extension activity, you can link ASL handshape knowledge to orthographical letter recognition. Give each student a card with a written letter (it could be just the letter or their name with their first letter underlined) and ask them to raise their card when they see the handshape that represents their assigned letter.

(MM) **Interactive Storysigning**

There are several names that teachers use to describe the activity of reading a book to children through signed language. Some prefer *storysigning* whereas some use *reading aloud*. These two terms are not to be confused with *storytelling*. ASL storytelling involves telling original stories in ASL, which, as mentioned, may include folklore, ABC, number, and handshape stories. Storysigning is different in that you are reading a book to the children while providing a "live" translation of print into ASL. We recommend both storytelling and storysigning to occur daily!

Some people think that storysigning just means signing the words in the book, but it is so much more. You will want to make the story come alive through animated facial expressions and body movements. When you make your storysigning highly interactive, not only are students more engaged but also their understanding of print

Teacher using both languages during storysigning.

and the story is strengthened. Storysigning is also a great time to model multilingual strategies by connecting the same concept to different languages (e.g., ASL, English, and children's home languages).

The first thing to do, of course, is to pick good books that are relevant to your themes! Do not forget to consider books with characters that represent diverse backgrounds (e.g., race, gender, disability, Deaf). Make sure to review the books first for positive and negative messages they might have and to be prepared to answer questions that children may ask. Here, we outline some key strategies you can use for a successful storysigning experience.

Demonstrate Both Languages   One of the 15 principles of reading with Deaf children (Schleper, 1997) is to always demonstrate both languages, ASL and English print, so that children have them both in their view at the same time. To do this, set up your book next to you to point to pictures, words, and sentences in between your signing. In this way, children are able to look back and forth between your ASL translations and the text/pictures.

Teach Key Vocabulary   Before you begin to read with your class, decide which vocabulary words to target that will help children follow the story. For example, if the book is about the farm theme, you could pick *rooster, hen, cow, farm,* and *barn* as your target words. You can pre-teach these words in ASL, English, and other home languages through pictures, videos, and/or role-playing. The familiarity of target words will help children connect more with the book. We suggest you set a limit of no more than five target words per book. You can expand your target vocabulary by also building on previously taught words.

Stick It Into Action!

Vocabulary- and theme-based units are a great way to provide multiple exposure in varied contexts to targeted skills. To get started, do the following:

- Introduce 5–10 new words per week related to your theme.
- Integrate target words in sign, fingerspelling, and English print multiple times in multiple contexts.
- Consider adding children's home languages.
- Children who have language delays may need more exposure to targeted words in multiple ways (e.g., role-playing, showing pictures, drawing).

Call Attention to Vocabulary   As you engage in storysigning, you can use a technique called *chaining* to highlight the vocabulary you are targeting in the story (Andrews & Rusher, 2010). Chaining is a multisymbolic, multilingual, and multimodal approach using multiple expressions to reinforce the understanding of the same concept or meaning, and it includes combinations of pointing, gesturing, drawing, showing images, fingerspelling, writing, signing, and speaking. Here, fingerspelling is a handy tool for bridging between signed and written languages. When you introduce a new word, make sure to sign it, define it, and spell it (while maintaining the fluid movement of fingerspelling). You may make a brief pause when there is a change in the contour of the handshapes (e.g., make a short pause between FAR and MER when fingerspelling). Encourage the children to improve their fingerspelling skills by copying you!

Concepts of Print   As we mentioned at the beginning of the chapter, emergent literacy skills involve the development of children's understanding that print carries meaning. This includes learning that reading English print follows certain rules, such as reading from left to right and from up to down. To stimulate children's emergent literacy development, you will want to model **concepts of print** during storysigning by demonstrating how books are handled and read. Children learn by observing you and seeing your explicit referencing, such as where the front of the book is, where the title is, who the authors are, and that pages are turned from right to left.

When introducing a book, point to the title with your finger underneath the printed words, fingerspell the title, and sign it. As you point, scan your finger from left to right, modeling reading direction. Call attention to the printed words that represent the title and those that represent the names of the people who wrote and illustrated the book. During reading, you can expose children to additional concepts of print by using vocabulary such as *word, sentence, page, page number,* and more. For example, you can sign, "Let's turn the page." Another important concept for children to learn is that the words *the end* mean *finish*. To model this, you can use chaining by signing FINISH, fingerspelling THE-END, pointing to the printed words *the end,* and signing FINISH again.

Ask Open-Ended Questions   Before jumping into the story, ask an open-ended question about the picture or printed words on the front of the book, such as, "What do you think will happen?" Be responsive to children's comments by expanding on their

Chew on This!

Did you know that . . . ?
Deaf children's understanding of fingerspelling develops in stages (Visual Language/Visual Learning, 2010).

- First, they perceive the fingerspelled word as a whole sign rather than as individual letters. When attempting to fingerspell a word, they mimic the movement without clearly producing the individual handshapes of the letters.
- Later, they understand that individual letters make up the whole movement of a fingerspelled word. They are able to fingerspell words using handshapes for each letter.
- Eventually, their fingerspelling fluency increases. This is called *fingerspelling synthesis*.

Dramatic play: pumpkin patch.

expressions and making connections to their past experiences or world knowledge. Throughout the story, you can pause to check for comprehension by asking questions to connect to students' personal experiences and/or to have them predict what may happen next. For example, while storysigning the book *The Very Busy Spider* by Eric Carle (1996), you can point to a picture of the spider and ask a yes/no question, "Is this a spider?" However, this type of questioning limits the depth of the conversation. We suggest that you use **open-ended questions** such as, "What is the spider doing?" Open-ended questions keep the conversation going between you and your student(s) and allow for sustained interactions with multiple turns. After you finish reading, you can ask follow-up questions like, "Why didn't the spider want to run with the sheep?" After several turns and scaffolding as needed, the conversation can lead you to say, "Yes! She was busy making her web." Extended conversations in multiple turns about a book not only get children to think but are also a critical language activity that helps children develop literacy skills and motivates them to read.

(MM) (DI) Stick It Into Action!

Checking for Comprehension

Always check for comprehension through questions. It helps when you add background knowledge and clues by pointing to pictures and encouraging role-playing. Be aware of how questions may vary in complexity. *How* and *why* questions are more complex than *what* and *do what* questions. Modify your questions as needed to ensure they fall within the reach of the children's level. The following dialogue is an example of how you can rephrase your questions to meet the child's language level.

Teacher	<u>Why</u> doesn't the spider want to go with the cow to eat grass?
Child	No response.
Teacher	<u>What</u> does the cow <u>ask</u> the spider?
Child	Grass eat.
Teacher	<u>What</u> is the spider <u>doing</u>?
Child	Spin web.
Teacher	Yes, the spider is too busy spinning its web. That's why it doesn't want to eat grass with the cow.

(MM) (CM) Transition Time

Transition time happens multiple times throughout each day, and it can be chaotic! Children dislike disruptions or being asked to stop what they are doing to move on to a new activity. It is why a review of what was just done and what lies ahead greatly helps everyone. Routines during transitions provide structure, consistency, and predictability for the children. You can use your schedule of the day to explain and reinforce routines as well as connect language to print. For example, you can say, "We just finished reading the story *The Busy Spider*. Now, let's look at the schedule to see what's next. Oh, it's exploration time!" Consider adding pictures, print (both English and any of your students' home languages), and signed words on your schedule.

When transitioning into a new activity, you can provide fun activities to make the experience less stressful for children. Be creative! Have children sign a cleanup or washing hands song, copy yoga poses, or do mindfulness activities. You can also connect back to your target vocabulary by integrating them into your transition activity. For example, show them the picture/printed word of your target vocabulary, *hen*, and say, "What animal is this?" "Yes, a *hen*! You are right! Let's walk like a hen to our exploration centers!"

(MM) (ES) Exploration Center Time

Remember, you will want to set up exploration centers connected to your unit theme and make books, videos, and other literacy tools accessible to children in each center (e.g., recipes, lists, environmental print, papers, markers, sticky notes, cameras, and more). We recommend having multiple centers open in addition to the reading and viewing centers and allowing children to choose which center they want to go to. It is why the centers are called "exploration": children are free to roam and explore freely.

If you are working on a unit about farm animals, you can have centers dedicated to dramatic play (e.g., role-playing as cows, pigs, and chickens), counting (e.g., counting the number of animals in the farm), drawing/writing center (e.g., drawing pictures of farm animals and/or writing their names), and a kitchen (e.g., looking at recipes, preparing food and serving people). Centers are also a great time for you to apply language strategies during child-led interactions, which is outlined next.

> "Dramatic play provides a beautiful opportunity to connect meaningful language with life experiences. One of our favorite examples, although there are many, is creating a grocery store. We observe students with carts or baskets full of food lining up in the checkout lane, not making a fuss, and proceeding without adult support, which is rare in other settings. We watch students using a barcode scanner and bagging groceries as if they'd worked at a food store their whole lives. They exchange money with ease and thank each other as they head out of the store. Adults in the classroom can join and model both directly and indirectly (incidental learning). Going to the grocery store is already a familiar task so it gives us an opportunity to attach meaningful language to what they already know about grocery shopping. We are able to meet each child where they are. Play, language, reading, and writing all become functional and meaningful.
>
> —April Rivera

Stick It Into Action!

Multilingual Chaining in Preschool

In this example, April and Courtney created a shopping list with items in Spanish. You could also add English text and other home languages and use chaining to connect languages like this:

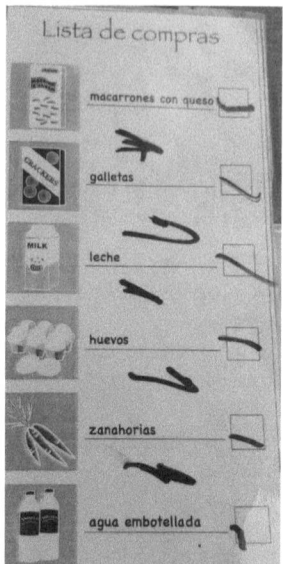

- Point to the picture of milk, sign MILK, point to English text *milk*, point to Spanish text that says *leche*, and then sign MILK in ASL again.
- Vary the order—play with it!
- Add multimodal strategies for children who have some access to spoken language (e.g., sign, finger-spell, speak, point to print).

Book Engagement We suggest keeping copies of your storysigned books in at least one of your exploration centers. If children choose this particular center, it is a great time to review the story and support active engagement. Here are some strategies to grab children's attention and keep their eyes on you while you reread the story together:

- Sit at eye level with your students.
- Encourage peers to help each other attend ("Can you tap ___?").
- Incorporate manipulatives such as toys or pictures that match the story.
- Use props like costumes and objects to encourage role-play.

Parallel Talk Sit with a child while they are playing with a toy or engaging in dramatic play and narrate to the child in ASL about what the child is doing. For example, as they are playing with a cow, follow the child's lead and provide signed phrases of what the cow is doing, "The cow turns right. The cow is walking. The cow is chewing grass." Through parallel talk, children are receiving language input that is meaningful because the conversation is about what they are doing.

Key Strategy

Think Aloud and Expansion

Thinking aloud means you are signing to yourself about what you are thinking while the child is looking at you. Children will observe you modeling language tied to the mental activity that you are engaged in. For example, in the math center, you could say, "Wow, there are many animals in the barn. There are two cows and five pigs. Are there more cows or more pigs? Hmm! Yes, there are more pigs!" Externalizing thinking processes helps children understand how others think.

If the child responds with a word or two, THIS COW, you can respond back by expanding on what they said, such as by saying, "Yes, this is a cow! It has black spots. It is big. It likes to chew grass." By doing this, you are providing new vocabulary that children can link to the concept of "cow," which they already internalized. This is demonstrated in April's Teacher Tale about a cow milking station in her classroom.

> "Field trips are a MUST for preschool because they provide our students with the lived experiences that make it easier to relate to concepts and skills such as those integrated throughout the farm unit. This is particularly true for students with limited language skills and/or limited experiences. During field trips, you can have discussions in ASL and connect to objects and print the children see during the field trip. Make sure to take lots of pictures and use them to make experience books, which you can use to read with the children later.
>
> —Courtney Hipskind

Teacher Tale

The cow milking station was highly popular among all students. It gave them the chance to act out what they'd seen in the cow milking videos that we shared during the morning meeting. I knew Michael loved chocolate milk, so one morning, while he was milking the cow, I took the opportunity to  explain how chocolate milk is made—by combining milk with chocolate syrup. I also took out my phone and showed a photo of chocolate syrup. His eyes widened with understanding and excitement. I pointed to the printed words and asked which he prefers, plain milk or chocolate milk, and he responded, CHOCOLATE MILK FAVORITE. I then responded by saying, "Yes, chocolate milk is your favorite. You like it better than plain milk." Then I asked him if he would like to make chocolate milk with the class during snack time, and he nodded his head vigorously, YES! WANT WANT! WANT!

—April Rivera

Snack Time

You guessed right: Snack time is also a time for language and emergent literacy! You can connect language to print by pointing to print on the wall beside the snack area, labeling the snacks, and pointing to print on the snack item (e.g., *milk carton*). For example, you can give your students animal crackers and ask them to identify the animal they are eating by signing, fingerspelling, and pointing to print on the animal cracker box. You can also make pictures of animals with the printed words available and have them identify their animals or play a matching game. We also suggest letting children read theme-related books if they have finished eating early (and have washed their hands!).

Chew on This!

Did you know that...?
Less than 25% of early childhood educators regularly include Deaf role models, ASL stories, and books with Deaf characters in early childhood settings for Deaf children (Golos et al., 2018). You can help to change this!

> "It is important that our students see themselves and others represented both in the books they read and in the classroom environment. We use the anti-bias education (ABE) approach (Derman-Sparks et al., 2020) to guide us in selecting books for the reading area and storysigning. Utilizing what we like to call the "ABE lens," we are careful to select books that reflect the diversity in our classroom and society and that provide accurate representations of race, culture, gender, bodies, disability, and Deaf people. This strategy also promotes the ABE goal of positive identity development."
>
> —Courtney Hipskind

(DI) Field Trips

Not everything in preschool happens inside the classroom. Field trips, like visiting a farm, are a great way to provide children with authentic experiences for them to talk about. Experiences are critical for introducing new topics and developing concepts and vocabulary. If you can find Deaf professionals or Deaf-owned businesses, such as Deaf farmers, the experience will be even richer with the presence of Deaf role models for your students!

(MM) (MT) ***Make Books and Videos of Your Field Trip Experiences*** Field trip photos and videos are always a big hit with children. Children love opportunities to look at photos or videos of themselves participating in the experience. You can encourage them to recount what they did on the field trip and provide them with language support as needed. You can make videos and books together using the following steps:

- Ask children to help you sequence the pictures or videos of the events.
- Ask them what happened in each picture or video.
- Film their ASL expressions.
- Translate their ASL expressions into simple English sentences.
- Make a video and book out of the pictures/videos and ASL/English sentences (you can add sentences in home languages as well).
- Watch the video and read the book with your class!
- Leave the book in the reading area and the ASL video in the viewing area so students can read/watch it independently.

Environmental print, exploration centers, storysigning/storytelling time, and other activities are all wonderful ways to integrate language and literacy throughout the day. In addition to language development, children also grow in other areas. Let's now take a look at **Core Recommendation 3** related to identity development.

(PI) (ABAR) (MT) Core Recommendation 3: Foster a Positive Sense of Self and Well-Being

Children begin to develop a sense of self and awareness of others in early childhood. Here we discuss how you can foster a positive sense of self in your students by providing linguistic and cultural role models along with anti-bias, social-emotional, and mindfulness activities. We also emphasize the importance of connecting with families.

Linguistic and Cultural Role Models
You can provide cultural and linguistic role models on a daily basis in your classroom by having children engage with peers, adults, books, and media that represent races, disabilities, genders, and cultural backgrounds that are both similar to and different from their own.

It is important to take into consideration the words you choose and the materials you integrate into the classroom. For example, using words like "hearing loss" instead of "Deaf" can subtly send a message to children that their identity revolves around "loss."[1] Steering away from negative labels is particularly critical during the early childhood years when children are first exposed to concepts related to who they are. Although you might think children are too young to internalize negativity associated with identities, research increasingly proves otherwise (Waxman, 2021). To nurture positive identity development, children need to see both themselves and others who are different from them portrayed in a positive light in multiple contexts and opportunities. This not only includes providing children's books and media with diverse characters (race, gender, hearing levels, bodies, abilities, and cultural backgrounds) but also frequently inviting Deaf adult role models from all walks of life into the classroom.

We have witnessed a preschooler wanting to be a janitor when he grows up because the janitor was the only person who looked like him in the classroom. Although being a janitor is a valuable job that should not be looked down on, this example shows the power of seeing adults who look like them in shaping children's aspirations. Another common experience is Deaf children thinking they will either grow up to become hearing or die before they become adults because they have never seen Deaf adults before. You have the potential to impact how children develop a positive (or negative) sense of self. Always be intentional and mindful about the books, media, and people you bring into the classroom!

  **Stick It Into Action!**

Deaf Role Models

Don't forget that if you are not a native or fluent signer of ASL, you will need to be intentional in your planning to provide Deaf role models. In addition to evidence-based interactive, educational videos that feature Deaf individuals, such as *Hands Land* or *Peter's Picture* (www.handsland.com; app.peterspicture.com), you can invite Deaf guests on a regular basis to chat with students about their life experiences. Also consider inviting Deaf guests virtually to broaden their exposure to Deaf people globally from diverse backgrounds (e.g., BIPOC, People with Disabilities, LGBTQIA+).

 Anti-Bias Learning

Choosing good books and providing diverse linguistic and cultural role models is of great importance. You can also do more to support positive identity development by providing anti-bias activities and engaging children in conversations about identities. Children as young as two years old notice differences in hair, eyes, bodies, and skin color (e.g., Derman-Sparks et al., 2020). Sometimes, they spontaneously make comments that are stated as a matter of fact: "I have straight hair. I am tan. You have curly hair. You are brown." Sometimes, their comments can demonstrate negative bias: "I don't like brown skin. I prefer friends who have the same color skin as me." Teachers are often stumped when children make such comments, but their silence can reinforce the misconceptions children have about the differences among themselves. It is

> "One of our goals is for our students to learn that Deaf people can do anything they set their minds to, and that includes pursuing different kinds of careers. We shared a few videos featuring Deaf farmers explaining the nature of their work. We explained that these farmers are Deaf and use ASL to communicate, just like us! Many of our students, like Wendy, were excited that they could relate to the Deaf farmers. Wendy said, "They sign just like we do!"
>
> —Courtney Hipskind

---

1. Most Deaf children are born deaf so the concept "loss" is not only untrue but it also does not make sense.

helpful to be proactive in talking openly about those differences, giving all children proper vocabulary, and modeling self-love and love for others.

Identities and multiculturalism can be integrated throughout your learning themes. For example, if you are focusing on colors, you can set up activities where children identify the colors of their skin, hair, and eyes. Their vocabulary knowledge can be expanded with the inclusion of these colors: white, light tan, dark tan, light brown, dark brown, and black.

Do not stop at recognizing and affirming diverse identities and multiculturalism! You can also design activities to teach children about unfairness or exclusion. For example, you can use dolls to act out scenarios relevant to their lives where unfairness or exclusion happens, such as boys telling girls that they cannot join in a ball game on the playground or girls telling boys that they cannot like the color pink. In this **Stick It Into Action,** we demonstrate a scenario that we have previously faced in the classroom and how we used dolls to teach about anti-bias.

  Stick It Into Action!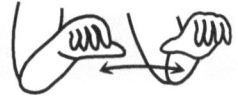

Using Dolls to Teach Anti-Bias
Teacher using dolls to role-play a conflict:

Doll 1	"I don't like brown skin. I prefer kids who have the same color skin as me."
Doll 2	"I have brown skin. I feel sad!"
Teacher	"Doll 1 is excluding Doll 2. Is that nice? Is that fair? What would you tell Doll 1 and Doll 2?"
Student 1	"You should not exclude people. All skins have different colors!"
Student 2	"Brown skin is beautiful. Tan skin is beautiful. Black skin is beautiful. White skin is beautiful."
Teacher	"Your suggestions are great! You are right, all skin colors are beautiful! If Doll 1 was a good friend, what would they do differently?"
Student 3	"A good friend would ask Doll 2 to play with you."
Teacher	"Okay, let's see what happens."
Doll 1	"I am sorry I hurt your feelings. All skins are beautiful. Can we play together?"
Doll 2	"Yes!"
Teacher	"That's great! Thank you for your help, class. If you notice unfairness or exclusion, what should you do? You say 'no, that is not right'! We can be good and kind friends. It is wonderful that we are different, and we can love each other's differences and care about each other!"

This dialogue also increases children's theory of mind, which is the ability to see things from other people's perspectives, understanding that they have their own beliefs and feelings (Shahaeian et al., 2023). Not only should children learn to care about others, but they also need to develop skills to recognize unfairness that they may encounter on the playground and will face throughout their lives. By giving children the tools and language to stand up for themselves and each other, they can grow to promote positive change in the world.

Social-Emotional Learning

Even though children are small, they have feelings as strong as adults' feelings! Imagine having big feelings inside and not knowing what they are or how to express them. How frustrating it must be! This is why toddlers are known to go through the phase of "the terrible twos" or even "the terrible threes." When children learn the skills of regulating their own emotions and become more empathetic, caring, thoughtful, and self-aware, they are undergoing a developmental process called *social-emotional learning* (Lawson et al., 2019). Learning social-emotional skills is a huge undertaking when children have not understood that what they feel inside are emotions that we call *sad, happy, fear,* or *frustration*. To help them begin to make these connections, you can engage in activities that raise awareness of what different emotions may look like.

Stick It Into Action!

Emotion Game

This is a game where students copy your exaggerated facial expressions, look at their faces in a mirror, and learn the vocabulary that matches the emotion.

- Demonstrate a facial expression: Provide the sign for the emotion that matches your facial expression and encourage students to do the same.
- Check for comprehension: You can "sabotage" the situation by making a sad face and then signing HAPPY to see how your students respond and if they can catch the mistake.
- When they correct you, it means they truly understand!

Here is a scenario that early childhood teachers know very well. A toddler sees another child with a toy that they want to play with. The toddler's heart races, their brain fires neurons telling them they must have this toy right now, and their hands immediately grab it out of the other child's hand. The other child starts to cry and attempts to take it back, and now they are locked in a tug-of-war! On top of needing to learn to identify and regulate their emotions and desires, children also need to learn the rules of social interactions, such as asking first, sharing, and taking turns. This means they need to learn vocabulary to negotiate with other people and to take into consideration what other people are feeling. Whew! Social-emotional learning is indeed challenging for our little ones.

You as a teacher can step in and use conflict as an opportunity to teach social-emotional skills. In your classroom, you will find some Deaf toddlers with escalated levels of frustration and behavioral struggles, which may be due to language deprivation and limited access to social experiences at home. It is critical that you are capable of producing clear and accessible communication while navigating these challenging interactions so that you are not contributing to children's experiences and frustrations with language barriers. You will want children to easily understand and internalize the language and behavior that you are modeling.

For example, you can sign aloud what each student may be thinking and feeling in the conflict and encourage them to imitate what you said such as, "I want the plane. Could we take turns, please?" or "I am sad." With plenty of practice and repetition, they will eventually learn important vocabulary to help them navigate conflicts that may occur with their peers as they play with each other.

Sensory Spaces   Social-emotional learning is not always about learning about differences or resolving conflict; it is also about learning to retreat and calm down. Children often experience anger, frustration, or exhaustion, but they may not have the skills yet to communicate those feelings with patience and language. This can lead to meltdowns with hurt individuals and broken toys, which is normal for children at this age. You can support children by teaching them how to take advantage of sensory spaces to help them calm down. These "safe spaces" function as a place where children, especially those who carry trauma (e.g., communication neglect) or have unique sensory processing needs (e.g., light or sensory sensitivity), can go to get their sensory needs met.

 **Stick It Into Action!**

Sensory Space/Calm Area
Set up a special sensory space with specific sensory toys to help reduce the sensory overload and stabilize the child for their and other children's safety with:

- extra-large beanbags
- suspended hammocks
- a small space to hide under
- weighted blankets or vests
- squishy stress balls

If a child asks for a break to go to a calm area, give them lots of praise for making the request, because it means they are regulating their emotions. If a child is not able to ask for a break even though they are visibly upset, you can guide the child to the calm area. First, help the child figure out which sensory aids help them feel better, and then set up a 2-min timer for them to stay with those aids. Eventually, the child will realize the benefits and be able to independently ask for a break.

 Mindfulness/Yoga
One way to help children calm down and feel good throughout their body is to teach them mindfulness and yoga. Mindfulness is a way to practice grounding the body and being present in the moment. This can happen through meditation or breathing activities such as counting breaths or paying attention to what we are smelling, tasting, and feeling. Did you know that mindfulness activities do not need to be long and can even be accomplished in less than a minute? Other types of mindfulness activities

may involve stretching our bodies and breathing in ways that can bring relaxation. Yoga exercises are an example of this kind of physical–mind activity. Such activities can help both you as a teacher and your students calm down, reconnect with your bodies, and feel relaxed both in and out of the classroom.

Deaf children who have experienced extended periods of communication isolation in inaccessible, nonsigning environments may exhibit trauma-induced emotions such as frustration, anxiety, and anger (e.g., Gulati, 2018). When Deaf children arrive in your classroom, it is important to be mindful and empathetic to the reality of trauma that may be impacting their minds and bodies. Children benefit from additional tools to regulate and soothe their brain's fight, flight, or freeze response. Research also shows that mindfulness and yoga can lead to increased self-regulation, executive functioning, prosocial behaviors, and engagement in learning (e.g., Thierry et al., 2016). Consider using a soft colored light to indicate that it is time to engage in mindfulness activities. You will find that if you carve out time for mindfulness and yoga, it will be worth it for everyone in the classroom. These skills come in handy in situations when children's emotions become unfocused or elevated.

 Stick It Into Action!

Yoga
When doing yoga with Deaf children, Jessalyn Akerman-Frank, a certified Deaf yoga instructor, has some suggestions for integrating yoga into the early childhood classroom to promote well-being.

- Show what you want children to do first before they close their eyes or look downward. You can have them count before they look back at you. For example: "Raise your hands over your head and move into a forward bend. Count to 5 and then slowly roll up."
- Always give students a choice whether or not to close their eyes. For some who have experienced trauma, closing their eyes may cause anxiety.
- If they are angry or need redirection, have them practice "lion pose" (i.e., making a big face with mouth open wide and sticking tongue out like a roar). It is a great way to get out angry feelings or extra energy.

Connecting With Families
It is best if school and home forces are working together to support children's well-being. When the world frames deafness as a tragedy, some families may need support and guidance in countering that message and celebrating their Deaf child's identity. For example, when you show excitement to families that their child is Deaf and say things about the child's bright future, this is likely to be in contrast to what families have been hearing from friends and medical professionals. Families also need to see Deaf role models, especially those with racial identities similar to those of their Deaf children, leading successful lives, so it is crucial for you to make an effort to connect families with Deaf adults. This can be accomplished by arranging ASL classes, Deaf

mentors, playdates, and events where families can interact with other Deaf families and Deaf role models.

When you go on home visits and/or have frequent contact with families, you will not only be putting on your mentoring hat, you will also be learning from families about their languages, cultures, and practices that may be different from your own. Your enthusiasm to learn from families and to include their languages, cultures, and practices in the classroom will show that the relationship is a two-way street. Families need to feel like they are respected and valued partners in supporting Deaf children's home language(s) and culture(s). For example, you can ask families to take pictures of their activities at home (e.g., cooking meals, playing games, going to events) to create a family book. You can make two copies of the book and label the pictures using ASL, English, and home language(s), and then leave one in the classroom and one at home. This is a way of recognizing and honoring families' cultures and customs. You can teach families how to talk about family activities with their Deaf children, using the book as a visual support. It is not an overstatement to say that many Deaf children rely on you to help make both home and school a place where they may thrive!

 ## Stick It Into Action!

Communicate Regularly With Families

- Use interactive apps (such as SeeSaw; https://web.seesaw.me/), class webpages, and weekly newsletters.
- Take pictures and share them with families.
- Share videos in ASL with captions.
- Share classroom activities that families can do at home.
- Direct parents to webinars and online videos.
- If families do not use English, make sure all the materials are accessible to them in their home languages.

Additional Things to Consider

Numeracy

Numeracy is also an important part of early childhood learning. Although it is beyond the scope of this chapter to go into the depths of numeracy, it is worth considering how you can include math in your language and literacy activities. You can take advantage of the visual-spatial features of signed languages to represent shapes, sizes, and patterns (Langdon et al., 2021). Here are some examples of how to integrate numeracy into a farm theme. You can use classifiers to discuss numbers of animals, such as signing "two pigs rolling in the mud" using the Bent-V handshape with both hands, and "many chickens running" using the wiggling 5 handshape with both hands. Play with size differences in the structures where the animals sleep (e.g., large barn, small-sized coop, medium-sized stable). Practice estimation by asking children to estimate how many cows they think could fit in your classroom. You can also give children toy farm animals and ask them to arrange them by size. There are so many options!

As an extension to the farm theme, April and Courtney created a pumpkin patch exploration center to target math skills in addition to language and literacy. You can see how they used pictures showing different pumpkin sizes, written words to indicate the size, and the costs of pumpkins for each size. They also used classifiers to convey pumpkin size (*small, medium,* and *large*) along with the equivalent words in written English. See the Teacher Tale for an account of how Courtney and April engaged with the students in a discussion around pumpkins and money.

Teacher Tale

Pumpkin Patch

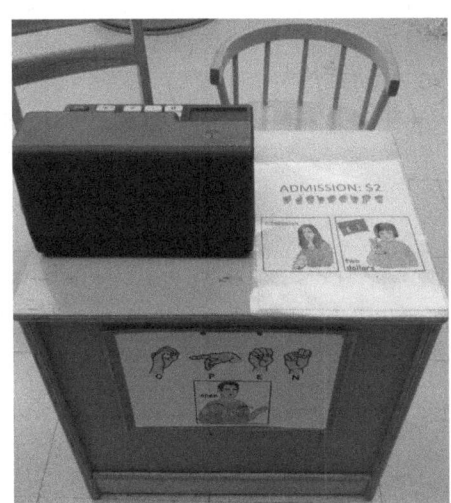

Admission station and printed labels.

One of our students named Charlotte sat waiting for a customer to pay admission to the pumpkin patch. Courtney approached and asked her how much admission costs and learned that it cost four dollars. The exchange continued as such:

Courtney (teacher)	Oh! Does it cost four dollars to get in?
Charlotte	Yes, four dollars.
Courtney	Okay, I want . . .
[April (teacher) interrupts]	
April	I just paid for admission. It cost me three dollars.
Courtney	What?! The price increased?
Charlotte	Yes, it was three dollars, but now it is four dollars.
Courtney	Okay, why did the price increase?
Charlotte	Because my farm needs more money.
Courtney	I understand! Okay, I will give you four dollars.

—*Courtney Hipskind*

Bringing It All Together: A Learning Unit

Teacher Tale

Theme-based unit planning is great because it allows us to integrate our objectives throughout the preschool day. For our farm unit, we read stories and share informational books with children related to the farm and teach targeted vocabulary and concepts such as farm, rooster, cow, barn, and chicken. The best part is going on a field trip to a farm (as well as urban farms and community gardens). We even watched a video of Deaf farmers in action. Throughout each day of the unit, we incorporated our target vocabulary and theme-based concepts in multiple ways: through exploration centers such as dramatic play, sensory time, science time, writing center, ASL media center, reading center as well as in morning meeting time, outside playtime, and snack time. We even tied in an ASL farm rhythm and rhyme song about a cow and acted out farm animal poses. Each of our centers always has print and books! The print is always at eye level for the children, and when the word is relevant to a topic that comes up, we call attention to it by connecting the meaning, pointing, signing, and fingerspelling. We always have a variety of fiction books, informational books, and media that are related to our theme, includes Deaf characters, and are from the ABE book list.

—*April and Courtney*

Let's take a closer look at the farm unit and see how the core recommendations are embedded throughout the activities. You can do some of these activities multiple times and/or rotate them depending on the length of the unit.

Teacher Tale

What Do Farm Animals Give Us?

We discussed the importance of being grateful to farm animals for what they give us. Students took turns opening up barn doors on a poster with printed words to reveal the resources each animal gives us such as eggs and milk. We also used props (e.g., toy farm animals, fake food items, clothing including printed labels, and informational texts) to make the content more concrete for our students.

—*April and Courtney*

Table 2.1. Daily Plan: Farm Unit

Activity and Time	Activity Description	Corresponding Skills	Core Recommendation (CR)
Circle time (10–15 min)	Sign ASL rhyme and rhythm song *Who's Here?* Connect sign, fingerspelling, print with attendance poster and name tags. Review schedule for the day.	Letter recognition Handshape recognition Relationships/Sense of community Vocabulary	CR 1, 2, 3
Storysigning (15 min)	Sign *The Little Red Hen* (Foresman, 1989) big book; support with picture/print card of target words: words *farm, barn, hen, cow, rooster*. Ask open-ended questions.	Concepts of print Story comprehension Vocabulary	CR 1, 3
Storytelling (10 min)	Sign farm-related ABC or number stories and encourage engagement.	Letter recognition, Handshape recognition Story comprehension	CR 1, 2
Center Time (45 min)	Have at least three centers for students to choose where to go. You can include barn, grocery store, cow milking station, pumpkin patch (extension unit). Include multiple books, writing materials, and print related to the farm!	Vocabulary ASL skills Social-emotional learning	CR 1, 2, 3
ASL rhyme and rhythm (10 min)	Sign together the ASL rhyme and rhythm song about cows playing. Ask children to come up with additional words using the Y handshape.	ASL phonological awareness	CR 1, 2
Snack time (15 min)	Give students animal crackers and ask them to identify the print/picture of the animal to match the animal cracker. Count the number of each animal before they nibble on it. Have farm-related books in the snack area that children can read when they are done (e.g., informational text, *From Cow to Carton*).	Following directions Numeracy Vocabulary in ASL/print	CR 1, 2
Outside time (15 min)	Create a scavenger hunt. Hide pictures/print of target vocabulary. When children find a card, ask them to sign or fingerspell what their picture is to check for comprehension.	Vocabulary Expressive/Receptive ASL	CR 1, 2
Guest farmer (15 min)	Invite a Deaf farmer(s) to your class or show a video of a Deaf farmer on their farm.	Identity development Positive sense of self	CR 2, 3
Goodbye time (5 min)	Sign an ASL rhythm and rhyme goodbye farm song and encourage engagement.	ASL phonological awareness Vocabulary	CR 2

Table 2.2. Additional Activities to Integrate Throughout Your Farm Unit

Activity and Time	Activity Description	Corresponding Skills	Core Recommendation (CR)
Transition (3 min)	Do short mindfulness minutes or yoga poses.	Letter recognition Handshape recognition Relationships/Sense of community	CR 1, 2, 3
ASL viewing time (ongoing)	Include media in your viewing center, like *Peter's Picture:* "Our Trip to Country Bob's Backyard," *Hands Land:* "Farm Animals on the Boat," and the video of your field trip. Encourage students to go there during center time.	ASL phonological awareness Vocabulary Sequencing Story comprehension Positive sense of self and others	CR 1, 2, 3
Reading (ongoing)	Include books and informational texts in the book nook related to your farm theme and encourage students to go there during center time. http://www.pareadysetgrow.org/book-list/	Concepts of print Comprehension Vocabulary Positive sense of self and others	CR 1, 2, 3
Field trip (1/2 day)	Take a field trip to a local farm.	Expressive/Receptive ASL skills Vocabulary Positive sense of self	CR 1, 2, 3

Your Turn to Practice!

Practice Activity for Teachers/Teacher Candidates

Now it's your turn! If you are already teaching, you can incorporate this into your classroom and modify as needed to fit your schedule. If you don't have your own classroom yet, that is all the more reason to practice now. During my (Debbie) early childhood methods course, I usually assign this final project to help students develop lesson objectives and activities around a theme, and practice teaching them. After their teaching day they reflect on their experiences evaluating themselves and their peers on what went well, what they would do differently next time and how well their students learned the targeted objectives.

Final Project!
You are required to work in groups to teach a 2.5-hour preschool day at a local Deaf program. First you will identify a theme (e.g., community helpers) and then plan your activities around your lesson objectives. Include each of the following activities as well as transitions to the next activity using mindfulness, yoga, or ASL rhyme and rhythm:

EARLY CHILDHOOD INSTRUCTION (AGES 3–5)

Table 2.3. Daily Plan Blank Chart

Time/Duration and Name of Leader (and peer assistant)	Activity (from bulleted list above)	Objective Areas (from bulleted list above)	Materials

- circle time with an ASL rhyme and rhythm to introduce your theme (10–15 min)
- storysigning time (15–20 min)
- ASL storytelling time (10–15 min)
- outside play time (15–20 min)
- snack time (20–30 min)
- exploration time including art, dramatic play, and book nook/viewing centers (15–20 min each)
- goodbye time with ASL rhyme and rhythm

For each activity, create objectives that target at least one of the areas in the following bulleted list, including outside and snack time! Make sure each objective includes an evaluative component to assess students' learning of targeted skills.

- vocabulary development in ASL and print
- expressive/receptive ASL skills
- story comprehension
- concepts of print
- letter recognition
- number recognition
- ASL phonological awareness
- positive sense of self

Create a chart as follows for each of your activities (see Table 2.5). Include who will take the lead on which activity. Each of you should lead an equal number of activities.

Recommended Readings/Viewings

For Teachers/Teacher Candidates

- *Anti-Bias Education for Young Children and Ourselves, Second Edition* (Derman-Sparks et al., 2020). This book, although focused on hearing children, provides anti-bias principles and examples of how to foster a positive sense of self and understanding of others in early childhood. See pages 180–181 for the checklist for assessing visual material in the environment.
- "Rethinking the Portrayal of Deaf Characters in Children's Picture Books" (Golos & Moses, 2013). This article summarizes messages about Deaf characters in children's picture books.

- "ASL Rhyme, Rhythm, and Phonological Awareness for Deaf Children" (Holcomb, 2020a). This article shares Leala's experiences engaging in language play with a multigenerational Deaf family.
- "The Benefits of Using Educational Videos in American Sign Language in Early Childhood Settings." Golos & Moses, 2015). This article shares research-based strategies you can use to teach language and literacy through interactive, educational media (see Chapter 12 for more).

To Use With Students

(MT) Books/Media With Deaf Characters

- *Moses Sees a Play* (Millman, 2004). This is a story with a Deaf character who goes with his family to see a play put on by the Little Theater of the Deaf.
- *Hands Land* (www.handsland.com). Created by an all-Deaf team, these videos provide ASL rhyme and rhythm songs to foster ASL phonological awareness skills.
- *Peter's Picture* app (https://app.peterspicture.com). This evidence-based interactive educational app includes three 40-min videos and four accompanying games per video to target ASL and English vocabulary, story knowledge, concepts of print, and Deaf cultural rules.
- *Before We Eat: From Farm to Table* (Brisson & Azarian, 2018). This is a story of how many people work hard to tend animals and grow food to eat.

Conclusion

Indeed, early childhood is a critical time for Deaf children. Early childhood teachers play an important role by providing a rich and accessible language environment in ASL and mitigating language deprivation experienced by many Deaf children through effective multilingual and anti-bias/antiracist practices. All teachers must understand the interconnectedness of language, literacy, and identity development and how early access impacts students' lifelong education. Similarly, anti-bias instruction also nurtures social-emotional learning and a positive sense of self. As a teacher, your power lies in the choices you make such as the people you bring into your classroom, the books and videos you choose, the activities you provide, and the discussions you have with your students. Never forget that you are valuable and can positively impact your students and their families' lives!

> "I have had many students in our teacher training program tell me they would never teach preschool only to email me later and say, "You will never believe this, but guess what? I'm now teaching preschool and I love it!"
> —Debbie Golos

Sticking Points

- Create a language- and literacy-rich environment by including various books, media, and environmental print in your students' home languages, ASL, and English.
- Implement theme-based units and field trips to connect experiences, languages, and emerging literacy skills throughout the day using multilingual strategies.
- Foster children's positive sense of self by regularly inviting Deaf adults from varying backgrounds into your classroom, including media in ASL and books with diverse and Deaf characters, and integrating mindfulness and yoga activities.

ASL Language Arts and ASL in Content Areas

Barbara Motylinski
Chris Kurz
Julie Stewart

As teachers or future teachers, you are most likely familiar with the language arts curriculum as it pertains to English. For those of you who have never taught it, you may have never heard of the term *ASL Language Arts* (ASLLA). In fact, ASLLA has historically been left out of the Deaf education curriculum. As mentioned in Chapter 1, Deaf children's access to American Sign Language (ASL) is critical for academic, identity, and social-emotional development. Language arts activities are essential not only to cultivate the development of language skills but also to foster an appreciation for the language and literature of both English and ASL. An important objective of the language arts curriculum is to develop literacy—that is, ASL and English—which is critical for helping students become lifelong independent learners. ASL language arts also include teaching about ASL variations, such as geographical-based and generationally based dialects. In addition, it is important to also honor students' home languages. We welcome the use of other spoken, written, or sign languages in preschool through Grade 12 (P–12) settings (e.g., Mexican Sign Language, Plain Indian Sign Languages, Black American Sign Language, and protactile American Sign Language) to enrich the global perspective of signed languages. This chapter highlights strategies for integrating ASLLA across the P–12 curriculum.

Key Vocabulary

ASL literacy is the skill to comprehend ASL in various genres and to effectively compose ASL (see Kuntze, 2008). This also includes appreciating and interpreting ASL literature.

Who Are We?

Before we proceed, we would like to introduce ourselves:

I (Barbara Motylinski) am an ASL/English bilingual coordinator at the New York School for the Deaf. For the past 3 decades, I have been teaching ASL classes, developing ASL curricular materials for kindergarten through Grade 12 (K–12) students, and sharing ASL assessment outcomes. I have used ASL literature in my lessons to promote awareness and appreciation of sign languages, and I have created a variety of multilingual strategies using technology and ASL genres, including strategies for vocabulary study, comprehension, and grammar study.

I (Chris Kurz) am a professor for the Master of Science in Secondary Education at Rochester Institute of Technology (RIT). Before working as a teacher trainer, I taught mathematics, science, and social studies at several locations, including the Kansas School for the Deaf. At RIT, I have taught structures of ASL and pedagogical methods of teaching academic subjects in ASL.

I (Julie Stewart) am an ASL specialist at Ohio School for the Deaf (OSD). In my 18 years as an educator, I have been a P–12 classroom teacher, an ASL teacher for Deaf students, worked with language teams (ASL specialists and spoken language professionals) as an educational consultant for the statewide services at OSD, and as the outreach specialist at OCALI (Ohio Center for Autism and Low Incidence).

Deaf Experiences, Perspectives, and Core Recommendations

Deaf people have developed, modified, and passed down ASL and its variations continually for more than 200 years. Their perspectives, knowledge, and arts are passed on through ASL from one generation to the next. To become heritage sign language users, Deaf children must be part of this cultural transmission. As teachers, we must help facilitate cultural transmission by bringing Deaf people from diverse backgrounds into the classroom, whether in person or virtually, to expose students to the various genres of ASL as well as the perspective and knowledge that the guest Deaf people have to share. It is also an important means of exposing students to signers who represent varying races, genders, cultures, and language variations. Although Deaf children acquire ASL naturally, learning about ASL literature and the linguistic use of ASL is more effective through direct instruction.

Historically, Deaf children did not have opportunities to formally learn about ASL, such as learning that linguistic rules and cultural norms govern ASL. Sometimes, they didn't learn about it until they were adults, and only then if they took ASL linguistics courses in college. Still today, teachers, whether Deaf or hearing, who have not taken these linguistics classes often have misconceptions about ASL. In addition, teacher preparation programs have not historically provided students with the opportunity to learn ASL linguistics and teaching methods for ASLLA. We emphasize that teachers of Deaf students must develop fluency in ASL to be able to teach ASLLA as well as the content areas (for further discussion, see Lang et al., 2006, and Pagliaro & Kurz, 2021). In addition, teachers should be familiar with technological tools that are available for viewing and producing signed literary pieces to teach students how to develop ASL literary projects (for examples of ASL literary activities, see Kuntze, 1993). These opportunities will help Deaf students to learn content better as well as appreciate the richness of ASL literature.

Chew on This!

Did you know that . . . ?

- ASL stems from a creolization of multiple languages, including home languages, local and Indigenous languages, Old French Sign Language, British Sign Language, and Martha's Vineyard Sign Language.
- Deaf people have published ASL literature, such as stories, poems, and plays, for more than 100 years (Supalla et al., 2014).
- Deaf children are catalysts for the evolution of ASL, including modifying existing words and creating new words (Barnard, 1835).
- Deaf children bring their own sign language style, including word choice and delivery. They should be embraced, not discounted or criticized, as they reflect the signers' personality and preference.

Handstamp Sample

Deaf student in an ASL literary contest.

Core Recommendations

In this chapter, we provide three core recommendations to integrate ASL language arts and literature into your instruction and support student learning of ASL and ASL literature.

1. Foster knowledge of grammar, mechanics, and usage of ASL.
2. Develop an appreciation for ASL literature.
3. Integrate ASL language and ASL literature across the curriculum.

Effective Practices for Deaf Learners

You may find that your school offers ASLLA instruction through ASLLA class, part of English language arts class, part of Deaf studies classes, or through an ASL specialist who comes into the class from time to time. We recommend as a first choice that you integrate ASLLA standards and lessons both into English language arts as well as across the curriculum (see the K–12 ASL Content Standards [Laurent Clerc National Deaf Education Center, 2018]; https://aslstandards.org/). In this section, we provide strategies and classroom examples of how to integrate each of our core recommendations into P–12 settings.

Core Recommendation 1: Foster Knowledge of Grammar Mechanics and Usage of ASL

Here, we highlight the instruction of ASL grammar mechanics and usage of ASL through three key areas: metalinguistic awareness, vocabulary building, and composition. **Metalinguistic awareness of ASL** is important for understanding the structure of ASL and

Key Vocabulary

Metalinguistic awareness of ASL is the awareness of the nature and structure of ASL that comes as a result of noticing, discussing, and learning the different ways ASL is used. This awareness enables students to explain why they use specific linguistic features in their expressions in ASL as compared to other languages (e.g., Mexican Sign Language, Plain Indian Sign Languages, English, Spanish).

monitoring whether it is used appropriately. The development of ASL vocabulary in all content areas includes the understanding and ability to use ASL vocabulary appropriately in varying types of discourse through ASL. The third area is to develop critical ASL viewing and composition skills.

Develop Metalinguistic Awareness of ASL Linguistic Structure

To support your students' development of metalinguistic awareness of ASL, have students view multiple and varied ASL publications and discuss the nature and structure of the language within these literary works. Metalinguistic awareness involves different levels of linguistics: phonology, morphology, semantics, syntax, and discourse. Teaching your students about each of these levels is crucial to helping them understand the overall structure of ASL, and you can have these conversations in any subject area. We touch on each in the following examples.

ASL Phonology   ASL phonological awareness involves understanding phonemes, the smallest contrastive linguistic unit, in the five parameters (i.e., handshape, location, movement, palm orientation, and nonmanual markers) of an ASL word and how they combine to create the phonology of a sign. One example of an activity to promote phonological awareness in social studies is illustrated in the following Stick It Into Action.

 Stick It Into Action!

Identification of ASL Phonology

1. Ask your students to identify the phoneme in each of the five parameters of the ASL word PRESIDENT.
   - **Handshape (HS):** start with HS-C on each hand and end with closing HS-S
   - **Location:** at both temples
   - **Movement:** outward movement
   - **Palm orientation:** palm orientation facing away from signer
   - **Nonmanual markers:** none
2. When each phoneme is identified, ask students to compare PRESIDENT with other ASL words that share one or more of the same phonemes:
   - SUPERINTENDENT (all phonemes are the same; it is a homonym)
   - BISON (all phonemess except the movement parameter are the same; it is a "minimal pair")
   - GOVERNMENT and CAPITAL (only the phoneme in the location parameter f and the phoneme in the handshape parameter for capital are the same as those for PRESIDENT)
3. Evaluate their learning by having students make a short video of what they have learned during the lesson or a video of the history of phonemes of the targeted ASL vocabulary with additional information for younger students, such as having them create their own "Did you know that…?"

You can incorporate ASL activities and publications (e.g., ASL word walls, ASL handshape games, ASL rhyme and rhythm) in your lessons to teach the phonological features (see Chapter 2).

ASL Morphological Awareness   ASL morphological awareness is the understanding that each sign is made up of separate units of meaning. Some signs have one unit of meaning whereas others may have more than one unit of meaning. These units are called *morphemes*. For example, the sign MONTH is one morpheme. The sign THREE-MONTH has two morphemes, and it is created by changing the handshape for *month* to the handshape representing the number *three*. Another example is using movement or facial expression to change the level of intensity of an adjective as shown in the following Stick It Into Action.

Chew on This!

Did you know that . . . ?

- The ASL word PRESIDENT stems from the shape of a hat called *bicorne* that was commonly worn by males in the late 18th/early 19th century.
- President James Monroe (1817–1825) wore this type of hat when he came to visit the American School for the Deaf shortly after it was founded.
- Laurent Clerc and the students at the school used classifiers depicting the shape of the bicorne hat to refer to President Monroe after he visited the American School for the Deaf.
- Both the handshape and the location used in the classifiers used to depict the shape of the tips of the bicorne hat changed over time to become a sign that becomes a new word for PRESIDENT, currently signed by moving the hands outward from both temples with handshapes changing from HS-C to HS-S.

Stick It Into Action!

Play With Morphology—Changing the Meaning Adjectives in ASL

1. Introduce the lesson by explaining that it is possible to modify the meaning of an adjective to convey varying levels of intensity.
2. Review how to sign different levels of happiness. First sign HAPPY (moderately happy) and then sign HAPPY (ecstatic). Ask students to explain what they noticed was different between those two ways you signed the word HAPPY. Students might respond by noting a change in facial expression and/or the tempo of the hand movement.
3. Explain that by changing the intensity of movement and/or intensity of facial expression, you modified the meaning of the word HAPPY and that you did this by adding the morpheme.
4. Have students practice modifying different adjectives and create a continuum for the adjectives (e.g., varying speeds of swimming and varying intensities of working). Have them add written English words to represent the signs on the continuum.

ASL Semantics   Semantics refers to the meaning of a word at the lexical, phrase, and sentence level. For this chapter, we focus on lexical (i.e., word-level semantics). One way in which students may develop a better understanding of lexical semantics in ASL is by learning about ASL words that are related in meaning and when it is appropriate to use one versus the other (see Chapter 10 for a discussion on FUNCTION-mathematics vs. TRANSLATION).

Stick It Into Action!

(MM) (MT) Practicing ASL Verb Semantics in the Elementary Classroom

1. Show a video of an animal doing a normal activity (e.g., walking, eating, playing).
2. Discuss the action (e.g., walking) that the animal demonstrates in the video and the ASL word for the action that is at a normal pace.

Stick It Into Action! (*continued*)

3. With the morphological intensity range image (shown earlier), have students come up with different morphemic additions (e.g., changes in movement and/or facial expression at various intensity levels) to the ASL word (e.g., walking really fast, walking really slow).
4. Discuss how morphological changes in the ASL word modifies the meaning (semantics) of the word.

ASL Word Order Variation Choosing the right word order is important for expressing ideas according to the pragmatics of what you want to say. One can create multiple word orders to express the same meaning. Word order flexibility is possible because of the morphological structure of some words and the use of facial expression.

a. YOU GIVE INDEX(girl) GIRL BALL (give the girl the ball)
b. GIRL INDEX(girl)(topic), BALL YOU GIVE(to girl)(raised brows) (give the girl the ball)
c. BALL(topic) YOU GIVE(to girl) GIRL (give the girl the ball)

You can show students how changing the word order along with the first word topicalized can subtly change the meaning:

a. GIVE(to girl) GIRL BALL, FINISH(raised brow)? (Did you give the girl the ball?)
b. BALL(topic) GIVE(to girl) GIRL, FINISH(raised brow)? (As for this ball, did you give it to the girl?)

In addition, you can show students how the same signs in the same word order can change meaning when you add a nonmanual marker at the end of a sentence (i.e., nod, headshake, raised eyebrow). Here is an example from science:

a. ZEBRA(topic), LION CHASE(nod). (Yes, the lion did chase the zebra.)
b. ZEBRA(topic), LION CHASE(headshake). (No, the lion did not chase the zebra.)
c. ZEBRA(topic), LION CHASE(raised eyebrow). (Did the lion chase the zebra?)

(MM) (DI) Strategies for Broadening Vocabulary

Broadening ASL vocabulary for all content areas is critical for learning. Here, we discuss five word-building strategies to support students' vocabulary development. You can use each of these strategies in any content area and modify them accordingly to use across the P–12 grade span.

(MM) *Word Wall* You can empower your students to become independent language learners by creating ASL word walls categorizing words based on ASL phonological features, such as locations (e.g., top half of head, bottom half of head, torso, arms/hands, and neutral space) and handshapes (e.g., HS-5, HS-3, HS-V). You can use each of these features as a basis for organizing the vocabulary on the wall. See the picture titled, "ASL Word Wall." With older children, ASL words may be categorized on a different basis, such as word meanings (e.g., synonyms, semantics; see additional examples in Chapters 7 and 10). After you and your students have defined an ASL word, it can then be added to the wall. Make sure to have students interact with word walls

ASL word wall and two close-ups of the group of signs made on the chest and/or shoulders.

regularly, and don't forget to check for comprehension of what each word means. The more you engage in discussions with your students about targeted ASL words, the more they will understand and use them precisely.

(MM) (DI) (MT) *Word Box* To encourage your students to learn new vocabulary, create a word box in your classroom for students to insert ASL words that they have seen and want to learn more about. Your word box can be a physical box where students can drop in the words (either written English words or a drawing of the ASL word) or a shared folder online where each student can make and upload a video of an ASL word(s) for the class to discuss its meaning. You can also have students add English words and words in their home languages so they can learn the ASL equivalent as well. Using this strategy, you can foster your students' curiosity and vocabulary building. This also allows them to feel comfortable sharing their daily incidental learning experiences for in-depth discussion.

(DI) (MM) (MT) (ES) *Classroom/Personal Vocabulary Dictionary* You can empower your students to become language learners by having them develop their own personal vocabulary dictionary that they can access anytime they want. As mentioned in Barbara's quote (p. 48), you can have your students create ASL words in GIF files for their ASL dictionary. They can also make a physical ASL vocabulary dictionary using pictures and drawings (see example in Chapter 8). Depending on the grade level you teach and the skill level of your students, each dictionary entry can include the ASL word, the ASL definition, and one or more of the following:

- ASL phonological information
- English equivalents, if any
- ASL definitions
- ASL sentence examples
- ASL synonyms
- ASL antonyms
- ASL word origin
- Information on variations (regional, gender, sexuality, generational, racial, and so on)
- Information on word families
- Grammatical information
- Supporting image/illustration

At the end of each unit, you can have each student pick their favorite word from the collection and explain why it is their favorite. You can also pick ASL words throughout the week to include in other activities. By continuing to create and use the ASL dictionaries and word walls over the course of the school year, students will begin to recognize that their ASL linguistic repertoire is expanding. You can also use this information as a formative assessment of evidence of their vocabulary growth.

(MM) (DI) (MT) *Semantic Mapping* Another way to build vocabulary knowledge is to encourage your students to connect a word or phrase to a set of related words or concepts through semantic mapping (e.g., SOFTBALL, FOOTBALL, WRESTLING, SWIMMING, and SPORTS) by following these steps:

1. Pick an ASL word (preferably in GIF) that you want your students to discuss (e.g., SPORTS).
2. Ask them to put the word in the center of the concept map on a slide (e.g., Google Slides, PowerPoint) and to add ASL-related words/phrases (also in GIFs) in the same word family as the target ASL word (e.g., field hockey is related to sports).
3. Finally, engage in discussions about the words in the map, having the students review the map as needed to reinforce the learning of the words.

> While showing one of Nathie Marbury's ASL stories to my students, we caught some unique ASL words in the story that I hadn't previously noticed. After defining what each word meant, we clipped those ASL words and converted them into GIF files (using Giphy) for our online ASL dictionary so that students can refer back to them and access them anytime and anywhere.
>
> —Barbara Motylinski

(DI) (ES) **Key Strategy**

Semantic Memory
Another strategy to strengthen your students' ability to recall ASL words/concepts is semantic memory. In this activity, give your students a concept (e.g., transportation) and have your students list as many ASL words as possible that connect to that concept within a specific time frame. When time is up, have your students compare their lists. Here are two ways you can engage in this activity, and you can do it in any educational setting.

Nathie Marbury, https://www.youtube.com/watch?v=ET_cO7bpM3Y

- Select an ASL handshape and ask your students to make a list of as many ASL words with the same handshape that are related to the same concept. For example, there are many vocabulary words related to the concept of graphing that use the same handshape as this: 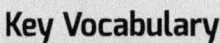 such as line, polygon, square, rectangle, intercept, *x-y* plane.
- Show a specific ASL word (e.g., ANGRY) and have your students make a list of ASL-related words that share similar meanings (e.g., MAD, FURIOUS, MIND-GONE, MIND-DISCONNECT).

In addition to these strategies for building vocabulary, exposing your students to new ASL words through storytelling or showing ASL stories, such as those by renowned storyteller Nathie Marbury, is one way to expose your students to new ASL words. The context in which the vocabulary is used in these and other ASL stories is great for in-depth discussion of what the words mean and how they may be used. Before showing an ASL story or other quality media, we recommend that you target five to seven ASL words per video. You can introduce them prior to viewing or you may ask students what they mean while viewing the story. Building vocabulary also helps with comprehending video content. Next, we share strategies for viewing comprehension.

(MT) Develop ASL Viewing and Composition Skills

ASL viewing and composition skills are to ASL what reading and writing skills are to English. Viewing ASL is not about watching videos. It is about building knowledge and understanding through comprehension of content presented in ASL on videos. You must understand how well your students comprehend in order for this to guide your instruction. Composing in ASL means planning and editing what you want to say in ASL.

ASL Viewing Comprehension Understanding your students' **viewing comprehension** in ASL is critical for their learning in all content areas. Just as with the role that reading plays in the development of writing skills, the development of comprehension skills from viewing ASL stories in different genres and signing styles will help with the development of ASL composition skills. And just as with reading, students' viewing comprehension ability will inform your instruction in all content areas (e.g. Golos & Moses 2013; 2015). Ask questions to elicit your students' background knowledge and to check for comprehension of content.

To maximize your students' **viewing comprehension** of an ASL story, you should ask questions at three different times: before viewing, during viewing, and after viewing, as demonstrated in the following Stick It Into Action.

> **Key Vocabulary**
>
> **Viewing comprehension** is the interpretation and understanding of content expressed in ASL. It involves information processing of content on video, including identifying key concepts and vocabulary, and connecting new information with prior knowledge.

(MT) Stick It Into Action!

Story Viewing Comprehension: Ask questions to check for comprehension

We demonstrate this strategy example using Jeremy Lee Stone's version of "The Three Little Pigs" (https://www.youtube.com/watch?v=J9HZ1JdV1Us).

Stick It Into Action! (continued)

- **Before viewing:** Show the first few seconds of the ASL story ("The Three Little Pigs"), then stop to ask questions such as, "What does the title tell you?" and "Do you know this story?" By eliciting responses, you can evaluate students' background knowledge about the story. Furthermore, you can foster their curiosity by discussing what they think will happen in the story. Encourage them to ask questions.
- **During viewing:** Stop from time to time while viewing the story, and ask comprehension questions. This is also a good time to evaluate students' understanding of different story elements, such as characters (e.g., How many pigs are in the story?) and setting (e.g., What is each pig's house built of?). Comprehension questions like, "Why does the wolf go to the pig's house?", "How do you think the wolf feels when the first pig says no?" or predicting questions such as "What do you think will happen with the third pig?" are important questions to ensure that students are engaging with the story at higher thinking levels.
- **After viewing:** Ask questions to evaluate your students' understanding and interpretation of the story (e.g., characters, story events, themes, main ideas), such as, "What happened in the third pig's house?", "Why did the third pig's house not fall apart when the wolf blew on it?", "What does the wolf do about his hunger after failing to eat any pigs?" or "How can the pigs help the wolf deal with his hunger?" Ask questions that encourage students to reflect, such as, "What is your favorite part of this story? Why?" You should also ask questions about how the story may be related to students' life experiences, such as, "When you are hungry and your parents are not around to cook you a meal, what do you do?"

Before-viewing questions.

During-viewing questions.

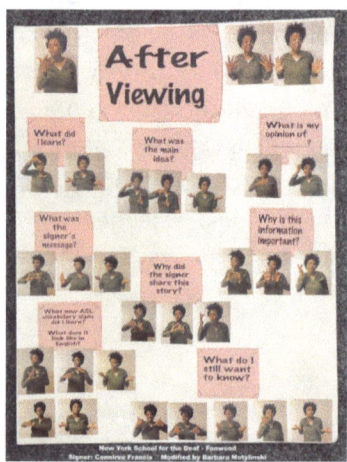

After-viewing questions.

In short, the pre-viewing questions are for you to understand and connect to students' background knowledge and to motivate them to view the story. The during-viewing questions allow you to check their understanding of the story elements and story events. They also help clarify any misunderstandings. Your students' responses to after-viewing questions are for you to evaluate their deep-level comprehension of the story, including theme, character development, story plot, and life applications. You can keep these generic questions posted throughout the year so that you and your students can refer back to them when you incorporate media in your lessons.

ASL Composition Skills   Make sure to give your students opportunities to create compositions in various genres and for various audiences such as children, peers, young adults, adults, and elders. Composition genres and possible topics are as follows (see Chapters 4 and 5 for more on composition strategies and skills):

- An informative essay about an archeological site
- A persuasive essay to justify the use of windmills for energy production
- An expository essay to describe the animal you want to become and why
- A narrative essay about your favorite family vacation
- A poem about a social justice issue (e.g., equity in voting rights)
- A slogan to emphasize the importance of arts for self-expression
- An advertisement about taking a vacation in a country in South America
- A creative fiction story with Deaf characters
- A children's story for young children

Offering your students these opportunities will help them develop composing skills (e.g., signing, revising, editing, citing sources, using mixed media) and understand how to vary ASL for different genres, audiences and age groups.

(DI) (MM) *Signing Process Checklists and Rubrics*   When you ask your students to create ASL essays, we recommend that you provide structured signing composition process checklists (e.g., completing tasks) and essay rubrics (e.g., evaluating the work) for your students. You can use or modify the following signing process checklist used at Metro Deaf School that incorporates the six traits of signing rubric as part of the composing process (i.e., idea, organization, sign choice, voice/style/affect, fluency, and structure/convention).

Some schools for the Deaf use the "six traits of signing" rubric as part of their expressive ASL assessments. It parallels a writing evaluation called 6+1 Trait writing assessment (e.g. Culham, 2003). There are various signing rubrics available. We recommend that you develop signing process checklists and rubrics appropriate for learning objectives and various lengths or composition genres (see Chapter 4 for additional suggestions related to Strategic and Interactive Writing Instruction, or SIWI). For example, with younger Deaf students, the checklist might have five steps with visual support and the rubric has emoticons for evaluation ("excellent" through "need to improve"). With these checklists and rubrics, your students can take the lead in their own process to plan, draft, revise, and share their ASL compositions.

You can also use these checklists to evaluate each student's vocabulary growth by evaluating their expressive vocabulary (in their ASL videos), for frequency and accuracy of signing target vocabulary, within individual publications as well as across publications analyzing the growth over time.

(MT) (PI) *Technological Tools for Composing*   Technological tools can become your best friend for both in-person and online learning when you have students create ASL

Signing Process Checklist
Name: _____

1. Think, plan, how and what to express
2. Brainstorm and organize your best ideas
3. Record your story
4. View your story
5. Note new additions, deletions, and changes
6. Feedback from teacher or student conference
   Focus on trait(s):
   - Idea
   - Organization
   - Sign Choice
   - Voice/Style
   - Fluency
   - Structure
7. Make another additions, deletions, and changes
8. Record the story again with new changes
9. View the story by yourself or with a partner
10. Record the final draft and add finishing touches (ex – add special effects, title, pictures, etc.)

Signing process checklist.

publications. The first step is for you to learn about available tools you can use to create ASL videos. This includes using proper cameras, finding a good signing space, and creating appropriate backgrounds for video shooting.

Next, you will need to become familiar and comfortable with ASL production tools. Some tools require basic skills—click for recording and sharing (e.g., Flip, YouTube). Other tools require advanced skills, such as video editing to add an image background, a picture in picture, or an animation. We recommend these free editing applications—CapCut, OpenShot, PowerDirector, and iMovie—or these paid editing applications—Final Cut Pro and Adobe Premiere—for video productions.

Furthermore, you can discuss with your students about how to critique and develop videos through a **Deaf lens**. This takes into account how to use filming techniques that capture the characters' signing and nonmanual expressions through a Deaf perspective that is aesthetically creative (Betts, 2010).

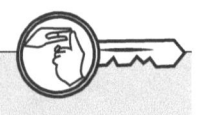

Key Vocabulary

Deaf lens is a creative concept that incorporates Deaf perspectives when it comes to cinematic techniques and editing in videos and films (Betts, 2010). This differs from the traditional techniques and editing (e.g., the signer in the middle of the screen and/or the one-color-tone background).

We recommend you review Brandon Hill's *SignLens* (https://smartasl.com/signlens/) as a guideline for using technology to produce, edit, and publish ASL videos. We also encourage you to learn about different video production apps (through professional development or training or resources) and integrate that into your curriculum. With those skills, you will be able to select appropriate tools to teach your students how to make videos based on their individual abilities. Ideally, you want to make your students aware of multiple available tools they can use to create ASL videos.

(MM) (ABAR) (PI) Core Recommendation 2: Develops an Appreciation for ASL Literature

As mentioned previously, members of Deaf communities have contributed to a rich body of **ASL literature**. It is important to develop students' appreciation for ASL literature not only by exposing them to its different genres but also by giving them opportunities to create ASL compositions in different genres such as ASL poetry, ASL stories, and other creative forms of ASL.

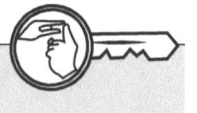

Key Vocabulary

We define **ASL literature** as a body of work in ASL that includes different genres (e.g., essays, stories, jokes and humor, poems, rhyme and rhythm, music, plays, arts) that are created by Deaf signers/artists.

Even at a young age, Deaf children can share voices, identities, languages, and cultures by discussing and learning about ASL literature (Bryne, 2013; Kuntze, 1993). Teaching ASL literature should align with the K–12 ASL Content Standards of literature, storytelling, and Deaf heritage. As a teacher, when selecting content for your students, you should also select literature that is reflective of Deaf people of diverse backgrounds, including marginalized groups. This fosters your students' identity development as Deaf individuals with multiple and intersecting identities and languages, as well as their ASL literary analysis and comprehension skills. As mentioned previously, your students should have multiple opportunities to develop creative pieces of ASL in various genres.

ASL Rhyme and Rhythm

ASL rhyme and rhythm is an innovative way to play with language visually while also developing ASL sign language phonological awareness (Holcomb & Wolbers, 2020). As mentioned in Chapter 2 on early childhood instruction, Deaf children enjoy visually based beats and visual rhymes that parallel hearing children's fascination with sounds, beats, and rhymes in songs. The Deaf community has been using visually based beats for decades. Signed words can also rhyme by putting together different signed words that share the same handshapes, locations, or movements. Rhyme can be created based on sentence structure that uses the 1-1-3 cycle. The following is an example about a tiger looking for food. Sign PAW (using a flat HS-B with fingers spread), alternating back and forth between each hand, and then sign LOOK (using a HS-V with both hands), from left to right and back.

1—PAW-left hand
1—PAW-right hand
3—LOOK-left direction LOOK-right direction LOOK-left direction

You can integrate ASL rhythm and rhyme into any content area or grade. Here is an example you can use in science related to the life cycle of a caterpillar. You can connect science, ASL, and reading with Eric Carle's (1994) book *The Very Hungry Caterpillar*. While the book is not ASL literature, you can use ASL literary principles to translate it, as demonstrated in the following Stick It Into Action.

 Stick It Into Action!

Rhythm and Rhyme in Science

As a pre- or post-storysigning activity, show *The Very Hungry Caterpillar* in ASL using rhyme and rhythm. You can make a video of this to show as well. Follow the strategies for before, during, and after viewing to check for comprehension and make connections among the ASL, book, and children's experiences.

CATERPILLAR HUNGRY
CRAWL CRAWL LOOK LOOK LOOK (looking for food)
LEAF LEAF EAT EAT EAT
APPLE APPLE EAT EAT EAT
ORANGE ORANGE EAT EAT EAT
BANANA BANANA EAT EAT EAT
COOKIE COOKIE EAT EAT EAT
... (You can use your students' suggested food and add EAT EAT EAT here.)
BELLY BELLY EXPAND EXPAND EXPAND
FULL TIRED CLIMB CLIMB CLIMB (finding a place to build a cocoon)
STRING-TIE STRING-TIE SLEEP SLEEP SLEEP (sleeping in the cocoon)
EYE-WAKE EYE-WAKE TEAR TEAR TEAR (breaking out of the cocoon)
OPEN-WING OPEN-WING FLY FLY FLY (flying as a butterfly)

ASL Handshape-Based Stories

In addition to rhyme and rhythm, you can have students view and create ASL handshape stories which students at any age or grade level will appreciate (see examples for creating ASL stories for early childhood in Chapter 2). When viewing the stories, check for comprehension of the actual story and then draw attention to the similarity of handshapes throughout the story to see whether they can identify what the signs have in common. These stories are based on the following four types of genres:

- **Handshape stories:** Stories using the same handshape(s) in all signs. Ask students to create a handshape story or poem about their favorite hobby (e.g., video games, sports) or a social issue (e.g., climate change, voting rights).
- **ABC stories:** Stories that use 26 signs in which the handshape of each sign corresponds to the handshape of each letter of the English alphabet. Each sign is to be used in the alphabetic order. Have students produce an ABC story about one of their favorite extracurricular activities, such as soccer.
- **Number stories:** Stories using sign handshapes that correspond to the handshape of numbers in numerical order. Encourage students to develop a number story about a family tradition.
- **Name letter stories:** Stories that use handshapes that follow the letters of a name. Have students come up with a name letter story or poem based on their own name that describes their personality.

(MM) (MT) **Additional ASL Storytelling Genres**

There are multiple additional ASL storytelling genres. In this chapter, we focus on four genres: visual vernacular, humor, poetry, and translated works. Start by having students view and discuss varying genres and then move on to having students create their own.

- **Visual vernacular:** This is a storytelling style that substantially uses classifiers and facial expressions that are blended in flowing movements. Role shifts and perspective shifts are also incorporated, and it often includes visual representations of cinematic effects (e.g., zoom in or out, fast or slow motion, panoramic view). For example, with young Deaf students, you can use visual vernacular to tell a story about a community helper or an animal. YouTube has numerous visual vernacular videos by Deaf artists such as Bernard Bragg, Lisa McBee, Justin Perez, Ian Sanborn, Dack Virnig, Ruthie Jordan, and Erwan Cifria that you can view and discuss with your students.
- **Humor:** There are different ways you can use ASL to convey humor. For example, there is a classic joke about a Deaf driver writing a note asking a railroad operator to open the crossing gate by writing, "Please but the gate." (The sign for "but" looks like railroad gates opening.) A different joke may be based on Deaf people's skills, such as the one about a tree that would not fall after the lumberjack cut it and yelled, "timber." A tree doctor who happened to be Deaf was summoned, and he diagnosed the problem. The tree was Deaf, so rather than yelling, the doctor fingerspelled TIMBER, and it fell down (see the *Signing Naturally* series for more humorous stories).
- **Poetry:** In sign language poetry, visual movement is central to the poem's structure. Signs are put together artistically and aesthetically, and patterned handshapes, movement, paths, space, and nonmanual signals are often incorporated to create rhyme, meter, and rhythm. You can find ASL poetry examples on the internet—*ASL Poetry Slam*, (https://www.aslslam.org) for example.
- **Translated works:** Translation of a story from one language (written language or signed language) to ASL requires the language skills to ensure that the original meaning is retained when translated to ASL. Often, cultural or historical context is considered as part of the translation process. There are some ASL translations of

Chew on This!

Did you know that . . . ?

Well known children's literature has been translated using ASL rhyme and rhythm.

- Barbara Motylinkski and Isabella Kogan at New York School for the Deaf Fanwood adapted the *Four for You! Fables and Fairy Tales Series* by Sign Media to create rhyme and rhythm skits. A valuable resource to support summarization and inferencing skills. https://www.youtube.com/watch?v=xFnrhgL-ROdM&list=UULFZriRcthWooq_CJ_c9QDacw
- Leala Holcomb translated *Hop on Pop* by Dr. Seuss into ASL rhyme and rhythm to support ASL phonological awareness skills. https://youtu.be/Lbqmnj9mGys?si=W09oLVAMX3JmklTB

classic works, such as the translation of Lewis Carroll's nonsensical poem "Jabberwocky" from *Through the Looking Glass and What Alice Found There* (1871). Here are two examples of that translation:
- Kyra Ayala and Courtney Hocog, students from California School for the Deaf, Riverside (https://www.youtube.com/watch?v=RO8_ipDLAll)
- Eric Malzkuhn, the original translator of ASL Jabberwocky (https://www.youtube.com/watch?v=AWfDFtyIBjU)

ASL Literary Analysis

You can expand the strategies for before, during, and after viewing to target specific literary skills (e.g., inferencing, interpretation, drawing a conclusion). This is called *ASL literary analysis* (see K–12 ASL Content Standards: College and Career Readiness Anchor Standards for Viewing; https://aslstandards.org/). It is important for you to provide multiple opportunities for your students to analyze and discuss content in ASL literature, and this should happen across grade levels. This includes but is not limited to discussing characters, story events, and storytellers' purposes and how the content is related to your students' life experiences. For example, when working with older students, show the video of Ben Bahan's (1992) *Bird of a Different Feather* (https://www.youtube.com/watch?v=Pn1wBlob6DE&t=38s) one chapter at a time. After using the strategies before, during, and after viewing to ensure that they understand the story, follow up by having students do a literary analysis. You can use the supplementary workbook that comes with the video as a discussion guide to help students to better understand how and why specific signs/phrases were used to convey meaning.

  **Stick It Into Action!**

ASL Literary Analysis
- Show a frozen frame of the title of Nathie Marbury's ASL video *Choir* (https://www.youtube.com/watch?v=ET_cO7bpM3Y).
- Ask students what they think the narrator will be talking about based on the video title *Choir* and if they have any experiences related to that title they can share (see p. 49).
- Play the video and stop from time to time to ask questions to check for comprehension.
- After the video ends, discuss the story by asking questions about specific parts of the story. The questions should include ones that ask the students to make an inference (e.g., "Why do you think she was placed in front of the choir?" "How do you think she kept up with the singing pace?" "Why do you think she wanted to deal with boredom at church?") and also that ask students to draw a conclusion (e.g., "Why did the narrator as a Deaf person want to share the story?").
- Extend the discussion by focusing on specific ASL vocabulary, including synonyms (e.g., BORED, EYE-WANDERING) and antonyms (e.g., DRESS-UP, OUT-OF-PLACE) and the use of complex sentence structures, especially the use of handshape (e.g., opening and closing flat HS-O to depict a hearing singer's mouth opening and closing, which the narrator's mouth also mimic).

Nathie Marbury, https://www.youtube.com/watch?v=ET_cO7bpM3Y

Stick It Into Action!

Jigsaw

Analyze Deaf literature through the jigsaw strategy, which is a cooperative learning strategy. Here are some steps:

- Assign students into groups of three and have them analyze a piece of Deaf literature to identify any of the following elements: Deaf experiences, views of the world, imaginations, and/or truths.
- Once they become familiar with a literary topic (theme, symbolism, figurative language, characterization, plot, mood, and so on), create new groupings. The new group will contain a student from each of the original groups.
- Have them create slides (Google Slides, PowerPoint, or other similar program) to write down their analysis.
- Each student in a new group takes turns sharing their short slide presentation of the literary analysis done in the previous group.

(MM) (DI) Core Recommendation 3: Integrate ASL Language and ASL Literature Across the Curriculum

Integrating ASLLA in content areas (e.g., science, mathematics, engineering and technology, social studies, arts, career, vocational and physical education, reading/writing, Deaf studies) can help enhance students' understanding of content and also develop ASL skills related to the content. By doing so, you can also teach students how ASL grammar and vocabulary are used in a specialized way relative to each discipline as well as connect ASL literature to content area topics. You can target ASLLA in any of your lessons regardless of the content area you teach. It is important for you to strategically design your lessons to ensure that Deaf students are introduced to grade-level concepts in ASL as demonstrated in the ASL K–12 Content Standards. If you teach at the elementary level, you can create interdisciplinary units that integrate ASLLA. In addition, consider collaborating with other subject matter teachers (e.g., arts, social studies, science) to figure out how to integrate ASL literature to reinforce student learning of subject concepts. See Chapters 7, 11, and 12 for examples of teachers collaborating on interdisciplinary units integrating ASLLA.

Progression of Vocabulary Complexity
One way to get started is to expand on the previously mentioned strategies for building vocabulary to introduce complex vocabulary within content areas. In the following Stick It Into Action, we describe how to introduce complex vocabulary into a science lesson on bacteria and viruses.

  **Stick It Into Action!**

Building Complex Vocabulary in Content Areas
Start a lesson with a live or recorded short story in ASL, such as the one below about bacteria and viruses.

> *(Translated from ASL to English):*
> Did you know that there are infinite numbers of small things everywhere that you cannot see, and that includes those on your hands, face, and skin, as well as things inside you, such as in the stomach and the lungs? Some of those small things are good for you, and some are not good. Some can lead to sickness, illness, and, unfortunately, death. But some are important for your health, like digesting food. These small things can be divided into two groups: bacteria and viruses. Bacteria are living and free and have a cell wall. They can live inside or outside a body. Viruses tend to be smaller in size compared to bacteria, and viruses are nonliving collections of molecules and have a protein covering. They seek host cells to infect for multiplication and mutation. Like bacteria, they can be found inside or outside a body.

- In the story, purposely include target ASL words (e.g., BACTERIA, VIRUS, CELL, PROTEIN, MOLECULE, HOST).
- Discuss with students the similarities and differences between bacteria and viruses in the story. Ask open-ended questions to check for comprehension.
- Have students compare and contrast bacteria and viruses by discussing their characteristics using a Venn diagram (see p. 58).
- Have students identify the difference in ASL words for BACTERIA and VIRUS, which show a difference in their behavior with respect to cells. BACTERIA is signed this way: the index finger (HS-1) moving to the fist (HS-S) and laterally on it (as if roaming between cells). VIRUS is signed by the index finger (HS-1) moving to the fist (HS-S) and laterally on it. Then, bend the index finger (HS-1) as if infecting the cell.
- They will eventually make a connection between the form of the ASL words for bacteria and virus and the manner by which each of them interacts with the cells: Viruses infect cells and bacteria take the spaces between cells. The structure of each ASL word will help students remember how viruses and bacteria behave and how they differ from each other.

 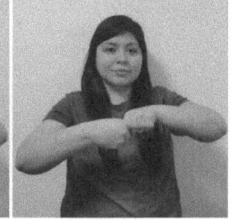

BACTERIA.

VIRUS.

Stick It Into Action! (*continued*)
- Provide opportunities for your students to use ASL vocabulary targeting different academic concepts in different contexts such as through class discussions or games.
- Use chaining or sandwiching to connect signing, fingerspelling, and written English equivalents (and additional languages as needed) to support the connections your students make between targeted vocabulary in ASL and English, which will help them relate to those concepts when reading. See Chapters 2, 4, 6, 7, and others for more on chaining.

Having students learn, recreate, and use the targeted concepts in both languages allows them to translate the concepts in ASL to English, or vice versa. As with writing, they need to have opportunities to recreate the information in ASL. Make sure to evaluate their understanding of concepts and their ability to express concepts in ASL.

ASL Learning Objectives in Content Areas

Here, we highlight how to incorporate ASL objectives in different content areas. When planning a lesson, consider which ASL objectives (e.g., grammatical uses, sentence mechanics, viewing/composing ASL literature) you want to focus on that align with ASL Content Standards. Ask students to demonstrate their knowledge/understanding of the content through a report, presentation, or demonstration in ASL to evaluate their learning. In this Stick It Into Action, we provide an example of how to embed ASL learning objectives into the lesson on bacteria and viruses.

 **Stick It Into Action!**

Embedding ASL Learning Objectives Into a Science Lesson

First, identify objectives for ASL language function—what would you expect your students to sign to show their understanding of bacteria and viruses? Let's say you choose to have students compare and contrast bacteria and viruses. Here is an example of an ASL learning objective: "Using ASL, students will be able to sign three similarities and three differences between bacteria and viruses." To integrate this into the previously mentioned lesson on bacteria and viruses, follow these steps:

- Select or develop a tool for language demand. For example, you can have them sign the differences and similarities between bacteria and viruses using a Venn diagram (tool).

- For young students, create a Venn diagram either with tape or using toy hoops on the floor for bacteria and viruses. The middle overlap is for characteristics that are common to both groups (see Chapter 13 for additional examples).

    Have students stand in the circle on the right (outside of the left circle) and video-record them signing the distinct characteristics of bacteria. Then, have them move to the left circle (outside of the right circle) and video-record them signing the distinct characteristics of viruses. Last, have them move to the overlap of both circles and explain the characteristics that bacteria and viruses have in common.
- For older students, instead of using the circles as a visual representation of the Venn diagram, they can use body shifts (i.e., left side, bacteria; right side, viruses; center, both).
- To integrate technology, have your students create a Venn diagram on a slide as a picture-in-picture within a video of their explanations in ASL. That would be your ASL language demand.

When you embed ASL language learning objectives in content areas, it is important that you clearly identify which language and modality (i.e., viewing, in-person signing, self-recording) you expect your students to use to demonstrate their knowledge and skills. Following are different samples of language functions and corresponding ASL language demands.

FUNCTION	DEMAND
Define	Sign definitions to vocabulary words
Assess	Sign 1-2 minute self-reflection
Compare	Use an ASL Venn diagram and fill sections with examples
Debate	Participate in a class debate in ASL
Construct	Create a multi-media project, explaining the concept in an ASL video
Apply	Solve word problems involving one variable and explain your work in ASL
Describe	Describe some characteristics of a main character in a novel in ASL

Let's look at an ASL objective example for mathematics:

Students will be able to identify each part of a fraction by signing the fraction statement and the fraction question appropriately while playing a card sequence game.

In this objective, the language function is to identify each part of the fraction, and the language demand is to sign the fraction statement and the fraction question as shown on the game card. During the card sequence game, you would evaluate your students' sign production (e.g., denominator, numerator, fraction, equivalent, less than, greater than, undefined, fraction, fractional numbers) as to whether they are able to convey the concept of fraction appropriately in ASL.

My fraction is $\frac{0}{7}$	My fraction is $\frac{14}{7}$	My fraction is $\frac{6}{0}$	My fraction is $\frac{5}{10}$
Who has the fraction with denominator of 7 and is equivalent to 2	Who has the fraction that is undefined	Who has the fraction with numerator of 5 and is equivalent to $\frac{1}{2}$	Who has the fraction that is equivalent to $\frac{2}{3}$

Fraction cards.

Here is another example for a science learning objective:

Given a selected organism, students will be able to correctly describe its traits in ASL according to the classification system. a (e.g., kingdom, phylum/division, class, order, family, genus, species).

Key Strategy

ASL-Centric Mnemonics

You can introduce the ASL memorization strategy **ASL-centric mnemonics**, as demonstrated in the following Stick It Into Action to help the student remember the classification system. If you want them to use both ASL and English, you can have them create a classification poster (e.g., using Google Slides) of a given organism (e.g., a horse or a ginkgo tree) with ASL GIFs/photos on the left and English text on the right (see Stick It Into Action).

> "I showed my students a video of a Deaf presenter who gave a brief ASL lecture on how the eye works. Then I asked them how many science terms were included in the lecture. Half of the students said none. A few students caught that the narrator fingerspelled LENS. I asked them what they learned from the lecture. They gave different parts of the eye and explained how it works. Eventually, they began to realize that science does not belong to English but that we can use any language to talk about science and that we have unique ASL words for different parts of the eye."
>
> —Chris Kurz

Stick It Into Action!

ASL-centric Mnemonics

ASL-centric mnemonics are learning tools that help learners recall larger pieces of information (e.g., characteristics, steps, stages) using ASL linguistic features (e.g., classifiers) and providing visual cues (e.g., use of space, movement). This differs from English-centric mnemonics, which use English letters to help learners recall (e.g., PEMDAS or Please Excuse My Dear Aunt Sally for the mathematical order of operations; My Very Educated Mother Just Served Us Noodles for the planets in the solar system; ROY G. BIV for the order of rainbow colors). ASL-centric mnemonics can be told as a story (a number story or a handshape story) as in the following examples:

- The mathematical order of operations using numbers (1–6): HS-1 for parentheses, HS-2 for exponent, HS-3 for multiplication, HS-4 for division, HS-5 for addition, and HS-6 for subtraction.

- The classification of organisms: moving downward from one level to another in one movement, telling a visual story: HS-5 AROUND for kingdom, HS-B DIVIDE for phylum/division, HS-C GROUP for class, HS-1 ONE+++ (palm orientation downward) for order, clawed HS-5 GROUP (smaller size) for family, HS-G SMALL+++ for genus, and HS-1 ONE-SPECIAL for species.

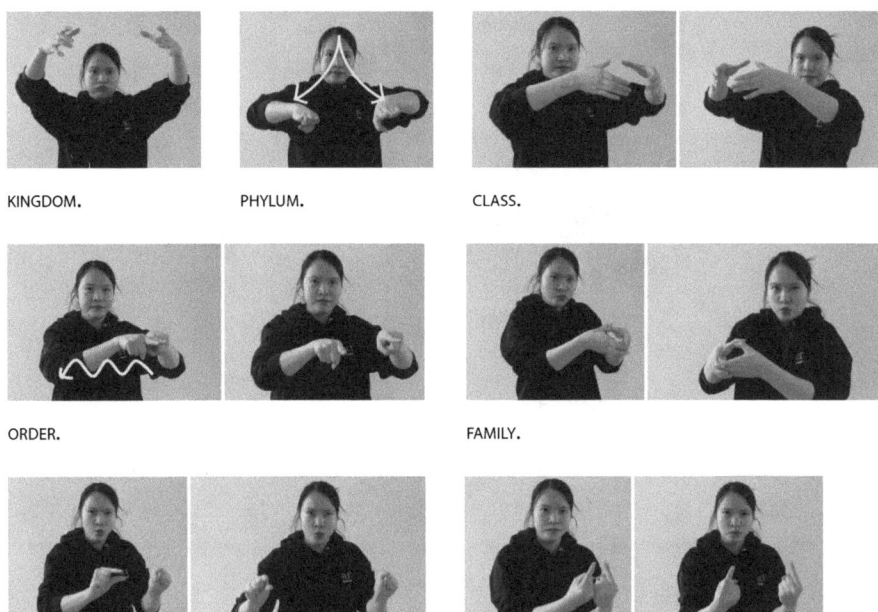

KINGDOM.   PHYLUM.   CLASS.

ORDER.   FAMILY.

GENUS.   SPECIES.

(MM) (DI) (MT) ASL Dictionary or Glossaries for Content Areas

In addition to the previously mentioned strategies for building vocabulary, you can reinforce vocabulary development in various content areas by adding new ASL words to the students' personal dictionaries and/or by creating **ASL glossaries** for each content area.

An ASL glossary differs from an ASL dictionary in that a dictionary provides not only a word in sign and print but also includes more elaborate information, such as at least one definition of the word; at least one example of the word in a signed sentence and its written sentence equivalent; information about the word class and other grammatical information; extra information on the form of the signed word, especially when it is presented in the form of a drawing or a picture; information on regional variations; and/or information about relationships to other signed words (Schermer, 2016).

The next figure depicts a glossary example that includes a list of social studies vocabulary in ASL and English based on HS-V and the location: head.

Key Vocabulary

An **ASL glossary** is a list of one-to-one translation between languages (e.g., signed word to written word, ASL word to Mexican Sign Language word, or Somali written word to English written word; Schermer, 2016).

HS-V vocabulary.

One of many benefits of having your students create their own personal dictionaries/glossaries is for students to have independent access to vocabulary definitions without having to repeatedly ask you for the meaning or how to spell equivalent English words. Similarly, you and your students can create an ASL dictionary/glossary and share it with other teachers and students to access anytime (e.g., Google Slides). See the following two figures for an ASL–English math glossary sample (using Google Slides with intra-hyperlinks):

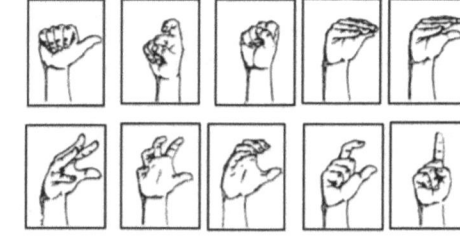

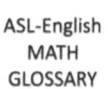

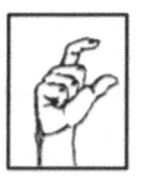

Evaluating Target ASL Word Use During Content Discussion

Evaluating how your students use target ASL words in content areas in a small-group or whole-class discussion will help you see whether they are able to use words accurately in context. One way of doing this is by tallying in a table how often they are using target ASL words (P, posing a question; R, responding to a question; and/or S, summarizing/stating), as shown in the word tally table below.

Class Discussion – Geometry – ASL Word Use

	Juan	Kim	Maya	Charlton
segments	R R	S	P	R
lines	P R	S	P R R S	
angles	S R	S	R S	R
parallel	P R	S	R R S	
rays	R	S	P R	
perpendicular	S	S		

P = posing a question   R = responding to question   S = summarizing/stating

Word tally table.

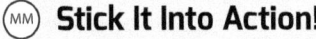 Stick It Into Action!

Geometry Word Use in ASL

Here is an example of an interactive dialogue you could have with your students when referring to the tally table for word use during a math discussion:

Teacher	Can you explain why that figure is a square?
Juan	It has four **lines.** All lines are equal in length. (R)
Charlton	It has four **angles**, too. (R)
Maya	I have a question. Are those not **lines**? (P) (looking at Juan) It should be called **line segments.** (R) Am I right?
Juan	They are the same. No different.
Maya	No, they are different. **Lines** mean nonstop. (R) Others have end points.
Charlton	Maya is right. **Line segments** have end points. (R)
Juan	I see. Okay.
Teacher	Kim, do you have any thoughts on the figure?
Kim	Okay, it is a square because it has four equal **line segments** and four equal **angles.** The **line segments** are **parallel** to their opposites and **perpendicular** to their adjacent **segments.** (S)
Juan	Yes, that is right. I see that the **line segments** are **perpendicular** to each other. That is why the **angles** are called **right angles.** (S)

Additional Things to Consider

(ES) Class Environment

Here are some ideas for you to set up your classroom/environment so that it is conducive to ASL teaching and learning. Ideally, your classroom should have a space where your students can create ASL publications. The space should include a mini studio with chrome green/blue background, a technology center for editing and exporting videos, and a large screen where ASL publications can be easily viewed and discussed. You can also use classroom walls and/or hallway bulletin boards for ASL words/phrases/sentences and to highlight your students' ASL works (see Chapter 2 for creating an ASL viewing center in early childhood).

(MM) (DI) (ES) (MT) Bring ASL Technology Outside of the Classroom on Field Trips

Another way you can foster ASLLA knowledge is by integrating technology on field trips. When your class is taking a field trip, you can have your students make ASL videos on site. For example, if your class goes on a field trip to a historical site, your students can use their mobile phones to create videos of ASL narratives describing different parts of the site. You can later view these videos to evaluate their ASL knowledge and skills.

(DI) (MM) Language Arts and Differentiated Instruction

It is critical for you to learn about your students' home cultures and languages so that you connect to them when teaching ASLLA in your classroom. For example, if students use additional languages in the home, provide opportunities for them to share their languages so you can make connections to ASL. For example, you can post pictures on the wall of the signs for colors in both their home sign language and ASL.

For students with language delays, who may not be ready for direct instruction of ASLLA, provide opportunities that allow them to engage in discourse through use of objects, pictures, and body language as much as possible. For example, you can show a toy fire truck and use body language and facial expression to describe the truck's physical characteristics. You can then model ASL words during this discussion. Use as many visuals as possible and relate them to students' background knowledge to help them connect ASL to concepts and build their repertoire (see Chapter 13 for additional examples). That will allow them to learn ASL language arts at their own pace.

Bringing It All Together

Here, we share an interdisciplinary unit plan about animals for fifth and sixth graders that incorporates each of our core recommendations for ASL language arts.

Unit Plan Example: Metamorphosis in Animals

Sample: ASL Content Standards

Viewing Standards for Informational Text (Grades 5 and 6)
- Determine the meaning of general academic and domain-specific words or phrases in an ASL text (i.e., video) relevant to a Grade 5 topic or subject area.
- Analyze in detail how a key individual, event, or idea is introduced, illustrated, and elaborated in an ASL text (e.g., through examples or anecdotes).
- Integrate information presented in different media or formats (e.g., visually, quantitatively) as well as in signs to develop a coherent understanding of a topic or issue.

Viewing Standards for Foundational Skills: Fluency (Grade 5)
- View and sign on-level texts with sufficient accuracy and fluency to support comprehension.

Standards for Publishing Signing (Grades 5 and 6)
- With guidance and support from peers and adults, develop and strengthen signing as needed by planning, revising, editing, re-signing, or trying a new approach. (Editing for structure should demonstrate command of Language Standards 1–3 up to and including Grade 5.)
- Conduct short research projects that use several sources to build knowledge by investigating different aspects of a topic.
- Sign informative/explanatory texts to examine a topic and convey ideas, concepts, and information through the selection, organization, and analysis of relevant content.

Sample: Learner Objectives
In the following areas, students will be able to:

- **ASL language arts:** identify ASL handshapes and facial expressions in an ASL story about an animal.
- **Viewing comprehension:** describe the story sequence of an ASL animal story.
- **Signing composition:** create an ASL story in different genres (e.g, ABC, poem, visual vernacular) about a fictional animal character that undergoes metamorphosis.
- **ASL literature:** publish ASL animal stories in two to three different genres (e.g., poem, visual vernacular).
- **Science:** describe metamorphosis as seen in ASL animal stories.
- **English reading:** Construct a narrative in ASL describing the life cycle of a fictional animal character (the life cycle information will be used for signing composition) using information from multiple reading materials.
- **English writing:** create a trading card (similar to Pokémon cards) with a short description of a fictional animal character's characteristics (e.g., body characteristics, living habitats, life cycle steps, eating habits).

This unit can take approximately 1–2 weeks, depending on the extent to which your students are able to complete each of the activities (see Table 3.1).

Table 3.1. Daily Plan for ASL Animal Metamorphosis Unit

Day	Activities	Core Recommendation (CR)

Day 1	• Show an ABC animal story (e.g., https://www.youtube.com/watch?v=q3VpazGowaI).
	  ▪ Discuss various linguistic features that the storyteller uses to convey images and actions.
	  ▪ Create a classwide ABC animal story (using different animals).
	  ▪ Make a video of the animal story.
		CR 1, 2

Day 2	• Show an ASL animal story (e.g., Ian Sanborn's *Caterpillar* [2014, March 30] or *The Squirrel Story* [2014, April 23]).
	  ▪ Discuss various linguistic features that the storyteller uses to convey images and messages.
	  ▪ Use viewing comprehension questions to elicit their responses about the story before, during, and after viewing.
	  ▪ Discuss the story and its connection to life experience.
		CR 1, 2

Day 3	• Introduce the concept of metamorphosis and relate it to the ASL animal story.
	  ▪ Discuss how the storyteller depicts metamorphosis in ASL (review *Caterpillar* from Day 2).
	  ▪ Read and discuss books with various metamorphosis examples (life cycle of different animals).
		CR 1, 3

Day 4	• Have your students create and draw their own fictional animal character and make up an animal name in ASL. • Discuss physical characteristics of their animal and how they can describe them in ASL. • Discuss what changes their animal character would experience (metamorphosis); have them create a visual life cycle. • Have them select a storytelling genre and complete a visual storyboard about their animal character.	CR 1, 3
Day 5	• Share visual storyboards for constructive feedback. • Have them create and practice the story in ASL, and provide feedback.	CR 1, 2, 3
Day 6	• ASL composition activity: Students create a video of their story, have it reviewed, and re-do if necessary. • Have students follow the signing checklist to ensure that they have all expected parts (e.g., ASL name, metamorphosis, visual life cycle).	CR 1, 2, 3
Day 7	• Have them create a trading card with a short description of their fictional animal character's characteristics (e.g., body characteristics, living habitats, life cycle steps, eating habits).	
Day 8	• Showcase their ASL works and trading cards.	CR 2

Your Turn to Practice!

Now, it is your turn! Develop, teach, and reflect on a lesson integrating ASLLA and ASL literature. You can integrate ASLLA and/or literature into any reading/writing or content area subject. You can develop a new lesson or modify an existing lesson by incorporating ideas from this chapter as well as other content area chapters.

Develop a Lesson

- Develop or modify a lesson plan.
- Select an ASL standard.
- Add an ASLLA objective(s) to your content area lesson that provides students an opportunity to demonstrate their ASL language skills or ASL literature skills (e.g., viewing, signing, composing).
- Select procedures (at least one of following):
  - A focused discussion about ASL linguistic structure (e.g., semantics, grammar)
  - Opportunity for the students to compose in ASL
  - Connect ASL litreature to personal experience

Teach Your Lesson

Teach in your classroom or in a mock setting.

Reflect on Your Instruction

Reflect on your teaching by considering the following questions:

- What went well?
- What would you change/do differently if you taught this lesson again?
- After assessing your students, how well did they learn the targeted objectives?
- What benefits could you see for your students, such as:
  - Understanding of targeted ASL linguistic structures
  - Appreciation of the targeted areas of ASL literature
  - Usage of ASL to convey content area concepts clearly and accurately
  - Connecting ASLLA, ASL literature, and content area knowledge

Recommended Readings/Viewings

For Teachers/Teacher Candidates

- *Discussing Bilingualism in Deaf Children: Essays in Honor of Robert Hoffmeister* (Enns et al., 2021). Although this book discusses the theoretical underpinnings of bilingual Deaf education and teaching strategies, it has several ASL-related chapters that can help with pedagogy.

- *The Routledge Handbook of Sign Language Pedagogy* (Rosen, 2019). This book focuses on sign language pedagogy for first- and second-language learners. There are multiple excellent chapters on sign language for first-language learners.
- *Signing the Body Poetic: Essays on American Sign Language Literature* (Baumann et al., 2006) This book discusses various genres in ASL literature.
- "Sign Language in the Production and Appreciation of Humor by Deaf Children" (Sanders, 1986). This article discusses how deaf children can appreciate and create ASL humor and jokes.
- Sign2Read (https://www.sign2read.com). This site is a good resource for ASL phonology activities (e.g., Sign2Read, Hands Up!, ASL Word Wall, and ASL Handshape Games).

To Use With Students

- World Around You (https://deafworldaroundyou.org). The website has children's stories in different genres in multiple sign languages. The reader interface allows Deaf readers to view the story one page at a time. The crowdsourced website provides an authoring interface where one can assemble a sign language book for free.
- Motion Light Lab (https://motionlightlab.podia.com/courses/asl-literacy-activities). The website has original stories in ASL and learning activities related to the stories.
- ASLized (https://aslized.org/). This website has ASL stories in different genres.
- ASL Bowl (https://www.ksdeaf.org/aslbowl). This website calls for ASL stories in different genres for Deaf students to submit competitively.
- YouTube has numerous ASL literature–related videos that can be used for viewing.
- Hands Land (https://sites.google.com/handsland.com/handsland/home).

Conclusion

By high school graduation, Deaf students should be competent in at least ASL and English and be able to use them in academic settings. You can support this goal by creating opportunities for students to learn and appreciate ASL language arts and ASL literature while connecting to their additional home languages. In this chapter, we have provided suggestions on ways in which you can incorporate ASL language arts objectives throughout P–12 grade levels within all content areas. Deaf students benefit from instruction on grammar, usage, and literature of ASL. Embedding ASL language and literature throughout your classes can enrich your students' learning experiences as well as make learning more engaging.

Sticking Points

- Incorporate focused instruction on ASL structure, including grammatical features, mechanics, and usage into lessons.
- Reinforce awareness, appreciation, and creation of ASL literature.
- Provide multiple ASL language and literature opportunities across the curriculum.

Writing

Kimberly Wolbers
Sarah Jerger McGaughey

Chapter 4

Hello, teachers! The first thing we would like to tell you is that writing instruction can be motivating for your students, effective, and fun! Current and future teachers often express to us that they are unfamiliar with resources to teach writing to Deaf students. In this chapter, we share with you just that—motivating, research-based, and multilingual approaches to writing instruction that can be used with Deaf students across the grade span. In particular, we will introduce principles from a framework called Strategic and Interactive Writing Instruction (SIWI), which will provide you with an organizational system for your planning as well as a guide for instructional decisions during writing. SIWI is built on years of evidence-based writing instruction research, and it is also designed to address the unique language needs of Deaf students. Our hope is that, after reading this chapter, you not only build a stronger understanding of effective writing instruction but you also feel ready to implement multilingual approaches in your own teaching context with diverse Deaf students.

Who Are We?

I (Kimberly) was previously a middle and high school teacher of Deaf students for English and language arts. Although it has been several years, I remember the

---

The research reported here was supported by the Institute of Education Sciences, U.S. Department of Education, through Grant R324A170086. The opinions expressed are those of the authors and do not represent views of the Institute or the U.S. Department of Education.

Chew on This!

Did you know that . . . ?
Writing is referred to as the "Neglected R" (of reading, writing, and arithmetic) because it is given considerably less time and attention compared to reading and arithmetic.

- *What do we know about writing instruction with hearing students?* Elementary teachers provide, on average, 30 min per day of writing instruction and practice, and it is recommended that they double the time (Cutler & Graham, 2008; Graham et al., 2012). In middle and secondary classrooms, the time spent on writing is even more limited—students receive only 3 min of writing instruction in a 50-min period (Applebee & Langer, 2011).
- *What do we know about writing instruction with Deaf students?* Elementary and secondary teachers report 2–3 hours weekly on average of writing/language instruction and practice. Many teachers report instructional approaches that are misaligned with evidence-based practices in the field (Wolbers et al., 2022), and two-thirds of them say that writing and reading (and sometimes American Sign Language [ASL]) are taught in the same block and that they focus mostly on reading instruction (Wolbers et al., 2023).

challenges of providing instruction that would lead to positive gains in students' writing and language. I remember feelings of satisfaction followed by feelings of bewilderment when students correctly practiced English grammar features I had taught them but then failed to integrate those same skills into real writing. Questions around why students were not transferring what they were learning to their writing led me to explore writing instruction for Deaf students in a doctoral program. Now, as a professor of Deaf education at the University of Tennessee, my work involves collaborating with teachers across the grade span to implement and study the effectiveness of writing instruction with Deaf students and to widely disseminate practices because we have evidence to support them.

When I (Sarah) entered the field of elementary teaching, one of the biggest challenges was motivating students to write. I was in constant search of resources to support Deaf students with writing, but all resources were geared toward hearing students. In addition, I often had students with diverse abilities, and I felt that I needed to work individually with students on writing. I found it challenging to motivate students to write with me as their audience. After a summer of SIWI training, my whole perspective shifted, and I started to accommodate diverse student needs during group writing instruction. My students were motivated by the interactive approach and by having an authentic audience. Later, as an elementary principal at the Marie Philip School, I saw more than half of our elementary teachers and several secondary teachers follow the same approach with their students, and they also saw an increase in motivation and engagement in writing.

With the multilingual complexities that Deaf students often navigate, it is essential that they receive consistent, evidence-based writing instruction and supported practice. One step you can take today is to increase the time and attention you give to writing! Writing instruction will not only have a positive impact on students' writing but it has been shown to have a positive reciprocal effect on reading as well (Shanahan, 2016).

We look forward to sharing with you what we have learned over the years from research and classroom practice.

Deaf Experiences, Perspectives, and Core Recommendations

It is common for American Sign Language (ASL) lexicon and grammar, or the features of other languages, to be observed in Deaf students' writing. Such an occurrence illustrates that a student is developing as a multilingual being who is drawing on their full linguistic repertoire to communicate meaning. This phenomenon, known as **translanguaging** (García & Lin, 2017), is a natural practice of people exposed to multiple languages, regardless of whether that language is Spanish, Arabic, or ASL.

You may see Deaf developing writers use signed expressions in their writing, such as "touch Florida finish" in place of "visited." They may also use ASL syntax to convey meaning (e.g., "house house all over" as a plural form of *houses*; for more examples, see Wolbers et al., 2014). In the following two handstamp samples, we show how Deaf students draw on their ASL linguistic resources to facilitate the expression of ideas in writing. In Handstamp Sample 1, written by a 12-year-old student, you can see the use of the topic-comment structure, whereby a topic (e.g., "my memory") is linked to a comment (e.g., "that fun/enjoy"). In ASL, the topic is accompanied by a forward lean and raised eyebrows; however, the student may not be aware of all linguistic features, such as nonmanual markers, present in their expressions or be able to convey an equivalent in written English. Near the end of the sample, you can see that the student uses a rhetorical question, "How?" which serves as a connective element between ideas in ASL. Last, you can see the possible use of ASL listing, which involves the student pointing to their fingers to list items (e.g., "1. Hold the ball").

Key Vocabulary

Translanguaging is a person's linguistic resources that are fluidly integrated or dynamically interacting during acts of meaning-making through written, signed, or spoken languages.

Handstamp Sample 1

Handwritten Sample of a 12-Year-Old Deaf Student

My special memory is … Bowling. When I was 7 age old ago I has a fun and my Mom teach me how to bowling to hit pins. When I was 11 age old ago I know how hits pins. My memory that fun/enjoy! And I was 7 age old ago I must use gramp because I can't thrown this ball too heavy ball and plus I must use bumper. And when I was 11 age old ago I know how ball to hits pins How? 1. Hold the ball. 2. Walk and thown hit floor will be straight.

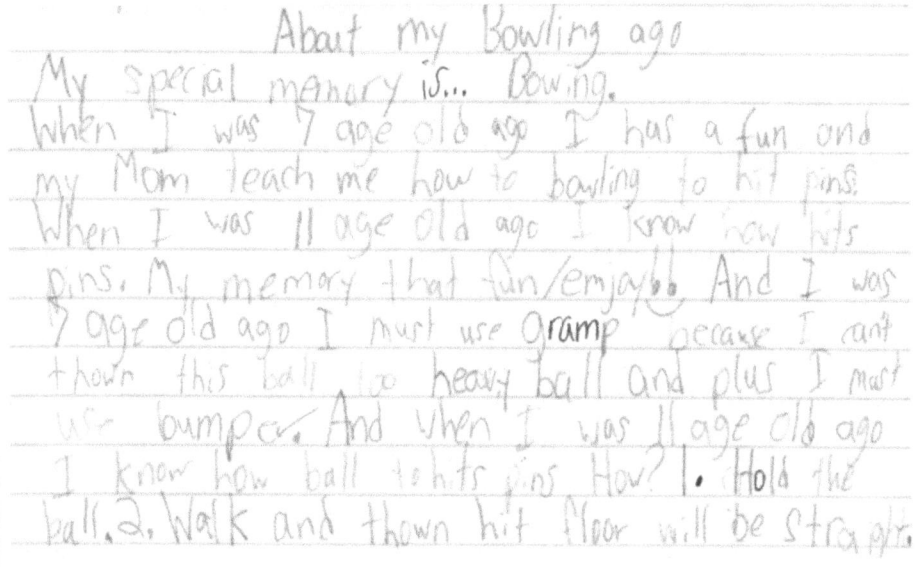

> Deaf students often express their ideas with an approach similar to anyone whose native language is not English. They sometimes use English words but follow their native language's grammar and syntax rules. They also occasionally use word-for-word translations that are not native-like. As a result, it can be helpful to step into their nonnative shoes in order to understand their writing. If something is unclear, I will "think in ASL," and that will often allow me to grasp its meaning. One such example is when a student wrote about the monster in Frankenstein, saying, "Now understand face ugly people hate me." Another is when a student wrote: "I remembered that never forget, I did broke my nose first time in my life!" By stopping and thinking in ASL or signing the sentence to myself, I can figure out what the student means.
>
> —Dynnelle Fields, secondary language arts teacher

In Handstamp Sample 2, a 14-year-old Deaf writer refers to two groups of students—those who are making fun of others (shown in boldface) and those who are on the receiving end of those jokes (shown as underlined). The writer provides loyalty and friendship to those affiliated with the underlined group while referring to the boldface group as working against others. Although the student's references to each group are not clearly conveyed in their writing, they are clearly communicated in ASL through the use of space and indexing (pointing). When signed, the student refers to each group of students on different sides of their body. In this case, the student was drawing on their knowledge of ASL to write English, and although clearly expressed in ASL, they were not fully successful in finding equivalent ways of expressing ASL linguistic features, such as body shifting, in English.

Handstamp Sample 2

Typed Writing Sample of 14-Year-Old Deaf Student
Well, **Someone was just Joke** to people and people don't Like it cuz they're sad. Sometime that problem Solve it and I want to be nice and **not to nice to destory to them. it their problem** with it. I want to work together with them "friendship." **yep! I challenge with them. yeah, but if they have solve a problem** and against us. We're friend not tell promise with anymore that your feel mood.

When writing, Deaf students draw on a full set of linguistic resources that has been developed over a lifetime of interactions and diverse language experiences. They may not be aware of socially constructed language boundaries (i.e., what is ASL, what is English, what is Spanish), and/or they may not have the linguistic tools to express their ideas fully in one language. As the linguistic competence of the multilingual student grows and as they increase their knowledge of languages as separate entities, their expressions over time will become more flexible to meet the demands of the communication situation (e.g., using ASL or English, or intentionally mingling languages when communicating with individuals who also know both). It follows that effective writing instruction with multilingual Deaf learners cannot focus solely on the teaching of English; rather, it must include, at a minimum, ASL and English language instruction. Teachers armed with translanguaging pedagogies—pointing out language boundaries, analyzing linguistic structures, comparing and contrasting languages' features, evaluating the equivalence of meaning in more than one language—provide linguistically responsive instruction that Deaf students need to become more flexible and knowledgeable language users (Wolbers et al., 2023).

Unfortunately, it is much less common for Deaf students to experience multilingual writing instruction compared to English grammar instruction. English grammar instruction with Deaf students, especially when decontextualized from authentic writing, has not provided much benefit to students. In our work with teachers of Deaf students, we often see grammar dominate the writing instruction time to the detriment of writing skill development. This leads to a situation where students may not show control over English grammar, nor do they effectively generate, organize, or convey their ideas to a reader. What is needed to combat this is a balanced, integrated approach—an approach that contextualizes multilingual instruction within meaningful and authentic writing. When you engage students in purposeful writing activities, you teach them to consider their reader's needs and naturally attend to both discourse-level writing (e.g., organization of ideas) and phrase-level language skills in order to communicate their ideas effectively.

Core Recommendations

In this chapter, we provide four core recommendations for writing instruction that will provide you with an evidence-based guide to multilingual writing instruction for Deaf students. The recommendations can be implemented with Deaf students at any level and for any type of writing. These recommendations align with four of the driving principles of the SIWI framework. For the full SIWI model, including additional principles, see the SIWI website (https://siwi.utk.edu).

1. Integrate **strategy instruction** with **visual supports.**
2. Apprentice students through guided, **interactive instruction.**
3. Build **metalinguistic knowledge and linguistic competence.**
4. Create **authentic** writing and published signing opportunities.

Effective Practices for Deaf Writers

In this section, we explain each of the four core recommendations for writing instruction with Deaf students and illustrate their meaning through classroom examples.

Core Recommendation 1: Integrate Strategy Instruction With Visual Supports

Strategy instruction in writing is one of the most high-impact approaches you can use, vetted in decades of research with hearing (Graham, 2006) and Deaf writers (Strassman & Schirmer, 2012). It involves explicitly teaching novice writers what proficient writers do when they write. You can make the ordinarily invisible cognitive processes of skilled writers accessible to your students by explicitly describing, modeling, and engaging them in supported practice. Further, by representing a writer's cognitive activities in visual ways, you can provide greater accessibility to new concepts. This is especially helpful for students developing multiple language competencies—to have, for example, writing concepts grounded in images bridging ASL, English, and other home languages. Although we will illustrate this through an example of teaching elementary students about the writing process, strategy instruction for writing in conjunction with visual scaffolds can be applied successfully at any level.

GOALS Writing Process
Strategy instruction of the writing process involves the explicit teaching of its recursive nature. Teachers can use a GOALS wall poster and individual student cue cards (see pictures). GOALS is an acronym that constitutes the writing processes:

Chew on This!

Did you know that . . . ?
- Contrary to what is traditionally taught in school, competent writers do not follow a sequence of separate and rigid writing stages (e.g., brainstorm, first draft, revise/edit, second draft).
- Rather, writing happens recursively, whereby the writer may generate initial ideas and then continually reread and revise their text while engaging in additional planning and generation.
- Writing processes are fluid and interactive rather than linear and ordered (Flower & Hayes, 1981).

- **G** is "Got ideas?" to represent the process of planning or brainstorming.
- **O** is "Organize" to prompt organizing one's ideas according to the genre text structure.
- **A** is "Attend to language" to remind students to incorporate language appropriate to the genre and writing purpose.
- **L** is "Look again" to cue students to reread the text they have generated and to make necessary revisions.
- **S** is "Share it" to represent publishing one's writing and sharing it with a reader.

> "My writing has improved . . . because the teachers would just tell us to write without any support. Now, we have a writing process that supports our stories and our English.
>
> —Sixth-grade student

In the center of the GOALS wall poster, there is a circle arrow around *WRITE*, which visually represents to students that writing can precede or follow any of the processes and that they can revisit any process while writing. Instead of progressing in sequence—first draft, reread, revise, second draft—students are continually prompted to reread and revise newly generated pieces of text. The teacher demonstrates recursive writing by moving a magnet atop the GOALS wall poster as the class zigzags and circles between different writing processes. They explicitly describe the process and make connections to the visual scaffold as they go, as demonstrated in the following Teacher Tale with fourth-grade students.

Teacher Tale

"Okay, we just wrote the second body paragraph (pointing to *WRITE* in the center of the GOALS poster). We reread the paragraph (pointing at *Look again*), and then Marquise noticed we forgot to mention how the skating accident happened. What do you say we brainstorm an idea (pointing at *Got ideas?*) and see where we can add it (pointing at *Organize*)?"

—Elizabeth Smith, fourth-grade teacher

The combination of expressed languages, visuals, and writing concepts, as provided in this example, is especially important for multilingual students. Through intentional linking of the signed summary to the words and visuals on the GOALS wall poster (or individual student cue cards), you can build conceptual understanding across languages.

GOALS wall poster for teaching the writing process.

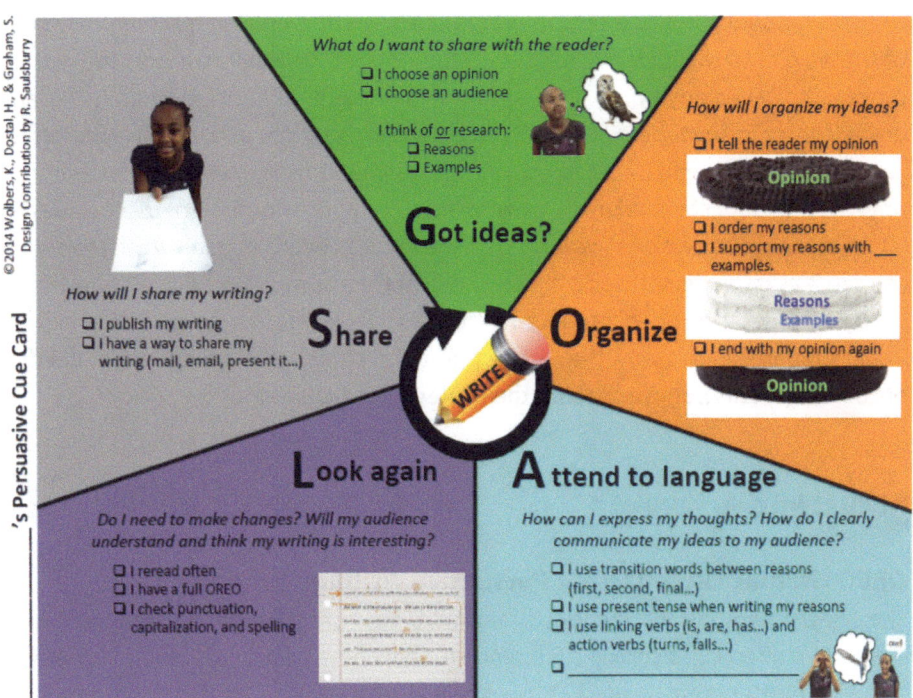

Individual student cue card for persuasive writing.

You can use individual student cue cards to accompany a writing process wall poster (like GOALS) and teach writing process strategies associated with specific genres of writing. (See picture for a cue card example of persuasive writing.) Encourage students to refer to the cue cards during group or individual writing. These cue cards have the same colors, pictures, and GOALS acronym as what is presented on the wall poster; in addition, there are checklists within each writing process to guide students' thinking and actions. You can also create laminated versions of the cue cards to allow students to erase and reuse them with each new writing project! Consider providing ASL-supported digital versions for your students as well (see https://prezi.com/rb3rjaixvdvj/asl-persuasive-writing-cue-card/). Cue cards are designed to prompt students to use more sophisticated composing process strategies than they do independently. It should be noted that cue cards can be provided for any type of writing at any level.

Graphic Organizers and Visual Scaffolds   During writing, you can provide students with graphic organizers to visually support them with the organizing process. Keep in mind that graphic organizers need to fit your students' current writing needs. The OREO graphic organizer (see Stick It Into Action) guides the writer to include the most essential elements of persuasive writing, which may be appropriate for beginners. As writers mature, the scaffolds also become more complex and may include, for example, counterclaims and rebuttals for each of the claims (see MILK figure), along with transition sentences between paragraphs. If you search "high school argumentative writing graphic organizers" online, it will instantly give you several good options. The key is to ensure that the level and complexity of the scaffolds align with your students' next writing objectives—not too high and not too low.

> "My kids took their FPMA (Florida Performance Measurement Assessment for Writing) today and for the FIRST time EVER, my students knew exactly what to do ... finding evidence, making their plan, etc., from two sources that are provided to them. They are confident with what they are doing and have a GOOD ATTITUDE about the whole procedure.
>
> —Krista Phelps-Elliot, elementary teacher

Visual supports like graphic organizers can be instrumental in teaching new skills or strategies to Deaf students. We just illustrated how to visually support the writing process; however, any number of writing or language skills, or genre traits (at any grade level or in any type of writing), can be explicitly taught and visually supported. For example, you might be teaching how to integrate sensory details or dialogue into one's writing of past experiences, how to include a counterargument in a persuasive letter, or how to reread one's writing with the reader's needs in mind. Visual supports can serve as reminders to apply the new skill at the appropriate time. With repeated practice, students will begin to internalize the strategies and become less reliant on visual supports. In this way, they are temporary scaffolds that are no longer needed once the students begin engaging the strategies independently.

Stick It Into Action!

OREO Graphic Organizer for Persuasive Writing

The OREO mnemonic (O, opinion; R, reasons; E, examples; O, opinion) is presented as a double-stuffed Oreo cookie to remind students how to structure their arguments and what elements are needed. This can be used along with a MILK graphic organizer if you observe that students are at the level of providing counterarguments.

Persuasive writing graphic organizers, OREO and MILK.

 **Key Strategy**

Compose in ASL

With multilingual Deaf students, it is desirable to draw on ASL strengths by teaching and practicing a wide range of skills and strategies in ASL. For example, writing process strategies (and the introduction of GOALS, genre-specific cue cards, and graphic organizers) can be incorporated into an ASL composing project aligned with the Published

Signing ASL Content Standards (Laurent Clerc National Deaf Education Center, 2018). For many Deaf students, they will develop knowledge and confidence in ASL and then be able to transfer what they know to writing English.

Share Mentor Texts

Another way to explicitly teach writing or language skills is to incorporate mentor texts such as books or ASL media publications into your instruction (see Chapter 5 for a definition of *mentor texts*). Students can see how other authors have communicated through writing/sign and try to adopt similar approaches. We recommend choosing publications that provide several examples of the students' targeted objectives for writing. When sharing publications, you play an instrumental role in explicitly pointing out writing or language features to students and encouraging them to imitate them in their own work. The same principles can apply to all levels. Even a postsecondary student who is working on a thesis will benefit from analysis of example text.

In this next Stick It Into Action, we provide an example of how you can use a storybook as mentor text for an elementary persuasive writing unit. *Dear Mrs. LaRue* (Teague, 2002) is about a dog named Ike who is sent to obedience school by his owner. Ike doesn't believe his behavior is as bad as his owner thinks, and he is insulted at being sent away to school. He sends daily letters to convince Mrs. LaRue to bring him back home. The letters are humorous and fun to read because they are from the dog's perspective. They serve as a good model on how to provide convincing reasons and examples in persuasive writing. In addition to modeling writing objectives, you can also use the text to illustrate language objectives.

Stick It Into Action!

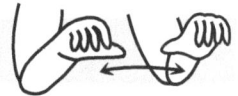

Share Mentor Texts

In the following excerpt from *Dear Mrs. LaRue,* the model language of focus is underlined. Here the teacher is working with students on using demonstrative pronouns (i.e., *this, that, these, those*) and modal verbs (i.e., *could, should, would*), which are frequently used in argumentative types of writing.

> Dear Mrs. LaRue (October 1),
> How **could** you do **_this_** to me? **_This_** is a PRISON, not a school! You **should** see the other dogs. They are BAD DOGS, Mrs. LaRue! I do not fit in. Even the journey here was a horror. I was very unhappy and may need something to chew on when I get home. Please come right away!
>
> Sincerely,
> Ike

- After reading the text together, you could explicitly point out the language features to students, using the contextualized examples from the book to aid understanding.
- You can then ask students to hunt for more examples.

You can also use ASL publications to explicitly discuss ASL linguistic features and their English equivalents. For example, in the ASL video *Yummy Cookies* (https://www.youtube.com/watch?v=99p00sX8L3A), Holcomb (2020b) models the use of *could, should,* and *would* in ASL. In the classroom, you might first explain how these are similar to and different from *can, need,* and *will.* You might also chain the signs to the written and/or fingerspelled versions of *could, should,* and *would* while discussing the story. In another example video, called *Let's Go for a Walk* (https://www.youtube.com/watch?v=m_ovqeVsEA8), Holcomb (2020b) demonstrates clear use of near versus far pointing, and singular versus plural pointing, which can then be related to demonstrative pronouns in English (*this/that* and *these/those*).

Core Recommendation 2: Apprentice Students Through Guided, Interactive Instruction

Learning a new skill on your own is very challenging. Whether we are learning how to ski, draw self-portraits, or solve quadratic equations, we often rely on the coaching and guidance of others who are more knowledgeable. Even though writing is often a solitary act, the process of developing new writing knowledge and skills is interactive, like learning to ride a bike.

Having just taught our children how to ride bikes, this analogy is fresh in our minds. You may recall your early biking experiences as well. When a child first gets on a two-wheel bike, they must learn how to pedal, stop, steer, keep aware of their surroundings, and, most important, balance. We would not send them off on their own to learn these skills; rather, we provide a substantial amount of support to begin. We stand close to the bike, perhaps with one hand on the handlebar and one hand on the seat, as they wobble to gain momentum. We talk with them about the biking process before, during, and after attempts at biking, all while providing encouragement and reassurance. As they begin to get a handle on various skills, growing in their biking confidence, we loosen our grip or reduce support to one hand on the seat. If at any time they start to lose control or call for help, we can move in quickly to provide stability again. After repeated practice with our support and coaching, they show increased independence and less reliance on us. They pull away without our assistance, and although we may run beside them for a time until we are certain of their skills, they demonstrate to us increasingly that they've got this!

Similarly, it is important that you provide sufficient support for your students in applying new writing skills and that you gradually decrease that support over time as they gain greater facility. During joint writing activities, for example, you (along with other students at times) will serve as more expert writers and will apprentice novice writers in the cognitive processes of writing. This is known as **cognitive apprenticeship in writing** and involves **thinking aloud during collaborative writing activity** (see definition on p. 79 and Chapter 2 for examples of thinking aloud in early childhood). Revealing cognitive processes during the act of writing makes the tacit knowledge of writers visible and tangible. Over time, novice writers increasingly appropriate the thought processes needed to direct writing activity.

You may think aloud, pair dialogue with modeled activity, engage students in supported problem-solving sequences, co-construct new understandings with students, or ask metacognitive questions such as "how" or "why" to get students to externalize their thinking.

> "I went from nothingness to kids that are excited about writing, and they feel confident. In all my years of teaching and struggling to figure out how to get kids to write, I don't know why I never thought of writing together. I guess I would have thought it was cheating, with everybody working together, but that's how you learn."
>
> —Kendra Grosso, elementary teacher

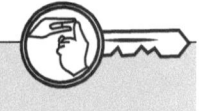

Key Vocabulary

Cognitive apprenticeship in writing is a significant tenet of sociocultural theory applied to writing instruction, whereby transfer of knowledge can occur through social interaction when the thoughts of expert writers are made accessible to novice writers (Englert et al., 2006).

Cognitive Apprenticeship

In SIWI, cognitive apprenticeship happens during group interactive writing as the teacher and students co-construct written pieces. From the initial brainstorming of ideas to final edits, students proceed through the writing process together. The teacher aims to keep classroom interaction at a level that is challenging for students but not frustrating or overwhelming. To accomplish this, we suggest grouping students of somewhat similar writing levels. (*Note:* You will be able to differentiate instruction for students who are at slightly higher or lower levels, but it will be difficult to do this if students are at very different levels.) It is recommended that you assess students' writing prior to group interactive writing and use ongoing formative assessment to select writing and language objectives that are slightly beyond students' current levels of performance. For example, you may begin with objectives for including sensory details and past tense action verbs in personal narrative (or recount) writing because students are not currently embedding these features accurately or independently. When writing together, much of the interactive dialogue and problem solving is focused around these objective areas. You "step back" to allow students to demonstrate control over learned skills and "step in" to model, think aloud, or co-construct understanding in unfamiliar areas (Englert et al., 2006).

Key Strategy

Thinking Aloud During Writing

This means sharing one's thoughts externally while engaged in writing. Teachers will think aloud to provide a window into their thought processes with the intention of encouraging similar cognitive activity among their students when writing.

Stick It Into Action!

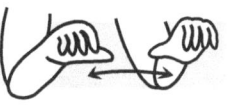

Thinking Aloud During Group Interactive Writing

Here is an example of thinking aloud during group, interactive writing.

> Teacher: I am thinking that our reader might be confused when we write *she* here (pointing to the text). We just talked about a mother and daughter. How will the reader know which person we are referring to? I wonder how we can make that more clear for the reader.

It is evident through this example that the teacher would like the students to review their writing with the reader's needs in mind and be able to locate spots that may cause confusion.

Guided, interactive writing provides a space where Deaf students can receive support with practicing the skills and processes of multilingual writers. Students receive help from the teacher and their class peers with finding words and phrases that

> "After multiple recount units written as a group with LOTS of rereading as we went, I noticed my students were finally starting to use "I" or "we" as the subject of their sentences (as opposed to using their own name), using their personalized resource binders of word banks to locate the spelling of these words. Even further, two of them actually began to independently write the subject without even looking in their resource binders!
>
> —Tori Wilson, elementary teacher

Student demonstrates greater writing independence to his teacher, Glennise Schlinger.

represent the meaning they hope to convey, or with translating ideas to English after expressing them in ASL. Whether generating language associated with one's ideas or finding meaning equivalence across languages, there is sufficient guidance (and thinking aloud) from more knowledgeable participants to promote greater language control and independence. As you observe students gaining independence over the targeted skills, you can swap the objectives for something more challenging. Group, interactive writing can be especially useful to multilingual Deaf students who will not only gain access to cognitive processes but also the language associated with the thought processes.

Shared Personal Reflections

> "I prefer writing with others. It helps me a lot.
> —Third grader

During guided, interactive writing, we encourage you to share with students your own struggles, confusions, or questions about writing. Show them when you are thinking or weighing options. They will begin to see that there are many ways to approach writing (as opposed to one right answer) and that writing can be challenging at times, even for the teacher. In our current and previous professions as professor, principal, and teachers, we have years of experience writing for various tasks—from professional emails to letters of recommendation to research manuscripts—and yet, we rarely see ourselves as fully competent writers. Rather, we view ourselves as "works in progress"! We know that writing takes concerted effort, time, and ongoing revision. When we look back on our earlier work, we see it as less developed than our writing now, and we predict we will have this same feeling 20 years from now when looking back on this chapter. Writing development is ongoing throughout our lives if we keep an open mind to continuous learning. Why not share this message with novice writers, especially multilingual students who are navigating complex language demands during writing? Although writing can be challenging, we can develop our skills with time and effort, which can be rewarding and enjoyable. Students who understand this begin to commit to the work, feel empowered that they are actively steering their development, and gain confidence and motivation for writing.

Teacher Tale

Across the year, I saw a change in the volume of off-task behaviors. For example, at the beginning of the year, students would quickly withdraw from writing activities if they perceived themselves to be wrong or if there was a possibility of being incorrect. Writing time in the classroom was, at first, a time filled with frustration and behaviors such as shoving papers off desks or looking away from signed communication. That changed as students began to understand that writing is complex and challenging for all of us and that we are continuously developing greater skill. In guided, interactive writing they learned there is no one correct way to write. There are many ways to effectively communicate our messages. They began to see that they were gaining the knowledge and skills needed to write through the active and interactive group writing. The more effort they put in, the more they took away. I remember the day a student told me, "Last week when you were absent, we decided we needed one hour to write." I thought to myself, "When did these students start to see themselves as writers?" Much later when reflecting on her own progress from the start of the year, Kasie said, "It was tough when I entered middle school, we didn't know how to write, but now that we know what authors do, we are authors."

—*Hannah Dostal, former middle grades teacher*

Core Recommendation 3: Build Metalinguistic Knowledge and Linguistic Competence

One of the most important things we can do to facilitate the success of Deaf writers is to support their language knowledge and development. The act of composing is more achievable when students have metalinguistic knowledge and a strong language foundation. Akin to constructing a new home, when there are cracks, crevices, or gaping holes in the foundation, the house built on that foundation is wobbly and unsteady. Instruction that builds students' (a) **metalinguistic awareness** and (b) linguistic competence can strengthen the foundation and stabilize the house of writing sitting on it.

Metalinguistic Awareness and Writing

Earlier in the chapter, we learned about translanguaging and how students utilized the knowledge they have across multiple languages to express their ideas in writing. Explicit language instruction can increase metalinguistic awareness of their languages' lexicon and syntactic structures, which helps them to compare/contrast and find equivalencies of expressions across languages. This approach has been effective with multilingual students and specifically with Deaf students to increase language knowledge of language boundaries (Wolbers et al., 2013).

An important step in providing explicit language instruction is first recognizing students' use of linguistically rich ASL. As a visual, spatial language, nuances in meaning can be conveyed through facial grammar, body language, repeated or enlarged sign movement, intensity, or concepts related in space. Meanings can also be expressed simultaneously rather than sequentially as in English. Take, for example, a person telling about a time they went bike riding (see p. 82). The same sign for bike riding is given additional meaning through facial expressions and/or sign movement

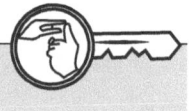

Key Vocabulary

Metalinguistic awareness is the ability to think about, talk about, and analyze language structure and use.

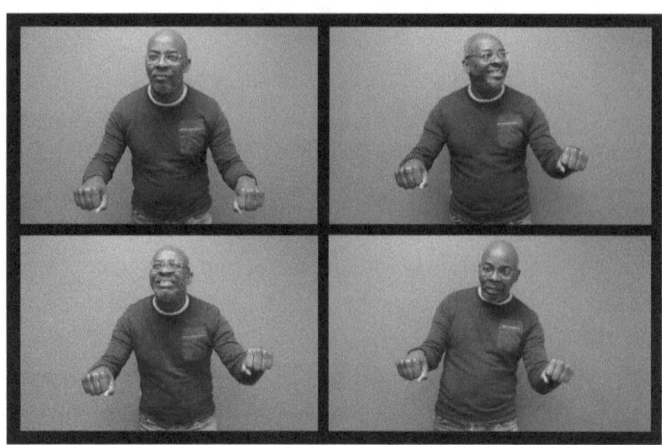

Nenio Mbazima, Deaf author and film producer, signs BIKE RIDING four different ways.

(i.e., clockwise, starting top left: determined bike riding, proud bike riding, challenging bike riding, nervous bike riding).

As mentioned in Chapter 3, you can heighten students' awareness of ASL by identifying the ASL linguistic properties in their expressions, or by modeling and explicitly discussing your expressions. Once you have brought attention to specific ASL language elements, you can guide students in a discussion of how variations add meaning, provide subtle distinctions, or change one's expression. You can discuss how the same concepts can be expressed equivalently in English. Through this process, students come to see the differences in grammars and are provided with supported practice in finding equivalences across languages. As a teacher participant, you are not only vital to apprenticing students in the development of writing skills through interactive writing, you are also instrumental in guiding translation processes and gradually transferring control to students as they increase their metalinguistic knowledge.

In the following Teacher Tale, Darcy McAfee shares how ASL and English equivalencies become the focus of instruction during group, interactive writing in her elementary classroom. During this lesson, one student served as the lead author, sharing his experience of sleeping over at a friend's house. The class worked together to compose a paper that recounted his experience. When the lead author described the sleeping arrangement using ASL classifiers for bunk beds, Darcy took the opportunity to provide specific ASL-English language instruction, using a space called the **language zone.**

You can see in this Teacher Tale how Darcy connected concepts to both languages through chaining (Humphries & MacDougall, 1999) of the picture, signs, fingerspelling, and the printed words. This practice raises students' metalinguistic awareness and highlights language equivalence (Swanwick, 2017). It also conveys to students that ASL is welcome in the writing space and can facilitate our thinking. Students come to see that even though ASL and English have different grammars, they are equally powerful, linguistically complex languages through which they can express their writing-related thoughts and knowledge.

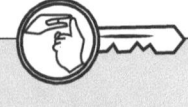

Key Vocabulary

The **language zone** is a three-dimensional space where explicit attention is given to language through drawing and labeling concepts; listing equivalent language options; role playing for clarification; or using concrete objects, pictures, or videos to anchor new language.

WRITING

Teacher Tale

Student 1	Did you sleep there?
Lead Student Author	Yes. [Signs one flat hand in space above his other flat hand.]
Teacher	How fun! You can climb to the top and sleep there! Those are so fun! What are those called?
Student 2	Bunk beds (voiced)

[Teacher begins drawing bunk beds on the easel while students in the classroom talk with each other about their prior experiences sleeping in bunk beds.]

Teacher	When you have two beds [pointing to picture], they're called bunk beds [fingerspelled]. [The teacher writes the words *bunk beds* on the easel next to the picture.] I know you slept [uses flat hands, one in space above the other]. In English, we call those bunk beds [pointing to picture and words while fingerspelling].
Teacher	Where did you sleep?
Lead Student Author	[Places one flat hand out to represent bottom bunk, points to himself, and then uses his free hand to show himself lying in the space above.]
Teacher	On the top? [Signing TOP? while pointing to the top bed in the drawing.]
Lead Student Author	Yes.
Teacher	[Teacher draws the student and his name on the top bunk bed and then writes *on the top*.]

—Darcy McAfee, Instructional Coach

> "SIWI has allowed them to finally identify that their language, ASL, is of value and unique, along with English. By validating their bilingual abilities, students' self-esteem improves, their excitement to express their ideas increases, and their willingness to participate soars. The students with whom I've seen the most success have been those who traditionally are considered low-language learners. [Translating from ASL to English] has been the most significant with that population of students, and they discover that they do have excellent ideas and thoughts to add.
>
> —Camille Benson, middle grades teacher

(MM) Linguistic Competence

In addition to increasing metalinguistic awareness, it's important to highlight the need for continued language acquisition and development. Linguistic competence is critical to creating clear and complex expressions, and it works in tandem with metalinguistic awareness to strengthen the foundation on which writing sits. In fact, you cannot possibly teach all aspects of language, so to a great extent, writers must rely on their "language gut." You can tell hearing people are using their language gut when they say things like, "That part doesn't sound right" or "Something sounds off here." They may not be able to tell you the name of the language feature or the specific language rule, but they can identify which part is wrong and needs to be changed. Deaf writers rely on a similar language gut—whether it's based on what sounds right, what looks right, or what feels right. In addition, simply having more options for vocabulary and phrases in one's language repertoire provides greater opportunity for communicating thoughts. Therefore, an important question for us to consider as teachers is, *How we can create opportunities for our students to grow their linguistic competence?*

Linguistic Competence in ASL We believe the highly interactive nature of SIWI contributes to growth in ASL proficiency. During guided, interactive writing, students are actively engaged in thinking about and talking about what needs to happen in the writing. At times, you provide language models through think-alouds, and at other times, you extend or guide class discussions. You can also ask metacognitive types of questions, such as "how" or "why," which require higher levels of critical thinking or reasoning, and therefore more advanced, complex language in students' responses. The focus and level of classroom dialogue, along with immediate feedback due to the threaded nature of the interaction, is known to advance students' ASL expressions.

Linguistic Competence in English   Even though English is not often the language of classroom discussion with Deaf students, there are opportunities to grow English linguistic competence during guided, interactive writing. One important writing process is rereading one's writing. Expert writers reread their writing several times during the composing process. In our experience working with novice writers, this is a skill that must be taught and practiced until they naturally engage in the practice themselves. During guided, interactive writing, you can continually prompt students to reread the last few sentences, the last section, or the entire co-constructed text to then make judgments about what revisions are needed or to generate the next ideas. In this way, they practice recursive writing. For Deaf writers, we believe that rereading the co-constructed text serves another important function—English language acquisition. Because the students generate, express, and discuss the ideas in the text, there is a shared understanding of what the writing means or communicates. In addition, in the guided, interactive writing space, you work together with students to advance and correct the initial English contributions. Thus, the English text that is continually reread is mutually understood, grammatically accurate, and at a slightly higher level than each student's initial contribution, which provides opportunities for growing English linguistic competence.

Core Recommendation 4: Create Authentic Writing and Published Signing Opportunities

Through collaborative writing, students can experience writing for real audiences with the support of the teacher and other students. Together, you can discuss what ideas to include and how to communicate them clearly so that the reader or viewer is effectively entertained, persuaded, moved, or haunted. Students soon learn that writing or published signing has the power to evoke emotion or action in others. This knowledge often leads to deeper engagement in the generating and revising process, and students become more involved in the decision making. Their interest in writing grows, especially when they have control over what they write, to whom, and for what purpose. This experience stands in stark contrast to artificial class assignments that carry no real purpose or relevance.

Having an authentic purpose for composing can be a motivating force. *Authentic* means having a real reason for communicating with a specified audience and sometimes receiving a reply. For example, one fifth-grade class wrote to an educational software company to inform them that their videos were not accessible to Deaf students and provided an argument for the addition of captions. Another Grade 7–8 class created ASL poetry about the grandparents or elders in their lives and then performed their poetry during a seniors evening at the Deaf Community Center. In these ways, students experienced what it is like to be published authors, interacting directly with

Chew on This!

Did you know that . . . ?
Prior research shows that students' ASL proficiencies (as measured by mean length of ASL utterances) and written English fluency (as measured by text length and number of clauses) significantly grow during SIWI implementation while unintelligible utterances decline (Dostal & Wolbers, 2014).

readers/viewers for the purpose of informing, persuading, entertaining, or emotionally moving them (see Chapters 3, 5, 7, and 12 for additional examples). As demonstrated in the following two Teacher Tales, one of the outcomes of an authentic approach to writing is that students begin to see the full utility of writing as they publish different types for a variety of audiences (Bruning & Horn, 2000). They can see the purpose and the power of published writing/signing in action.

> **Teacher Tale**
>
> I contacted Rochester School for the Deaf (RSD) and they connected me with another third-grade teacher who taught there. I informed her that my students would be sending a letter to her students sharing a fun educational activity related to prepositions. She was enthusiastic about the collaboration. My students played Follow the Leader in which they followed exactly what I did across campus, inside and outside (e.g., crawled through the tunnel at the playground, skipped around the playground, slid down the slide, hopped over the lines). They then wrote about the activity in a letter format with pictures and sent it to the third-grade students at RSD. RSD sent them a response letter thanking them. The RSD students did an activity where they looked for their Deaf stuffed animal friend "Walter the Wolf." When they found him in different places, they wrote down full sentences with a preposition in each and then sent a letter to my students about their experience. My students were thrilled to read their letter. This experience was highly motivating for my students and the RSD third graders, which helped them understand prepositions, past tense irregular verbs, and writing a recount letter.
>
> —*Jennifer Jones, elementary teacher*

(MM) Balancing Language and Writing Instruction

Another benefit of authentic writing in classrooms with Deaf multilingual students is that when you write for real purposes and audiences, it can help you keep your instruction balanced. This means that you are providing apprenticeship opportunities addressing both writing and language skills. Deaf students have a history of receiving instruction that is unbalanced—too heavily focused on English grammar, English vocabulary, and spelling due to errors in their written language that are different from native English users. Using the majority of instructional time on grammar instruction squeezes out opportunities for students to learn about process, craft, voice, and genre traits, and there isn't much evidence to support decontextualized grammar instruction. Rather, grammar instruction when contextualized in student writing has proven beneficial (Berent et al., 2007). Furthermore, engaging in purposeful writing and having a reader in mind forces students to reflect on whether their ideas are powerful and well organized, as well as whether they are communicated clearly in English. In our research and experience, we have found that a balanced approach—with grammar instruction contextualized in authentic writing—is effective in producing gains in both grammar and writing skills among Deaf students (Bowers et al., 2018; Wolbers et al., 2018, 2022).

Teacher Tale

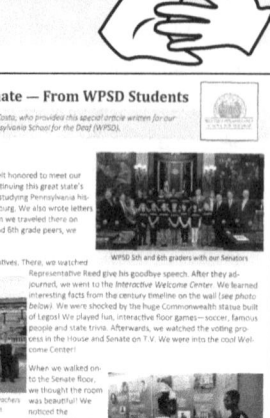

One year, my sixth-grade students were impassioned to change a school policy that an adult must accompany them during class changes. They observed that seventh- and eighth-grade students were allowed to transition independently and wanted to do the same. They were fueled and motivated by this desire to change what they considered to be an unjust rule. They determined that they could write to persuade the school administrators to make a change. Their argument was that the sixth graders are demonstrating responsibility and the know-how to transition to and from various points on campus without an escort. They worked to include several reasons and examples to support their claims. They also included counterarguments they anticipated receiving back from administrators—for example, why the policy was put in place—and then offered strong rebuttals.

Thank-you note from Western Pennsylvania School for the Deaf students published in the Pennsylvania Secretary of the Senate's *Dispatch*.

They worked very hard to ensure they were heard. In the end, the administration granted them the ability to change classes independently while also stressing that the privilege could be revoked again if there were any mishaps. Students were elated that they were successful in evoking this change and started to see the power of their own writing!

Another time, we visited Harrisburg to meet the students' senators and representatives. During our walk on the Senate floor, we noticed a senate publication. We asked for a copy and how we could write for it. Together, we wrote a thank-you note in the form of a recount. It was an exciting day. They published it in the next issue with photos of us!

—*Mary Nochese, middle grades teacher*

Additional Things to Consider

 Setting Up the Classroom for Instruction

Here are some tips for setting up your classroom space so that you can integrate strategy instruction and language support into your guided, interactive writing with Deaf students.

1. A main whiteboard or smart board is often used for the co-construction process. With older students, you can pass around a wireless keyboard for students to add their thoughts or edit throughout the writing process.

> "High school students want their teachers to know what motivates them to write. "When we get to choose what to read or what to write about, it's easier to get interested in something."
> —Lauraliz (Cushman, 2005, p. 106)

2. To the side of the shared writing space is a language zone. The language zone includes a drawing/writing surface and floor space for individuals to role play, gesture, and so forth. Having the language zone nearby allows students to be able to fluidly enter and exit the zone throughout the writing process. Some teachers have opted to set up an easel or whiteboard, whereas some teachers use a flipboard. Using large sheets of paper allows teachers to post the language zone after writing is complete and use it for extension activities such as vocabulary, spelling, or ASL/English phrase equivalencies.
3. You might provide each student with a small whiteboard at their seats to jot down quick ideas and thoughts to share with the class.
4. Visual supports, such as GOALS and a graphic organizer, are close by for the class to use throughout the writing process. These can be class-size posters on the wall or projected electronically. When students are working independently or in small groups, they may use small laminated versions in their writing binders or write on printed copies.
5. Some teachers set up a graduation wall for students to hang accomplished objectives or visual scaffolds that are no longer needed. This is one way the class can celebrate and reflect on their progress.
6. With emergent writers, you might collect pictures from students' home lives. The pictures capture events they experience and can be used to generate ideas for writing. This is a great way to integrate students' home lives, cultures, and traditions. Pictures can also be used in the language zone to facilitate the chaining of concepts and languages.
7. You may also create a space for posting responses from your readers.

> During a school break, I asked each of my students to take pictures of activities they did at home with their families. (For some students, this meant visiting a haunted house, going bowling, or having a family night in with dinner and a movie!) The students then got to bring their family experiences into the classroom and share with their peers.
>
> —Tori Wilson, elementary teacher

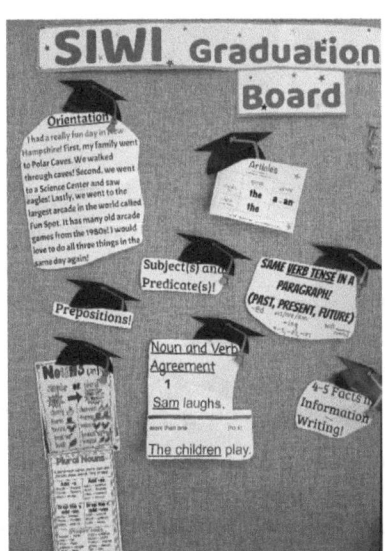

Elementary teacher Jennifer Jones has a graduation wall in her classroom.

Elementary teacher Stephanie Alves de Lima has a reader response board in her classroom.

Writing and Language Delays

When teaching writing to students with language delays, the instructional approach must center on language acquisition and development first and foremost. Commonly, students who write unintelligible phrases or scrambles of letters/words exhibit large gaps and crevices in their language foundations and do not demonstrate age-appropriate competencies in any expressive/receptive language—ASL, English, or otherwise. For example, one middle school student writes, "I want be need do know" and another writes, "My is my dad how ball." An elementary student writes, "cat you ah is so is pay so is so you is you yes is pay is yes." Unintelligible written utterances such as these do not resemble English or ASL, or any other language.

During guided, interactive writing, when a student's contribution is not understood by the others, or your suggestion is not understood, you can work with the class using the language zone to get to a point of shared understanding. You can identify breakdowns in communication as they occur by continually assessing students' expressed thoughts or responses. The language zone offers many options for repairing breakdowns and getting everyone on the same page! You might:

- Ask a student to draw or act out what they are trying to communicate.
- Use a concrete object, a picture, or a website to confirm a student's expression.
- Involve another student or adult to act as a middle person. (The middle person may understand more because of shared experience, context, or knowledge of the student.)
- Ask open-ended questions. (Avoid leading questions that contain ideas or language the student may not understand, which can result in further breakdowns in communication.)

In the following Teacher Tale, we take a look into Katie Leith's classroom to see an example of how language zone approaches are applied during guided, interactive writing.

Teacher Tale

Yasmeen was the author of the day and she wanted to tell us about a time when a pan of chicken caught fire in her kitchen. She started by telling us, "the chicken burn off." To help the author give enough information and to help the other students think of questions to ask the author, I had *Who, What, Where, When, Why,* and *How* written in our prewriting space. Yasmeen started to answer. She told us her mom put the "yellow hot" in the pan. I did not want to assume to know what she was describing, so we asked her to explain further. She said that her mom "give the pan the yellow hot" and "give the pan the chicken." When writing verbatim what Yasmeen said, I underlined "yellow hot," and we tried to figure out another word that would give the reader more info. Yasmeen answered some questions from other students, and we figured out that it was something her mom put in the pan first. Using the smart board, I quickly searched images that the whole class could see. I showed them an image for butter, but it was wrong. Yasmeen was gesturing that someone was pouring as she explained again the "yellow hot." Another teacher in the room guessed it. I looked up a picture of vegetable oil on the computer, and we had a winner! We took a few minutes for every student to express "vegetable oil" and tell about a time they saw it used in the kitchen. We kept the image on screen while Yasmeen told the rest of her story.

—Katie Leith, former elementary teacher

When you persevere through communication breakdowns and ensure understanding among members, there is an opportunity for language growth. Ultimately, you are building a stronger foundation of writing for your students. In the example from Katie's class, the teacher and peer students worked to ensure everyone understood. Once they had a mutual understanding, the teacher intentionally paired language with the concrete meaning in the language zone—in this case, the picture of vegetable oil. From this point forward, the students of the writing community used the newly learned language, and they repeatedly chained the picture with writing and signed, spoken, and/or fingerspelled expressions.

(ABAR) (MM) Bringing It All Together

Here, we share one fifth-grade teacher's unit on Martin Luther King Jr. (MLK) to illustrate each of the core recommendations in practice. The unit is broken down by day to show how the class progressed, from establishing a purpose and audience for their writing to final publication. You can learn about what was happening before and after the writing unit from the teacher in the Teacher Tale.

Teacher Tale

Anti-bias teaching was a big focus in my fifth-grade classroom all last year. We discussed bias in other people as well as bias within ourselves. We discussed segregation, Jim Crow, peaceful protests, nonpeaceful protests, and touched on the Black Panther Party. We discussed the Black Lives Matter movement and how it is not appropriate for force to be used against peaceful protesters. After a very long unit on racism in the United States, and reading about Black people like Rosa Parks and Frederick Douglass, we then co-constructed an information report on Martin Luther King, Jr. using SIWI. With the MLK group construction, they researched information individually and in pairs to fill in the popsicles (or subtopics; see information report graphic organizer on p. 91), and then we wrote together. Students also independently wrote information reports about different Black Americans. After we went remote due to COVID-19, George Floyd was murdered. We talked about it as a group (what they saw, what they knew, questions they had, feelings), and we read an article together that Scholastic News released. We discussed the history of slavery, past racism in America, and current racism in America. These were all used to compare what is happening today in America to what happened in the past. After all of the articles, class discussions, and teaching, students

> "I used SIWI with a group of middle school students who had very little first language, which meant instruction was carried out in slow and careful ways. Our first guided, interactive constructions included gestures, dancing, anything we could do to express our meaning. The language zone became our best friend. We lived there, we slept there, we ate there. Moving from their understanding of gestures to language was slow but it happened. The students never took total control of an entire publication, but that was okay. After co-constructing together for some time, students could start to write independently at the word and sentence level and then those became part of the construction. Realizing that students can write independently, even if that means at the most basic level, was empowering for them and for me.
>
> —Casey Spencer, middle grades and secondary education teacher

> were asked to write a reflection piece, using guided questions, on what is currently happening in America while thinking about America's past.
>
> —*Suzanne Lippy, elementary teacher*

Table 4.1. MLK Unit Daily Activities

Day	Activities	Core Recommendation (CR)
Day 1	I introduced a new writing topic (MLK biography). I shared two different MLK biographies as mentor texts to illustrate and discuss text features. I provided explicit instruction on the differences between writing recounted experiences (familiar genre) and information reports (unfamiliar).	CR 1: Strategic
Day 2	We used GOALS scaffold to begin the writing process. We determined the audience and purpose together. We used the organizational scaffold with popsicles to brainstorm the facts we knew. We created possible subtopics together.	CR 1, 2, 4: Strategic and visual supports, interactive, authentic
Day 3	Pairs of students chose one subtopic each. Each pair researched a subtopic. They took notes in English together and later shared the ideas in ASL with the full class.	CR 2, 3: Interactive, metalinguistic/linguistic
Day 4–5	The class added more facts to the popsicle organizer from the paired research. Students worked together to create sentences that represent the ideas in the graphic organizer. I typed the language students gave me. We discussed some language differences or confusions as they arose. We continually reread and revised the text while generating next ideas.	CR 1, 2, 3: Strategic and visual supports, interactive, metalinguistic/linguistic
Day 6	We continued to reread and revise the text. We added and edited text to clarify our message for the readers.	CR 2, 3, 4: Interactive, metalinguistic/linguistic, authentic
Day 7–8	Students reread the writing in pairs. Each pair was assigned to review a piece of the report with an editing checklist. They used laptops and made changes to the shared online document. Students reread with the audience in mind, adding and revising information for greater clarification.	CR 2, 3, 4: Interactive, metalinguistic/linguistic, authentic
Day 9	Each pair explained the edits they made. I guided further revision where needed. A final report was printed to share with the readers (see Handstamp Sample).	CR 2, 3, 4: Interactive, metalinguistic/linguistic, authentic

MLK Unit in Suzanne Lippy's Fifth-Grade Classroom

Purpose: To inform about MLK (see Table 4.1).
Audience: The school's students, staff, and visitors. In the hallway, there was a bulletin board to honor MLK. Various classes contributed and learned from the board.

Handstamp Sample

Suzanne Lippy's Class Publication on Martin Luther King Jr.

We will discuss about Martin Luther King, Jr. and how he made the USA a better place. His great protests were peaceful and he tried to change America.

Martin Luther King Jr. was born on January 15, 1929, in Atlanta, Georgia. His father was a minister in a Black church. He taught Martin all about religion and believed in him that he could change the world. Also, MLK had a very good white friend. They always played together outside until the white boy's parents told him he couldn't play with Martin anymore because he was Black.

In 1944, Martin graduated from T. Washington High School. He skipped his freshman and senior year of high school and graduated when he was 15 years old. He was also quarterback of his football team. In addition, he competed in many public speaking competitions during high school that helped him become more skilled with his powerful words. After graduating, he enrolled at Morehouse College in Atlanta and graduated with a degree in theology. After Morehouse College he got a scholarship at Crozer Theological Seminary in Chester, Pennsylvania to study theology. He was elected student body president. He graduated as valedictorian, the top student in his

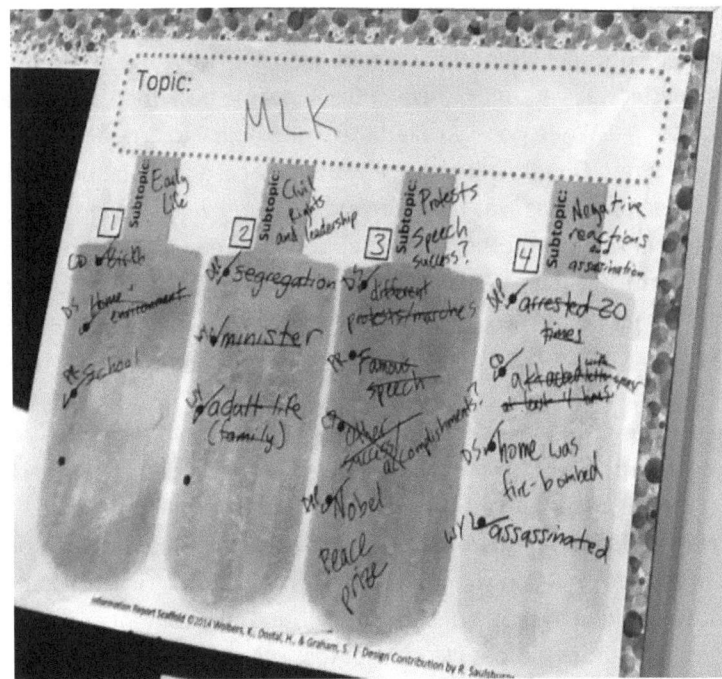

Information report graphic organizer used to organize the group's ideas on MLK.

Handstamp Sample (*continued*)

class, and won the Pearl Plafker award. Next, he went to Boston University and got his Ph.D. in theology and became Dr. Martin Luther King Jr.

At Boston University, he met his future wife, Coretta. They were married on June 18, 1953, in Marion, Alabama at his wife's parents' house. In 1960, they moved back to Atlanta where Martin Luther King Jr. was a pastor with his father at Ebenezer Baptist Church. They had a total of four children named Yolanda "Yoki," Martin III, Dexter, and Bernice.

Martin Luther King Jr. lived through segregation. In about 1880's the word "Segregation" started to spread around U.S.A. Black people were not equal as white people but Martin he was the part of breaking segregation. He helped people to support to make any humans equal. But now the community starting to grow and make both equal.

Therefore, Martin Luther King Jr. took part in many protests. First, I will start with the Freedom riders. Black people rode all over the 50 states to protest about freedom. Sadly, they were abused, mugged, and killed. Martin was in jail this time, when he heard about the abuse of the group, he became more determined to protest more. Second, The Fast Food protest was in process at the same time. The Black sat on the whites' only front seat row. They wouldn't move until they served them food.

Last, he was struggling with the Black power group, each time he tried to protest they shot people, hit them with clubs, and sadly, they were crazy enough to kill many people. They kept going on and on until MLK Jr. called out to them to stop the violent acts. They wouldn't stop the violent acts. For example, setting cars on fire and flipping the cars on the top. Finally, he got peace from protesting so much that America saw the mistake they made

Martin Luther King Jr. was also arrested about 20 times from multiple protests. One of them was that a white policeman just didn't like Martin in 1963. Martin was a very good civil rights activist and people wondered why people wanted him to go the prison. Martin was very supportive of Black people back then and white people hated Black people. White people called the white police to arrest him. He was also attacked four times. One time he was seriously attacked and stabbed with a letter opener. The person's name was Izola Curry. Izola Curry was arrested from trying to kill Martin Luther King Jr. Another attack happened when Martin Luther King was at a missionary circle meeting to plan their next protest. His wife and three kids were at their home when someone got a wine bottle, a towel, and lit it on fire and threw it into MLK's home. Luckily, nobody was badly hurt, but his home was destroyed in the explosion.

All these protests and speeches from Martin Luther King Jr. were finally changing. Racism was declining (but not fully). There was one famous speech that changed everything. On August 28, 1963, Martin Luther King Jr. delivered the all-time famous speech, "I Have a Dream" that altered America and all of our history. In his famous speech he said, "I have a dream that my four little children will one day live in a nation where they will not be judged by the color of their skin but by the content of their character." Two hundred fifty thousand people were at that speech. Martin helped change the lives of all African Americans from that day forward. Next, in 1964, he won the Nobel Peace Prize at age 34. At that time, he was the youngest person to get that award.

> Martin Luther King Jr. died in 1968. He was killed at age 36 in Memphis, Tennessee. He was staying at the Lorraine Motel. Martin just finished getting ready for dinner with his friends. He went to the balcony and leaned over the rail to tell his friends he would go downstairs. At the same time, James Earl Ray used a rifle and shot and killed MLK.
>
> We want to thank Martin Luther King Jr. for making a huge change in the USA by fighting against segregation and helping to reduce racism against Black people.

Your Turn to Practice!

Now it's your turn! The core recommendations in this chapter can be practiced by implementing guided, interactive writing instruction with your students. For those in teacher training programs, this can be implemented in your field placement, or can be mock instruction with your classmates taking on the student roles. With mock instruction, you will not have time to teach a full unit (from establishing audience/purpose with your students to publishing), so you will choose one lesson from a unit to teach. Your lesson is limited to 30 min of class time. This means you will need to take your classmates into the middle of the unit, explaining what has already happened in earlier lessons.

 ### Develop Your Lesson

Your lesson must include (a) guided, interactive writing, rereading, and revision, and (b) the explicit teaching of writing processes.

1. Begin planning for instruction by determining the following:
   - Purpose for writing
   - Genre and graphic organizer
   - Audience
   - Language of publication (e.g., ASL or English)
   - Topic
   - Grade level and writing level
   - Class writing and language objectives
2. Choose one or two writing objectives and one or two language objectives that will challenge but not frustrate the class. These should be aligned with your state's content standards, ASL standards, and/or individual education program objectives. If you are a classroom teacher, you can determine the instructional level for your unit by evaluating your students' independent writing samples. You may have student/s who are performing above or below the others in the class. In this case, you will also have differentiated objectives for select students to challenge them at their respective levels. If you are a teacher candidate and practicing in a mock setting, you may envision your students and select objectives for them.
3. Prepare your materials. Plan for strategy instruction by creating at least one visual support for a writing or language objective. Then, set up your writing

space. At a minimum, you must have spaces for the co-constructed writing (or sign language), the language zone, and the visual scaffolds.

SIWI Indicators to Incorporate

Here are selected indicators of instruction you should aim to incorporate (see Dostal & Wolbers, 2015, for a complete list of all 53 indicators). Review the indicators repeatedly throughout your lesson or unit to reflect on your progress.

Strategic Instruction Indicators

- Teach strategies for writing processes in the context of producing text.
- Approach the writing process as recursive (e.g., write-reread-revise-write more) rather than rigidly sequenced (e.g., write first draft-revise-write final draft).
- Explicitly discuss text structure associated with the genre of writing.
- Give attention to the purpose or audience when constructing text (e.g., "Will Jill's mom understand?" "With this expository writing, we want to inform our audience by …").

Interactive Instruction Indicators

- Invite students to take active roles in the construction, monitoring, and revising of text.
- Position yourself as a learner or community member (e.g., "What could we do next?" "I'm not sure. How could we figure that out?" "I learned something new").
- Stimulate and challenge students without overwhelming or frustrating them.
- "Step back" to transfer control to students by asking open questions (e.g., "What do we do here?" "What should we do next?" "What do you think?").
- "Step in" gradually when students struggle by providing more and more support.
- "Steps in" fully when students are stuck (e.g., thinking aloud, modeling, explaining).

Metalinguistic Knowledge Indicators

- Engage students in identifying, comparing and/or distinguishing grammatical features of ASL and English.
- Engage students in chaining and pairing of ASL and English. Languages are clearly distinguished (e.g., different colors or spaces).

Teach Your Lesson

Teach your lesson using guided, interactive instruction in a real classroom or mock setting.

Reflect on Your Teaching

Reflect on your teaching by considering the following questions:

a. What went well?
b. What would you change/do differently if you taught this lesson again?
c. After assessing your students, how well did the students learn the targeted objective?

d. Reflect on your incorporation of the SIWI indicators.

Recommended Readings/Viewings

For Teachers/Teacher Candidates

- "'We Are Authors': A Qualitative Analysis of Deaf Students' Writing During One Year of Strategic and Interactive Writing Instruction" (Dostal et al., 2015). In this article, you can read about the development of author identity and writer motivation.
- "The Language Zone: Differentiating Writing Instruction for Students Who Are Deaf and Hard of Hearing" (Dostal et al., 2019). Read more on the language zone, including classroom scenarios.
- "Beyond the Pen: A Functional Grammar Approach to Evaluating the Written Language of Deaf Students" (Kilpatrick & Wolbers, 2020). Here, you can learn about assessing Deaf students' written language.
- "Getting Students Excited About Learning: Digital Tools to Support the Writing Process" (Saulsburry et al., 2015). This article describes various technologies that support writing instruction.

For Students

- *Dear Mrs. LaRue: Letters From Obedience School* (Teague, 2002). This book demonstrates convincing reasons and examples and persuasive language.
- *Yummy Cookies* (Holcomb, 2020c). This ASL story models the use of *could, should,* and *would*.
- *Let's Go for a Walk* (Holcomb, 2020b). This ASL story models near/far pointing and singular/plural pointing and can be used to teach demonstrative pronouns.

Conclusion

The core recommendations in this chapter can be applied at any grade level to support the learning of any genre of writing. As you begin writing instruction, or as you incorporate changes to your current practice, we encourage you to remember that it will take time to gain confidence enacting the chapter suggestions, but it is worth it! Start with integrating one or two approaches consistently until you feel comfortable, and then expand your practice by adding other recommendations. We often see teachers master certain instructional recommendations before others. This is a natural process. Through continual reflection and revisiting the recommendations, you will broaden and deepen your practice over time.

We also encourage you to actively engage your students in the writing process to the fullest extent possible. Create the space during guided, interactive writing for students to lead the construction as well as follow, and allow ample opportunities for them to express as well as receive. The more opportunities your students have to contribute their thinking, comments, or actions, the more they will grow in their writing and motivation and benefit from the apprenticeship experience. You can do this. Write on!

Sticking Points

- Provide explicit instruction for writing strategies, process, and skills, and use visual scaffolds to support practice. [*Strategy instruction with visual supports*]
- Remember that learning to write is similar to learning how to ride a bike! Apprentice novices. [*Guided, interactive instruction*]
- Heighten student awareness of English and ASL and additional home languages. [*Metalinguistic knowledge*]
- Motivate your students by having real purposes for writing/signing as well as real readers/viewers. [*Authentic writing*]

Writing in the Content Areas

Hannah Dostal
Shannon Graham

Language and literacy are common topics in Deaf education. However, there has been limited discussion of the applications of language and literacy in discipline-specific content areas (e.g., mathematics, science, social studies, art, Deaf studies). In this chapter, we encourage you to see how these domains of learning naturally connect. By integrating the writing tasks that are central to each academic discipline, your students have the potential to develop content knowledge, language, and literacy.

Who Are We?

When I (Shannon) taught middle and high school science, I focused on content delivery and learning, but I also incorporated writing in authentic ways. Even though my undergraduate degree is in biology, I did not fully grasp the literacy-related elements of scientific research until I worked with several scientists experiencing scientific inquiry firsthand and completed my own research. Through these experiences, I became familiar with formal written communication and presentations in the various domains of science. Proposals and reports differ in content and format from the written representations used during data collection and analysis. When I intentionally implemented science units that fostered discursive practices, including writing, student engagement, interaction, and language use, the inquiry process was considerably more dynamic. Some years later, when I was in the scientific research field and before starting my current role as curriculum and assessment coordinator, I conducted my last scientific research project and invited three science teachers of Deaf students

Chew on This!

Did you know that...?

- Teachers more frequently provide scaffolding for *basic* literacy skills and less often scaffold students as they attempt to acquire *disciplinary* literacy skills (Athanases & de Oliveira, 2014).
- Basic literacy skills and DL skills can be taught simultaneously, or a focus on DL skills can be a catalyst for learning basic skills.

Key Vocabulary

Central concepts of **disciplinary literacy** include the existence of "specialized literacy practices of a given disciplinary domain (e.g., science, math, social studies)" (Moje, 2015, p. 256) and the need to teach the practices, strategies, and habits of expert readers and writers to developing readers and writers (Shanahan & Shanahan, 2008).

---

to participate as research assistants. Similar to my experience early in my teaching career, the goal was to immerse them in the work as scientists and to see first-hand the importance of literacy. This pivotal moment is when I realized I wanted to work with content area teachers to more fully engage students in the discipline.

When I (Hannah) was a middle school English/language arts teacher, I quickly noticed that my students needed content to write about that was meaningful and substantive in order to be engaged—just like all writers need. Since students were already deeply engaged in discussing and thinking about meaningful topics in their mathematics, science, history, Deaf studies, and art classes, I decided to collaborate with content area teachers. Partnering writing in my English/language arts class with the concepts students had from going to other classes provided a set of shared experiences and meaningful topics to write about. It also expanded opportunities to develop language and literacy throughout the day as students revisited these concepts in other classes. This was particularly important for my students, many of whom had more ideas and insights than they were currently able to convey in writing and who would need writing to demonstrate their knowledge and competence later in school and in the workforce. The change in engagement, growth, and achievement was so significant that I have continued to study and refine writing instruction as a researcher.

Knowing one's audience and purpose for writing is one of the most powerful guiding forces. As with other chapters, we view the audience for this chapter as (a) those in Deaf education teacher training programs—thinking about what we (Shannon and Hannah) would have liked to know on our first days in the classroom—and (b) current teachers in the field who have spent time investing in the development of Deaf children—considering what we have learned through our own practice and research. In addition, our purpose for writing is to honor the knowledge, capacity, and creativity of our past and future Deaf students. We see disciplinary literacy (DL) as a perspective that positions students as knowledgeable and encourages them to use and develop reading and writing skills in authentic and meaningful ways. Disciplinary literacy instruction (DLI) directs you (teachers and future teachers) to set high expectations and provide instruction that is content-focused and content-rich. When you engage in this approach, your students will have greater opportunities to demonstrate and develop their strengths and contributions in schools, communities, and workplaces. To enter and thrive in these fields, Deaf students must build and practice related literacy skill sets, and we have an obligation to integrate DL practices to open more opportunities for Deaf students.

In this chapter, we provide an overview of and rationale for multilingual practices in DLI specific to writing with Deaf students, and we describe the application of writing practices and skills in history, science, mathematics, Deaf studies, and other subject matter (Shanahan & Shanahan, 2008). More specifically, we will share strategies for generating authentic writing opportunities in content area classes and demonstrate how writing can be a part of and integrated into the disciplines, rather than as an additional layer.

Deaf Experiences, Perspectives, and Core Recommendations

Incidental learning is crucial to any child's development and world knowledge; however, this presents challenges for Deaf learners in an auditory-reliant society. External cues in spoken languages are not easily accessible. In addition, incidental learning is paired with social engagement. The majority of Deaf learners are from hearing families, and those families often have limited understanding of how to make incidental learning opportunities explicit. As a result, Deaf learners may have gaps in their content knowledge and vocabulary as well as written discourse.

This may present challenges for you in your current or future teaching. With instructional planning and limited time for formal education, you may find yourself simultaneously providing a content-rich learning environment and trying to address these gaps. Often, Deaf learners are taught content-specific concepts similar to learning English as a second language or other language without much attention to communicating such ideas through writing (e.g., Graham, 2012; Lane-Outlaw, 2009). We recommend that by maximizing the learning environment and instructional time by using a few DL writing-related strategies, you can encourage content learning (e.g., teaching subject-specific discourse through writing). In addition, using American Sign Language (ASL) as the language of instruction while considering additional home languages, discussion, and/or demonstration of knowledge can allow students to use the known to learn the new and therefore discuss and participate more readily using ASL and written English.

In the following example, we share how one teacher addresses challenges to integrate writing into math while maximizing incidental learning. This is a description of an elementary student, Mekell (pseudonym), and her process with a math problem using her first language (ASL) to build content knowledge and make connections to print and using mentor text to support the writing process.

The lesson, originally developed by Raye Schafer, a kindergarten/first-grade teacher from Washington, was designed to support students' writing about their study of local school bus routes. Raye designed the lesson with the idea of how mathematicians, and those conveying mathematical ideas (e.g., to summarize consumer reports, to report attendance trends), use math-specific representations (e.g., numbers, graphs, symbols) to demonstrate their thinking about content-specific concepts and sometimes to show the steps necessary to answer or explore a problem. Unfortunately, not all teachers learn these strategies in their training. To address this, we begin by providing you with strategies to integrate writing into your content area instruction.

> "Writing is like the roof of a house. It depends on strong walls, a good foundation. We build the foundation through modeling our thought processes in ASL, and build the walls by doing the tasks with grade-level ASL receptive and expressive tasks. When I know the foundation is strong, and the walls have set, that's when we can build the roof. We transfer those already developed skills, into the students' second language, in the writing tasks. Any time I've done a writing assignment within a content area, and it looks like a "collapsed roof," the first thing I do is go back and check my foundation and my walls.
>
> —Raye Schafer, kindergarten/first-grade teacher, Washington School for the Deaf

Core Recommendations

Here are three core recommendations on how to integrate writing into content areas.

1. Write to learn.
2. Write with a purpose in a content area.
3. Model disciplinary discourse and thought processes in ASL.

Teacher Tale: Elementary Math

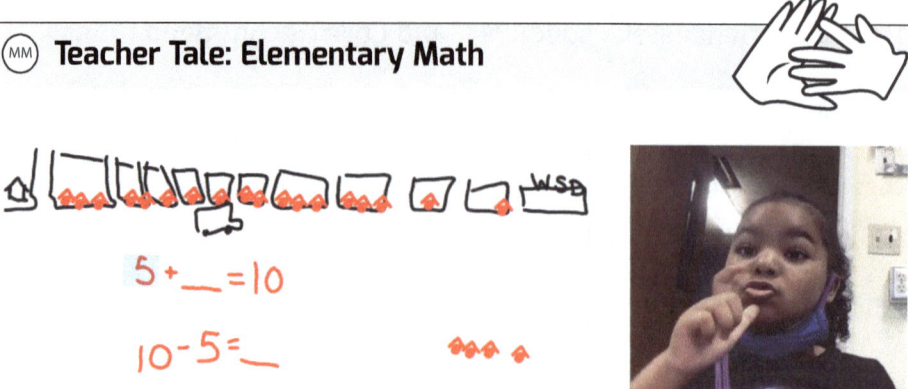

Benny rides the bus to school. The school is 10 blocks away from his house. Benny's bus has gone 5 blocks. How many more blocks to his school?

I used Mekell's first language (ASL) to ensure understanding of these concepts, modeled a think-aloud during the writing process, and used mentor text as a strategy to include information usually gained from incidental opportunities.

Mekell and I then talked about Benny's bus route from his house to Washington School for the Deaf (WSD). Mekell completed drawings to capture a sequence of events that required computation. This allowed her to visualize the math story problem she would be sharing with a peer (first in ASL and then in writing). [Discussions on math stories are through the students' first language (ASL) because the focus is on math concepts and skills. Once students have internalized the elements of math stories, I shift the focus to expressing math stories and watching/answering their peers' examples, also in their first language. This critical phase is necessary before making connections to print.] The drawing provided a permanent representation of ideas so Mekell could reference her image as she began to add math representations (e.g., numbers, symbols). Linking the drawing with ASL throughout the process continued to build content-specific vocabulary, allowing Mekell to flexibly use the discourse of the discipline and build a deeper understanding of the math concepts. She demonstrated the four modes used to explore a math concept: ASL, written English, images, and mathematical representations.

—*Raye Schafer, kindergarten/first-grade teacher*

> "The math in print will look different in English. Students refer to my examples as mentor text and use them to support the writing of their math stories.
> —Raye Schafer, teacher of the Deaf

Effective Practices for Deaf Learners

Cognitively, it is more efficient to learn about communication patterns, conventions (i.e., a way something is typically done in a discipline), and structures of a discipline (e.g., how to present findings, how to record data) in an accessible/first language than it is to attempt to learn through the second language exclusively (e.g., Goldenberg, 2008). This is partly because each discipline or subject area has its own specific vocabulary, syntax, and ways of using language to communicate. You can invite students to explore some of these ideas and content concepts in their first language (e.g., ASL) as a bridge to a second or additional language(s) (e.g., written English) so that they are not tasked with learning language while exploring content and convention. If the first language can be used for exploration and supported translation by modeling disciplinary discourse and thinking in ASL, students can develop language, literacy, and content simultaneously.

When you provide students with the opportunity to compare languages when learning a new concept and related vocabulary, they can create bridges among their existing linguistic competence (Echevarria et al., 2008) in ASL, English, additional languages, and subject-specific language skills in mathematics, science, Deaf studies, and so forth, that allow for more efficient integration. In other words, you should recognize and use the language and content skills students have as they build new understandings of content by considering the type of work that professionals in various fields engage in. Similarly, when you purposefully activate students' prior knowledge based on their previous relevant experiences, students integrate new concepts and ideas more efficiently. Here, we share strategies on how you can use writing to support learning rather than through discussion or demonstration alone. You do not have to wait to introduce DL skills and advanced content. Writing can be taught within these contexts using tools that provide scaffolds for language and literacy development.

Core Recommendation 1: Write to Learn

When teaching, you might ask students to write to demonstrate that they understand something rather than as a way they might come to understand. Students are often asked to write notes in content area classes to capture information and to write answers on assessments to show what they know. However, the process of writing can be a learning experience unto itself if students are creating texts that represent their knowledge as it emerges. This involves providing your students with a variety of different kinds of writing opportunities that allow them to practice using the specific vocabulary, structures, conventions, and text types associated with their new knowledge. You can use these strategies and approaches in all content areas.

Not all writing has to be formal or organized in paragraphs. In fact, you can incorporate informal writing in content areas that use a variety of formats (e.g., lists, diagrams, observations, sketches, dialogue) to capture and enhance students' learning as it emerges in real time. In addition, you can provide informal writing opportunities to allow students to work across languages as they discuss and reflect in ASL while taking written notes to capture their ideas. Working across languages (e.g., ASL, written English, and other languages) provides students with guided opportunities to refine their content-specific ASL skills (e.g., register, vocabulary, organization), while also using ASL as a foundation for developing writing skills by comparing and contrasting languages through translation work.

For example, even before you ask students to begin a science experiment during your science class, you might encourage them to list the materials and procedures needed for an investigation in both ASL and **text,** and in doing so, discuss in ASL and write the vocabulary specific to the instruments and tools related to this task. Similarly, asking students to create a timeline of events from a film shown in social studies class not only demonstrates what students learned from watching, but also it allows them to write, read, organize, and examine the sequence of events from a certain historical time period. Or, as seen in the following Handstamp Sample, your students can develop graphs to visually represent data read about and discussed in class. This writing sample was created by Ezra (pseudonym), a high school student at a school for the Deaf, during a unit on water levels and weather patterns in an environmental science class. His teacher assigned this writing task as a way for Ezra and his classmates to further develop their understanding of data representation and interpretation

Key Vocabulary

Text is "[t]he symbolic representation of ideas... In this way, a math problem without words, an image without a label, can be viewed as texts" (Dostal & Gabriel, 2016, p. 30). Examples include text message, textbook, agenda, calendar, diagram, graph, chart, icon, logo, note.

rather than as a demonstration of knowledge (**Core Recommendation 1**). Writing was used to promote content learning. Following Ezra's sample is a table that highlights the features of science writing that he integrated with suggested next instructional steps.

Handstamp Sample

Secondary Science Writing

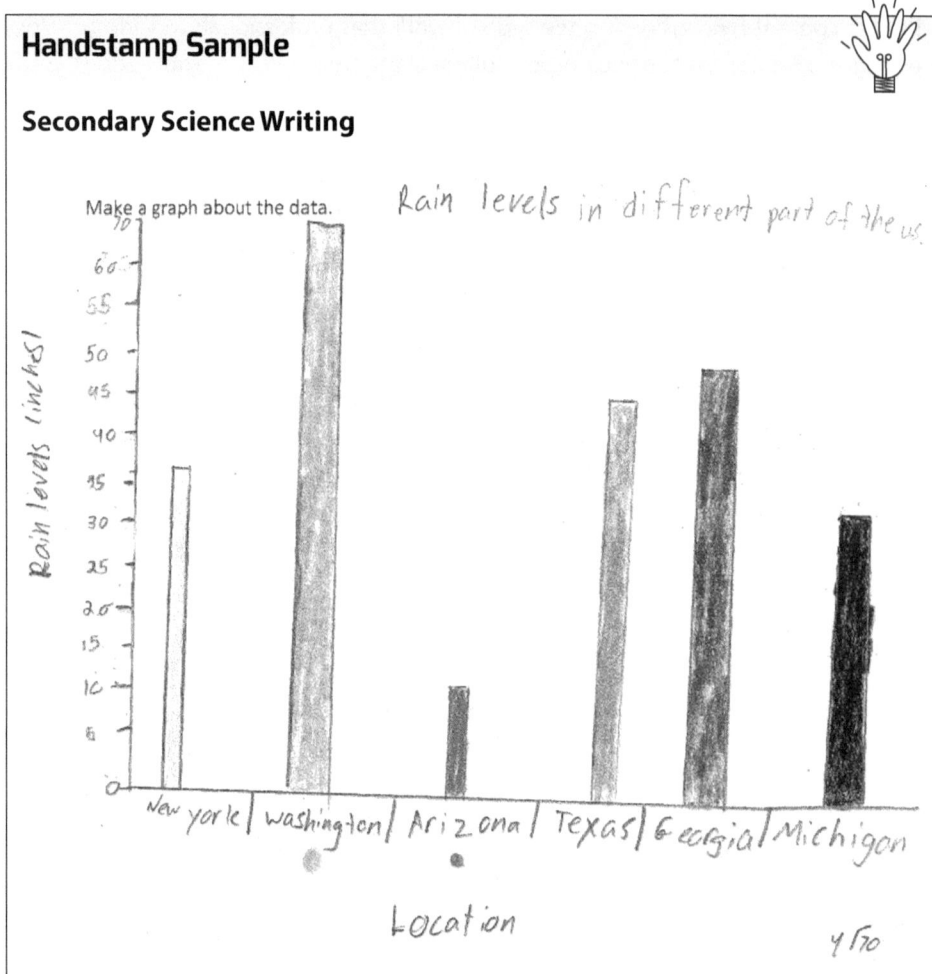

Make a graph about the data.

Rain levels in different part of the u.s.

Explain your graph on page 2.

This bar is about Rain levels in different parts of the u.s. The lable is New york, washington, Arizona, Texas, Georgia and Michigan. The number lable is 36, 32, 9, 44, 48, 69. The heighest is Washington has number 69. The lowest is Arizona has number 9. The middle is New york, Texas, Georgia and Michigan have number 32 to 48. the Side table number is 70 to 0.

Table 5.1. Science Writing Features That Ezra Integrated

Conventions of Science Writing	Examples of Conventions Demonstrated in Ezra's Text	Next Instructional Steps
Replicate and disseminate knowledge in a format that matches the way an expert communicates for this reason.	Ezra compares data using a bar graph and knows that it is necessary to pair a visual representation with an explanation.	The bar graph was used to represent categorical data. He is ready to create a graph with continuous data.
Embed modes of representation and discipline-specific text features.	He demonstrates an understanding of the significance of the labels by the placement of the data (e.g., the independent variable is on the *x*-axis, the dependent variable is on the *y*-axis), and represents the data using equal units of measure.	The next step is to transfer this understanding to a graph using a different kind of data (e.g., continuous).
Interpret content knowledge for the intended audience.	Ezra systematically explains his labels and the amounts of rainfall in each state, and he follows up with an interpretation of his graph, noting the highest and lowest rainfall amounts and the median.	He is set up to create a hypothesis and predict trends by analyzing the data for patterns.
Include content-specific vocabulary.	Scientific vocabulary that is key to interpreting the visual is emerging through the use of terms such as *rainfall levels*, *location*, and *x*- and *y*-*axes*.	The use of *middle* demonstrates understanding of the concept of *medium*. Continue pairing concepts in ASL and English.

Core Recommendation 2: Write With a Purpose in Content Areas

There are many reasons we write outside of school settings: to remember information or ideas, to convey a message to someone, to demonstrate knowledge to others, and more. Two elements that make writing tasks authentic and meaningful are having a clear purpose and an audience. This is also true of writing in any academic discipline: Although formats, topics, and even the symbols used for writing may vary across classes, writing requires a purpose and an audience.

Often, understanding the purpose and audience for a particular piece of writing allows students to learn more about the topic they are studying and the disciplinary community in which it is understood (Dostal & Robinson, 2018). For example, if students learn about probability in mathematics class, they may be limited to writing the computation associated with solving problems. However, you can explain to your students that many professionals use this knowledge to do important work in the world and convey it in specific formats to certain audiences. If you ensure that students (a) not only went through the steps of an isolated mathematics problem, but also engaged with news stories that examined probabilities, and wrote their own story problem; or (b) engaged with graphic representations of probabilities related to stock prices and then drafted their own; or (c) wrote advertisements based on certain probabilities, they would be using their mathematical knowledge in contexts where it is meaningful. At the same time, you will increase students' exposure to relevant vocabulary, conventions, and ways of presenting that knowledge so that they are more likely to remember, use, and be able to flexibly apply it in the future (as in these examples). In addition, and importantly, purposefully considering how Deaf professionals create and disseminate information highlights the ways professionals leverage multilingual practices to understand and disseminate content-specific information. These ideas and practices can be used by students.

By positioning students as participants in ongoing activities that use or produce knowledge rather than learning about content or processes contained in the curriculum, students learn to use content or processes to do things in the world. This kind of use almost always involves some form of written communication. Therefore, by writing in each content area class, students are learning more about the content, in context, while they also develop the language and literacy in both ASL and print that are required to communicate content-specific ideas.

When you have students write for a purpose in content areas, you should do the following:

- Identify purpose and audience associated with instructional targets that require students to use discipline-specific writing practices to communicate.
- Examine examples of writing that integrate the instructional targets and discipline-specific writing practices to see what they include, how they are created, and what they are used for. Share these elements with students.

In the following Stick It Into Action, we demonstrate these steps in action in a middle school science class.

> "Using discursive practices is reflective of what scientists do in the field. As a Deaf scientist, I reviewed articles, engaged in discussions with other scientists on all aspects of the inquiry process, recorded notes and observations, and produced a published piece presenting the scope of my inquiry. This information was shared in various forms (article, presentation, infographic, and so on). As a teacher, I used these strategies to replicate the work of scientists, including but not limited to, modeling the practices of scientists through ASL and writing, selecting purposeful writing tasks (e.g., producing an article in the school newsletter about a scientific inquiry), and assessing competence using all means of discourse in ASL and writing.
>
> —Shannon Graham

Stick It Into Action!

Writing in Science

This is an example of a performance task for a middle school life science unit on sea turtles and conservations.

Performance Task (Step 1)

Students will create an infographic and narrative of the infographic in ASL for the school website with information about sea turtles and conservation efforts. Scientists often use infographics as a format that shares results with community members.

Learning Goals

Students will use informative elements and language to communicate with their audience through writing by

1. stating three facts about sea turtles, three threats they face, and one related conservation effort that can be accomplished locally;
2. including one heading and at least two subheadings, at least two graphics and one graph or chart with figure captions, and three statistics with references; and
3. using infographic and design elements (e.g., layout, use of visuals).

And through ASL by

1. stating all of the content on the infographic in logical order by subtopics;
2. including an explanation of the graph or chart and statistics; and
3. using ASL grammar, sign production, delivery of concepts in conceptually accurate ways, and space referents to highlight and distinguish facts presented on the infographic.

Read and Examine Texts About Sea Turtles and Conservation Efforts (Step 2)

1. Interview with a Deaf sea turtle biologist about sea turtles and conservation efforts, https://www.youtube.com/watch?v=Vajaxwgz1vc&t=146s
2. Volunteer opportunities with a Deaf sea turtle biologist, https://marinelife.org/blue-friday-asl-edition/
3. Infographic on an environmental issue and conservation efforts, https://d3n8a8pro7vhmx.cloudfront.net/boomerangalliance/pages/231/attachments/original/1464851954/MicroPlastic-Infographic-Final-2016.jpg?1464851954

Core Recommendation 3: Model Disciplinary Discourse and Thought Processes in ASL

DL instruction includes the **discursive practices** that are used within each discipline. Such strategies include modes of communication (e.g., visual, signed, written) and the ways information is conveyed within specific disciplines (e.g., methods of discussing, debating, arguing, explaining). Language used within disciplines facilitates such activities and amounts to a linguistic practice in and of itself (Wallace et al., 2004). You can capitalize on multilingual teaching strategies by addressing skills that may not be acquired incidentally, and thus need to be explicitly taught to Deaf students. This leads to Core Recommendation 3, which is focused on modeling disciplinary discourse and thought processes in ASL.

One example, as demonstrated in the next Teacher Tale, is to think out loud to model content-specific skills (e.g., using particular types of evidence to support a claim, using primary or secondary documents to answer questions, comparing data points on a graph). Another example is to invite students to make connections between languages as they learn new concepts and terms. In addition to using ASL for introducing a specific vocabulary word, you can use ASL as students engage in processes and procedures for activities so that related vocabulary and ways of using language are presented in addition to key vocabulary.

In addition, providing students with opportunities to share their thinking as they draft a written piece allows and encourages students to work between languages (i.e., writing in English but discussing the writing and content in ASL). For example, you may ask students to share with the class evidence that sets up their argument (as demonstrated in the following Teacher Tale) in order to receive peer and teacher feedback in ASL before drafting text. This allows the ideas and presentation of the information to be refined to align with the discursive practices of the discipline. In this way, students engage in content-focused thinking that both refines the way ASL is used in a discipline-specific setting and sets them up to write in the discipline.

Key Vocabulary

Discursive practices are practices that highlight ways information is communicated within a specific field (e.g., reporting, disseminating, debating) and how information is conveyed across modalities, including signed and written.

Teacher Tale

I plan lessons to ensure that students do activities similar to what scientists do: observing, valuing evidence, and communicating claims and evidence. Even though I do not explicitly talk about the works of scientists, I am building students' initial problem-solving skills that scientists use in their line of work. Recently, I taught a unit that focused on what we wonder about snails after observing them in their controlled habitat.

Here is an example of what I used to keep a record of our observations and questions derived from observations.

With snails, we have observed the following:

- They have shells.
- Their back half is soft.
- Snails are slow.
- They have eyes.
- We wonder about snails:
- Why do their shells curl?
- What are the tentacles for?
- Why don't snails have legs?
- Can they jump?

- We wonder about how their bodies move.
- We wonder if the shells are hard or soft when they are still on the snail.
- We wonder why their back half sticks out behind them instead of staying inside the shell.

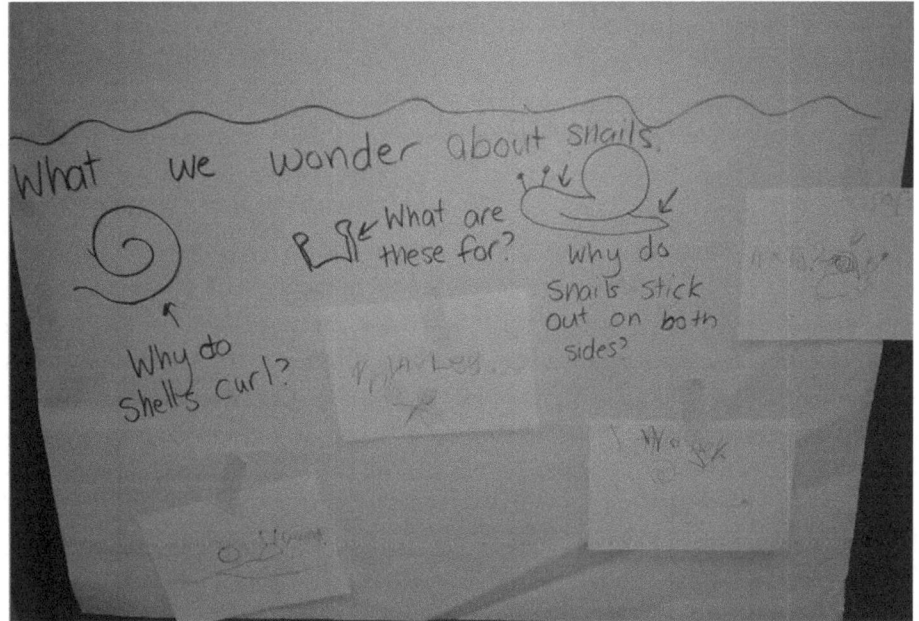

If a student makes an assumption about a snail that is inaccurate or does not rely on evidence, I will wait until the next instructional opportunity and state, "I wonder…" and insert an actual misconception from a student (because those types of misconceptions have meaning to students).

For example: "I wonder if snails do not like vegetables?"

Think Aloud. Next, I will model how the students can approach the question as scientists. My think-aloud will include what scientists do: observe, question, experiment, communicate results, and so on.

For example: "Scientists wonder and observe to find their answers, so that's what I am going to do. I will add cucumbers, lettuce, and carrots in the aquarium and see if snails eat them. I will check the vegetables and observe them three times a day for 5 min. While I am observing, I will write down if snails eat the vegetables or not."

I will also model correction of claims through additional observations and revisit the original claim/evidence. Again, I incorporate the inquiry process, which is reflective of what scientists do.

For example: "I observed snails for one week. The lettuce and cucumber became smaller. The carrot is still the same. I wanted more information, so I asked my friend who studies snails. She said snails like to eat vegetables. Because some of the vegetables in the aquarium became smaller and my friend in the aquarium said that snails eat vegetables, I am going to fix this statement here and write, 'Snails like vegetables.'"

—*Raye Schafer*

(MM) Additional Things to Consider

(MM) (MT) Connecting Text Sets and Writing for Content Area Classes

In this section, we will demonstrate how you can use text sets to support writing in the content areas through an example of writing to advocate for changes in a local community.

We are naturally surrounded by texts that offer multiple representations of the content with which we engage, whether it is having multiple tabs open on an internet browser with different representations of information we seek or exploring different sections of a product page when considering a purchase online, including a set of reviews, descriptions, images, and comparisons for that item. Creating and providing your students with a set of texts related to a central concept or task provides access to students with varying strengths, interests, and literacy levels. In addition, it mirrors the way professionals in math, science, social studies, and other disciplines approach tasks (or elements of a larger task) outside school settings (see **Core Recommendation 2**). Writers often benefit from multiple representations of content and must develop the flexibility and synthesis skills to extract information and integrate into more comprehensive understandings and texts.

In the following elementary social studies example, the teacher has selected texts at various levels and in different modes with the goal of building students' content knowledge and confidence. **Text sets** usually include text that address content standards/topics and serve as **mentor texts** for writing. We suggest that you pair texts that use challenging content-specific knowledge and language with texts that are likely to be more accessible to students (e.g., less text, more visuals, different modes; Lewis et al., 2014; Lupo et al., 2018). A text set that you create might include books, websites, videos, posters, and more. In addition, the texts you include in your set should be informed by the purpose and audience for the piece your students are writing (**Core Recommendation 2**).

Key Vocabulary

Text sets are a collection of texts of varying complexity curated by the teacher that are all related to a central concept or task to provide students with varying strengths, interests, and literacy levels a way to engage with the content. In content area classes, text sets mirror the way professionals in math, science, social studies, and other disciplines approach tasks.

Mentor texts are any signed or print-based material (e.g., books, poems, websites, articles, posters, videos) that students can use to emulate when crafting their own writing. Teachers carefully select these texts to highlight features that are well crafted and can be used as models for students as writers.

(MT) (ABAR) (MM) Teacher Tale

Text Set for Upper Elementary Social Studies
In this text set, I selected four texts that support students as they explore discipline-specific ways to communicate about social and current issues.

Unit Overview
This is an upper-elementary social studies unit focused on cultivating students' identities as activists and allies. During a series of lessons, students learn about the history of Indigenous peoples and cultures as a way to explore identities and allyship. They then reflect on their own identities to compare and contrast the concepts of identities and allyship. In this unit, students advocate for changing the school district's celebration of Columbus Day to Indigenous Peoples' Day, which requires them to write a letter and make a short, related presentation to the local school board.

The learning goals that guide the writing element of this unit include the following: "Students will use persuasive elements and language to communicate with their audience through both ASL and writing by

1. stating a clear opinion;
2. including at least three reasons to support their argument;
3. using emotive language in their writing; and
4. including connectives associated with reasoning."

Developing these skills in ASL and writing highlights for students and readers/viewers that bilingualism is a strength when sharing and exploring identities, including Deaf identities. Further, using ASL to communicate ideas about allyship and identity with community leaders and members provides students with opportunities to use and develop ASL (e.g., register, presentation, word choice). Written communication for advocacy purposes is important because it has the potential to open doors for collaboration and communication in new communities (in this activity: school board members).

Table 5.2. Established Purpose, Audience, and Format

Purpose for Writing	Audience for Writing	Format
To advocate for changing the school district's celebration of Columbus Day to Indigenous Peoples' Day	The local board of education	Following the social convention of communicating about local issues via letter to community representatives, students will develop letters.

Text 1. Drew Daywalt (2013). **The Day the Crayons Quit.**
Although *The Day the Crayons Quit* does not center on Indigenous peoples, it does highlight labor strikes as a form of civic activism. In addition, it does an effective job providing examples of (a) stating a clear opinion, (b) providing reasons to support an argument, (c) using emotive language to support an argument, (d) including connectives associated with reasoning (e.g., see the Green Crayon's dialogue).

Text 2. Anna Lee Rain Yellowhammer. (2016). **Letter to the Army Corps of Engineers.** https://americanindian.si.edu/nk360/plains-treaties/dapl

This text is a letter written by a 13-year-old who is part of the Standing Rock Sioux Tribe. In this activity exploring identity and allyship, it is important to use texts created by kids similar to the students' ages to serve as a source of inspiration and connection.

This letter presents elements of history and explores power and equity (Muhammad, 2020). It is written by an Indigenous person about an issue pertaining to Indigenous people. This text also works to advance students' understanding of a people and culture. This text is especially important as it challenges the common stereotype or racist notion that Indigenous people's issues are a thing of the past. Given that this

Teacher Tale (*continued*)

unit focuses on the historical aspects of Indigenous peoples and Columbus, this text re-grounds and expands student thinking to current social times as well.

The author, Anna Lee, clearly states her opinion by writing, "I am writing this letter to stop the Dakota Access Pipeline," which models stating a clear opinion for constructing persuasive text. Anna Lee also shares four reasons that support her argument in her middle paragraph (i.e., her familial connection, agriculture, clean drinking water, time and cost to clean), which demonstrates a way to state a clear opinion.

Text 3. Teacher-Created Mentor Text by Kiana Foster-Mauro

The following text is a student-friendly version of a real letter that I wrote to a local city council. This adds to the authenticity of the text, as my students can see how I applied the skills that they are working on in real life. It serves as an appropriate selection for this text set for several reasons. First, it is connected to the topic/issue that the unit addresses: Indigenous issues and Columbus. Secondly, it is written in the style of a letter, which is the format that my students will be using. Additionally, it addresses the learning goals set for this persuasive piece (listed above).

Dear New London City Council,

My name is Kiana Foster-Mauro and I am writing this letter to you about the Christopher Columbus statue in downtown New London. I believe that the Council should vote to permanently remove the Christopher Columbus statue.

The first reason that the statue should be removed is that Christopher Columbus never actually came to North America, which means he never came to Connecticut. When Christopher Columbus set sail, he landed in the Caribbean and never reached the mainland of the U.S. If we have statues, we should have them for people that were important to our community.

The second reason is that Columbus did a lot of terrible things to Indigenous peoples. When Columbus sailed to the Caribbean, he hurt the Indigenous peoples there and many of them died. In New London, we live very close to two Native American reservations of the Mashantucket Pequot and the Mohegan tribes. New London also has many Puerto Ricans in the community. Puerto Rico is one of the islands that was hurt by Columbus' actions. Having a statue celebrating him is hurtful to these members of our community and makes them feel not welcome.

The third reason that you should vote to remove the Columbus statue is because if we remove it, we can put up a statue to people who did good and came to New London. For example, we could replace Columbus' statue with a statue for the Africans on the Amistad ship who landed in New London and freed themselves from slavery, which I learned about at the Mystic Seaport!

I know that the Columbus statue was a gift from the Italian community to celebrate all of the ways that Italians have helped New London, but there are other ways we can celebrate the Italian community. We can hold a festival in the summer or even paint a mural that celebrates Italian members of the New London community who were kind. Please vote to permanently remove the Columbus statue.

Sincerely,
Kiana Foster-Mauro

Text 4. Traveling Morning Star/James Wooden Legs (2019). **Native Cultural Stories.**
https://www.youtube.com/watch?v=zKLmJ1E83Vs
This text is a video created by Traveling Morning Star, or James Wooden Legs, from the Northern Cherokee Tribe in which he tells stories passed down to him by his family. The first story counters the legend of Columbus naming the Americas. Although this text is a narrative, and not a persuasive piece, it serves to build students' understanding of various perspectives that exist about a topic, in this case the discovery story of the Americas (**Core Recommendation 3**). In addition, it demonstrates the intersection of identities: Deaf and Cherokee.

—*Kiana Foster-Mauro, elementary teacher*

Did you know that . . . ?

- The number of children's books that specifically tackle and provide examples of persuasive writing through a focus of civic activism, with Black, Indigenous, and/or People of Color, is incredibly lacking.
- The Cooperative Children's Book Center reported that in 2020 only 52 out of 3,299 children's books received by the center were about Indigenous peoples, and only 37 were written by Indigenous peoples (School of Education, University of Wisconsin–Madison, 2021).

 Bringing It All Together

Unit Overview

This is a high school social studies unit that integrates each of the core recommendations of this chapter. It was created by J. Piper Gallucci, a Washington teacher, focusing on relating the 9/11 attacks and the Deaf survivors and victims of these attacks. Students learned about the events of 9/11 and explored how these attacks impacted the Deaf community.

Common Core State Standards Addressed

The following common core standards (National Governors Association Center for Best Practices & Council of Chief State School Officers, 2010) are taken from the History/Social Studies component of the English Language Arts Standards, Grades 6–8, and from the ASL Content Standards (Laurent Clerc National Deaf Education Center, 2018), Standards for Published Signing, Text Types and Purposes, Grades 9–10.

- *CCSS.ELA-LITERACY.RH.6-8.2:* Determine the central idea or information of a primary or secondary source; provide an accurate summary of the source distinct from prior knowledge or opinions.
- *CCSS.ELA-LITERACY.RH.6-8.8:* Distinguish among fact, opinion, and reasoned judgment in a text.
- *CCSS.ELA-LITERACY.W.6.2:* Write informative texts to examine a topic and convey ideas, through the selection, organization, and analysis of relevant content.
- *CCSS.ELA-LITERACY.W.6.4:* Produce clear writing in which the development, organization, and style are appropriate to task, purpose, and audience.
- *ASL Content Standards:* Sign informative/explanatory texts to examine and convey complex ideas, concepts, and information clearly and accurately through the effective selection, organization, and analysis of content.

Students viewed and read news articles, interviewed Deaf survivors and/or families of Deaf victims, and engaged in disciplinary writing opportunities to expand their knowledge on this topic (**Core Recommendation 1**). The result was to compile findings into a presentation in ASL and a one-page informational report, as a reporter might, to inform and teach middle school students about Deaf survivors and victims of the 9/11 attacks (**Core Recommendation 2**). The development of the one-page informational report can be facilitated in ASL to introduce or review elements of 9/11. A think-aloud can be used (e.g., deciding if a source is primary or secondary) that would allow for the integration of discursive strategies in both ASL and writing (e.g., using content vocabulary in context, interviews as primary sources) (**Core Recommendation 3**).

Learning Goals

Students will use informative elements and language to communicate with their audience through ASL by the following:

1. Stating the historical events of 9/11 with support of citations
2. Including a photo and at least three facts about the events
3. Using ASL grammar, sign production, delivery, and space referents to highlight and distinguish these facts

and through writing by the following:

1. Stating a historical event and person of interest associated with that event
2. Including at least three facts about this person of interest
3. Using emotive language in their writing

Table 5.3. Established Purpose, Audience, and Format

Purpose for Writing	Audience for Writing	Format
To inform about 9/11 events and Deaf survivors or victims	Middle school social studies classes	ASL presentation and one-page informational report

Learning Plan

1. Select mentor texts (e.g., *The Daily Moth*, ASL; *Newsela*, writing) to introduce the events of 9/11 to prompt student inquiry and use throughout the unit. *Note:* Newsela pulls facts from primary sources into meaningful pieces in five different reading levels without losing content information!
2. Use these mentor texts to demonstrate how the presentation of historical information through craft and structure impacts the viewer and reader of a text. Point out ways to convey facts and analyze sign and word choices—in ASL and English—used by the authors to inform viewers and readers.
3. Divide the class into two reporting groups and select one student to lead each group. The student leading each group becomes the lead reporter and

facilitates the development of their group presentation in ASL and one-page informational report using the mentor texts and visuals as a guide.
4. Each group presents to one middle school social studies class and shares their informational report and answers questions, if applicable.

This next Handstamp Sample demonstrates the reporting group's content knowledge through academic writing, even though they are still developing their knowledge of English through writing. For example, this reporting group let the intended audience and purpose of their writing inform the format (i.e., informational report) and related techniques (e.g., addressing the reader, using first person). In addition, they included discursive moves that build a connection with Deaf readers of their report by integrating personal information about one of the Deaf victims, Nick, among facts related to the event. Please note that when integrating lessons about historical topics that are based in trauma or loss, be aware of and sensitive to students' potential responses to the topic. Find resources about trauma-informed approaches and school personnel who can support you with navigating conversations about these topics.

> **(PI) Handstamp Sample**
>
> **Secondary Social Studies**
>
> Deaf Victims of 9/11
> By Adhira, Sunya, Lucia, Jon, and Martin
>
> November 10, 2020
>
> On September 11, 2001, which was 19 years ago, four planes were hijacked by terrorists and used as missiles to attack several buildings in New York City and Washington, DC. More than 2,500 people did not survive the attack. Of those who died, a few were Deaf. Our Contemporary World History class picked one Deaf person to research. We picked Nick Pietrunti.
>
> We reached out to Nick's family to learn more about him and provided our condolences. Nick's siblings shared his workplace and interest. Nick worked in Tower One of the World Trade Center as a data entry clerk. He loved to talk about sports and food. He was a funny person and always made his friends smile. He was only 38 years old.
>
> His name and obituary can be found online. However, reaching out to his family made the experience more authentic. We did not experience 9/11 ourselves but we can see it was such a catastrophic event! We are sad that so many people died. Some of them were Deaf.
>
> If you ever go to New York City, be sure to visit Ground Zero at the World Trade Center and find Nick's name on one of the plaques. This is one way to show your support for the Deaf community.

> "Providing students with an authentic audience for their writing increases their investment. Students begin to see their writing as an author and a reader. They care more about what they write and how they write. When the students wrote to the siblings of a Deaf victim of the September 11 terrorist attacks in addition to writing an informational report, they went beyond a typical professional letter. They wrote deeply and tenderly about what they knew of the terrorist attack. Most important, they connected with the siblings by writing about themselves, their life experiences, and how they felt connected to the Deaf victim. None of that would have occurred if the class bulletin and letter were just writing exercises with me as the sole audience.
>
> —J. Piper Gallucci, social studies teacher

Your Turn to Practice!

Text and Language Roundup

Now it's your turn to practice! This assignment/activity provides you with an opportunity to explore discipline-specific text types and purposes for writing that are associated with the discipline(s) you teach (or will teach) (Part 1) in order for you to create and teach your own authentic writing assignment in content area classes (Part 2). After you develop and teach your lesson, reflect on your experience.

Part 1: Interview Professionals

Begin by identifying three people to interview. They should be professionals who use content you plan to teach in their work in different ways. For example, if you plan to teach a unit on weather, you might interview a boat captain, weatherman, scientist, travel planner, pilot, or someone else who uses weather information in their everyday work. *Your goal is to understand the contexts in which content knowledge is used outside of school.* You are encouraged to find a Deaf professional with experience in this field to consider their experiences and to explore ASL texts.

Each interviewee should have a slightly different job description (e.g., do not interview three biologists). They will need to agree to answer questions for you. The interview should not require more than 15 min, but feel free to expand on the questions if you want to and have time.

The following questions are suggestions for what you could ask in the interviews. Please ask additional questions and/or paraphrase these.

1. How does your work relate to _____ (insert the topic, area, standard you chose to investigate)?
2. What types of texts do you use in your everyday work? Or when do you write things down or read things as part of your everyday work?
3. What formats do you use to keep track of or share information (e.g., ledgers, sketches, notes, texts)?
4. How did you learn to use/create these texts?
5. How do you engage with this topic and these texts?

Once you have interviewed three people, write about what you have learned in a brief summary memo (approximately a half page) and create a list of the texts and purposes for writing identified in your interviews.

Part 2: Create a Writing Lesson

After you have interviewed three professionals, develop and teach a writing assignment. Draw on the information you learned about texts these professionals use and create, the reasons they write, the writing formats they use, and the writing practices they engage in while creating texts.

The writing assignment you create for your students should include the three elements listed next. These elements can be presented in a one-page document using lists, tables, and/or connected text. You can decide the overall format, but each element must be labeled and presented in your lesson plan. After developing the lesson, practice teaching the lesson (either with your own students or in a mock situation). Reflect on each component—what went well and what you would do differently.

1. **Overview information.** State the discipline (e.g., mathematics, Deaf studies), course topic (e.g., geometric measurements, Deaf artists), grade level, and content-specific instructional goals based on the Common Core State Standards or local standards and ASL standards.
2. **Write to learn.** Describe in a brief paragraph one writing/composing activity your students will engage in that will support them as they *learn* about the disciplinary content reflected in your instructional goals. The purpose of this short writing/composing activity is to capture and enhance students' disciplinary learning as it emerges. This task should prepare students to engage in the more comprehensive writing assignment you create (see the next step below) by increasing their content knowledge.
   - Consider having students create a timeline, draft notes, list materials and procedures needed for an investigation, and so forth. See **Core Recommendation 1** *for ideas.*
   - Students should be provided with opportunities to work between ASL and English. See **Core Recommendation 3** *for ideas.*
3. **Writing task.** Create a discipline-specific writing task informed by the professionals you interviewed and linked to your instructional goals.
   - Describe the *purpose* for writing and the *audience* and *format* of the writing. Examples of this are provided throughout the chapter (e.g., marine debris, history of Indigenous peoples and cultures; *see* **Core Recommendation 2** *for ideas).*
   - Students should be provided with opportunities to publish in both ASL and English. See **Core Recommendation 3** *for ideas.*

Part 3. Teach the Lesson
Teach the lesson in a real or mock setting.

Part 4. Reflect on Your Teaching
Consider the following questions:

- What went well?
- What would you change/do differently if you taught this lesson again?
  - After assessing your students, how well did they learn your targeted objectives?
- Reflect on your incorporation and effectiveness of DLI in your lesson?

Recommended Readings/Viewings

For Teachers/Teacher Candidates

- "A National Survey of Teachers of the Deaf on Disciplinary Writing" (Dostal et al., 2018). This article shares results from a survey of teachers of the Deaf across the United States.

- "Developing the Science Writing of Deaf Developing Bilinguals" (Scott et al., 2021). In a study of the analysis of Deaf and Hard of Hearing students' science writing by scientists and educators, the authors found that discipline-specific literacy practices emerge in students' writing when their attention is drawn to features of the discipline.
- "Making a Case and a Place for Effective Content Area Literacy Instruction in the Elementary Grades" (Moss, 2005). In this article, the authors describe why and how literacy should and can be integrated into the disciplines throughout the elementary grades.
- WNDB (We Need Diverse Books; https://diversebooks.org/). This website provides suggestions for selecting and integrating texts into content area lessons.

To Use With Students

- Atomic Hands (https://atomichands.com). This website introduces students to Deaf STEMists and provides rich science content for expository writing.
- Facing History and Ourselves (https://www.facinghistory.org). This website engages diverse perspectives about current and historical events and can be used with students as they develop persuasive writing in history class.
- Cornell Lab of Ornithology (birds.cornell.edu/home). Cornell Lab of Ornithology's website provides access to videos and interactive summaries about nature and access to the largest bird community in the world. This site can be used for research for writing and sharing of writing in science classes.
- Seek the World (seektheworld.com). Learn about new places and visit different countries by joining a Deaf traveler on his adventures. Use this website as a way to connect students to Deaf writers and ways that content-specific information is shared from a personal retelling.

Conclusion

We hope to have provided you with an overview of disciplinary writing instruction with multilingual Deaf students. Remember that authentic writing opportunities should parallel the work of professionals in fields and subfields of mathematics, science, history, and Deaf studies. Specific to a Deaf multilingual teaching environment, we have shown how you can encourage the use of ASL to teach new concepts and to engage students in disciplinary discourse and written English to bridge learned concepts to literacy skills. Considering the three core recommendations presented in this chapter through a DLI lens will broaden Deaf students' content knowledge and build writing skills in multiple languages simultaneously.

Sticking Points

- Integrate writing and content area topics so students are learning while they write and writing while they learn.
- Create opportunities for students to write with a disciplinary purpose.
- Model in ASL disciplinary-specific ways of thinking and communicating about content.

Reading

Marlon Kuntze
Jessica Scott
Stacey Katz Shapiro

In this chapter, you will learn how to create an environment that enables Deaf students to develop a joy for reading and how to offer multilingual and culturally relevant strategies before, during, and after reading that will contribute to improved comprehension development.

Who Are We?

First, we will introduce ourselves. I (Marlon Kuntze) am a professor who retired from Gallaudet University, and my academic interest is in the language, communication, and literacy of young Deaf students. At the beginning of my career, I taught high school English at the California School for the Deaf, Fremont. I became a bilingual/bicultural education coordinator at the school largely as a result of my experience using American Sign Language (ASL) to support students' English development. I (Jessica Scott) am an associate professor of Deaf education at Georgia State University. I taught English to high school Deaf students in Alaska. Later, I became a reading specialist for Deaf students in Grades K–8 in Massachusetts. I (Stacey Katz Shapiro) was an administrator at the Atlanta Area School for the Deaf for more than 15 years and am presently the director of online programs at the American School for the Deaf. I began my career as a middle school teacher at the California School for the Deaf, Riverside, where I also was the bilingual/bicultural co-coordinator. I then worked

Thank you to the following staff at the Atlanta Area School for the Deaf for their contributions: Reginald Bess, Terynce Butts, Helen Gazda, Amanda Lee, and Tyler Stone.

at Maryland School for the Deaf in early intervention and co-coordinated the bilingual program.

In each of our assorted roles over the years, we have experienced the challenges of teaching reading, and we understand the task teachers of Deaf students undertake every time they enter the classroom. However, we also have seen the sense of accomplishment that success in reading brings to students.

It is impossible to cover within one chapter all that is required for the successful literacy development of Deaf students. This chapter focuses mainly on reading comprehension from kindergarten through Grade 12 (K–12) education. Our approach to the development of reading comprehension is based on two assumptions. The first is based on an important characteristic of Deaf people whose orientation is, by nature, visually based. Their eyes provide the best access to the world. Tapping into the visual strengths of Deaf students is essential for enhancing the development of reading skills, and it represents a significant paradigm shift from the conventional views of teaching reading. The second assumption, and thus an important claim underlying this chapter, is that learning to read is a product of the meaningful experience of reading.

In this chapter, we frame our suggestions using two reading models. First, Kuntze and colleagues (2014) provide a model highlighting ASL as an important factor because communication that is rich, socially satisfying, and intellectually nourishing is key to successful reading outcomes. The cognitive skills needed for reading comprehension are also needed for comprehending stories in ASL (Kuntze, 2023), a finding that empirically supports the notion that the comprehension skills acquired through one language will help with comprehension in another language. The second model is based on the notion of reading comprehension as a product of "simultaneously extracting and constructing meaning through interaction and involvement with written language" (RAND, 2003, p. 2). In other words, successful reading involves a reader, a text, and the activity of reading. We propose that the facilitative role played by ASL helps catalyze the interaction among those three elements.

You will see throughout this chapter how the infusion of ASL in reading instruction may lead to a deeper appreciation of reading, as well as provide students with the access and opportunity necessary to become successful readers.

Did you know that...?
The better your comprehension, the more you are willing to read, and the more you are willing to read, the better your comprehension will become. Cognitive skills, linguistic competence, and knowledge are intertwined, and reading comprehension is what connects them (Stanovich & Stanovich, 1995).

Deaf Experiences, Perspectives, and Core Recommendations

To design appropriate and empowering instruction, you need to take into account Deaf students' experiences and strengths. Consider the following:

- *Most Deaf students have less access than their hearing peers to positive and language-rich reading experiences at home.* While some families read books with their Deaf child, others do not. They either may not do it for their children (Deaf or hearing), or they might not read with their Deaf child because they do not know how. Researchers encourage families to read books with their Deaf child regardless of their ASL ability. They can use visual strategies (e.g., role play, connect to pictures, gesture) to engage their Deaf child. The most important thing is that they spend time together in shared reading). The experiences Deaf children have

> "Although children learn the mechanics of reading in the early elementary grades, reading with understanding and meaning is a skill that needs to be nurtured over many years.
> —Roberts & Roberts, 2008, p. 125

with books at home may influence their perception of reading—whether it is feelings of disconnection or frustration or with feelings of pleasure or enjoyment.
- *Deaf students are diverse in many ways.* This includes ethnically, culturally, racially, and linguistically, on top of wide variance in family socioeconomic status and in physical, mental, and hearing abilities. This means that students in the same classroom are likely to have varying sets of knowledge and language experiences and be at varying levels of readiness for reading instruction.
- *Deaf students are fully capable of becoming independent learners.* Teachers have historically spoon-fed answers when Deaf students struggle, which can lead to feelings of inadequacy and dependency. Independent learning is an essential skill to develop, and it comes through challenging but supported learning experiences.
- *Deaf students do not need to know spoken English before starting to read.* Students experience improved English when they are engaged in reading with ASL support. English growth takes place when students experience reading instruction in this way.
- *Deaf students can develop, through ASL, the cognitive skills that are needed for comprehension.* These skills do not develop exclusively through reading. Rather, they can be practiced and honed through ASL (see Kuntze, 2023).
- *Deaf students' struggle when learning to read is not predicated simply on being Deaf.* It is rather a result of the limited communication access they have had with people in their lives. The development of knowledge and curiosity about the world is a product of rich and satisfying communication with adults, which is too often missing in the lives of many Deaf children.

Core Recommendations

We provide the following core recommendations based on best practices and the experiences and strengths of Deaf students:

- Model joy. *[Joy]*
- Boost cognition. *[Cognition]*
- Ensure meaningfulness, impact, and engagement. *[Meaningfulness]*
- Use ASL translation during reading instruction. *[Translation]*
- Build comprehension skills. *[Comprehension]*
- Address equity issues in the classroom. *[Equity]*

Effective Reading Practices for Deaf Learners

In this section, we expand on our core recommendations. You will notice that although we explore each as a separate construct, many of these concepts overlap and build on one another. As a result, there are times when a discussion related to one core recommendation incorporates ideas that are also pertinent to other core recommendations. We indicate this by italicizing words in brackets (as shown in the core recommendations).

Chew on This!

Did you know that . . . ?
- Deaf students are no different from hearing students in that they will not be in the right mindset to work if their basic needs such as full communication access are not being met at home.
- If Deaf students' physiological, safety, and love/belonging needs are met, they will move into the esteem and self-actualization domains (see Maslow's Hierarchy of Needs; Maslow, 1943), whereby motivation and functioning are known to increase and readiness for learning becomes more evident (Tracey & Morrow, 2017).
- Awareness of and sensitivity toward students' needs fosters the environment necessary for success in reading.

Core Recommendation 1: Model Joy

Many children can associate warm, loving feelings with reading to a time when they snuggled with their caregivers as they read a bedtime story. These often become treasured times of love for children and their caregivers in the hurried world in which we live. With most Deaf children coming from hearing families, these intimate experiences at a young age may not include books. When Deaf children enter school, sometimes their first truly accessible experience with books is with their teacher. These positive reading experiences can be pivotal in creating joy of reading.

While ASL as a key factor in Deaf students' reading development seems obvious, what is sometimes overlooked is the power ASL holds to make literature joyful. Incorporating ASL read-alouds (also called *storysigning*; see Chapter 2) into the reading curriculum helps to keep students engaged at any age. Watching a book come to life in ASL can captivate the attention of the most unwilling of students. Leaving students with a cliffhanger at the end of a chapter leaves them wanting more.

You can model and create joy for reading in multiple ways. Let students see you reading for pleasure. Choose books that align with your students' interests. Share your joy of stories and literature. Creating a classroom that makes reading fun and encourages students to be curious about books and stories helps motivate them to read. When children are young, this may mean making reading a positive time of close connection. As students get older, it may be having them select material they are excited to read, helping them to connect and relate to characters in a story, or providing a read-aloud where they anticipate with excitement what comes next in a book. As a teacher, you can help create that joy.

Core Recommendation 2: Boosting Cognition

Increasing cognitive skills is key to building students' ability to comprehend what they are reading. You can do this by talking with students about ideas, problems, and solutions. Lesson plans, whether related to reading or not, should be designed with opportunities for developing higher order thinking skills such as making inferences, asking questions, and solving problems. For example, through ASL discussion you can model the process of inferring. This might involve asking open-ended questions, using what students know to help them make sense of new information, asking about characters' and authors' perspectives, clarifying unfamiliar words, and modeling how to summarize the plot or the main idea. These skills are important for helping students develop independence as readers, which in turn fosters reading comprehension.

The cognitive skills for reading can absolutely be taught before a student has begun to read in earnest. Regularly, teachers of preschool, kindergarten, and first-grade students watch their classes engage in stories that are read aloud to them. In fact, these are prime opportunities to model and support higher order thinking strategies. Even teachers of older students may find that reading a book to their class allows students to focus more energy on comprehension.

> "Whether it is a very young child who takes my hand and drags me to the bean bag chairs or climbs into my lap with a pile of books for me to share, a middle-grades child who asks about having a read-aloud, or an older student who shows up to my classroom early after lunch wanting to talk about a novel they can't put down, the phenomenon of students developing a love of reading is one of the very best parts of being a reading teacher. It is when I know I have done a good job.
>
> —Former multilevel reading teacher

Teacher Tale

As a high school teacher in a bilingual program, I was always looking for ways to help my students use critical thinking skills during reading. Once, I had a student who learned early on that a great strategy for answering reading questions was to look for the words in his book that matched the words in the question. He would then use a sentence with those words as an answer without understanding what it meant. I wanted him to work on his cognitive skills to answer questions about what he was reading. One day in my class when we were reading *Glass Slipper, Gold Sandal* (Fleischman, 2007; reading level approximately third grade), I wrote a question for him to answer: "What do you think about the stepmother's choices to keep Ashpet away from the King?" He came up to me and shook the book in frustration. "It's not in here!" I took the book from him and told him that the answer could only come from thinking about it from his perspective. From then on, I always used these kinds of questions for reading discussions.

—*A high school English teacher*

Scaffolding to Boost Cognition

Scaffolding is an important teaching skill and is helpful for fostering reading comprehension. One way of providing scaffolding is to answer students' questions with a question. A simple "Well, why do *you* think that happened?" or "What do *you* think about it?" can lead students to use thinking muscles instead of relying on an adult for the answers. The goal of this strategy is to encourage students to think for themselves versus always looking to adults for answers. In addition, sharing your own thought processes of how you came to certain opinions or understandings during reading can serve as a cognitive model for students. They see how someone else's thoughts work when solving a problem or making a deduction. These are approaches that help fill in gaps that are created as a result of communication deprivation that stymied the development of early thinking skills. Keep in mind that when you provide opportunities for students to strengthen their cognitive "muscle," you are providing opportunities for them to think and solve problems.

 Stick It Into Action!

Scaffolding to Support Comprehension

There are many ways that you can use scaffolding to support reading comprehension in the classroom:

- *Think-alouds.* As you work with students who are navigating text, model how to problem-solve when encountering difficulty by thinking aloud (see Chapters 4 and 5 for examples). Show them your thought processes when you encounter an unknown word or a confusing passage as well as the steps you take to resolve the challenge you are experiencing. [*Cognition*]
- *Activate prior knowledge.* Before students engage in reading, get them thinking about what they already know about the subject of the text. [*Meaningfulness*]

- *Use visual supports.* Show students pictures, videos, and even real-life objects representing important concepts in the text. You can do this before reading to build background knowledge but also during reading to help jog their memories.

Students require the mental tools to plan, problem-solve, and remember what they are taught. You should create an exploratory environment, rich with language and experiences from which to develop these tools. For example, during a read-aloud with a lower elementary class, you could sign the wrong word to the class (e.g., when referring to the story *Goldilocks and the Three Bears,* tell the class that Goldilocks ate chicken instead of porridge) and let students catch your error. Together, you can problem-solve any reading and comprehension errors by looking for the solutions or evidence in the text (see Chapter 7 for additional examples of searching for evidence in text). This is a versatile activity that can be modified in many ways to be appropriate for your students by class or grade level. Remember, you are encouraged to engage students in thinking activities outside of reading text as well. Giving students relatable problems to solve at a variety of complexities is important. For example, you could ask them about and discuss the consequences of going outside without shoes when it is raining. Engaging students in thinking skills and teaching them how to draw on their competencies across languages can strengthen the cognitive skills needed for reading. However, not all students have the same experiences and backgrounds, which requires us to consider how to provide meaningful and engaged learning opportunities for all.

(DI) (PI) (MT) Core Recommendation 3: Meaningfulness, Impact, and Engagement

Students who struggle to read may have a limited understanding of why people read or how reading will benefit them. You can help students understand the many benefits of reading, such as developing advanced language skills, escaping into the world of a story, learning new facts about the world, keeping up with the news, or even planning a trip. To this end, reading activities should be meaningful, impactful, and engaging.

Making Reading Meaningful
Building students' background knowledge is one thing you can do to make reading *meaningful*. To tap into or build students' background knowledge before they read, there are a number of approaches that can be taken. Some of these require a great deal of planning and time, such as bringing students on a field trip to visit a zoo before they read about animals or visiting a historical site before reading about historical events. However, there are other valuable activities that take less planning that also develop background knowledge and allow students to connect to what they will be reading. For example, you can capitalize on resources available online. Tours, videos, and places that students have not seen firsthand are accessible visually through the internet. Take time to find meaningful and relevant videos in ASL and students' home languages that provide background knowledge that all can access. Students may have the background knowledge but need help in making the connection. Asking students about whether and when they have seen certain things or talking about books with

similar content that the class has read in the past are also effective ways of connecting to background knowledge. [*Cognition*]

Making Reading Activities Impactful

Reading activities should also be *impactful*. A dynamic and robust classroom discussion is essential in Deaf education and is especially important for reading. We have discussed ways you can use scaffolding to foster cognitive skills; here, we demonstrate how you can use scaffolding to make learning impactful. Discussion is key to filling in gaps of knowledge by honing in on what students already know; it is also when you try to scaffold to new information. Students coming from homes where communication is limited will have had fewer high-level discussions about events they experience or phenomena they see, and they will require more interaction about topics in the classroom. In addition, students who have home languages other than ASL or English may have knowledge in these other languages that you can capitalize on (Wolbers et al., 2023; for more on translanguaging see Chapters 4, 10, and others). For example, the term *rite of passage*, which appears in *Hatchet* (Paulsen, 2006), may not be something a student knows, but when discussion begins they realize they have the vocabulary for a similar event (e.g., a quinceañera), and they can share details of that experience they had or their sibling(s) had. By making connections between your students' languages and experiences and the content they are learning in school, you can create a strong foundation for continued learning.

We recommend that you incorporate discussions both before and after reading a text. Before reading, you can engage students in discussion as a preview of the vocabulary and concepts they will encounter in the assigned text. Discussions after reading are also crucial because they help reinforce and/or deepen comprehension of what they read. Include opportunities for your students to have discussions about the text, both with their peers and with you. These types of conversations are both socially satisfying and intellectually nourishing.

Teacher Tale

I remember when Maya told me she was going to join the book club because her friends were doing it. Despite her parents sharing that they read with her at home, she had never been willing to read a book for enjoyment or that was not attached to some required assignment. I remember when she came into class early after book club and was sitting with friends, still discussing the book with such excitement and talking about the characters as if they were their friends. She's in high school now, a strong student and avid reader, and when I asked her what changed and made her like reading, she actually said, "Book club in fifth grade."

[Joy]—A fifth-grade teacher

 **Engaging Students in Reading**

One final aspect of this core recommendation is that reading should be *engaging*. You can create book clubs to encourage engagement with reading in your classroom. We recommend pairing students in buddies or groups with varying ages or reading

Author Nic Stone visits the Atlanta Area School for the Deaf.

levels. Students in these clubs can then share with their peers their reactions to what they have read. With the advent of social media and the continuing advancement of videoconferencing technologies, it is becoming more and more possible for teachers to reach out to and invite authors and illustrators of students' favorite books and stories to meet your students. These interactions also keep students engaged and can be a motivating factor for reading a text. If your school doesn't already have an event, try to set one up—with certified interpreters. See the picture of author Nic Stone visiting the Atlanta Area School for the Deaf (AASD). She discussed the process of becoming an author and shared her book, *Dear Martin*, with a captivated audience of students. Students found the book, which is about race relations, to be relevant and meaningful. This contributed to their motivation to read and discuss it, which again emphasizes the importance of students feeling connected to what they read. Let your students know in advance that they will be meeting with the author so they can have a built-in meaningful, impactful, and engaging reason for reading. Have them create questions ahead of time that they want to ask the author about the story or the writing process.

Interactions do not have to take place in the here and now to be engaging. You can have your students create book reviews that can be written in English or produced in ASL and made available to classmates on a tablet or computer. You can also set up a reading pen-pal exchange center where two students from different schools or classrooms read the same book and exchange video messages or written letters. These videos can be recorded using tools such as Flip, which provides a user-friendly platform for you to post a video prompt and for students to film and share their comments with their classmates. There are also filters and features that are similar to many of the social media platforms your students are likely accustomed to using, which makes it highly motivating.

Core Recommendation 4: Using ASL Translation During Reading

Translating an English word, an English sentence, or even an English passage in ASL is a common cultural practice in the Deaf community. It is how Deaf adults introduce their children to the world of print. Translating stories from English to ASL does not only help ensure comprehension but will also help instill an appreciation of the content. [Joy] You can ask readers to translate in a few ways during reading, such as translating individual words (signing RED when reading the word "red"), translating short phrases (signing the single sign GET-UP when reading the phrase "gets up"), or translating full sentences or paragraphs. You can also use ASL translation by initiating a dialogue to clarify meaning or to boost comprehension. By no means should students be encouraged to sign to themselves while reading unless it is for the purpose of giving the adult access to how students are processing the text. Here are some suggestions to see how students are comprehending text at varying reading levels.

- **Emergent readers:** Ask a beginning reader to sign some of the individual words on a page, with the purpose being to check their word recognition. This will help you to determine whether a book is at an appropriate level and see what words they are reading correctly as well as incorrectly.
- **Intermediate readers:** Once readers have the basics down, translation should get more complicated. Ask students to sign portions of what they read to themselves and then have them summarize the meaning—but only after they have read it silently for comprehension. In addition to determining the appropriateness of the book, this activity can also help you determine whether students are selecting the correct meanings of multiple-meaning words using context clues or appropriately translating idiomatic language or phrases (e.g., signing SIT UP as one sign instead of two).
- **Advanced readers:** Once students are proficient readers, the act of translation should happen automatically in their heads. They should not translate everything they read. Translation is best utilized as a strategy when trying to make clear sense of what they are reading. Even if they are reading well, it may be good to check in by asking them what an entire paragraph or chapter was about and use their signed translation as a gauge to check for comprehension or to pinpoint the source of miscomprehension. You may find that there are confusing or complex grammatical structures in the text that you may want to check to ensure the student comprehends.

We recommend that you pre-identify words with multiple meanings, difficult phrases, figurative language, and/or complex grammatical structures that have the potential to cause comprehension breakdowns for your students. While students are actively reading, you can interrupt when you notice they have arrived at parts of the text that may be problematic. Asking them to translate or explain what a given word, phrase, sentence, or paragraph means will help you know how they make meaning of the text. Then, you can actively support students with comprehension strategies as needed.

Core Recommendation 5: Build Comprehension Skills

Often with Deaf children, comprehension can take a "back seat" to building other skills. Some may mistakenly think that foundational skills need to be in place before work on comprehension strategies may commence. However, this is not true! Deaf children can and should learn to use comprehension strategies from an early age. Not only does this build reading skills, but comprehension is what brings *joy* into the reading experience. In this section, we focus on comprehension monitoring, comprehension strategies, and the use of **dialogic reading** during the reading process to support comprehension.

Monitor Comprehension

One thing that good readers do is monitor their own comprehension and apply strategies as needed. We have all experienced a time during reading when we realize our mind has been somewhere else, or we have not understood what we read. There are a few ways you can teach students to pay attention to what and how they are comprehending. First, you might pre-identify places in the text for students to stop reading and to comment on what they have read so far or to make a prediction about what may take place in the next part of the text. If the student understands the story but is not able to make a prediction, you can make an absurd prediction that students will know is not possible, such as, "What do you think will happen when the girl goes to the toy store? Do you think she will buy fruit?" Sometimes, a discussion about what cannot happen helps students to make stronger, more likely predictions. It is also important to have a system in place to guide students, such as a checklist for unfamiliar words (see Stick It Into Action). Giving students strategies to identify unknown words allows them to continue reading instead of waiting for you to translate the word. These teaching strategies support independence and help build confidence.

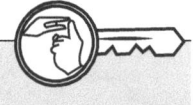

Key Vocabulary

Dialogic reading is a form of reading instruction that uses intentional interactive activities to support comprehension.

Stick It Into Action!

"What to Do" List

You can use this list to help students try different strategies prior to asking for assistance when they encounter unknown words. You can also modify this by adding strategies as you teach new ways to approach unfamiliar words.

Name: _____

When I'm reading, if I get stuck on a word:

1. STOP, stay calm, and read it again.
2. Look at the picture.
3. See if the word is on our QR code list.
4. Check the word wall.
5. Look in your word cards.
6. Use an online dictionary.
7. Write it down, skip it, and read the rest of the sentence. Make a guess. Does that make sense?
8. Keep reading.

_____ p. # ____
_____ p. # ____
_____ p. # ____
_____ p. # ____
_____ p. # ____

When you have five words written on your paper, ask a teacher for help.

Key Strategy

Dialogic Reading

Another good multilingual approach to building comprehension skills with Deaf learners is dialogic reading because of its natural incorporation of ASL dialogue during the reading process. This not only can boost comprehension but also allows you to identify misunderstandings or errors students are making. With dialogic reading, you will often use specific types of questions, and we illustrate this using the book *Corduroy* (Freeman, 1968). Here, we provide examples of different types of questions. We provide ASL glosses to give you one example of how you might sign these questions along with the English equivalent.

Completion questions (ask a child to supply a missing word in a sentence)
- CORDUROY LIVE WHERE (rhetorical[1]), BIG STORE. IN STORE (topic[2]), WHICH DEPARTMENT WHICH (furrowed eyebrows)?
- (English equivalent) Corduroy lived in the _____ department of a big store.

Recall questions (ask the child to remember key facts or details from their reading)
- CORDUROY LOSE, WHAT POINT-ON-EACH-FINGER (FURROWED EYEBROWS)?
- (English equivalent) What items does Corduroy lose?

Open-ended questions (ask the child to elaborate on questions related to events in the story)
- REMEMBER CORDUROY RIDE-UP-ON-ESCALATOR ARRIVE-AT-TOP (topic), CORDUROY AMAZED. WHY? WHAT HE SEE (furrowed eyebrows)?
- (English equivalent) Why was Corduroy amazed when he got to the top of the escalator? What did he see?

Wh-prompts (ask the child to answer *who, what, when, where, why,* and *how* questions)
- CORDUROY GO HOME WITH WHO (furrowed eyebrows)?
- (English equivalent) Who did Corduroy go home with?

Distancing questions (ask the child to make connections between the events or circumstances in the reading and their own lives (Lonigan & Whitehurst, 1998)
- HAVE FAVORITE TOY QM[3]? WHAT YOUR FAVORITE TOY (furrowed eyebrows)?
- (English equivalent) Do you have a favorite toy? If so, what is your favorite?

Although there is limited research on the use of dialogic reading with Deaf children, the practice shows promise for vocabulary acquisition (Fung et al., 2005; Trussell & Easterbrooks, 2015) and comprehension of content area texts (Scott & Hansen, 2019). These activities boost comprehension and make reading more meaningful.

---

1. Underlined words are signs that are accompanied by a nonmanual marker. In this example, a rhetorical question nonmanual marker is what accompanies those signs.
2. Different grammatical nonmanual markers are used. Here, a topicalization nonmanual marker is used.
3. QM is a shorthand for QUESTION-MARK (flexing index finger) used in yes/no questions.

Literature Circles

You can set up **literature circles** in your classroom as another way to bring ASL into reading comprehension, which can make the text more accessible and enjoyable for students. [*Joy, Meaningfulness, Comprehension*] Although commonly used with upper elementary and older students, there is evidence that literature circles can be successful at the earlier elementary level as well (see Schlick & Johnson, 1999, for in-depth information on how to set up literature circles). You can begin by modeling how literature circles work and then have students take on the responsibility of leading the discussions with you providing support as needed. (For a more in-depth exploration of how to set up literature circles, see Hill et al., 2001.) The use of literature circles helps make reading more relevant and meaningful by encouraging students to reflect on what they read. You can also use them to enable students to learn and benefit from the knowledge and experiences of others in the circle group while also providing opportunities for discussion in ASL, which helps to boost comprehension. For example, if a literature circle group was reading a book about Mexico and one group member had personal knowledge of Mexico (e.g., through previously visiting or living in Mexico), this student may choose to be the leader in their group and provide the students with background knowledge to help them better understand the text.

Key Vocabulary

Literature circles are groups of students who have chosen (via a limited selection provided by the teacher) a book they all wish to read. During literature circles, there are structures in place to support their abilities to understand and discuss the book.

Graphic Organizers

Graphic organizers can be extremely helpful for providing Deaf students with a framework to discuss and think about different aspects of learning, particularly the reading and writing process (see Chapter 4 for additional examples). They also provide information that can help you monitor student comprehension. Graphic organizers help students organize their thinking in various ways. You can use these with your students in small groups by asking them to brainstorm and predict what a story is about, identify cause and effect, retell a story, sequence events, compare and contrast characters, and make analogies. When comprehension activities are completed, leaving these graphic organizers visible in your room can support many other learning activities related to the reading. You can use these across grade levels and reading levels. In the following four Handstamp Samples, the teachers use a graphic organizer program called Thinking Maps (Hyerle & Yeager, 2007) to support students' comprehension of a range of stories. However, there are many different graphic organizer programs and models that can create these visual supports for thinking about information.

These examples show ways you can use these kinds of graphic organizers to support students who are reading at various levels. In the circle map, you can see the group recall the characters and their characteristics from *Quick as a Cricket* by Audrey Wood (1982) using word and picture prompts that young students can physically manipulate to add to the circle map. This can be done by providing a list of characters and adjectives that were both in the story and not in the story for students to select and add to the circle map. (Those not included in the story are not visible in this photo.) In the bubble map, you can see student-elicited words to describe the traits of a character from *Amal Unbound* by Aisha Saeed (2020). Older students independently chose their favorite character and then identified their traits. After completion, students took turns presenting and discussing why they chose this character. In the double bubble map, students compared and contrasted two characters from *The Rooster Who Would Not Be Quiet* by Carmen Agra Deedy (2017). Several examples are provided here to show different ways you can meet varying student levels using different modalities. Some students used only pictures, some used written words, and some used plates and pipe cleaners to make things more kinesthetic, but all compared and contrasted the characters Don Pepe and the Rooster. In the flow map, students sequenced events that happened in *The Mitten* (Brett, 2009) after the content was reviewed in a class discussion.

Handstamp Sample

Graphic Organizers to Support Comprehension

Student responses to the book *Amal Unbound* by Aisha Saeed in a circle map (Hyerle & Yeager, 2007).

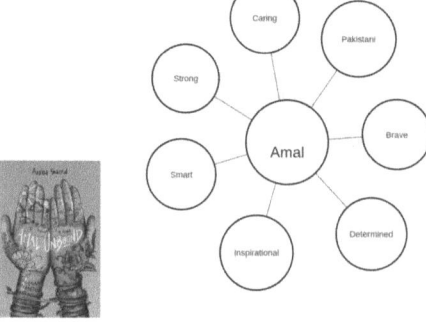

Student responses to *Amal Unbound* in a bubble map (Hyerle & Yeager, 2007).

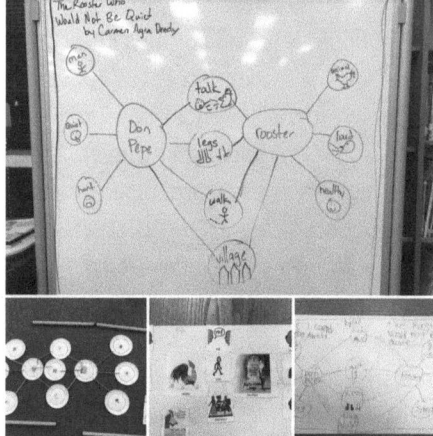

Student responses to *The Rooster Who Would Not Be Quiet* by Carma Agra Deedy in a double bubble map (Hyerle & Yeager, 2007).

Student responses in a flow map (Hyerle & Yeager, 2007).

(SEL) (ABAR) (DI) Core Recommendation 6: Address Equity Issues in the Classroom

When exploring issues of equity, our intention is for you to take the whole child into account. Here, we explore how classroom instruction and activities can reflect the backgrounds and experiences of students in your class on a variety of factors (e.g., race, language, gender), and how you can use an anti-bias, antiracist framework to guide teaching and material development. Not every student will come to your classroom with the same level of access to language, experiences, knowledge, and external resources for getting support for reading outside school. Whereas *equality* simply means that everyone is treated the exact same way, *equity* means that everyone receives what they need to succeed, which is often different for individual students. Creating an equitable environment for the teaching of reading will serve all of your students.

It is important for you to recognize your students' home and family situations rather than making assumptions about their lived experiences. Their cultural and social backgrounds shape the kind of prior information and experiences they have, and you should keep them in mind when preparing your classroom instruction and activities. As a result of these diverse experiences or lack of experiences, your students may have an abundance of background knowledge in some areas and much less in other areas. Creating opportunities to tap into students' funds of knowledge as well as building needed background knowledge together as a class, prior to attacking a text, can be a source of discussion and a way to develop common understandings. However, you will need to be thoughtful when asking about background information. For example, for students living in poverty, what may seem like a benign request from a teacher, such as asking, "What color is your toothbrush?" when reading *Brush, Brush, Brush* by Alicia Padron (2010), can result in embarrassment for a student who doesn't currently have a toothbrush. When you ask questions about students' lived experiences, provide them with a shared experience (e.g., getting a dentist to donate toothbrushes to each student in the class), and then ask about these experiences, to help build the needed prerequisite knowledge. It is your responsibility to think about different factors that go into planning and to create a reading environment that is safe, equitable, and supportive.

Increasing your own awareness of racism and bias, evaluating your classroom culture, understanding the history of racism, and acknowledging your own personal biases and privilege will help you to address equity issues in the classroom (see Chapters 8 and 14 for more). Over time as you become familiar with the backgrounds and knowledge that your individual students bring to the classroom, you will increase your ability to identify the causes of comprehension breakdowns and support students' understanding of what they read. It is also important to use an anti-bias, antiracist lens when selecting books and other materials in the reading classroom. This includes selecting books with positive narratives versus trauma-focused narratives (or preparing students to engage in these narratives before you choose these types of books) and making sure to choose books with diverse characters to provide your students multiple opportunities to be able see themselves and others throughout texts. In addition, make sure to review material ahead of time so you are aware of all potential messages within the text and are prepared to guide conversations accordingly (Golos et al., 2021; Williams, 2020). Remember that when students see themselves in books, not only does it influence their own identity development but it also motivates them to engage in reading.

It is essential for you to create an environment that is supportive and safe for students from a wide range of languages, backgrounds, and cultures. Reading is one of the activities that Deaf students may have adverse feelings about. Students enjoy activities in which they excel and feel confident in, and they resist activities in which they feel they will not succeed. Risk-taking is critical for students to build reading skills, and when students do not feel safe with the notion that they are able to make mistakes, they will refrain from pushing themselves. As students are learning new reading vocabulary, information, and skills, it is critical that you be cognizant of your reactions to errors, how you provide feedback when students struggle, and when and where you provide feedback (privately versus in a group). It is important to begin with activities that allow students to experience success and enable confidence building.

Additional Things to Consider

Vocabulary and Reading

We have purposefully excluded vocabulary from the core recommendations. This chapter has limited space, and it is our perspective that vocabulary teaching and learning should be embedded in various comprehension activities. For example, when you carry out activities related to some of our core recommendations (i.e., using ASL translation, boosting cognition, and building comprehension), there will be natural opportunities for vocabulary development in both English and ASL. That said, we want to acknowledge the critical role vocabulary plays in reading development and would like to highlight a few strategies to foster vocabulary development. You can use a multilingual and multimodal approach to expand and deepen the students' vocabulary knowledge. As mentioned in the early childhood chapter (Chapter 2), you can pre-teach vocabulary to students at any reading level using strategies such as chaining (i.e., expanding on the meaning of a word; connecting a word in print to signs, visual representations, and/or fingerspelling) or sandwiching (i.e., fingerspelling a word, signing it, and then fingerspelling again; see Humphries & MacDougall, 1999, and Padden & Ramsey, 1998). Both approaches connect concepts that students know and link them to English (and additional languages when possible). Keep in mind that there may not be a one-to-one correspondence between the words of each language as in the case of two-word phrases (e.g., *look at* or *get out*), which have one-sign equivalences. Further, intentional chaining helps reinforce students' understanding of a concept through different modes in which it may be represented (see Chapter 4 for translanguaging examples). In addition, refer to Chapters 3 and 10 regarding ASL word families and translations, which are examples of how students' understanding of a concept may be deepened and enriched.

Another important element of using multilingual strategies during vocabulary instruction for Deaf learners is to provide them with opportunities to learn the varied meanings of words in both English and ASL (and additional home or heritage languages). When a word has multiple meanings, it is not sufficient to teach only the most common or most basic meaning of that word. The Frayer Model (an approach to teaching vocabulary that asks students to generate word definitions, examples, non-examples, and characteristics using a graphic organizer; Frayer et al., 1969) is a good approach for teaching multi-meaning words.

Also, vocabulary teaching should not be limited to individual words. It is important to teach meaning conveyed through a multiword level of representation, which is important for understanding meaning at the phrase level. For this and other methods specifically designed for teaching multiple meaning words for Deaf students, check the following resources: the Bedrock Curriculum (https://bedrockliteracy.com), Bilingual Grammar Curriculum (https://www.bgcasl.org), Fairview Reading (https://www.fairviewlearning.com), and ASL Standards (Laurent Clerc National Deaf Education Center, 2018).

It is essential to create an environment that fosters word consciousness (in both English and ASL as well as other languages as appropriate) among students. This might be fostered through classroom games and activities where students share new words with their peers. The words can be displayed in word walls (see Chapters 3 and 7) and become a classroom resource. When considering words to choose, select words for their *meaningfulness* to expand knowledge, enhance communication opportunities, and directly support comprehension during reading for Deaf learners.

Multimodal Strategies

If the student's ASL skills are emerging and the student has some spoken language skills, consider how you can expand on activities described throughout this chapter to include spoken English and/or a spoken home language. One strategy we suggest is to chain the sign, printed word, and spoken word. Consider the following when implementing multimodal strategies:

- Ensure that learning opportunities are equitable. Consider the needs of students with emerging ASL skills as well as the needs of students who are or are not developing spoken English.
- Use spoken English in ways that support those that benefit from sound but do not diminish learning for students who do not benefit from spoken English.
- Be purposeful in your language planning (see Nover, 2006). The appropriateness of these language practice opportunities is key and should reflect individual students' needs.
- When possible, take into consideration students' home and heritage languages as well.

This type of purposeful planning and communication is essential for maintaining respect and equity.

Selecting Appropriate Materials

When you are establishing and selecting materials for reading with your students, you have to keep in mind the students' varying reading levels. The challenge of ensuring that those at lower reading levels maintain positive self-esteem and confidence in their reading abilities is no small feat. It is important that you seek material that is of high interest to students because it helps provide motivation. Educational newspaper and magazine articles can be a good resource as some tend to be written at more accessible reading levels but contain topics that are relevant or of interest to older students (see Chapters 4, 5, and 7 for additional examples). Further, there are programs such as Achieve 3000 and Delta Explore that differentiate levels but provide consistent content. It is important that you provide students at all levels with resources that contain age-appropriate themes. Further, providing reading materials representative of a diversity of perspective, such as authors and characters from various races, genders, hearing levels, abilities, and cultural backgrounds, is essential for providing students with reading materials that not only reflect their own experiences but also broaden their understanding of other people's experiences. Try whenever possible to think about diverse perspectives in both the selections of the readings and in the discussions that ensue. As demonstrated in the following Teacher Tale, you as a teacher can make a difference in each of your student's experiences in class by creating a safe and supportive environment for all of your students. [*Equity*]

Teacher Tale

Jon was a student who came from a hearing household and started learning ASL when he began attending a school for the Deaf. As he was ending elementary school, his behavior grew concerning. He threw desks, used bad language, and was labeled a behavior problem by the time he was in sixth grade. It was the middle of that year that I started teaching. I worked hard to provide him a safe and supportive environment. By ignoring his negative behaviors and focusing on his positives, I discovered that Jon was acting out to avoid school work because at 11, he really couldn't read and he was socially aware and embarrassed. Jon could see the differences between the work he was assigned and the work assigned to others, and he didn't want work that looked babyish compared to his peers. He especially did not want his peers to notice. His other teachers and I began to modify the look of his assignments, and we made sure that reading assignments for him looked similar and covered similar content, which helped Jon access age-appropriate content that was still at his reading level.

—*Sixth-grade teacher of Deaf students*

(DI) (MM) (ES) (SEL) Bringing It All Together

When developing reading lessons, keep in mind that each reading lesson should be structured so that students receive (a) preteaching (before they read) designed to prepare them for reading, (b) activities that occur during reading to engage students in the meaning-making process, and (c) post-teaching in the form of a culminating discussion, activity, or task that occurs once reading is done. These before, during, and after elements of reading will need to be incorporated into the overall structure of your classroom. You will find that schools often provide directives for how much time should be spent on different aspects of a balanced literacy program (vocabulary work, guided reading, read-alouds, writing about what you read, and so on). Work as best you can within these parameters to include each of our suggestions. Here, we provide examples of reading lessons for both younger and older students that integrate each of the core recommendations and emphasize before, during, and after reading activities.

Lesson Plan With Younger Students (Range: Grades K–3 with modifications as needed)

The following sample lesson is from the beginning part of a unit plan on *Corduroy* by Don Freeman (1968), a classic story about a teddy bear waiting to be chosen as a child's stuffed animal. You might select this book to read as part of a unit about favorite things. [*Meaningfulness*] In using this book, you might provide a variety of toys and give students the choice to either bring something from home or select a favorite thing from your collection. [*Equity*]

Lesson Objectives: *Students will . . .*
1. Identify some characteristics of each of the main characters: Corduroy, girl, mother.
2. Define key vocabulary and concepts: corduroy, overalls, button, escalator, mattress, strap, friend.
3. Make predictions prior to reading the book.
4. Make inferences at the conclusion of the story.

Note that your lesson objectives should align with the Common Core Reading Standards for Literature as well as the ASL Content Standards, Viewing Standards for Literature. We encourage you to invoke the cognitive strategies in multiple languages.

Before Reading
To introduce the book, ask students to bring in (or choose from your collection) beloved toys or objects to share (and you should bring in one as well). [*Joy*] Use this to connect to the content of the book and create excitement with the class. After you have discussed the illustrations on the cover and back of the book, discuss key vocabulary words. It is helpful to have the words visible on the board or on a flipchart when discussing the meaning. Any pictures or drawings you add as prompts are helpful. Finally, engage the students in making predictions about the story using the following questions:

- What do you think the story is about based on the cover illustration?
- What do you think will happen when the security officer sees the toys (like we can see in the picture)?

During Reading
Students have been given their own copy of the book and are moving through literacy centers at this time. Each center focuses on different reading activities such as guided reading, vocabulary work, and thinking maps. You may need to create modified text with picture support for students with disabilities or language delays. During guided reading, make sure that you ask questions while the students are reading to monitor

their understanding. [*Comprehension*] Also, make sure to assist students with word attack strategies and in breaking down more challenging sentence structures.

After Reading

Once all students have rotated through time with you and the centers, have them come together as a class to discuss the story and answer inferential questions. Below are some open-ended questions you can ask that require higher order thinking [*Cognitive skills*]:

- How did Corduroy feel at the beginning of the story? What evidence do you have to support this?
- Why do you think the mother would not let the girl get Corduroy at first?
- How did Corduroy feel at the end of the story? What evidence do you have to support this?
- What was different about living in the store compared to living in his new home?

At the end of each reading lesson, students are required to write, sign (recorded on a tablet), or draw something related to what they read. In this case, they were asked to explain something they have experienced themselves that is the same as in the story (e.g., big store, escalator, buying a stuffed animal, mom telling you no, feeling like a toy is your friend) and also to mention and something from the story they have not experienced.

Lesson Plan With Older Students: (Range: Grades 8–10 with modifications as needed)

The following example covers what might be the first few chapters in a unit on *The Hunger Games* by Suzanne Collins (2008), a high-interest book for middle and high school students. This book can be taught using a variety of grouping approaches (individualized, small group, or whole class) based on student needs. This is an example of a book that might be selected by the students as a result of having seen family members and/or friends read it or having seen the movie. [*Joy*] The book emphasizes themes that are relatable to young people such as inequity between rich and poor, sensationalizing challenges and suffering, and the importance of appearances. [*Meaningfulness*] Before asking the class to begin reading the novel, discuss these themes. The discussion is not only to help you assess background knowledge but also to help students become aware of the themes that will be present throughout the book. Students who struggle or those with disabilities or language delays may benefit from the addition of picture support or text that you have modified in advance.

Lesson Objectives: *Students will . . .*
1. Identify some characteristics of each of the main characters: Katniss, Prim, Gale, Mother, Effie, Haymitch, Peeta.
2. Define key vocabulary and concepts: District 12, poaching, trespassing, peacekeepers, reaping, tribute.
3. Make inferences to answer questions about the first two chapters.
4. Make predictions about what will happen in Chapters 3–5.

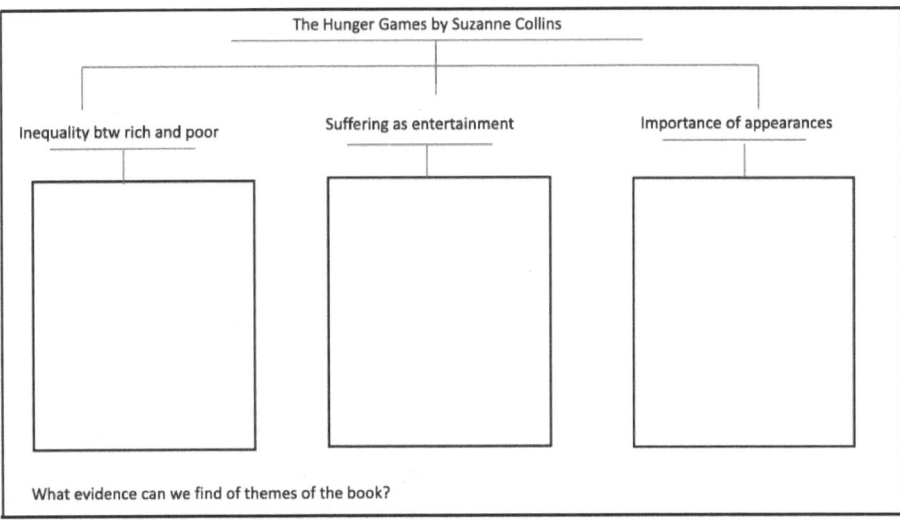

Example of a thinking map/tree map graphic organizer (Hyerle & Yeager, 2007).

Before Reading

Just before reading, review the target vocabulary for the targeted chapter(s) via a PowerPoint presentation that includes the English print and a picture or group of pictures that represent the meaning of each word. On each slide, ask the class for the sign and/or translation, and provide it if it is not known. Have students then add new vocabulary to the word wall.

During Reading

There are several different approaches for during-reading instruction. One approach is to sign a chapter aloud, making occasional check-ins for comprehension. Give each student a graphic organizer to keep notes to document evidence of the themes in the book (see example of a thinking map).

Another strategy during reading is for students to read independently. When doing this, you can pre-divide the chapter at places where comprehension of the story is crucial for understanding before moving on with the chapter. Ask the class to read to a specific page and then when everyone has reached that point, pause the class and discuss comprehension questions. The following comprehension questions are from the first two chapters of *The Hunger Games*. They should be presented to students in ASL (through signing the questions) while simultaneously projecting the written questions in English:

1. How did Mother feel when Katniss volunteered as tribute?
2. How did the people of District 12 feel about the Hunger Games?
3. Why would someone be a part of the Peacekeepers?

Questions for discussion can be differentiated for students. For those who may struggle to answer *how* or *why* questions, you can include *what*, *where*, or *when* questions (see Chapter 2 for additional examples). You should also be prepared to provide additional scaffolding for the questions you have asked. For example, for Question 1, you might ask your students to look in the book at a specific paragraph to identify some words that would give a clue about Katniss's mother's feelings or make the question into a more concrete question (e.g., What did Katniss's mother do after she saw Katniss volunteer as tribute?).

After the discussion, have students continue reading. You can have some students continue reading independently while having others rotate in pairs for a turn reading a section of the chapter with you or another adult. This ensures that you are providing students with opportunities for reading activities in large-group, small-group, and individual formats. When rotating to read with students, you are able to see their reading processes as they move along in the chapter, identifying areas where they may need additional support. This may result in adding words to the vocabulary lists and/or the word wall. By periodically reading one-to-one with your students, you can formatively assess their comprehension of and progress through the chapter. This gives you the opportunity to design instruction that is tailored to the individual needs of each student. [*Equity*] You should also encourage students to keep a list of words that they skip or to record the page numbers where they struggled to understand (see "What to Do" List on p. 127).

Here are some sample questions you can use to probe comprehension:

- Can you summarize what you just read?
- Where have you seen this word before? What does it mean?
- (When a student is confused) What is a strategy you can use to figure out what's going on?
- How would you sign this phrase in ASL?

After Reading

After your class has finished reading the assigned section, facilitate full-group discussions with students designed to engage them in inference-making and making predictions in ASL. Again, you should differentiate the difficulty of your questions to challenge your students at the appropriate levels. Next are sample questions to ask during a discussion like this after they have read Chapters 1 and 2:

- Why do you think Gale and Katniss discuss running away?
- Why do you think the term *tribute* is used?
- When Prim's name is drawn, how do you think she feels? Her mother? Katniss? Gale? And why do you think they feel this way?
- How do you think a Deaf tribute would adapt in *The Hunger Games*? What would the benefits be to being Deaf in that setting?
- Will Katniss make friends? Why will that be or not be important?
- How can Haymitch and Effie help Katniss?

You can close the lesson by asking students to make a connection between their experiences as Deaf individuals from diverse backgrounds to the experiences of the characters in the book so far. At the end of the reading lesson, students' "ticket out the door" is a prediction. Have students identify one defining event from what they read that day and then ask them to predict two or three possibilities of what they think will happen next. This can be in the form of drawing a picture, writing, or making a short and quick video on a tablet. You can also ask students to consider alternate endings or scenarios and discuss what those would look like (e.g., what would have happened if...?). Lastly, you might require students to reflect on what they have read and how it makes them feel either through writing or creating an ASL video (see Chapters 3 and 12).

 Your Turn to Practice!

Now it's your turn to try planning a reading lesson that incorporates all of the core recommendations using three phases of reading instruction: before, during, and after reading activity. If you are a teacher, plan a lesson for your students. If you are a teacher candidate and do not have access to a class, you can engage in mock teaching in a college class, imagining you are working with six fifth-grade students who do not read at grade level and vary in reading levels in the kindergarten to fifth-grade range. Imagine the students also range in their experience with ASL—from having been born and raised in a signing environment to that of having started to learn ASL within the last few months. First, read the book *How to Eat Fried Worms* by Thomas Rockwell (1973) with your students. Here is a template to help you develop a lesson that uses "before, during, and after" reading activities.

Develop a Lesson

Before Reading
- My lesson objectives for my students are _____.
- I will adapt the book and create supplemental materials for those who need it by (doing what?) _____.
- I will get students excited to read by _____. (Remember to find ways to talk about and model the joy of reading.)
- My preselected vocabulary words are _____ (choose 5–10 words). I will introduce preselected vocabulary by _____.
- I will activate background knowledge by _____.

During Reading
- I will monitor students' comprehension by _____. I will be prepared with guiding questions that help students make connections for comprehension and alternative questions to meet individual language needs.
- I will provide opportunities for students to apply reading strategies by _____.
- I will use the following graphic organizers to help students take notes and organize thinking during reading: _____.
- I will ensure that students increase independence during reading by _____.
- I will ensure that students get the individual support they need during reading by _____.
- I will include ASL in the reading process by _____. I will remember to use dialogue to support the reading process.

After Reading

- I will provide an opportunity for students to interact with others about the content of the book by _____. [*Meaningfulness*]
- I will challenge my students to think about what they are reading by _____. [*Cognition and Comprehension*]
- I will call my students' attention to figurative language in the text and how that same language is presented in ASL by _____. [*Translation*]
- I will facilitate connection with the content by _____. [*Meaningfulness*]
- I will allow for the opportunity to engage in creative expression about what was read by _____. [*Joy*]
- I will connect what we have read with other content areas by _____. [*Meaningfulness*]
- I will relate something from the reading to my students' cultural, social, and/or linguistic experience by _____. [*Equity*]

Teach Your Lesson With Your Students or in a Mock Setting

In your classroom, student teaching placement, or one of your classes in your teacher preparation program, try to use the template to develop then teach the lesson. Then reflect on it using the procedures explained next.

Reflect on Your Instruction: Questions for Post-Lesson Reflection

The perfect time to reflect on your lesson and think about what was successful and what you might change is right after you do the lesson (see Table 6.1). What did you do well? If you taught it again, what would you do differently? How well did your students learn the targeted objectives? Here are some questions to ask yourself.

Recommended Readings/Viewings

For Teachers/Teacher Candidates

- *Strategies That Work: Teaching Comprehension for Understanding and Engagement* (Harvey & Goudvis, 2007). This text explores the implementation of comprehension strategy instruction in the K–12 classroom and also provides sample lesson plans and activity ideas for teaching these strategies to students. [*Comprehension*]
- *Oxford Handbook on Deaf Studies in Literacy* (Easterbrooks & Dostal, 2021). This text covers diverse research-based topics such as literacy development with DeafBlind students, major elements of literacy learning (e.g., reading fluency, vocabulary development, morphological awareness). [*Comprehension, Equity*]

Table 6.1. Teacher Post-Lesson Reflection Sheet

Questions to ask yourself about your *before*-reading activities	Questions to ask yourself about your *during*-reading activities	Questions to ask yourself about your *after*-reading activities
Did you build enough equity and provide enough background knowledge prior to reading? ___ Yes ___ No Next time, I will _____.	Did you teach students strategies to enable them to maintain independence while reading? ___ Yes ___ No Next time, I will _____.	Did all students contribute to the discussion? ___ Yes ___ No Next time, I will _____.
Did you intentionally build your students' vocabulary knowledge? ___ Yes ___ No Next time, I will _____.	Did you have time in your schedule to provide reading independently and in pairs or small groups? ___ Yes ___ No Next time, I will _____.	Did the students have the opportunity to apply what they learned? ___ Yes ___ No Next time, I will _____.
Did you succeed in connecting the reading material to something currently relevant to students? ___ Yes ___ No Next time, I will _____.	Did you ask comprehension and additional types of questions that build higher order thinking skills? ___ Yes ___ No Next time, I will _____.	Did you ensure adequate comprehension through translation activities on selected parts of text or by providing supplementary background information and visually based materials? ___ Yes ___ No Next time, I will _____.
Did you select material that is motivating for students? ___ Yes ___ No Next time, I will _____.	Did you create experiences for you to read aloud? ___ Yes ___ No Next time, I will _____.	Did students enjoy the reading activity? ___ Yes ___ No Next time, I will _____.
Did you consider diverse backgrounds and experiences? ___ Yes ___ No Next time, I will _____.	Did you call on everyone to participate? ___ Yes ___ No Next time, I will _____.	How did you model a love of reading for your students? ___ Yes ___ No Next time, I will _____.
Score yourself and see how many YES responses you have out of 15!		

For Using With Students

Books to Use With Students

To emphasize planning for equity and to ensure meaning and engagement, we have put books that reflect diversity as the examples here. Note that schools vary in the books that they allow when it comes to controversial topics, and it is important to check with your school librarian for direction on resources.

- *The Family Book* (Parr, 2003). This book can be used with younger students to present a variety of diverse options for what a family can look like. [*Meaningfulness, Equity*]
- *Wonderstruck* (Selznick, 2011). This book, appropriate for middle and high school students reading at a Grade 4–6 level, contains two stories (one in pictures and one in words). The stories occur 50 years apart and are told by two different characters, one of whom is Deaf.
- *All American Boys* (Reynolds & Kiely, 2017). This book for high school students follows two characters as they navigate racism, switching between the perspective of a Black boy and a white boy. [*Meaningfulness, Equity*]

(MT) **Media to Use With Students:**

- Subscribe to YouTube channels. Rocky Mountain Deaf School (https://www.youtube.com/channel/UC7clP2oTJlzKjNTba7APp2A) and the California School for the Deaf, Fremont (https://www.youtube.com/@csdeagles) provide videos of Deaf adults reading stories, and the Atlanta Area School for the Deaf Veditz Studio provides stories and lessons via the Accessible Materials Project (AMP) www.youtube.com/AMPresources. [*Joy, Cognition, Comprehension*]
- Storybook apps published by Visual Language/Visual Learning (VL2) are available for download at https://vl2storybookapps.com/ [*Joy, Cognition, Comprehension*]

Note: The use of media certainly helps with making stories come alive and supports increasing the comprehension and joy of reading. Asking children questions about the videos they view before, during, and after is a critical component that requires adult interaction and mediation (see Chapters 3 and 12 for before, during, and after viewing strategies).

Conclusion

In this chapter, we highlight the importance of using ASL in reading activities especially as part of the strategy to support your student's understanding of what they are reading. Communication in ASL during reading also makes the process enjoyable and rewarding both for you and your students and also can provide you a keen understanding of the background, languages, and cultural knowledge that each student brings. Certainly, the task of teaching reading can be daunting but, as with many things, there are multiple paths to achieve reading success while creating joy for reading. Throughout this chapter, we have offered approaches to teaching reading that build on students' strengths and provide independence and feedback that enables

> "Reading was always just okay for me growing up. It wasn't until I was older that a colleague asked if I would be willing to be part of a book discussion related to racism. My serious interest in the topic had me surprisingly finish the book *Stamped* by Ibram X. Kendi and Jason Reynolds in just two days. I started to see the power that came with reading. I could support my beliefs with facts. I could have real debates with people about things. Teachers now are so lucky to be able to use social media and so many other materials to help find content that is highly motivating for students. Now I see the serious importance of making sure that what students read is relevant to their lives. Reading is power. Teachers really need to make sure students understand that.
> —Black Deaf teacher/behavior specialist/doctoral student

them to take risks and grow. When you create opportunities for discussions that take into account what matters to students, it not only develops their higher order thinking skills but can also help them see the value and purpose of reading. When you help students be successful readers and find that power of reading, there is joy—not only in fostering a lifelong love of reading for your students but also in fostering joy in your teaching. Teaching reading is challenging and rewarding! Connect with your fellow teachers and work together to create a great reading program in your own classroom and at your school. Don't worry, you've got this!

Sticking Points

- **Model joy.** Make reading FUN! Show students you love to read. Encourage curiosity through reading. Joy is essential.
- **Boost cognition.** Discuss, discuss, discuss. Do not underestimate the value of dialogue that has sufficient challenge and support to make students think.
- **Ensure meaningfulness, impact, and engagement.** Create opportunities for student engagement by selecting materials that are relevant to them. Their engagement is a reflection of your planning.
- **Use ASL translation during reading instruction.** ASL is critical! The use of a Deaf child's natural language(s) to access a text cannot be overstated, and ASL should be present throughout the reading process.
- **Build comprehension skills.** Ask questions to check for understanding and build comprehension skills.
- **Acknowledge the need for equity.** Your students are diverse and have a range of experiences! Make sure they see themselves in the materials you select and the topics you discuss.

Reading in the Content Areas

Chapter 7

Debbie Golos
Susan Outlaw
Sarah Jerger McGaughey

If you teach science, math, social studies, art, drama, or Deaf studies, you may not think too much about teaching reading and writing. Still, you don't have to be a reading or language arts teacher to include language and literacy instruction in your content area(s). In fact, doing so can provide increased benefits to your Deaf students, particularly those who have experienced language delays. This chapter is beneficial for all content area instructors to show how you can integrate reading in ways that are motivational. We will discuss multilingual strategies for reading in the content areas and why this is critical for Deaf students. We start by sharing a bit about ourselves.

Who Are We?

As a former sixth-grade reading/writing teacher, I (Debbie) often included theme-based units to integrate reading across the curriculum. I always loved to start with a book such as *Shiloh* (Reynolds Naylor, 2000). After reading the story, we would do a mock trial called *Preston v. Travers* to determine which of the two main characters would keep the dog, Shiloh. We would begin the unit with a field trip to the local courthouse. We would then return there at the end of the unit to conduct a mock trial in the actual courthouse. Another sixth-grade class would be invited to serve as the jury. Seeing the success of how reading could be integrated with social studies, science, writing, performing arts, ASL, and Deaf studies was an eye-opener for me. The students loved it! Now, as an associate professor of Deaf education, I use this project as a model in a language and literacy across the content area methods class; then, teacher candidates develop and teach their own interdisciplinary unit.

I (Susan) am the executive director at Metro Deaf School in Saint Paul, Minnesota. I have had more than 25 years in the field of Deaf education as a teacher and administrator and as an assistant professor. As a teacher from preschool to 12th grade, I developed interdisciplinary units with connections between the standards, the curriculum, and students' everyday lives. While an assistant professor, I taught courses related to language and literacy instruction in the content areas for preservice Deaf education teachers. A passion of mine is helping teachers from all content areas realize and embrace that they are, in fact, language and literacy teachers of their subject area.

When I (Sarah) entered the field of elementary teaching, our literacy block was 90 min on a daily basis. I depended heavily on textbooks to guide my instruction. I noticed that it was hard to engage my students due to varying factors—their background knowledge, their motivation and interest in the story, and their ability to make connections. During a health lesson, we were discussing fire safety. Their level of motivation and desire to know more about the content led me to connect this topic with literacy. After choosing a book about firefighters, we reviewed key vocabulary and discussed background/content knowledge. I read the story to the class, and then we took turns reading together. To allow them to continue to make connections after reading, we took a trip to the fire station. This experience as a new teacher allowed me to see how important it is for students to make language and literacy connections in the content areas. I quickly realized the benefits of interdisciplinary units!

Deaf Experiences, Perspectives, and Core Recommendations

Deaf students often arrive at school with limited world knowledge and language (e.g., Hall et al., 2017). As educators, it is important to provide an environment that is fully accessible and designed for students to make connections between their experiences and new language. Furthermore, literacy is essential to accessing and participating in the world around them.

Too often, we have seen Deaf students interested in varying professions, such as veterinarians, teachers, or business managers, but they aren't aware of the literacy skills needed to succeed in those jobs. Let's say you have a student who is great at building things and wants to be a construction worker; they will need to be able to read and interpret blueprints, review code specifications, and provide written documentation for billing purposes. To succeed in future careers, disciplinary literacy skills are critical (see Chapter 5 for more on disciplinary literacy skills). Yet, due to pervasive language delays among Deaf students that have impacted literacy development, content area teachers of science, math, Deaf studies, or social studies may focus more on conceptual knowledge of the subject devoid of any real integrated application of reading and writing. This approach of circumventing the students' literacy challenges may be viewed as responsive instruction by some; however, we take the position that it is further hindering students' growth and future opportunities. Further, students need to see how disciplinary literacy skills are important for their future and how reading skills in particular are needed to make sense of and apply content learning to their daily lives.

> "When I was in elementary school, I always loved math and reading. That changed once I got to middle school. I loved reading but when the concept of $a + b = c$ or "x" was introduced, I just couldn't understand the purpose or concept of having letters in math. Seeing children's picture book stories out there today that integrate math, I think, "Wow, I would have loved that!" I remember one day I was struggling with the "x" and "y" formulas and asked my teacher, "This makes no sense. When would I ever need to know this?" I also clearly remember to this day that she couldn't answer the question. She just told me that I needed to "focus harder on my work." I think it was at this point I gave up on math. I wonder how things would have gone differently if she would have been able to answer that question, making real-life connections or connections to stories!
>
> —Debbie Golos

We propose an interdisciplinary approach to integrate content knowledge and literacy. In this chapter, we describe the intentional integration of reading; for integration of writing, see Chapter 5.

Core Recommendations for Integrating Reading in Content Areas

We have identified three core recommendations that guide and support multilingual reading practices along with content learning:

- Connect print, American Sign Language (ASL), and content to build world knowledge.
- Implement critical thinking strategies.
- Create interdisciplinary units.

Effective Practices for Deaf Learners

Have you ever struggled with using textbooks with your K–12 Deaf students? Do you sometimes deliver content primarily in ASL because it provides easier and more direct communication with your students? We have too. Grade-level textbooks can be challenging to read or inaccessible to students, which makes presenting information in ASL ideal for developing content knowledge. However, learning how to read informational texts is critical for your students' futures in postsecondary programs or careers and independent living skills. There are now more high-quality informational books and stories than ever before that are available at varying reading levels. You can use texts such as these to supplement your instruction, connecting content in the texts to hands-on experiences such as field trips or experiments to build background knowledge and increase motivation. In this chapter, within each core recommendation we share suggestions and examples of how you can integrate reading into various subject areas from elementary through high school.

(MM) (ABAR) (DI) Core Recommendation 1: Connect Print, ASL, and Content to Build World Knowledge

In building students' world knowledge, you'll want to help them make connections between print on the page and ASL (and other home languages). We share ways you can do this through field trips, use of fiction and informational texts, and teaching target vocabulary.

Field Trips to Build World Knowledge

As mentioned in other chapters, it is important to provide authentic experiences such as field trips to help students build connections among what students are seeing in ASL and additional languages, reading in English, and experiencing. Field trips in a broader sense include experiential activities such as integrating a guest speaker, a video, an experiment, and opportunities to interact with real objects or pictures in and out of your classroom. These activities allow all of your students to share an experience and engage in related discussions in accessible language. It is an opportunity

Chew on This!

Did you know that . . . ?

- Content learning is optimized when students have regular access to a combination of informational texts, stories, and hands-on activities (Hoover et al., 2012; Vacca et al., 2016).
- When teachers thoughtfully choose texts that align with student interests within content areas, they are more motivated to engage in learning and reading (Rolston & Cox, 2015; Vacca et al., 2016).

for you to connect content with targeted vocabulary in ASL, fingerspelling, written English, and students' home languages. These opportunities provide students with world knowledge and connected languages to prepare them for reading in the content areas.

(MM) (MT) Teacher Tale

When beginning the book *Shiloh* (Reynolds Naylor, 2000) with my sixth-grade class, I would set up a field trip to the courthouse. An officer would guide us on a tour of the courthouse, showing us the judge's bench, the witness stand, and the jury deliberation room. We would meet the bailiff and learn about what their job entails. I would also invite a lawyer to join us at the courthouse to share with the students about their job duties and responsibilities. (If possible, we recommend inviting a Deaf lawyer, Deaf police officer, and/or other Deaf people so students see Deaf models.) After returning from the field trip, I would show them a video of a mock trial from a former class and let them know they will be doing their own mock trial in the actual courthouse. When I introduced the court- and trial-related vocabulary, they were able to connect the written word and ASL to their shared experience. The field trip led to increased world knowledge. They had developed the language and content-related experiences essential to engaging in meaningful discussions and preparing for their own mock trial.
—*Debbie Golos, former sixth-grade teacher*

(MM) Making Fiction and Nonfiction Connections

Whereas some students are motivated to learn by reading fictional stories, others are more motivated by reading informational text (e.g., Correia, 2011). Incorporating both into your content areas is not only a great way to motivate students to read, but it is also a great way for them to build world knowledge. For example, let's say you are teaching third grade. During recess, one of your students was looking at an ant on the ground and another student wanted to step on it. You can connect this to your upcoming science unit on bugs, incorporating a lesson on ants with the following embedded science and reading standards:

- **Science Standard from Common Core State Standards (CCSS)**
  Being part of a group helps animals obtain food, defend themselves, and cope with changes. Groups may serve different functions and vary dramatically in size.
- **ASL Content Standard/Viewing Standard for Literature Third Grade and CCSS Reading Standard: RI.3.1**
  Ask and answer questions to demonstrate understanding of a text, referring explicitly to the text as the basis for the answers.

One way to start this unit is by reading "aloud" in ASL (i.e., storysigning) the story *Hey, Little Ant* (Hoose & Hoose, 1992). In this story, a boy finds an ant on the ground that he wants to squish. Throughout the story, the ant shares how they have families and all work very hard. At the end, the book leaves the reader with a question: Should the boy step on and squash the ant? You can ask your students this same question and record their responses by making tally marks for those who would and those who wouldn't step on the ant. Then, to supplement this, over the course of a week you can read aloud from various informational texts about ant habitats, families, and so on, such as *Ants, Ants, and More Ants* (Roberts, n.d.) or *Amazing Ants* (Cooley Peterson, 2019).

Remember to use multilingual strategies to connect languages while reading aloud from informational texts as well as fiction (e.g., showing ASL and English simultaneously and using chaining to bridge languages). You can also call your students' attention to the differences in structures between informational texts and stories. This is a great way to reinforce structural aspects of informational texts across all content areas (e.g., directions, table of contents, figures, tables, indexes, glossaries, headings). These will help students understand how to access content and locate information within informational texts. If your focus is teaching content area knowledge, you may overlook these words and sign them in ASL without reference to the written words. Don't assume that students have learned these words in previous grades. It is important that you double-check that your students are not only learning the meaning of words in ASL but also recognizing them in fingerspelling and written English. In addition, you can guide them to develop an understanding of their meaning by examining examples in varying types of texts. Ask them to locate information such as, "Show me where the table of contents is" (fingerspell *table of contents*), "Can you point to the word *glossary*? Show me where to find the glossary? What information goes there?" (See Chapter 3 for information on creating ASL glossaries.)

 Stick It Into Action!

Teach Parts of Informational Text

You can make connections between fiction and nonfiction texts while also teaching students strategies for locating details in informational texts (Don't forget to follow up any yes/no questions with open-ended questions). For example, after reading *Hey, Little Ant,* you could say:

Teacher	Do you see on this page it says, "My nestmates need me because I'm strong"? The ant is saying he lives in a nest, but it shows a picture of the ant lying in bed reading a book with other ants. Do you think ants have beds like you do in their nest?
Student	No, not like us.
Teacher	Where do you think they sleep?
Student	On the ground.
Teacher	Well, let's check to see if you are correct. I have another book here; this one isn't a story but an informational text. It's called *Amazing Ants*. What did we learn about the difference between fictional stories and informational texts?
Student	Informational texts have facts.
Teacher	You are correct. They have real facts about ants. Now let's check to see if we can find where ants live. Remember that with informational texts we don't always have to start at the beginning. Where can we look to find information about ant nests?

Student	At the end.
Teacher	Correct at the end. Remember this is called an *index*. The index is one way we can look up information. Let's look up the word *nests* together and see what we can find out about what an ant nest looks like. (They look up the word and find a picture of an ant nest.) What do you notice?
Student	That is different from where I sleep. They are not in beds.
Teacher	Right! It is different from where people sleep. Ants sleep in nests rather than in beds. Great job! Let's add that to our concept map.

At the end of the bug unit, reread the book *Hey, Little Ant* and ask students open-ended questions to check for comprehension (e.g., "Where do ants live?"). Target the ASL and reading standards by asking them to support their reasoning with supporting details from both the story and informational texts. You can then extend the lesson on ants by providing various informational texts on different bugs, such as spiders while posing similar questions and engaging students in similar strategies.

One thing to keep in mind, though, before choosing your texts (whether informational or fiction) is to make sure to review them for accuracy and potential misunderstandings that students may have, both in the text and in illustrations. This way, you can consider what is needed in terms of additional prereading activities or pretaught vocabulary. To confirm science conceptual understanding and engage students in a close examination of the written texts, you can provide a graphic organizer for them to compare and contrast the differences in ant habitats portrayed in the fictional and factual texts. This is particularly critical for students with language delays and limited prior experience with comparing/contrasting. For example, the written text in the fictional book says, "I'm on my way with a piece of pie" (with a picture of the ant carrying a piece of pie on a plate). You can have students contrast this with the types of food and ways that ants actually eat. Other fictional stories might not accurately illustrate the correct number of legs for a spider, or correct color. When selecting informational texts, it is best if texts are accurate. When choosing fictional stories, be aware of the inaccuracies depicted so you can call attention to these and utilize them to stimulate critical thinking skills and develop conceptually accurate content knowledge.

There are many ways of incorporating reading and increasing disciplinary literacy skills while achieving content standards. While the bug unit example is specific to science, you can create similar connections between English print, ASL, additional languages, and content learning in math, social studies, or Deaf studies. For students who love stories, incorporating fictional and informational text can be one way to help your students engage in both content and literacy learning. There are many great informational picture books and chapter books at all grade levels and all content areas, including math.

  **Stick It Into Action!**

Reading Area for Content Teachers

Create a library or book nook in your classroom (see Chapter 2 for more on book and ASL nooks). Keep a variety of informational texts and stories related to the content area

Stick It Into Action! (*continued*)

Student making connections with an informational text and globe.

topics you teach. These can be in the form of posters, magazines, pamphlets, books, and primary sources and can be provided at varying reading levels. You should also set up an ASL media area where children can watch informational ASL videos. If you have a math or science lab area, make sure to provide an ample variety of materials for students, including informational charts, journals, articles, graphs, and other texts.

Word Learning in Content Areas

Another way to help students build world knowledge in content areas is by helping them understand the meaning and origin of words. This can be done in any content area and in any subject. In the following Teacher Tale, Kristin Stai, a high school science teacher at Metro Deaf School, demonstrates how she engages students in word study in science by exploring parts of English words (e.g., roots, suffixes, prefixes) and then relating these to ASL signs. These short mini-lessons in her high school science classes help students begin to recognize root words in larger words they see every day and in their science textbook and materials.

 Stick It Into Action!

Word Study in Science

Here is an example of word study in science during a lesson on heat and temperature:

Kristin   The root word "therm" is related to heat. [Teacher *fingerspells "THERM" and writes the word on the whiteboard.*] Can you get into pairs and list all the words that you can think of that include the root "therm"?

Root Words

Acid- a substance with a sour taste	E/Ef- out or without	Hypo- under or below or low
Allo- other	En- to cause (a person or thing) to be in	Hydr- water hydrogen
Alpha- first, beginning	Endo- inside	Im- not or in
Amino- chemical compound formed from ammonia	Equ- equal	In- inside
	Erg- work	Iso-equal
Amph-both sides or both kinds	Exo- outside or outer	Kilo- one thousand
	Ferr- iron	Kine- movement
Anti- against or opposite of	Fiss- cleft	Lipo- fat
Aqua- water	Fract- to break	Lys- break out
Baro- pressure	Gen- 1. informal term for information	Macr- large
Bi- twice or two or pair		Malle- shaped by hammering
Bio- life	2. make or beginning	Mer- part
Carb- carbon	Glyc- 1. sugar	Met- change
Co/Com- with or together	2. gylcogen	Meter- measure
Cry-cold	Graph- 1. variant of -graphy	Micro- small
De- do or opposite of not	2. write	Milli- one thousandth 1/1000
Dens- thick	Halo- salt or combined halogen	Misc- mix
Di- two		Mono- one
Did/Dis- not, apart, or away	Hetero- different or other	Morph- form shape
	Homo- same	Neo- new
	Hyper- over or excessive or more	Nom- name

Word study poster in a science classroom.

Students get into pairs and then think about, discuss, look up, and write various words on chart paper, such as *thermostat, thermometer, thermos, hypothermia, endothermic,* and *thermal.*

Kristin   Does knowing the meaning of the root word "therm" help us better understand these words?

—*Kristin Stai*

In addition to giving students the root word and having them come up with examples, you could also give them a word and ask them to tell you what the root word is and what they think it means. For example, Kristin gives students a list of words for a science unit that she will be discussing related to transportation, but she also includes words students have learned in previous units, such as *transportation, transcontinental, transmission, transparency,* and *transatlantic.* Then, she asks them to discuss the meaning of each word and checks to see if students can figure out what the root word "trans" might mean. She also keeps a list of science-related root words on the wall for students to refer to throughout the year. You can do this for any subject you teach.

Here is an example of an ASL word study focusing on root words. This bulletin board was created by a Metro Deaf School second-grade teacher, Katarina Isola. She uses the bulletin board to classify ASL signs by handshape, location, and movement, just as English words can be categorized into families. Students are involved in studying ASL signs in a similar way to studying word families with English words. This allows students to independently use an ASL resource using the handshape and location of signs, similar to finding English words in an alphabetically ordered dictionary. Students

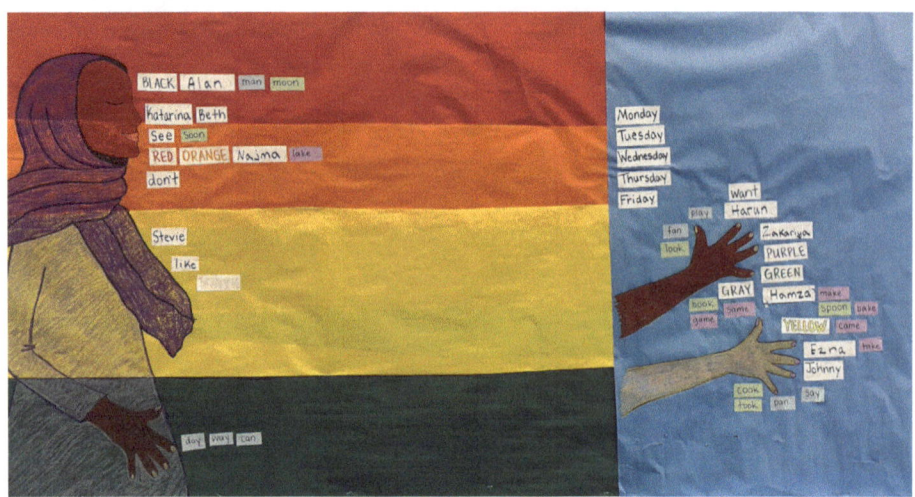

Sign study bulletin board by ASL parameters.

can then refer to the bulletin board when doing English reading and writing activities. Katrina expresses how it helps her students increase their metalinguistic awareness skills and helps develop pride in both languages.

At Marie Philip School for the Deaf, the first-grade team uses a digital and interactive picture-based ASL dictionary. The dictionary was developed by a teacher in a digital format for students to use on tablets. It is organized by the ASL parameters of location and handshape and is used as a word bank resource for students to foster independence with reading and content learning. The following Teacher Tale demonstrates how one teacher uses this interactive dictionary to support content learning.

Teacher Tale

Using an ASL Picture Dictionary in Social Studies

This is an interaction between a first-grade teacher, Anne Marie, and one of her students during a social studies class related to the theme of "community helpers." It illustrates how an ASL picture dictionary can be used to learn targeted vocabulary during social studies and foster students' independence in finding English words using their ASL knowledge.

Anne Marie	Can you name some people who provide services to our community?
Student	(raises hand and signs) Doctor.
Anne Marie	Yes, doctor. That is a great example of someone who provides services to people in our community. Go ahead and write down that word under the column "Services" (points to column "Services").
Student	I don't know what to do.

Identify ASL handshape locations by color.

READING IN THE CONTENT AREAS

Anne Marie	Remember, you can look in the ASL dictionary. What is the first step?
Student	Look for the color! (Student uses the ASL dictionary, which shows ASL locations by color.)

The student signs DOCTOR to themself and identifies the sign location color as green. The student clicks on the green portion of the ASL dictionary, which is located on Google Slides. This then leads the student to the next slide, which shows different handshapes for signs in that location.—Anne Marie Smith, a first-grade teacher

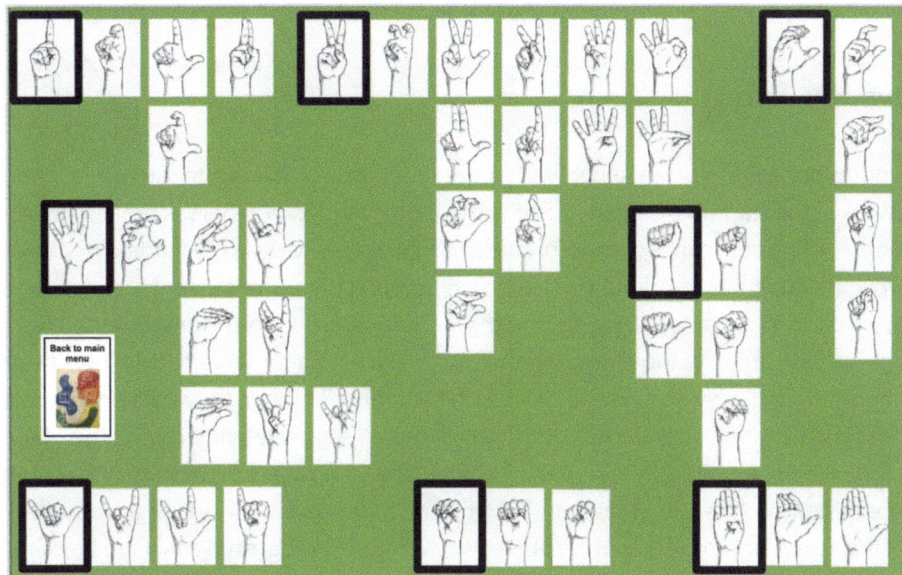

ASL handshapes by location.

The student identifies the handshape being a D handshape and clicks on it. The next slide shows different signs related to the handshape selected. The student then sees a picture of a doctor and sees the related English print.

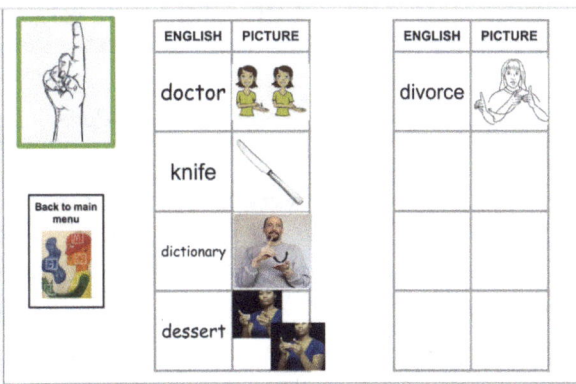

Signs related to ASL handshape location with picture and print.

The student then writes down the word *doctor* under the column "Services."

Modifying Materials for Reading Levels

No matter what subject you teach, you are likely to encounter students with varying language and reading levels. To make connections between ASL, content, and print, it is important to have materials that align with students' reading levels. How often have you found materials for a grade-level topic you wanted to teach, but the reading level of the materials was too high for some of your students? This often means that as Deaf educators, you have to select multiple materials or modify/create your own. In the following Teacher Tale, I (Debbie) will share how I was able to target both social studies and reading objectives by selecting materials appropriate to students' varying reading levels.

Teacher Tale

During one year, students involved in the mock trial unit were reading at varying levels. Some students read on or above the sixth-grade level, whereas other students were reading at second- or third-grade levels. I was able to diversify reading materials while maintaining the same content learning objectives. The students reading at a second- or third-grade level served on the *Preston v. Travers* jury (from *Shiloh*) and were able to participate without reading the same text. In fact, to serve on the jury, it was important that they were not familiar with the story. That way, they could deliberate as a jury member solely based on what they observed and learned during the trial.

Students serving on the jury then participated in a different mock trial based on *The Three Little Pigs* story that had text written at their levels. I was able to address all of the same content and reading objectives with a mock trial on *Wolf v. Pigs*. Students read the books *The Three Little Pigs* (Seibert, 2001) and *The True Story of the Three Little Pigs* (Scieszka, 1996). (*Note:* Make sure to pick a version of *The Three Little Pigs* where the wolf doesn't die at the end, because he needs to be a witness at the trial!). These books are at a lower reading level, but students still search for details within the illustrations and words of the texts to find evidence to use in the trial (e.g., a cup of sugar to support the reason the wolf went to the pigs' homes). They also used the information to develop their questions for witnesses (e.g., "Why did you, Alexander T. Wolf, go to the pig's house?"). The students go through the whole trial process, hitting on the same reading and content objectives.

—*Debbie Golos*

When creating or modifying materials, make sure to review the directions to ensure that they are at your students' *independent* reading levels. With assigned homework, even if you explain what they are supposed to do in class, students need to be able to reread the directions at home on their own, so all materials you develop or modify should be at your students' independent reading levels. If they are not yet reading multiple paragraphs, you wouldn't want to give them homework that has directions in multiple paragraphs with complex sentences or include vocabulary that they aren't familiar with. Also, consider the type and size font you use. With younger students or students reading at lower levels, you will want to use a clear font that is a bit larger. Also, don't forget to include the word *directions*—a key vocabulary word for all content areas! Here is an example of modified directions for an assignment related to the mock trial.

Stick It Into Action!

(DI) Modifying Materials

In this assignment, I first asked students to list their top choice of who they wanted to be in the mock trial (i.e., lawyer or witness, and if a witness, which one). For those reading and writing at grade level, the directions read:

Directions: In complete sentences, explain (a) why you want this role, (b) what you think your responsibility will be during the trial, and (c) why I should choose you for that role (followed by an empty space for them to respond).

I then modified the language for those reading below grade level and also typed it in a larger font.

Directions: List three reasons I should choose you for this role.

1. _____
2. _____
3. _____

(PI) (SEL) (MM) Mindfulness in Content Areas

One topic not often considered in content areas is connected to mindfulness. Although little research has been conducted in classrooms with Deaf students, many benefits have been documented for teachers and for hearing students regarding integrating mindfulness into the classroom, such as increasing engagement, focus, and a positive sense of self, which are bound to have a positive impact on content and literacy learning (e.g., Cheang et al., 2019; Thierry et al., 2016) as well as prevent teacher burnout (e.g., Taylor et al., 2021). You can start by doing regular mindfulness activities in ASL at the beginning and end of each class (see Chapters 2 and 8 for additional ideas). They don't have to take up much time; they can vary from 30 sec to 1 min long, such as asking students to take a few deep breaths, or up to 5 min on days you have more flexibility. You can then integrate mindfulness texts that connect to your content lessons to build world knowledge about your content while also increasing student engagement and awareness of mindfulness activities.

For example, let's say you are doing a lesson on the water cycle. You can open and/or close your lesson with the "rainstorm" and "cloud" activities from the book *Breathe Like a Bear* (Willey, 2017). As described in the following Stick It Into Action, you can use the cloud activity to inspire creativity while also providing visual/kinesthetic ways to practice expressing conceptually accurate meanings (e.g., imagine you are a rain cloud; snowstorm; big, puffy cloud) and also to help them release frustration and/or be more prepared to focus. You can use ASL and written English to highlight targeted vocabulary (e.g., *cloud, raindrop, storm*) in your unit and then engage your students in the following mindfulness activity. It can also offer you, as a teacher, a way to maintain patience and be more present.

 **Stick It Into Action!**

Mindfulness Moment in Science

You seem frustrated. I understand. Let's practice mindfulness. It can help you to breathe easier and let go of your frustration. Remember the word *raindrop*? (Remind students of the meaning of the word and then use chaining to point to the written word, sign it, and fingerspell.) Now, imagine you are a dark gray storm cloud. You are so full, you feel like you will burst. Take a deep breath and, on the exhale, let all the raindrops go. Imagine your angry raindrops just falling away. Slowly breathe in and out three times. Let's do it together. Breathe in. Breathe out. Breathe In. Breathe out. Breathe in. Breathe out. Did you feel your angry raindrops falling away? Great, now let's learn more about the different types of clouds that have raindrops.

Core Recommendation 2: Connect Critical Thinking With Content Area Reading

Fostering the development of critical thinking skills can help students not only to have a deeper understanding of your target content but also help them to develop skills needed for successful lifelong learning and ultimately increase their independence in accessing new information. You can extend each of the previously described examples during content area reading by building in time for developing critical thinking skills such as higher order questions, inferential skills, cause and effect, synthesis, and evaluation. By providing your students with opportunities to engage in both small- and large-group discussions in ASL, it can push your students to think critically.

For example, let's go back to the *Hey, Little Ant* book (Hoose & Hoose, 1998). After reading the story and learning facts about ants through the informational texts, revisit the students' responses on whether they would or would not squash the ant. Work together to create a cause-and-effect chart. Have students take turns responding to the question, "What would be the effects if they did or did not squash the ant?" After completing the chart together, ask each student if they want to keep or change their answer. Then, ask them to support their reasoning with information from the chart. This teaches them the critical thinking skill of connecting cause and effect while also reinforcing the reading skill of identifying supporting details. Further, it provides an opportunity to monitor and deepen comprehension on what they learned about ant behaviors and habitats.

Critical Thinking in Social Studies

Recall that in Chapter 5, Dostal and Graham describe an upper-elementary history unit focused on cultivating students' identities as activists and allies. The class discusses Columbus Day and whether it should be changed to Indigenous Peoples' Day. Let's explore their unit further by adding reading activities. First, you can have students read books about Christopher Columbus from varying perspectives through books such as *Encounter* (Yolen, 1992) and *Columbus Day* (Gardeski, 2000). These texts provide students with access to content knowledge about Christopher Columbus from two perspectives: the perspective of Christopher Columbus and/or those with him, as well as the perspective of Indigenous people.

Key Strategy

Then, using a strategy called "**literature detectives**" (Henning et al., 2006), have your students engage in critical thinking skills (see Stick It Into Action). Your students become detectives, identifying what perspectives are shown and how some perspectives might be missing. For each book, have students respond to the following questions in a graphic organizer: Who talks in the book? What is shown? What is described? What is the author's perspective? Often missing from history books is the perspective of Indigenous peoples. The literature detective's strategy provides students with opportunities to analyze potential stereotypes that may be depicted in these stories. It is also an excellent way to practice reading skills for content-learning purposes and to build critical thinking around historical events like the arrival of Christopher Columbus.

In addition, you can connect to Deaf studies by including books with Deaf characters and Deaf people to discuss where and how Deaf people fit in time with the historical event and/or what a Deaf perspective to the event might be (see Chapters 2, 8, and 9 for more on books with Deaf characters/people). Think about ways you could implement this activity across grade levels and other content areas.

Stick It Into Action!

(ABAR) (MM) Literature Detectives

Let's apply the literature detectives' approach with another example on the topic of the Underground Railroad (see Table 7.1). You can have your students examine this topic using texts from various perspectives such as a Deaf perspective, a Black perspective, a Black Deaf perspective, and a white hearing perspective. Prior to reading and discussing these with your students, it is important to review what stereotypes may be present related to Black people and Deaf people. Encourage them to look for both positive and negative messages they may find in the texts (e.g., Golos et al., 2012).

One thing to keep in mind is that lessons related to slavery and racism may be traumatic for some students. Topics like this should not be isolated but integrated into a larger thematic unit, in this case, that also includes the history of Black people, Black Deaf people, resilience, revolution, and so on. When you engage in tough conversations, it is important to create a space where students feel they can share their perspectives bravely and learn from one another, and where those who have been oppressed are not blamed for their oppression and others are not judged for their lack of experience or knowledge (see Chapter 8). Also, be considerate of students who have witnessed or lived through similar experiences of disempowerment, because they can be triggered by classroom conversations and/or material. Make sure you are prepared to engage in these units before taking them on. Keep in mind that preferred word choices are ever evolving in communities (e.g., *enslaver, enslaved* rather than *slave, master*). We suggest reviewing terminology and best practices for anti-bias and antiracist instruction as well as trauma-informed approaches to education before you

Table 7.1. Literature Detectives

	Signing Black in America (Language & Life Project, 2020) https://youtu.be/oiLltM1tJ9M	*Secret Signs: An Escape through the Underground Railroad* (Riggio, 2003)	*Henry's Freedom Box: A True Story From the Underground Railroad* (Levine, 2007)	*Unspoken, A Story from the Underground Railroad* (Cole, 2012)
Who speaks/signs in the book/film?	Black Deaf people	White hearing people	Black hearing people who are enslaved	White hearing people
What bias/stereotypes or negative messages about people are shown in the illustration?	N/A	Deaf in danger	N/A	No representation of enslaved people
What bias/stereotypes or negative messages are portrayed in the text?	N/A	Deaf character as brave; Black characters saved by white character; no perspective of enslaved people	N/A	Assumption that the reader would identify with white abolitionists; no perspective of enslaved people
What positive/cultural messages are shown in the illustrations	Real-life interviews/videos of Black Deaf people and Black schools	Deaf character using sign	Black character as courageous; realistic depictions	White child character has sense of morality
What positive/cultural or accurate messages are described in the text	Sharing narratives of history of Black ASL; accurate depictions and historical accounts of Black Deaf people	Deaf and hearing communicating using sign	Black characters as smart and courageous; enslaver as abusive; other white characters as allies	N/A
What is the point of view of the author?	Black Deaf creators, actors, and producers	White hearing author and illustrator	White hearing author Black illustrator	White hearing author

begin (see Recommended Readings/Viewings and https://transformingeducation.org/resources/trauma-informed-sel-toolkit/).

In the next Teacher Tale, we demonstrate how you can promote critical thinking in high school by analyzing primary sources.

> **Teacher Tale**
>
> **Primary Sources to Foster Critical Thinking in High School**
> When teaching high school content areas such as social studies, my students are often very engaged with the topics but come to the class with a wide range of English literacy skills. I use a number of strategies to assist students with analyzing primary sources. Lessons with primary sources encourage critical thinking skills (e.g., reasoning, inferring, predicting) and foster language and literacy development in the content areas. I typically bring in visual primary sources, which provide less of an English barrier for some students and allow me to focus more on their ASL development and critical thinking skills before transferring the same skills to English. Thoughtful use of primary source analysis can address multiple state and Common Core reading, ASL, and social studies standards.
>
> For a lesson on civic engagement and intersectionality, I curated a collection of primary and secondary sources about the 1977 protests to enact Section 504 of the Rehabilitation Act (prohibiting discrimination based on disability). Some were photographs such as images from the 504 sit-in in San Francisco, others were combinations of text and images such as a news article about the sit-in from the Black Panther Intercommunal News Service, and still others were text-only such as published interviews with organizers. Students analyzed the primary and secondary sources for the civic engagement strategies that activists used. Students then organized the strategies according to how much of a personal risk was at stake for each type of action. After that, students looked for examples of strategies used by activists in current events, and then choose an issue about they wanted to take civic action on themselves.
> —*Wendy Harris, high school social studies teacher*

(MM) (ABAR) (PI) (MT) Core Recommendation 3: Incorporate Reading Into All Content Areas With Interdisciplinary Units

Developing robust interdisciplinary units is one way to connect learning happening across content areas. You can integrate reading into interdisciplinary units through topic-relevant texts, stories, and experiences. But where do you start? First, select unit topics and materials that are interesting for your students to increase their motivation to engage with learning and reading! The students' learning can be deepened when they have exposure to content that is repeated through multiple contexts. Provide them with a combination of hands-on and mind-on experiences, field trips, stories, and various types of informational texts (e.g., newspapers, recipes, magazines) connected to your unit topic (Hoover et al., 2012; Vacca et al., 2016). If you teach elementary school, you might teach all subjects, which makes it easier for you to plan and implement interdisciplinary units. However, even if you don't teach all subjects, you can collaborate with other teachers to work together on a unit (see Additional Things to Consider). I'll tell you a bit more about how I (Debbie) implemented the interdisciplinary unit on the mock trial, and in the Bringing It All Together section, you can read more about how to integrate multiple content areas into the unit.

Teacher Tale

In the book *Shiloh* (Reynolds Naylor, 2000), the main character Marty Preston finds a dog covered with ticks and whose ribs are showing. He keeps the dog hidden and cares for it as he nurses it back to health. However, the man who owns the dog, Judd Travers, wants the dog back. There are many ways to connect reading in the content areas. For science, you can have students read about nutritional health in dogs and ways to identify whether a dog is undernourished. In my class, students used what they learned to support their statements as witnesses in the mock trial (*Travers v. Preston*) and this supported their argument as to who should keep the dog.

—*Debbie Golos, former sixth-grade teacher*

In another example described in the following Teacher Tale, Amy Garvey, a fifth-grade teacher, created an interdisciplinary unit on food trucks. Her students had seen a food truck, asked questions about it, and wondered what it would take to run one. These questions initiated the unit. Amy gathered informational texts on food trucks for students to read as a class, and she selected and taught targeted vocabulary on the topic. To initiate the unit, they took a field trip to an area that had many different kinds of food trucks. Then, she presented an assignment that would include having students design their own trucks, including the types and amounts of food to make for the trucks. The food trucks unit was interdisciplinary, integrating math, health, and reading.

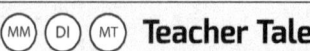 

Teacher Tale

At the time of this project, the trend of food trucks was starting to take off. When asking students about their knowledge of food trucks, most of them were only able to identify those with hot dogs and ice cream. This led to watching the *Great Food Truck Race* on the Food Network to help build students' knowledge about the current food truck trend. In addition, students read a book, *Food Trucks,* from Reading A–Z; https://www.readinga-z.com/book.php?id=3160), which provided great examples and pictures of the variety of food trucks. The colorful photographs of real trucks (as opposed to illustrated, fictional ones) excited the students and inspired their final projects to be full of color and character. Students put time and effort into designing their trucks, choosing the cuisine, learning about the associated cultures, and designing uniforms and logos that reflected the culture appropriately. One student decided she was going to create a menu with foods related to her own nationality.

This class of students was very resistant to learning math with a mindset of "When am I ever going to use this stuff?" The food truck unit showed them firsthand how often we use math in the real world. The students were responsible for developing their budget and hiring all of their staff, from drivers to chefs and managers. They gave consideration to pricing, expenses, and profits among many other responsibilities that come with owning a food business.

A typical fifth-grade perspective is that a customer walks up to the counter, orders food, food gets thrown into a bag, and then they are on their way. After this project, students had further insight into how many "hands" it takes to create even just one inexpensive fast-food meal. The question educators normally get from students—"When am I ever going to use this in real life?"—became obvious during this project. From a career education standpoint, learning how many roles are involved in even a small business taught students that future job opportunities in the food industry can go beyond being a cashier or cook. The students talked about their own personal interests and how those skills could be turned into long-term careers. For instance, the student who enjoyed building their truck and designing their logo and uniforms learned about career opportunities in construction and graphic design, whereas the student who enjoyed figuring out how to get the largest profit in the class learned about careers in finance. This project was long and included many parts, but each student was able to take away something, and all students experienced how reading and math are applied to real-world situations.

—*Amy Garvey, fifth-grade teacher*

There are many ways you can create opportunities to incorporate fiction and informational texts throughout a unit like food trucks. For example, you can read books about food trucks, local articles, interviews, menus, maps, recipes, schedules, and real-world math problems. Students gain background knowledge and vocabulary while learning the content.

 Stick It Into Action!

Reading and Food Trucks
See the many ways you can incorporate reading into content instruction on the topic of food trucks.

Reading and Math (together as a large group or small group activities)
- Read and research about food trucks in the area. Create a pie chart of the number and types of food trucks.
- Develop simple surveys for food options and graph the results.
- Read recipes together and have students decide what food you will make.
- Solve word problems to predict how many customers they will have within 1 hour.
- After reading an informational text about graphs, have students graph their supply and demand based on sales data.
- Read one recipe and practice halving or doubling it.
- Create a list of ingredients they will need and go shopping on a budget.
- Read the ingredients of items with different brands. Compare which is healthiest and least expensive.

Stick It Into Action! (*continued*)

Reading and Health and Nutrition
- Read and review the food pyramid and government health guidelines. Read food labels and discuss what is healthy (or not) about the food items. Discuss what foods you will serve from your food truck and how healthy they are.
- Hand out pictures of various food items with labeled sentences for students to read (this is particularly beneficial for students who are new to this country or who have language delays).
- Have students create a balanced menu for your food truck. Include pictures and print for each item.
- Make a recipe book of your food truck items.

Reading and Social Studies
- Read informational books about food trucks and visit local food trucks.
- Bring informational texts for students to research where different foods come from and read about these cultures. Discuss various types of food and where different foods originated from.
- Find locations on a world map and place pictures of various foods on the map to show their origins. Bring in or make some of the foods discussed.

Note: Be mindful of any allergies or other food restrictions and communicate with families before sharing food with the class.

Reading and Art
- Read *Chef Roy Choi and the Street Food Remix* by Jacqueline Briggs Martin and June Jo Lee (2017). Discuss how art is integrated throughout the book to represent food. Explore the artwork used on food trucks and ask, "How does the art make you feel?" and "What is the relationship (if any) between art and food?"

Deaf Studies
- Read about Deaf-owned restaurants and view videos of interviews in ASL with the owners.
- Read about the names and designs of Deaf-owned restaurants. Discuss what students would name their trucks that represents their own language(s), race, or culture(s). Consider the design of the food truck and menu.
- Read a couple of example communication policies. Have students develop one for their food truck and discuss what language(s) their menu will be in and if they will have a sign posted for their communication policy.

Project-Based Learning
Another way to do interdisciplinary units is through project-based learning (PBL). PBL is an instructional method in which students gain knowledge and skills by planning and executing a project over an extended period of time. This is a student-centered project that allows for investigating and responding to an authentic student question, problem, or challenge. It allows students to explore real-world issues and fully engage in a topic connecting languages, informational texts, stories, and content

areas. It often ends with a culminating event or project of the students' choice. There are many different ways to approach a culminating event that can be related to the unit topic. It could be running a science fair, creating a food truck, going on a camping trip, cleaning up a park, and so on. PBL differs from interdisciplinary units in that it is student driven, meaning students bring their interests and experiences to the project. It allows students to explore real-world issues and fully engage in a topic (see Duke, 2014 for more on integrating informational text and project-based instruction).

The *Shiloh* unit is an interdisciplinary unit that originally stemmed from a question initiated by the students while reading the book. They wanted to learn more about how to fight to keep a dog that was being abused by its owner. The culminating event for the *Shiloh* unit was conducting a mock trial. We invited other sixth-grade classes to sit on the jury. Students were empowered to take leadership and excited to participate in the trial. It also had real-world implications for them because it taught them how to identify signs of a dog being abused and how they could look for evidence to support an argument to fight for justice.

(PI) (MM) (MT) *Project-Based Learning in High School*   Here, we provide an example of what a high school PBL experience with Deaf students can look like. In this example, students were taking an elective course titled "Project-Based Learning." The students started by brainstorming issues that bothered them. The topic of dating and going to restaurants came to the forefront of the discussion, and students knew they wanted to explore this further. Students felt that servers often didn't communicate food options with them, such as specials for the day, how they would like their meat cooked, options for sides, or salad dressing or sauce options at restaurants. They also shared a common complaint that waitstaff would not check on them during service. Some students felt that the waitstaff were scared to interact with them. Many felt that the service they received was poor.

After discussing the problem and their experiences, they worked together to develop a plan and timeline for the project, which was submitted to their teacher for approval. The teacher's role was to guide the PBL as a teacher facilitator. The teacher helped support their learning with mini-lessons on related topics (e.g., Deaf studies, reading, statistics) and helped keep the students focused with some clear timelines.

Students read about other members of the Deaf community who had similarly negative experiences at restaurants. From there, they decided to create and administer a paper-and-pencil survey to distribute to Deaf community members to learn more about their specific experiences. First, they read about how to format and develop a good survey and then they developed and shared their survey with their teacher for feedback. Then, after finalizing their survey, they went to a large Deaf community event, distributing and collecting more than 150 completed surveys. Once they had their data, the next step was to learn how to analyze it. The teacher facilitator conducted mini-lessons on statistics to guide students on how to analyze their data by applying mathematical concepts. Students concluded from their results that negative restaurant experiences are not isolated events but rather commonly shared experiences of Deaf people. In general, respondents felt that restaurant staff do not know how to work directly with Deaf customers.

As a follow-up, each student interviewed a Deaf community member on video and transcribed it. Translating from the ASL on video to written English was a learning experience for all students. These transcriptions allowed students to document and analyze their interviews, find common themes, and have it in written English ready to use in a grant application. By that point, the students better understood the problem and they could begin to explore how to be a part of the solution.

The teacher shared information about a national competitive grant to gain funding support for high school students looking to make a difference in their communities. The students didn't know much about grants, let alone how to write a grant. The teacher invited a professional from a local university to discuss the nuts and bolts of grant writing. Once students had a draft written, he reviewed their grant narrative and provided feedback for revisions before their final submission. The students were in fact awarded the grant, which allowed them to partner with a national restaurant chain to make short training videos on how to successfully work with Deaf customers. The students engaged in literacy and content learning during their project while also gaining real-world knowledge and experiences that can create systemic change.

Additional Things to Consider

 Collaborate With Other Teachers

There are many ways to integrate interdisciplinary units, and your approach may depend on what grade you are teaching and which subject(s). Some of you might be able to do an interdisciplinary unit on your own. For those of you who do not teach all subjects, you might consider the benefit of collaborating with other teachers. There are multiple ways to do this when you take an interdisciplinary approach. The first step is to identify other teachers you want to collaborate with and meet with them to determine a topic. You might need to discuss schedules with school administration to ensure that you have time to regularly collaborate. It is important to select a topic that is based on your students' interests or a question they have. You can also consider incorporating a culminating activity to have the students work toward. Make sure to infuse language arts and literacy into each content area and discuss as a group who will be responsible for instruction of what skills and objectives. Keep in mind that it is important for you to have a good understanding of your students' instructional and independent reading levels. We encourage you to communicate regularly with your students' reading teacher.

For example, when creating an interdisciplinary unit on astronomy, teachers (of science, Deaf studies, social studies, math, reading, and writing) can work collaboratively to design the unit, giving consideration to the related and necessary learning objectives in their content areas as well as reading. The culminating activity could be a camping trip. As a group, you can brainstorm camping trip activities and discuss which teacher will take the lead on what part (see Chapter 12 for ways to extend this unit to include the arts).

There are many ways you could incorporate reading into the content areas for this unit. For science, you could teach astronomy and the stars and then engage in stargazing on the trip. You could have students read books about Katherine Johnson (there are multiple books at varying reading levels about her). Two examples are *Hidden Figures* (Shetterly, 2016) and *A Computer Called Katherine: How Katherine Johnson Helped Put America on the Moon* (Slade & Miller Jamison, 2019). Science objectives could relate to the moon orbiting the Earth, as well as traveling to the moon. For math, you could reread the book about Katherine Johnson while focusing on the vocabulary related to math, geometry, and plotting graphs. Aligned with reading objectives, you could teach about biographies and the differences between biographies and autobiographies. You could then connect to Deaf studies, writing, and ASLLA by having students interview Deaf people who are Black, Indigenous, and People of Color (BIPOC) and working in STEAM (science, technology, engineering, arts, and mathematics) fields and create a written or ASL publication of their biography. On the camping trip, students can share the biographical information they learned from their interviews with others. An alternative idea for older students is to have them read mythology related to constellations and how constellations have been used and described through history. For writing and ASL, students could create their own mythology for a constellation.

To plan for the trip, have students write "to do" lists for things that need to be done, what they would need to bring, who would be responsible, and when each task needs to be completed by. Additional readings could include informational text with the rules of the campground, environmental safety, and the types of plants or animals they might see (e.g., Ruurs, 2004).

Bringing It All Together

 Mock Trial Interdisciplinary Unit

Throughout this chapter, we have highlighted examples from a mock trial unit. Here, we share more details from this interdisciplinary unit. You will find each of our core recommendations integrated into this cohesive unit.

Unit Plan Broad Goals

The purpose of this sixth-grade social studies interdisciplinary unit is to develop an understanding of how a court trial works and who the key players are. Students are taught to critically analyze texts (Core Recommendation 2) for key evidence and prepare witnesses for a trial based on evidence presented in the *Shiloh* novel (Reynolds Nayler, 2000). Throughout the unit, ASL is connected to print and concepts to build world knowledge (Core Recommendation 1). Reading is connected throughout this interdisciplinary unit (Core Recommendation 3) along with content goals that include learning about healthy diets for animals and humans and exploring the education and skills required for future jobs.

Targeted Social Studies Vocabulary: judge, prosecution, defense, evidence, guilty, not guilty, courtroom, witness, trial, lawyer, bailiff
Sample: Learner Objectives (aligned with State Standards):
- **Science:** Given a list of attributes of healthy diet and exercise, students will be able to identify at least five attributes of healthy diet and exercise for humans and five attributes for dogs.
- **Reading Comprehension:** Using the text *Shiloh*, students will be able to identify three facts or evidence (supporting details) for Judd, Marty, and each additional witness.

- **Social Studies:** Students will participate in the democratic process of a mock trial in a real courtroom and will be able to follow at least nine out of 10 of the given courtroom procedures appropriately.
- **Math:** Using the text *Shiloh*, students will work together to recreate the dog pen Marty kept Shiloh in, following the same dimensions described in the text.
- **Deaf Studies:** After interviewing a Deaf veterinarian, students will be able to list at least five qualifications for the job accurately.
- **Writing/Language Arts:** Students will write three questions for each witness in complete sentences with fewer than three grammatical errors in their final drafts.
- **ASL:** Students will sign each of their questions/responses using appropriate ASL grammar conceptually accurate vocabulary.
- **Performing Arts:** Students will assume roles in mock trial dramatizations, staying in character for at least 90% of the time they are in front of the judge/jury.

This unit can take approximately 3–6 weeks depending on the extent to which you are able to allocate daily time to each of the content areas. It culminates with a mock trial in the courtroom (if you have reserved it) or in your school (see Table 7.2).

Your Turn to Practice!

 Create an Interdisciplinary Unit Plan

Now it's your turn! Work in a group (either with other students in your teacher preparation program or colleagues at your school) to create an interdisciplinary unit that integrates Deaf studies and at least two other content areas of focus (e.g., math, social studies, science). Each content area must include objectives for reading in addition to objectives for the content. Include at least one activity using the literature detectives strategy that examines varying perspectives of fiction and informational texts. Take into consideration at least one or more of the following: race, culture, gender, Deaf people, languages. Consider also including a mindfulness activity. Make sure that you have clearly identified an overall unit goal, objectives for each content area, ASL, reading and writing/language arts objectives (within each content area) that align with your state standards and ASL standards. Create materials for one lesson at two different reading levels. You will then individually teach a lesson from the unit (at least 30 min) and reflect on your teaching experience.

As a Group

- Choose an interdisciplinary unit goal and grade level.
- Choose four subjects: one subject as your primary focus (e.g., science), Deaf studies, and at least two additional subjects. (e.g., social studies, math). Reading and writing, ASL/English language arts should be integrated into each. Decide who will teach which subject.

Table 7.2. Mock Trial Unit Sample Activities for Days 1–3: Each Activity Targets All Three Core Recommendations (Connecting Real-Word Knowledge, Critical Thinking Skills, Interdisciplinary Unit)

	Interdisciplinary Study and Activities
Day 1	**Social Studies Integrating Reading:** Introduce project. View past trial video. Introduce trial vocabulary with definitions.
Day 1	**Science Integrating Reading:** Review the *Shiloh* text to brainstorm questions for the veterinarian (e.g., What are problems caused by a dog having ticks? How do you know if a dog is underweight?).
Day 1	**Deaf Studies Integrating Reading:** Analyze the *Shiloh* text to identify the characters' jobs (e.g., veterinarian, mail carrier). Create a concept map with different types of jobs students might want to pursue in the future. Include additional informational texts about these jobs and identify Deaf people for them to interview (Maze, 1999).
Day 1	**Reading Integrating Social Studies:** Review the *Shiloh* text to identify potential witnesses and evidence to be used for the trial. Make a list of witnesses and evidence for both prosecution and defense
Day 2	**Social Studies Integrating Reading:** Review court vocabulary in ASL and written English. Discuss the role of the jury.
Day 2	**Science Integrating Reading:** Ask previously developed questions (from Day 1 Science) to the guest veterinarian. Encourage students to take notes. You can also video record the lecture so students can review the ASL afterward to complete their answers.
Day 2	**Deaf Studies Integrating Writing:** Prepare for the Deaf attorney to visit class. Review targeted trial vocabulary and brainstorm questions as a group in ASL. Model the questions in the equivalent for written English. Then, have students write their own questions individually.
Day 2	**Reading Integrating Writing:** Have students complete the assignment titled "Who do you want to be?" Ask them to write what roles they want to play in the trial (prioritizing their top three choices) and state why they would be good for each. They must use information from *Shiloh,* targeted trial vocabulary, and the informational texts on various jobs to support their answers.
Day 3	**Social Studies Integrating Reading/Writing:** Discuss the role of witnesses in court (review past trials regarding questioning of witnesses). Analyze *Shiloh* text to suggest witnesses and defend which witnesses will be for prosecution vs. defense. Create questions for witnesses in ASL and written English.
Day 3	**Science Integrating Reading:** Complete a cause-and-effect paper together in pairs or small groups analyzing the *Shiloh* text and information shared by the guest speaker about the physical conditions of dogs.
Day 3	**Deaf Studies Integrating Reading:** Guest speaker—Deaf attorney. Reread your questions you developed from Day 2 Writing integrating target vocabulary and information from texts. Practice signing them in conceptually accurate ASL.
Day 3	**Language Arts Integrating ASLLA:** Announce who was chosen for each role. Students chosen for each role will present in ASL their reasons from their "Who do you want to be?" paper, demonstrating their understanding of court-related vocabulary using conceptually accurate ASL.

- Decide on a topic or culminating activity that fits with standards of your grade level and is of interest to your students (e.g., Earth Day, community service project, De'VIA Day, voting rights day).
- Decide on one authentic field trip. (Your culminating activity may include a second field trip). How long will your field trip be? (A half day? Or the whole day?) What will it entail?
- Choose a book on the required reading list for students' grade level that aligns with the unit topic. Choose an alternate book that aligns with the unit for those reading below grade level.
- Choose additional reading materials to be covered by the content area teachers (e.g., informational texts, primary sources).

Individual Goals for Teacher Candidates/Teachers

Create an Activity Chart
- Write content-specific and reading/writing objectives for the subject you will teach.
- List the standards from the state core curriculum and ASL content standards to which your objectives align.
- For your subject, you will create a 3-week plan. You must align each lesson with the interdisciplinary unit topic and demonstrate connectedness with the other content area lessons.
- Create an activity chart with your weekly activities:
  - List the materials, books/additional texts, and videos you will use.
  - List the strategies you will use to promote reading in content areas and critical thinking.
  - List target vocabulary.
  - Include activities for your field trip related to your content area (e.g., have students write a list of questions to ask the field trip guide).
  - Make sure to include pre and post activities for field trips and guest presenters

Develop One Complete Lesson
Develop a lesson from the first day of your unit. You should all be aware of what each person will be teaching. Make sure that you connect to what was discussed in the other subjects (or will be discussed in other classes).

Teach Your Lesson
Teach in a real or mock setting.

Reflect on How Your Teaching Day Went
- What went well?
- What would you change/do differently if you taught this lesson again?
- After assessing your students, how well did they learn the targeted objectives?

Recommended Readings/Viewings

For Teachers/Teacher Candidates

- *Reading and Writing Informational Text in the Primary Grades: Research-Based Practices* (Duke & Bennett Armistead, 2003). Although this book is targeted toward hearing students, it has recommended strategies for reading in the content area that can be implemented with Deaf students.
- Teaching for Change (https://www.teachingforchange.org/). You can select books with social justice and multicultural themes to align with your interdisciplinary unit at varying grade levels.
- Described and Captioned Media Program (https://dcmp.org/learn/366-black-deaf-culture-through-the-lens-of-black-deaf-history). This website provides information and additional readings on Black Deaf history and Black ASL.

To Use With Students

- *Round Is a Tortilla: A Book of Shapes* (Thong & Parra, 2015). This is a good book for younger children to use to teach shapes.
- *The Girl With a Mind for Math: The Story of Raye Montague* (Mosca & Reilly, 2020). This is also an excellent book to use for math or science.
- *Counting on Katherine: How Katherine Johnson Saved Apollo 13* (Becker & Phumirk, 2018). This is a story about an African American mathematician who worked for NASA during the space race and is a good way to incorporate reading in math and/or science.
- Talking Black in America: *Signing Black in America* (https://www.talkingblackinamerica.org/signing-black-in-america/). This is a documentary about Black ASL in the United States that can be used in middle school or high school social studies and/or Deaf studies classes.

Conclusion

Content area teachers have a lot to teach! We understand that your priority is focusing on content area standards. You might be thinking, "I have to do all that and include reading too? How can I do it all?" Here, we hope to have provided you with some ways you can integrate reading and ASL into each content area. Remember, it's important to provide hands-on, minds-on experiences and field trips to build world knowledge. Then, you can connect these experiences to language and content-specific objectives. Also, keep in mind that some students prefer informational texts, and it is a great way to draw them into the content as readers. Don't be afraid to try interdisciplinary units. There are so many ways you can use multilingual strategies to make things meaningful for your students. Connect to real-world knowledge, and let students see how they can apply what they learn in your content area to their future. These meaningful, integrated opportunities can go a long way to supporting students' development in the disciplines. And, who knows, you might be teaching the next astronaut, engineer, lawyer, or mathematician! The content-based reading experiences you provide today can impact your students for a lifetime.

Sticking Points

- Connect world knowledge developed through content learning, field trips, and hands-on experiences to various types of ASL and English texts (e.g., informational and fiction books, articles, primary sources).
- Foster critical thinking skills with reading in each content area.
- Integrate interdisciplinary units into your classroom with objectives for reading, ASLLA, English language arts, and the content areas, or collaborate with other content area teachers for interdisciplinary units of study.

Deaf Identities and Social/Cultural Perspectives

Chapter 8

Marlon Kuntze
Chris Kurz
Debbie Golos

Much of the content in this book would not be possible without first considering the multiple and intersecting identities of ourselves and our students. Healthy identity development is a foundation for teaching and learning. With this foundation, you can build cultural and social awareness and understanding to align with the principles of social justice. The content in this chapter provides a foundation for all of your instruction. We draw on the principles of anti-bias/antiracist (ABAR) pedagogy (see Chapter 1 for definition) and the resources of Deaf studies scholarship and use them to help you develop a perspective that will help you become a facilitator of the journey of self-discovery and self-identification that your students will embark on. It is important for all teachers to be conscious of the attitudes, values, and beliefs of the lived experiences of Deaf people and understand that every Deaf student is unique. By teaching about Deaf people through a multilingual lens, you can help your students understand themselves, their history, and their languages and cultures and learn about the lived experiences of diverse Deaf people. As you consciously create space in our classrooms and schools for families, students, and colleagues who use languages other than American Sign Language (ASL) and English, we can also collectively contribute to a more inclusive society. Whether you are a preservice, novice, or an experienced educator, this chapter provides strategies to teach about Deaf people and use the knowledge to foster identity development through various lessons across the curriculum.

Who Are We?

We introduce ourselves by including our social identities to acknowledge the different identities within the field:

Marlon Kuntze is a white cisgender male raised in a Deaf family. He helped establish a Deaf studies curriculum at the California School for the Deaf in Fremont in the early 1990s. He also taught and helped expand Deaf studies coursework at various colleges and universities.

Chris Kurz is a Deaf white man from a large mixed Deaf-hearing signing family. He has taught at various kindergarten through Grade 12 (K–12) and postsecondary educational institutions, including Deaf studies courses at the University of Kansas.

Debbie Golos is a white, cisgender, hearing woman who has taught in various K–12 and university Deaf education settings for 30 years. She has been striving to transform teacher preparation by integrating the development of multiple and intersecting identities, ABAR, and well-being practices.

We also want to recognize important contributions made to this chapter by Amy Parsons and Shira Leitson-Grabelsky. Amy Parsons is a Black mixed-race Deaf woman raised as an only—and only Deaf—child in a close-knit, large extended family of hearing people with beginner-level signing fluency. The granddaughter of teachers, Amy is a lifelong activist for language and educational equality, advancing anti-oppression frameworks within educational and community systems for the past decade. Currently, Amy is working with organizations to incorporate anti-bias, anti-ableism, and anti-oppression practices.

Shira Leitson-Grabelsky is a DeafDisabled white woman who identifies as a Deaf and Little Person. She grew up as the only Deaf individual in a hearing signing family. Her prior and current work in the nonprofit sector, K–12 education, and community education is strongly influenced by personal experiences and far-reaching dialogue about multiple identities, autonomy, and evolving identities.

We would also like to acknowledge and thank Doralynn Folse, who contributed to the foundational information for this chapter.

Deaf Experiences, Perspectives, and Core Recommendations

Deaf studies started out as an etic study of Deaf lives. The term *etic* refers to scholarship in which crosscultural differences are the focus. The interest was in comparing Deaf people with hearing people. However, more recently, an *emic* study of Deaf people has been emerging in which the focus is more from within the culture. The emic contributions of individuals from different communities (e.g., Deaf, DeafBlind, DeafDisabled, Hard of Hearing [DDBDDHH]) have influenced the more recent transformation of Deaf studies. The lived experiences of the Deaf community that are shared in conversation, literature, and social media are foundational to both the growing body of research and discourse about Deaf studies and to our fundamental understanding of what it means to "be Deaf." While the etic study of Deaf people was key in recognizing Deaf people as a distinct cultural group, the emic perspective continues to be an important

---

Chew on This!

Did you know that...?
Deaf scholars and activists are shining new lights on Deaf identities:

- Dunn's work on Black Deaf identities (Anderson & Dunn, 2016; Dunn, 1992, 1998, 2020; Dunn & Anderson, 2019)
- Simms and Thumann's (2007; Thumann & Simms, 2009) work on positing culturally sensitive paradigms in Deaf education
- Ladd's work (2005, 2007, 2008, 2022) on positioning the field as resistance in response to colonialism
- Also check out Deaf activists, including Ashanti Monts-Tréviska, Victorica Monroe, and Anna Lim Franck

source for developing a rich understanding of the lives of Deaf people with multiple and intersecting identities.

There is a lot to celebrate about the lives of Deaf people as a group as well as the diversity in the lives of individual Deaf people. At the same time, it is important to understand the oppression that Deaf people have been fighting against not only from outside the community but also from within the community. It is important when you teach about Deaf people that you attempt to broaden it to a societal level and do it through an ABAR lens. All teachers need to consider how to best teach students to strive toward change—the change needed to improve equity and justice in the lives of all Deaf people. Deaf students within preschool through Grade 12 (P–12) need access to these conversations, knowledge, and evolution so they can learn about the history and lives of Deaf people, including cultural and social awareness of Deaf people on a global scale. In some P–12 settings, Deaf studies may look like a course or unit of study, or it could be integrated into any subject, especially social studies and language arts (see Chapters 5, 7, and 9). If your school program does not include it or has limited resources, you can start building and integrating Deaf studies into your lessons.

As a teacher, it is your responsibility to teach Deaf studies and do it in a way that fosters a positive development of your students' sense of who they are as Deaf people as well as your understanding of their multiple and intersecting identities. In doing so, it is important to keep in mind that you will have students who are Deaf signers, Deaf nonsigners, DeafBlind signers, DeafBlind nonsigners, DeafDisabled people, and Deaf people who are Black, Indigenous, and People of Color. You will also have students who come from hearing nonsigning families, hearing signing families, nonsigning Deaf families, and signing Deaf families. Look at each student not only as a part of the larger Deaf community but also, importantly, as an individual. They need to be recognized and understood as being complex, possessing multiple, intersecting identities, and coming from different backgrounds. Consciously engaging in this practice on an individual and a collective level will shine a light on traditionally underrepresented identities and experiences within Deaf studies.

Regardless of what Deaf studies classes may have looked like in the past or whether your school has established Deaf studies as a core component of its instructional philosophy, there is much value in getting as many teachers as possible to be conscientiously committed to incorporating Deaf studies into their classroom in all subject areas and across the P–12 grade span. One way to get started is by teaching about the lives and identities of Deaf people.

Core Recommendations

Here, we present three core recommendations for fostering students' awareness, understanding, and appreciation of their identities across P–12.

- Enrich positive perceptions of self as a Deaf person.
- Teach the history, literature, and lives of diverse Deaf people.
- Increase cultural and social awareness.

Effective Practices for Deaf Learners

As a teacher, you have the power to make your classroom a safe and nurturing place for all students. Each core recommendation complements the others to build an even stronger foundation. These strategies can be incorporated in ways you feel most comfortable within your teaching. We recommend that when you develop lessons, incorporate the social justice standards within the anti-bias education framework. See the Southern Poverty Law Center's Learning for Justice frameworks (https://www.learningforjustice.org/frameworks), which gives a rationale for connecting to all four domains: identity, diversity, justice, and action.

(PI) Core Recommendation 1: Enrich Positive Perceptions of Self as a Deaf Person

Here, we will share ways you can use to foster the positive development of your students' multiple and intersecting identities. It is important to remember that although we have chosen to use the term *Deaf* in this book (see Chapter 1 for definition), we need to keep in mind that we use it as an inclusive term that represents all DDBDDHH people. This means that the curriculum, pedagogy, and expectations need to match the rich diversity of your students. It also starts with you getting to know yourself.

(ABAR) Critically Examine Your Own Social Identities

As a teacher, before you can more fully understand the diverse needs of your students and how to best create space to foster their identity development, you need to examine yourself and understand who you are. One first step is to explore your own personal and social identities. When we talk about personal identities, we are referring to things such as your name, attributes of your personality, what you like to do, who is in your family, and so on. Like each of your students, you also have multiple and intersecting **social identities** and have formed your own values, beliefs, and biases. There are resources in *Anti-Bias Education for Young Children and Ourselves* (Derman-Sparks et al., 2020) to help you get started on your anti-bias journey as a teacher.

(ABAR) Know Yourself, Your Beliefs, and Your Privileges

Once you have explored your personal and social identities, the next step is to start exploring your knowledge, beliefs, and biases. Think about what your beliefs are. What privileges do you carry? Privileges are what you have as a member of a dominant group in our society (e.g., male, white, hearing, straight, ablebodied). For example, what privileges do you carry as a teacher if you are a white hearing woman, and how do these differ from those of a white Deaf woman? A Black Deaf man? *This Book Is Anti-Racist—Journal* (Jewell, 2021) is a good resource to use not only for your students but also for yourself. Before getting started implementing activities in your classroom, we recommend that you first complete these activities yourself. In doing so, make sure to consider how the questions within the journal activities connect to Deaf people. That way you will not only have the opportunity to explore your own beliefs but you also can share them with your students as an example of how one might answer the question. We also recommend that you become familiar with additional literature on

Key Vocabulary

Social identity is the sense of self that is based on memories, experiences, and relationships that are derived from a person's place in the world. Social identities are in relation to the society in which people live and include cultural identity, professional identity, gender identity, disability identity, Deaf identity, language identity, racial identity, ethnic and national identity, religious identity, and so on.

ABAR education (see Recommended Readings/Viewings at the end of the chapter). Remember that this is a journey, an ongoing part of professional development.

 Stick It Into Action!

Explore Your Identities and Beliefs
The following activities will help you explore your own identities and beliefs:

- Complete the social identities portrait (in Jewell, 2021, p. 32) and the follow-up questions that are provided.
- Complete pages 14–19 about your social identities.
  - Add your identity related to Deaf (DDBDDHH) or, if you are hearing, your identity as a hearing teacher in Deaf education.
  - Add in your preferred languages/modalities.
- Complete pages 24–25, 28–29, and 34–37 in the journal about your ethnicity, culture, and who holds power in your world.
  - Consider additional questions related to your school such as: Are Deaf people in power within your school? Your communities? At what levels?
  - Share and discuss your responses with a colleague or friend in the field of Deaf education.

After completing these activities on your own, we recommend having your students complete some of them (modify as needed based by age and grade level). It will help serve as a reminder that the exploration of identities, both for you and your students, is an ongoing process of understanding who you are and that identities are fluid and ever-changing according to where you are at that moment in time and with whom you are interacting. Keep in mind trauma-informed approaches to education as you engage in these conversations (see, for example, https://transformingeducation.org/resources/trauma-informed-sel-toolkit/ and https://ies.ed.gov/ncee/edlabs/regions/appalachia/events/materials/04-8-20-Handout2_menu-trauma-informed-programs-for-schools.pdf).

(PI) (ABAR) (CM) (ES) **Create a Nurturing and Supportive Environment**
The classroom should be a place for students to explore their identities in a nurturing and supportive way. At the beginning of the year, it is important that you create an environment where students feel comfortable communicating their feelings with one another and do so without worrying that they will be judged or harmed in any way. This helps them develop a healthy sense of self and feel good about who they are. It will also help them learn that they can stand up and advocate not only for themselves but also against injustices involving others. Having such a system in place can help support students when you engage them in conversations that may be triggering or upsetting to those who have experienced oppressions (e.g., racism, audism, ableism) while providing space to encourage students to get comfortable with uncomfortable conversations.

One way to get started is to have guidelines that you can create with students at the beginning of the year. Here are some suggested ground rules to get you started:

- We will respect one another, whoever we are. This includes preferred languages, modes of communication, hearing levels, abilities, gender, skills, interests, values, and experiences.
- We acknowledge that audism, ableism, sexism, classism, racism, heterosexism, and other forms of discrimination exist (see Derman Sparks et al., 2020 for more on "isms").
- We will make sure that everyone has equitable access to communication.
- We will not "put down" others for their experiences or lack of experiences (e.g., being from a Deaf vs. a hearing family, having exposure to a language versus no exposure, having a language proficiency versus limited language proficiency).
- We will hold each other responsible in not repeating misinformation or offensive behavior once we have learned otherwise.
- We will challenge the idea or the practice—but not the person.
- We will commit to learn about the diversity in the lives of all people.
- We will commit to actively combat myths and stereotypes about DDDBDDHH and other Deaf-related groups.

Be open to other ground rules that the class would like to add.

You can also modify the complexity of the written sentences in your guidelines to meet your students' languages and grade levels. For example, you can simplify rules such as the following:

- Take care of and respect yourself.
- Engage respectfully with one another (students, staff, teachers, etc.).
- Take care of and respect school spaces and materials.

It is important to reflect on these guidelines throughout the year and change them as you see fit. They can also be modified according to the age level and language abilities of your students. Also, consider adding the additional home languages of your students.

(SEL) (PI) Integrate Well-Being Practices Into Your Classroom

As we mentioned in the early childhood chapter (Chapter 2), there are many benefits of integrating well-being practices into the classroom for you and your students (e.g., mindfulness, yoga, self-care). One aspect of creating a nurturing space is fostering compassion for oneself and one another in your students. As with everyone, your students may experience struggles at home or in society due to a lack of accessible communication, language delays or deprivation, microaggressions, or other negative experiences. When you provide strategies for your students to manage their feelings, they learn coping tools, which also help to strengthen a positive sense of self. As described in Chapter 2, mindfulness activities are one way to do this. Building compassion helps build a strong classroom community and also helps them be compassionate toward others when engaging in challenging conversations about topics such as racism, ableism, or audism. Encourage them to practice mindfulness

DEAF IDENTITIES AND SOCIAL/CULTURAL PERSPECTIVES

Welcome sign in a school hallway. (Drawn by Tamara Frijmersum and Linda MacDonald, parents of Deaf children at the California School for the Deaf, Fremont.)

at school and at home. Although some mindfulness practices are sound-based, have discussions with your students on how you can modify mindfulness practices to meet their individual needs—visual and/or kinesthetic. Ask your students questions like the following:

- What is the best way to start and end mindfulness activities visually? Light? Scent? Vibrations?
- What can we call our "talking stick" (i.e., an object that they take turns holding to indicate it is their turn)?

See the following Stick It Into Action for suggestions on getting started. Review Chapter 3 for the explanation of ASL mnemonics.

 Stick It Into Action!

Mindfulness to Foster Positive Sense of Self

Here are some suggestions for mindfulness activities you can try out in your classroom to help ground both you and your students and increase engagement.

- Begin and end your class with a short mindfulness activity, such as taking deep breaths.
- View or create short mindfulness videos in ASL to share (see Recommended Readings/Viewings).
- Use visual and/or kinesthetic cues to start/end mindfulness activities, which can include the following:
  - Soft light/dimming lights
  - Changing light colors

Stick It Into Action! (*continued*)
- Vibrations from beating a drum
- Essential oils such as lavender for calming
- Integrate yoga practices. As mentioned in Chapter 2, make sure to explain what you want students to do before they look away (e.g., go into Downward Dog, count to 10, and then come up). For more examples, check out https://www.facebook.com/DeafNorthYoga/videos).
- Go on mindful walks in your building or outside to help to be present in the moment.

> " In our teacher preparation program, we integrate mindfulness and self-care practices throughout our program (e.g., self-care check-ins, mindfulness moments to begin and end each class). It helps teachers learn how to be grounded and present, maintain balance in their lives, and prevent burnout once they become a teacher. Providing opportunities for teacher candidates to integrate these practices into their lessons helps give them tools they can use to foster well-being. We are increasingly seeing how self-care practices help teachers create a welcoming space for all students to actively engage in learning about one another, themselves, and the content. Once we have these practices in place, we begin to explore the complexities of our own social identities through identity projects (personal, then social) and then practice anti-bias approaches to teaching and activities to foster the development and awareness of multiple and intersecting identities of their future students.
>
> —Debbie Golos

 Key Strategy

ASL Mnemonic for Calming and Grounding

You can modify the BCOOL strategy (Srinivasan, 2014) in ASL using the 5 handshape to help your students remember what to do to help when they are upset or frustrated. Encourage them to practice this at school and at home.

- Breathe (ASL = BREATHE).
- Calm yourself down (ASL = CALM DOWN).
- Know that you are okay (ASL = AWARE).
- Observe what is happening inside yourself (ASL = REFLECT [flickering fingers-at-head with closed 5 handshape]).
- Hold it with love (ASL = LOVE with unspread 5 handshape).

(SEL) *Practice Self-Care*   In addition to mindfulness, make sure to model and practice self-care. One way to do this is to demonstrate what you do for your own self-care; mindful eating, sleeping, drinking water, yoga, exercising, and engaging in activities that bring you joy are all excellent self-care practices. You can also integrate self-care minutes in your classroom (e.g., look out the window at the sun, drink water, stop and breathe). By encouraging self-care check-ins regularly with your students, you are also fostering a positive sense of self by encouraging them to explore self-care practices that bring them joy, calm them down, help them sleep, and so on. Developing these practices also helps them identify what they enjoy and what is important to them.

(ABAR)   **Exploring Identities**

Fostering your students' positive perceptions about themselves is an opportunity for you to know who your students are and what is important to them. One activity to get you started learning about your students is to have them complete an All About Me project (see also Chapters 9 and 12). See the following Stick It Into Action for one way to introduce an All About Me project at the beginning of the year to learn about each other's identities. It is also a way for you to evaluate how well your students are able to follow directions by asking them to include different items along with a different number for each question about themselves (e.g., 4 favorite things, 3 hobbies, 2 goals).

Make sure you pre-teach target vocabulary as needed (e.g., hobbies, activities, self-care goals). (See Chapters 3 and 6 for strategies for introducing target vocabulary.) You can also make a video in ASL and in other languages, as needed, to explain the project so your students can review it when they get home (see Chapters 3, 4, and 12). They can also connect to ASL within their posters as demonstrated in the "All About Me" poster.

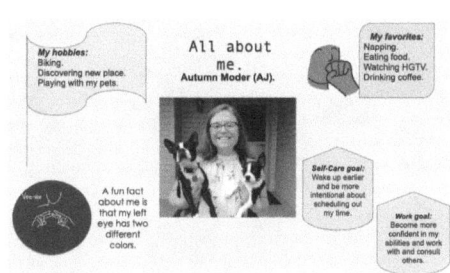

Early childhood Deaf teacher: "All About Me" poster.

We recommend doing variations of these types of projects throughout the year. In this example, we demonstrate *personal* identities. As you begin engaging in conversations in your classroom, where students start to feel comfortable sharing their *social* identities, you can then start to ask them to reflect on other questions related to preferred languages, cultural activities, race, gender, and so forth. Provide multiple ways for them to engage in different types of identity projects where you explore social identities, such as creating poetry in written or signed languages or an art project. See Chapter 12 for ways you can have students create them through multiple mediums (e.g., visual arts, performing arts, and media arts). Once you believe your students are ready, have them complete their pages like you did from *This Book Is Anti-Racist—Journal* (Jewell, 2021).

Another great activity for students is to create a Social Identity Wheel, shown in the following Stick It Into Action. For background information, explore the University of Michigan's College of Literature, Science, and the Arts website (https://sites.lsa.umich.edu/inclusive-teaching/social-identity-wheel/), which you will need to modify to be inclusive of ASL and additional languages that students use. Also, make sure to add their Deaf identities there as well. Let students be creative in the colors, languages, and ways they create their wheel. For students with language delays and/or disabilities, it is important to allow them multiple options (see the *many media, same message* strategy, and the section titled "Differentiating Instruction in the Arts" on p. 309 in Chapter 12).

 **Stick It Into Action!**

Social Identity Wheel
Have students create their own identity wheels.

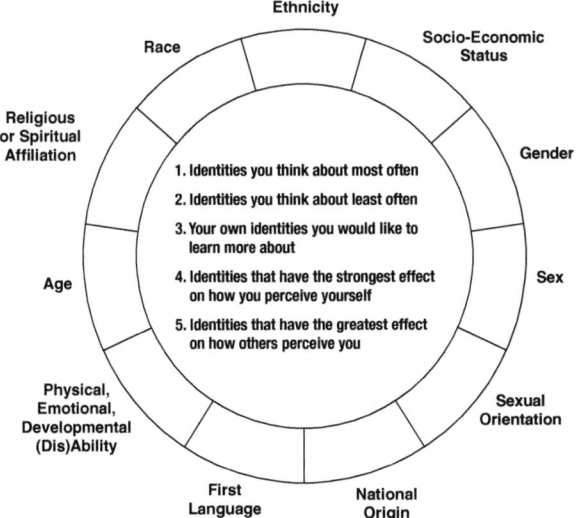

After completing the Social Identity Wheel project, have students return to activities in *This Book Is Anti-Racist—Journal,* such as "How Diverse Is Your Universe?" (pp. 20–21) in which they explore who is in their family, community, school, etc. Encourage them to notice what they see. You can ask questions like, "Which parts of your identities are inside and outside of the dominant culture?" and "Who holds the power?" (see pp. 34–38). Allowing students opportunities to explore and notice these situations in the world helps them better understand who they are and how to work to make change (see Chapter 5 for sample unit on cultivating allies and activists).

> In early childhood, much of the narratives have a stark binary line, "boys like this and girls like that." However, if a boy wants to wear a dress in the drama area, then so be it! Our jobs are to foster positive outlets of creativity and identity, not inhibit them. This is similar to how we want to foster students' development of a positive identity as a Deaf person. In order to do that, we must embrace and nourish all aspects of our students' lives.
>
> —Autumn Moder, Deaf early childhood teacher

Name Signs Our names are a huge part of who we are and how we identify ourselves. As you begin to discuss more complex aspects of identities, students may start to rethink how they identify themselves and that may include changing their pronouns or their names. Just as with names in other languages, some Deaf people decide to change their name signs to better reflect who they are and how they identify themselves. As you review the cultural rules of forming name signs, it is important to be sensitive to the ones your students were given, particularly those whose name signs do not follow the cultural rules. You can start by discussing name signs of well-known people from diverse backgrounds before discussing their own, such as how the name sign for *Kamala Harris* was created. Here is a good resource to get you started: https://www.nytimes.com/interactive/2021/07/16/arts/kamala-harris-name-sign-language.html. See the following Teacher Tale to connect to the importance of names and people's identities when reading the book *The Giver* (Lowry, 1993) and consider what life would be like without names.

Teacher Tale

A middle school reading class read Lois Lowry's *The Giver*. Instead of names, the characters in the book are recognized by their assigned number. Names are a valuable part of our identities, and a tangent lesson was created to explore this. This lesson, "Say Their Names," brought to the table discussions about the value of names, the value of our own names, and why it is significant to correctly say or sign the names of people we know or do not know, both while they are alive and posthumously. As examples of the latter, the class discussed "Say Her Name," a direct call to action to the Black Lives Matter movement centering on Black female lives lost. This lesson helped develop a sense of what it means to live in the dystopian world of *The Giver* in which nobody has a name.

—*Middle school teacher*

Trying on Identities The more you provide your students with opportunities to explore who they are and allow them to try on different identities, the stronger their positive sense of self will be. Just as historically male children have been labeled as *boys* and females as *girls* from birth, Deaf children have often been labeled according to their audiogram. Some may grow up with that label without questioning it. It is up to you to provide them with opportunities to see others' lived experiences through books, media, and interactions, learn from them, and play with their identities. This exploration may occur through role-play, starting in preschool with simple activities such as trying on different clothes and onward to more complex activities such as communicating in different languages. These activities should continue all the way through high school. The activities can be through the arts (as we describe in Chapter 12) and through discussions about different content (which is discussed more in the section on **Core Recommendation 2**).

By engaging in these experiences and discussions for students to try on multiple and intersecting identities, you may start to see your students' identities change over time. You may see students who were labeled as Hard of Hearing start to identify as Deaf or vice versa. You may see students start choosing to stop wearing hearing aids or cochlear implants. You may see students change their pronouns from *he/she* to *they*. You may see a student who begins to identify as both Black and Deaf. Opportunities to explore without being subjected to judgment by others are critical to developing a healthy and positive sense of self.

(SEL) (PI) (ABAR) **Creating a Classroom Environment to Reflect Humanity and Provide Role Models**

The tangibility of identities in classroom materials also helps create a place where each student can feel a sense of belonging. As demonstrated in the following Stick It Into Action, it is important for you to create an inclusive environment and provide many quality materials, because students need to be able to see themselves and diverse others in the books, media, and people they interact with in your classroom (e.g. Cawthon et al., 2016). Make sure to preview any material you include for potential stereotypes or bias.

(PI) (MM) (ES) (MT) **Stick It Into Action!**

Create an Inclusive Classroom Environment
- Include quality stories, informational texts, and media with diverse people represented (e.g., Deaf, abilities, race, gender, religion, cultures, sexual orientation).
- Make signed languages visible and accessible. This can be done by playing videos on loops, creating QR codes for access to videos, and/or creating dedicated spaces for sign/word walls reflecting languages used in the classroom (see Chapters 3 and 7).
- Include additional home languages of your students in materials and on classroom walls.
- Invite Deaf people from diverse backgrounds into your classroom, live and virtually, on a regular basis to share their **lived experiences**. Ask them to share about their own identities and how they may have changed over time.

Key Vocabulary

Lived experiences are the firsthand personal experiences of people that often inform their worldviews.

There are increasingly higher quality materials for reading and viewing related to anti-bias to include in your classroom (see Recommended Readings/Viewings). For example, when teaching about respect for personal boundaries, including those who have experienced microaggressions, *Don't Touch My Hair* (Miller, 2019) is an example of a good book to use (see the ASL translation https://youtu.be/SIPH4Wg7uNQ?si=GqSjvT1Q1ubhBTur). One example of a microaggression against a Black student would be if a white student asked about touching a Black person's hair (or worse, doing it without permission). The discussion on boundaries can be expanded to cover additional situations such as how to respond to someone who grabs you by the chin to get your attention or wants to give you a hug when you don't want one. It is important to empower your students to say "no" anytime they are uncomfortable if someone crosses a boundary or tries to get into their personal space.

It is also important to provide opportunities for interactions with diverse Deaf adults and have them share their lived experiences and also provide positive role models for your students. See Stick It Into Action for a possible activity related to this objective.

 Stick It Into Action!

Get to Know Deaf People in Your Community
Create activities for your students to meet Deaf people in your community, such as the following:

- Have students research a local Deaf community member from a local Black, Indigenous, or Person of Color (BIPOC) community.
- Invite a local BIPOC Deaf person to your class (live or virtually).
- Have students discuss and prepare questions ahead of time and use them to learn about the lives of the guests, what they do, their stories and experiences, challenges they have faced, and advice they have for the students.

Spend Time With Students Outside of School
To really get to know your students and their families, make an effort to spend time with them outside of school. This not only deepens teacher–student relationships but also allows you to learn more about students on a personal level, including how they interact with their families and friends and what languages they prefer to use when they are in varying social settings. Knowing your students, their families, and where they live can also help you better select appropriate materials as well as be better prepared to engage in conversations about them (see Chapters 9, 11, and 12 for additional examples). For example, if you are teaching a unit on gardening, choose books that represent varied homes and areas that match the homes where your students live as well as demonstrate that not everyone's home/yard looks the same. In *Green Green: A Community Gardening* (Lamba & Lamba, 2017), for example, children living in a city come together to build a community garden.

 Stick It Into Action!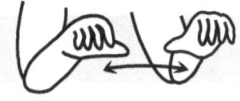

Searching for Diverse Materials
When searching for materials online, use search terms that reflect diversity in Deaf communities:

- Search "child + wheelchair" to generate specific images of children using wheelchairs.
- Use search terms specific to each of the multiple identities of Deaf people, such as *Deaf, Hard of Hearing, Deaf Black, Black ASL, DeafDisabled, Deaf Latinx,* and *Deaf*

LGBTQIA+ [Lesbian, Gay, Bisexual, Transgender, Queer or Questioning, Intersex, Asexual, or more].
- Review materials for potential bias and stereotypes.
- Allow for student choice when possible.

As you start to implement these strategies consistently, you will see tangible effects on your students' sense of self as they increasingly engage in discussing pictures, stories, and themes that reflect communities both within and outside your classroom.

(PI) (ABAR) (MM) Core Recommendation 2: Teach the History, Literature, and Lives of Diverse Deaf People

As we have mentioned, the study of Deaf people has often been left out of the curriculum. If offered, it is often presented through a **keyhole perspective.** It is crucial to Deaf students' identity development that they learn about the experiences of diverse people, especially Deaf people, through their stories and as participants in events, places, and societies throughout history. In this section, we discuss how you can integrate the history and literature of Deaf people in various content instruction throughout the P–12 curriculum.

Key Vocabulary

Keyhole perspective means perceiving the world or experiences with a limited scope, similar to when we view something through a literal keyhole.

Infuse Deaf History

You should infuse Deaf history into some of your lessons regardless of the subject you teach (e.g., math, science, English/language arts) because it can help make learning more interesting and meaningful for your students. Deaf history has traditionally been passed to younger generations by storytellers in sign language, especially those that were captured on film, video, images, or in writing. However, it is up to you to determine how to best integrate the available resources into your instruction. As with any history, Deaf history is tentative in that it undergoes constant changes as new artifacts come to light. As mentioned in the other chapters (see Chapters 5, 7, and 9), seek out primary sources for all subjects, including Deaf studies. As teachers, you can provide opportunities for your students to locate and use primary sources related to Deaf history for their projects, including artifacts (e.g., letters, diaries, films, videos, photos, arts, newspapers, journals) (Von Bitter & Turley, 2018). We present suggestions on how to implement this in the following Stick It Into Action.

Stick It Into Action!

Examining Deaf Student Life in the Past

In the past, almost all residential Deaf schools published periodical newsletters, which they also shared with all other Deaf schools. Those newsletters came to be known as "The Little Paper Family." Deaf students during that time enjoyed the newsletters because they offered them a window into the lives of their peers in other schools. Your students can also enjoy learning what students at their school did in the past by reviewing their school's archival copies of the Little Paper Family publications. Here is how to get started:

Stick It Into Action! *(continued)*

- After assigning your students to groups, have them select a decade in the past (e.g., 1890s, 1930s) to collect examples of Deaf student life at their school.
- Show students how to locate sources or archives of their school's old newsletters.
  - For example, Rochester School for the Deaf has its own newsletter, *The Rochester Advocate*: http://archives.rsdeaf.org/about_archives-advocate.asp
  - Have students find the newsletters that were published during their selected decade.
- Have them make notes about student life activities (e.g., classes, after-school activities, letters from home, school changes).
- Have students present their findings with text and pictorial evidence comparing similarities and differences of what it was like to be a Deaf student during their selected decade with the present time (consider social justice topics for discussion).
- Have them share their findings with younger students. They can use Theater in Education (see Chapter 12) to dress up like students in the past.

Chew on This!

Did you know that . . . ?

There are online resources containing primary Deaf history sources (see additional resources in Chapter 9):

- Gallaudet University has been archiving many old newspapers, journals, and videos (e.g., *The Silent Worker*, the *Deaf-Mute Journal*, National Association of the Deaf old films, Deaf President Now videos). Check them out at https://gallaudet.edu/archives/
- Gallaudet Center on Black Deaf Studies has a website: https://gallaudet.edu/center-black-deaf-studies/
- There are several excellent websites related to Black Deaf history: https://www.nbda.org/black-deaf-history/, https://dcmp.org/learn/366, https://www.blackdeafcenter.com/
- Check out the back issues of *American Annals of the Deaf and Dumb* (1847–1886) and *American Annals of the Deaf* (1886–2022) at https://www.jstor.org/journal/amerannadeaf
- Deaf Rochester Institute for Technology librarian maintains a list of guides for different Deaf-related information: http://infoguides.rit.edu/prf.php?account_id=43304
- The Library of Congress has been archiving thousands of Deaf-related items: https://www.loc.gov/

You can also collaborate with other teachers to set up a list of digitally available primary sources appropriate for varying grade levels and/or students with various abilities.

No matter what your and your students' views are, it is important to provide students with information and opportunities to see and discuss a more complete picture of each era, whose perspectives are included and whose are missing (see Chapters 5, 7, and 9). This means teaching them the importance of searching for as many sources of evidence as possible. Understanding how and why events occurred and looking at them from multiple perspectives helps your students achieve a more solid understanding of the current world they live in. For example, if you are teaching the Holocaust to fourth to sixth graders, you can include Deaf perspectives by having them read *Signs of Survival: A Memoir of the Holocaust* (Hartman & Greene, 2022). It is about two sisters, one Deaf and one hearing, from a Deaf family in Czechoslovakia who were caught by the Nazis and brought to concentration camps.

We encourage you to read Chapter 9 and other chapters for ideas of how Deaf history can be incorporated across the curriculum. When creating these lessons, you can incorporate objectives from the anchor standards of diversity and justice. One critical thing to remember (as mentioned in Chapters 7 and 9) is that historical events can be triggering or traumatizing for some students (e.g., the Holocaust, slavery, segregation). Before engaging in such conversations, as previously mentioned, make sure to consider trauma-informed approaches to teaching and that you have already created your ground rules for conversations and practiced engaging in mindfulness and compassion activities, as mentioned in **Core Recommendation 1**. In the following Stick It Into Action, we revised an activity mentioned in *This Book Is Anti-Racist—Journal* so it would connect to Deaf studies.

 Stick It Into Action!

Investigating History

If you could learn about or rewrite history to include stories from marginalized groups that were excluded, whose stories would you include? Here are some ideas:

- Complete an activity using the literature detectives strategy (see Chapter 7).
- Invite Deaf people from diverse backgrounds to share something from their histories.
- Give students a specific event and have them interview a member of the Deaf community to learn about their culture/history, such as a Native American Deaf person in America.
- Have your students learn about Black Coyote, who was Deaf and one of the Lakotas who were massacred by soldiers of the U.S. Army during the Wounded Knee Massacre on the Lakota Pine Ridge Indian Reservation on December 29, 1890.
- Have your students learn about a Black Deaf family who was enslaved by a Deaf man, John Jacob Flourney, in Georgia.
- Have your students learn about the desegregation of Deaf people, including information about and the perspective of a Black student who attended a school in Washington, D.C., which later moved to Niagara Falls, New York, before the Civil War.
- Explore additional historical events for opportunities to consider the perspectives of Deaf Alaska Native Americans; Deaf Asian Americans; Deaf Hispanics, Deaf Latinos, Latinas, or Latinx; and Deaf Native Hawaiians.

In addition to discussing Deaf perspectives on different historical events, you can also celebrate with your students by recognizing the accomplishments of diverse Deaf people. Create opportunities for your students to share the accomplishments of diverse Deaf people with others, such as younger students, caregivers, families, school staff, and/or local community members.

  Infuse Deaf Literature

In addition to Deaf historical events, you can also incorporate Deaf literature across the curriculum to promote understanding and appreciation of diverse Deaf cultural perspectives. Deaf literature includes various genres (e.g., fiction, nonfiction, poetry, drama, folktales) and consists of works by authors/artists who are Black Deaf, Deaf-Blind, DeafDisabled, Deaf Hispanic/Latinx, Deaf Native Americans, LGBTQIA+, and so on. They usually reflect Deaf experiences that provide differing views of the world and

Chew on This!

Did you know that . . . ?

We have local, national, and international celebrations to recognize the accomplishments of Deaf people.

- National Deaf History Month is recognized and celebrated every year in April.
- The first International Day of the Deaf was celebrated by the World Federation of the Deaf (WFD) in 1958. It was extended to a full week, becoming the International Week of the Deaf (IWD). It is celebrated annually by the global Deaf community in the last week of September.
- The Sign Union flag to represent the global union of Deaf communities and sign languages communities, designed by Arnaud Balard, has been flown in six continents since 2014.

Deaf-inspired imaginations, and they are rich in ways of enlightening students about the lives of Deaf people, both in the past and the present.

You can include works created by diverse Deaf people documented in various mediums, including print, video, images, and the arts. Here are some examples: Adrean Clark's *The Cost of Heaven* (2022), a graphic comic about her own experiences attending both public schools and Deaf schools in North Carolina; poems and/or essays by John Lee Clark, a well-known DeafBlind poet who shares his lived experiences as a DeafBlind person in *Where I Stand: On the Signing Community and My DeafBlind Experience* (2014) and *Suddenly Slow* (2008). They are wonderful resources for helping your students develop empathy by understanding what others think or feel. As you develop these lessons, we suggest you also review strategies presented in other chapters on teaching literary works, such as scaffolding, modeling, cooperative learning, independent reading, and literary response. In the following Stick It Into Action, we provide an additional strategy that you can use to engage in conversations about varying works in Deaf literature.

Key Strategy

Use RAFT to Create or Recreate!
RAFT stands for Role, Audience, Format, and Topic/Tone/Theme. As a writing strategy, it gives students a useful framework for crafting effective and purposeful pieces of writing and to create or tell their own stories.

 ### Stick It Into Action!

Implementing RAFT
Have your student recreate media (music, short videos [e.g., TikTok, plays, poems, vlog essays]) using new roles, audiences, formats, or topics/tones/themes.

- Select a poem (e.g., "Dream the Impossible Dream" by Dr. Nathie Marbury [2017])
- Encourage students to recreate the poem in different formats (e.g., print, video, social media posting, artwork, drama), to a new audience (e.g., teenagers, artists, senior citizens), or perform it with a different tone (e.g., joy, anger, sadness, fear).
- Publish and share students' works with others in your school or community.
- Discuss students' experiences working with media design.
- Relate the discussion to how Deaf authors produce their literary works.
- Discuss the power of connecting the old with the new in authentic ways to share knowledge with modern users.

We recommend that you develop interdisciplinary units, including Deaf literature, regardless of the subject you teach (see Chapters 5, 7, and 9 for more on interdisciplinary units). You can use a thematic focus to promote discussion of literary themes related to the human condition, such as civil rights, identity, resilience, redemption, coming of age, relationships, love lost, revenge, good versus evil, technology, dreams, courage, and heroism. For resilience, one example of literature you could use that connects both English/language arts and social studies includes *Once Upon a Twin*, a book of poems by Raymond Luczak (2021), a Deaf gay author and poet who explores the loss of his twin and *Sounds Like Home: Growing Up Black and Deaf in the South*, a memoir by Mary Herring Wright (1999), who wrote about her experience at a segregated school for the Deaf and her disappointment that, at that time, Gallaudet College did not accept Black Deaf students and that Historically Black Colleges did not have the financial resources to provide sign language interpreters. Related to science and technology, you could include Nick Sturley's (2008) science fiction book, *Milan*. Having your students engage in discussions related to works by Deaf authors can broaden your students' understanding of experiences faced by different Deaf people and connect them to their own experiences. See the following Stick It Into Action for ways to engage in conversations about these themes with your students.

(ABAR) (MT) Stick It Into Action!

Create classroom-only (or grade, if appropriate) private social media–based Deaf literature discussions/clubs.

- Establish a hashtag that anchors yearlong discussion threads of certain creators (e.g., authors, ASL storytellers, artists, music makers) or themes.
- Remind students about your classroom ground rules (e.g., **Core Recommendation 1**, a safe space to engage in these conversations and respect each other) and that they also apply to online learning and only accept those who have engaged in those discussions and who are committed to adhering to the guidelines.
- Have students use the hashtag to share their thoughts, feelings, and interpretations.
- Make visual graphics of the hashtag by the end of the year for your students to identify trends.

You can also use the jigsaw strategy (see Chapter 3), which can provide a great opportunity for your students to review specific aspects of Deaf literature.

By providing opportunities for your students to analyze Deaf literature, you can help your students not only appreciate the works left behind by Deaf people like them but also be prepared to create their own literary works in the future (see Chapters 3, 4, and 12 for more on creating ASL works of literature).

(DI) (PI) Infuse Lived Experiences of Diverse Deaf People in All Content Areas

When you provide students with opportunities to recognize, accept, and celebrate the similarities and differences among people, they will learn to break down walls and value each person as an individual. As discussed in the first core recommendation, the All About Me personal and social identity projects help students appreciate each other by learning more about one another and their lived experiences. You can then connect to your students' individual and common interests throughout your lessons.

(PI) Stick It Into Action!

Integrate students' interests throughout content area lessons:

- Learn about your students' interests:
  - Take inventories of students' favorite role models, sports, video games, shows, holidays, colors, and food.
  - Ask questions that invite them to share their emotions and feelings about different things (e.g., social justice issues, neighborhood activities, technology, viral videos).
  - Invite students to share memories and lived experiences.
- Integrate the students' interests, emotions, feelings, memories, and lived experiences in your lessons and units.
  - Make a reference to something your student has shared. This helps students see the connection between learning and their lived experiences. For example, when you discuss Deaf contributions to science, you can mention that one of your students recently visited the Kennedy Space Center.
  - Ensure that you do this often so that students are engaged as they connect their stories to the content being learned (see the First Salmon Feast in Chapter 11).

By inviting diverse Deaf people to share their lived experiences, integrating Deaf history and literature, and connecting to your students' interests, students will be able to learn about multiple perspectives in an inclusive learning environment where unique perspectives are valued and respected. Include Deaf history and Deaf literature in your instruction whenever possible. That will motivate and engage your students as they connect the lived experiences of Deaf people with the content being learned.

(ABAR) Core Recommendation 3: Increase Cultural and Social Awareness

People have made and continue to make assumptions about Deaf people—their abilities, preferred languages, preferred modes of communication, and interests. It is important that you intentionally teach about cultural and social awareness. This also includes practices of social justice, which we will address within this next core recommendation.

(PI) (MM) Prioritize and Highlight Languages and Cultures Used Within the School and Community—Beyond ASL and English

When we recognize how interconnected we are, we want to build on these networks of connections to sustain our relationships. This means genuinely welcoming your students' families and communities and expanding your perspectives to include the range of languages and cultures in your school and community. You can play a significant role in facilitating language and cultural access by engaging in these conversations as well as developing and maintaining relationships with families.

Stick It Into Action!

Develop Relationships With Families

Here are some ways you can develop and maintain relationships with families:

- **Make intentional connections.** Reach out to families by finding out their preferred ways to communicate. Invite families into the classroom to share their knowledge and expertise on a range of topics.
- **Value languages and cultures.** When languages and cultures are given places in school, connections to cultures, values, and languages are also fostered. It is important to remember that your perception of your relationships with families may not match the families' perceptions of their relationships with you (Miller et al., 2016).
- **Meaningful engagement.** Create relevant and meaningful activities to engage families. These take time to develop and require frequent dialogue to check in. These relationships are strengthened when you involve colleagues and administrators in the process so that the effort does not remain isolated in a single classroom.

Teach About Different Cultures   You can teach about different cultures throughout the curriculum in many ways. As one example, we share pictures of multiple bulletin boards that were created and posted in the hallway. These bulletin boards are filled with information related to a specific culture with pictures of well-known Deaf people who are members of that culture. You can collaborate with multiple classes in elementary school and ask each class to take a turn studying about a culture and then take the lead on a month-long focus on that cultural heritage. Each class is responsible for updating the cultural heritage bulletin board and preparing a videoconferencing presentation (e.g., via Zoom) for the whole school related to the culture. Here are some examples of bulletin boards about different heritage cultures and identities:

Bulletin boards. Women, gender/sexual identity, and different cultural heritages with pictures of well-known Deaf people on them. (Posted in the Elementary Department building hallways at the California School for the Deaf, Fremont.)

Please note that the example in the following Stick It Into Action is about a specific cultural heritage done in a given month and that a similar activity takes place for each cultural heritage throughout the year. However, we recommend that cultural heritages not be limited to one month and that they continue to be integrated as much as possible throughout the year. We also recommend regularly reviewing and incorporating information from these organizations:

- National Black Deaf Advocates
- American Association of the Deaf-Blind
- Council de Manos
- Deaf Women United
- National Asian Deaf Congress
- National Association of the Deaf
- National Hispanic Latino Association of the Deaf
- Sacred Circle (Indigenous people of the Americas)

Chew on This!

Did you know that ...?

- Research shows that children have working theories about how the world works and that they evolve over time and are influenced by those around them (Davis & McKenzie, 2017).
- Students want and need a space where they can discuss challenging topics, such as race, without getting any repercussions (Vetter & Hungerford-Kresser, 2014).
- As teachers, you need to actively counteract the processes and beliefs of prejudice, hatred, and discrimination that develop when children are young by providing them opportunities to "take risks" that may feel challenging or uncomfortable (Robinson, 2005).

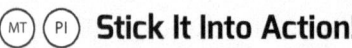  **Stick It Into Action!**

Cultural Heritage Throughout the Year

Here is an example related to a Lunar New Year activity:

1. Give an introduction. Have students watch this video: https://youtu.be/4hfl4uHLsa8?si=BYtcUPwuzMWGJ6ms
2. Invite students to share about their heritage and how they celebrate New Year's in their homes!
3. Invite a representative of a local or national Asian Deaf association to make remarks.
4. Provide a brief explanation of related art activities for all students to do.
5. Have students engage in follow-up art activities, such as making paper lanterns.

Additional Things to Consider

 ### Engage Rather Than Stay Silent

We are living together in this world. Humanity is nestled in the present time, influenced by the past and possessing the ability to direct our future trajectory. To develop and shape our understanding of the world means treating knowledge and learning as an inalienable right. Many topics may seem sensitive or advanced for younger students or too complex even for older students. However, the perception that many topics are too complicated or taboo is often perpetuated by those who desire to maintain the status quo and do not commit to the transactional nature of transformative education. Silence can be the culprit in diminishing your students' curiosity and questioning process. If you offer a response in the form of silence, some messages may be miscommunicated, such as the following:

- Students may think the vocabulary related to asking about things that are confusing or troubling to them is not appropriate. This leads to increasing their reluctance to question, initiate, or continue conversations about topics they wonder about.
- Students may think it is better for them to figure out things on their own rather than engage others in learning about the world.
- Students may think the root of their wondering is a fearful matter and should not be broached. They may also think that the topic is disconcerting to adults, meaning that nobody should talk about it.
- If you keep silent, students may be relying on other sources for information (e.g., other children, the media, adults around them) and these may be inaccurate or include bias or stereotypes (Derman-Sparks et al., 2020).

Any and every topic can be discussed and shared, regardless of the student's age; it is the manner by which they are discussed that can make content developmentally appropriate and accessible. Your students will not outgrow their curiosity to understand the world unless they have been taught not to be curious. Once you have created a nurturing space in your classroom, as mentioned in **Core Recommendation 1**, you will be better able to address these topics. In the following Teacher Tale, Shira models how you can respond to an inappropriate comment.

Teacher Tale

I am a DeafDisabled woman who is a Little Person. Very often, the younger students will approach me and measure their height against mine and exclaim how short I am. Educators may respond with "No, that isn't appropriate!" whereas I will respond with, "Yes, I'm very short." This generates dialogue about how people are different and the various ways we can observe and discuss differences, and we open the space for students to dialogue about important topics.

—*Shira Grabelsky*

Promote a Transformative Atmosphere

Rather than staying silent, you can engage in challenging topics to promote change. In doing this you are confirming that all topics can be discussed and to as much extent as possible so no question will go unanswered. There are increasingly more and more resources to address how to tackle challenging questions like racism. As educators, you will often be confronted with questions or issues raised by students. Understanding that silence can be a harmful response, it helps to prepare how you can respond, especially when you don't know the answer, don't feel well-equipped to continue the conversation, or perhaps feel uncomfortable with a topic. And it's okay if you don't know what to say. In this Stick It Into Action, we demonstrate how you can respond if you are unsure.

Stick It Into Action!

How to Respond If You Don't Know

Here are some ways you can respond:

- "That is a good question that I don't have the answer to. I would like to learn about it too. Can I get back to you after lunch/tomorrow?"
- "This seems to be something that is troubling you. I'd like to chat more about this. Can we discuss this during our next period together?"
- "Would you feel comfortable asking _____ about their thoughts on this? This person knows more about this than I do, and I want to be sure you get information that is accurate and helps you think more about this."

Bringing It All Together

   Unit: Social Justice Quilt Project

We present a unit called Social Justice Quilt[1] (see photos on pp. 193–194) to highlight our core recommendations. Two middle school teachers worked together to develop two units (one for sixth and another for eighth grade connected to the Social Justice Sewing Academy, a nonprofit organization that helps young people engage in social justice topics through creating quilts. We also recognize that not everyone will have the resources to create their own quilt, so we have provided some alternative suggestions.

Sixth-Grade Goal

Choose one activist from the teacher-provided list. Research the life and work of the activist and use the information related to the activist to learn the importance of activism and about the issue the activist was working on.

Essential Questions   Who was I? How do I deal with challenges? and How did I become self-sufficient? (See Chapter 9 for more on essential questions.)

Eighth-Grade Goal

Choose one social justice topic that each student is personally invested in and that is also based on individual interest, life experience, and prior learning.

Essential Questions   How do my values align with those of my communities? How do our actions impact the future? How can we become or support leaders to help improve the world?

Objectives Related to Content Areas

- Students will explain their research on activists or social justice issues (English, social studies, and Deaf studies).

1. The authors want to thank Adele Ann Eberwein and Keila Simos of the California School for the Deaf, Fremont, for sharing the unit on the Social Justice Quilt.

- Students will be video-recorded explaining the content on their quilt squares in ASL or Heritage SL. (ASL standards for organizing and giving presentations)
- Students will create a quilt square to address a social justice issue. (Arts, mathematics, Deaf studies)
- Students will create geometric shapes for their quilt squares. (Mathematics)

Social Justice Standards
- Students will recognize stereotypes and relate to people as individuals rather than as representatives of groups.
- Students will recognize unfairness on the individual level (e.g., biased speech) and injustice at the institutional or systemic level (i.e., discrimination).
- Students will recognize their own responsibility to stand up to exclusion, prejudice, and injustice.

Lesson Sequence

This lesson can be created over several weeks (see Table 8.1). You can create alternatives to quilting by modifying activities according to an individual student's needs and abilities and the available resources. Some alternatives are to make a wall or flags or to make a picture or art book with students' quilt squares.

Teacher Tale

A student, who was an emergent ASL signer and new to the school, used gestures to express his likes for singing groups, and I wanted to focus on activism rather than the "celebrity." We spent more time researching different singers and finally reached the activism part. Time spent was powerful to me as a teacher because I learned so much more about the student and his life experiences.

—*Keila Simos, middle school teacher*

Handstamp Sample

Sample pieces on the middle school Social Justice Quilt. The QR code takes you to the quilt collection on the internet (https://gallaudetupress.manifoldapp.org/projects/58-in-mind/resource-collection/social-justice-quilts)

Handstamp Sample (continued)

Social Justice Quilt examples.

Table 8.1. Social Justice Weekly Quilt Project Plan

Lessons and Core Recommendations (CR)	Activities
Week 1: Introduction CR 1, 2, 3	1. Review classroom ground rules and how to make and keep a positive classroom community (CR 1, 3). 2. Read and discuss *The Keeping Quilt* (Polacco, 2011) as a class and review social media from groups such as National Black Deaf Advocates, Council de Manos, National Asian Deaf Congress, Deaf Women United, Sacred Circle, and others. 3. Review activists (https://www.tolerance.org/classroom-resources/one-world-posters; https://www.thefamouspeople.com/activists.php) and other additional websites/books on Deaf activists. 4. Have each student choose one square in a Social Justice Quilt and learn about it and why the artist created it.

Week 2: Select a topic
 	
CR 2, 3
	1. Post different areas you think students will be connected to or be inspired by.
	   a. **Activism:** animal rights, women's rights, environment, human rights, children's rights, peace, civil rights, politics, etc.
	   b. **Social justice topics:** gender discrimination, LGBTQIA+ experiences, mass incarceration, rise in hate crimes, gentrification, charged political language, etc.
	   c. **Deaf rights:** education, language deprivation, employment, etc.
	2. Have students select a topic and research. After they have enough information, they can draft a design for a piece on the quilt that captures the topic.

Week 3–4: Create a quilt CR 2	After the drawing is finalized, it is then translated into fabric with appliqué techniques (this may take more time). Alternatively, you can give each student a square cloth, a poster, or a piece of paper and have them draw on paper, pencil-draw a square, cut the shapes for the square, and permanent-draw/write on the quilt or square.

Weeks 5–6: Create a video
 	
CR 1, 2, 3
	Finally, have each student create an ASL (and/or heritage language) video using Flip or videos submitted over Google Classroom. Students follow these steps:
	1. Write or record a draft of responses to the following questions:
	   • Their names
	   • Topics they picked
	   • Description of their squares
	   • Why their issue is important to them
	   • Their ideas for a solution
	2. Seek feedback from you.
	3. Revise the draft (see Chapters 3 and 4 for revision process).
	4. Convert them into a QR code for display (see the pictures).

Week 7: Presentations and reflection CR 2, 3	To wrap up the unit, have each student do the following: 1. Present their videos to the class. 2. Share what they learned with elementary school students, their families, and/or the school community. 3. Do a final reflection.

Teacher Tale

Teaching the social justice unit related to the quilt project was powerful because of the conversations it created among peers, teachers, and students about different social justice topics. It created a natural atmosphere where we could examine our own biases (adult and student), wrestle with our thoughts and the perspectives of our communities, and ultimately be given full rein to design and express our point of view through an art medium.

—*Keila Simos, middle school teacher*

 Your Turn to Practice!

Now, it's your turn! Develop, teach, and reflect on a lesson that integrates identities and cultural and social awareness into a content area subject. You can modify a lesson you have previously developed or create a new lesson. If you are currently teaching, try it out with your own students. If you are a teacher candidate, you can practice with real or mock students.

Here are the steps to follow:

Develop a Lesson

Develop or modify a lesson plan for a content area (e.g., science, math, Deaf studies, social studies, reading, writing, ASL, and English language arts).

- Add a Deaf studies objective related to at least one of the core recommendations in this chapter.
    - How will you modify it based on students' varying language levels and abilities?
    - How would you modify the lesson for varying educational settings (e.g., one-to-one, group)?
- Add a mindfulness activity to your lesson (to begin and/or end the lesson or within the lesson).

Teach the Lesson

Teach the lesson to your students or in a mock setting.

Reflect on Your Teaching

After teaching the lesson, reflect on your experience. Consider the following questions:

- What went well?
- What would you change/do differently if you taught this lesson again?
- What benefits could you see for your students?
  After assessing your students, how well did they learn the targeted objectives?
- In what ways did your Deaf studies objectives promote a positive sense of self and/or justice in society? (**Core Recommendation 1**)

Recommended Readings/Viewings

For Teachers/Teacher Candidates

- The Early Childhood Education Assembly (https://sites.google.com/view/ecea-ncte/resources) provides resources for teachers to learn about ABAR.
- California School for the Deaf, Fremont, CORE department (https://sites.google.com/csdeagles.net/core-learning-channel/home) includes several great sites with the following titles: Black Lives Matter Resources, Latinx/Hispanic Resources, Asian American/Pacific Islanders Resources, Diversity & Equity Resources, and Deaf Studies.
- *Deaf Identities* (Leigh & O'Brien, 2020). This book presents chapters on varying Deaf identities, including race, LGBTQ, and religion.
- *Teach, Breathe, Learn: Mindfulness In and Out of the Classroom* (Srinivasan, 2014). This book presents strategies on ways for teachers to include mindfulness activities in the classroom as well as outside of the classroom.

For Using With Students

- *This Book Is Anti-Racist—Journal* (Jewell, 2021). This journal provides activities for you to use with your students to help them explore their identities and impact on positive change in society.
- The Conscious Kid (https://www.theconsciouskid.org/antiracist-childrens-books) website provides books you can use in your classroom with students on varying topics of social justice.
- Complex: *32 Young Activists Who Are Changing the World* (https://www.complex.com/life/young-activists-who-are-changing-the-world) provides information on various young activists.

Conclusion

The field of Deaf studies keeps evolving to represent diverse experiences of the history, literature, and lives of Deaf people. Our hope with this chapter is that you will look at ways to integrate these experiences of Deaf people into your instruction regardless of the grade or content you teach. When you integrate resources from Deaf studies with resources on social justice and ABAR pedagogy, you will have a wealth of tools to help each of your students explore their multiple and intersecting personal and social identities as a Deaf person, be it Deaf, DeafBlind, DeafDisabled, or Hard of Hearing, as well as increase their understanding of others. Doing this work means you also need to develop an awareness of yourself as a teacher, critically examining your relationship with each student and understanding who they are. Language and culture are inextricably connected (Petrová, 2013). By honoring students' backgrounds and identities through a multilingual and multicultural lens along with a commitment to social justice, you will have a ripple effect—as you change yourself, it will enable your students to flourish.

Sticking Points

- Create a nurturing and welcoming space in your classroom to foster students, positive sense of self and understanding of others' multiple and intersecting identities.
- Integrate the history, literature, and lives of diverse Deaf people through a multilingual lens across the curriculum to foster a schoolwide commitment to do the same.
- Provide multiple opportunities for your students to learn about and practice cultural and social awareness.

Social Studies

David H. Smith
Kathleen K. Mockus

One of the best things about social studies is that it incorporates not only traditional topics like history, geography, and civics but also language arts, philosophy, architecture, career education, and STEAM (science, technology, engineering, arts, and mathematics). Nearly every current or past event studied in social studies is a perfect source for inquiry-based instruction, and social studies can be a vibrant learning experience for Deaf students. As teachers, you can make history, current events, and social and cultural issues come alive through a Deaf studies lens and the use of multilingual and multimodal approaches. When students are able to actively participate in discussions about past and current events, it promotes language development, critical thinking skills, and the empowerment needed to act when injustice is happening.

Who Are We?

Before we move on, we would like to introduce ourselves. I (Dave Smith) have been involved with Deaf education for more than 30 years at the kindergarten through Grade 12 (K–12) and higher education levels. I taught social studies and STEAM topics at the California School for the Deaf (CSD), Riverside for 8 years prior to going into Deaf education teacher preparation. I am currently a research professor at the University of Tennessee.

I (Kathleen Mockus) am a credentialed teacher in Deaf education and cultural, linguistic academic development, and have been teaching Deaf students K–12 at CSD

Fremont for over 25 years. With a background in history and anthropology, I support others teaching history/social sciences, science, and health as a mentor teacher and curriculum specialist.

In this chapter, we give an overview of social studies instruction across the K–12 spectrum for Deaf students. Using a Deaf-centered lens, we address various instructional strategies specific to social studies as well as how instructional approaches can be applied to social studies, such as developing inquiry-based units, cooperative learning, differentiating instruction, and incorporating anti-bias/antiracist (ABAR) topics. Learning about equity, fairness, and respect for diversity is a critical part of a social studies foundation.

Handstamp Sample

This third grader proudly shows off Black Lives Matter signs. Students' pictures and letters were sent to (then) California Senator Kamala Harris, creating an authentic purpose for their activity.

Deaf Students and Social Studies

One goal of social studies is to develop civic competence and skills for students to become actively engaged in their communities. Civic education is more central to social studies than to any other subject area. It provides the information and learning experiences necessary to empower students to actively participate in their diverse communities and in our democracy. In an increasingly fractured society, it is essential that students are given knowledge, critical thinking skills, and awareness of and respect for diverse peoples to sustain a democratic society (National Council for the

Social Studies, 2013). For Deaf children, this includes learning about ways they can be involved in advocating for the rights of Deaf people via local and state Deaf organizations as well as the National Association of the Deaf and other national and international organizations.

Because social studies includes cultural, philosophical, historical, and geographical topics, there are ways to integrate Deaf studies to increase the cultural relevance for Deaf children, as well as their engagement and participation. In the following section, we briefly outline some core recommendations as applied to social studies in classrooms with Deaf students.

Deaf Experiences, Perspectives, and Core Recommendations

It is important to expose Deaf students to the history, geography, and culture of Deaf people to provide them a locus of their roles in society as well as within their own Deaf community. These roles have been defined over the millennia by societal views, laws, and educational practices, most of which were quite oppressive in nature. With the civil and disabilities rights movements in the United States during the 1960s and 1970s and the recognition of signed languages, there was a dramatic shift in the understanding of Deaf people's role and place in society. This led to a rise of pride within the Deaf community and efforts to cast off institutionalized oppression such as the Deaf President Now movement that caught the attention of the general public. Given the changes that followed, Deaf people have been less likely to be relegated to an inferior status. However, we still have quite a way to go toward equity in terms of recognizing the intersecting identities of Deaf people, particularly those who are Black, Indigenous, and/or People of Color (BIPOC), DeafBlind, Lesbian, Gay, Transgender, Queer or Questioning, Intersex, Asexual, or more (LGBTQIA+), DeafDisabled, and other marginalized groups. This also extends to some languages, such as Black ASL and Indigenous Sign Languages, and communication modalities, such as Protactile Sign. Deaf students need to learn and critically reflect on these topics. They should have opportunities to participate in dialogues about ABAR topics more broadly as well as those specific to the Deaf community.

(MM) Deaf Students' Experiences With the World Around Them

Deaf students often show up at school with a wide range of skills in language, critical thinking, theory of mind, and executive functioning. The variation in their world knowledge and experiences may be due to a lack of access to incidental language occurring around them. It can also be due to the socioeconomic status of their families or where they live. City-based children may have never visited rural areas, and rural children may have never gone out of the areas of their own neighborhoods and schools. The students who experience language deprivation arrive at school without the foundational language required to think critically, and the impacts are felt academically, socially, and ultimately in their lives and careers unless addressed (Hall et al., 2017).

Social studies lends itself to using differentiated instructional methods to meet students' learning needs within classes. As with other subjects, your instruction should involve language planning for multilingual and multimodal teaching strategies, as you will likely be working with students who have a variety of knowledge, skills, and abilities in the same classroom. This includes social skills, literacy, and linguistic fluency as well as academic and developmental readiness for their assigned grade levels. Also, Deaf students are diverse in their home and heritage backgrounds, and we need to be sensitive to the wide variations among students on several intersecting layers. A few things they all have in common are a need for direct and accessible communication, a healthy self-identity, and a right to self-determination (Holcomb, 2013). All good multilingual/multimodal Deaf education programs will provide communication access. A good social studies teacher can go a long way toward developing a Deaf student's identities and self-determination (see Chapters 2 and 8 for more on identity development). Given these skills, along with instruction in critical thinking and appreciation for the rich history and diversity of human cultures, your students will be ready to face the world as responsible and thoughtful citizens.

Core Recommendations

We offer the following recommendations (and associated multimodal and multilingual strategies) for teaching social studies. In all areas, make critical thinking and language goals in ASL and English a priority.

- Incorporate inquiry-based learning that integrates Deaf studies and ABAR topics.
- Use cooperative learning activities and practice civil discourse.
- Provide authentic learning experiences.
- Integrate a wide variety of text, geographical, and media sources (original and/or adapted) related to historical and current events.

Effective Practices for Deaf Learners

The context and content of a social studies class provides a means to work on the language and thinking skills required for literacy, social, and self-advocacy skills while empowering your students toward action in their community. Framed this way, it is not the content that's paramount, it is what students *do* with it and *how* it's acquired that is key. Any social studies lesson can be turned into a critical thinking skills and literacy lesson when framed in this way. In this section, we highlight our four core recommendations that all integrate critical thinking, as well as language goals in ASL and English. We like to think of the question, "What do social scientists DO?" when considering lesson plans and developing materials (see list of skills in this Stick it Into Action).

Stick It Into Action!

Skills Involved With DOing Social Studies
Include these skills in your social studies instruction. This list includes "but is not limited to" the following:

SOCIAL STUDIES

Chronological thinking
Map reading
Analyzing artifacts (guided visual analysis of images or objects)
Problem solving
Explaining cause and effect
Summarizing main ideas
Distinguishing between details
Analyzing perspectives
Weighing costs/benefits
Discussing difficult topics effectively and politely with others who may disagree
Conducting research

Spatial thinking
Categorizing information
Performing analysis of a signed or written text
Comparing and contrasting ideas
Reading for detail
Interpreting claims
Determining points of view
Evaluating alternatives
Sharing information
Working effectively and respectfully with others who are different from you
Distinguishing fact from fiction or fact from opinion

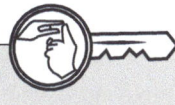

Key Vocabulary

Primary source documents include firsthand witness accounts of events, discoveries, and time periods, such as documents, diaries, photos, and videos.

While addressing these skills, expose students to as many types of **primary source documents** as possible in both ASL and English. Depending on your content and objectives, visual resources can include historical photographs, artwork, architecture, maps, graphic information systems, graphs, film clips, artifacts, filmed storytelling, political cartoons, historical clothing, and so on. Text resources can include diaries, news articles, eyewitness accounts, letters, inventories, and more. With consistent exposure to these documents, you can contribute to your Deaf students' depth of knowledge and critical thinking (see Chapter 7 for additional connections with primary sources and critical thinking) through a variety of activities involving the skills mentioned here that will serve them in all other areas of their lives.

In this section, we draw on these skills as well as the use of primary sources within each of the four core recommendations. Consider which of the myriad skills lends itself to the social studies content you need to teach. For each lesson, ask yourself, "Which skills will it be?" No matter which grade level you're teaching, you can focus on the skills (that you determine through assessment and observation) that your Deaf students need.

  ### Core Recommendation 1: Incorporate Inquiry-Based Learning

Students creating stained-glass replicas on windows.

Teacher Tale

My seventh graders had been learning about the architecture of the European Middle Ages as part of their required World History course. When they learned that stained-glass windows were created to tell stories to people who could not read or understand the language around them, it became a natural extension for us to paint "stained-glass" windows depicting stories of the history we'd learned (see photo on p. 203). In cooperative groups, students developed questions and researched literature such as Robin Hood, or retold stories such as that of Eleanor of Aquitaine or Charlemagne. Based on these stories and research, students designed and painted my classroom windows to create "stained glass." The colored light streamed through their designs into my classroom. They'd beg to come in at recess and before and after school to continue to work on their paintings. When they finished, their cooperative groups proudly presented to a group of prominent people from the community. I do not think they even realized that they had just completed a rigorous inquiry-based unit involving European Medieval art, architecture, history, and literature.

—*Kathleen Mockus*

Deaf students should be offered rich opportunities to participate in inquiry-based learning projects. According to the College, Career, and Civic Life (C3) Framework for Social Studies State Standards (National Council for the Social Studies, 2013), inquiry-based learning involves (a) developing questions and planning inquiries, (b) applying disciplinary concepts and tools, (c) evaluating primary sources and using evidence, and (d) communicating conclusions and taking informed action. Each of these steps requires careful language instruction and provides rich opportunities that are often not offered to Deaf students. You can also find support for planning rigorous language-focused instruction in Gallaudet's ASL K–12 Content Standards (Laurent Clerc National Deaf Education Center, 2018), your state's English language standards, and social studies frameworks.

(MT) (ABAR) Developing Questions and Planning Inquiries

We recommend that inquiry topics be based on state social studies standards for grade levels and include **essential questions.** Such inquiries can cut across other subject areas and be combined with their standards as well. These standards may be based on history, cultures, and geographical locations (e.g., state, nation, world). When designing unit plans, your guiding questions should revolve around one or two main concepts. For example, a fifth-grade unit on early North American history could revolve around the essential questions of expansion during the postcolonial period, such as, "What happens when we encounter newcomers?" Because much of the historical canon in textbooks is based on Eurocentric perspectives, alternative views need to be presented, including those with ABAR and Deaf studies lenses (see the literature detectives strategy in Chapter 7). For example, you could include not only the development of early Deaf education during this period but also information about Black Deaf schools or the lack thereof. Later, in the Bringing It All Together section, we show how to take a theme that begins with essential questions and plan out unit lessons with whole-class activities, multilingual/multimodal strategies, and differentiated instruction components.

Key Vocabulary

Essential questions are important questions used to guide inquiry-based units that are broadly applicable, timeless, and recur throughout one's life—for example, "How do we overcome prejudice?" "When does the government have the right to limit people's freedoms?" or "What makes a good friend?"

Applying Disciplinary Concepts and Tools
Given the focus on increasing state test scores in language arts and mathematics, inquiry-based units are a way you can also integrate social studies. Many social studies standards start with geography, family, school, and community experiences in the early grades, which can be used as themes for units that allow learning across multiple subjects. As the grades progress, the social studies standards start to expand to the state, nation, and world, which have combined elements of history, geography, government, and economy. Themes can be based on exploration, colonization, democracy, foundations, development, expansion, resources, industrialization, globalization, and so on. You can also interweave historical connections, figures, and perspectives of the home cultures of your students. Because many themes revolve around the form and functions of social units of community and how they work, a good place to start in the primary grades is to organize a classroom community (see **Core Recommendation 3**).

(ABAR) (PI) *Empower Your Students* As you implement inquiry-based learning, educate your students for empowerment. This is important for identities that have been historically marginalized, of which being Deaf is just one among several intersecting identities your students will have. Educate your students about the history of oppression, how dominant groups work, and about past and current social or revolutionary movements to overcome oppression. From this, show your students various ways they can self-advocate for their needs and rights.

Most of us know that history is not always the varnished version depicted in texts or media for young children. The effects of colonization, as in subjugation and/or marginalization of Indigenous peoples, is one example. Having knowledge of this injustice toward Indigenous peoples and others, including LGBTQIA+, immigrants, enslaved people, Deaf people, women, and more, is the basis of beginning to learn about social justice. Good teachers will carefully consider students' developmental levels and lived experiences when teaching about oppressive historical or current events and about social justice. "Messy" history is usually addressed as students become more mature and ready to discuss complex historical events from different points of view. Role-playing historical figures, whether Deaf or hearing, is a key tool for Deaf students to achieve this. Be careful not to appropriate cultural activities by not actually involving members of that particular culture (e.g., Native American Pow Wows). At the elementary level, students are learning chronology and spatial relations, and they are just beginning to understand multiple perspectives. Therefore, instead of using outdated depictions of Thanksgiving, such as the "discovery" of America by European colonizers and other popular myths, have students investigate these events from various perspectives. Use primary sources and **artifacts** whenever possible.

(ABAR) **Evaluating Primary Sources and Using Evidence**
State standards are trending toward requiring students to engage more directly with primary source documents and artifacts, not just textbooks. You can have your students find answers to the essential questions of your inquiry-based unit by investigating and analyzing texts, photos, and artifacts. Including ABAR questions will go a long way toward ensuring a balanced, non–Western-biased curriculum. Examples of these questions or ideas might be, "Is democracy fair for everyone?" "Why do so many people not vote in our country?" "What can we learn about enslaved and freed people

Key Vocabulary

Artifacts are a type of primary source: human-made objects of historical or cultural significance (e.g., pottery, clothing, metalware).

through photographs?" "What are the symbols of equity and justice that activists for women's rights/LGBTQIA+/civil rights/Deaf rights use?" Some texts/curricula do give recommendations on addressing heritage cultures but are less likely to mention heritage languages, so be sure to include that component through exposure to Black ASL, LSM (Lenguaje de Señas Mexicana), Spanish, and other home and heritage languages of your students through media you choose or by inviting visiting guests to your classroom (live or virtually).

(ABAR) (MM) Communicating Conclusions

All historical inquiry should include a lens on the lived experiences of Deaf people and Deaf history and be inclusive of ABAR topics and materials. By exploring essential questions, and using relevant primary documents, media sources, and graphic organizers, the subject matter will become much more engaging and relevant to students' lives. In the following Teacher Tale, you can see an example of how embedding primary resources used for student inquiry into varying timelines helped students communicate conclusions about the question, "Why did Black ASL develop?"

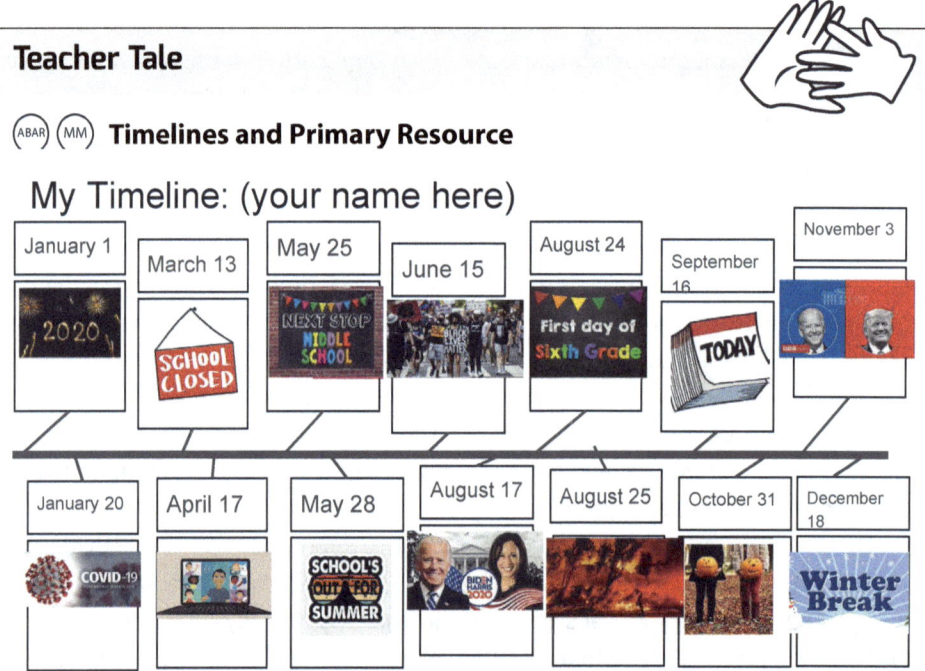

> **Teacher Tale**
>
> **(ABAR) (MM) Timelines and Primary Resource**
>
> This timeline bulletin board used primary sources to help third graders answer the question, "What were some important events in the country this year?"
>
> I scaffolded my language-deprived students' understanding of chronology by first introducing the concept of timelines through personal timelines. I then overlapped with country timelines (shown here), before moving on to teaching about world history timelines as required by state standards. I include the primary resources while studying these topics such as pictures of events and campaign material. My essential questions were: "What are timelines used for?" and "What were the most important events in the country during my life this year?"
>
> —*Autumn Lutge, sixth-grade teacher*

SOCIAL STUDIES

Inquiry-based learning, along with applying active engagement with primary documents, is an excellent way to make history and the world around them relevant to the lives of your students. The bonus of this approach is that it is a lot more fun for all involved. Our next recommendation shows you how to combine this inquiry-based learning with interactive activities.

(DI) (ES) (MM) Core Recommendation 2: Use Cooperative Learning Activities and Practice Civil Discourse

One reason we recommend you implement cooperative learning activities with your Deaf students is that it is quite adaptable to differentiation. Freeman et al. (2016) have pointed out that those learning English as a second language (such as Deaf students) benefit from learning collaboratively in groups. Peer interaction naturally encourages receptive and expressive language development and problem-solving skills. Specifically, Deaf learners show improvement in sign language, literacy, and communication when involved in collaborative learning projects (Aristizábal et al., 2017). When well planned and executed, these activities can be an enjoyable and motivating approach to teaching and learning that promotes **civil discourse,** social cohesion, improved cognitive development, and enhanced learning (Slavin, 2015). Deaf students also benefit from being partnered with other Deaf students who can impart language and knowledge specific to Deaf culture, to which they may not otherwise be exposed. There are many resources available on instructional strategies to use with cooperative groups, so we focus on how they can be used to facilitate learning for Deaf students in social studies classes.

Social studies content requires analysis skills and geographical and chronological skills. It also involves building discipline-specific literacy skills (see Chapters 5 and 7 for more on disciplinary literacy skills) and developmental readiness. We would never ask students who are just learning their ABCs to read and analyze the poetry of William Shakespeare, but that is often what social studies teachers are faced with. You may be asking students who may be just learning ASL to then view or even participate in a meaningful debate on economic growth and justice or the development of the rule of law. This is asking them to deeply understand social justice issues and historical periods that they may never have seen pictures of or experienced. Direct instruction in combination with cooperative grouping helps to bridge these gaps.

We recommend that cooperative groups be mixed by the language and the academic skills of the students. This helps take advantage of support and modeling from more knowledgeable peers as a form of differentiated instruction.

Key Vocabulary

Civil discourse is discussion in which students learn to share different viewpoints while respecting others' perspectives. Different from a debate, the point is not to necessarily convince or "win" the argument but for students to understand that issues are often more complex than they had previously thought.

(MM) (MT) Stick It Into Action!

Cooperative Learning in Social Studies

When beginning cooperative groups, consider the following for your Deaf learners:

- Assign roles according to students' talents and needs; give choices when possible.
- Act out what you expect the students to do within those roles—Do's and Don'ts—using picture supports as needed.

Stick It Into Action! (*continued*)
- Use multimedia visual reminders of each of the assigned group roles (e.g., photos of the students signing the role along with the written word).
- For *civil discourse*, model in both ASL and English the vocabulary and language students will need as well as how to make group decisions or vote. Role-play what to do if disagreements arise. By training students to use accountable talk sentence starters (e.g., "I disagree/agree, because...") to provide reasons for their viewpoints, they learn tools to agree, disagree, clarify, discuss, paraphrase, and support their opinions with evidence.
- Post and practice rules of respectful discourse with picture supports.

(CM) Teacher Tale

During my first year of teaching sixth grade with two other team teachers, we decided to teach social studies using cooperative learning groups. At first, it was a disaster as none of the students had ever worked together to complete activities. There was no civil discourse, they had no clue how to interact nor apply team strategy skills, and in typical 11- and 12-year-old behavior, they started having serious disagreements. We remembered that one of the physical education teachers was an outdoor leadership specialist, so we asked him to help us. He led the class in outdoor team activities in their assigned cooperative groups an hour a day for 1 week. I participated with my team teachers so that our group could serve as a model of civil discourse and problem-solving for the class. After that week, things went a lot more smoothly, and the students looked forward to group time. One takeaway from this is that teachers just starting to implement cooperative groups can do something similar with physical education, art, or other team-building activities until students are comfortable working together.
—*Dave Smith*

Cooperative activities help students improve their communication, social skills, and accountability to each other within the group, allowing for fuller civic discourse engagement.

(DI) (CM) (ES) (PI) (MM) Core Recommendation 3: Provide Authentic Learning Experiences

Deaf students especially benefit from authentic learning experiences in social studies as they provide language-learning opportunities and real audiences with which to communicate outside the typical classroom environment. Here, we highlight three authentic experiences you can use in your classrooms: classroom communities, field trips, and mock events.

(ES) Classroom Communities

A classroom community is an excellent way to help students understand the structure and roles of various agencies and economies. Setting up working communities involves having the class "founded" (as a new city). With your students, you can establish the classroom city name and government, a city hall, and a court system. Elections can be held periodically for mayor, council, judge, et cetera, so students can have an opportunity to experience each of these roles. You must include your students in the development of roles and responsibilities so that they can experience more authentically how democracy works.

We recommend that you create visual charts of your city's rules and laws to help your students understand their roles, classroom expectations, and rewards/consequences. Referring to these charts facilitates more in-depth discussions of the societal reasons for rules and laws, which will exercise students' critical thinking and language skills related to concepts such as cause and effect. This is also a great way to include civics lessons and activities on topics such as community activism and election campaigns.

Stick It Into Action!

(MM) (ES) (PI) **Classroom Community Helpers**

So often, adults do things for Deaf kids that it creates learned helplessness. Instead, empower your Deaf students to learn responsibility for your classroom community by assigning classroom helper roles. You can simultaneously teach community roles, civic duties, and if thought out carefully, expose them early on to future careers and help them find their hidden talents (see Chapter 14 for additional suggestions). Here are the steps to get started:

- Prepare a visual chart including images, signs, and English words for each role you choose. Include additional home/heritage languages when possible.
- Be creative to match students' interests and your needs. Classroom Gardner, Recycling Expert, Classroom Ambassador, Kindness Chief, and Newsletter Reporter are good examples of jobs that feel important and offer opportunities for learning independence. You can also match them to the theme being studied.
- Introduce the responsibilities for each community helper with a careful role-play of what to do and what not to do.
- Make sure to rotate the roles. Kids are sticklers for fairness!

Token Economies   You might also consider developing a classroom community with a token economy, which involves students earning tangible items like tokens (or credits) that they can later exchange or "cash in" for a desirable reward. Tokens can come in all sorts of forms: imitation currency with denominations (which is good for teaching about money), points or credits on display in the classroom, rubber stamps on cards, tally marks, and so forth.

(PI) (CM) Stick It Into Action!

Setting Up a Token Economy in Your Classroom

One idea is to create a currency with images representing famous and diverse Deaf people to visually and cognitively emphasize their roles in Deaf history. You can

Stick It Into Action! (*continued*)

informally assess students by asking them whom the image represents and what they did. Students can save or accrue these tokens until they reach a certain goal. You can also set up "bank accounts" for students to save and spend and a store that sells snacks, trinkets, comic books, trade books, and also "high-ticket" items like lunch with the teacher. Less tangible items for sale can be allocated as well, such as time with toys, games, technology, and other desirable activities. There is a lot of potential for creativity! Token economies not only provide behavior and learning incentives, but students also learn the basics of how an economic system works.

 Field Trips

Most Deaf students miss out on overhearing their families and the media discuss matters of the world. Through field trips, you can provide your students with vocabulary and language opportunities connected to social studies. For younger students, these may involve outings to grocery stores or banks, experiencing farms, trying different modes of transportation, or taking cultural trips to restaurants. Social studies field trips for older students may involve visits to museums, historical sites, businesses (including Deaf-owned), and government agencies. We also recommend that students visit their local Deaf service agencies and/or Deaf schools because some also have small museums. These trips should combine a number of subject areas to maximize the benefits of the time, effort, and expense involved (see Chapters 2, 7, and 12 and others for additional field trip ideas). To ensure learning retention, have your students provide a follow-up summary report about the trip and thank you notes to their respective hosts, interpreters, and docents. This can be done as a *cooperative learning activity* where, as a group, students produce a written or signed report about what they saw, with references to what they learned along with photos and videos (see Chapters 4 and 5 for more on writing/signing publications for a purpose). This can be given as a presentation to the class by the group reporter.

Teacher Tale

Authentic learning activities often lead to wonderful and surprising outcomes. One of my students' most memorable trips included taking a ferry to the Angel Island Immigration Station, the West Coast's version of Ellis Island, to learn about the challenges and oppression of the Asian immigration experience. The museum within this detainment center was both heartbreaking and a rich historical experience for the high schoolers. But what turned out to be most memorable for many of them was that it was their first opportunity ever to be on a boat! This bit of shared background experience ended up changing their understanding, adding to their schema as they encountered historical figures' experiences, and gave them reference as they learned about the opening of the West to newcomers—all while building confidence and opening up minds to new experiences. Students interacted with the boat operators, each dealing with tickets and schedules, and asked questions of tour guides along the way.

—*Kathleen Mockus*

SOCIAL STUDIES

Students use real voting booths as part of an authentic learning experience in a mock election. (*left*)

Students celebrate at a Barack Obama inauguration event. (*above*)

(MM) (PI) (MT) Mock Events

Mock events are great ways to provide authentic experiences that can also be used as *culminating end-of-unit activities* as a way for students to display what they learned. When possible, we encourage you to give these situations a Deaf "twist."

- **Mock trials** give Deaf students the opportunity to practice self-advocacy as well as see and express multiple points of view, and the chance to practice persuasive language in front of an audience. In the early grades, trials can involve defendants such as literary characters like Goldilocks (see Chapter 7 for a mock trial example in middle school). As students become older, historical figures such as Alexander Graham Bell can be put on the stand. Legislative sessions can involve not only Deaf issues ("Should courts be required to provide an ASL interpreter for Deaf people to participate in juries?") but also other social justice issues such as, "Should teachers be allowed to teach from the 1619 Project related to the first enslaved Africans in the United States?" "Should Deaf students whose parents are not yet citizens receive voice relay support?"
- **Debates** are typically about historical or contemporary issues. You can create debates about controversial topics, such as signed versus oral education or the pros and cons of cochlear implantation in infants. Learning how to debate formally is another great place for Deaf students to practice the language of accountable talk and civil discourse.
- **Archaeological mock excavations.** One example of this rewarding learning activity is to set up an archaeological dig site on a school campus or within your classroom. This activity exposes Deaf students to the concept of combined careers in STEAM and history. For an outdoor site, a very large sandbox can be built and "artifacts" can be buried within the box. Or partner with a local university to teach your students about archeological dig techniques and processes while conducting an excavation. Have students carry out activities like recording locations on a grid, drawing pictures of the objects and/or photographing them, removing and preserving the objects, setting up a display, and writing a report to be presented to their peers.

Students participating in a mock archaeological excavation.

Reenactments

Reenactments are also extremely rewarding. You can have students create materials, costumes, and other artifacts during classes or outside of school for the specific time period of the unit, such as with historical Deaf events like Deaf President Now, Deaf Way, Deaflympics, or even Greek Deaflympics. Reenactments create opportunities for Deaf students to put language and vocabulary learned in content areas into practical use as well as create fun, memorable ways to learn about historical perspectives (see Chapter 12 for more on theater in education).

Service Learning Projects

These are excellent for instilling a volunteer spirit in your students that can carry over to adulthood. Start with simple school community service activities at the elementary level and move to the local neighborhood and wider community as students rise through the grades. You can encourage them to come up with project ideas and implementation planning. Encourage students to consider ways projects might benefit the Deaf community (e.g., creating a website with resources in ASL, collecting Deaf elders' stories on a particular topic to share with others, serving at the local Deaf senior assisted living center). When students plan and execute them, these projects become unforgettable authentic experiences that benefit the community and students alike. Deaf students are empowered through the experience by learning the value of giving back while gaining a deeper understanding of citizenship. This process is ideal for helping students apply new knowledge and language using critical thinking skills.

The key to creating authentic learning activities is making them hands-on and "minds-on." Have your students document these activities in portfolios with student-made artifacts, pictures, and videos. Students filming themselves in ASL and then viewing each other's responses is a great way to document the activity and target ASL standards while cementing newly acquired vocabulary and content in their minds. It also helps to build community and confidence (See more on filming in ASL in Chapters 3 and 12).

(MM) (DI) (ABAR) (MT) Core Recommendation 4: Use of Text, Media, and Geographical Sources

As mentioned previously, most standards require that students be exposed to a variety of primary documents and demonstrate how they can show varying points of view. You can discuss how these documents are used to "write history." There are many

Deaf-related primary documents and historical films available online, such as the digital collection at the Gallaudet University Archives (https://gallaudet.edu/archives/) and the National Technical Institute for the Deaf archive (https://library.rit.edu/archives/Deaf-studies-archive). Some state schools may also have their own museums and archives (See Chapter 8 for additional examples).

You'll want to expose students to as many types of resources as possible in ASL and English. We have already mentioned the use of **primary resources** and will expand more on secondary sources such as texts, media, and geographic sources here.

(DI) (MM) (ABAR) Use and Adaptation of Social Studies Textbooks

Textbooks have been the standard approach for providing reading materials to Deaf students in social studies. Yet, for many Deaf students, relying on these texts as a sole reading source is ineffective. In addition, there have been criticisms that some textbooks do not represent accurate histories or perspectives of BIPOC, Deaf, and LGBTQIA+ communities. You can consider supplementing with other materials or adapting the textbooks to address this. Note that if you do decide to forgo using a textbook, it is important that the alternatives are provided at students' reading levels in order for them to become fluent bilinguals, developing ASL, written English, and disciplinary literacy in social studies. Here, we highlight ways to use traditional texts, alternative informational text options, and media sources for social studies. (See Recommended Readings/Viewings for additional suggestions as well as Chapter 7 for more on primary sources and modifying materials.)

Despite their shortcomings, social studies textbooks can be a useful resource for teaching, assuming your students are reading at or close to the grade level for which the books were created. However, many Deaf students will need some sort of scaffolded approach to using textbooks. This includes providing explicit instruction and strategies for navigating them, such as teaching your students how to use the table of contents, glossary, index pages, graphs, and captions to help find main ideas (see Chapter 7 for more on informational texts). Even students who cannot access the entirety of the text will benefit from a discussion of the pictures and captions. Students should be given the pleasure and "joy of ownership" of the textbooks that their age-level peers get (see Chapter 6 for more on joy and reading). High-interest/low reading level and leveled texts related to social studies topics are available, some created specifically for struggling readers and others for English learners. These also benefit Deaf readers because they include increased picture-to-text ratio, fewer idioms, and intentionally chosen vocabulary. Some publishers offer the same content at four different reading levels. There are also apps and online platforms for adaptive texts as well. Differentiated text from Newsela, for example, provides reading passages on almost any topic, including current events, adaptive to different lexile levels. History books formatted as graphic novels are becoming increasingly popular for Deaf students and easier to find. An internet search using terms like "leveled texts for social studies" or "history through graphic novels" will lead to publishing sites with various text options. (See Recommended Readings/Viewings for a few current places to find leveled text and Chapter 6 for more on high-interest books.) And now, at this writing, teachers are even beginning to harness the power of artificial intelligence (AI), such as chatbots, to modify texts to different grade-level reading.

Examples of graphic novels in publication. *Truth: Red, White, and Black* is a series of comics written by Robert Morales and drawn and inked by Kyle Baker. It was published monthly by Marvel from January 2003 to July 2003. *Colorblind: A Story of Racism* is a graphic novel by Johnathan Harris, illustrated by Donald Hudson, and inked by Fahriza Kamaputra. It was published in 2019 by Zuiker Press.

There are also many ways you can adapt social studies texts yourself! At the time of writing this chapter, chatbots have given us the power of AI to adapt texts for any level. For example, using simple video-recording programs such as Loom or Screencastify, you can create visual textbooks that show both the printed word and images from the text along with ASL translations and guiding questions. Because many texts are colorful and dynamic with sidebars and pictures included, you can connect to this information while doing a live read-aloud (i.e., storysigning) of passages in ASL or using prerecorded videos (see Chapters 3 and 12).

Another approach is to have your students who are more fluent bilinguals do a live storysigning and create their own videos to share with the class. For example, government class seniors at CSD Fremont have been researching and translating passages of the U.S. Constitution into ASL. By engaging in this activity, their knowledge and understanding of the Constitution have deepened while also giving others access to a primary source document of our nation's history through ASL (see Recommended Readings/Viewings).

Use a Wide Variety of Texts

There are few textbooks that can compare to reading well-crafted stories found in nonfiction and historical fiction books in their ability to draw students' interest. Here, we share some nonfiction books that depict Deaf history and culture. Jack Gannon's classic *Deaf Heritage* narrative history was first published in 1981. This has been followed by a number of historical narratives and biographies, including some related

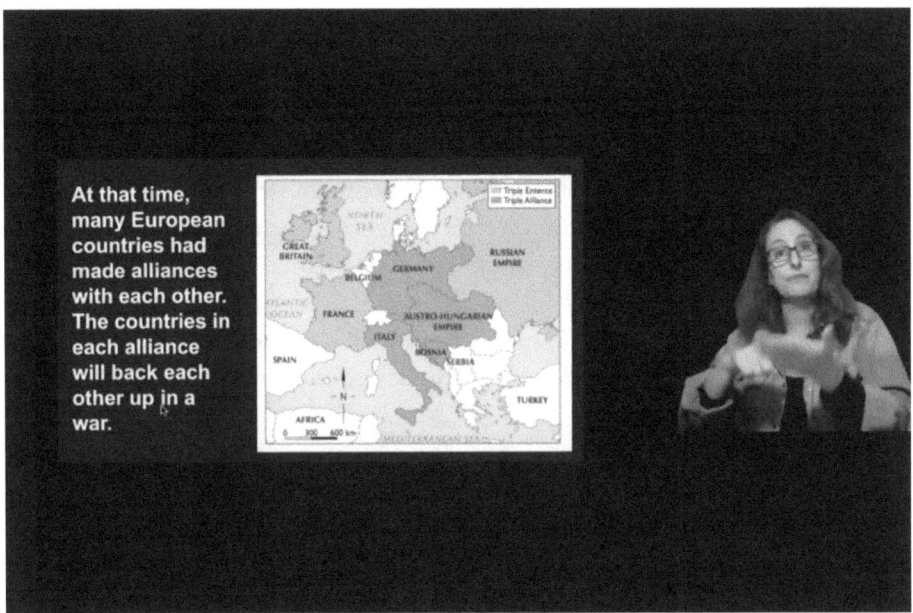

A CSD high school teacher, Stacy Eilbert, creates ASL "textbooks" using main ideas from the English text and elaborating in ASL.

to Black Deaf people and Deaf women during the Nazi Holocaust (see Chapter 8 for additional examples). Most of these are appropriate for older readers. For general history, there are a number of nonfiction biographies and historical fiction available at varying reading levels for students. These are not only in print form, but also additional versions are available as comics or graphic novels, which provide visual depictions of events. Biographies are readily available in picture book format for emergent readers and increasingly as wordless picture books and graphic novels. We recommend illustrated texts for Deaf students because they support students with language delays and conceptualize the text; in addition, many people, including proficient readers, enjoy illustrations.

Historical fiction can be an interesting and engaging way for students to learn about historical eras and events. For younger children, *Secret Signs of the Underground Railroad* (Riggio, 2003) is a fictional picture book that includes a Deaf character (see Chapter 7). When selecting any book, we recommend you evaluate first for biases and be prepared to discuss stereotypes and messages about Deaf people with your students (see Chapter 2; Golos & Moses, 2013). *Dad, Jackie and Me,* written by a child of a Deaf adult (Coda), Myron Uhlberg (2005), is a lovely picture book for younger students that shares the story of Jackie Robinson.

Because of the traditional Eurocentric focus in history, you should intentionally expose students to various biographies and historical fiction from different viewpoints, such as BIPOC authors, women, Deaf people, disabled people, LGBTQIA+, and other historically marginalized groups. *The Lions of Little Rock* by Kristin Levine (2012) is a wonderful novel regarding race, segregation, and standing up for what you believe. In addition, we recommend *Singing Hands* by Delia Ray (2006), *Sounds Like Home: Growing Up Black and Deaf in the South* by Mary Herring Wright (1999), and *Haben, The Deafblind Woman Who Conquered Harvard Law* by Haben Girma (2019). These are all examples of biographical and historical fiction you can share with older students.

(MM) (MT) **Teacher Tale**

With graphic novels, make sure you always front-load key vocabulary words and find ways to scaffold students' understanding. Simply handing students a graphic novel and a worksheet isn't gonna cut it because a lot of better-known graphic novels are often philosophical and thoughtful in their approach. Conclude with a fun project.

With graphic novels, first pre-teach the following terms in both ASL and English:

- Panel: An individual frame capturing a single moment frozen in time
- Word balloon: A bubble besides a character's head showing what a character is saying, signing, or thinking
- Narration box/caption: The panel in which a narrator gives a third-person viewpoint or information about the story's previous or upcoming panels

Here are some fun project ideas I have found to be successful when using graphic novels:

- Act out a scene from a graphic novel.
- Create your own autobiographical graphic novel. (This was a lot of fun after reading *March* by John Lewis et al. [2013].)
- Make a graphic timeline based on events from a graphic novel. There are many timeline generators online to choose from where students can insert graphics from the novel they are reading.

—*Michael Sidansky, CSD Fremont high school teacher*

 (PI) **Stick It Into Action!**

Storysigning in Social Studies

Unlike creating textbooks in ASL, storysigning (also called *reading aloud*; see Chapters 2 and 6) is another way to engage children in learning social studies by telling stories about people from a variety of cultures in ASL. It allows younger students to be exposed to a variety of points of view, and multilingual literacy. *Viva Frida* is a story about Mexican artist and activist Frida Kahlo. The storysigned video includes LSM, ASL, Spanish, and English: https://www.youtube.com/watch?v=R1H1oYSU1WQ. Remember when sharing storysigning videos that it is important not just to have students view it but to engage in discussion before, during, and after viewing (see Chapters 3, 5, and 12).

The use of a wide variety of texts as described not only makes content accessible and differentiated across the students in your classroom, but it is also more enjoyable than the standard and often dry history texts that many of us endured.

SOCIAL STUDIES

A virtual library for students to explore and click on storysigned books at a variety of levels for Black History Month. (Created by CSD elementary teacher Carley Carbin.)

(MT) (DI) **Use of Visually Accessible Media**

Many sources are available online for teaching factual and fictional accounts of history. There are some older video series in ASL, such as the *American Freedom Speeches* (Sign Media, 1994). Today, more and more social studies content is being produced in ASL and shared online through sources such as *Deaf History That*, *Seek the World*, and news sources such as *The Daily Moth* and *DPAN*. An excellent spot to find cultural, historical, and many other video resources in ASL that have been curated for you is at CSD Fremont's CORE Learning Channel (https://sites.google.com/csdeagles.net/core-learning-channel/home).

Using graphics, GIFs, and short videos in ASL allows you to differentiate instruction in your classroom. This helps all students but is especially useful for students who struggle with reading English or learning abstract concepts or critical thinking skills. Have students respond in their preferred languages and encourage them to use written responses as well (see Chapters 3, 4, and 12 for more examples).

Chew on This!

Did you know that...?
There are additional multilingual resources on the CSD core learning channel to teach about history lives and cultures of and/or by BIPOC Deaf people?

- Latinx/Hispanic Resources: https://sites.google.com/csdeagles.net/core-learning-channel/latinxhispanic-resources
- Asian American/Pacific Islander Resources: https://sites.google.com/csdeagles.net/core-learning-channel/asian-americanpacific-islanders-resources
- History/Social Studies Resources: https://sites.google.com/csdeagles.net/core-learning-channel/history-social-studies

(MM) (MT) **Teacher Tale**

This is an example of an online resource created by a teacher with video links to ASL biographies and works by current Black changemakers. For example learn about Laurene Simms: https://www.youtube.com/watch?v=dB-pVQ-PCcD8, Andrew Foster: https://youtu.be/rpqVYm_G8cU?si=-uA45cqaE6eon7V1

Although both of these examples celebrate Black History Month, you should incorporate these books throughout the year so students have multiple opportunities to learn about Black Deaf people. What is attractive about these platforms is that they allow flexibility for student choice.

When selecting video media for social studies, don't forget to check for captioning! Although most available published video sources are now captioned, it is still important for you to confirm they are captioned before using them in your classroom. The Described and Captioned Media Program (DCMP, see https://www.dcmp.org) has free streaming videos available on a wide variety of topics (including social studies) for teachers, students, or families. Brainpop.com and Brainpopjr.com are subscription-based websites with short, captioned cartoons about many topics, including current events and visual supporting materials.

When using historically accurate captioned videos or clips of historical periods to give Deaf students the visual support needed to understand characters' motives, be sure to expose them to the language of the era and provide additional information about the lived experiences of the time. Such pedagogy requires discussions about fact versus fiction and historical accuracy (see Chapter 7 for more on fiction and nonfiction connections). Although videos make for excellent sources of learning, simply having students watch a video and then answer questions on a worksheet is ineffective pedagogy. A more effective approach may be to translate the captions into ASL for students when differentiation is necessary. In this way, you can help students connect both images and ASL to the printed words in captions. You can pause to point out key vocabulary, places, and people's names (see Chapters 3 and 12 for more on strategies for viewing before, during, and after). With shorter clips, consider having students read the transcripts after instruction to connect the printed word with topics they have already learned in class in ASL. Be sure to discuss videos immediately after viewing or take periodic breaks every 15–20 min to discuss longer videos. Students will retain the material better when asked to respond to prompts about what they saw.

 **Use of Geographical Resources**

These include maps and other diagrammatic representations of spaces. Places and events need to be placed in the context of the location at which they occur, which helps students have a better understanding of spatial relationships. In addition, being able to interpret a map or globe is a critical thinking skill needed for independence in navigating the world. If you teach lower grades, you can start with a map of the school. Most schools will have theirs on a wall as well as online. Then, you can move onto maps of communities and the rest of the world. **Deaf geography** presents a unique way of helping students locate Deaf places, whether they are historical or current. Some examples include having students locate and identify founding/closing dates of Deaf schools and Deaf clubs in the country and internationally, plus highly concentrated historical Deaf populations (e.g., Martha's Vineyard, Sandy River in Maine, Hennicker in New Hampshire). Additional locations that would be beneficial to have your students locate are the segregated Black schools for the Deaf in the South, which gave rise to Black ASL between the time of the Civil War and the 1960s and 1970s. Once students understand the use of geographical locations or features on a map, you can lead them in applying data (population, elevation, climate, and more) to computer-based graphic information systems.

Key Vocabulary

Deaf geography is the study of Deaf cultures, languages, and spaces in geographical locations and the history of how they emerged, how they evolved, and where they may have migrated, adapted, or became extinct.

Student using a relief map with raised surfaces along with Google Earth on a tablet as a graphic information system (GIS) source.

(MT) Evaluating the Quality of Media and Online Sources

With the advent of the internet and widespread use of social media and unchecked news sources, we must teach our Deaf students to become critical thinkers and skeptics. Media literacy, such as evaluating the reliability and accuracy of online websites and historical documents, is an important skill. You can start with a work of historical fiction and ask students to determine which events are fictitious and which actually happened. Through guided and supported discussions, students can begin to recognize that not everything they see is necessarily true. There are website credibility checklists and rubrics available online for you to use. Many library websites have links for educators regarding "Currency, Reliability, Authority, and Purpose/Point of View." To compare various news sites and media, provide students with reliable resource sites for fact-checking, such as Snopes.com, Politifact.org, or FactCheck.org. You can also assign students to check the validity of information posted on wiki sites. Modify information as needed when it is above students' independent reading levels (see Chapter 7). Teach students how wiki sites are created by individual contributors, some of whom may have agendas other than simply providing factual information. Even young students can learn about the trustworthiness of images representing concepts while doing vocabulary searches. Create vocabulary charts for students to do online image/video searches and then guide them through the process. They can practice searching for pictures of the vocabulary related to a particular unit independently and insert them into the chart. In doing so, they are exposed to multiple images of the concept, and then you can discuss which images are untrustworthy. This technique is especially effective for students with language delays and/or deprivation.

If students begin discerning an author's or director's purpose from an early age, they will also become more critical users of media. Now that news media resources are readily available in ASL, you can focus on the analysis of content rather than constantly creating your own materials in ASL as teachers have had to do in the past.

Additional Things to Consider

(MM) (MT) (DI) (ES) K–12 Classroom Setup and Environment

Here, we provide some suggestions for setting up your social studies classroom to align with our core recommendations and provide a better context for learning.

We highly recommend using standard wall maps appropriate for grade levels that you can leave up and refer to as needed. Relief maps and atlases colored by altitude are even better. For DeafBlind students, use relief maps because they are tactile and accessible. Plus, many other students may benefit from feeling maps too. A good-sized globe is definitely an essential 3-D learning resource for you to keep in your classroom, not only for geography but also for STEAM topics like earth science, measurement, astronomy, and ecology.

Content vocabulary associated with social studies should be posted on word walls or word charts for students to learn (consider adding words in students' home/heritage languages in addition to ASL and English). Ideally, have your students be involved in the creation of the postings, especially at the elementary level (e.g., use photos of students signing the vocabulary). Once posted, bring the vocabulary alive by referring to it during lessons and engaging with it regularly in order to make it meaningful and memorable (see Chapters 3, 6, and 7 for more on word walls).

You can also create a fixed timeline in your classroom with your students as you go through the school year, beginning with your earliest units of study, and gradually have students add to and refer back to it during instruction. It just might snake all around your entire room's upper walls by the end of the year. Create opportunities for students to interact with it and to make additions. This supports their understanding of the general chronological order of events—first, this happened, then that happened—rather than the specific dates. Allowing students to take charge of the timeline by adding visuals and labels helps them apply chronology concepts rather than relying on teaching through rote memorization.

Display as many visuals as possible—posters, pictures, artifacts, magazines, books, and so on—related to each topic to immerse the students in the studied time and place, changing them as you change topics. These help to provide context and create curiosity for students. We, of course, also need to emphasize the importance of displaying photos and paintings of Deaf and BIPOC people both as social scientists and as historical figures.

(PI) (DI) (MM) (MT) Bringing It All Together

Here is an example of an empowering inquiry-based learning unit developed for a small class of first and second graders at the CSD in Fremont that ties together each of our core recommendations. Multilingual language goals in ASL and English are front and center in the unit planning. You will also see that over the course of the unit, several subject areas are integrated into this inquiry-based social studies unit, including language arts, science, social-emotional learning, and a positive sense of self. Deaf studies is at its heart, and the teacher has worked carefully to ensure that multiple racial groups are represented. While it is targeted at students with language delays, it can be differentiated for any student. The unit focuses on *doing*. Students are actively engaged through cooperative learning and authentic learning experiences, and instruction is differentiated through the use of an array of media and text sources. The culminating project involves choice, allowing students to research topics of their own interest. And although less evident in the write-up of this unit, the teacher aims to intentionally model the vocabulary and language(s) students will use during their discussions and presentations.

Deaf Like Me! Heroes Biography Unit

Inquiry Essential Questions
Let's find out: How do we form and shape our identities? What makes someone "heroic"? Who are the people who make a difference in the lives of others? What language(s) does my community use to share our culture(s)? Who are some heroes who are Deaf like me?

Selected Standards/Objectives
History-Social Science Standard   Understand the importance of individual action and character and explain how heroes from long ago and the recent past have made a difference in others' lives.
- Students will be able to use the calendar to express time concepts and can identify locations on a simple map.
- Students will be able to research and collect data through simple interviews and internet searches.
- Students will be able to analyze artifacts. (*Note, in this case, posters in the hall of Deaf heroes of multiple races and genders.)

K–12 ASL Content Standards (https://aslstandards.org/): Discourse and Presentation for Kindergarten   Ask and answer questions in order to seek help, get information, or clarify something that is not understood.

English Language Development Standards   Note that in our case, these are interpreted as ASL language development in signing, attending, and viewing.
- Exchanging information and ideas: Contribute to conversations and express ideas by asking and answering yes/no and *wh-* questions and responding using gestures, words, and simple phrases.
- Listening actively: Demonstrate active listening to read-alouds (storysigning) and oral presentations by asking and answering yes/no and *wh-* questions with oral sentence frames and substantial prompting and support. (*Note:* Beginnings of learning civil discourse.)
- Presenting: Plan and deliver brief oral presentations.

Teachers' Language and Literacy Goals
- Writing/signing in third person point of view and past tense
- Summarizing main ideas

> "This Deaf Awareness unit is for students with language delays due to having experienced language deprivation. Although the primary focus is social studies, it also follows the state science requirements and incorporates learning experiences on "sound." While it opens with students learning about the medical term *deaf*, understanding their own audiograms, and meeting with the school audiologist, the main focus of this unit, however, is for students to learn about the rich diversity of the Deaf community and how people identify with the cultural and linguistic meanings of Deaf community. This is a powerful way for students to connect with Deaf role models in real-world situations. The goal by the end of the unit is for students to understand the importance of individual action and character and be able to explain how heroes from long ago and the recent past have made a difference in others' lives, including Deaf heroes.
>
> —Bianca Hamilton Miller, elementary teacher

- Learning features of biography text: past tense, third person point of view, chronological order
- Understanding vocabulary: autobiography, biography, Deaf, hearing, hero, birth date, birthplace, language, culture, occupation, facts

Lesson Sequence

We have provided an estimated number of days each lesson may occur. However, these should be modified according to students' needs (see Table 9.1).

Handstamp Sample

This is a student autobiographical poster leading to the study of Deaf heroes. A hole is cut for her to insert her face.

Example of the rubric for the Deaf biography.

Criteria	3	2	1
Name	Included full name—both first and last names	Included either first or last names	Did not include both first or last names
Portrait	Created a portrait and included one prop that is easily seen	Created a portrait	Did not create a portrait
Birthdate/place	Included both birthdate and birthplace	Included with birthdate or birthplace	Did not include both birthdate and birthplace
Facts	Included 3 facts	Included 1–2 facts	Did not include facts
Zoom Presentation	Signs clearly	Signs clearly sometimes	Did not sign clearly

Table 9.1

Lessons and Core Recommendation (CR)	Activities
Lesson 1: What Are Deaf and Hearing? (1–2 days) CR 1: Inquiry based (whole class)	Use PowerPoint as a visual guide to discuss: • What the terms *Deaf, deaf, Hard of Hearing*, and *hearing* mean • How the ear works • Role of an audiologist Guest speaker: School audiologist • View bright, colorful versions of each student's individual audiograms (connect to the science unit on sound). • Practice expressing to each other what they can or cannot hear.
Lesson 2: Who Is Deaf or Hearing in Our Community? (1–3 days) CR 1: Inquiry based (whole-class discussion) CR 2: Cooperative learning (group activity)	Whole-class discussion: Deaf people as a cultural group; ask students the following questions: • Do you know a Deaf person? • What can you say about that person? (Age, how they communicate, languages used at home, race, culture(s), occupation, hobbies, special equipment they use, etc.) Group activity: What can students say about themselves? • Provide sentence frames to practice simple exchanges asking if they identify as Deaf or Hard of Hearing: Have students interview each other about languages used at home/school, racial heritage, and cultures. • Have students conduct a scavenger hunt to find out about others on campus and their families.
Lesson 3: Autobiography and Biography (2–3 days) CR 2: Cooperative learning (group activities) CR 3: Authentic learning	Provide sentence frames and graphic organizers with a head cut out of the portrait so students can put their own face in to create an autobiographical poster. • Have students work in three group centers over the course of a day with support via teacher modeling, questioning, and writing scaffolds to design their poster. Students apply questions from Lesson 2 to themselves with explanations of expectations and assessment rubric. • Information to include: full name, date of birth, birthplace, Deaf/hearing identity, occupation (student), and three facts about themselves • Add this information to their poster and present it to the class.
Lesson 4: Deaf Biography (3–4 days) CR 1: Inquiry based (whole class) CR 2: Cooperative learning (group activities) CR 4: Use array of text/media	Engage students in class discussion. What makes someone heroic? Can students think of any superheroes? Why do people look up to them? Share preselected photos of Deaf people of various ages, genders, and racial and cultural backgrounds. Use large photos with simple occupation descriptions and use graphic organizers to support students' research projects. Have students each choose a current Deaf hero to research for their poster. Students view ASL videos about their heroes and generate questions about them.

Table 9.1 (continued)

Lessons and Core Recommendation (CR)	Activities
	Differentiate for students' choice of video text, ASL difficulty levels, and short teacher-made written texts. After you model, have students work together using graphic organizers previously used in Lesson 3 to find required information about their chosen Deaf hero. Have students use internet sources to research information and enter that onto their graphic organizer and writing scaffolds. Then, they arrange the information on posters representing their Deaf heroes.
Lesson 5: Poster Presentations (2–3 days) CR 3: Authentic learning	Have students practice presenting their poster using the third-person point of view and explain how their hero makes a difference in people's lives. Provide feedback. Then have students revise their presentations based both on peer feedback and your feedback. Students present their posters to their classmates and ask each other relevant questions. These presentations are filmed to share with each other and a larger audience. Student's hero videos are shared to educate the larger elementary community during assembly.

Handstamp Sample

A second-grade student presentation of his final Deaf hero biography poster.

SOCIAL STUDIES

 Your Turn to Practice!

Now it's your turn! Create inquiry-based learning goals and a lesson sequence that develops critical thinking skills and language skills on a historical topic interweaving a Deaf studies topic and using an ABAR lens. During the unit, students should participate in aspects of civil discourse and cooperative learning. Your unit must incorporate a variety of texts/media/geographical resources throughout. You will also fully develop one lesson that incorporates cooperative learning and teach it in your classroom or in a mock setting if you are a teacher candidate. After you have taught the lesson, reflect on how it went. We describe the process in detail next.

Develop Your Inquiry-Based Unit

Start by developing the unit topic around essential questions, and let the questions guide the development of your learning outcomes. The topic for the unit needs to be engaging, expansive, and relevant to your students, with real-life implications. It should invite students to dive into the subject matter and create opportunities for in-depth critical thinking. Although guided by open-ended essential questions, it should also support guided inquiry projects for which the students come up with their own questions. These inspiring units should be guided by questions like, "How do we make our community a better place?" "Can people live just anywhere?" "How are gender roles assigned?" "What is a 'good fight'?" and "What would it take for you to stand up for what you believe?"

- **List of standards addressed:** In addition to listing social studies standards, include ASL standards and standards for other subject areas, especially for reading, writing, and STEAM (e.g., science, math). *Also, do not forget to find ways to integrate Deaf studies topics.* These could be related by the era, civilization, geographical location, concept, or a combination of these.
- **Unit topics:** Choose a unit topic that allows you to focus more on *inquiry-based*, higher level thinking skills (rather than facts/skills).
- **Unit goals and objectives:** Consider which higher level critical thinking skills you wish to have your students develop, such as compare and contrast, distinguish cause and effect or fact from opinion, or recognize bias or points of view. Your objectives should include active verbs such as *analyze, assess, determine, value, defend, recognize,* or *respond to*. You can easily find a list of Bloom's Taxonomy action verbs online for more ideas.
- **Instructional strategies used:** Integrate our core recommendations throughout your unit and lesson plans. These include cooperative learning with civil discourse; providing authentic learning experiences; and using a variety of text, video, and media. Remember to incorporate the use of primary documents. Also, feel free to use strategies from other chapters in this book as appropriate.
- **Lesson sequence list:** Make a list of the lessons and the instructional strategies with a brief one-paragraph description for each. The lessons should culminate with a mock event designed to showcase what the students learned as well as the artifacts they created.

Develop Your Lesson Plan(s)

Develop at least one complete lesson plan (using whatever format is required by your school or university). In addition to the typical sections, include each of the following sections:

- Differentiated instruction
- Language planning including multimodal/multilingual approaches
- Deaf studies content
- Assessment/evaluation

Assessments: For each student assignment, you will need a way of measuring outcomes. You can use rubrics, learning contracts, or objective agreements that outline what students are expected to do in order to get a certain grade.

Practice Teaching

Teach at least one complete lesson to your students or to a mock class of students.

Reflect on Your Teaching

Reflect afterward on your lesson (and unit). Overall, the main questions to ask yourself are "What worked as well or better than I thought?" "What surprised me or the students the most (good or bad)?" and "What revisions will I make based on my answers?"
   Additional questions to ask yourself are:

- Use of inquiry-based learning with ABAR and Deaf studies topics: In what ways were my students excited and engaged in critical thinking, or were they bored and detached?
- Use cooperative learning activities and practice civil discourse: How well did my students work together using civil discourse? Did they have enough objectives and direction to make good decisions?
- Provide authentic learning experiences: Did I provide the right kind and amount of authentic experiences or was it too overwhelming for the students?
- Integrate a wide variety of text, geological, and media sources (original and/or adapted) related to historical and current events: Were there enough primary documents? Were they differentiated across the skill level of my students? Were they able to use these independently to produce learning artifacts after some guidance?
- Assessment/Evaluation: How well did students learn what I intended them to learn according to my lesson objectives?

(MM) (ABAR) (DI) (MT) Recommended Readings/Viewings

For Teachers/Teacher Candidates

- *Seeing the Whole Through Social Studies* (Lindquist, 2002). Although not specifically about Deaf students, this little book includes tips, inspirational lesson plans,

and strategies for elementary and middle school, with many examples and photos for language learners.
- *Lies My Teacher Told Me: Everything Your American History Textbook Got Wrong* (Loewen, 2018). An excellent ABAR resource for teachers and their students that takes a critical look at popular and inaccurate depictions of American history.

Leveled Text Resources
- Online: Getepic.com, ReadingA-Z.com, Newsela.com, Studysync.com, CommonLit.org
- Print materials: Wieser Educational, National Geographic, Saddleback Publishing, Savvas, High Noon Books

To Use With Students

This is just a sample of a variety of texts available. We recommend browsing the Gallaudet University Press catalog for more topics.

- *The William Hoy Story: How a Deaf Baseball Player Changed the Game* (Churnin, 2022). An award-winning illustrated book for young readers.
- *Sounds Like Home: Growing Up Black and Deaf in the South* (Wright, 1999). For young adult and adult readers, this is an autobiography about life at a segregated Deaf school in the South.
- *Deaf People in Hitler's Europe* (Ryan & Schuchman, 2002). For young adult and adult readers. This is a collection of essays based on the 1998 international conference of the same name in Washington, D.C.
- *Deaf Heritage: A Narrative History of Deaf America* (Gannon, 1981/2011). For young adult and adult readers. This is a classic volume covering Deaf history in the United States from the 18th century to 1980.

Conclusion

The four core recommendations in this chapter are intended to address how to teach social studies as a dynamic subject involving *critical thinking and language goals* and to demonstrate that there are ways to incorporate it into the daily curriculum, even in an era with tremendous focus on high-stakes test scores. If you're teaching K–8 social studies, inquiry-based units could very well serve as the driving force behind integrating all of your subject matter across the curriculum. You can also apply a Deaf studies and/or ABAR or social justice lens to topics. Subtopics can be introduced chronologically by eras or organized by essential questions or topics. Because historical topics were traditionally male-oriented and Eurocentric, the contributions of women, BIPOC, Deaf people, and those with disabilities have often been overlooked. Intentionally incorporate a variety of materials, especially primary documents, that demonstrate their struggles for equity. Although it seems that we are reaching a transformative period with more inclusive curricula, it is imperative to make sure alternative points of view are presented. Finally, we recognize that developing and teaching inquiry units requires careful planning, time, and effort, especially the first time you teach a unit.

However, even though it may not happen right away, knowing that you play a part in the development of Deaf students in becoming knowledgeable and responsible citizens with an awareness of social justice can be quite rewarding; authentic experiences and cooperative learning approaches enhance this development. Empowering students to embrace their diverse cultures, languages, and Deaf heritage and be prepared to work actively toward change in the world is the greatest joy a teacher can have.

Sticking Points

- Make critical thinking and language goals in ASL and English priorities in your social studies classes.
- Guide students through inquiry-based learning and units to integrate subject areas, including Deaf studies and ABAR topics.
- Facilitate active learning of civics using cooperative learning activities and civil discourse rules of respect.
- Provide authentic and experiential learning activities to ignite a passion for learning and keep students engaged.
- Integrate a wide variety of social studies–related text, media, and geographical resources that can be adapted to the current skill levels of your students.

Mathematics

Samantha Braidi
Brenda Call
Chris Kurz

Hello, teachers and teacher candidates! We are excited to share this chapter on best practices for teaching mathematics to Deaf students of diverse backgrounds (e.g., linguistic, cultural, race, gender, abilities). Even though there is no one-size-fits-all approach to teaching math to Deaf students, the strategies that we will describe have been implemented with a high rate of success. By the end of this chapter, we hope you will expand your knowledge of how to communicate and teach mathematics effectively. We also hope you will be able to foster a mathematical mindset in all Deaf children, and see that mistakes are a critical part of their learning and should be celebrated.

Who Are We?

Now, let us introduce ourselves. Teaching mathematics to students has always been our passion. We, all Deaf, have a combined total of more than 50 years of experience teaching mathematics to Deaf students. I (Brenda Call) am currently the kindergarten through Grade 12 (K–12) mathematics coach at California School for the Deaf (CSD), Fremont. At CSD, I have taught mathematics in the middle school department for more than 20 years; for 14 of those years, I was also the lead math teacher. I (Samantha Braidi) have been teaching high school mathematics at CSD, Fremont, for 9 years and have given professional development workshops on teaching mathematics to Deaf children. I have a bachelor's degree in applied mathematics. I (Chris Kurz) have taught mathematics to Deaf and hearing students (through interpreters) at different school

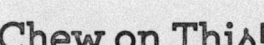 

Chew on This!

Did you know that . . . ?
- Deaf children are natural-born mathematicians.
- Deaf children rely on tactile-spatial and visual-spatial association to learn early mathematical concepts.
- Deaf children can learn grade-level mathematics even with basic American Sign Language (ASL) literacy and/or English literacy skills.

Chew on This!

Did you know that...?
Some mathematicians have taken more than 20 years to solve one problem.

> "I have noticed that Deaf children are usually placed in math classes based on their English proficiency. We should not rely on English proficiency for math placement. We should rely on their mathematical knowledge to place them in correct math classes. I know some Deaf students who are capable of explaining advanced mathematical concepts well in ASL. They should be placed accordingly.
>
> —Samantha Braidi,
> high school math teacher

Key Vocabulary

Mathematical talk is a conversation between a child and an adult about math. Its purpose is to stimulate the child's mind to think about math, and it can take place at home, in the classroom, or in the community.

settings (a public school, schools for the Deaf, a community college, and a university) for almost 20 years. I am currently preparing teacher candidates to become mathematics and science teachers at National Technical Institute for the Deaf. Like Samantha, I have a degree in applied mathematics.

Our teaching experiences with Deaf students tell us that even before Deaf children arrive at school for formal education, they have a natural and innate curiosity about the mathematical world. If they are provided with language-rich environments at home, in school, and elsewhere that allow opportunities for natural, structured, and unstructured, consistent, and sporadic activities, they will build on these experiences to develop mathematical knowledge, skills, and literacy (Kurz, 2006, 2008; Langdon et al., 2021).

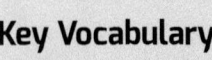 Deaf Experiences, Perspectives, and Core Recommendations

As one of the three Rs (aRithmetic, Reading, and wRiting), mathematics has been a significant part of the academic curriculum with a long history of formal schooling. Students have learned arithmetic for centuries, and if they decided to advance further in higher education, they learned higher branches of mathematics (e.g., algebra and geometry). During the majority of the 20th century, rapid computation (e.g., mad minutes, timed worksheets) was often the chief goal for students in school, and the media fell in love with those who could compute in less than a second. In reality, mathematics is not about solving problems as fast as possible, and it should not be that. It is about understanding and defining a problem and coming up with possible solutions. It is also about deeper learning—seeking patterns and relationships and engaging in mathematical thinking.

Early Concepts of Mathematics

Because not all Deaf children have full access to language at home, some arrive at school unprepared to learn mathematics (Kritzer, 2009). In the early years at home, children observe their environments and can interact with others about colors, sizes, basic shapes, and basic numbers, which all work to create a foundation for math learning later in school. However, Deaf children often do not have access to mathematical concepts through language at home. Ideally, Deaf children should be engaged in early **mathematical talk** as well as visual-spatial and tactile math, which promote finger tracing and counting (Langdon et al., 2021; Nunes & Moreno, 2002; Nunes et al., 2006); however, this is often not the case. As such, as a teacher, it becomes important to build relationships with families throughout students' schooling to help support this process. Yet, these strategies are often not included in teacher preparation programs.

Educational Professional Preparation

Increasingly, we are aware of the benefits of multilingual and multimodal approaches to Deaf education, and this includes mathematics. Deaf students benefit when teachers provide opportunities for students to discuss math through multiple languages as well as multiple modal approaches that infuse multiple representations to teaching math. However, teachers of the Deaf (as well as educational interpreters) lack training in mathematics pedagogy—curriculum, instruction, and assessment (Pagliaro, 2010). They also have limited ASL knowledge and skills in mathematics (Kurz et al., 2020). Only a small percentage of mathematics teachers of Deaf students have college degrees in mathematics (Pagliaro, 2010); yet the more teachers know about math and the better their pedagogical and language proficiency, the better Deaf students perform in math. Bridging ASL and English for mathematical learning requires having vocabulary repertoires in math in both languages. For example, Samantha Braidi was very fortunate to have sign language interpreters who were knowledgeable in mathematics when she entered college to study applied mathematics. Yet, teachers of Deaf students need these skills as well.

Core Recommendations

We have four core recommendations for teaching mathematics to Deaf students using effective multilingual practices that address the Deaf-specific needs described previously.

- Infuse multiple representations and methods in instruction.
- Optimize all languages (ASL, English, and additional languages) to learn mathematical concepts.
- Collaborate with caregivers and family members.
- Address mathematics in a diverse world.

> "I did not realize how big of a difference it made for interpreters/teachers working with Deaf students to have had specialized math training until I watched the ASL interpreters in my Multivariable Calculus class during college. They used conceptually accurate math signs and took advantage of the visual space in front of them. I was mind blown as it was the very first time I made a meaningful connection between ASL and math concepts.
> —Samantha Braidi

Effective Practices for Deaf Learners

In this section, we explain each of the four core recommendations for math instruction with Deaf students through classroom examples.

(MM) (DI) Core Recommendation 1: Infuse Multiple Representations in Instruction

When you are planning your lessons, it is important that you consider incorporating opportunities for your students to interact with mathematical concepts. Because math is a critical thinking subject, your goal as a teacher is to support your students' mathematical practices, which requires them to think and talk about mathematics in their languages. That usually starts by aligning your lesson objectives with **mathematical practices** and the associated state content learning standards for mathematics as well as the language content standards (e.g., ASL, English).
Here are some examples of mathematical practices:

- Make sense of problems and persevere in solving them (e.g., encourage students to represent their thinking while problem solving).
- Reason abstractly and quantitatively (e.g., facilitate opportunities for students to discuss or use representations to make sense of quantities and their relationships).
- Construct viable arguments and critique the reasoning of others (e.g., provide and facilitate opportunities for students to listen to the solution strategies of others, discuss alternative solutions, and defend their ideas).

Key Vocabulary

Mathematical practices are ways students develop procedure and understanding as they interact and engage in their critical thinking processes with mathematical concepts throughout their preschool through Grade 12 (P–12) years.

- Model with mathematics (e.g., use mathematical models, such as manipulatives, variables, equations, and graphs).
- Use appropriate tools strategically (e.g., use appropriate physical and/or digital tools to represent, explore, and deepen student understanding).
- Attend to precision (e.g., checking your work, sense-making, and resolving any inconsistencies).
- Look for and make use of structure (e.g., provide activities in which students demonstrate their flexibility in representing mathematics in a number of ways).
- Look for and express regularity in repeated reasoning (e.g., engage students in discussion related to repeated reasoning that may occur in a problem's solution).

With an emphasis on mathematical practices in your lessons, you might notice that your students talk, think, and interact with mathematical concepts more. You may learn new things by watching them as they go through their thinking process.

Mathematics is not only the study of quantities, spaces, structures, and patterns, it is also about understanding relationships. As a teacher, you might have a tendency to teach mathematics the way you learned it when you were younger, which was probably based on drill practices and one or two representations (Roman numerals and mathematical symbols). However, mathematics instruction has advanced over the years to deepen students' understanding through multiple representations. Deaf children need to be able to understand mathematics in these multiple representations as well as be able to transition between **semiotic representations** (Pagliaro & Kurz, 2021). We will highlight strategies for infusing multiple semiotic representations in instruction, starting with the teaching of multiplication.

Multiple Representations and Operations

Using multiple approaches will provide your students with greater opportunities to understand and explain mathematical processes. For example, when teaching multiplication, it is critical to show other ways of multiplying in addition to the traditional vertical method (see Stick It Into Action). Each of these various methods has its advantages. The area model, for example, is applicable to nearly all numbers and polynomials. The Japanese sticks method provides visual support for understanding place values while multiplying. Deaf students can become fluent in any one of these when they are given the time to practice and understand.

Key Vocabulary

Semiotic representations are external mental representations for communication purposes. People use representations (languages, images, movements, actions, and objects) and attribute them with meanings.

Stick It Into Action!

Multiplication Methods

Here are pictures of different multiplication methods (the vertical method, area model, and Japanese sticks method) that can be taught to be used with multiplication problems with two or more digits.

- The vertical model is the more traditional model with which you may be most familiar.
- The area model shows the multiplication array for 54 × 32. In the area model, the columns represent 50 and 4, which makes 54, and the rows represent 30 and 2,

which makes 32. Each cell is a multiplication of numbers in each row and column. The resulting numbers are then added to make 1,728.
- The Japanese sticks model shows the multiplication for 54 × 32. Fifty-four is split into 5 horizontal sticks on the top left (each stick representing 10) and 4 sticks on the bottom (each stick representing 1). The same goes for 32, which is shown by 3 vertical sticks on the left (each stick representing 10) and 2 sticks on the right (each stick representing 1). Each leftmost crossing point (represented by a dot where the two sticks cross) represents 100, or a 10 stick times another 10 stick. In this example, there are 15 leftmost crossing points, equaling 1,500. Each top or bottom crossing point represents 10 (or a 10 stick times a 1 stick). There are a total of 22 crossing points (10 on the top and 12 on the bottom), totaling 220. Each rightmost crossing point represents 1, and there are eight rightmost crossing points, representing 8. The sum is 1,500 + 220 + 8 = 1,728.

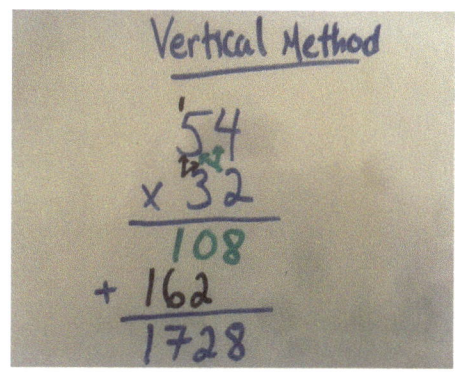
Vertical method.

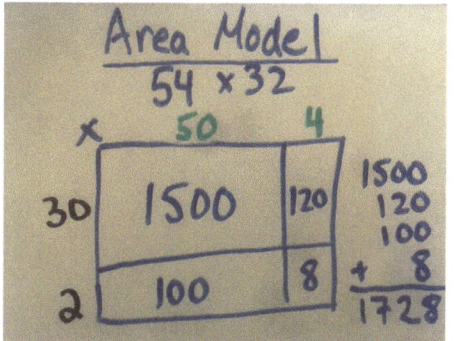
Area model.

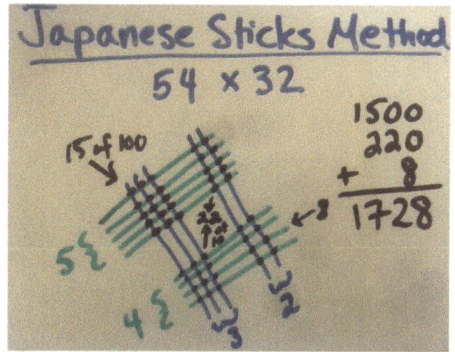
Japanese sticks method.

As we have demonstrated, there are many different ways to teach your students how to multiply. One advantage of teaching the area model for multiplication is that it can be used for all numbers (including fractions) and expressions with variables (e.g., $2a$, $5x - 4$, $8y^2 - 3y + 5$). You should not limit your students to using one method for rapidity because each student may differ in how they come to understand multiplication concepts. This applies to other types of calculations as well. As in multiplication, there are many different ways to add, subtract, and divide. In the following Stick It Into Action, we demonstrate how you can foster critical thinking in math by asking students to think about different ways to add.

  **Stick It Into Action!**

Critical Thinking in Math
Ask your students to think about and come up with one or more ways to add 38 and 54.

Teacher	(to students) "Think and show us one or two different ways to add 38 and 54."
Student A	Walks to the board and draws her number line where she explains that she starts at 38 and adds 50 to 38, which makes 88. She then adds 4 to make it 92.
Teacher	"Very good. That is one way to add the numbers by using a number line."
Student B	Walks to the board and writes 38 as 30 + 8 and 54 as 50 + 4, and then she writes 30 + 8 + 50 + 4 = 80 + 12 = 92. "I break 38 into 30 and 8 and 54 into 50 and 4. I then add 30 and 50 because they are tens, and 8 and 4 because they are ones. That makes 80 for tens and 12 for ones, so it is 92."
Teacher	"[Student B] used a different way to add the numbers, and she used expansion by breaking the numbers down into the tens and ones and adding them together."
Student C	"I have another idea. We can take 4 from 54 and then add it to 38, which makes 42 (38 + 4), and then add it to 50. That makes 92."

Stick It Into Action! *(continued)*

Teacher	"Yes, that is another way to add the numbers by taking some from one number and then adding that to the other number."
Student D	"We can use tens blocks and ones blocks to show the addition."
Teacher	"Yes, that is also correct. How would you do that?"
Student D	"38 is 3 tens blocks and 8 ones blocks. 54 is 5 tens blocks and 4 ones blocks. We then have 8 tens blocks and 12 ones blocks altogether. That makes 9 tens blocks and 2 ones blocks, which makes 92."
Teacher	"Some people use visual aids to compute, and [Student D] showed you how you can do that with tens blocks and ones blocks."
Student C	"I have a different idea: We can also take 2 from 54 and add it to 38, which makes 40 and then add it to 52. That makes 92."
Teacher	Great! These are all great examples of different ways to add.

Key Strategy

Concrete–Representational–Abstract (CRA) Approach

Here is a multiple representation strategy that has become popular in STEAM (science, technology, engineering, arts, mathematics) classrooms (Hughes et al., 2014), and can be beneficial to Deaf students. With this strategy, representations can be depicted concretely (**C**, using real objects), representationally (**R**, using images/illustrations), and/or abstractly (**A**, using symbols and words in ASL, English, and additional home languages when possible). You can set up learning stations to allow opportunities for teaching and practicing math using these different representations. For example, you can set up one station with manipulatives (e.g., counters, linking cubes, base 10 blocks), one station with pictorial forms (e.g., number lines, ten frames, arrays, base 10 shorthand, hundred grids), and another station with sign and print languages (e.g., flashcards with English words and/or ASL words, standard notations, and standard algorithms). You can also add students' home languages as well on the cards (e.g., Spanish, Mexican Sign Language/Lengua de Señas Mexicana [LSM]).

 **Stick It Into Action!**

CRA—Patterns

Here are ways to integrate CRA into your classroom to practice with patterns after you have taught about them.

- **C:** Ask students to arrange solids, foam blocks, or beads (in different sizes and colors). They can create or follow a given pattern.
- **R:** Ask students to create pictures, drawings, or graphs of different kinds of patterns (e.g., colors, shapes).
- **A:** Ask students to write a patterned statement in English (e.g., ABAB, 1212, blue-green-blue-green). Have students film their patterns in ASL.

Handstamp Sample

CRA

Young Deaf Students Doing Mathematics Using Montessori Materials at Metro Deaf School.

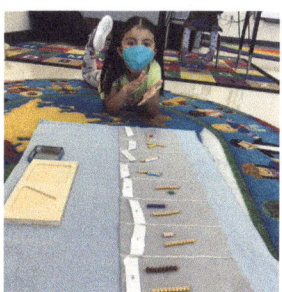

Concrete activity. A student arranging number sets of beads.

Representational activity. A student using an area model for addition.

Abstract activity. Students putting numbers in Arabic numerals in order. (Photo credit: Susan Lane-Outlaw.)

CRA With Older Students For upper elementary and middle school, you can give each student a paper with three columns—concrete, representational, and abstract—like this.

Inequality
Fill the blank with one of the following symbols (<, =, >).

2 □ 5   4 □ 4   3 □ 7

CONCRETE	REPRESENTATIONAL	ABSTRACT

Blank CRA chart for older students.

Ask students to use the manipulatives to show their concrete understanding of mathematical inequality. To show their representational understanding, they can draw tallies/circles/squares or use a number line for comparisons. In the last column, they can use mathematical notations (i.e., numbers and symbols) and write and/or insert a signed video.

Handstamp Sample

Completed CRA

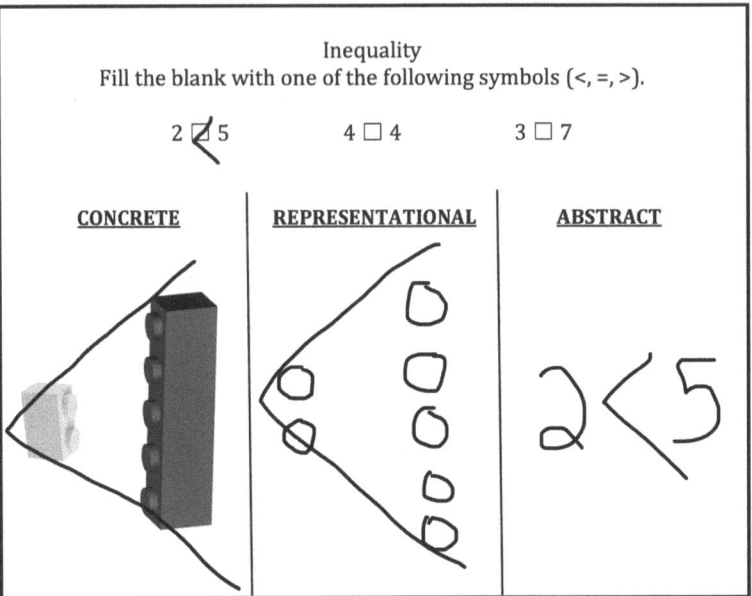

Ideally, abstract learning is built on representational experience, which is built on concrete learning. Each of the three representations may not be feasible or needed in all situations (e.g., finding a matrix determinant). Yet, opportunities to practice transitioning between representations is a crucial aspect in developing students' understanding of relationships (Witzel et al., 2008).

Teacher Tale

One of my favorite activities is having students do a discovery activity where they find the circumference through physical activity. First, I ask students to decide how much floor space they will need on which to make a large circle. They can use chalk or tape to mark a visible dot as a center point on the floor. After they mark their dot, I ask them to use a string to create their circle on the floor. Then, they tape both ends of the string together to complete their circle. They can tape some points of the string to help secure their string-created circle on the floor. Then, I ask them to measure the radii from different points on the circle to the center point to make sure they are all equal. Students then remove the tape holding the string, and they straighten and measure their string to find its length. They compare the length of the string to the number they previously computed on paper using the previously taught circumference formula. I then have them compare how close the length of the string is to the calculated answer. We have a discussion afterward on the relationship between the circumference and the diameter—that is, the value of pi (3.14159...)—and different ways we use the relationship for different circle-related measurements. Perspective sharing!

—*Brenda Call, mathematics coach*

Math Talks

When teaching students multiple representations for solving equations, it is also important to provide opportunities for them to explore their understanding through meaningful multimodal discussions about mathematical concepts (i.e., Math talk). The first step is to create a welcoming classroom environment where Deaf students with diverse language backgrounds and communication skills can explore freely, ask questions, and share ideas with one another. This is a great way to observe their mathematical thinking and analysis skills. As mentioned previously, Deaf students might not have had as many opportunities to talk about mathematics at home, so it is important to provide these opportunities in your classroom. Here are some strategies to promote math talk in the classroom.

Key Strategy

10-Minute Math Talk

You can show students a math concept or problem and ask an open-ended question to start a discussion (e.g., "What formula do you think you should use to solve this?"). As students begin to share their thinking using mathematical language, you can further extend the conversation with additional questions such as, "What is your reasoning for using this formula?" "Do you agree or disagree with what that student said? Why or why not?" and "What is a possible counterexample that makes this false?" For example, before you introduce the concept of negative exponent, show a slide like this: $3^3 = 27$; $3^2 = 9$, $3^1 = 3$. Ask your students to think about what the next two numbers in this sequence might be and have them take turns sharing their thoughts.

Key Strategy

Number Talk

This is an excellent activity for younger children to help them develop **number sense.** This will help them start to connect numbers to objects or see patterns and relationships in numbers, each of which is an important foundation for mathematical learning. To implement this, you can show your class a card with the number 9 and ask them questions like, "What two numbers can make 9?" and "Can you show me something in this classroom that represents or makes 9?" You can also use this strategy to ask your students to make an estimate. "I wonder, how many elephants do you think would fit in this room?" "How many people do you think are in this building?" "How many coin tosses will I need to get 10 heads?" "How long would it take you to complete this task?" "How many candy hearts are in this jar?" Estimation is critical to the development of **number sense,** especially when it comes to evaluating a solution to a problem. We make estimates every day.

Key Vocabulary

Number sense is the ability to understand quantities and work with numbers, including, but not limited to, counting (e.g., order of numbers), comparing (e.g., more or less, larger or smaller), and using symbols that represent quantities (e.g., 7 in ASL means the same as 7 in Arabic numerals).

Key Strategy

3 Acts Talk

This is a math talk that consists of three acts and a reflection. In Act 1, you ask students to identify and talk about a central conflict; in Act 2, you ask students to select a method and make progress on solving the conflict; in Act 3, ask students to reflect on their solutions and resolve any inconsistencies in their responses. This is a great opportunity for students to compare and contrast what they did throughout the whole process (see https://blog.mrmeyer.com/ for more on 3 acts talk).

 Stick It Into Action!

3 Acts Talk

Here is an example of steps for a 3 acts talk discussing a real-life photograph on a smart board. The picture shows coconuts spilled from an overturned tractor-trailer on a road.

"Coconut Truck Accident, General Santos City, Mindanao" by Gary Lee Todd, CC PDM 1.0.

- Have your students look at the picture and talk about any mathematical concepts that are related to the content in the picture.
- Act 1: Ask them to describe possible conflicts depicted in the picture and then narrow them down to one central conflict for Act 2. For example, how many coconuts were spilled? How fast did the truck go before it overturned?
- Act 2: Have students solve the selected conflict mathematically. If it is, "How many coconuts were spilled?" provide the students with the truck's dimensions and have them figure out the volume of the trailer. Then, you can provide students with a small-scale replica containing four coconuts, and they can use the volume and number of coconuts in the replica to set up an equivalency equation to calculate the total number of coconuts in the overturned truck. This can be done individually or in groups.
- Act 3: Ask students to check and reflect on their solutions and how they can resolve their solutions if they don't match the correct answers (i.e., identify mistakes in their procedure and solve the problem correctly).

Next, we discuss how to communicate multiple representations of mathematical ideas through multiple languages.

Core Recommendation 2: Optimize All Languages (ASL, English, and Additional Languages) to Learn Mathematical Concepts

Language plays a critical role in learning mathematics. Deaf children naturally use all languages in their linguistic repertoire to develop literacy, including mathematical literacy. It is natural for them to switch among languages, such as ASL, English, and home languages, to communicate their ideas. A student might sign the ASL phrase *Pythagorean theorem* and then fingerspell *Pythagorean* to emphasize the spelling of the English term. A Deaf student whose home language is LSM might use ASL words for the mathematical operation (e.g., *add, subtract*) and then use LSM words for numbers, and then go back to ASL words for calculation. It is normal for students to use this tactic of translanguaging to navigate thinking (Wolbers et al., 2023; see Chapter 4 for more on translanguaging).

As a teacher, it is your role to embrace and model languages and maximize opportunities for your students to connect languages and math. When you provide Deaf students with many opportunities to express what they have learned in both signing and writing, they will be able to better generate and explain their mathematical understanding. You can ask your students to sign and write how they get to their solutions and/or a sentence that explains what the solution means. For example, in a given story problem where there are four dog sleds with five dogs each, tell students that they must multiply to get the total number of dogs. After solving the problem, you can then ask them to explain the answer in their preferred languages (e.g., There are 20 dogs in four teams of five dogs). In this way, students are engaging in mathematical meaning-making across their languages.

Mathematical Lexicons

Although mathematics is universal, each language has its own way of communicating mathematical concepts. Arabic, for example, has its own set of vocabulary to describe a mathematical concept. ASL, LSM, and English each have a different set of vocabulary to describe the same mathematical concept as well. For example, when we are talking about $a^2 + b^2 = c^2$, we refer to it in English as the "Pythagorean theorem." In ASL, we refer to it as (ASL word, handshape [HS]-V on HS-1) as shown here.

ASL word for *Pythagorean theorem*.

Words With Multiple Meanings

As in any language, some words have multiple meanings, and it is important that appropriate language is used to refer to the mathematical concept or relationship. One example is the English word *function*, which has different meanings in different contexts. In mathematics, it represents a special relationship where each input has a single output. There are also multiple ASL words that represent the different meanings of the English word *function*. To refer to the mathematical relationship in ASL, the signer uses HS-1 on both hands and bonds them at the knuckles. The hands rotate back and forth to the top position.

This ASL word appropriately illustrates the mathematical concept that the value of *x* acts as an input to produce a single value of *y* when applied to an equation,

ASL word for *function*.

as you might see in the *x-y* table figure. Each *x*-value corresponds to one and only one *y*-value.

Advantages of ASL or Any Sign Language as the Language of Mathematics

There are many benefits of using sign language to communicate visual-spatial aspects of mathematical concepts. Here we provide recommendations for ways to sign common mathematical terms in ASL so they are conceptually accurate. For example, the *x-y-z* coordinate plane can be depicted with an upward HS-3 hand with the middle finger pointing forward. The advantage of using HS-3 is that you can show a 1-D line, a 2-D plane, or a 3-D solid within the *x-y-z* graph using the other hand.

x	y
−3	6
−2	0
−1	−4
0	−6
1	−6
2	−4
3	0
4	6

x-y table.

The use of depiction features in ASL (e.g., classifiers, depicting verbs, visual descriptions) adds more information, such as textural, locational, positional, or instrumental characteristics (Kurz et al., 2018, 2020). Similarly, the ASL word for *quadrilateral* is depicted with two HS-1 hands with palms facing each other (depicting the vertical sides), and then transitions to two HS-1 hands with palms facing downwards (depicting the horizontal sides). This movement allows the hands to represent all sides of the quadrilateral. The same approach of using the HS-1 classifier to represent a side of a figure can be used for all 2-D polygons. An octagon would be depicted by two HS-1 hands facing and touching each other. The hands move in an arc from the bottom to the top of the polygon until all sides have been represented, and the "1" fingers touch at the top. This can then be followed by the ASL word for *eight* to indicate that an octagon has eight sides. You can use HS-1 for all 2-D shapes and HS-5 for all 3-D solids.

ASL HS-3 for *x-y-z* coordinate plane.

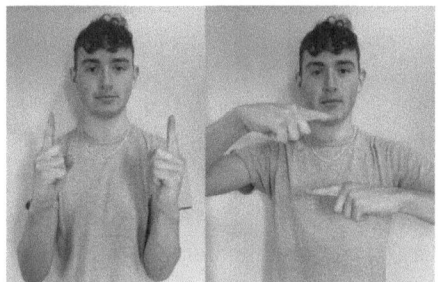

ASL word for *quadrilateral*.

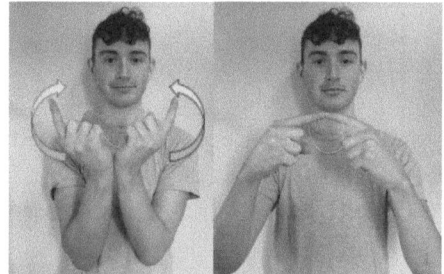

ASL word for *polygon*.

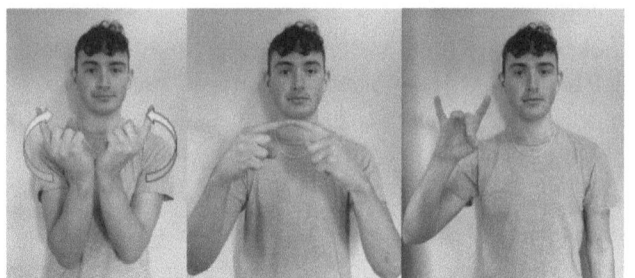

ASL word for *octagon*.

ASL word for *base*.

MATHEMATICS

ASL word for *exponent*.   ASL word for *variable*.

In the next images, the bent HS-L classifier is used to convey fractions. A proper fraction is a fraction that has a larger denominator, and an improper fraction is a fraction that has a larger numerator. The ASL word for *proper fraction* shows a smaller bent HS-L in the numerator and a larger bent HS-L hand in the denominator, and the ASL word for *improper fraction* shows a larger bent HS-L hand in the numerator and a smaller one in the denominator.

ASL word for *proper fraction*.   ASL word for *improper fraction*.

Another benefit of using ASL in math is the ability to use depicting verbs when a mathematical situation includes plurality in action. Consider the following example: "A Deaf girl put 40 ASL cards in five bins. Each bin has the same number of cards. How many cards were in each bin?" You can use depicting verbs with your students to depict the action of "putting cards in bins one at a time" repeatedly (flat HS-o). This depiction helps with the associative concept of "each" in this situation.

ASL Finger Counting Although there have been debates regarding the benefits of finger counting going back to the 19th century (Kurz, 2006, 2009), we highly recommend it as a strategy to integrate into your math instruction. Finger counting strategies are a physical extension of abstract thinking in ASL, and it can be natural for Deaf people to use their hands to compute numbers in ASL. When Deaf learners use this approach, their hands hold their ASL numbers while their brains process and make the next decision on how to calculate or solve. One benefit of using finger counting is that you can show your students how to use ASL finger-counting strategies to compute numbers beyond tens. You should promote using both finger counting and mental calculation creatively. Your students can then choose to continue or discontinue finger counting after achieving fluency with mental calculation.

Chew on This!

Did you know that . . . ?
In ASL, handshapes can denote word families in math (see Chapters 3 and 7 for more on word families).

- You can use HS-1 to represent a side of a figure for all 2-D polygons.
- The advantage of this approach is to show that all polygons depicted in ASL belong to the same word family, sharing similar language characteristics.
- This is similar to the suffix "-agon" in English, which denotes various numbers of angles in a closed figure.
- You can use the bent HS-L for many math concepts of value, number, magnitude, and/or placement, including fraction, proper fraction, improper fraction, mixed number, base number, exponent, coefficient, place value, subscript, factor, composite number, prime number, natural number, integer, rational number, irrational number, real number, complex number, and variable.

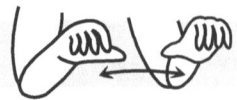

Stick It Into Action!

 ASL Finger Counting

Finger counting can be fun for your students, and it allows them to be active participants in learning. For example, ask your students to think about different ways to use their fingers to add 3 and 4 using ASL. Here are some responses you might see:

- **Student A:** With 4 on your passive hand and 3 on your active hand, start counting up from 3 by touching each of your passive hand fingers that are extended to the active hand.
- **Student B:** Use the same approach except start with 3 on your passive hand and 4 on your active hand.
- **Student C:** With 4 on your passive hand and 3 on your active hand, give one of the 3 fingers to the passive hand to make it 5 and reduce the number of active fingers to 2. Then, add 5 and 2 mentally.

You can also ask them to think about how to add 8 and 5 using ASL finger counting because in ASL it's possible to hold numbers greater than 10 on one hand. You can also show your students how to use their fingers to multiply. For example, to multiply 3×8, they can start with 3 on their passive hand and use their active hand to multiply each finger by 8, placing 8, 16, and 24 on each of their passive hand fingers.

  Word Study and Fluency in ASL and English

When teaching P–12 mathematics, you will want to incorporate ASL–English word study for vocabulary and phrases. Word study includes the explicit examination of word parts as well as word meanings. ASL word study involves bringing attention to the five phonological features (i.e., handshape, location, movement, palm orientation, and nonmanual markers; see Chapter 3 for additional information), root/family words, and synonyms and antonyms. Going back to HS-1 and bent HS-L, we have already mentioned ways you can use handshapes to represent 2-D polygons as well as number word families. In an elementary classroom, you can put up an ASL root/family word wall that categorizes ASL words based on its ASL handshape features or ASL location features (i.e., top of the head, bottom of the head, torso, arms and hands, and neutral space; see Chapters 3 and 7 for additional examples).

Here's how you can use it when teaching math:

- If a student knows the ASL word but cannot recall its equivalent English word, you can suggest they go to the ASL wall, search for the ASL word's location category, and then search for the target ASL word by picture to locate its equivalent English word (see Chapter 7 for pictures modeling this).
- You may also engage your students in analyzing, comparing, or using vocabulary in academic contexts across languages. As mentioned previously, the English words for polygons (i.e., pentagon, hexagon, septagon, octagon, nonagon, decagon) combine a Greek-derived numerical prefix and the root word "-agon." In ASL, students can also note patterns of expression by identifying how the HS-1 classifiers depict sides.

- Consider adding your students' home languages to your word wall as well.
- Bridging ASL and English (and additional languages) at the word and phrase level enriches the learning of mathematical language and concepts.

To increase your Deaf students' word fluency, we recommend you provide opportunities for them to practice using math words (in ASL, English, and additional languages) in both contextualized (e.g., words in story problems) and decontextualized (e.g., words only) situations. They can demonstrate fluency in ASL by showing the correct sign production for a word and using it in a sentence appropriately. Similarly, you can check your students' fluency and comprehension in English by asking them to write the concept in a sentence. You can increase their word fluency through games such as Wordopoly.

 Stick It Into Action!

Wordopoly in Math

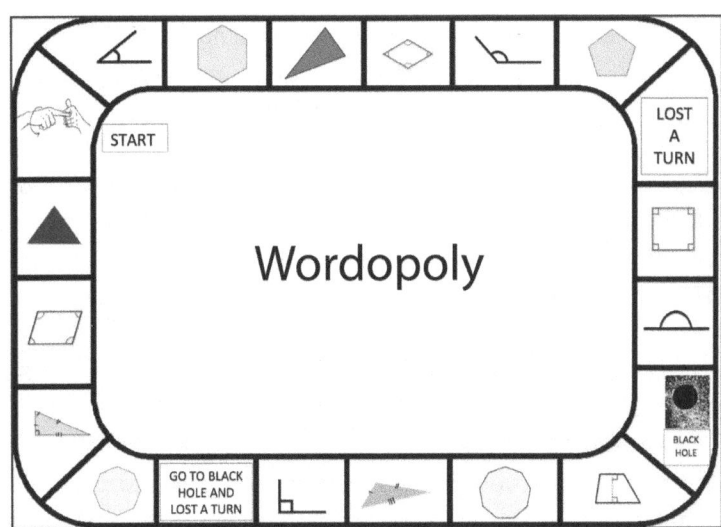

Directions: To play Wordopoly, students roll a die (can be one die or two dice) to advance their tokens around the path on a board, such as the one shown here, until they sign all ASL words and/or write English words on their paper correctly.

Core Recommendation 3: Collaborate With Caregivers and Family Members

Although math is formally learned at school, there are also plentiful opportunities for children to learn mathematics concepts and language(s) at home.

You can promote caregiver engagement by hosting family fun math events (e.g., mathematical festivals, math night) and showing them how to provide structured and unstructured mathematics talks to promote development in younger Deaf learners (Langdon et al., 2021). For example, you can demonstrate to families how to do

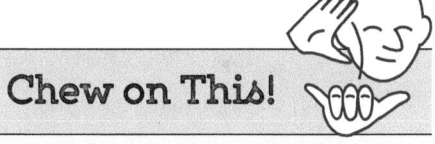

Chew on This!

Did you know that...?

- Children's number knowledge is predicted by their early experiences with number language. (Gunderson & Levine, 2011)
- Parent math talk has a positive impact on children's number sense and mathematical abilities (Gibson et al., 2020; Susperreguy & Davis-Kean, 2016)
- When providing math-related tablet computer games, parent–child mathematics talk can be enhanced by providing brief parental support and guidance (Zippert & Rittle-Johnson, 2020).

photo scavenger hunts for numbers, shapes, and patterns around the school building (or their home). Or you can introduce them to the idea of embedding these concepts in the game I Spy. You can "spy a large red circle" or "a bird with four stripes" and then have the children look for the object. Another possibility is asking families to bring cultural heritage quilts, crafts, and/or other items to the classroom and supporting them to discuss line segments and shapes with students (e.g., square, triangle, pentagon, hexagon, rhombus, octagon, trapezoid). This provides a hands-on and supportive opportunity for families to learn ASL math words and become more comfortable talking about math concepts that appear in their daily lives. If you teach middle or high school students, you can introduce physical or online games and puzzles to families that can be used at home. You can also use this time to talk with them about math learning trajectories, curriculum, pedagogies, and assessments.

We also recommend that you encourage caregivers to spend time with their children reading math-related storybooks. Even caregivers who are not yet proficient in ASL can share math-related storybooks with their children. For example, Rocky Mountain Deaf School has produced several translated stories on its YouTube channel, such as *A Kids Book About Money*, *Sir Cumference and the Dragon of Pi*, *Math Curse*, and *Magic Pi*. You can also encourage families to read aloud (i.e., storysigning; see Chapter 2) these math-related storybooks with their children at home. You can then use them in the classroom to promote mathematical discourse by connecting concepts to children's books and informational texts (see Chapter 7 for additional suggestions connecting fiction and nonfiction).

Engaging caregivers and family members in their Deaf children's school activities (family math nights, math festivals, and family games) will allow them to learn how to play games with their children, talk math everywhere (at home, at work, and on the road), and build relationships with both their children and their children's teachers.

(ABAR) Core Recommendation 4: Address Mathematics in a Diverse World

Diversity in ideas and skills is valuable to the field of mathematics. Rather than giving students rigid formulas, you can help them discover mathematical concepts and equations. Students with diverse experiences bring diverse ideas that can be applied to math analysis and discourse. Here are some topics and strategies to promote perspectives and help your students understand diverse populations who contribute to the mathematical fields.

(PI) (ABAR) Gender and Sexuality in Mathematics

You may notice that when discussing mathematical contributions, male mathematicians (e.g., Sir Isaac Newton, Leonardo Bonacciare [aka Fibonacci], Archimedes Pythagoras of Samos, Euclid of Alexandria) are often the ones mentioned most frequently. However, many female mathematicians have also contributed to the field of mathematics, and it is important that you teach your students about them. You can share or have your students research female mathematicians such as Hypatia, Sophie Germain, Ada Lovelace, Sofia Kovalevskaya, Emmy Noether, and Dorothy Vaughan (one of many female and Black, Indigenous, and People of Color human computers working for aerospace, defense, and intelligence government agencies: NASA, Department of Defense, Ministry of Defense).

Chew on This!

Did you know that...?
Recent statistics show that 28% of those in the STEAM fields identify as female. Of those, 42% are in mathematics fields (computer and mathematical occupations) (U.S. Bureau of Labor Statistics, 2020). However, female students are often called to participate less and receive the following negative messages in math class:

- Math is not for girls (or those who identify as girls).
- Think faster.
- This class will be too hard for you.
- You shouldn't count with your hands.
- You overthink the problem.
- You're not a math person.

You can help change who participates in math by raising your awareness of the biases as well as the perceptions you may even harbor of your own math capabilities. Math is for everyone, and there are many ways to do math.

You can create a learning environment that is welcoming and inclusive of gender and sexuality by using appropriate language (e.g., preferred pronouns) and content related to mathematics (e.g., using nongender-stereotyping activities). Doing so can help your students develop their "can do" attitude when tackling mathematical problems. You can also share information about organizations for LGBTQIA+ (Spectra: The Association of LGBTQ+ Mathematicians) and women (Association of Women in Mathematics) as well as stories and contributions of Queer scientists (https://500queerscientists.com/). Diversity in mathematical ideas should be appreciated in the classroom.

(PI) (MM) Deaf-Related Mathematics

You can also make mathematics more Deaf friendly and empowering for your students. One way is to develop or modify problems using their names and Deaf cultural information. For example, consider the wording in a typical math problem: "Abby is driving from City A to City B. After 2 hours of driving at the same speed, she noticed that she covered 90 miles, and she had 30 more miles left to City B. If she continues driving at the same speed, what will be her total driving time from A to B?" You also can add Deaf-related information as in the following example: "[name of one of your students] is driving from Kansas School for the Deaf to Iowa School for the Deaf. After 2 hours of driving at the same speed, she noticed that she had covered 150 miles and still has 50 more miles left. If she continues driving at the same speed, what will be her total driving time from Kansas School for the Deaf to Iowa School for the Deaf." This modified story problem is more personalized and has Deaf-related information to help students learn more about Deaf heritage. Sometimes, all you need to do is to add *Deaf* to a story problem, and the problem becomes more relatable for your students, such as changing "a farmer has two cows..." to "a Deaf farmer has two cows..." Connecting back to gender, you can also change the pronoun *she* to *they* to be more inclusive.

Another way to connect Deaf-related mathematics is by sharing information about Deaf mathematicians. For example, you can incorporate information on James Michael David when teaching about topology. James Michael David, a Black Deaf mathematician, earned his doctorate in mathematics at the University of Chicago in 1977 and is currently a professor at Howard University's mathematics department. He has published in the area of differential topology. If teaching about velocity, you can talk about Konstantin Tsiolkovsky (1857–1935), who was a Deaf math teacher in Russia and is known as the "father of rocketry" because he published on topics of rocketry, space shuttles, and space stations all before we got in the space race. He also created a formula that computes the required escape velocity for a rocket to leave the gravity of Earth. The derivatives of his formula are still currently being used by our space organizations (i.e., NASA, SpaceX).

You can also have your students do projects on Deaf individuals from diverse backgrounds who have contributed to the field of mathematics and math-related studies. For example, you can share with your students about Charlotte Angas Scott (1858–1931). She was born in England and earned master's and doctoral degrees from the University of London. She eventually became a professor and the first mathematics department head at Bryn Mawr College in Pennsylvania in 1885. She mentored three female doctoral students in mathematics before 1900; at the time, they represented

> "I am one of the first Deaf female students to graduate with a bachelor's degree in applied mathematics from the Rochester Institute of Technology. While I was studying mathematics, I got constant looks of dismissal from my professors and other people just because I was female and Deaf. Some of them ignored me completely or encouraged me to look elsewhere for my study. I was very fortunate to have a few female professors, and they were very welcoming and made me feel included. I was more motivated when I had them. If you look at the faces of our international and national award winners in the past 100 years, they were primarily male. That does not mean there were no female mathematicians. We have plenty. We need to break down those societal walls and make math more inclusive of students of all genders and marginalized groups.
>
> —Samantha Braidi

one-third of all American female mathematicians. She also was a coeditor of the prestigious *American Journal of Mathematics* for 27 years.

Mathematics is a collection of ideas from diverse representations from all around the world, including the Middle East, Africa, and South America, and you can and should introduce them to your students to show that Deaf people can contribute to the field of mathematics and math-related studies. Mathematics does not belong to the majority population. Everyone of diverse populations, including Indigenous, contributes to the field (see https://indigenousmathematicians.org/ and https://indigenous.mathnetwork.educ.ubc.ca/resources/). You can use this information to share resources about Indigenous mathematics and mathematicians.

(ABAR) (MM) Equitable Mathematics

We strongly encourage you to address current societal issues with mathematics. At the time of writing this chapter, the COVID-19 pandemic, the Black Lives Matter movement, presidential elections, and environmental waste are frequent newsmakers. By understanding statistical information, for example, students can better identify data-based versus made-up news (see Chapter 9 for more on identifying accurate information online). You can relate mathematics to current societal issues and allow students to apply mathematics to better understand the issues (e.g., graphing trends and gaps) as demonstrated in the next Stick it Into Action.

(ABAR) (MM) Stick It Into Action!

Address Societal Issues With Math

Analyze societal issues with your students mathematically by having them do the following:

- Select a meaningful social issue (e.g., racial profiling, environmental deterioration, attitudes and behaviors toward students of marginalized populations).
- Collect numerical data related to the issue.
  - Encourage students to conduct a survey on their selected issue where they ask their peers, school professionals, family members, and others for opinions (see Chapter 7 for a survey example).
  - Have them analyze their surveys and graph their data.
  - If possible, have them also share an article that uses graphs or numbers to support their survey findings.
- Present findings and/or solutions.

As a teacher, it is important that you reflect on your personal and professional bias toward Deaf people, including Deaf people of marginalized groups. Do you have any beliefs or thoughts on their capabilities to learn and do mathematics? Are you lowering your expectations for them just because they are Deaf or of a specific marginalized group, and you do not know how to teach them effectively? Are you using various methods to reach out to your students? Do you allow them to express their mathematical ideas in ASL as part of their summative assessment responses? Do you

---

Chew on This!

Consider Equitable Assessments. Did you know that . . . ?

- Using ASL to assess mathematical knowledge is not giving students the answers. It is good to remember that English words also carry mathematical meanings (e.g., tri-"angle"; "ratio"-nal number, "in"-put, "out"-put; Higgins et al., 2016; Kurz et al., 2018, 2020).
- Although Deaf students might understand a math problem when it is given in ASL, it does not mean they know how to solve it. They must have the content knowledge to be able to do so (Cawthon & Leppo, 2013).
- Current math standardized assessments are not inclusive for Deaf students, especially Deaf students from marginalized groups. In the standardized assessments that have ASL videos, the majority of signers are white and male, or they are translated into ASL by interpreters and/or teachers who are second-language learners of ASL.
- Timed assessments may not be equitable for students who need time to demonstrate their mathematical thinking.

allow them to support their responses with additional home languages and language variations?

Every student needs to have an equitable opportunity to demonstrate their mathematical knowledge and skills and to have access to similar resources for learning mathematics. Your goal is to ensure that they receive the resources they need to succeed in school and after graduation.

As with other content areas, to provide equitable assessments in math, we encourage you to collect preassessment data for each student when they enter your classroom because all Deaf students have different backgrounds related to math knowledge and skills. Using information from preassessments, you can then identify a list of topics to target for each student. This will help with proper class placement or math-level placement. If your assessment goal is to measure your students' mathematical knowledge and skills, you will want your assessment to optimize their language repertoire, whether ASL, English, additional languages and/variations , or visual representations.

Additional Things to Consider

Although we would love to cover everything in this chapter, we cannot, but we will discuss some important areas for you to consider while preparing to teach Deaf students mathematics.

 Growth Mindsets

The saying "To err is human" is crucial to understanding how children learn. Making mistakes is natural for humans and is critical to learning. Would you be where you are now if you had not made any mistakes? Do you remember how long it took you to develop fluency with multiplication tables? Carol Dweck, an American psychologist, has studied people's mindsets when it comes to learning (Dweck & Yeager, 2019), and she named two types of mindsets that people develop during their formative years: the fixed mindset and the growth mindset. The fixed mindset is a belief that skills, intellect, and talents are fixed and unchangeable. The growth mindset is a belief that skills, intellect, and talents can be developed through practice and perseverance. Boaler (2022) then incorporated Dweck's mindset theory into the mathematical learning context as demonstrated here.

 Technology

Technology has become an integral part of mathematical learning. You can use various technological tools (manipulatives, apps, calculators, online programs)

Recognize the Difference Between Fixed and Growth Mindsets. Did you know that . . . ?

- Samantha Braidi could have easily changed her undergraduate study after receiving messages that she could not achieve in mathematics. Her growth mindset helped her persevere and achieve her goal.
- A mother who says, "I am not good at mathematics. Ask your father for help" can solidify the female child's fixed mindset that mathematics is for boys only.
- Timed tasks limit students who may need time to calculate and/or solve problems. Excessive use of timed tasks can build fixed mindsets.
- If you do not ask your student to elaborate after they give a wrong answer, they will not have an opportunity to catch their mistake. They may develop a fixed mindset if they do not get feedback.
- Praising a certain student as "the best math student" or "the math person" can stop other students' growth mindsets. Instead, praise them on specific learning achievements, such as, "You checked your work, and it helped improve your accuracy," "I see you asked for extra help when you were stuck. That is a good strategy to talk it through with another person," or "I notice you used a different way to solve this problem. That shows flexible thinking."
- Instead of saying this problem is "hard" or "easy," say this problem is a "challenge that you can figure out a way to solve."

to teach mathematics. Students need to learn how to access and use them as well. Graphing calculators can be expensive for some students whose families have less than moderate means. Consider other graphical tools that you can use that are inexpensive or free, such as DESMOS, a free online app that provides many features that are similar to those of graphing calculators. Integrate popular personalized learning platforms that are commonly used in schools for the Deaf: ST Math (a visual math instructional program for P–8 students leverages the spatial-temporal reasoning ability to solve problems with its penguin avatar) and IXL Math (a personalized learning platform with practice problems that follows Common Core standards). In addition, you can provide classroom activities where students can participate in online number talks, such as through TikTok or Flip videos. You can also use virtual math-related tools and manipulatives or make digital cartoons about concepts or procedures to allow your students to express their mathematical thinking creatively. As of this writing, there are apps that can translate and solve a mathematical problem for you. Imagine that! There are many benefits of using technology in math, but remember to continue to have your students talk about mathematics rather than only writing down their answers.

Financial Literacy

Financial literacy should be part of mathematics education for all K–12 grades because all of your students need to learn personal finance concepts whether they are in elementary, middle, or high school. The reality is that many Deaf students might not learn finance concepts at home where communication is limited. As early as elementary grades, you should be teaching students about money, its value, how to save and spend, and how to invest. You can do a simulation in the classroom to reinforce your students' learning about finance (see Chapter 14 for additional discussion on life skills).

Teacher Tale

After teaching a class of ninth-grade students on general mathematics for a year and learning that their next year's mathematics curriculum was pretty much similar to the recent one, I decided to revamp that curriculum to include finance concepts and run a simulation classroom (using mock money) as a one-stop center for all transactions that my students would learn throughout the year—they learned about understanding money and its value in multiple ways:

- Writing checks
- Earning money by completing recently taught mathematical tasks
- Paying bills (e.g., housing, electricity, groceries, waste management)
- Using coupons and rebates to save money
- Investing money in stocks
- Understanding late payment fees and accrued interest
- Knowing how to not waste money (e.g., paying past their due dates can result in fees)
- Understanding the benefits and downsides of using Social Security Disability Insurance (SSDI) benefits and Supplemental Security Income (SSI)

As a result, these students became literate in personal finance throughout the year. Most schools do not include personal finance education, and it is likely that Deaf students do not get the education at home. I believe that it is our responsibility to teach them personal finance concepts in their most accessible language. If I were to run that simulation now, I would include online and mobile apps for them to keep track of their expenses and revenues.

—*Chris Kurz*

We encourage you to collaborate with other elementary teachers, middle school math teachers, and high school teachers to embed financial education in K–12 for Deaf students.

Story Problems in ASL and English

Most Deaf students automatically put up a wall as soon as they see a story problem on the board in the classroom because they see their second language, English. One strategy that can break through this "wall" is called the **3-Read Protocol.**

Key Strategy

The 3-Read Protocol

This strategy was designed to address bilingual learners' struggles with story problem solving at all grade levels (San Francisco Unified School District, 2015). It places emphasis on *understanding* the problem rather than rapidly trying to solve it. This strategy incorporates having students read a math scenario three times with a different objective each time:

- First read = Understand the context of the story in their L1
- Second read = Understand the math in the story through L2 with the support of their L1
- Third read = Obtain inquiry questions based on the scenario with both L1 and L2

Stick It Into Action!

The 3-Read Protocol

The 3-Read Protocol can be used throughout all grade, language, and math levels. To implement it, start with the "problem stem" of a word problem, which means presenting the word problem *without* the question at the end. Here is an example of a problem stem:

- "You own a popular ice cream shop in DeafTown. Your menu offers the container choice of a cup, a cone, or a bowl. It also offers a choice of three different flavors (cotton candy, orange, and strawberry) and four different toppings (marshmallows, sprinkles, gummy bears, and coconut)."

Chew on This!

Did you know that...?

- Children's number knowledge is predicted by their early experiences with number language. (Gunderson & Levine, 2011)
- Parent math talk has a positive impact on children's number sense and mathematical abilities (Gibson et al., 2020; Susperreguy & Davis-Kean, 2016)
- When providing math-related tablet computer games, parent–child mathematics talk can be enhanced by providing brief parental support and guidance (Zippert & Rittle-Johnson, 2020).

Stick It Into Action! (*continued*)

Then, set up three columns labeled with *Read 1*, *Read 2*, and *Read 3* on a whiteboard like this.

Table 10.1. Blank 3-Read Protocol Chart

Read 1	Read 2	Read 3

First Read: ASL Viewing

- Narrate the problem stem to your students in ASL using a storytelling style without any written input. Animatedly tell the story in first-person point of view as if it was your own story (see ASL stories by Nathie Marbury (see Chapter 3) for an example). Deaf students learn to view your math story in ASL.
- After the students view your math story in ASL, ask them, "What do you remember from this story?"
- In the *Read 1* column, write everything on the board that the students reconstruct the story in their own words.

Second Read: Student ASL Signing[1] and Guided English Reading

- Present the problem stem in English on the board for the students and call on a student to translate the problem into ASL (sometimes, students understand their peers' ASL better than their teacher). This is where the first read helps as the students see the ASL-English associations.
- Mention that math stories usually have information about quantities/units and then ask the next question: "What are the quantities in this situation?"

Once the numerical quantities (e.g., three flavors; a cup, a cone, or a bowl; four toppings) are mentioned by the students, record student responses in English in the *Read 2* column. After filling out the second column, explain the difference between implicit (words) and explicit (numbers) quantities in English. In addition, ask them to pinpoint which quantities are considered "unnecessary information." The goal behind the second read is to help students understand words in the story that denote mathematical concepts.

1. Storysigning is a process of translation of the print text of a story into the target sign language (see Chapter 2).

Third Read: Independent English Reading and Question Writing
- Allow students to take the time to reread the problem stem in English on the board and think to themselves, "What is missing to make this a good math problem?"
- Ask the students the following question: "What mathematical questions can we ask about the situation?"
- This is when students' critical thinking skills start brewing in their brains, and they often come up with the most fun, creative questions! After writing all the possible questions in the *Read 3* column, challenge each student whether or not their question could be answered with the information from this story.
- Finally, reveal the preset question: "How many different combinations result from choosing a cone, a cup, or a bowl; one kind of ice cream, and one topping?"

As soon as the actual question is revealed, have students work in collaboration to solve the problem with little or no support from the teacher because they already spent time together analyzing the word problem from reading it "three times" (see Table 10.2).

The 3-Read Protocol helps Deaf learners tackle language complexity in mathematics story problems with at least two languages (Braidi, 2017) and four modalities (viewing, signing, reading, and writing). Because it provides students the opportunity to focus on both the contextual and mathematical information thoroughly before solving the problem, it helps address the potential linguistic and mathematical roadblocks that the students might face. Using this approach with a story problem might take the entire class time, so we recommend that you only use this approach once in a while.

Table 10.2. Completed 3-Read Protocol Chart After the Third Read

Read 1	Read 2	Read 3
Ice cream shop	1 shop ("a" means 1)	Students' questions:
Menu has different choices:	1 cup/1 cone/1 bowl ("or" means pick only one)	• How many customers come to my shop? • How many different combinations can I
Cup/cone/bowl	Three flavors	make from choosing one container, one
Flavors: cotton candy, orange, and strawberry	Four toppings	kind of ice cream, and one topping?
Toppings: marshmallows, sprinkles, gummy bears, and coconut		• How many scoops does a cone have? • Can I choose two toppings for my ice cream? • How many different mixtures do I have for my 1 container, 1 flavor, and 1 topping?

 **Bringing It All Together**

Here, we provide a sample lesson on rectangular prisms that incorporates the 3-Read Protocol. It also integrates each of the core recommendations by including multiple representations (**Core Recommendation 1**), multiple modalities in ASL and English (**Core Recommendation 2**), and promoting diverse perspectives (**Core Recommendation 4**) on the topic. Your students can bring their products home to share and talk with their families, or you can demonstrate this lesson in front of your students' parents during a family math event (**Core Recommendation 3**). This lesson takes place over one class period (40–50 min).

Sample 3-Read Lesson Plan

Objectives
- Use and apply the volumes of rectangular prisms.
- Solve a real-world problem involving the volume of rectangular prisms.

Standards Covered
(California) CCSS.MATH.CONTENT.5.MD.C.5
- Relate volume to the operations of multiplication and addition and solve real-world and mathematical problems involving volume.

ASL Content Standards, Language Standards
- Use the full breadth of signing frame space.
- Use frequently occurring descriptive classifiers and other adjectives.

Procedures: Follow the 3-Read Protocol
1. READ 1
   - Provide the story problem in ASL (modeling ASL language standards), preferably in a fun, entertaining storytelling mode (first person point of view). (**Core Recommendations 1, 2**)
   - Ask students what they recall about the story while writing their words in Column 1. (**Core Recommendations 1, 2**)
2. READ 2
   - Project the following story problem stem on the board (**Core Recommendations 1, 2**):

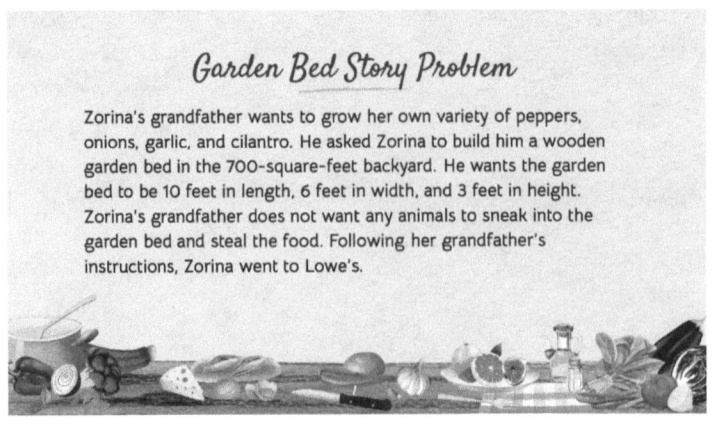

Garden Bed Story Problem

Zorina's grandfather wants to grow her own variety of peppers, onions, garlic, and cilantro. He asked Zorina to build him a wooden garden bed in the 700-square-feet backyard. He wants the garden bed to be 10 feet in length, 6 feet in width, and 3 feet in height. Zorina's grandfather does not want any animals to sneak into the garden bed and steal the food. Following her grandfather's instructions, Zorina went to Lowe's.

- Ask one student to sign the story problem in ASL for the class. Make sure the student reads the problem to themselves first before retelling in ASL. Provide support for ASL language objectives. (**Core Recommendations 1, 2**)
- Ask students what quantities are given in the story problem and record their responses in Column 2. (**Core Recommendations 1, 2**)
- Ask them which of the quantities listed in the column are considered relevant to concepts taught in previous lessons, and which quantities are not. Why? Why not? (One possible irrelevant quantity in the story problem is the garden bed being 700 square feet.) (**Core Recommendation 2**)

3. READ 3
   - Have students read the story problem again on their own for a few minutes and ask them to think of a mathematical question. Have them write down their questions in written English and record their creative questions in the *Read 3* column. This will bring different perspectives on addressing the same problem mathematically (**Core Recommendations 1, 2, 4**)
   - Have them guess which one of these questions is most likely to be the actual question based on the content that they recently learned in previous lessons.
   - Present the next slide with the actual question and point out similarities and differences between their generated questions and the question on the slide.

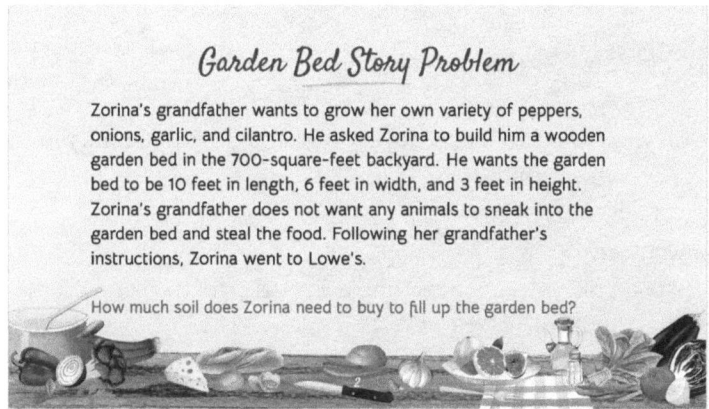

- Distribute the Garden Bed Story Problem handouts to the students. Have them solve the problem individually or in groups and discuss how they solved the problem with the whole group. This allows the students to bring and share their knowledge and skills in solving a problem. (**Core Recommendation 4**)
- If time permits, have students solve selected student-generated questions that are relevant to previous lessons (e.g., What is the area of the garden bed? What is the perimeter of the garden bed? How much would it cost to buy wood to build the garden bed if a foot of wood costs $1.75?)
- As a follow-up activity, read Jayden's *Impossible Garden* together as a class (https://youtu.be/vM7APYysnYo) and create a new story problem for creating a garden bed in a city setting. (**Core Recommendation 4**)
- Give the students a similar problem to take home and work with their caregiver(s). (**Core Recommendation 3**)

 **Your Turn to Practice!**

Now, it's your turn! In this section, we will ask you to develop, teach, and reflect on a lesson incorporating our core recommendations. If you are a teacher candidate, you can implement this in your current classroom, one-to-one with a student, or in a mock situation.

Develop a Lesson Plan

Develop a lesson plan that includes a math and an ASL objectives and create a story problem that allows for contextualized practice of the objective areas. Be sure to integrate Deaf-related content into your story problem.

- Use the 3-Read Protocol to guide students in their understanding of the problem in both ASL and English.

Teach Your Lesson Plan

Teach your own students or in a mock setting.

Reflect on Your Teaching

Reflect on what went well and how you would do it differently in the future. Ask yourself the following questions:

- What went well?
- In what ways did you effectively implement each of the core recommendations? The 3-Read Protocol?
- What would you change/do differently if you taught this lesson again?
- After assessing your students, how well did they learn the targeted objectives?

Additional Activity

Develop a unit plan that includes concrete, representational, and abstract activities for a targeted mathematical concept. Teach a selected activity to real students or in a mock setting and then reflect on what went well and how you would do it differently in the future.

 Recommended Readings/Viewings

For Teachers/Teacher Candidates

- *Mathematical Mindsets* (Boaler, 2022). This book focuses on growth mindsets in a mathematical learning context.

- YouCubed (https://www.youcubed.org). This website has resources related to growth mindsets for learning mathematics.
- *Elementary and Middle School Mathematics: Teaching Developmentally* (Van de Walle et al., 2018). This textbook is good for preservice P–8 teachers because it covers best practices for teaching mathematics through hands-on, problem-based activities.
- National Council of Teachers of Mathematics (www.nctm.org). This website has resources related to teaching and learning in mathematics, including learning standards, professional development, lesson plans and activities, journals, and many others.
- *Family Math II: Achieving Success in Mathematics* (Coates & Thompson, 2003). This book has strategies and tips to engage the family in math activities and promote math talk.

To Use With Your Students

- *Deaf Persons in the Arts and Sciences* (Lang & Lang-Meath, 1995). This book includes biographies of Deaf mathematicians who have contributed to the field.
- Read Brightly (https://www.readbrightly.com/). This site, features children's books related to mathematics and STEAM fields.

Conclusion

Math teachers not only need strong mathematical content knowledge, but they also need to be able to use all languages—ASL and English (and additional home languages)—in academic settings. In this chapter, we gave recommendations to help you provide opportunities to engage your Deaf students in mathematics at school and at home in ways that are multilingual, multimodal, and integrative of multiple representations. This will lead to them gaining a deeper mathematical understanding and greater ability to apply math in everyday situations. By increasingly including your students in math conversations and thinking, it will result in deep learning and they will increasingly make sense of patterns and relationships and how math applies to various real-world situations. It is every teacher's job to make math lessons meaningful and accessible through multiple forms and languages. By doing so, you can help foster a love for mathematics in all your students.

Sticking Points

- Infuse multiple representations of mathematical concepts in your instruction.
- Optimize ASL and English and additional languages through multiple modalities to teach mathematical concepts.
- Create opportunities to collaborate with families in math activities through math nights at school or activities to do together at home.
- Incorporate role models of Deaf people from diverse backgrounds in STEAM fields in your discussions and math-related materials.

Science

Elizabeth Henderson
Scott Cohen
Chris Kurz

When children are asked what scientists do, they may say that they work in a lab dressed in a white lab coat while wearing safety glasses and making stuff explode. Popular media reinforces the stereotype of scientists as white men in lab coats who are often villains or heroes. Many children share this misconception, and this may be even more prevalent among Deaf children, who have limited access to science and exposure to Deaf role models in science. Our job as science educators is to broaden children's conceptions of scientists so that they work in a variety of settings other than labs, including space/air/water mission control rooms, ships, hospitals, forests/parks/ecosystems, universities, governmental facilities, and so forth. As a teacher, it is your role to ensure that science is engaging, interesting, minds-on, hands-on, and applicable to many things in their daily lives. This will foster an understanding that the work of scientists is diverse and that scientists can look like the person they see in the mirror—themselves. In this chapter, we share multilingual and multimodal strategies and tips for you to use when teaching science to Deaf students. Before we dive into the content, let us introduce ourselves.

Who Are We?

Hello! I am Elizabeth Henderson. I have been teaching science in middle school for more than 10 years at the California School for the Deaf (CSD), Riverside. I was a recipient of the 2018 Presidential Award of Excellence in Mathematics and Science Teaching in California. I believe that incorporating deep scientific learning opportunities gives Deaf students a more holistic science learning experience.

Greetings! I am Scott Cohen, a former science teacher at Atlanta Area School for the Deaf and a doctoral candidate in science education at Georgia State University. My research focuses on improving science learning experiences for Deaf students through formal and informal science education. The recommendations in this chapter reflect my experience as a former science teacher as well as current scholarship in science education.

Welcome! I am Chris Kurz, a professor of science and math methods courses for the Secondary Education teacher training program at Rochester Institute of Technology. After earning a bachelor's degree in mathematics with an emphasis in physics, I taught mathematics and science to kindergarten through Grade 12 (K–12) and postsecondary Deaf students for 20 years. Along with Scott and Elizabeth, I will share best practices with you based on my experience as a STEAM (science, technology, engineering, arts, and mathematics) student, teacher, and teacher-trainer.

This chapter synthesizes our collective experiences, insights, and knowledge about teaching science to Deaf students. We aim to communicate principles of teaching and learning that are multilingual and multimodal in nature and that engage students in deep learning about science. We provide guidance on how each of your students, who are diverse in communication skills and thinking, may be included in classroom conversations in ways that can help them become more enlightened about science.

Our recommendations here align with Three-Dimensional (3-D) Learning, a pedagogical practice highlighted in the Next Generation Science Standards (NGSS) and by the National Science Teaching Association (NSTA). This includes connecting to students' backgrounds, languages, and experiences (e.g., inquiry-based learning, activating funds of knowledge). Thus, 3-D Learning provides a foundational pedagogical framework for transforming the science classroom from static to dynamic learning, which supports active engagement and leverages up-to-date teaching practices (National Research Council, 2012). It is structured as a spiraled curriculum that increases conceptual and linguistic complexity as students progress to higher grades, and it emphasizes the integration of three elements of science education shown here: practices, crosscutting concepts, and content.

Although it is beyond the scope of this chapter to explain the 3-D Learning framework in depth, we believe it is important to mention that the approaches to science education discussed in this chapter follow this framework. We encourage you to review both the NGSS and NSTA websites to familiarize yourself with 3-D Learning and its three elements (practices, crosscutting concepts, and content).

Chew on This!

Did you know that . . . ?
The utmost objective of the NGSS is not to have all students become scientists or engineers but rather to have students develop and use their scientific understanding to participate productively as citizens in society (McElhaney et al., 2019).

Deaf Experiences, Perspectives, and Core Recommendations

Many Deaf students face challenges and barriers to science education due to limited background knowledge due to lack of access to language and curriculum (Borron, 1978; Molander et al., 2001). Although they make observations about the natural and material world and their surrounding environment, their understanding of those experiences varies depending on who explains or clarifies what they observe. Their understanding of science ranges from well-developed to fuzzy or inaccurate. The filter through which they learn about science at home may be shaped by the level of communication access they have had with others, and it may be informed by the cultural experiences of their family. Historically, science curriculums do not include perspectives of Black, Indigenous, and People of Color (BIPOC), women, People with Disabilities, Deaf people, and other marginalized groups. Science may come across to these students as being "socially sterile, authoritarian, non-humanistic, positivistic, and absolute truth" (Aikenhead, 1996, p. 10). When there is a disconnect among students' backgrounds, lived experiences, and the science curriculum, as may happen for marginalized students, they may feel distanced if their teachers do not break down culturally based barriers to science.

As teachers, it is important to be aware of the knowledge about science that students bring from home that is provided through their family culture. This is called **funds of knowledge**. It is a good idea to become familiar with this concept because it can inform your science instruction by making connections between the knowledge about science each student brings to your classroom.

In addition, Deaf children's natural abilities have often not been tapped into during science. Deaf children are natural observers and will notice aspects of nature, machines, and how things work—this allows them to gather a lot of science information visually and kinesthetically. Although they are curious about how things work in our world, it is important that you tap into these natural abilities during science instruction. You can also leverage technology to aid scientific investigation and provide opportunities for your students to communicate their science ideas through multiple modalities, which is particularly beneficial for students with language delays.

Indeed, the challenge of learning science may be compounded when a Deaf student has limited language skills stemming from different factors, including home communication and inaccessibility to public information. For example, talking about a **science phenomenon** and providing minds-on, hands-on lab activities to help students better understand the phenomenon is a good approach you can use to nurture thinking and reasoning skills, which will help make science fun, engaging, and relevant. Talking about science also helps your students develop vocabulary, language, and critical thinking skills. Finally, it will help you learn the extent of your students' science understanding as well as their misconceptions. As you teach science and engage with your students about what they know, you can make your classroom a place where they develop a more informed and refined understanding of science.

Core Recommendations

We focus on the following three core recommendations for teaching science to Deaf students:

- Connect students' languages, backgrounds, and lived experiences to science.
- Engage students in talking about and doing science.
- Leverage technology in science instruction.

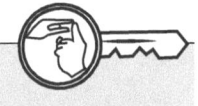

Key Vocabulary

Funds of knowledge are the background knowledge (here related to science) that children informally acquire outside school, which can directly or indirectly be connected to formal science learning.

Key Vocabulary

A **science phenomenon** is a natural or synthetic (human-made) occurrence that makes people think, wonder, and question. Some examples are coral reef erosion, snow fences, earlobes, and rusting.

Effective Practices for Deaf Learners

As mentioned, when your students enter the classroom, some of their science ideas may be underdeveloped (or "spontaneous," as Dixon-Krauss [1996] wrote). These ideas, however fuzzy, provide valuable information to help you guide the direction of their science education (Molander et al., 2001). It is essential that you provide your students the space to share their science ideas without fear of criticism or the expectation that they have to be "right." Each of the core recommendations discussed in this chapter encourages you to draw on your students' funds of knowledge and to use this to connect with targeted scientific concepts.

(MM) Core Recommendation 1: Connect Your Students' Languages, Backgrounds, and Lived Experiences to Science

Working with Deaf students calls for the use of culturally relevant pedagogy, a pedagogical approach grounded in the students' lived experience, particularly those from multilingual and multicultural backgrounds. It will help you tap into the funds of knowledge the students bring to your class, which may come from their family, community, and culture(s) (Seriki & Brown, 2019). When you are aware of your students' backgrounds, you can use examples that are relevant to their lived experiences to give context to connect science to social, linguistic, and cultural contexts.

> "We often forget that children themselves are a walking science curriculum. They bring to the classroom their family heritage, cultural knowledge, worldview, and lived experience related to science. They are curious observers, experimenters, and consumers in our natural and human-made world."
> —Chris Kurz

(MM) (ABAR) Develop Culturally Relevant Teaching in Your Science Lesson

You can develop culturally relevant science lessons by centering them in the language(s) and culture(s) of your students. When you combine the 3-D Learning practice of talking and doing science with the "spontaneous" knowledge your students have about science, along with their cultural perspectives, you can help frame your teaching lens through your students' cultural knowledge to make it more attainable to learn science. Further, using a critical lens to scrutinize the assumption that traditional science learning is the only way to learn science will help you to reach a wide range of students with multiple and intersecting identities. Embracing students' cultural knowledge may also make them feel more included and able to trust that their science ideas will be validated. It will also help them see how they can participate in local, national, and global scientific events and conversations. Here are some practices that will help you get started integrating culturally relevant teaching into your science classroom:

- Seek to understand as the student explains their thoughts and perspectives in their own words (including words in their home languages). Respond to and expand on their ideas (rather than correcting their language) by encouraging them to give examples or create visuals, such as by asking them to draw (e.g., draw a habitat of squirrels on the board) or through role-playing.
- Foster a safe and welcoming environment for all languages (e.g., offer an option for a student to make and share videos about their tribe's view of the relationship between the Sun and the Earth in the language(s) of their choice).
- Invite Deaf adults from diverse backgrounds, such as those who are Native American, Latinx, Black, LGBTQ+ (Lesbian, Gay, Bisexual, Transgender, Queer or

Questioning, and more), and so forth, to your classroom to talk about science or to serve as a mentor during the school year.
- Create opportunities for your students to investigate the scientific knowledge and practices of different cultures, such as:
  - Plant-based medication (e.g., Indigenous natural medicine; Eastern medicines)
  - Planting and harvesting (e.g., spacing cornstalk leaves for maximum light exposure)
  - Astronomy (e.g., the Mayan perspective of astronomy)
  - Sustainable use of harvested animals (e.g., some Native Americans use the body parts of a bison)
- Include children's stories and nonfiction books related to science that illustrate diverse cultural knowledge and practices (e.g., *We Are Water Protectors*, *The Boy Who Harnessed the Wind*, *Hidden Figures*, *Black Pioneers in Science and Invention*).
- Challenge your students to see that there is more than one correct way of knowing in science and that scientific knowledge continues evolving with diverse ideas and discoveries (e.g., dinosaur family tree, subatomic particles, germ theory).
- Ask your students questions about their lived experiences, and find ways to relate their experiences to science lessons (see Teacher Tale for an example).

 **Stick It Into Action!**

Culturally Relevant Dialogue in Science
Here, we model a discussion you could have with a student in a third-grade class that connects the students' lived experience as a member of the Blackfoot Tribe to a lesson on fish habitats.

Teacher	Today, we will be discussing fish that live in rivers.
Student	I love to fish. My tribe has an annual First Salmon Feast and we catch many fish and have a feast to honor the salmon.
Teacher	Oh, your tribe has a celebration related to catching and eating salmon? Are there different kinds of salmon that your tribe catches? Can you describe to the class what they look like?
Student	Yes, we catch fish that are different in size and color. I once caught a salmon that was red, long, and sleek. My mother caught a different salmon that was, like, gray and short.
Teacher	So, there are salmon in different colors and lengths. How does your tribe catch them?
Student	Salmon are swimming upriver from the ocean. We use a pole with a net to catch them.
Teacher	So, salmon come to the river from the ocean. Why is that?
Student	They go back to where they were born. After they become mature enough, they go out to the ocean. As adults, they return to breed babies.

Teacher	(to students) Thank you, (insert student's name), for sharing your family tradition. When we have more time, we'd love to learn more about the First Salmon Feast. Your salmon example shows that fish like salmon can live in both freshwater in the river and saltwater in the ocean. They have to acclimate their bodies for the change of water salinity—that is, the amount of salt dissolved in the water—as they travel from freshwater to saltwater and then back to freshwater.

By drawing on your students' knowledge and lived experiences, you can extend their knowledge by making a comment related to science, such as the discussion about the life cycle of salmon. You can foster a more equitable science classroom by intentionally engaging your students' language(s) and culture(s) in your science lessons.

Remember, your students bring knowledge and skills related to science to your classroom that you might not be aware of or familiar with. Allow them to share their personal and cultural viewpoints related to science while avoiding tokenizing a student. If the student is interested, we encourage you to invite members of your students' families and/or communities to share their lived experiences, such as the First Salmon Feast. This practice will help bridge your students' families/communities to the school community, increasing possibilities for students to make connections between school and their home lives. Science belongs to everyone, and everyone in the classroom and community has the ability to contribute to your students' holistic understanding of science in their lives.

(MM) (DI) Core Recommendation 2: Engage Students in Talking About and Doing Science

Here, we share strategies for developing students' scientific knowledge and skills. These include activating your students' scientific knowledge, engaging them in learning, and checking their comprehension throughout each lesson. In our experience, the more opportunities students have to actively participate in science activities, the better they will understand science and learn the content.

(DI) (MM) Activate Science Ideas

At the beginning of each science lesson, you can spark students' interest and curiosity by introducing a **science phenomenon** through videos, pictures, articles/stories, or demonstrations (physical or virtual). For example, if your lesson is about the weather, you can show a video of a tornado or physically demonstrate the motion of a twister in the classroom. The phenomenon serves as a conversation starter as you ask your students to share their observations and thoughts. You can include specific prompts to connect their funds of knowledge to the phenomenon and check for initial comprehension.

> "It is challenging to create instruction that includes culture in science lessons because we do not want to offend or misrepresent the cultures we intend to respect. So, instead of creating lessons based on what you think you know about a culture, you should establish a safe and welcoming classroom for your students to share their cultures, perspectives, and materials and then find ways to connect these with science. The goal is for your students to see a personal connection to science, rendering science learning meaningful.
>
> —Scott Cohen

Key Strategy

ESRU Protocol

Another strategy you can use to activate students' science ideas about tornados and other phenomena is the **ESRU protocol**. ESRU stands for **E**licit responses from your **S**tudents, **R**ecognize their comments, and **U**se the information from their comments to support their science learning (Araceli Ruiz-Primo & Furtak, 2006). It is essential that you have ways to encourage thinking and sharing of ideas. This is a great strategy to connect to your students' background knowledge and experiences while allowing them to drive their scientific understanding.

 Stick It Into Action!

ESRU Protocol

- **E**licit responses from your **S**tudents:
  - Ask students to formulate explanations or provide evidence of their experiences with a phenomenon.
    - For example, show your students a bottle that holds different liquids of varying densities and ask them what makes the liquids separate from each other.
- **R**ecognize their responses:
  - Repeat or rephrase students' responses for confirmation of the students' intended meaning and for other students.
  - Ask students to elaborate on their responses to their peers.
    - For example, your students might use words like *heavy, light, different weights, mass,* and so forth to describe liquids in the bottle. You can ask them to elaborate on their word choice and how it relates to their scientific understanding of the phenomenon.
  - **U**se the information from your students' responses as a starting point:
    - Discuss the science behind the phenomenon, starting with the information from their responses, and initiate group or individual learning activity.
    - For example, you can explain the concept of density by connecting to and expanding your students' word choices (e.g., "Tanita says that the oil is lighter. We can also say that it is less dense. What made the oil lighter?").

In the following Teacher Tale, we demonstrate how you can use ESRU to activate and monitor your students' understanding of the phenomenon of living and nonliving things.

This Teacher Tale provides an example of how to activate students' science ideas about a phenomenon (here, living and nonliving things). Students' observations and thoughts touched on several different scientific concepts, such as fertility, gas exchange, and cell division. In their investigative groups, they worked to make sense of these concepts, and each group had an opportunity to discuss different characteristics of living and nonliving things. Using the ESRU protocol, you can facilitate scientific discussions to help you identify your students' scientific knowledge backgrounds. You can deepen scientific knowledge by collecting and sharing evidence about a phenomenon with their peers and engaging them in scientific discussions.

Teacher Tale

Integrating ESRU in a Lesson on Living and Nonliving Things
I hooked my students into a lesson about the growth and development of organisms by first asking them to crack an egg without interlocking their fingers. My students loved the challenge and eventually collaborated with their classmates to plan and investigate different ways to crack the eggs. Some groups broke the egg, whereas others did not. Either way, they began to analyze egg cracking scientifically. I then started the ESRU protocol to get my students to ask questions about the phenomenon of living/nonliving things with a prompt on the board to elicit responses (E): "Is the egg a living or a nonliving thing?" I explained the prompt to the class and then observed the whole-group discussion (S) that followed. The discussion helped me identify their understanding of the phenomenon and potential misconceptions. Some thoughts they shared were, "Yes, it is living because we eat eggs for energy, and living things have energy," or "Yes, it is living because the egg has its mom and dad's DNA in it." In contrast, others answered, "No, the eggs are nonliving because I have a chicken coop that only houses hens, and none of our eggs can hatch chicks because there is no rooster" or "No, it's not living because it's not breathing, and living things need to breathe." I noted correct and incorrect information and then extended their responses in the next lesson (R) in which the students observed differences and similarities between the yolk from two eggs: one from my chicken coop with a rooster and one egg from the store. Some students noticed differences in the white spots or reddish marks on the yolk, such as a distinctive bulls-eye shape in the middle of the yolk. I then used (U) their information to provide a lesson on fertilized versus unfertilized eggs, which is one of the characteristics of living organisms (i.e., they must have the ability to reproduce). Some science ideas from the students started to emerge as they referred to comments from a previous lesson that gas exchange was one of the characteristics of a living thing and argued that because the egg was airtight, it should then be a nonliving thing. They connected these two ideas as evidence that the egg was a nonliving thing.

—*Elizabeth Henderson*

  ## Key Strategy

Using SWRL to Communicate Students' Science Ideas
Signing, Writing, Reading, and Listening (i.e., Viewing; SWRL) is a teaching strategy that involves multiple language modalities used to promote scientific discourse. The combination of signing (American Sign Language [ASL] and/or other sign languages), writing (English and/or other written languages), reading (English and/or other written languages), and listening/viewing (i.e., ASL and/or other languages) integrates each language domain that you and your students use in the science

Key Strategy (*continued*)

classroom to help them communicate their scientific understanding (Settlage et al., 2017). Allow your students to choose language(s) in which they are comfortable with expressing their ideas and questions. We encourage you to integrate at least two if not all, components of SWRL in each of your daily lessons. In doing so, you can also integrate objectives for reading, writing, viewing, and signing along with science objectives into daily lessons.

Stick It Into Action!

SWRL in the Science Classroom

- **Signing:** Provide opportunities for students to share their thoughts in signed language by
  - sharing personal stories about their experiences with science
  - engaging in constructive arguments based on data and evidence
  - giving class presentations and video recording their responses
- **Writing:** Provide opportunities for students to write (see Chapters 4 and 5 for more on implementing writing strategies) what they have learned by
  - taking notes in their notebook/journal
  - producing investigative reports
  - creating letters to local leaders on socioscientific issues
- **Reading:** Provide times for the students to read during class:
  - Make sure you include varying types of texts at varying reading levels in your science classroom, including the following:
    - Newspaper articles, scientific magazines, science fiction novels, stories, informational books, and scientific websites (see Chapter 7 for more on informational texts and Chapter 9 for more on primary sources).
- **Listening/Viewing:** Provide opportunities for your students to observe other people's comments and discussions by
  - participating in small-group and whole-group discussions
  - viewing signed videos (see Chapters 3 and 12 for viewing strategies)
  - watching guest speakers (Deaf adults when possible)

As you can see, the options for language usage and translanguaging in your classroom are endless (see Chapters 4, 10, and others for more examples of translanguaging). However, you need to intentionally embed SWRL in your lessons to empower your students to use languages to learn and express their science ideas. For instance, you can give your students a pretest on a science unit in the students' preferred language(s) and modalities to determine what your students already know about or don't know about a targeted topic, as demonstrated in the following Handstamp Sample. Here, both signed videos and written texts were embedded in the pretest to present the students with multilingual and multimodal opportunities to respond to a question about boiling water. This allows your students to use their preferred language(s) and modalities to demonstrate their knowledge. If students struggle with the questions, you can do one-to-one interviews with them to evaluate their knowledge.

Handstamp Sample

SWRL Responses

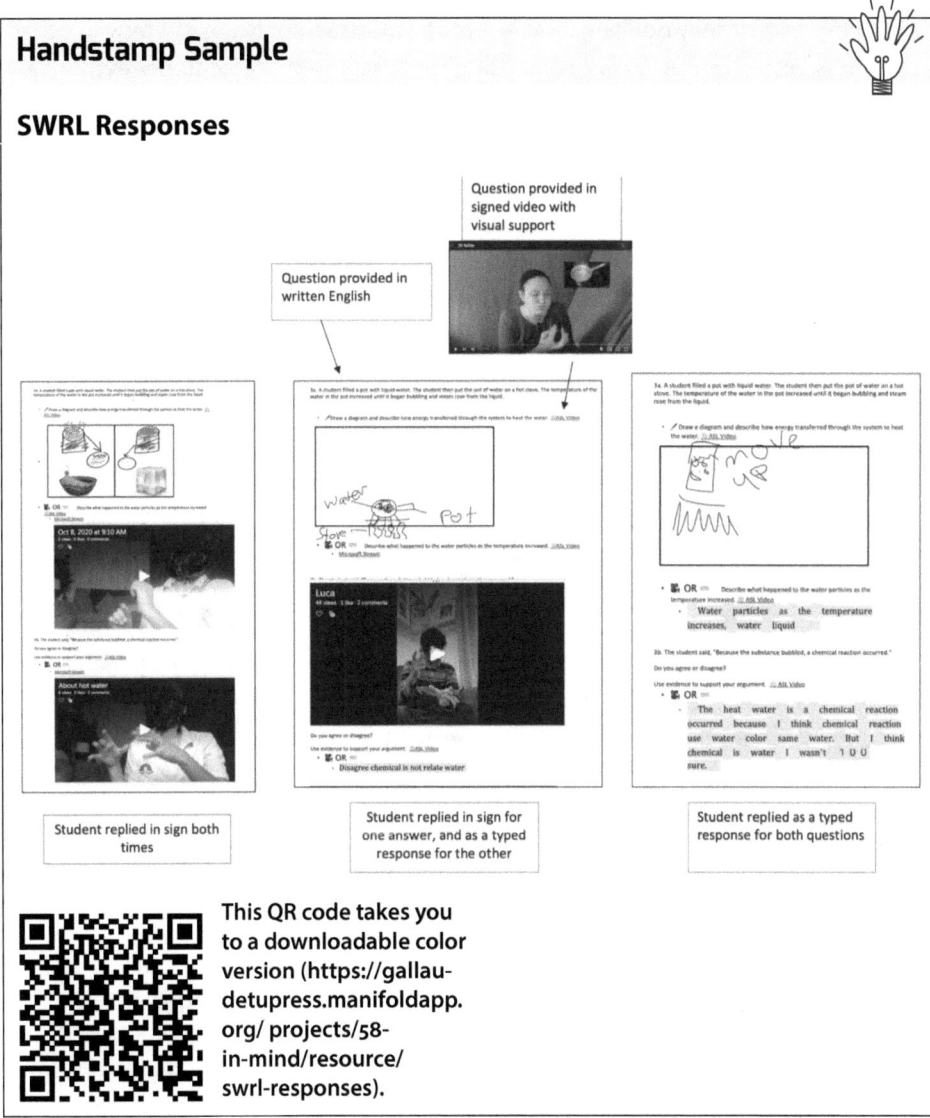

Integrating SWRL into your lessons allows students to develop skills to communicate scientific terms and concepts in signing and/or writing modalities. Deaf students naturally utilize translanguaging practices when discussing science (or other subjects), and they should be provided every opportunity to develop their language skills in different languages and modalities during science lessons. When implementing SWRL, we recommend you use concept expansion (elaborating on a concept) in combination with sandwiching (sign–fingerspell–sign) and chaining (image–sign–fingerspell–print–other modality) to support vocabulary development (see Chapters 2, 4, 6, and others for more examples of chaining).

Engage Students in Scientific Argument: The Cornerstone of Scientific Practices

Of course, not all students will become scientists, but you can help them come to understand how scientists engage in their work and communicate their understandings with other scientists and the general public. Scientists are trained to engage in constructive scientific arguments to build a case for their claims. You can support your students in developing the art of justifying their claims by using evidence and reasoning. Even if they don't become scientists, they can apply this strategy to other situations. To do this, we recommend using the teaching strategy, **claim–evidence–reasoning (CER).**

Key Strategy

Claim–Evidence–Reasoning (CER)

This strategy includes making a **claim** that answers a question, producing **evidence** using data, and **reasoning** why the evidence supports the claim (McNeill & Krajcick 2008).

Using the CER strategy, you can model the steps involved in developing a scientific argument. To do this, begin by providing a guiding question for your students to consider and to come up with a claim. Guide them in the collection of data they need for constructing an argument to support their claim. Finally, support them in how to develop an argument based on data and the scientific reasoning behind the interpretation of the data. Allow students to share differing claims and evidence that encourage them to listen to each other's arguments and reevaluate their initial claims as they see fit. This is an iterative activity where students can refine their thinking through scientific dialogue during their investigation.

Stick It Into Action!

Making a Point

In science discussions, we suggest you use an ASL-signed word equivalent to the phrase "the point is ..." (it is a larger version of the ASL word POINT made with an emphatic movement) instead of debate/argue. This signed word is handy for the following reasons:

- It is about making a point (claim) backed with data and evidence, not for the sake of arguing.
- You do not want to mislead your students into thinking they are arguing to prove that they are right.
- Instead, you want students to learn to decide which claim has the best scientifically reasoned evidence to support it as well as how one claim compares with another.

Teacher Tale

I reserved one bulletin board in my classroom for a CER activity with my middle school students. At the beginning of the unit on living and nonliving things, students were given pictures of different items which they categorized as living, nonliving, or unknown. First, they had to make a claim for each categorization they made. Then, students engaged in investigations, readings, discussions, and research to gather evidence for each claim they made. They recorded a video of themselves summarizing evidence to support the claim of the item in question. If they found contradictory evidence, they were required to provide a reason for moving the item to a different category. Every Friday, the class reviewed the CER video submissions and discussed the potential rearrangements. The item in question needed a vote from two-thirds of the class before we changed its category. The students got to see firsthand that robust reasoning could sway the number of votes. They then had an opportunity to reflect on how they could look for better evidence and reasoning to support a claim.

—*Elizabeth Henderson*

As described in Elizabeth's Teacher Tale, her students developed their skill on scientific argumentation by utilizing the CER strategy. They repeatedly were provided opportunities to practice this skill throughout the year in every unit by creating as many videos as they wanted and as often as they wanted. Here is a Handstamp Sample displaying the instructions and classifications on the bulletin board mentioned in the Teacher Tale board.

Handstamp Sample

CER Strategy With Living and Nonliving Things

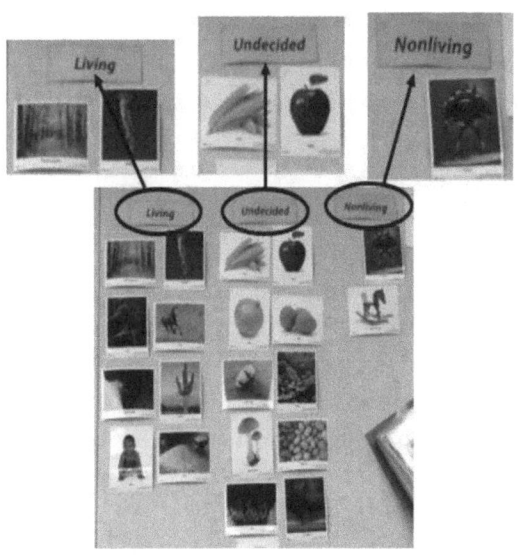
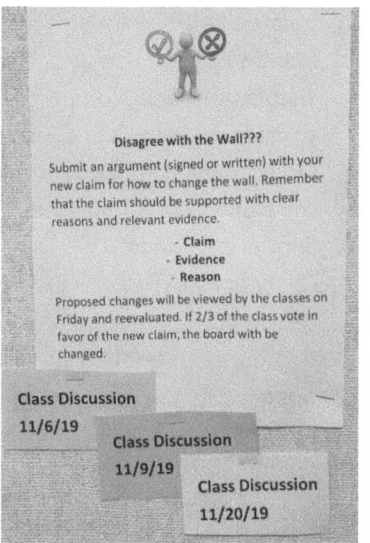

https://gallaudetupress.manifoldapp.org/projects/58-in-mind/resource/cer-strategy-with-living-and-nonliving-things

You can also use the CER strategy in a laboratory setting by having your students work in small groups to collect data, formulate arguments, and produce investigative reports. In the following Stick It Into Action, we outline steps for applying the CER strategy in small groups. The roles are designed to help students make their contributions to the claim and to push the group's thinking forward as they construct and evaluate their CER board. You can have a culminating activity of a poster showcase where one student from each group presents their poster; other group members can then visit other CER boards to ask questions and critique their findings.

 Stick It Into Action!

Implementing CER in Small Groups

To implement CER in small groups, have each group follow these steps:

1. Each student assumes a role in the group. Students can hold more than one role after they have a fundamental understanding of each role. Some ideas from Tools for Ambitious Science Teaching (https://ambitiousscienceteaching.org/tools-scaffolding/) include:
   - Group leader: Focuses on the big ideas.
   - Clarifier: Monitors the group's understanding of the content.
   - Questioner: Repeats and rephrases questions from members of the group.
   - Skeptic: Identifies weaknesses in the evidence and reasonings.
   - Progress monitor: Checks in on finished tasks and tasks needed to be completed.
2. Identify questions, issues, or situations about the phenomenon (all groups should have one prompt for the first few times they use the CER before allowing them to develop their own prompts.)
3. Collect data to construct evidence.
4. Develop reasoning for how their evidence is supported by data.
5. Formulate a claim.
6. Construct a CER poster including questions, claims, evidence, and reasoning.
7. Decide which group members will stay and present their poster first and who will rotate to see other posters. Continue to rotate until all groups have had the opportunity to view other groups' poster presentations.
8. Return to their small groups and debrief what they learned from other posters. Identify evidence and reasoning that they need to revise and refine in their group's poster.

The following Handstamp Sample shows an example of middle school students' slides portraying evidence and reasoning supporting their claim that fewer bacteria in the stomach affects one's health. The students used graphs from data collected in labs.

Handstamp Sample

Student CER Examples From a Microbiome Unit

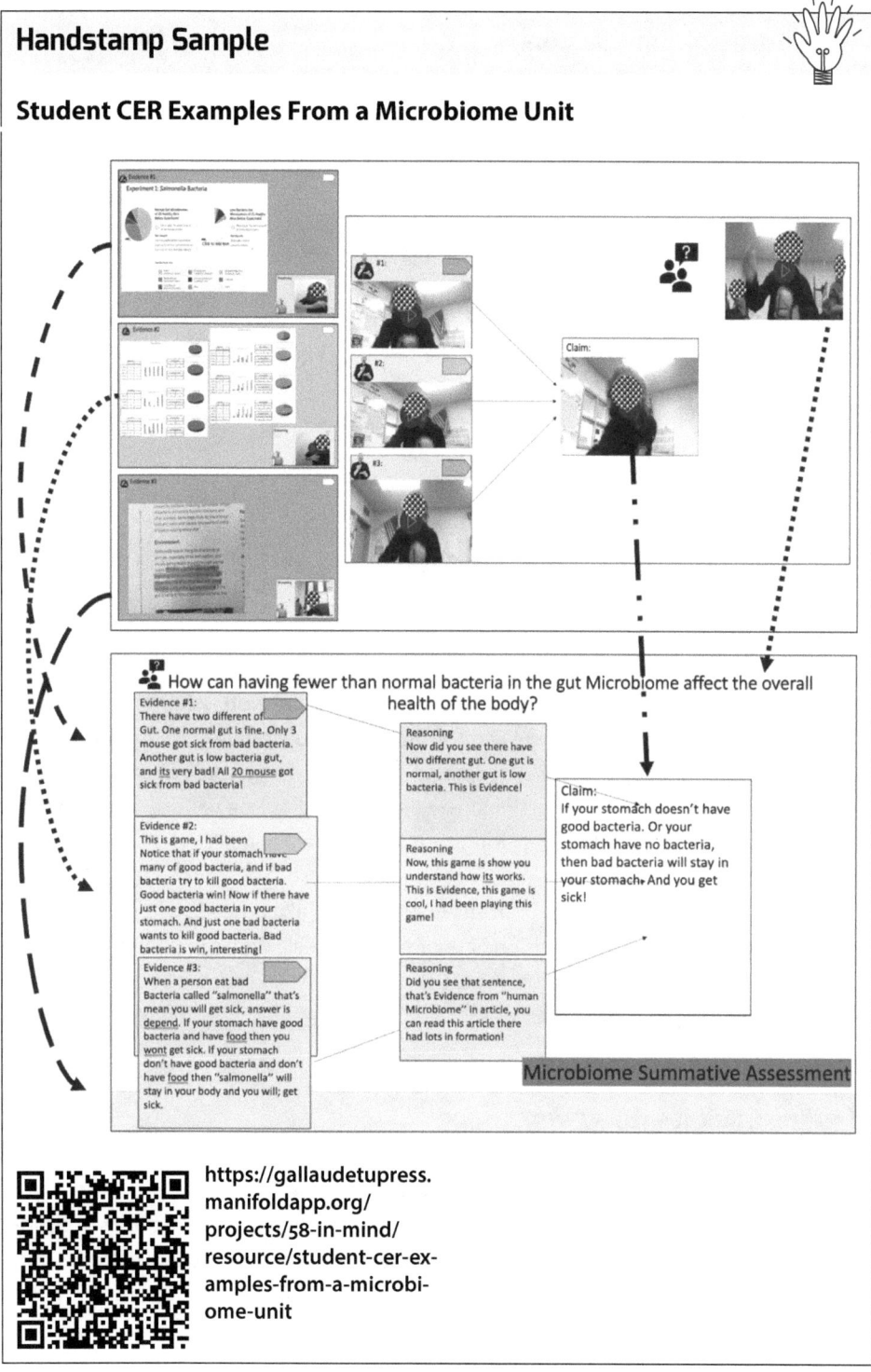

https://gallaudetupress.manifoldapp.org/projects/58-in-mind/resource/student-cer-examples-from-a-microbiome-unit

After they are done, each student should create an investigative report (written or recorded ASL; see Stick It Into Action). Doing this gives students the time to digest and reflect on their learning experience from the CER and also another opportunity for you to assess their learning.

Chew on This!

Did you know that ... ?
Some might suggest that children need to have language mastery *before* learning science, but increasing evidence disputes this claim, suggesting that students, including Deaf students, can learn science content and language simultaneously (Borron, 1978; Settlage et al., 2017).

You can encourage students' engagement in science activities and discussions by providing them with multiple CER opportunities. This helps them learn that scientific knowledge grows through questioning, exploring, observing, and discussing. As your students become more comfortable expressing various science ideas and questions, it will be helpful to have a system for tracking their evolving science thinking.

(MM) (MT) Stick It Into Action!

Produce an Investigative Report
Have each student produce an individual investigative report by doing the following:

- Choose whether they want to write a paper or make an ASL video of their investigative report.
- Create a presentation slide for each component of the CER from their poster with a picture-in-picture screen (see 1–3 in the previous Handstamp Sample) where they recorded their CER responses in ASL.
- View their ASL narrative and translate it into written English on each CER slide accordingly.
- Review and revise their investigative report to confirm that it connects to their science idea.
- Write or sign the formal investigative report.

(DI) (MM) Track Students' Evolving Science Ideas

One of the hallmark practices in science is note-keeping. Note-keeping allows students to keep track of information (e.g., numeric and qualitative data, drawings) and journal their thoughts, ideas, and questions. Scientists make notes of their observations, interpretations, and reflections. They are trained to use various tracking systems to organize their data sets throughout their experiments for data analysis and interpretation.

We strongly encourage you to have your students take notes as often as possible to track the evolution and expansion of their science ideas. They can do this by writing in a composition book or an online notebook, where you can encourage your students to video record their notes in ASL.

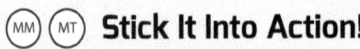

(MM) (MT) Stick It Into Action!

Journal Prompts and Sentence Starters
Table 11.1 contains prompts and sentence starters for students to choose from. We suggest you give students a choice in how they record their science ideas (e.g., write, sign and/or draw). Encourage them to practice using one or all of the columns.

Table 11.1. Prompts and Sentence Starters

Clarification on Science Idea	3-D Learning Connection	Home Cultural and Language Connection
• I don't understand ... • What would happen if ...	• Are there any patterns? • How did the matter change?	• Where do I see the phenomenon at home?

Table 11.1. (continued)

Clarification on Science Idea	3-D Learning Connection	Home Cultural and Language Connection
• I wonder … • I need more information about … • Is there another perspective? • Why does … • I noticed …	• How is the energy being used? • What system is it operating under? • This phenomenon is related to … • What are the constraints (limitations)?	• What is the cultural significance of the phenomenon to my family? • How would the phenomenon be described in another language and culture?

It is essential to provide students time to record their notes. After a class discussion, for example, you can pause and ask students to spend approximately 5–10 min writing or recording their thoughts generated from the class conversation. The focus should be on capturing their everchanging scientific ideas and thinking, and this can happen in many ways, such as jotting down a list, writing in English and/or their home languages, or drawing pictures. They may use technology to include images or record their thoughts by signing, typing, or drawing with a stylus.

To summarize, note-keeping has three benefits. First, your students practice documenting science learning as their science ideas develop and evolve. Documenting allows students to transfer ideas in their minds into a tangible, trackable form. Second, you can occasionally review your students' notes as a formative assessment to evaluate students' strengths and gaps and then use this information in subsequent lesson planning. Last, note-keeping plays an essential role in investigative activity when engaging in the work of scientists. Your students can review their notes to evaluate their learning, use them as references, and support/revise their scientific reasoning.

As you can see, centering your science lessons around your students' languages and modalities can lead to meaningful learning experiences to help them better understand the world around them.

Core Recommendation 3: Leverage Technology in Science

Technology has greatly enhanced access to multilingual and multimodal information about science, such as by sharing videos, using a computer or mobile device to find information on the internet, communicating information, collecting data, building models, and running simulations. You can use technology to create multimodal instructional materials in science. For example, you can add a QR code to a handout to direct students to access web-based information that may be signed in ASL, which will help the students better understand the content presented in English. Students can then use their phones or tablets to scan the QR code and open a video of a signed translation of the content. That way, students would not be stuck if they could not understand the written instructions.

(MM) (MT) **Stick It Into Action!**

Integrating QR Codes Into Science Labs

These instructional handouts (the first handout is on organisms in vials; the second is on ascorbic acid) include QR codes, which give students access to the ASL translation of the targeted sections of the English-based text.

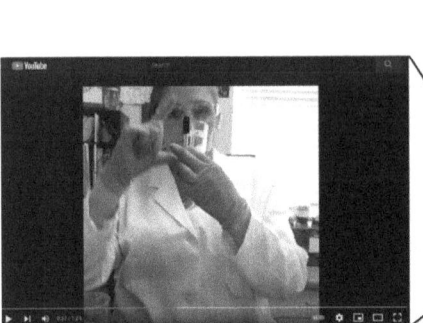

https://gallaudetupress.manifoldapp.org/projects/58-in-mind/resource/integrating-qr-codes-into-science-labs

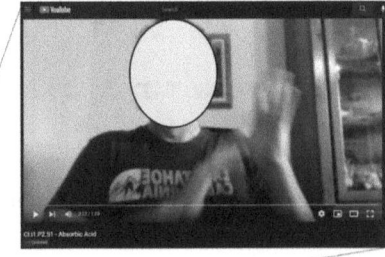

https://gallaudetupress.manifoldapp.org/projects/58-in-mind/resource/integrating-qr-codes-example-2

We recommend that you include QR codes or links to signed video translations on all of your handouts. You can also include links for additional languages for students who have home languages other than English and ASL. That would empower your students by providing opportunities to use translanguaging strategies as they become more active participants in their learning at their own pace. You can also create a checkpoint for your students to check in before advancing to the next step, which will also help you keep track of their progress and provide the opportunity for you to offer feedback as needed on their investigation plan. You can use checkpoints whether the students are working individually or in small groups.

As demonstrated in the previous CER Handstamp Sample, technology also allows students to provide responses in multiple modalities. In this additional Handstamp Sample, Elizabeth encouraged her students to practice responding through multiple modalities (e.g., mathematical, signed, and written) to explain the natural phenomenon of why a bowling ball floats in the Dead Sea but sinks elsewhere (due to the high-density ratio of salt to water).

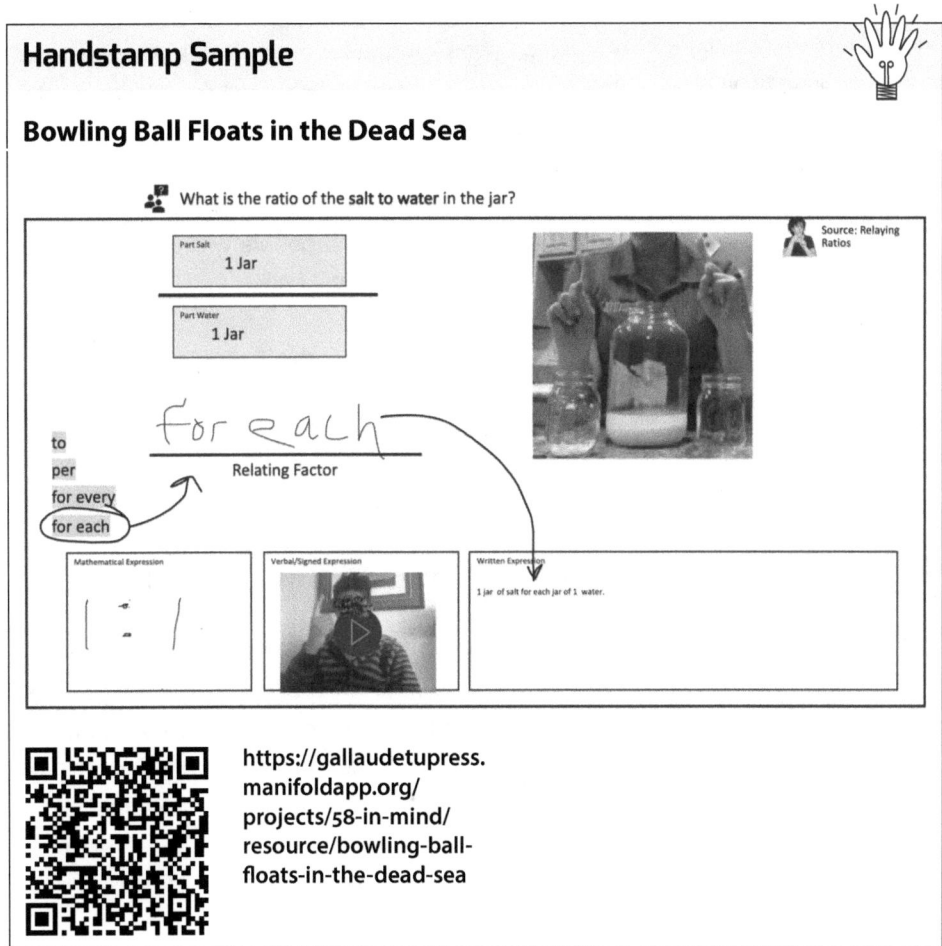

Additional Things to Consider

(PI) (MM) (MT) Incorporate Deaf Perspectives and Experiences in Your Science Lessons

If you ask your students who their Deaf role model in science is, they may say, "I do not know," "My Deaf science teacher," or "I don't have one." Although it may feel challenging to introduce Deaf role models to your students in science, there are Deaf people in a wide range of science-related fields whom you could introduce to your students in person, through videoconferencing, or via media. By introducing the work and life experiences of Deaf scientists, you can help your students visualize themselves doing science. In addition, the number of science-related programs, camps, and competitions for Deaf students across the country is growing, which provides Deaf students with opportunities to engage in science with both Deaf peers and adults.

There are also websites with videos that show Deaf people talking about science in ASL and/or other signed languages that you can include in your instruction. For example, the **Atomic Hands** website (https://atomichands.com/) has a library of Deaf scientists explaining science ideas in ASL (see Recommended Readings/Viewings). You can use these videos to model to your students how to talk about science in ASL like Deaf scientists do.

Providing opportunities for your students to interact and collaborate with Deaf people who are in science-related careers has multiple benefits:

- They can expose your students to current scientific technology and tools used in their fields.
- Your students can communicate directly with Deaf scientists without an interpreter.
- They can inspire students to consider possible careers related to science and serve as Deaf role models to look up to for advice and mentoring.

In addition to meeting Deaf scientists in person or online, you should also expose your students to stories about Deaf people who have made contributions to science, such as Annie Jump Cannon, a Deaf female astronomer, and the Gallaudet 11, test subjects who participated in NASA experiments for space travel. These are examples of Deaf people that you can teach about as part of a lesson on astronomy.

As mentioned previously, Deaf students are diverse, and your classroom can become a site of cultural and knowledge exchange. Thus, incorporating Deaf perspectives in addition to students' home cultures and languages in your teaching is the key to making science learning meaningful, relevant, and engaging. It also helps your students connect science to their identities, including their Deaf identity.

> "I didn't begin my teaching career as a science teacher. Originally, I was primarily an English language arts teacher, with only one life science class in my schedule. The middle school science teacher in my school was amazing at mentoring, observing my teaching, and meeting after school to help set up the labs. He made science hands-on and applicable to real life. That experience provided the catalyst for me to pursue science teaching. I quickly connected to science organizations, such as the NSTA and CASE (California Association of Science Educators), and fervently attended their science workshops and webinars. Once NGSS rolled out, I was ecstatic! I took many NGSS-related workshops with NSTA and CASE because they provided valuable information and strategies for using 3-D learning in the classroom. I also gained invaluable networking experience because it connected me with other amazing and innovative science teachers. Eventually, I became a recipient of the Presidential Award of Excellence in Mathematics and Science Teaching, where phenomenal teachers from across America are recognized and share their innovative work in science teaching, including treasured resources! I may not have a college degree in science, but being passionate about keeping up to date with the latest practices and research in science teaching has transformed me into an expert science teacher. There is zero doubt that any Deaf educator, regardless of background, could become a master science teacher with proper resources and support!
>
> —Elizabeth Henderson

SCIENCE

 ## ASL Science Vocabulary

All content areas have specific vocabulary and concepts that can be expressed in any language. You should become familiar with how science concepts are expressed in ASL as demonstrated in the following Stick It Into Action (see Kurz et al., 2020, for further information).

Stick It Into Action!

Conceptually Accurate Scientific Vocabulary in ASL
When you introduce a scientific word in English or other languages that is not familiar to students and does not have a lexical equivalent in ASL, you should then do the following:

- Discuss what the term means.
- If you are knowledgeable in science content and a native signer, you could discuss ways to express specialized scientific concepts in ASL after your students understand the concept. If you are not a content expert and/or native signer, you should reach out to and invite someone who has content expertise and is a native signer of ASL to help you and your students express the scientific term.
- Use the specialized ASL science vocabulary in your lecture and encourage students to use it in their presentations or when participating in science discussions with their classmates.
- Use chaining or sandwiching strategies to reinforce vocabulary development in multiple languages and modalities.

> ### Teacher Tale
>
> One of my student teachers, Emily Sidansky, developed a card game for her biology class to teach the concept of mitosis. The cards include images/English texts of the stages of mitosis from a single cell to the daughter cells and cell destructions. The objective of the game is to play the cards according to the order of stages of mitosis. Each student gets five to seven cards, and the person with the first card places their card face up to start the order. They must play either stage by stage or skip one or more stages in the order. They can start over by going back to the beginning of the mitosis stage order (e.g., the prophase stage) by placing a cell destruction card (i.e., cancer, apoptosis). As the students play their cards, they need to sign and fingerspell the stage of mitosis or cell destruction on the card while the rest of the students check for the correct signed word and explanation. If the signed word and explanation are correct, the next student takes their turn. If not, the student has to take the card back. Students take turns in a clockwise direction and continue to play until one of their hands is empty. The students loved playing the game as they became more confident in communicating their science ideas in ASL with each other.
>
> —*Chris Kurz*

Professional Development With a Professional Organization in Science Teaching

Finally, we encourage you to seek resources and professional development opportunities such as the NSTA. If you become a member, you can participate in workshops and webinars and learn more about 3-D learning and how to implement high-quality science teaching and learning. They also publish assessments and evaluative resources, such as formative assessments.

All of us are NSTA members and have attended NSTA conferences as well as National Deaf Education Conference events. The National Deaf Education Conference provides workshops and presentations that align the Deaf perspective with contemporary training in science education.

(MM) (ES) (MT) Bringing It All Together

In this section, we present a unit plan derived from Elizabeth's middle school science unit on states of matter that integrates each of our core recommendations. Although the lake in this unit is specific to the geographic area where she teaches, you could modify it to be any lake near where you live. In this unit, she used Flip, a digital platform for students to share their video responses in ASL, but other technologies can be used. She also provided students with video responses in ASL, including supplemental documents such as images, drawings, and PowerPoint slides. In this example, each class was 50 min long.

Big Idea: Unit Plan on States of Matter in Folsom Lake

Students explored how changes in states of matter (i.e., gas, liquid, and solid) affect the water levels in Folsom Lake. Students learned that matter is made of invisible tiny atoms or molecules that change from one state to another based on energy transfer and molecular attraction. For example, the energy released from the sun during droughts creates increased evaporation rates of water (i.e., change from liquid to gas) and results in less condensation of water back in the form of precipitation (i.e., change from gas to liquid).

3-D Learning Performance Expectation (NGSS)
- Students investigate phase change at the macroscale and molecular scale (scale, proportion, and quantity) using physical and digital models and hands-on experiences to construct explanations about how energy transfer and molecular attraction determine whether a substance will change phase (energy and matter).

The unit covers the core ideas of the role of water, its physical structure, and human impact on it. Students will ask questions and define problems, build and use models, analyze and interpret data, and engage in arguments based on evidence (see Table 11.2).

ASL Standards

- Comprehension and Collaboration
  - Engage effectively in a range of collaborative discussions (e.g., one-to-one, in groups, teacher-led) with diverse partners on topics, texts, and issues, building on others' ideas and expressing their own clearly.
- Presentation of Knowledge and Ideas
  - Present claims and findings, emphasizing salient points in a focused, coherent manner with relevant evidence, valid reasoning, and well-chosen details; use appropriate eye contact, appropriate signing space, and clear production.
  - Integrate multimedia and visual displays into presentations to clarify information, strengthen claims and evidence, and add interest.
  - Adapt signs to a variety of contexts and tasks, demonstrating command of formal ASL when indicated or appropriate.

Materials

- Readings (news articles related to Folsom Lake, articles related to energy and matter in the water cycle, and documents related to current water issues [water footprint, water conservation, water scarcity, water pollution, and water sustainability] and human activity, and the school's middle school life science textbook)
- Videos and pictures of Folsom Lake (2011–2014)
- Lab tools for experiments

Description of Days 1–8 of the Unit

Table 11.2. States of Matter: Energy Transfer

Class Period	Activity Summary
Day 1	**Introducing "Natural Phenomenon: States of Matter"** • Show videos, news articles, and images of Folsom Lake between 2011 and 2014, with proximity to students' communities. (CR 1) • Implement the ESRU protocol to discuss the phenomenon of the drought in California. (CR 2)
Day 2	**Teacher facilitates experiment on evaporation/condensation** • Identify several experiments from NSTA resources to do with your students. • Assign students to CER investigative groups and have them take notes on procedure, setup, and observation. Leave experiments on display for the duration of the unit as students continue to record their observations at the beginning of each class. (CR 2)
Day 3	**Lecture on energy transfer/phase change** • Show and discuss the aslclear.org ASL lecture video on matter. (CR 3) • Implement ESRU discussion on matter. (CR 2) • Have students respond on Flip by explaining the experiment and elaborating with home/life examples of water phase change. (CR 1)

Table 11.2. (continued)

Class Period	Activity Summary
Day 4	**Student-led experiment on energy transfer/phase change** • Have students explore phase changes and water cycles with an interactive simulation website such as PhET.colorado.edu. (CR 3) • Implement ESRU to discuss the phase changes and water cycles of the lake. (CR 2)
Day 5	**Reading and writing about energy transfer/phase change** • Present articles for students to read and implement SWRL to discuss the role of energy and matter in the water cycle. Have students record their thoughts in their notebooks. (CR 2)
Day 6	**Create a CER poster on the processes of water cycle that contribute to drought in California** • Have students create their CER poster responding to the guiding question (using evidence from Day 5 readings) "What process of the water cycle is likely to contribute to drought in California?" (CR 2)
Day 7	**Engage in an argument using a CER poster** • Small-group CER poster showcase. (CR 2)
Day 8	**Produce an investigative report** • Students create an investigative report (CR 2) using PowerPoint or digital poster embedding CER. (CR 3).
Day 9	**Water cycle application: Water sustainability SWRL** • Provide students handouts and readings on current water issues (e.g., water footprint, water conservation, water scarcity, water pollution, water sustainability) and human activity. (CR 1) • Read and discuss water issues to identify an issue the class would like to turn into a social media campaign. (CR 2)
Day 10	**Water cycle application: Water sustainability SWRL** • Have students produce ASL videos and write about water awareness that includes scientific background about water at the molecular level and energy transfer among phase changes influencing the drought conditions in California. (CR 2) • Design a social media campaign as a class, embedding their ASL videos and writing. (CR 3)

Note: CER = claim–evidence–reasoning; CR = core recommendation; ESRU = **E**licit responses from your **S**tudents, **R**ecognize their comments, and **U**se the information from their comments; NSTA = National Science Teaching Association; SWRL = signing, writing, reading, and listening.

SCIENCE

Handstamp Sample

This is a student diagram explaining the process of water separating from sugar molecules in a water–sugar mixture. The diagram is based on one of the class experiments where gas rises from the water solution.

Your Turn to Practice!

Develop a Unit Plan About a Scientific Phenomenon

Now, it is your turn! Develop a unit plan that includes multiple lessons about a targeted phenomenon. You may follow a unit plan template from the school where you work or from your college methods course if you are a teacher candidate. Otherwise, feel free to design your own format for your unit plan or refer to unit plan examples in other chapters. Follow these steps:

- Identify the content topic and its natural or artificial phenomenon for your unit and a targeted grade level.
- Identify the NGSS 3-D learning standards or state core learning standards as well as ASL Standards.
- Create an outline of the unit that includes at least one strategy from each of the core recommendations.
- Select several formative assessments and a summative assessment from the NSTA resources that reflects each component in the SWRL recommendation.

  Keep in mind the following questions as you develop your unit and lessons:

- How are you centering your students' languages and cultures?
- Do your students have opportunities to express their science ideas in multimodal and multilingual ways?
- How are you planning to engage in scientific discussion with your students?

Develop Your Lesson Plan From Day 1 of Your Unit

- Create a lesson plan for Day 1 of your unit. You may follow a template provided by your school or professor if you are a teacher candidate. Include the following:
  - Lesson objectives aligning with state standards (including objectives for both science and ASL)
  - Procedures
  - Materials for class activities and science experiments
  - Guiding questions developed by you or your students
  - At least one of the core recommendations with one strategy in this chapter. Provide details on how you will use the strategy with your students.
  - Several ways to assess your students. Allocate time for evaluating the progress of student learning during the lesson, and ensure that you give feedback to each student.

Teach Your Lesson

Teach the lesson with your own students or in a mock setting if you are a teacher candidate.

Reflect on Your Teaching

After you have implemented your lesson, it is important to reflect on your experience. Consider these questions:

- What went well?
- What would you change/do differently if you taught this lesson again?
- After assessing your students, how well did they learn the targeted objectives?

You cannot plan the next lesson without knowing where your students stand with their science learning. It is important to keep track of your students' evolving science ideas. First, however, you need to reflect on how students responded to your lesson. Reflect on these additional questions as you review the lesson you implemented:

- Was the phenomenon meaningful to my students?
- Were the strategy and resources/materials appropriate for the level of my students' science ideas?
- How could I improve the strategy or resources/materials for next time?
- How did I promote my students to use their languages and linguistic repertoires to construct their science ideas?
- What cultural connections did I make in the lesson, and were they used appropriately?

Recommended Readings/Viewings

For Teachers/Teacher Candidates

- *Teaching Science to Every Child: Using Culture as a Starting Point* (3rd ed.) (Settlage et al., 2017) is a valuable handbook on contemporary science teaching.
- STEM Teaching Toolkit (http://stemteachingtools.org/tools). This is a free online resource that aligns NGSS with professional development modules and many different tools that would help you fine-tune your pedagogical technique.
- *Silence of the Spheres: The Deaf Experience in the History of Science* (Lang, 1994). This is a comprehensive list of biographies of Deaf people contributing to science.
- *Seeing Students Learn Science* (https://www.nap.edu/catalog/23548/seeing-students-learn-science-integrating-assessment-and-instruction-in-the-classroom). This free PDF from the National Academies of Sciences, Engineering, and Medicine offers guidance on developing assessments that are aligned with 3-D Learning.

For Using With Students

- Atomic Hands (https://www.atomichands.com/). Atomic Hands is the Deaf-owned enterprise of two Deaf women, Dr. Alicia Wooten and Dr. Barbara Spiecker, with more than 130 videos on various science topics, from scientific concepts to current events to their journey to becoming a scientist.
- CSD Learns: STEM Education Resources (https://csdlearns.com/). CSD Learns developed resources on STEM education for Deaf/Hard of Hearing teachers and students, including toolkits featuring Deaf role models.
- *Wild Saga With Call* (https://www.youtube.com/@wildsagawithcall6689). Some refer to Brandon Call, the leading biologist in *Wild Saga with Call,* as the Deaf version of Steve Irwin. He produced this episodic series exploring nature and wildlife while explaining it in ASL. He has a YouTube and a Facebook page that you and your students could follow about wildlife.

Conclusion

The practices we have described in this chapter are based on both research and experience. We hope this guide provides you with the foundation to become an effective science teacher and that you will find science teaching enjoyable and rewarding. Just remember that when teaching science, it is vital to build relationships with each of your students. Integrate their cultural heritages, languages, and world viewpoints into your science lessons to help them make connections to science. Cultivate your students' science understanding by thinking, discussing, and learning about it. Deaf students need to be provided with multiple opportunities to communicate their science ideas through ASL, English, and their home languages daily. Be intentional about using multilingual, multimodal, and multicultural approaches in lesson planning. Your teaching practice will evolve as you continue to use the strategies we have recommended in this chapter. Remember to keep updated with the growing body of scientific knowledge and skills as well as with the current science pedagogical practices through professional development from NSTA or your state science teacher association. Ultimately, the experiences you provide your students in science class can make positive and lifelong impacts whether or not they become scientists. By implementing the skills provided in this chapter, you are providing them with foundational tools they can apply in everyday life and learning.

Sticking Points

- Incorporate your students' cultural heritages and worldviews into science lessons.
- Foster diversity by promoting multilinguistic, multimodal, and multicultural science learning.
- Integrate technology to broaden their scientific knowledge and connect to scientists, including Deaf scientists.

Incorporating the Arts Across the Curriculum

Chapter 12

Fred Michael Beam
Scott Gentzke
Debbie Golos
Chris Kurz

If you teach a subject area such as science, math, reading/writing, or social studies, you may wonder how to incorporate the arts or even wonder *why* it is essential to do so. There is unlimited potential to tap into the arts regardless of what grade or subject you teach. Not only can the arts motivate your students to engage in learning, but they can also foster a positive sense of self through creative expression. In addition, because the arts provide kinesthetic, tactile, and visual ways to communicate, they support communication access and development for Deaf students, particularly among those experiencing language delays or language deprivation. In this chapter, we show you how to include the arts in preschool through Grade 12 (P–12) by expanding on examples previously provided in other chapters and by providing additional examples from Deaf artists and us. Ultimately, this chapter offers strategies for teachers to integrate the arts across the curriculum to support their students' learning.

Who Are We?

As authors, we have a variety of experiences within visual, performing, and media arts, including how to incorporate them into instruction across the curriculum. An experienced performer, dancer, director, teacher, ASL director, and choreographer with many acting credits that include *Fall Out Shelter* at the Kennedy Center, *Othello* at Gallaudet University, and *I Didn't Hear That Color,* the first Black Deaf play ever produced, I (Fred Beam) am currently the outreach coordinator for Sunshine 2.0 at the

Student from St. Mary's School for the Deaf experimenting with fingerpainting.

National Technical Institute for the Deaf (NTID). I have also toured nationwide in one-man shows and established the Leadership Training in Theater Arts for Deaf and Hard of Hearing People of Color.

After earning a bachelor's degree in illustration and a master's degree in art education, I (Scott Gentzke) taught visual arts for students in prekindergarten to age 21 at Rochester School for the Deaf for 10 years. I was also a resident advisor at Delaware School for the Deaf and a principal and dean of students at St. Mary's School for the Deaf for several years. In both roles, I was able to incorporate the arts to support students in developing creative problem-solving skills and becoming more aware of how they observe the world. I am currently a faculty member for the Master of Science in Secondary Education for Students Who Are Deaf or Hard-of-Hearing department at Rochester Institute of Technology's National Technical Institute for the Deaf and obtained my doctorate from the Critical Studies in the Education of Deaf Learners program at Gallaudet University.

As a professor with a background in creative writing and theater and a former sixth-grade reading/writing teacher, I (Debbie Golos) have always tried to incorporate the arts in education, including teacher training. My research focus is on language, literacy, well-being and identity development, and developing and evaluating the effectiveness of interactive educational media in ASL. Through my experiences, when given opportunities to engage in the arts, I have seen Deaf students' creativity and identities flourish!

While teaching STEM (science, technology, engineering, and math) and methods courses, I (Chris Kurz) have always sought artistic creativity in expressing academic concepts. This includes working with art and media teachers to develop and implement shared units on science, technology, engineering, and math (STEM) concepts (e.g., fractals, transformations, atomic structures, time–space fields). This reinforces the importance of STEAM, with the *A* being the arts.

Deaf Experiences, Perspectives, and Core Recommendations

There is a long history of connecting American Sign Language (ASL) and the arts in Deaf schools, Deaf clubs, and Deaf theaters. For example, storytelling in ASL has been a tradition for more than two centuries, and Deaf people have been telling ASL stories through media for more than 100 years (see Chapter 3). Although some of these treasures were lost (e.g., old stories in Black ASL, ASL folklore), we are increasingly finding ways to preserve this rich heritage.

Schools serving Deaf students often share these traditions by providing opportunities for the students to become involved in plays, storytelling, and visual arts, through after-school activities as well as through art and drama classes in ASL. Through the arts, there are many opportunities to provide diverse Deaf role models, support students' language development and learning, and encourage students to explore and express themselves, which can lead to a positive sense of self. However, this rich artistic heritage has often not been tapped to its fullest by teachers of the Deaf and across the P–12 curriculum.

As mentioned in other chapters, Deaf children need access to Deaf role models from diverse backgrounds—whether live, virtual, or through media and literature (Cawthon et al., 2016). Yet, there has not always been enough access to these role models through media, art, and literature. One reason for this is that Deaf people haven't often been portrayed from a cultural perspective, such as being shown within a Deaf environment or communicating with other Deaf characters in ASL (e.g., Golos, 2010). This is a result of limited opportunities being made available for Deaf people in the writing, development, and production processes. For example, although Deaf actors have been filmmaking and/or have been on television for more than 100 years (e.g., Bernard Bragg's *The Quiet Man*, a weekly television show in San Francisco; Linda Bove's recurring appearance on *Sesame Street* [1971–2003]), few roles were written, developed, or directed by Deaf people. Deaf people were not often provided opportunities to engage in these leadership roles or even consulted when their languages, cultures, or communities were portrayed.

However, this has improved in recent years with an increase in television and literature incorporating positive Deaf characters. For example, AMC's *The Walking Dead* introduced Connie, who uses ASL to communicate with other characters on the show and is portrayed by multiracial Deaf actor Lauren Ridloff. Ridloff also portrays Makkari, the first Deaf superhero, on the silver screen in 2021's *Eternals* from Marvel Studios. Black Deaf actor CJ Jones created the Na'vi sign language for the indigenous species who live on Pandora in *Avatar: The Way of Water*.

Another reason Deaf students have not had access to role models through the arts is that Deaf role models, in general, have not been widely integrated across the P–12 curricula. Recent research has indicated that teachers are not regularly inviting Deaf adults into the classroom or incorporating books/media with Deaf people or ASL into early childhood classrooms (Golos et al., 2018). As such, there are many missed opportunities to share the work and experiences of diverse Deaf artists. Deaf children need

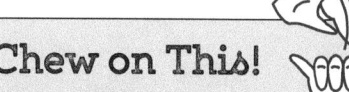

Chew on This!

Did you know that . . . ?

- Children, by nature, are artists! They just need opportunities to let their creativity shine.
- Art can be used to strengthen Deaf students' language and literacy skills and promote self-expression.
- Despite what many may think, Deaf people enjoy dance and music. Deaf artists who are well-known for their musical talents include The Wild Zappers and the National Deaf Dance Theater (Deaf dance companies), NTID Sunshine 2.0 (Deaf educational theater troupe), Warren "WaWa" Snipe (rapper, writer, and performer), Rosa Lee Timm (performing artist), Justina Miles (ASL performer), Bob Hiltermann (drummer), and Sean Forbes (rapper).

Proud to Be Deaf. A bulletin board mural created by elementary students at St. Mary's School for the Deaf.

exposure to role models and particularly those who are Deaf and/or Black, Indigenous, or People of Color (BIPOC). With intentional integration of the arts into your teaching, there are many opportunities to include diverse Deaf role models!

In addition to Deaf role models, providing Deaf students opportunities to engage in the arts is particularly important for the many arriving at school with language delays. As mentioned throughout this book, the impacts of language deprivation are significant and long-lasting (e.g., Gulati, 2018). By providing opportunities for students to participate in the arts, Deaf students gain not only an outlet for their feelings, motivations, and frustrations but also an additional means of communication.

As educators of the Deaf, we must value Deaf students' languages, cultures, and histories, and this includes Deaf artists. You can help enhance the role of the arts in Deaf students' education by exposing students to diverse Deaf artists, including those who are BIPOC, DeafBlind, and Lesbian, Gay, Bisexual, Transgender, Queer or Questioning, Intersex, Asexual, and/or more (LGBTQIA+), and provide opportunities for them to engage in creative expression. In doing so, you help foster positive identity development while also supporting their language development and learning.

Core Recommendations

In this chapter, we provide two core recommendations to integrate visual, media, and performing arts (subsequently referred to as "the arts") into content areas across the P–12 curriculum.

- Provide role models from diverse backgrounds through the arts.
- Embed opportunities for creative expression to engage, motivate, and learn.

Effective Multilingual Practices for the Arts

In this section, we provide examples of how you can integrate our core recommendations throughout the curriculum. We also illustrate how you can align these recommendations with three out of the following four National Core Arts Standards (creating, performing, and connecting).

National Core Arts Standards

1. *Creating:* Conceiving and developing new artistic ideas and work
2. *Performing/Presenting/Producing:*
   Performing: Realizing artistic ideas and work through interpretation and presentation
   Presenting: Interpreting and sharing artistic work
   Producing: Realizing and presenting artistic ideas and work
3. *Responding:* Understanding and evaluating how the arts convey meaning
4. *Connecting:* Relating artistic ideas and work with personal meaning and external context

We also encourage you to review your state standards for the arts and try to integrate objectives from those standards, along with ASL and content area standards, into your lessons as well.

(MM) (ABAR) (PI) (DI) Core Recommendation 1: Provide Role Models from Diverse Backgrounds Through the Arts

Deaf students need to be able to see themselves and diverse others represented through media, theater, and the arts to reflect on who they are and learn about the world around them. You can do this by (a) viewing and discussing diverse Deaf art/Deaf artists and (b) integrating interactive media in ASL with Deaf role models into your instruction.

Handstamp Sample

Learning to see themselves
St. Mary's School for the Deaf students show their De'VIA self-portrait project with Deaf artist Nancy Rourke.

(PI) Chew on This

Did you know that . . . ?
There are many diverse Deaf artists:

- Michelle Banks and Alexandria Wailes were the first Black Deaf actors who performed with Michael Davis, a Latino actor, in the musical *Big River* at the Mark Taper Forum in Hollywood, California, in 2002. Christina Dunams joined the cast with returning actress Alexandria Wailes to be the first Black Deaf actor to perform on Broadway in New York City at the American Airlines Theatre in 2003 (https://playbill.com/article/deaf-wests-big-river-shines-on-broadway-as-roundabout-revival-opens-july-24-com-114432).
- In 2017, NTID exhibited the artwork of more than 50 Latinx Deaf artists, including Claudia Jimenez, Miguel Diaz Calderon, Rolando Sigüenza, Iris Nelia Aranda, and Drago Renteria.
- Alaqua Cox, a Native American Deaf actress from Menominee and Mohican American Nations, is the first to play an Indigenous character who is Deaf and uses ASL: superhero Maya Lopez/Echo in the Marvel Cinematic Universe.

View and Discuss Deaf Art and De'VIA

It is important for you to provide opportunities for your students to learn and appreciate Deaf art and Deaf artists so they have Deaf role models they can look up to who are artists, actors, performers, and directors. This is a great way to target the art standard of connecting art in meaningful ways by providing role models who are DEAF SAME, which can inspire students to see themselves as artists. One way you can get started is by introducing De'VIA.

First defined and recognized as an art genre in 1989, De'VIA stands for Deaf View/Image Art, which is art that emphasizes the Deaf experience and what it means to be Deaf. It is defined as:

- art that is representative of Deaf experiences
- artistic strategies that highlight color contrast and centralized focus
- visual fine arts and alternative media
- not exclusive to Deaf artists (e.g., Codas)
- not inclusive of all Deaf artists

We recommend you review https://deviacurr.wordpress.com/devia-curr/what-is-devia/ for suggestions on how to integrate De'VIA into the content areas. They present some excellent examples of how you can connect De'VIA to history, science, and other subjects to help your students learn about Deaf experiences and the world around them. In the following Teacher Tale, I (Scott) demonstrate how you can discuss Pop Art and the standard of connecting to the Deaf experience by integrating handshapes into art. Although I did this as an art teacher, you could also connect this to social studies class when discussing the Deaf experience and current trends in popular culture.

Teacher Tale

When I was an art teacher at Rochester School for the Deaf, one of my favorite topics to teach was Pop Art and what it might look like in the eyes of a Deaf person. I would talk about how pop artists are not interested in creating anything new, but rather they want to take what's already been produced and make a statement about it. One thing pop artists do is make "larger-than-life" sculptures of everyday objects. One year, I had my students work in small groups to make pop art using objects that were important to them but with a twist—they had to incorporate De'VIA into their work. One group made a sculpture of a partially unwrapped Hershey's Kisses using a Hula Hoop, chicken wire, paper-maché, paint, and aluminum foil for the wrapper. The students made handshapes representing the letters in the word *Kisses* with plaster wrap, painted them brown, and then attached the three-dimensional letters to the exposed part of the chocolate so it looked like the chocolate was spelling "Kisses" on the side. Another group made a giant Apple laptop out of cardboard boxes and paint. The keyboard had drawings of handshapes instead of letters in text, and on the screen, they made a "Word document" that said "ASL" in handshapes.

—*Scott Gentzke*

Building off of this Teacher Tale, you can further connect to Deaf experiences, such as making a sculpture with a hand-to-the-mouth signing KISS-FIST (i.e., love that!) made of Hershey's Kisses. Also, consider ways you can connect to the Deaf experience not related to language. For example, in social studies, you and your students can create a diorama of a scene from a Deaf club or a scene from a family experience (e.g., at the dinner table).

In addition to De'VIA, it is also important to introduce Deaf art, which is a separate concept from De'VIA. Although De'VIA specifically emphasizes the Deaf experience, Deaf art can be any art created by a Deaf person but does not necessarily represent or portray the Deaf experience (e.g., natural landscapes, fruit stills). Let's revisit the example in the social studies chapter (Chapter 9) when the students created stained glass while learning about the European Middle Ages. This would be a great opportunity to introduce students to Deaf artists who work in that medium, such as Barbie Harris, Beulah Hester, and Betty Taylor. (See Recommended Readings/Viewings to learn more about them and other Deaf visual artists.) When students see Deaf artists presenting their own work, they can see how they could also grow up to be artists or how art could play a part in their lives as Deaf adults.

Handstamp Sample

Deaf Artist in Action
A student sketches the statue of Abbe Charles-Michel de l'Épée at St. Mary's School for the Deaf.

When possible, invite Deaf artists to your classroom live or virtually. A Deaf artist-in-residence program is a great way to get the entire school involved in a cross-curricular project, as described in the following Teacher Tale. St. Mary's School for the Deaf has invited Deaf artists to work with their students as part of their Deaf artist-in-residence program.

Chew on This!

Did you know that...?
There are many ways for you to integrate BIPOC Deaf artists into your classroom!

- *Deaf Artists in America: Colonial to Contemporary* (Sonnenstrahl, 2002) showcases more than 300 works from over 60 diverse Deaf artists.
- Have your students explore the National Technical Institute for the Deaf at the Rochester Institute of Technology exhibitions that spotlight the works of BIPOC Deaf artists Latinx/Hispanic, Black, and LGBTQ+ community; https://www.rit.edu/ntid/dyerarts-exhibitions) and extensive Deaf arts collections that highlight many Deaf artists of varying cultural, racial, and ethnic backgrounds.
- Teach about BIPOC Deaf artists such as Burton Bird, Shawn Richardson, Nancy Rourke, Gayle Sanchez, Mia Sanchez, Christine Sun Kim, and other well-known Deaf artists such as Chuck Baird, Matt Daigle, and Guy Wonder.

Teacher Tale

When St. Mary's School for the Deaf and Rochester School for the Deaf hosted their Deaf artist-in-residence programs, they invited a Deaf artist to implement a schoolwide project and work with various teachers and students by creating artwork that incorporated not only the arts but also history, math, ASL, English, and so on. This also gave the students a connection to Deaf artists in a more tangible way. When students meet a Deaf artist they have been learning about, they begin to see the significance of the arts and also develop deeper connections to Deaf history and culture. The best part is that the schools ended up with a beautiful piece of artwork that many in the school community contributed to.

—*Scott Gentzke*

Deaf artist Nancy Rourke in front of a mural she helped Deaf students create at St. Mary's School for the Deaf.

A student pauses to look at his progress on the mural.

St. Mary's School for the Deaf also invited Ellie Zusi to their Deaf Artist-in-Residence program. Ellie discussed intersectionality and the Deaf and LGBTQIA+ community and also provided the school with an ASL dictionary of LGBTQIA+ signs.

View and Discuss Diverse Deaf Artists

There is a long history of Deaf BIPOC and LGBTQIA+ people in the arts. To provide role models for Deaf students, it is important for them to see and learn about artists from diverse backgrounds. For example, well-known Native American Deaf artist Nancy Rourke spent a few weeks at St. Mary's as staff, students, and other members of the school community participated in De'VIA workshops and collaborated on a large mural that is now permanently on display in the hallway.

Let's consider Black Deaf theater.

INCORPORATING THE ARTS ACROSS THE CURRICULUM

Deaf artist Ellie Zusi working with students virtually at St. Mary's School for the Deaf.

Stick It Into Action!

History of Black Deaf Theater

You can integrate the history of Black Deaf theater into social studies, Deaf studies, language arts, and other STEAM classes. Here are some key points to include:

- 1972: A one-act play, *The American Dream,* had the first all-Black Deaf cast.
- 1973: First all-Black Deaf cast in a full-length play is *Ceremonies in Dark Old Men*.
- 1977: National Theater for the Deaf had three Black Deaf actors playing the lead roles in their play, *The Three Musketeers*. This was the first dominant Black lead role in mainstream theater or Deaf theater.
- 1990: Michelle Banks, a Black Deaf actress, founded the Onyx Theater Company in New York City, the first Deaf theater company for People of Color.
- 1990: First all-Black Deaf play about the Black Deaf experience was *I Didn't Hear That Color*.

You can connect to your students' experiences as Deaf people when viewing or discussing art in any subject area. For example, in language arts and/or Deaf studies, you can have students read, analyze, and discuss a graphic novel by Awet Moges, a Deaf artist, and then create their own graphic novel. You could also have your students analyze the meaning of song lyrics and create an ASL music video, which would be a great way to study and analyze the genres of ASL literature as well as introduce Deaf performers such as The Wild Zappers, National Deaf Dance Theater, NTID Sunshine 2.0,

Rosa Lee Timm, Warren "Wawa" Snipe, and Justina Miles (see Core Recommendation 2 and Chapter 3 for additional examples of creative expression in content areas).

Also, if possible, consider taking your students on field trips to see Deaf artists perform in local or national touring productions. For example, if you are teaching Shakespeare in social studies or language arts, look to see if there are any local Deaf theaters putting on performances of his works, like the annual Oregon Shakespeare Festival, which includes Deaf plays. It is a great way to make literature come alive for your students.

In this next Teacher Tale, Leala Holcomb shares their experience about how growing up in a Deaf family led Leala to found an all-Deaf company, Hands Land, that creates and produces ASL rhyme and rhythm media (see www.handsland.org for more information). Sharing Leala's story can empower students to believe they too can create their own business integrating art and education.

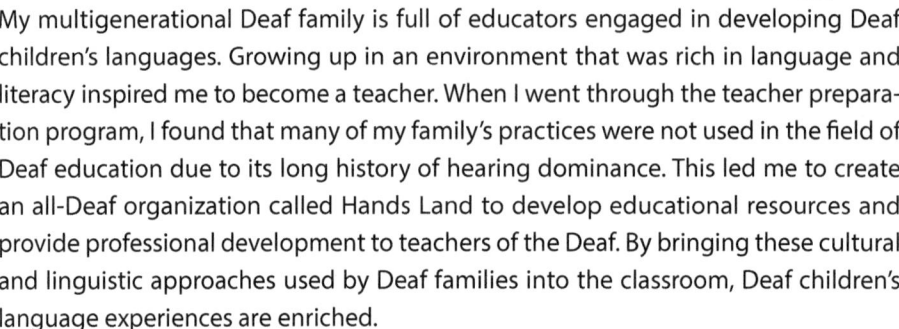

(PI) (MM) Teacher Tale

My multigenerational Deaf family is full of educators engaged in developing Deaf children's languages. Growing up in an environment that was rich in language and literacy inspired me to become a teacher. When I went through the teacher preparation program, I found that many of my family's practices were not used in the field of Deaf education due to its long history of hearing dominance. This led me to create an all-Deaf organization called Hands Land to develop educational resources and provide professional development to teachers of the Deaf. By bringing these cultural and linguistic approaches used by Deaf families into the classroom, Deaf children's language experiences are enriched.

—*Leala Holcomb, former preschool teacher*

> "For 17 years, I have spent one week a year with Deaf children from mainstream programs to engage them in the theater. Every year, I watched how engaging in the arts with Deaf adults and peers has helped them grow and shine. They become more confident, open, creative, and proud of who they are. Their teachers say the children always talk about their time with me throughout the whole year. This has always touched my heart. Deaf children need role models to inspire them through the arts. With creativity and strong identities, they can achieve their dreams of who they want to be!
>
> —CJ Jones, Deaf actor, producer, and director

Exposure to diverse Deaf role models of varying backgrounds who are working in various artistic fields is critical to fostering students' positive and intersecting identities. Providing models of and opportunities for students to express their content understanding by connecting to their experience as a Deaf person leads to positive self-identity. It also increases opportunities for deeper, richer, and more meaningful learning experiences when students can connect them to their own personal experiences. Make sure to provide models where diverse Deaf experiences are not only recognized and uplifted but also become central to learning in any educational settings.

(MM) (MT) (PI) (ES) Incorporate Interactive Educational Media With Deaf Artists to Provide World Knowledge

Deaf children learn more when they connect with characters they see or read about in books and media. Did you know that Deaf children can learn from interactive educational media in ASL and learn even more with teacher support (e.g., Golos et al., 2013)? As explained in Chapter 14 with Deafverse (deafverse.com), as well as in Chapter 3, you can connect media in any content area or through interdisciplinary units. In doing so, you can also integrate the standard of connecting art to the Deaf experience by including media with diverse Deaf role models. Deaf children may start to receive messages from an early age that they need to be "fixed" or are not good enough. When Deaf children see Deaf people in the media interacting in everyday experiences, it can help them start to develop a positive sense of self. This also increases their engagement in learning, as demonstrated in Christina's Teacher Tale using the evidence-based, interactive educational media from the *Peter's Picture* series, starring well-known Deaf actor and storyteller Peter Cook (see Recommended Readings).

  Teacher Tale

I teach K–3 Deaf students. I remember the first time they found out that Peter and the other children in the *Peter's Picture* series were Deaf themselves. They could not believe it. They looked at each other in excitement, signing, "DEAF?? THEY'RE DEAF???" It was very sweet, and I could see it positively impacting their identities. I also noticed the attention that they had during the episodes. Many of my students struggle to watch me or other signers for longer than a few minutes. Yet, when I turned on *Peter's Picture*, they were glued to the screen. And the students giggled all the way through each episode. While laughing along with Peter, Rika Roo, and the other characters, they are learning so many new valuable things in a natural and age-appropriate way. They had no problem watching the entire episode, and I was amazed; they were able to recall the words they learned after viewing the episode when playing the *Peter's Picture* app games afterward. *Peter's Picture* is a must-have for any teacher working to close the gap of language deprivation in our Deaf and Hard of Hearing students.
—*Christina Skahen, early childhood/elementary teacher*

As we have mentioned throughout the book, viewing educational media with Deaf people along with field trips are excellent ways you can help students learn about the world around them, particularly when they don't have the language to connect with their experiences. When using interactive media, we recommend integrating the viewing comprehension strategies (questioning before, during, and after viewing) described in Chapter 3 and the reading comprehension strategies discussed in Chapter 6. Here we provide an example that can be used with students from preschool through third grade as well as with older students who exhibit language delays. It is a great resource for building world knowledge (e.g., farms, libraries, restaurants) by viewing Deaf characters in ASL. You can use the following viewing strategies with any educational media in any educational setting.

  Stick It Into Action!

Viewing Strategies
Let's say you plan a field trip to the library for students. You can view evidence-based, interactive educational media such as the *Peter's Picture* "Our Trip to the Library" episode to teach story knowledge and targeted vocabulary, here library-related

Stick It Into Action! (*continued*)

vocabulary, as well as how to behave in a library (See Golos & Moses, 2013; Golos et al., 2015) for additional viewing strategies).

- **Before viewing:**
  - Introduce target vocabulary: *library, librarian, borrow, library card.*
  - Introduce the main characters and theme.
  - Let children know it's okay to engage during the video by
    - moving along with the main character
    - copying their signs or fingerspelling
    - asking questions
- **During viewing:**
  - Have children watch the video without teacher interaction.
  - Watch the video again and encourage active engagement.
  - Encourage children to sign along with the main character.
  - In subsequent viewings, pause, question, and discuss. Encourage children to ask questions and interact with the print on the screen by signing or fingerspelling the target written word and asking them to point to the correct word on the screen.
- **After viewing:**
  - Have students sequence pictures, add sentences, and make a book.
  - Storysign the book in ASL and record your students on video.
  - Reenact scenes from the videos.
  - Interact with the four *Peter's Picture* app games (app.peterspicture.com)
    - Vocabulary matching game
      + Sign to picture
      + Sign to print
      + Fingerspelling to picture
      + Fingerspelling to print
    - Play a sequencing game: putting key events from the story in order
    - Play a word game: match the target word to the word in a sentence
    - Read an eBook of the story in the movie
  - Go on a field trip to the library. Bring along students' books and/or pictures of the vocabulary words and support their learning.
    - Take pictures and video record the trip with students explaining what they are doing during the trip.
    - When you return, follow the same "after viewing" steps by making a book of your own trip!
    - Create your own library with books and videos of all the trips you take during the year.

Viewing and discussing Deaf artists through multiple contexts and mediums lays a great foundation for students to begin to explore and express themselves and demonstrate their learning through their creative expression.

(MM) (MT) (PI) (DI) (ES) **Core Recommendation 2: Embed Opportunities for Creative Expression to Engage, Motivate, and Learn**

As teachers, you know that drawing on students' prior knowledge and experiences is important when teaching any new content. The arts can provide a medium to engage students in learning as well as ways of making meaning of the world through Deaf eyes. Here, we revisit some strategies and examples from other chapters as well as share additional resources you can tap into to provide your students with opportunities to engage in creative expression in the arts. You can target the art standards of creating, connecting, and/or performing these activities. As mentioned in Chapter 2, it is never too early for you to have your students begin to explore who they are and what is important to them. In fact, the sooner, the better! You have an important role to play in fostering a positive sense of self and awareness of their multiple and intersecting identities across all ages and grade levels. When you empower students to express themselves creatively, students not only learn about themselves but also become actively and personally engaged in learning.

(DI) **Theater in Education**

Theater in Education (TiE) uses interactive drama practices to help aid the educational process for students of all ages. In TiE, teachers have students use acting, role-play, and movement to learn a concept, express understanding, and reinforce learning. See the following Stick It Into Action for an example in science.

Stick It Into Action!

TiE and the Digestive System

To integrate TiE into a science lesson, follow these steps:

- Assign your students a part of the digestive system (e.g., teeth, tongue, esophagus, stomach).
- Have them research their assigned part for its function(s) and come up with body movements to represent the function(s).
- Allow them to move around and find their adjacent part(s), such as the large intestine, which should be next to the small intestine and rectum.
- Have another student check the system for accuracy.
- Select a student who is not in the system to become a cookie and have them go through the system from the mouth to the anus.
- Discuss each part's body movements and functions and how they work together as the digestive system.

> "One of my earliest memories as a student was when I was 3 or 4 in preschool, and we were learning about colors. I remember being excited to learn how to identify my favorite color, orange, along with the other colors. This is the moment I connected my love of working with colors and started a lifelong relationship with art. From there, I spent my childhood coloring, drawing, and poring over artwork in comic books (which led to a love of reading), and eventually, I became an art teacher. Positive connections to the arts can create powerful memories and build a foundation for learning and identity development.
>
> —Scott Gentzke

Teacher Tale

My students really like TiE because they can move around and demonstrate their learning differently. When we discuss abstract ideas, such as different bodily systems, we use TiE to express them visually and kinesthetically. The students become actively engaged and motivated in understanding how each part in the system works. I also use TiE when teaching history. Each of my students selects and researches a Deaf person of historical significance. We then have a Deaf Celebration party where every student (including the teacher—me) dresses up like their Deaf person and makes a short biographical presentation or acts out a biographical play.

—*Chris Kurz*

TiE: Deaf persons of historical significance.

> "Growing up Deaf, I struggled with my identity as a Gay person. Every time I could get into a role and fly with it, it felt like an escape. However, through the process, I fell in love with the art of acting, and it gave me the confidence to embrace my identity every time I stepped out of a role.
>
> —Justin Jackerson, Deaf actor, ASL teacher, creator of The ASL Lab

(PI) (MM) (MT) Exploring Identities Through Creative Expression

There are so many ways you can integrate creative projects to encourage students to think about who they are and what is important to them or to build confidence, as Justin shares in his quote. One way to get started is through "All About Me" projects (see Chapter 8 for more information), which can be incorporated into your classrooms no matter what grade you teach. It's never too early to start and you can use so many different mediums for this. Have students reflect on their personal and social identities to reflect on who they are, what they like, what is important to them, who the people are who have shaped them, activities they enjoy doing, and/or for self-care or well-being, what they value, and so on.

For older students, you can have them create biographies as discussed in Chapter 9 or other projects that represent their multiple and intersecting identities. For example, you can have them create a poster or an online slide with embedded art, drawing, picture collage, and so forth, and then have them make a video of themselves to share with others. You can embed technology by requiring students to also include a GIF of themselves doing something they love (see Chapters 3 and 11 for more on leveraging technology). This is a great project to introduce at the beginning of the year, with opportunities to return to it throughout the year with modifications or updates. You can modify it for any grade level. Your students can learn about themselves, each other, and you as their teacher. In the following Teacher Tale, Judy demonstrates how students explore their identities and target the art standards of creating and connecting with Deaf studies through the arts.

Teacher Tale

When I was teaching Deaf studies, I did several art projects with middle school Deaf students to help them explore and discover their multiple and intersecting identities as a Deaf person. For one project, we made papier-mâché masks showing two perspectives: on the front, what they felt to be the hearing/public perception of them, and on the inside, the mask showing their true feelings, their perspectives as a Deaf person. In another art project, students traced their hands in crayon and then drew pictures/wrote words expressing their thoughts about ASL and the value of their hands. Afterward, they covered their drawing with black ink. In the end, they scraped their chosen words, such as *proud, sacred, beautiful,* on the black ink, exposing the drawings/words from behind. I saw how powerful the art projects were for the students. It truly helped them become more proud and positive about their Deaf beings.

—*Judy Pratt McGuigan, Deaf teacher*

(PI) (DI) Tap Into Your Students' Strengths in Creativity for Self-Expression

At the start of each year, as you welcome new students, it is important to get to know them and develop an awareness of their diverse backgrounds—not only their race, cultures, languages, and academic skills, but also what brings them joy and motivates them. In the reading chapter, one of the core recommendations is joy (see Chapter 6). Here, we highlight how tapping into your students' creative strengths can bring both joy and motivation for them to engage in learning. One way to do this is by offering them opportunities to express themselves through drawing, as I (Scott) highlight in the following Teacher Tale. For students with language delays, expressing through arts offers them alternative ways to engage in the classroom content and contribute their ideas to class discussion. It also gives them opportunities to share their strengths and develop confidence in their abilities.

Tapping into students' strengths, particularly for students with language delays, is not only a great way to build confidence but also a way of building language and literacy skills across multiple languages. For those of you who teach reading/writing, you have probably seen students who shut down when they come to your class because literacy may have been a frustrating experience for them throughout schooling. In the following Teacher Tale, Debbie shares how she addressed the art standard of creating by allowing a student to use his strength as an artist to engage in reading/writing class.

> **(MM) Teacher Tale**
>
> I used to assign "Questions of the Week" journal responses for my middle school students when I was an art teacher as a way to promote literacy in the arts. Although this may seem like most journal assignments, the students used "write and draw" journals (which can be found online, or you can have students create their own). The pages are half blank at the top and have lines for writing at the bottom. This gave the students the opportunity to respond to the question of the week using some sort of artistic expression on the top half, accompanied by their written responses on the bottom half. This way, students who struggled to express themselves in writing could use their art skills to support their responses and sometimes students benefit from having something they can see on paper to help develop their written responses. Although this was a weekly assignment for art class, this could easily be done in language arts as well as any other classes that involve journaling/written responses (e.g., reading, ASL, science, math). Students who struggle with writing may be able to better express themselves artistically, which promotes participation and boosts their self-esteem.
> —Scott Gentzke

> **(MM) (DI) Teacher Tale**
>
> **Author/Illustrator**
> As a reading/writing teacher, I worked with my students every year on creating their own stories. I often found that the students who had delayed literacy skills due to having experienced language deprivation did not want to do this project. One year, I noticed a student who had amazing artistic skills. He loved to draw and would often doodle or draw whenever the opportunity presented itself. I paired him with another student who had better writing skills and enjoyed writing more than drawing. Together, they worked to create an amazing story. While they discussed the story in ASL and worked on the writing and drawing together, one took the lead on writing while the other took the lead on illustrating. It allowed them the opportunity to be creative in developing a story together while building off of each of their individual strengths. They were motivated every day to come to class to write, create and draw!
> —Debbie Golos

> "The *Shiloh* mock trial not only allowed me to understand the story and trial process through real-life experience, but it also gave me a new way to analyze literature through acting.
> —Justin Jackerson

Engage in Role-Play Another way we can tap into students' strengths is by providing them opportunities to engage in role-play. We have seen time and again that when students are provided opportunities to act, it allows them to try on different roles (e.g., different genders, personalities), explore potential future jobs they may have, or step into different family relationships or dynamics. For example, when teaching about animals to preschool students, you can role-play different animals as seen in the following image of Sunshine 2.0.

You can engage in role-play with your students at any grade level. When I (Debbie) was teaching middle school, I incorporated role-play as a component with most of the books I taught. I often saw that students thrived when having the opportunity to play a role, and it provided them another way of deepening their understanding of

INCORPORATING THE ARTS ACROSS THE CURRICULUM

Sunshine 2.0 with preschool students. Role-play as an animal.

what they were reading, as Justin illustrates regarding his experience participating in the *Shiloh* mock trial in sixth grade (see Chapter 7).

Teacher Tale

As described in Chapter 7, my sixth-grade students would put on a mock trial every year, taking on the roles of witnesses, lawyers, or jury members. I remember I was surprised when one student, who was quite shy, put "lawyer" on her "Who do you want to be?" list (see Chapter 7 for the description of the *Shiloh* trial). Through this role, I saw her truly shine; I could see her leadership skills blossoming as she practiced her part as the prosecuting lawyer trying to fight for Marty Preston to keep the dog. As the students worked in small groups to prepare, she took the lead in preparing for this activity. She made sure all the witnesses had practiced and were ready for trial day, and she double-checked that the evidence was labeled and organized. When it came time for the mock trial day, she came prepared and ready to take on the role of presenting her opening and closing arguments and questioning the witnesses. She was one of the best lawyers I had in the trial.

—*Debbie Golos*

Not only can taking on role-play foster students' strengths in academic areas, you can also target the art standard of performing by providing students opportunities to practice and get feedback on their performances. Sometimes, it takes us as teachers to believe in them and see their inner sparkle, as demonstrated by the following Teacher Tale about performing the story of *The Little Prince* (Saint-Exupéry, 2000).

Teacher Tale

I love seeing unity and confidence being built through theater. I remember one time when I directed *The Little Prince*, the student playing the Little Prince was absent a lot

Teacher Tale (*continued*)

and not committed to the role. I picked out one of the crew members, a bright, timid freshman, to temporarily take over during rehearsals. I quickly noticed her memorization, translation, and acting skills. Within 3 weeks, she ended up taking over the role, and I replaced the original actor with the crew member. She did a fabulous job! I believe that she continued to participate in theater for years after. I know that children need good and sincere people to believe in them and to find the hidden gems within the students and encourage them to thrive. I always root for underdogs—keep them under your wings in the beginning, and then watch them soar!

—*Judy Pratt McGuigan, Deaf teacher and theater director*

(PI) Incorporating Your Own Creative Abilities Into Your Teaching

Sometimes, as teachers, we are so focused on what our students need that there is no time to think about ourselves and what our own strengths for creative expression are that we can bring to our classroom. However, your passion can shine through you, and this can inspire students in their learning. Do you like to draw or paint? Tell or write stories? Create poetry in ASL or other languages? Rap? Dance? Act? Play drums? Then include that in your teaching! You don't have to be an expert to share your love for the arts. Students enjoy seeing their teachers use their own hidden artistic talents in their lessons. In language arts, I (Debbie) would sometimes come to class dressed up as characters in the books I was teaching, and the students loved it. Here, I (Scott) share my experience sharing my art with my students.

Teacher Tale

As an art teacher, obviously I would use my art skills when working with students, such as sketching something for them as a reference or showing them different methods of painting with a brush. However, they were always most excited whenever I would share examples of my own artwork with them as if it helped them realize that they could learn to do the same thing. It would be an extra-special treat when some of my colleagues who taught other subject areas would come visit the art room and share their artistic creations or talk about their art. Seeing teachers from a different perspective helps the students humanize them and see them as more than a teacher, strengthening their relationship. It also shows students that it is good to develop a wide variety of skills and outlets for creative expression.

—*Scott Gentzke*

You can share your creative expression no matter what grade or content you teach. In the social studies chapter (see Chapter 9), we show a picture of a timeline responding to the question, "Why did Black ASL develop?" If you love poetry, create a poem with your students to highlight key events that align with the timeline. If you love to rap, create a math rap when teaching about exponents (see examples from ASL in Chapters 3 and 10). There are so many ways for you to connect your own passions for the arts in your classroom to motivate and engage your students in learning. In this picture, we see members of the Sunshine 2.0 company signing a rap song about the order of operations in mathematics.

The Sunshine 2.0 order of operations video screenshot.

(MM) (PI) (MT) **Create Opportunities for Creative Expression in All Content Areas**
In addition to modeling your own passion for the arts and connecting it to content areas, it is also important to provide ways for your students to express themselves creatively. Think about the assignments that you give your students. Is there room for flexibility? When you have assignments requiring responses to questions, you could provide them with options on how to respond, as I (Scott) demonstrated in my previous Teacher Tale. As we also mentioned in the science chapter, there are several strategies for allowing students to respond in multiple languages and modalities, such as through ASL and drawing. Students could also demonstrate their learning through an art project, a poem in ASL, or creative dance. For example, in science class, they could create an ASL video combining dance and sign language to explain how planets orbit the sun. In social studies, they could role-play interviews with famous Deaf people in history and create props, backdrops, and a funny but historically accurate script. Allowing students to have options in how they interact with or respond to class material can increase motivation, engagement, and learning.

(MM) Key Strategy

Let's take a look at the strategy "many media, same message." With this strategy, you can offer options for students to demonstrate their learning in one of several different mediums (e.g., drawing, video, acting) as described in the following Stick It Into Action.

(MM) (MT) Stick It Into Action!

Many Media, Same Message
You can integrate the strategy "many media, same message" (Jones & Lapham, 2004) into assignments in any content area at any grade level. Here, we give an example

Stick It Into Action! (*continued*)

from Deaf studies with students learning about the Deaf President Now movement. Give students the option to choose from one of the following and then share their presentations with the class:

- Reenact the Gallaudet students stating their demands to the board.
- Create an interpretive dance demonstrating the key events of Deaf President Now.
- Draw a map of where the key events occurred. Create a legend to identify key locations and people.

- Write and illustrate a picture book demonstrating key events in the order they occurred.
- Create an ASL poem or story about what Deaf President Now means to you, and record yourself on video telling the story.

Using strategies such as this provides students with additional ways of communicating, which can support students' understanding of concepts and promote language learning. When students are struggling with a concept, think about ways you can integrate the arts to expand on meaning. For example, in the book *Maniac Magee* (Spinelli, 1999), the main character's favorite food is Butterscotch Krimpets (note: make sure to review anti-bias and trauma-informed approaches before teaching this book as it addresses racism; see Chapters 7 and 8). It is repeated throughout the book, and none of my (Debbie) students had ever seen them before. At the same time, in writing class, we were also working on persuasive writing. In the following Teacher Tale, I describe how we connected reading, writing, and ASL with the arts standards of creating and performing.

  **Teacher Tale**

Throughout my time teaching sixth grade, I must have walked away with boxes of videos of my students' performances. We incorporated acting or production into almost all of our units. And sometimes, they stemmed from questions from the students. I remember one of the students asked whether Butterscotch Krimpets were real. We researched together as a class and found out they were made in Philadelphia. The students had the idea of creating commercials acting like the main characters advertising their favorite treats. Once they found out that they were real but that we couldn't buy them in California, we wrote a letter to the Tasty Baking Company (now called Flowers Foods). We let them know the book we were reading and asked if they could send us a sample to make our commercial. Imagine the students' surprise when they sent us 10 boxes! Students worked together in small groups to create storyboards and make commercial videos. It helped them to see the real-life benefits of persuasive writing. In addition, it also helped them better understand the characters and key content in the story. We connected reading, writing, art, acting, and film production, and the students had a blast!

—*Debbie Golos*

INCORPORATING THE ARTS ACROSS THE CURRICULUM

Creative Expression Through Storytelling and Poetry Creating stories, ASL rhyme and rhythm, and ASL poetry can be fun and help develop sign language skills, cognitive skills, and problem-solving skills, as well as target the art standard of creating. You can have students do these activities as individuals or in a group. Consider Leala's Teacher Tale about their experience engaging and motivating students in an early childhood classroom. As we mentioned in Chapter 2, you can build off of their motivation and engagement by asking students to come up with new signs with a specific handshape to create a new rhyme.

Teacher Tale

Every time I use ASL rhyme and rhythm, my students' faces look like they have seen something magical. No matter what their language skills are, they often smile, giggle, bob their heads, and sing along with their little hands. They are truly absorbed in the delightful experience! It is my favorite part of teaching.

—*Leala Holcomb, former preschool teacher*

You can offer storytelling opportunities in any content area for your students to be expressive and use their imaginations while engaging in the course content. For example, let's say you are studying legends in social studies. You can create an interdisciplinary unit connecting to science, English language arts, and ASL language arts and a book such as *The Legend of Gravity: A Tall Basketball Tale* (Palmer, 2022) to explore the ways the main character is a legend. As an extension, you can have students create stories of themselves as legends or Deaf heroes (see Chapter 9). You could add a performance activity by having them tell their stories live or prerecorded.

Teacher Tale

As a creative writing activity in our legend unit, students created stories of their lives as Deaf legends. One of my students created a story where he became a famous Deaf basketball player whose legendary activities were raising money for basketball camps for Deaf youths. I remember that throughout the unit, he showed up early for school, so he had extra time to work on editing and revising his writing. His writing improved, and the unit became more meaningful for him by allowing him the opportunity for creative expression. As a culminating activity, we showcased each of the students' legends through storytelling in ASL.

—*Debbie Golos*

You can have your students do individual or collaborative storytelling activities. For example, in this picture, students collaboratively create a story related to science content using their bodies to demonstrate Newton's laws of motion.

Creative Expression in STEAM Here, we provide some examples from NTID Sunshine 2.0, a professional traveling theater troupe based at NTID in Rochester, New York. The troupe provides performances and activities for Deaf students that highlight the fields

Students create a story for science about flying with their bodies.

of science, technology, engineering, arts, and math (STEAM), as well as educational topics connecting to the Deaf experience. The following Stick It Into Action describes a workshop provided by Sunshine 2.0 on Newton's laws of motion that illustrates all three arts standards introduced in this chapter: creating, connecting, and performing.

 Stick It Into Action!

Newton's Laws of Motion

The virtual workshop presentation (created by Bianca Ware of Sunshine 2.0; https://drive.google.com/file/d/1_TqGfjJBrIoWt7TK14GtES756-BA4seu/view) is shown on video. It is designed to be a 20-min lesson plan, and the objectives with emphasis in arts are for students to be able to do the following:

- Demonstrate the laws of motion through body movement and in ASL.
- Define vocabulary words in different modalities.
- Do an experiment embodying the laws of motion through arts.

Follow these steps to implement this lesson:

- Ask students if they know about the laws of motion.
- Ask where they may see the laws of motion in action; have them role-play their examples (e.g., planes, driving, balls).
- Introduce the three laws of motion individually with video and demonstrations.
- Have students tell a story, in character, of Newton and describe how you (Newton) came up with the laws.
- Review Law 1 (play video).
- Provide visualization through movie clips or plays with class participation.
- Have students use body movement or dance to define vocabulary words they need to know before moving on to Laws 2 and 3 (i.e., Force [show sign] = push or pull in a specific direction; velocity [show sign] = speed of something in a given direction).
- Follow these steps with the next two laws.

INCORPORATING THE ARTS ACROSS THE CURRICULUM

Bianca Ware of Sunshine 2.0 giving a lesson on Newton's laws of motion.

- Follow-up activity: Have students create their own lyrics and production (dance, acting, poetry, or songwriting) to summarize an interpretation of the laws of motion.

The Sunshine 2.0 troupe: (from left to right) Bianca Ware, Zain Ahmed, Fred Beam (coordinator), Shiann Cook, Tyler Fortson.

Creative Expression and Nature Taking your students outside is a great way to connect to the arts. Not only is it grounding, but it is also good for students who need to move, such as those with challenges with attention. You can implement many activities outside in any subject or grade level. For example, if you are doing a project on the solar system, take the students outside and make a sundial. There are many craft kits for this, or you can create your own. Go on a nature walk with the class to learn about animals, plants, trees, and the land around them. You can have them take pictures along the way, make a movie of their experience, and/or create a book when they return. Have them create a poem about an animal they saw in ASL, English, or other languages (see Bringing It All Together and Chapter 7). You can also have students collect flowers such as lavender. These can be dried to create a collage or scrapbook. A great way to start engaging with nature is through short mindfulness practices. Regularly going on a mindfulness walk with your students is a great way to do moving meditations, helping them to stay present, engaged, and grounded (see Chapters 2, 7, and 8 for more on mindfulness). This will help your students feel more connected to nature, sense what they want to select for their art projects, and be more present and engaged in their learning in general.

Handstamp Sample

Using Nature as a Theme Is a Great Way to Introduce Color Theory!

Handstamp Sample

A Tinfoil Monoprint of a Rainbow by an Elementary Student at St. Mary's School for the Deaf

In doing any of these activities, consider also collaborating with teachers of the arts in your school to create a crosscurricular unit where you each cover your respective subject areas but work together to have the students create a project that incorporates both content and the arts. The arts are often dismissed as "special" or as something that is not a core class, and you can help change this by working together with teachers of the arts. They are usually more than happy to collaborate with other subject area teachers!

(PI) Teacher Tale

One year, I was introducing eighth graders to the concept of tessellations, which is when a shape is repeated throughout the design like a tile without any overlapping or gaps like a puzzle. The students told me that they just started learning about tessellations in math class as well. Right after class, I reached out to the math teacher to see if we could find a way to combine our lessons. Students created their own tessellations and, as a result, ended up with a stronger and more cohesive understanding of the concept. At the end of the unit, they were excited to show off their artwork to their math teacher.

—*Scott Gentzke*

Showcasing Students' Artistic Works

There are many ways you can share your students' work. Display students' artwork in a public space so they can revisit concepts they learned, and you can also invite their families to see them. Tap students' creative literary expression through performing, role-playing, and skits. You can host an ASL bowl, ASL slam, and/or ASL storytelling night for your students to demonstrate their ASL literary skills. The goal is for students to apply their knowledge and skills by creating their own ASL essays, stories, poems, and skits. When you showcase students' work, it not only makes your students feel good about themselves, but it is also a way to engage with families by sharing and appreciating their children's work and enjoyment of art.

Handstamp Sample

Elementary Students' De'VIA Artwork on Display at St. Mary's School for the Deaf

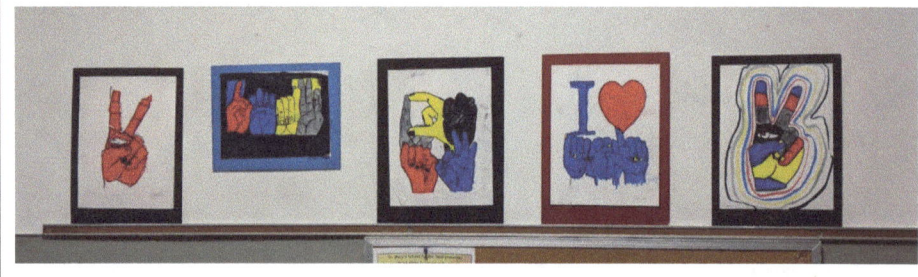

Additional Things to Consider

   Differentiating Instruction and the Arts

It is very important to create opportunities for all of your students to engage in the arts. Deaf students with disabilities can create artwork in any medium. They can also understand how other works have been constructed. Although they may require differentiated instruction and accessible accommodations with the process and even the type of materials they are using, it is critical that you see them as artists, creative problem solvers, and capable learners. Make sure to provide opportunities for hands-on activities that involve various media tools, such as using a tablet to make a short video of what they just did or learned. You can also have them feel and touch art materials and media equipment before doing an activity. They should be empowered to make choices and decisions, such as picking colors or mediums.

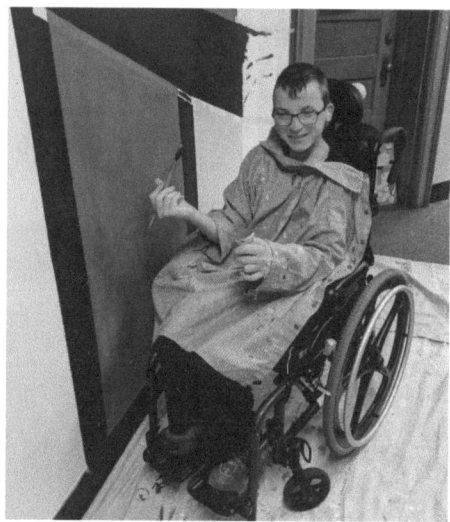

Student at St. Mary's School for the Deaf painting a De'VIA mural.

For some students with disabilities, arts may be their only way of communicating their understanding, needs, wants, and emotions. This also may be true for Deaf students with language delays. Communicating through the arts helps them develop language skills through self-expression and concept understanding. By being actively engaged in arts-related activities, they are learning ways to communicate their feelings and thinking while developing language skills.

Stick It Into Action!

Differentiating Instruction in Art

You can purchase adaptive materials for students who struggle with fine and gross motor skills. Here are some examples:

- Instead of regular crayons, you can purchase thicker crayons or handwriting grips that are fitted onto crayons that are designed for those who struggle to hold things.
- For students who are DeafBlind, many materials can be used to provide accessibility to creating art: Sponge 'Ums for tactile painting, scented markers to develop a color association with smell, light boards, paint pallets with braille labels, neon paint, and purple glue that will dry clear.

There are no limits for your students!

   Bringing It All Together

If you recall, in Chapter 7, we suggested an idea for an interdisciplinary unit for middle schoolers on astronomy that included a culminating activity of a camping trip. This included students studying the stars, moon, and sun and reading books about

Katherine Johnson, such as *Hidden Figures* (Shetterly, 2016) or *A Computer Called Katherine: How Katherine Johnson Helped Put America on the Moon* (Slade & Miller Jamison, 2019). We have expanded here to align the camping trip with our core recommendations and the theme of "Hidden Figures." In this unit, students can explore multiple meanings of the term and what it means for Deaf people through creative expression by connecting to the art standards of create, connect, and perform.

Unit: Hidden Figures

Prior to the camping trip, students will have completed the following activities within their content area classes.

Content Area Objectives

- **Language arts:** Read and analyze the book *Hidden Figures* using graphic organizers and the before, during, and after comprehension strategies outlined in Chapter 6. View the movie *Hidden Figures* using the viewing comprehension strategies outlined in Chapter 3.
- **ASL language arts:** Have students create a 1-min social media-like video of the multiple meanings of the term *hidden figures,* including as it applies to racial justice, geometry, and science. Sign concepts accurately in ASL. (**Core Recommendation 2**)
- **Social studies:** Read and analyze primary sources about the civil rights movement and "women in computing." Engage in civil discourse discussions as outlined in Chapter 9. Have students compare and contrast facts and fiction with the *Hidden Figures* movie and primary source documents (see Chapter 7 comparing fiction/nonfiction).
- **Deaf studies:** Identify and interview a BIPOC Deaf role model in STEAM fields (e.g., Emmanuel Perrodin-Njoku, David James, Ashley Fisher, Nadmionor Casiano-Berrios). Have students create a video summarizing why they are role models to Deaf people (see Chapter 9 on biographical information). (**Core Recommendation 1**)
- **Math:** After learning about geometric shapes in nature, explore and take pictures of hidden geometric shapes or numerical digits in nature. Have students create a new natural object with hidden shapes or digits.
- **Science:** Study the seasonal appearances of constellations. Engage in claim-evidence-reasoning (outlined in Chapter 11) to predict how constellations will appear during the camping trip. If it is cloudy, use a constellation projector in the dark classroom. Have students compare and contrast the hidden figures in the night sky with their predictions.

Camping Showcase

Students will present one of the following for the evening showcase to demonstrate the arts objective by reinterpreting what *hidden figure* means to them with one of the following options: visual art project, ASL poem/storytelling, or media art project (see Table 12.1).

Table 12.1. Hidden Figures Unit Evening Showcase

Subjects	Evening Showcase Activities and Core Recommendation (CR)
Math, science, arts, media, ASL	**Nature walk:** Share a media poem, story, video, or play of their nature walk: Hidden Figures in Nature. (CR 2)
Social studies, science, Deaf studies, reading, ASL arts	**Storytelling/visual art/media share:** Perform their story, skit, or poem on what *hidden figures* means to them related to their own identities and/or the Deaf adults they have interviewed or researched. (CR 1, 2)

- Students perform their story, skit, or poem on what *hidden figures* means to them. Their stories can connect to their own identities and/or the Deaf adults they have interviewed or researched.

This unit can take approximately 3 to 4 weeks, depending on the extent to which you are able to allocate daily time to each of the content areas. The camping trip could be a one- or two-night trip and take place in the fall or spring, depending on where you live. As an alternative to overnight camping, you could do a day trip to a local park or nature center.

(MM) (PI) (DI) (ES) **Your Turn to Practice!**

Now, it's your turn! Develop, teach, and reflect on a lesson that integrates visual and/or performing arts and media into a content area subject. You can modify a previously developed lesson or create a new one. If you are currently teaching, try it out with your own students. If you are a teacher candidate, you can practice with real or mock students. Here are the steps to follow.

Create a Lesson

Develop or modify a lesson plan for a content area (e.g., science, math, Deaf studies, social studies, reading/writing, ASL, language arts).

- Add a visual or performing arts objective(s) to your lesson that provides students an opportunity for creative expression (e.g., creating, performing, connecting):
- A discussion about Deaf artists (if possible, invite a Deaf artist to the conversation either in person or through video conferencing)
- An opportunity for the students to engage in the creative expression of their choice (e.g., drawing, painting, viewing, production, theater, dance)
- A way of connecting their engagement in the arts to personal experience

Teach Your Lesson

Teach your lesson to students in your classroom or in a mock setting.

Reflect on Your Teaching

Reflect on your experience. Consider the following questions:

- What went well?
- What would you change/do differently if you taught this lesson again?
- After assessing your students, how well did your students learn the targeted objectives?
- What benefits could you see for your students?
  - Creative expression
  - Development of multiple and intersecting identities
  - Those with language delays
  - In varying educational settings (e.g., one to one, group)
  - Motivation? Engagement? Other?

(MM) (MT) Recommended Readings/Viewings

For Teachers/Teacher Candidates

- De'VIA Curriculum (https://deviacurr.wordpress.com/) is a website where you can access lesson plans, curriculua, and materials about De'VIA art and artists.
- Sunshine 2.0 (https://www.rit.edu/ntid/sunshine) for more information about workshops and performances including ASL poetry, storytelling, skits dance, and basic performing skills.
- "Creating and Using Educational Media With a Cultural Perspective of Deaf People" (Moses et al., 2018). Read more on best practices for creating and using educational media ensuring that Deaf people are taking the lead in the process.
- "The Benefits of Using Educational Videos in American Sign Language in Early Childhood Settings" (Golos & Moses, 2015). This article shares research-based strategies you can use to teach language and literacy through interactive, educational media in ASL.
- "Supplementing an Educational Video Series With Video-Related Classroom Activities and Materials" (Golos & Moses, 2015). This article shares strategies for teachers for pre-, during, and post-viewing of educational media in ASL.

For Using With Students

- Deaf Art (https://deaf-art.org/) is a website featuring more than 100 Deaf artists and their works. It also has numerous resources and materials that are excellent for students to research and present.
- *Unfolding the Soul of Black Deaf Expressions* (Terry, 2016). This book covers illustrations of artworks by Black Deaf artists.

- *Peter's Picture* (https://app.peterspicture.com) is a website that includes three interactive educational videos from the *Peter's Picture* series, each with four aligning games.

Conclusion

In this chapter, we provided resources and suggestions on ways you can introduce Deaf artists and embed the arts throughout P–12 grade levels (and transition) in any subject area. Doing so can have many positive impacts on your students, from fostering a positive sense of self and understanding diverse perspectives of others, to motivating them to engage in learning. When students, particularly those with language delays, are given multiple opportunities to express themselves through a variety of different artistic mediums, you are providing them with multiple avenues for meaning-making through creative expression. Whether theater, drawing, dance, music, or media, students often find at least one of the arts they connect to. Embed the arts in your classes, and you will be amazed at the positive impact on your students' engagement and enjoyment in learning!

Sticking Points

- Introduce and discuss diverse Deaf role models in performing, visual, and media arts to foster students' multiple and intersecting identities.
- Provide multiple opportunities for creative expression in visual, performing, and media arts across the curriculum.

ASL Immersion I and II

Petra M. Horn-Marsh
Kester Horn-Marsh

Chapter 13

After reading other chapters in this book, you may still be wondering how best to teach academics to your current or future Deaf students who have language delays due to language deprivation. You may be thinking, "How can I improve their language abilities to maximize their learning?" These students need dedicated time and space to immerse themselves in American Sign Language (ASL). In this chapter, we will share strategies from an ASL immersion curriculum that is spreading and becoming more established in programs for Deaf students, driven by the expanding literature on the impacts of language deprivation. All preschool through Grade 12 (P–12) teachers should learn about ASL immersion regardless of student age or the content they teach. Whether or not your school has an ASL immersion program, you can implement activities in your classroom that help support ASL development.

Who Are We?

Looking back on my childhood, I (Petra) realized I had functioned as a tutor to many peers that I grew up with. Now I understand why. I grew up with German Sign Language, which I acquired from my Deaf immigrant parents. Even though I learned ASL later in school, I was already ahead of many peers in world knowledge because I already had a language foundation. Many times, when my classmates did not understand their teachers, I would fill them in on background knowledge through ASL. I also found that my role as a tutor extended well beyond the classroom. I spent passionate but grueling hours in the dormitory halls teaching some Deaf schoolmates reading. More concerning, I routinely acted as a peer tutor when the teacher's back was turned, providing **asides** to help my classmates figure out what the teacher was talking about. Currently, I work as an associate professor in the ASL and Deaf studies program at the University of Kansas Edwards campus after a 15-year stint at Kansas School for the Deaf, first as the bilingual specialist and then as the early childhood/elementary school principal.

I (Kester) grew up as the only hearing child in an entirely Deaf family, many of whom were working in the field of Deaf education. As a result, working in an ASL/English bilingual setting was a natural way for me to get involved in the field. As a high school English language arts teacher, I later ended up teaching a HILL (High Interest, Low Level) class with Petra for students who had experienced language deprivation. Although they had full control of conversational ASL, they still needed ASL skills for academic discussions. We also quickly realized that many students had little background knowledge needed for reading comprehension. For example, when reading an article on Martin Luther King Jr., we found that several of our Deaf students were completely unaware of Black people being enslaved, let alone the history of Jim Crow. Having to go back and reteach parts of American history made me realize that language deprivation, left unchecked, could have detrimental impacts. Now, working as the bilingual specialist at Kansas School for the Deaf, I assess students' expressive and receptive ASL skills and provide ASL services such as ASL immersion classes, ASL tutoring, and language facilitation.

The concept and practice of ASL immersion classes discussed in this chapter stem from a combination of my (Petra) personal experience as a consumer of the Deaf education system and my (Kester) childhood as a child of Deaf adults (Coda). In addition to our team-teaching experience in a ninth- and 10th-grade English language arts class and working with students who struggled in reading and writing, we have witnessed the value of ASL after seeing our students learning to read after progressing in ASL development. Subsequently, the Kansas School for the Deaf administration created an ASL immersion class with me (Petra) and the assistant bilingual specialist, Sherry Gabel, taking the lead. This chapter will highlight strategies and effective practices we have learned over the years teaching Deaf students in ASL immersion classes. We believe these practices can be incorporated into any content area and grade level you teach and are more effective than pull-out and push-in tutoring or in-class language coaching.

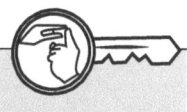

Key Vocabulary

Asides involve explanations and explicit life experience examples typically found in naturally occurring **incidental learning** opportunities to which approximately 90% Deaf children lack access (Bailes, 2001).

Chew on This!

Did you know that...?
In social situations, students may appear fluent in ASL making minimal errors. However, they may struggle expressing themselves in new situations or academic contexts due to gaps in vocabulary and grammatically complex phrases (Cummins, 2006; P. Horn-Marsh & K. Horn-Marsh, 2010).

(MM) (MT) (ES) (DI) (PI) Deaf Experiences, Perspectives, and Core Recommendations

Approximately 70% of Deaf children experience such severe language deprivation and language delays that their ability to learn and participate in school is impeded (Mitchell & Karchmer, 2004, 2005; Scott & Dostal, 2019). To mitigate these delays, they must be immersed in a fully accessible language environment (Hall et al., 2019).

ASL immersion classes have helped students make incredible leaps in ASL acquisition and knowledge development (Cummins, 2006; P. Horn-Marsh & K. Horn-Marsh,

2010). The introduction of a concept and expanding on it by talking about it encapsulates the main principle of the ASL immersion curriculum: Deaf students with language delays learn best when they are presented with opportunities to interact in ASL about things or concepts while also being supported by visuals including props, pictures, and videos. Unlike their same-age peers who have early access to language, these students need help catching up by having concepts explained and named, as demonstrated in the following Teacher Tale.

(MM) (MT) Teacher Tale

One January, during the second month of ASL immersion class implementation, we developed a 2-week unit on "ice," but instead of the intended 2-week unit, the unit continued for 1 month.

The first 2 weeks of the unit started with introducing the concept of "ice" in ASL. We used a graphic organizer displaying ice cubes, icicles, and the process of water turning into ice. A drawing of a popsicle was broken down by several illustrations showing how it is composed of different parts. Next, we had the students conduct a mini science activity in which they learned how to make their own popsicles by freezing grape juice. Many discussions, coupled with modeling ASL vocabulary and phrases, took place. As a result, the students began acquiring not only an understanding of the concepts but also the ASL for expressing them. The lesson ended with students reflecting on their experience and explaining what they learned on video and in ASL.

The second 2-week lesson started by showing another graphic organizer of animals (including penguins) and people living in the Arctic and Antarctica. Students in kindergarten and first grade went wild when a drawing of a penguin was on the whiteboard because *Happy Feet* (2006), an animated film, had recently come out in movie theaters. They recognized the flightless birds who lived in really cold waters, but they lacked the language and concepts to talk about them. So, over several days, we watched the movie *March of the Penguins* (2005) as a class, with us signing (using translanguaging rather than interpreting; see Chapters 4, 10, 11 and others for more on translanguaging), pointing to certain words in the captions and stopping to expose new sign vocabulary, discussing images and actions in the film, and explaining relevant background information. We took breaks from watching the film to engage in language-based activities that were thematic and hands-on (e.g., going outside with a thermometer before and after snow hit the ground to see temperature changes). At the conclusion of the movie, we returned to discussion and asked students to review what they had learned from the hands-on activities. We ended the month-long unit with the students making a class model of a penguin home and creating a penguin show-and-tell on video to share with their families.

—*Petra Horn-Marsh and Sherry Gabel*

ASL immersion teaching practices are based on the Vygotskian principle that interaction with peers is an effective way to develop language and learning strategies. According to Vygotsky (1962), language plays two critical roles in cognitive development: Language is the main means for adults to transmit information to students, and language itself becomes a powerful tool for expression. Through cooperative learning exercises, less-competent students acquire and develop ASL skills through social interaction with more skilled peers and adults in a conversation that is within the students' zones of proximal development.

Core Recommendations

Here, we highlight our core recommendations for incorporating ASL immersion strategies throughout K–12:

- Create opportunities to learn about self and the world through ASL.
- Scaffold comprehension of topics from concrete to complex ASL.
- Engage in a broad range of topics through a variety of ASL discourse.

(ES) (MM) (MT) Effective Practices for Immersion

This chapter presents activities highlighting each of our core recommendations for two different levels of ASL immersion: ASL Immersion I and ASL Immersion II. We recommend that you incorporate practices from both ASL immersion levels into your classroom. The main focus of ASL Immersion I is for young children to acquire and begin to develop ASL in a setting that is rich in context providing many cues (e.g., visuals, materials, scenarios) to assist students in their understanding of vocabulary and concepts, as well as to facilitate communication with others. In this class, students engage in creative play, enjoy watching **storytelling and storysigning**, are introduced to topics presented in still as well as moving images (e.g., drawings, photos, models, videos), and interact with others about the topics through visual- and language-rich activities (see Chapters 2, 3, and 4 for more on storytelling and storysigning).

ASL Immersion II is typically offered at the secondary level for students who transfer from mainstream and public school settings to a Deaf school or program that uses ASL. The focus of ASL Immersion II centers on students' development of ASL to discuss academic content. Students are presented with information through ASL and visually (e.g., drawings, photos, videos) to support their development of vocabulary and phrases in ASL for discussing academic content, including storytelling and storysigning. They also learn how to form different types of questions and develop the confidence to participate in language-rich and interpersonal discussions, fine-tuning their ASL to make it more colorful (Cummins, 2006; P. Horn-Marsh & K. Horn-Marsh, 2010).

The model that we have found most successful is when students from several different grade levels are placed in an ASL immersion class (e.g., in small schools: K–2 ASL immersion class, Grades 3–6 ASL immersion class, middle school ASL immersion class, and high school ASL immersion class; in large schools: the number of grade levels in an immersion class varies) with the optimal number of up to six students per class. If there is no ASL immersion class in your school, you can still integrate these practices by creating language-rich and real-world lessons and environments in your own classroom to support your students' acquisition of ASL.

Key Vocabulary

Storytelling involves oral stories passed down by storytellers, whereas **storysigning** involves translating written English by "signing it aloud" in ASL, making language and modality changes as needed (Center for ASL/English Bilingual Education and Research, 2004).

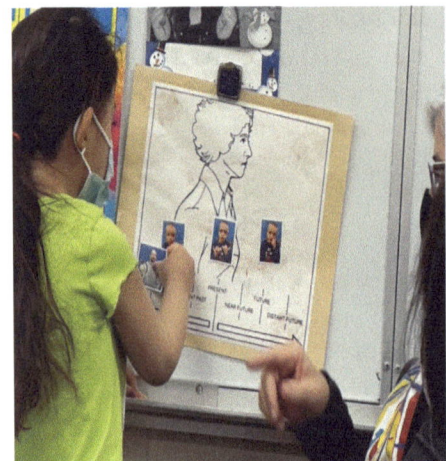 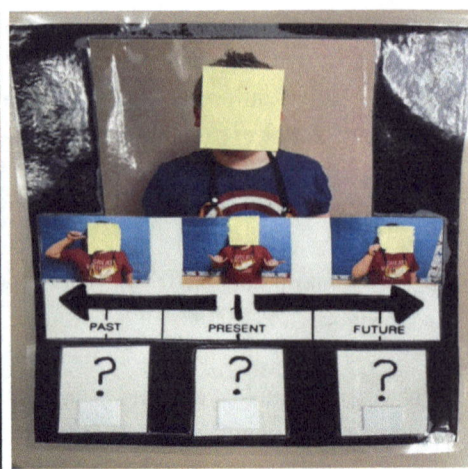

Students practice with time vocabulary by changing handshape or movement (i.e., ASL morphology) to add more detail to basic signs like year, month, week, and the days of the week (e.g., signing PAST-YEAR or 2-WEEK-LATER).

> ... developmental approaches for deaf children should prioritize healthy, expected development of all developmental domains (e.g., cognitive, academic, socio-emotional) that comes with the guaranteed full acquisition of a *fully accessible* first-language language foundation....
>
> —Hall, 2017, p. 364

In this section, we provide strategies for integrating each of our core recommendations in both ASL Immersion I and Immersion II settings. As mentioned, you can modify these strategies for any K–12 classroom setting.

(MM) (DI) (SEL) (MT) Core Recommendation 1: Create Opportunities to Learn About Self and the World Through ASL

In ASL Immersion I, opportunities are created for students who, due to language deprivation, have not had naturally occurring opportunities for authentic and spontaneous communication and imaginative investigation of self and the world. To get started, we recommend that you select topics based on concepts students need to develop. For many, these concepts may be very basic, such as naming the family members they interact with every day (e.g., mom, dad, siblings, grandparents, aunts, uncles). They often also may not have the ability to tell their ages or their birthday, and some may not even know their own names. They also may not know ASL signs for colors, clothes, and seasons and may struggle with time concepts (e.g., days of the week, months of the year, minutes, hours). When a new concept is introduced, not only do students need vocabulary, but they also need frequent and extended conversations related to the concept in order to develop it.

Calendar Time

Calendar work is one of the first units for ASL Immersion I students, regardless of their age. Here, we recommend that longer periods of time be allotted for discussing topics related to the calendar because the development of the concept of time is fundamental to the development of complex grammar, time management, and planning skills (Fellinger et al., 2005; Gulati, 2018; Hall et al., 2019). For younger children, you can start the unit with a children's book, such as *Today Is Monday* (Carle, 1993), *Monday Is One Day* (Levine, 2011), or *Saturdays Are for Stella* (Wellins, 2020). For students of any age, you can integrate stories from children's books to introduce and/or review varying

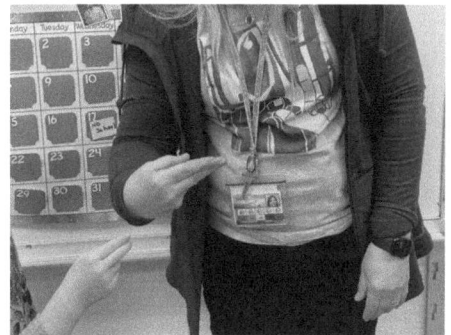

Here, Ivelis Bauman, an ASL Immersion teacher at Kansas School for the Deaf, guides students on how to fingerspell as well as sign. Each student is expected to name the next peer to go up to the calendar and to sign to the next student to let them know that it is their turn.

time concepts and related vocabulary like *family, celebrations, holidays, traditions, colors,* and *seasons.*

It is important to integrate calendar time daily, but you can vary the amount of time spent on it depending on student comprehension. Not only will your students benefit by learning past, present, and future temporal vocabulary through personalized picture cards of themselves signing the vocabulary, but you can ask them to apply their knowledge daily by attaching their picture cards (e.g., using Velcro) to the appropriate day of the week.

There are many activities you can do to help students build awareness of self and the world (see Chapters 7, 8, and others). You can then use drawings, enactments, and retells as formative assessments through teacher observations, video recording documentation, and student work (drawings, graphic organizers, and student–teacher conferences).

(MM) (DI) (SEL) (ABAR) (CM) Core Recommendation 2: Scaffold Comprehension of Topics From Concrete to Complex ASL

Have you wondered how to make your classroom represent environments that can model the world outside of the classroom? You can create this context in your classroom so that your students can apply their prior knowledge to the learning activities needed to move up to the next level. One way to do this is through scaffolding. Scaffolding gives the students the needed context to help them walk along a continuum where cognitively challenging topics, issues, and scenarios are increasingly

Chew on This!

Did you know that . . .
During the early stages of language acquisition, communication is more basic and is aided by the context where communication is happening. Cummins (2006) calls these *basic interpersonal communication skills*; children need to have enough of them before engaging in more complex language interactions.

understood with less contextualization (see Chapters 4, 5, and others for more examples on scaffolding). Here are some suggestions to get you started.

Stick It Into Action!

(CM) Moving From Concrete to Complex Language

Here are multiple approaches to help students move from concrete to complex language:

- Model how to protest appropriately (e.g., "Please stop pushing me," "Please wear your mask. If you don't wear your mask, you might get me sick").
- Model active listening skills (e.g., "I can see you're upset because your friend took your toy. What do you suggest we do to solve the problem?").
- Model positive conflict resolution (e.g., "I want to sit somewhere else because I'm in a bad mood" instead of "I don't want to sit by him").
- Model correct negotiating behavior (e.g., "I'll trade you this ball for your toy car" instead of "Give me the car!").
- Model creating and maintaining worlds of make-believe (e.g., a student asking another student to play the role of a horse and a cow arguing over a pile of hay. Continue beyond this argument, all staying in character, to see where the story goes).

Community Helpers

Here, we will highlight integrating scaffolding into a unit on community helpers from a K–2 social studies curriculum. To implement this, guide your students in creating a mini metropolis containing streets, businesses, people, and so on. Have students then play with the town while you create situations requiring them to communicate with each other. For example, while the students are going about their day in school or work (invented role-play), you might flash the lights and announce a fire at the post office. Students have to react and work together to find a solution by communicating with each other. Before creating such scenarios, though, it is important to use trauma-informed approaches, avoiding situations that may be triggering for students (e.g., do not choose a fire scenario if one of your students has had experiences with fires) and setting up ground rules for problem-solving to respect one another's varying backgrounds (e.g., race, culture,

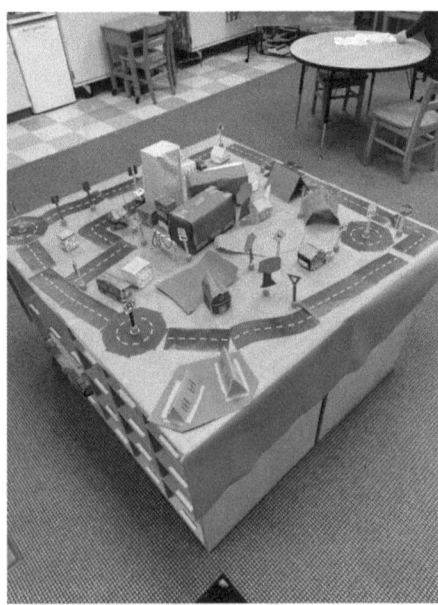

Community helper model.

languages, gender; see Chapter 8 for more on setting up ground rules). In the following Stick It Into Action, we demonstrate how you can bolster communication interactions by using the strategy of "Sabotage" (see Chapter 2 for additional examples).

 Stick It Into Action!

"Sabotage" Your Community to Encourage Communication
You can create a situation in which students need to communicate with each other by following these steps:

- Before class starts, block access to one building or street in your mini metropolis, thereby "sabotaging" the students' ability to navigate around the city.
- Students then must work together to figure out how to solve the problem of lack of access to the street or building. Draw on your students' experiences with seeing road construction but never having had labels, actions, or reasons explained to them in an accessible language such as ASL.
- Guide students' vocabulary development by introducing concepts such as *tar*, *steamroller*, and *orange barrels*. Guided actions can include shoveling asphalt, driving big machines, holding signs, or moving orange barrels to different parts of the street.
- After they have solved the problem, ask students to discuss the purpose of keeping roads well-maintained and why it is important to have workers holding signs and moving orange barrels or cones around.

Deaf children benefit from a visual setup like the mini metropolis to acquire various language skills like protesting, labeling, making simple requests, making requests for a broader range of objects and services, and communicating about the location of objects or barriers to objects. Activities that involve manipulating objects give children an opportunity to develop grammatical skills in which ASL classifiers are used and to enrich their language by using adjectives. These structured activities help keep the conversation focused, making it rich while building multiple areas of ASL grammar.

Venn Diagrams for Concept Development

The use of Venn diagrams (Venn, 1881) is a wonderful tool in ASL immersion class. They give visual support for concept development and help students integrate context and mediation that the teacher may need to add (see Chapter 3 for additional examples). This activity uses pictures to compare and contrast wants and needs.

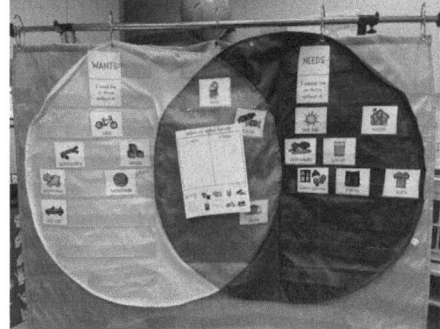

Using a Venn diagram to compare and contrast.

Stick It Into Action!

(MM) (DI) Venn Diagrams in the Immersion Classroom

Here are steps to use Venn diagrams to compare and contrast:

- Step 1 (Day 1): Ask your students what the difference is between things we want (but that are not necessary for survival) and things we need (things we must have to survive).
- Step 2 (Day 1): Lay out picture cards and ask each student to direct you where to place each picture on the Venn diagram following the students' direction, regardless if they are correct or not, until all the cards are exhausted.
- Step 3 (Day 2): Ask students if all of the picture cards are in the right place or if some of them should be moved to a different spot. Discuss together and confirm whether they are correct.
- Step 4: On subsequent days, ask your students to place pictures on the Venn diagram independently; their peers are expected to object if they see something out of place and explain why certain pictures belong in a different area of the circle.

This activity creates a reason for your students to debate with each other because they have to explain why a picture belongs in a certain spot and not another. Eventually, some students will start to ask questions about the differently colored space where the two circles overlap. Students then learn that there are gray areas in which some objects or concepts can belong in two different areas simultaneously. This is a great example of how you can scaffold your students' comprehension by moving them from simple to complex concepts.

Throughout this entire unit, one overarching skill you should continually emphasize is for students to communicate with each other while seated. They often want so badly to approach and interact with the diagram, but it is important for them to learn how to explain to others what to do by communicating only through ASL. Although this activity targets beginning ASL skills such as identifying objects on request or repeating what was just said by others, you can build on these skills by asking why people are doing certain things, conversing in hypotheticals, and influencing the opinions of others. Practicing interacting through complex dialogue is necessary to support development of more complex ASL skills.

(MM) (DI) (MT) Core Recommendation 3: Engage in a Broad Range of Topics Through a Variety of ASL Discourse

Development of language skills that are increasingly context-reduced and cognitively demanding are important for academic achievement and literacy development. One way of developing these kinds of language skills is by providing opportunities for varying types of discourse that cover different topics; the development of skills to narrate, argue, or describe also means an opportunity to broaden the vocabulary, morphology, and syntax of ASL.

Although it is essential to use ASL both in person (live) and in text (through videos), we recommend in-person activities as often as possible. Interacting in person is a more natural way of learning a language, and it also has many advantages for you as a teacher. Through interactive activities, you can create collaborative cooperative learning groups, observe students' interactive language skills, and modify the complexity of discourse on the spot. With ASL text, however, the difficulty level of discourse is frozen. To build students' receptive skills, you need to plan for viewing activities that highlight parts of a story, vocabulary, and other elements (see Chapters 3 and 12 for additional viewing strategies). For students' expressive ASL to grow, it is important to have students plan what to say before video recording themselves. This provides a learning structure for them to develop their ASL skills through two avenues: live attending/live signing and video viewing/video recording.

Building Knowledge of Story Elements and Structure
One way you can support ASL development through different discourses is to have your students practice telling stories that include characters, a beginning, middle, and end, descriptions of the setting, and dialogue between characters. You should also encourage them to discuss how a problem in the story is resolved. As an introductory activity, give each student a different wordless book to peruse. The advantage of this is that there is no English dictating the direction they are to take; there are only pictures depicting the action, characters, and scenery. With no distractions of written language, students are more able to construct their own versions of the story freely and are also able to focus solely on ASL. I (Kester) created a graphic organizer called **"Unlock the Text With a Key"** that we have found very useful for providing scaffolding for the students. This is a particularly beneficial strategy for Deaf students, who are visual learners, for helping them "see" the components of a story.

Stick It Into Action!

 **Unlock the Text With a KEY**
Here's what you can do to implement this strategy:

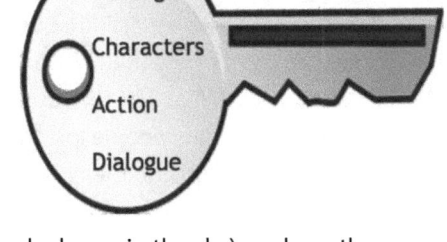

- To "see" the setting in a story: First, view the opening scenes of a movie with which all of your students are already familiar.
- Explain how opening movie scenes help to set up the story; for example, the camera panning over an area showing the landscape (e.g., city, countryside, ocean), the time of day (e.g., clock, sun in the sky), and weather (e.g., rainy, sunny, hot, cold).
- When the camera zooms in on the characters, discuss how the physical aspects and personality of the characters are revealed.
- Describe how students can identify the characters through their actions and dialogue.

Stick It Into Action! *(continued)*

- Prominently display the KEY graphic in your classroom any time the students are expected to tell stories in ASL because the graphic helps remind them how to narrate a story for others.
- Remind your students to approach discourse with this strategy and explain when it may or may not apply (sometimes, ideas or actions do not lend themselves to the key).

Another wonderful activity is to take a book that has been storysigned, in which the content is already familiar to the class, and assign roles such as characters, setting, and narrator to each student. Then, have them become the characters and reenact the story as a group. The person assigned the role of "setting" is responsible for narrating what the viewer sees in the way of landscape, weather, time, and so on. The student in the narrator role steps in and out of scenes to provide backstory and explicit information or to explain the lesson or moral of the story. Have the class put on a play together and then film the play as a culminating activity to demonstrate their knowledge of story structure. You can then evaluate students on whether the meaning of the story content was intact and whether they used appropriate ASL features (structure) and conceptually and semantically accurate ASL.

When you have students who are working on more complex ASL skills, you can take this one step further by explicitly teaching targeted skills through storybooks, reenactments, scenarios, viewing and signing videos and presentations, and other activities. In this Teacher Tale, we highlight an example from an ASL teacher in a secondary school monitoring students' ASL comprehension. Remember to use trauma-informed approaches when discussing topics of death and devastation.

  Teacher Tale

One good activity for finding out the extent to which my students are able to comprehend new information in ASL is by selecting a current event that I know will captivate their interest. One example I used was the tsunami that hit parts of Asia in 2007. Most of the students had no idea what had happened, the root cause, or the complete devastation resulting from it. I started the lesson by scrolling through pictures showing the tsunami's aftermath before starting a question-and-answer discussion session for about half an hour. Students were then given a quiz in ASL to assess their comprehension of the discussion (e.g., "What was the cause of the tsunami?" "In which world region did it occur?" and "How many people lost their lives?"). It was also evident that when students are in charge of driving their own discussion, they are more motivated to learn.

—*Sherry Gabel, ASL teacher*

  Key Strategy

Brief and Extended Constructed Response

These activities involve asking students an open-ended question that begins with a prompt and having students arrive at a conclusion based on their knowledge about the topic. You can then have them respond in one of two ways with a brief or extended constructed response. The brief constructed response (BCR; Tankersley, 2007) involves the student restating the teacher's question and the student's answer about the topic. The extended constructed response (ECR; Tankersley, 2007) takes considerably more time and thought. It requires students not only to give an answer but also to do so in as much in-depth detail as possible. In some cases, students not only have to give an answer and explain the answer, but they also have to show how they arrived at that answer (see Appendices C, D, and E, on https://gallaudetupress.manifoldapp). The graphic outlining the steps involved in performing a BCR or an ECR should always be present to support the student's presentation.

A BCR can become a daily bellringer activity for practicing complex ASL. You can also use it at the end of your lessons as a way to evaluate students' ASL development. You can ask your students to perform the BCR on different academic, technical, or procedural topics. Topics may be drawn from a stack of cards or from a list projected on the whiteboard and could include, for example, the life cycle of a frog, how to cook spaghetti, how to post a YouTube video, the underlying factors causing the American Civil War, or the efforts farmers take in soil and water conservation.

You can record yourself presenting information on a complex topic in the form of a BCR or an ECR, using technical and fingerspelled vocabulary you know is difficult for the students to grasp without scaffolding, preteaching, or extrapolation. Ask students to keep a tally of the number of things they did not comprehend and then use the list to guide the class discussions. Conversely, you can have students view the same videos but give each student a turn holding the remote control or mouse. Every time a student does not understand something, be it a vocabulary word or concept, have them pause the video and ask for clarification. After viewing your BCR or ECR (via video or in person), peers challenge each other's opinions by trying to poke holes in their arguments; they must defend their opinions with supporting evidence (see Chapters 9 and 11 for additional strategies, such as the strategy CER, on making a point and supporting a claim). For students to master this skill, they must defend their position with details as well as explain how they arrived at their position. At the time of this writing, we recommend PowerPoint as the preferred method for students to present their information.

Stick It Into Action!

 **Making an Argument**

When engaging in an ECR, it may be helpful for students to practice making an argument. Here's what you can do to help them practice:

- Model yourself making an argument (e.g., using a teacher- or student-selected topic, live signing in front of the class, or via video).
- Show students that making a claim requires evidence (e.g., facts, quotations, statistics).
- Practice with students how to gather evidence they can use to support their claims.
- Show students how to organize their arguments using a graphic organizer.
- Give students time in the classroom to create their PowerPoint presentations.

Stick It Into Action! (*continued*)
- Have students practice presenting their arguments with peers and/or with you providing feedback.
- Have students record themselves presenting their arguments.

Keep in mind that all of these discussions or performances mentioned in this section should be recorded on video and viewed again with your students to discuss what worked well and what could be improved. This is the essence of ongoing learning and formative assessment.

Additional Things to Consider

 Entering/Exiting ASL Immersion

So, what are the qualifications for entering and exiting ASL immersion class? The Kendall Conversational Proficiency Level (P-Level) scale is an ideal instrument for identifying students' conversational proficiency levels in ASL according to their chronological age (see P-Level Assessment, Appendix A, available on https://gallaudetupress.manifoldapp.org). Technically, although developed with Deaf students in mind, the P-Level instrument can be used to assess students' conversational proficiency levels in any language (French, 1999a).

In elementary school, instead of attending social studies and science in their regular classes, *identified*[1] students could go to ASL immersion class during that time and return to their regular classes for the rest of the day. Lessons in ASL immersion can follow the social studies and science state standards where instruction on social studies and science themes are then taught. If the student is age 5 or older, and they have not mastered all of the communication skills on Level 4, they would automatically qualify for an ASL immersion class. Once they achieve a P-Level 4, they exit the class and their ASL goals carry over to pull-out ASL tutoring. A few students may need continued support beyond their time in ASL immersion if they have not yet mastered age-appropriate expressive ASL skills to convey academic concepts. They would then begin receiving ASL tutoring services directly related to the ASL goals identified in their individualized education program.

In secondary school, the ASL immersion curriculum loosely follows the important life events of students, including school events, extracurricular events, holidays, seasons, and so on. This class is targeted toward students who have been identified[2] at a

---

1. Identified elementary school students are those with a P-level of 0–4, which are levels for basic interpersonal communication skills, or social ASL. For more information on P-Levels, see Appendix. These students receive support for quick acquisition of social ASL skills. This type of class can occur at the elementary and/or secondary levels. Spoken and printed English are not to be emphasized during this class, but English may be found attached to pictures or other materials used in lessons. Students are encouraged to draw or gesture to express ideas not yet acquired in ASL. The instructor is also expected to draw until students achieve higher levels of ASL proficiency.

2. Identified students are typically those at the secondary school level (P-Levels 5–7), which refer to *cognitive academic language proficiency*. Students are encouraged to use social ASL as a means to circumnavigate when they express academic ideas not yet developed in ASL. The instructor is expected to start lessons on familiar topics before delving deeper into new topics.

P-Level 5–7 for ASL development. ASL Immersion II can be offered as an elective class at this level, and no grades should be given.

Our observations and student results show that student growth has indeed been exponential. Often, multiple students have the same goals, making them easier to address in a group setting, thereby saving an immense amount of time that would be lost due to being pulled from other core classes for tutoring. You may read this and think that these ASL communication skills should already be covered in an ASL class. Indeed, they should! Yet, unlike English language arts, ASL language arts (ASLLA) is not widely and consistently available for Deaf students (see Chapter 3 for more on ASLLA and ASL literature across the curriculum). To address the repercussions of language deprivation and delays, we recommend a language immersion class in ASL; however, at minimum, ASLLA and ASL literature arts should be integrated into the P–12 curriculum to support and facilitate ASL acquisition and development for all students.

Bringing It All Together

In this section, we provide examples of instructional activities from both ASL Immersion I and II units. Each unit also includes all three of our core recommendations. We have broken down activities from each unit by day to show how you may progress.

ASL Immersion I

The following ASL Immersion I unit example is appropriate for elementary students with language deprivation and delays (P-Levels 1–4):

(MM) (DI) (PI) (SEL) (MT) **Baking Bread Unit in ASL Immersion I Class**
Purpose: To learn multiple skills including measurement, sequencing, time, and team communication.

One favorite activity each year is baking bread. Some students may have never been given the opportunity to cook with their caregivers or siblings at home, let alone acquire the vocabulary for measurements, cooking utensils, ingredients, etc. It is truly exhilarating to see many of these students run around the room gathering ingredients and utensils to make something together that they can call their own (see Table 13.1).

Ivelis Bauman models the sign for *flour*.

Picture cards on a ring are made available to each group. They should also be projected on a screen both before the activity and as a review.

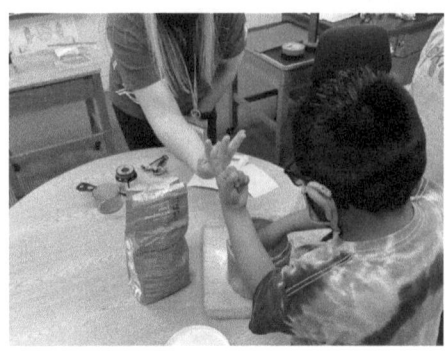
Explicit monitoring while student counts how many tablespoons to add.

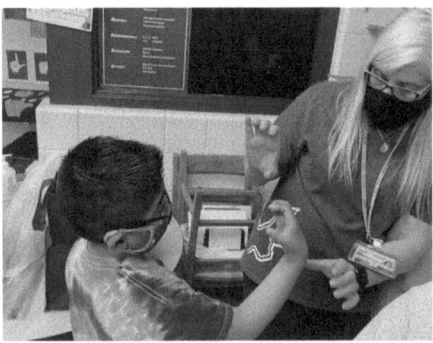
Modeling correct palm orientation.

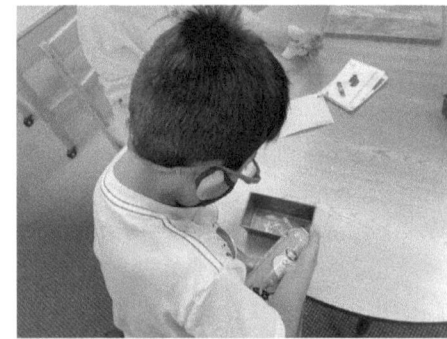
Student independently adding grease.

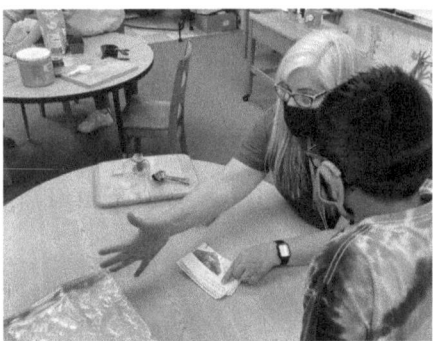
Explanation of what each card says.

Incorporating time concepts in cooking.

ASL Immersion II

This unit example is appropriate for secondary students in an ASL Immersion II and/or for those with limited ASL skills (P-Level 4) or who have already completed ASL Immersion I class but still need to catch up to their same-age peers.

(MM) (PI) (SEL) (MT) **Children's Story Classics Unit in ASL Immersion II Class**
Purpose: Develop receptive and expressive signing skills using grammatical aspects and ASL literacy features during ASL storytelling (see Table 13.2).

Table 13.1. Daily Plan for Baking Bread Unit for ASL Immersion I

Day	Activities	Core Recommendation (CR)
Day 1	Open the unit by storysigning the books *Bread Around the World* (Serrano, 2010) and *Pop Pop and Me and a Recipe* (Smalls, 2012).	CR 1
	Ask your students if they have ever cooked with a caregiver (keep in mind that some of your students may have never had this experience).	
	Ask your students if they'd like to try it in school.	
Day 2	Review the vocabulary for measurements (e.g., cups, tablespoons, teaspoons), ingredients (e.g., flour, grease, oil), and cooking utensils (e.g., plastic zipper bag, pan, oven).	CR 2
	Teach new vocabulary by having students view a pre-made video demonstrating in ASL how to bake or cook a dish using the targeted vocabulary related to measurements and cooking.	CR 3
	We recommend you make your own video so you can determine appropriate vocabulary and content to include.	
Day 3	Divide the class into groups so that more students have an increased opportunity to communicate with each other and to physically complete sequenced steps in this hands-on activity.	CR 2
	Give each group their own set of measuring instruments, cooking utensils, and ingredients.	
	Start with pre-made cards with pictures and labels attached to a ring.	
	Give each group their own set of cards to manipulate and follow (keeping a duplicate set for yourself).	
	In a dry run, demonstrate each step from start to finish while the students follow along with their own sequence cards, viewing the steps only.	
Day 4	Tell the students to wash their hands before starting to make their bread, and then tell them to carefully follow the recipe according to sequenced instruction cards.	CR 1
	At this point, you no longer guide the students. Only ask students questions such as, "Have you added the water?" and "How many tablespoons of oil have you added?"	CR 2
	Ask students to keep track of how many tablespoons have been added or need to be added.	

Table 13.1. (*continued*)

Day	Activities	Core Recommendation (CR)
	Encourage students to think about and respond to questions.	
	Model correct use of ASL vocabulary when needed.	
	If needed, remind students of specific vocabulary for measuring that they learned earlier.	
	Support students as they perform each step by themselves whether they make mistakes or not.	
	If the students make errors, they need to experience the fruits of their labor (eating bread made with a tablespoon of salt added rather than just a teaspoon).	
	Keep asking questions to make students think, weigh their options, or ask for help.	
Day 5	After all groups have completed the steps laid out in their sequence cards, review time concepts for how long it takes to bake bread.	CR 2
	Because the bread can't be baked in the same class session, you may have to do the actual baking. However, the steps in baking can be explained using a smartphone timer.	
Day 6	After you bake the bread in the classroom oven, bring the students back, later in the day, to taste and to bring home their creation.	CR 1
Day 7	Ask students to rate the taste of their bread and to debate what went wrong if it didn't bake correctly or if it tasted peculiar.	CR 1
		CR 2
	Finally, give each student a simple recipe (can be the same one or contact their family for their bread, naan, or other recipes) and ask them to bake it at home with family or friends, reviewing the signs for everything they learned in the lesson.	CR 3

Well-known books and stories (classics like *The Three Little Pigs, The Tortoise and the Hare,* or *Goldilocks and the Three Bears*) are chosen initially because these students have usually been exposed to these stories. Since the students are already familiar with the storyline, they are better able to focus on their storysigning. That makes it easy for them to focus on incorporating all key elements of the story (e.g., important events, characters, setting) while incorporating targeted ASL vocabulary, morphology, grammar, or structure. Because ASL immersion does not focus on reading English print, it is important to choose books or stories with plenty of pictures that provide enough nonverbal information to help the students follow the storyline more easily.

ASL IMMERSION I AND II

Daily Plan for Unit

Table 13.2. Daily Plan for Children's Story Classics Unit for ASL Immersion II

Day	Activities	Core Recommendation (CR)
Day 1	Sit with your students in a semicircle with you sitting next to a large-print book on an easel, engaging students by asking questions.	CR 1, 2, 3
	Highlight the following details: Point out and describe the setting; introduce and describe the characters with rich details (e.g., through the use of constructed action mimicking the action of the characters) and dialogue (what the characters say and how they say it).	
Day 2	Start by modeling the first page. That will help orient the students to what is expected from them and will help get the activity rolling.	CR 2, 3
	Assign a student to sign the next page, and then randomly choose students to sign subsequent pages (rather than following a predictable order).	
	If the student starts to read the English text, ask the student to detach from the text after reading it and face the class. The students should retell the story from what they remember (i.e., free translation).	
	Provide feedback as needed with particular attention to facial expression, use of constructed action, and details.	
	Choose a new student to sign the next page.	
	Each student should have a turn and do more than one page, continuing in this manner until the class is finished with the book.	
Day 3	Have the students take control of the whole book.	CR 2, 3
	Students are assigned as "peer editors" to provide feedback to the person who retells a given part of the book (3–4 pages at a time per student).	
	After one student has completed the assigned pages, the peers then give feedback on what can be improved or changed.	
	Your role is just to encourage and guide discussion.	
Days 4–7	Have individual students retell the whole story and receive feedback from peers at the end.	CR 3
	Based on peer feedback and your observations, decide which skills to target in subsequent mini lessons: a. How to role-play characters using constructed action and constructed dialogue b. How to make a more detailed description of the setting	

Table 13.2. (continued)

Day	Activities	Core Recommendation (CR)
Day 8	Each student is recorded signing the story for formative or summative assessment. This can be done with a laptop and a constructed backdrop behind the student. Consider constructing different backgrounds to accommodate different scenes in the story. One idea is to assign each group of students to construct a background. Archive all recordings to show students their growth at the end of the year. It is not only a fun activity but the recordings can also be used as models for future students.	CR 2, 3

Teacher demonstrating what not to do (read English text).

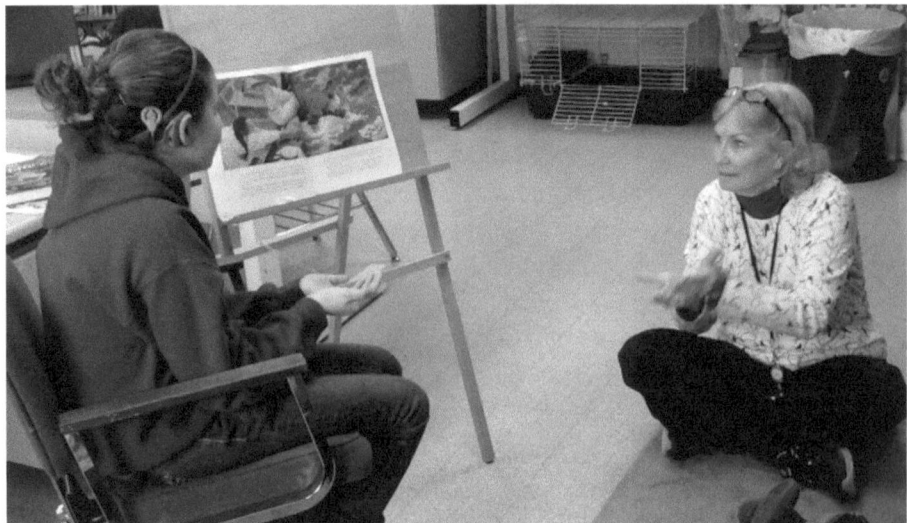

Teacher provides feedback on classifier movement.

Your Turn to Practice!

Now it's your turn! You can practice implementing the core recommendations in this chapter by exploring the topic of community living we described previously (see Core Recommendation 2) with your current students, in a mock setting, or within a pull-out class situation approved by your school's administration or faculty instructor. The objectives you identify for expressive and receptive ASL skills should follow an ongoing assessment tool, such as a teacher observation record, rubrics, and/or the P-Levels. Essentially, formative assessment can be used daily to monitor progress in students' communication skills in ASL. Because you will have students with different levels of ASL mastery, you will need to provide differentiated instruction. In this lesson, as with every classroom activity throughout the year, you should always provide opportunities for students to resolve conflicts. Begin with role-playing and modeling, with the goal of students ultimately being able to independently resolve conflicts using appropriate vocabulary.

Plan Your Lesson

Create a mini-metropolis and implement the sabotage strategy (see **Core Recommendation 2**). After observing students interacting and identifying areas to target, you can create your next lesson.

- Plan for instruction by determining the following student skills:
    - Which ASL language objectives will you target? (See ASL Standards)
    - What vocabulary will you target? (Choose five words)
    - What background knowledge does each student need for your lesson?
- After determining your lesson objectives, take into account the possible situations that may arise when you have multiple students working either together or in opposition to each other.
    - Identify possible opportunities to sabotage.
    - Set up conflicts for students to practice resolving.

Teach Your Lesson

Teach your lesson in a real or mock setting.

Reflect on Your Instruction

- Reflect on your teaching of the lesson. In what ways did you effectively incorporate each of the core recommendations?
    - What went well? What would you do differently if you teach it again?
    - After assessing your students, how well did they learn the targeted objectives?

Recommended Readings/Viewings

For Teachers/Teacher Candidates

- *Have You Ever Seen . . . ? An American Sign Language Handshape DVD/Book* (Smith & Jacobowitz, 2006). Students discover and discuss ASL handshapes in environmental pictures. The DVD provides expanded background in Deaf culture and history.
- *Pursuit of ASL: Interesting Facts Using Classifiers* (Petrone Stratiy, 1998). This is a fantastic DVD for viewing brief constructed responses in ASL, and it can also be used for finger-reading skills and acquiring/learning classifiers.

For Using With Students:

- VL2 Storybook Apps (https://vl2storybookapps.com). Students enjoy viewing these original works (i.e., *The Baobab, The Giant Turnip,* and *Evon Discovers Black Pride*).
- *The American Sign Language Handshape Game Cards* (Bahan & Paul, 1988). These cards can be used in various ways, but distinctions can be made between initialized signs, regular signs, and classifiers.
- YA Books Central (https://www.yabookscentral.com/search/tag/publisher/asl-tales/?criteria=2). ASL Tales books with videos (e.g., *The Princess and the Pea* and *Annie's Tails*). Students can view and practice storysigning and learn to apply ASL linguistic features.
- American Society for Deaf Children: ASDC Video Archives (https://deafchildren.org/category/asl-videos/). You can expose your students to (as well as share with their families) this wonderful free ASL resource on various cultural holidays and traditions, daily life, stories, and ASL learning.

Conclusion

We recognize that teachers and future teachers of Deaf students, like you, have much to juggle with standards-based content and skill instruction delivery, not to mention working with students on meeting their individualized education program goals. You may worry about not being able to do all of these while providing time and space for your students to acquire and develop their ASL. Keep in mind that students' language skills and ability to communicate about academic concepts are the cornerstone of their learning successes. You can integrate standard-based content and skills with ASL-specific objectives using an interdisciplinary approach. Utilizing the strategies we provide here, along with others, can make units comprehensible and meaningful for your students. Connect to real-world knowledge visually and through hands-on activities, and allow students to acquire and develop ASL communication and language skills. These meaningful and comprehensible integrated opportunities can go a long way to supporting students' language development that is fully accessible to them.

Sticking Points

- Connect students' personal information, the world, and content through visuals, literature, and activities to students' varying ASL language skills.
- Apply students' prior knowledge to the learning activities which they need to move up to the next communication and language level. Use scaffolding as needed.
- Create opportunities for peer interaction in different discourses and expose them to ASL texts to broaden students' language skills and learning strategies.

Transition

Carrie Lou Bloom
Kristin Ryan

Although the concept of "transition" may seem like something that can be limited to a book chapter, a course, or a presentation, we suggest that this concept is foundational to everything you do in educational environments. The goal of transition is to ensure that students are ready for life after high school. That means transition goals should consist of incremental milestones like increasing self-advocacy skills and larger milestones like completing degrees or certifications and getting jobs. Transition goals are deeply personal and individualized—and often, they change over time. As educators, researchers, and community members, we want to ensure that Deaf students are prepared for the next step in their lives. This is the ultimate goal of education. As members of Deaf communities ourselves, we believe deeply in the success of Deaf people and Deaf communities. When we uplift one, we uplift all.

Who Are We?

For most of my childhood, I (Carrie Lou) wanted to be an art teacher. But a middle school field trip to the Gulf of Mexico, where I dissected squid, along with visits to see dolphins at SeaWorld, led to a brief period of time where I wanted to become a marine biologist. Eventually, I combined my interests in education and science to become an educational researcher. In my work with the National Deaf Center on Postsecondary Outcomes, my main job is making sure people understand that we need to improve systems so Deaf people can reach their goals—not that we need to "fix" Deaf people.

As a child, I (Kristin) wanted to be a social worker. After several years in the mental health field working with clients who needed to improve their independent living skills, I saw the need for intervention in all areas of transition earlier in their lives. I returned to school and obtained my degree in education. I also obtained my work-based learning coordinator license and helped establish a transition program at our high school. I am currently the transition coordinator at Metro Deaf School, where I work with ninth to 12th grade students to help them start thinking about and preparing for life beyond high school.

As educators, researchers, and community members who are part of the system, we each must do our part to increase our knowledge and readiness to support transition preparedness for Deaf students, and we must advocate for changing the systems in which Deaf students navigate. This chapter offers a mix of evidence-based practices, professional experiences, and practical examples to give you the tools you need to support Deaf students. Schools and programs vary widely in how transition planning is embedded in school systems—this depends on available resources, district guidelines, school structure, interagency collaboration, state regulations, and the expertise of school staff. Some programs have dedicated transition courses and specialized staff, whereas others discuss transition planning only during the individualized education program (IEP) process, and others have a mix of approaches. Because we believe that transition is foundational to education, we believe that *all* teachers and school staff should become familiar with the core recommendations in this chapter, not only "transition" staff.

Deaf Experiences, Perspectives, and Core Recommendations

Although many Deaf students want to complete high school, receive college degrees or certifications, and get jobs, fewer Deaf people reach these goals than hearing people. Deaf students are slightly less likely to complete high school when compared to their hearing peers, but they are much less likely to complete college degrees or certifications (Bloom et al., 2023; Garberoglio & Cawthon, 2020; Garberoglio et al., 2019b). Employment rates are also lower among Deaf communities; only 53.5% of Deaf people were employed in 2021 compared to 70.4% of hearing people (Bloom et al., 2022). These gaps are also visible within Deaf communities. Black, Indigenous, and Latinx Deaf people, DeafDisabled, and DeafBlind people are less likely to complete degrees or certifications and be employed than are their white or nondisabled Deaf peers (Bloom et al., 2023; Garberoglio et al., 2019a, 2019b). These gaps are indicative of systemic deficiencies, not individual deficiencies. Systemic deficiencies include language deprivation, reduced access to social opportunities, negative attitudes and biases about Deaf people, and the lack of qualified and experienced professionals (National Deaf Center, 2017). Systemic barriers prevent Deaf people from achieving their goals, and this is what needs to be changed.

At its core, transition is about reaching our goals, dreams, and aspirations. This is a highly individual process. Your students form their goals based on who they are and who they want to be. Newer perspectives of transition have shifted beyond standardized checklists and milestones toward a way of understanding transition as a design for life—as an active and ongoing construction of our lives (Nota et al., 2015). This

Chew on This!

Did you know that . . . ?
Only 21% of Deaf adults ages 25 to 64 in the United States have completed a bachelor's degree in 2021 compared to 36.9% of hearing adults (Bloom et al., 2023). Let's change that!

Chew on This!

Did you know that...?
Stronger self-determination and autonomy have been linked to living independently, college enrollment, higher earnings, and more opportunities for career advancement for Deaf young adults (Garberoglio et al., 2014, 2017). Ask yourself how you can strengthen your Deaf students' self-determination skills!

process must be student-centered and also Deaf-centered. Deaf people need to be free to create their own goals and make plans for reaching them in ways that align with their values, needs, and experiences.

Student-centered decision making ensures that students take an active role in planning their future. This recognizes the reality that many Deaf students have reduced access to formal, structured support systems after they leave high school. As teachers, it's your job to make sure that you equip Deaf students with the tools they will need for the rest of their lives. After all, Deaf students must be not *just as* prepared but *more* prepared for challenging situations than their hearing peers. Your students will face many potential conflicts on a daily basis—fighting for appropriate accommodations, deciding when to stand up for their rights, identifying strategies to be included in group conversations, and advocating for job promotions and raises. However, this preparation doesn't always happen in classrooms, and it's time to change that.

Deaf people often talk about the importance of self-determination in our lives—the ability to make things happen in our own lives that align with our goals. Students who have stronger self-determination skills are more comfortable making their own decisions, managing their time, solving problems, advocating for themselves, setting goals, and making plans; these are all key transition outcomes (Landmark et al., 2010; Shogren et al., 2015; Test et al., 2009; Wehmeyer et al., 2012). Although all people have the potential to develop self-determination skills, Deaf students need actual *opportunities* to develop and practice those skills (Nota et al., 2007). This needs to be a key consideration in transition planning—to ensure that we center Deaf students in this process and create real opportunities for them to develop self-determination.

The attitudes and beliefs of families and educators have a big influence on what Deaf youth believe about themselves and their ability to reach their goals (Cawthon et al., 2015; Crowe et al., 2015). As a teacher, it is your role to do whatever you can to counter the negative assumptions about Deaf people's potential for success and prepare Deaf students to do the same for themselves. Encouraging autonomous decision making, scaffolding increasingly difficult challenges, and allowing space for growth are all part of raising expectations for Deaf youth. This should happen within supportive environments where students feel like they have the space to learn and grow even while making mistakes. Teachers with optimistic expectations about Deaf students are able to support social-emotional development and self-advocacy (Smith, 2013). At the end of the day, students need to know that the adults in their lives believe in their potential to reach their goals. This is what matters—not so much what the specific expectations are but knowing that someone believes in them.

When thinking about how to raise expectations for Deaf students, recall that strengthening self-determination skills requires the *opportunity* to develop and practice these skills. Raising expectations for Deaf students means you must ask yourself if you are doing things *for* Deaf students. Encourage students to make their own choices whenever possible. As teachers and role models in students' lives, you should be mindful of how adults tend to intervene when you see students making poor choices. Students need to be given opportunities to learn, even if that means making mistakes along the way. Furthermore, you also need to be mindful of what you base their expectations on. Are you basing their expectations on your students' true abilities, or are you subconsciously comparing those students to their idea of what Deaf students can and cannot do? As an example, Deaf students without any Deaf adults on their transition planning team may be praised for doing mediocre work because those transition team members may not have access to Deaf role models, robust benchmarks, or established standards that they can use to gauge the students' abilities.

Transition planning for Deaf students must be not only student-centered but also Deaf-centered. This means that transition planning must center on the lived experiences, specific challenges, and needs of Deaf people. Transition objectives should be written specifically based on these experiences, challenges, and needs. For example, Deaf students will need to become knowledgeable about the range of assistive and accessible technologies that may be a good fit for their needs and goals, their legal rights, and how to request accommodations. Students also need to see real-life examples of how Deaf people navigate the world across a range of settings and contexts. People learn best in community, from one another. Involving Deaf adults in transition planning for Deaf students is critical, particularly as an opportunity for incidental learning.

Did you know that...?
Deaf high school students who looked for jobs on their own had stronger employment outcomes later in life than those who found their jobs with support (Garberoglio et al., 2017). Ask yourself how you can encourage more autonomy in the job search process.

Core Recommendations

We provide four core recommendations, framed around the core concepts of being student-centered and Deaf-centered, as you prepare Deaf students to reach their transition goals:

- Raise expectations.
- Set good goals.
- Rely on community resources.
- Develop a strong collaborative team.

Effective Practices for Transition

In this section, we integrate research with practice as we dive deeper into the four core recommendations for transition planning. These recommendations are built around the idea of being student-centered and Deaf-centered. Each recommendation is based on evidence-based practices in the field and will have examples from practice that you can use in your classroom or transition program now.

(DI) (PI) Core Recommendation 1: Raise Expectations

Raising expectations for Deaf students is key to preparing youth for their future and encouraging self-determination development. Do not be afraid to set realistic expectations that are age appropriate and, if necessary, incorporate lessons on social skills. You can raise expectations by (a) checking your biases and assumptions, (b) providing real-life opportunities, (c) encouraging students to lead their IEP meetings, and (d) evaluating appropriate course placement.

❝ The best way to learn is often through authentic real-life experiences and examples.

—Kristin Ryan, transition teacher

 Check Your Biases and Assumptions

This is the first step in the process of setting and raising expectations. Each of us has differing levels of privilege, which comes with a set of assumptions about others who do not share the same privileges. Maybe you are a hearing teacher who subconsciously believes that Deaf students need a little extra help and thus takes away opportunities for them to do things themselves. Maybe your whiteness is influencing your biases about which of your students you should recommend for a leadership opportunity, where you might be more likely to believe that your white students are more "qualified." Maybe ableism is underlying your assumptions on which jobs your DeafDisabled or DeafBlind students should aim for, thinking it is in their best interest to decide for them instead of taking the time to learn more about their individual goals and how you can best support them. Maybe monolingual bias hinders your ability to value non-English languages such as ASL and Spanish equitably. Take some time to consider how understanding your privileges should be a part of your ongoing professional development plans (see Chapter 8 for additional examples). There are many workshops and articles about unpacking our privilege as educators—we suggest starting with Learning for Justice (www.learningforjustice.org). Just as you expect your students to set goals and make plans, you should do the same for yourselves!

Teacher Tale

Another staff person (Hard of Hearing, fluent in ASL) and I brought a group of students to a store to purchase individual bus passes for each student. Some students needed a new bus pass, whereas others needed a specific amount put on the card they already had. I wanted each student to go through the experience of purchasing and loading their bus pass. Because of how our school rules are set up, I had all of the money needed to facilitate individual transactions. I wanted to explain to the clerk what was going on before calling each student up to take care of their business. The clerk was confused and having a hard time understanding why I didn't want just to do the whole thing in one single transaction. The other staff person I was with was getting agitated because this was not normal for them. They came and took over the discussion, and they were able to finish everything up in one entire transaction. My whole goal for the outing was pretty much canceled out. It was clear to me that the other staff person was not used to having to navigate, explain, and clarify. I almost feel like the other staff person was embarrassed for us. Their discomfort took over, and the students missed out on an opportunity to see how that whole situation could have been handled in a different way.

—*Kristin Ryan, transition teacher*

Provide Real-Life Opportunities

To practice autonomous decision making while being allowed space to make mistakes is a key component of raising expectations for Deaf youth. Hands-on experiences out in the community are key, whether through field trips or on-the-job training. If that is not feasible, seek out online resources to expose students to real-life examples of how to navigate the world as a Deaf person. In the following Teacher Tale, Kristin describes taking the lessons students learned in a real-life experience riding a bus and how those lessons helped the students understand that mistakes and surprises happen in real life. Through that experience, students learned that situations usually work out even when things don't always go as planned. Students also learned about the importance of paying attention to details.

Stick It Into Action!

Have Students Plan a Field Trip

Have students take the lead in planning a field trip. This can include having them look up bus route information, fill out a worksheet with step-by-step instructions for taking public transit to a destination, and then follow those instructions. Staff can tag along but should not help at all, even if the student(s) are way off base.

Teacher Tale

While on an outing a few years ago, on our way back, a group of students got on the bus, but it was going the wrong way—they were supposed to get on the bus that was going eastbound instead of westbound. All of the other information was correct—correct bus stop, correct intersection, correct bus number, correct route number except for the one letter that indicates whether it was going E or W. I was hoping that one of the students would notice their error before we got on the bus. As we waited, I made several comments, trying to drop hints, to no avail. As the bus approached the bus stop, I was going to tell the students what was going on, but at the very last minute, I changed my mind. As we got on the bus, I told myself that the students would notice their error within a block or two, and we could just get off, cross the street, and catch the other bus. We got on the bus and rode along for a while. The students were busy chatting, so they didn't notice that we weren't passing the usual landmarks. As a teacher, I had a very hard time not saying anything. Internally, I was FREAKING OUT and wondering if I would still have a job at the end of the day. By the time they realized their mistake, we were already 15 minutes into the ride. Getting off, crossing the street, and then waiting for the next bus in the opposite direction put us an hour behind schedule. As a result, they didn't get back to school until after their buses left for the day. Their parents had to come to pick them up. Even though the students were clearly very stressed out after they realized their mistake, ultimately, they learned how to manage their stress and understood that it was not the end of the world. Although it was hard to maintain my expectations for them, being able to accomplish the goal on their own, I stuck with it, and they learned a much stronger lesson than if I had intervened. I don't think I could have "planned" this lesson better!
—*Kristin Ryan, transition teacher*

(PI) Encourage Students to Lead Their IEP Meetings

IEP meetings are an important part of transition planning—and a great opportunity to raise expectations for Deaf students. Student-led IEP meetings are a well-documented, evidence-based practice in transition (Martin et al., 2006; Seong et al., 2015). Students should be encouraged to be active participants in their IEPs as early as possible. Starting in ninth grade, students should be introduced to the concept of leading their own IEP meetings with their case manager's support. Whether you are their teacher or transition specialist, be sure to prepare students for leading their IEP meetings by doing things like asking them questions about themselves and their goals, setting up prep meetings in advance, and sharing slideshow templates that the students can use for these meetings. Having students actively participate in their IEP meetings helps them build their self-confidence. Their increased self-confidence, in turn, leads to empowerment, which plays a critical role in developing their leadership skills.

Teacher Tale

One student, who I was assigned as a teacher advocate, declared to the team (including his grandparents) that he wanted to become a professional basketball player. They laughed at his comment, dismissed it, and asked him to "be real." He became upset. I asked him to explain how we could support his next steps to becoming a basketball player. He was a great basketball player. He explained the WHOLE nine yards (AAU [Amateur Athletic Union] tournaments, sending video recordings to college coaches, attending scouting tryouts, etc.). The team was shocked that he knew his stuff. They (his grandparents did not use signs) assumed he knew nothing and that it was only his dream. I had to tell the IEP coordinator to write down what he said. After that was done, I asked the student what he would like to pursue while he does those things (e.g., sending video recordings to coaches, playing in tournaments). He said he would like to be a car mechanic. He ended up going to a local vocational school to take classes during his senior year, and even though basketball didn't pan out, he is now a great car mechanic. After this experience, I wondered how many dreams were dismissed or shot down by ignorance, bias, and/or assumptions.

—*Chris Kurz, teacher advocate*

(DI) Stick It Into Action!

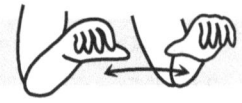

Develop an IEP Meeting Template

Develop an IEP meeting template to have students going into ninth grade complete prior to their IEP meeting; or, at the very least, ask students some guiding questions before their IEP meetings so they feel comfortable sharing information about themselves at the meeting. It is best to ask open-ended questions and allow students to express their thoughts freely. Raising expectations for Deaf students needs to be done concurrently with giving them concrete guidance. Following are some examples of questions to ask:

- "Tell us about yourself."
- "What do you like to do? What do you dislike?"
- "What are your strengths? Challenges?"
- "What do you want to do in the future for school? For work?"
  - Postsecondary options: "What options are you thinking of attending? What programs are you interested in?"
- "What other things do you want to do in the future that are not related to school or work?"
  - Examples: Travel, live in a specific region, et cetera.
- "What volunteer experiences and paid work experiences do you have?"
- "Tell us about your independent living skills."
  - Examples vary, based on the specific student's unique circumstances, but can include reading bus route information, requesting accommodations, understanding bank statements, understanding gross versus net income, good and bad credit, et cetera.
- "What things do you feel you need to learn or need more practice with?"

The information that the student shares with the IEP team should be included in the IEP, and this should be used to help develop their own transition goals. Ultimately, you can raise expectations for your students.

(ES) Evaluate Appropriate Course Placement

Evaluate appropriate course placement during high school as a key element of college and career readiness. Many Deaf high school students are placed on vocational tracks and complete less-rigorous coursework than their hearing peers (Garberoglio et al., 2019c; Nagle et al., 2016). In some cases, this may be indicative of lower expectations at play for Deaf students and what they are capable of. When appropriate, you should encourage your students to take specialized, rigorous, and academically challenging coursework during high school, particularly college-level courses. Consider ways to work with community colleges in your area or online programs to provide greater access to specialized coursework for your students. For example, Texas School for the Deaf initiated a partnership with their local community college to provide dual-credit courses in welding and computer science, and Metro Deaf School collaborates with several local high schools and postsecondary institutions. In addition to academic benefits, students learn how to navigate a large campus and advocate for and use accommodations. As a teacher or future teacher, you can take some time to become more familiar with the options available to your Deaf students for taking college-level courses. Explore what courses are offered at your local community colleges. Seek out the contact person at these colleges and explore opportunities for partnerships. Can you work with a local community college or an online course program to offer more options for your Deaf students?

In summary, we must emphasize the importance for Deaf students to know, as early as possible, that people believe they can succeed in their goals. Everyone in their life (parents, teachers, counselors, coaches, extended family, and more) should be actively involved in their education journey and provide opportunities to learn, make mistakes, and grow. As teachers, you have a significant role in the process of raising

Chew on This!

Did you know that . . . ?
Deaf students who take college-level courses during high school are less likely to need developmental coursework in college (U.S. Department of Education, 2018).

expectations for your students. Learning is not just about academics. Teach students that they have a voice and ensure that they have multiple opportunities to be active participants in their learning experience.

Core Recommendation 2: Set Good Goals

Setting good goals is a key element for your students to plan for the future. Goal setting within transition planning for Deaf students should be four things: (a) student-led, (b) Deaf-specific, (c) data-driven, and (d) realistic. As a part of best practices for transition, you should provide opportunities for and encourage your students to set their own goals, develop action plans, and evaluate progress (Loman et al., 2010; Raley et al., 2021; Wehmeyer et al., 2012).

Student-Led Goals

Student-led goals are essential to the transition process—built on students' ambitions and dreams. Developing these goals should be a highly collaborative process between you, your students, and their transition team. Before any IEP meetings happen, the student should have several opportunities to meet with their case manager, transition teacher, or transition coordinator to discuss their interests, skills, and strengths. Meet with the student ahead of their IEP meeting to help them come up with some talking points and ideas to bring up at their meeting. Often, students become overwhelmed at larger meetings with several adults in attendance. Set up mini-meetings with your students to give them the opportunity and time to think through and discuss what goals they want to work on. You can suggest that members of a student's transition team assist the student and make suggestions if needed. Doing this ahead of the IEP meeting helps reduce the student's anxiety and greatly increases the chances of the student being actively involved in their meeting. Even if you aren't a transition teacher, you can help support your students in this process.

Although transition goals should always be student-driven, additional input from professionals and families can help strengthen and clarify these goals. Any assessment or evaluation data should be part of this process as well to give each student as much information as they can use to identify their goals. Ensure that your students understand the IEP process and are prepared for the IEP meeting. This helps them think about their long-term goals and which objectives can help them achieve them. For example, if a student expresses interest in attending a specific postsecondary program, you may want to include objectives to explore the named program's minimum admission requirements. If another student is interested in working as an auto mechanic, include objectives to explore local programs that offer training in the field of automotive technology. The IEP should clearly state how students will be involved in developing their goals and the specific objectives that allow them to reach these goals through language that identifies how students will explore, research, identify, or learn about their goals. For example, an objective could address program options and read as follows:

- "Sam will research and identify three different programs in the metro area that offer degrees in the field of automotive technology, as documented by the transition team."

Another objective could focus on minimum program requirements,

- "Sam will identify at least two requirements for acceptance into the automotive technology program as documented by the transition team."

Use language that explicitly states what the student will explore, research, identify, or learn. This serves as a reminder and an affirmation that students are leading the process of developing their goals and how to reach these goals. You can also work with your students to create a timeline and checklist for their planning. Here is one Kristin developed for meeting with college-bound seniors (see Stick It Into Action).

 Stick It Into Action!

Create a Timeline and Checklist

To best prepare for transition planning, meet with students on a regular basis as soon as they start high school, not only right before their IEP meeting. These intervals vary based on the student's unique circumstances and where they are at in their educational journey.

Name: _____ Date: _____

Parent signature: _____ T. Coordinator Initials: ____

Senior Timeline and Checklist

Your senior year in high school can be one of the most pivotal and life changing steps into adulthood. It is important for you to meet with the Transition Coordinator on a regular basis during your Senior year to make sure that things are moving along in a timely manner.

Senior Timeline				
	September	Date	Student Initials	T. C. Initials
1	Meet with the Transition Coordinator (T. C.) to develop a plan			
2	Have a group meeting with the T. C. and parents			
3	Meet with the T. C. and VR Counselor			
4	Have your parent sign this timeline and checklist			
5	Explore postsecondary options and fill out comparison sheet			
6	Make sure the postsecondary options offer programs in the field you are interested in			
7	Explore postsecondary requirements and make sure you meet the minimum requirements			
8	Tour the postsecondary options (live or virtual)			
9	Interview other people who have attended the programs that you are exploring.			
10	Write a practice college essay			
11	Let Melissa know if you want to retake the ACT test			
	October	Date	Student Initials	T. C. Initials
12	Meet with the Transition Coordinator to check in			
13	Finalize college options to 4 or 5			
14	Inform T.C., VR counselor and parents your of final choices			
15	Research application timelines, tuition costs and financial aid options for final choices			
16	Set up a Google Folder for all of your application paperwork			

#		Date	Student Initials	T. C. Initials
17	Complete FAFSA with your parents the first week of October			
18	Ask teachers for letters of recommendations			
19	Obtain a copy of your transcript			
20	Retake the ACT test, if applicable			
21	Start working on your Transition Portfolio			
	November	Date	Student Initials	T. C. Initials
22	Meet with the Transition Coordinator and VR Counselor			
23	Set up meetings with the T. C. and the admissions counselors of the postsecondary options you are interested in applying to			
24	Finalize your college application essays			
25	Inform T. C. and VR counselor of new ACT test scores, if applicable			
	December	Date	Student Initials	T. C. Initials
26	Meet with the Transition Coordinator to check in			
27	Apply to the colleges that you are interested in. Make a note of when you should expect to hear back from each college			
28	Verify with the T. C. that your transcripts, letters of recommendation, and test scores have been sent to your prospective schools			
29	Make sure you will meet all the requirements for HS graduation. If you have any classes you still need to take, let Melissa know			
	January	Date	Student Initials	T. C. Initials
30	Meet with the Transition Coordinator and VR Counselor			
31	Send an email or make a phone call to make sure your colleges have received your application. While you're at it, check to see that they have everything else they need, including your transcripts and financial aid material			
	February	Date	Student Initials	T. C. Initials
32	Meet with the Transition Coordinator to check in			
33	Request that the T. C. send your first semester grades to every college you applied to			
34	Research and apply for scholarships			
	March	Date	Student Initials	T. C. Initials
35	Meet with the Transition Coordinator and VR counselor - Your parent should also attend this meeting			
36	Finalize your FAFSA with updated tax information			
37	Once you've received all of your responses from all of the colleges, make your final decision			
38	Email the T. C. and your VR counselor with your final decision			
39	Research the scholarship options at the college and apply for scholarships			
40	Finalize your Transition Portfolio			
	April	Date	Student Initials	T. C. Initials
41	Meet with the Transition Coordinator to check in			
42	Your Financial Aid Award Letter will be mailed to you			
43	Verify your financial aid before you make any college budget decisions.			
44	Develop a plan for paying for college			
45	Inform the college that you intend to register for classes			
46	Inform the other colleges that you will not attend			
47	Contact the disability office at the college to make arrangements for accommodations			
48	Make your announcement to the HS team on College Celebration Day during the last week of April			
49	Once you've been admitted to a college and accept the invitation to attend, you'll receive all sorts of information on course scheduling, housing, orientation sessions, and financial aid disbursement. As a responsible young student, it's your job to get these forms back to where they came from as soon as possible.			
	May	Date	Student Initials	T. C. Initials
50	Meet with the Transition Coordinator and VR counselor			
51	Take a look at your college admissions checklist - Is everything checked off?			
52	Check your financial aid checklist - Is everything in order?			
53	Double check to make sure that you met all the HS requirements for			

 Deaf-Specific Goals

Deaf-specific goals should address students' experiences as a Deaf person in the transition process. These goals should be individualized to each student's needs and experiences. Not all Deaf students are the same. Each student will have their own preferences, such as preferred languages, communication modalities, and accommodation needs. In your lessons, you should create opportunities for students to learn more about the range of accommodations and assistive technologies available to them. For example, you can have students review the accommodations listed on their IEP and have them explain how those accommodations help them. This will give them the tools they need to be able to advocate for what they will need in postsecondary education and training, in the workplace, or in community settings. Don't forget to educate yourself about the range of accommodations and assistive technologies that may be a good fit for DeafDisabled and DeafBlind students.

In general, your students will need to learn strategies to navigate the world as a Deaf person. As mentioned throughout this book, many Deaf students are the only, or one of few, Deaf students in their school, and thus they have reduced opportunities to learn from other Deaf peers or Deaf adults in their environment. This means you will need to be intentional about sharing specific tips, tools, and resources that, as Deaf

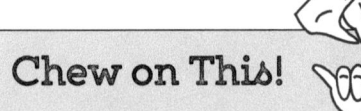

Did you know that . . . ?
Many Deaf students use accommodations for the first time after they leave high school (Palmer et al., 2020).

people, they will need to be aware of in order to advocate for themselves in adult life. For example, you should teach students about the options for using relay services to make calls and encourage students to apply for vocational rehabilitation (VR) services to get support for achieving their career goals. Think about how you can reach out to Deaf adults in the community—maybe even recent graduates from your school—to share more tips with your students.

You can also work with your Deaf students to set goals to prepare them to advocate for themselves and be familiar with their legal rights across various settings. If students plan to go to college, they will need to know how to request accommodations and what legal rights they have in that setting. And when students start applying for jobs, they will need to figure out when to disclose their disability, when to request accommodations, and how to address discrimination in the workplace. You can provide them with opportunities to practice requesting accommodations and advocating for themselves. Skills that do not fit under postsecondary options or employment skills can be addressed in the independent living skills area of the transition IEP. For example, as part of the community participation portion of the independent living skills area of the IEP, you can have your students explore local organizations that relate to their multiple identities as a Deaf person (e.g., Lesbian, Gay, Bisexual, Transgender, Queer or Questioning, Intersex, Asexual and/or more [LGBTQIA+] organizations, National Black Deaf Advocates [NBDA], Junior National Association for the Deaf); students are not only Deaf but also have many other identities that are formative to their life.

Stick It Into Action!

 **Deaf-Specific Objectives**

What are some Deaf-specific objectives that you can integrate into transition planning? Review the sample objectives in the table to help you write some of your own. Make sure that the objectives, although Deaf-specific, are individualized to fit the individual student's specific needs and unique learning style.

Table 14.1. Deaf-Specific Objectives

Topic	Example Objective 1	Example Objective 2
Assistive technology	Develop a chart with technology devices that will be needed for living independently. Include information on where to get devices and how much they will cost.	Identify at least two speech-to-text apps that students can use when they interact with hearing people in the community.
Interpreter	Explain at least one appropriate procedure for filing a complaint about an interpreter.	Identify two local interpreting agencies and add contact information to a file of resources.

Table 14.1. (*continued*)

Topic	Example Objective 1	Example Objective 2
Deaf interpreter	Identify two situations where they can request a Deaf Interpreter.	Explain the process of requesting a Deaf interpreter.
Video remote interpreting	Name at least one situation where a video remote interpreter might be used instead of a live interpreter.	Explain the difference between using video relay service and video remote interpreter.
Video relay service	Sign up for a video relay service number.	Make a video relay service call to request information from a business.
Advocacy and resources	Research at least three entitlement programs (e.g., Social Security benefits, housing assistance, Medicare) and add eligibility and contact information to a file of resources.	Identify a minimum of two laws that protect their rights as a Deaf person.
Vocational rehabilitation or state services for the Blind	Explain at least two things that vocational rehabilitation (or state services for the Blind) can do for them.	Meet with their vocational rehabilitation or state services for the Blind counselor at least two times during the IEP year.

(MT) Stick It Into Action!

Deaf-Specific Objective for Using Video Relay

Here is an example of how you can carry out the objective for "Make a video relay service call to request information":

- Have students call organizations to make inquiries using a video relay service (examples include calling a workplace to inquire about job openings and qualifications, calling a local bakery to inquire about gluten-free items and prices, or ordering a pizza for a group lunch to celebrate after a successful lesson).

(DI) (MM) **Data-Driven Goals**

Data-driven goals are an accurate reflection of where a student is in the transition process, and these allow for individualization based on differentiated needs. During the student's initial transition assessments, it is important for you to collect data about their abilities, strengths, and areas of growth that support the development of goals and objectives. You can obtain data from multiple resources: the student, their parents, and other teachers. Each IEP includes an assessment of the student's present levels of academic achievement and functional performance (i.e., PLOP [present level of performance]) that informs transition planning. This section should include data from all relevant assessments and tests, and the information must be accessible to the student and the transition planning team, including the student's family (and in their preferred languages).

When you are collecting data to inform transition planning, be sure to include both formal and informal assessments. Do not rely exclusively on tests and quantitative measures; make sure you also include observations, sample work, interviews, or performance-based tasks. Be sure data are collected from at least two or three different types of assessments. It is best practice to use at least one formal assessment (e.g., Brigance Transition) and one informal assessment (e.g., caregiver interview and student interview). Don't forget to consider social and emotional development (e.g., self-advocacy skills, organizational skills) in this process in addition to academic skills. Transition evaluations are a collaboration among teachers, transition specialists, and the school social worker, counselor, and/or psychologist, and often these evaluations are done in conjunction with a social-emotional and behavioral assessment. The right assessment tools and approach depend on each individual student's specific circumstances. A multiple-measures approach to understanding your students' strengths and areas of growth is often necessary because many assessments are not accessible or are not a good fit for Deaf students (Cawthon, 2015). Ideally, the perspectives of Deaf adults should be included in assessing and evaluating data about your students, because these adults may be more familiar with additional contexts that need to be considered.

Work with your student and the transition team to ensure that all transition goals and objectives are measurable so the transition planning team can rely on an iterative process of data collection and evaluation and adjust accordingly. These data are usually based on actual tasks that the student can perform (e.g., test scores, performance tasks such as contacting a postsecondary program to get more information or attaining a specific percentage on an assessment). Strong objectives should also include benchmarks, timelines, and a specific number of trials/opportunities to demonstrate skills gained.

Here is an example of a high school junior's measurable/realistic postsecondary transition goal and related objectives:

Goal Alex will move from a level of not developing a timeline for applying to the National Technical Institute for the Deaf (NTID), not filling out an application to NTID, and not filling out a Free Application for Federal Student Aid (FAFSA) to a level of doing all of those tasks with support by March 2022.

- **Objective 1:** Alex will develop a timeline that lists the necessary steps and a due date for each step required in the process for applying to NTID, as documented by the transition team.
- **Objective 2:** Alex will fill out an application to NTID by the due date, with the intention of enrolling and attending NTID in the fall of 2022.
- **Objective 3:** Alex will fill out the FAFSA application with family support and share any financial aid award letters with the transition coordinator and VR counselor, as documented by the transition team.

In the postsecondary goal area, be sure to include data about the student's test scores (for districtwide, statewide assessments, etc.), starting in ninth grade. This will give the IEP team a good idea of the student's academic abilities and what is realistic for the student. Don't forget to add data from informal assessments as well.

(DI) (ABAR) (MM) (PI) **Realistic Goals**

Realistic goals that are a good fit for each student are an important part of the transition planning process. In addition to being data-driven, your students' transition goals should also be reachable and achievable. Goals should be deeply individualized—what one person views as being the pinnacle of success is not the same for everyone. What matters is that these goals are a good fit for each person and are actually something your students can achieve. Becoming an astronaut who goes to the moon, a multimillionaire chief executive officer, or a professional tennis player is out of reach for most people. However, if you have a student with those interests, they could set incremental goals to study astronomy, gain business management skills, or explore careers in athletics and physical education. As described previously, these goals should be based on data collected throughout the transition assessment and planning period. At the beginning of the transition process, the planning team should have a good idea of the realistic options for the student. If the student does not demonstrate grade-level skills or test scores, that should be discussed with the family as soon as possible. Ideally, these sensitive discussions should occur outside of and before the student's first transition IEP meeting so the family doesn't feel blindsided. Be sure to take into consideration the diverse backgrounds of families and the importance of understanding the student's home cultural practices and additional languages spoken and/or signed in the home before engaging in these conversations with families. Although education is important, it is vital to remember that college is not always the way or the answer for everyone. Transition goals and objectives should be individualized for each student.

Teacher Tale

A student who has a secondary mild/moderate developmental coordination disorder (DCD) diagnosis in addition to being Deaf really wanted to be a nurse. Her test scores and ability to retain information indicated that going into nursing was not a realistic option for her. In one-to-one discussions with the student, it was determined that she really wanted to work with people in a caregiving role. She said she also enjoyed cleaning because that makes people happy. In the end, after several discussions, she agreed that she wanted to obtain a job as a housekeeper in a hospital setting. She made it clear to the IEP team that she did not want to be a housekeeper in a house or in a hotel. That is a great example of how sometimes a position in one setting is very different from the same position in another setting. Because we were able to work together to figure out what she really wanted to do, she was able to identify the setting and the tasks that she enjoyed doing that also fit her skills and abilities.

—*Kristin Ryan, transition teacher*

Stick It Into Action!

Set Good Goals

Work with students to set goals, develop plans, and use data to evaluate progress toward strengthening self-determination by using these resources. Start the process as soon as the student enters middle school. These suggestions can be helpful even if you are not a transition teacher or if you teach younger students:

- Read the teacher's guide for the Self-Determined Learning Model of Instruction (https://selfdetermination.ku.edu/homepage/intervention/) to learn more about how to set good goals while strengthening self-determination.
- Have your students take the Self-Determination Inventory: Student-Report (https://nationaldeafcenter.org/resource-items/self-determination-inventory/), an ASL-accessible measure of self-determination, to get an individualized report of their strengths and areas of improvement. This online assessment asks how youth feel about their ability to be self-determined: to make choices, set and go after goals, and make decisions. Designed for youth between the ages of 13 and 22, it takes approximately 10–15 min to complete.
- Download the Choose Your Own Adventure Activity Kit (https://nationalDeafcenter.org/learn/Deafverse), a handout to help Deaf high school students identify their goals and make a plan for reaching their goals that builds on their strengths, interests, and needs.

Core Recommendation 3: Rely on Community Resources

Community resources, expertise, and knowledge can help strengthen student readiness for life after high school (Trainor et al., 2012). You and your transition planning team should be familiar with resources and services available in the community, particularly those that are beneficial for Deaf students (NASDSE, 2018). For example, job opportunities may be found at Deaf-owned or Deaf-friendly businesses or while networking at Deaf community events. Some ways you can build a stronger reliance on community resources are (a) building relationships with diverse Deaf role models and mentors, (b) encouraging extracurricular involvement, and (c) identifying local resources and services.

Stick It Into Action!

Mock Job Interviews
Present students with opportunities to use their communication skills in the community: with hearing and Deaf adults, through mock job interviews, and by encouraging them to communicate with a store employee when looking for a specific item, and so on.

Key Strategy

Transition Binder/Portfolio

Starting in ninth grade, have students create a transition binder or portfolio that includes subfolders. Students can create their portfolios using hard copies of materials organized in a binder or online storage tools like Google Drive. Some suggestions for subfolders are as follows: About Me, Personal, Education, Work, Medical, Financial, Misc., and Resources. This portfolio should also identify important community resources. They should complete their portfolio by the time they graduate. At graduation, ownership of the portfolio can be transferred to the student's personal account.

(MM) (PI) (ABAR) (ES) Build Relationships With Diverse Deaf Role Models and Mentors

Building relationships with diverse Deaf role models is a way to strengthen Deaf students' development of identities, language(s), and social skills (Cawthon et al., 2016). Deaf students benefit from seeing Deaf adults across a range of professions and from a variety of backgrounds and how they interact with each other. Students also benefit from seeing Deaf adults in a variety of settings and how they interact with their hearing peers or other individuals from diverse communities. This helps students understand what is possible for them. Deaf role models and mentors can also share real-life examples of experiences, such as requesting accommodations at work, communicating with coworkers, and/or dealing with conflict on the job. Take a close look at each student's situation—if there are not enough Deaf adults in their life, think about some ways to connect them with Deaf adults as a part of transition planning. Consider ways to build relationships with Deaf role models or mentors by reaching out to local organizations (e.g., the local Deaf club, a local college) for volunteer opportunities, collaborating with other schools with larger numbers of Deaf professionals, inviting guest speakers or creating job shadowing opportunities with Deaf professionals. There may be cases where you will need to consider building these relationships virtually to broaden the opportunities available in your area for your students. When building these relationships, remember that Deaf youth have multiple identities and are not only Deaf (see Chapter 8 for more). Relationships with role models and mentors who share their identities—race, ethnicity, gender, sexual orientation, and disability—are an important part of the transition process as Deaf youth develop a stronger sense of their own identities. Although shared identity relationships are deeply valuable, ensuring that Deaf youth have opportunities to learn from adults that have identities different from their own can also strengthen their skills and abilities to work in solidarity with other communities, which may be important for white and/or nondisabled Deaf youth.

Stick It Into Action!

(MM) (ABAR) (MT) (PI) **Include Videos of Deaf Role Models**
Find videos of successful Deaf adults talking about their work experiences to show your Deaf students.

- You can start with the #DeafAtWork videos (https://www.nad.org/resources/deafatwork/) from the National Association of the Deaf, or the #DeafSuccess videos (https://www.youtube.com/hashtag/deafsuccess) from the National Deaf Center on Postsecondary Outcomes.
- Search out stories from Deaf people who are Black, Indigenous, and People of Color (BIPOC), DeafDisabled, and DeafBlind to ensure diverse representation.

Seek out resources for diverse Deaf youth that can strengthen identity development and support systems. These resources may be found within your local geographical area but also virtually. Whereas some communities have robust affinity groups like the Deaf Muslim Community in Minnesota or local chapters of NBDA, many geographical areas do not have a large enough Deaf community to sustain support groups such as for Deaf students who are LGBTQIA+. In those cases, seek out national organizations with which students can connect on social media or get involved virtually, like the Deaf Queer Resource Center. If no resources are immediately available, think about ways you can create these opportunities for your students. For example, at my (Kristin) school, one of the school counselors, who is a Deaf Person of Color, hosts a weekly lunch for Deaf students who are BIPOC.

Stick It Into Action!

Connect with NBDA
Connect with your local NBDA chapter. Visit this link, www.nbda.org/local_chapters, to identify whether your area has a local chapter of NBDA that you can learn more about.

(SEL) (PI) **Encourage Extracurricular Involvement**
Encourage extracurricular involvement with athletics, theater, advocacy groups, or peer support groups to build deeper relationships with community networks. Extracurricular involvement also creates opportunities to develop important skills like leadership, teamwork, and communication. Participation in extracurricular

activities during high school has been linked to stronger postsecondary outcomes for Deaf youth (Schoffstall et al., 2016). Extracurricular involvement is also a good way to strengthen students' resumes as they prepare for applying to college or jobs. You should be familiar with the extracurricular activities available to your students in your school and in your local community. If you have a specific passion or skill, think about ways you can develop a new program, club, or activity, or volunteer to coach or mentor Deaf students in these activities. Many Deaf-centered organizations and programs offer opportunities for students to get involved in activities that interest them. Summer camps and programs for Deaf, DeafBlind, and DeafDisabled youth are also important ways to build stronger support systems and peer relationships with other youth like them (e.g., Youth Leadership Camp at the NAD, Y.E.S! Youth Empowerment Summit at the NBDA, the DeafBlind Camp of Texas).

(MT) (PI) Identify Local Resources and Services

Identify local resources and services that Deaf students can use to reach their goals. When students leave high school, they should be familiar with the resources available in their community, what support is available, and how to get involved with organizations or make requests. Encourage students to actively research these resources and compile the resources they find rather than just providing them with a list. For example, students should know about resources to help them search for and get jobs, including employment agencies, VR services, and job opportunities that they might want to pursue. As teachers, try to build a rapport with your school's assigned VR counselor. Find out which employment agency the VR services contracts with. Invite both the VR counselor and a representative from the employment agency on a regular basis to develop connections with the students.

Your students will need to be familiar with a range of resources and services to help them achieve their plans after high school. Provide opportunities for them to learn about these services. For example, they should be knowledgeable about continuing education and training opportunities that are relevant to their goals (i.e., adult basic education courses, specialized certification and training opportunities, community colleges, or 4-year college options). As part of transition planning, ask your students to explore these continuing education and training opportunities as well as the housing options that fit their circumstances and needs. When students get involved with the community or apply for jobs, in some cases, they are expected to know whom to reach out to when accommodations are requested. They should be familiar with how to connect with interpreting agencies when that happens. Community-based organizations are also an important asset for developing community relationships and building networks that could lead to job opportunities—have students learn more about their local Deaf club or association for the Deaf. Also, think about mental health support—seek out counselors, therapists, or substance abuse counselors available in your area and virtually that use ASL. Consider supports for well-being such as yoga, mindfulness, and fitness instructors who are Deaf and/or use ASL (see Chapters 2, 7, and 8 for more information on yoga and mindfulness). Have your students explore and research those resources starting in ninth grade and throughout their high school journey. Students should organize all of the information that they collect, which becomes a part of their transition portfolio, so they have it available when needed (see Handstamp Sample).

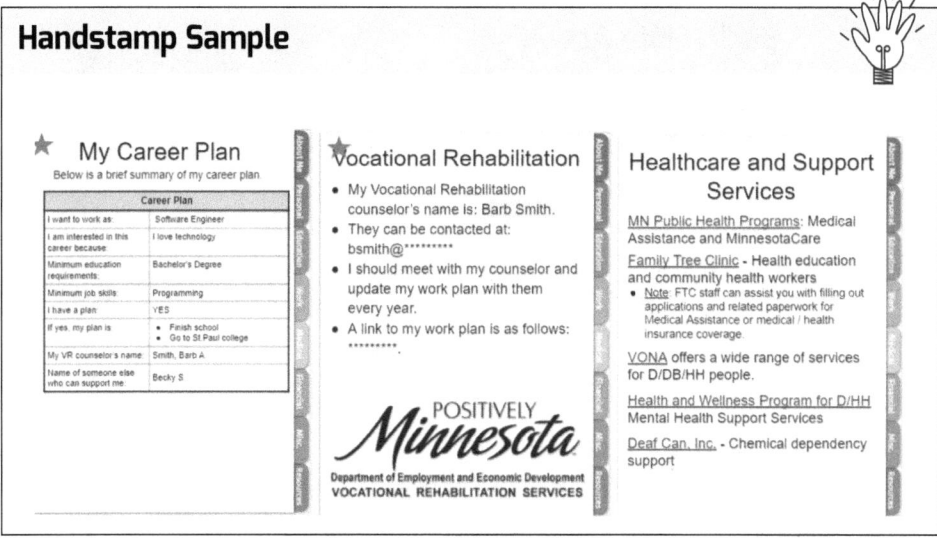

Core Recommendation 4: Develop a Strong Collaborative Team

A collaborative approach to transition planning that includes students, teachers, families, and community members leads to stronger outcomes for disabled students in general (Gothberg et al., 2019). For Deaf students, it becomes even more important to have strong collaborative efforts within transition teams that are able to meet the specific needs of each student, especially for DeafDisabled students and multilingual learners (Bruce et al., 2008). Take a close look at each student's transition team to be sure that the right people are at the table. You will need to be intentional about inviting people with the right backgrounds, experiences, and expertise. For example, it is deeply valuable to invite members of the transition team who can speak/sign the languages used in students' homes and ensure that students' home languages and cultures are represented in transition planning. In addition to the students, it is key that the transition planning team includes (a) a transition teacher or specialist, (b) relevant agencies, and (c) the students' families.

Build Relationships With Families

Building relationships with families is a key component of transition planning. It is vital that you check in to see whether families have a solid understanding of their child's abilities and interests. This should happen as early as possible, ideally by ninth grade at the very latest. These discussions should happen outside of parent–teacher conferences and IEP meetings. Encourage families to learn more about their child's goals and talk to their child about their own experiences in the workplace. Be aware that the transition process can feel technical and inaccessible to families. Seek out resources that help demystify the transition process, and use plain language when you communicate with families about transition planning, especially when discussing data. Make sure your program has resources available for translating all materials and providing interpreters as needed, so families have access to all information being discussed in their preferred language. In some situations, it may be appropriate for you to request an interpreter for transition planning meetings so students and/or their families can fully engage with the content being discussed.

Stick It Into Action!

ASL-Accessible Resources
Use ASL-accessible resources with students and families to ensure that transition planning information is accessible. For example, *Plan Your Future: A Guide to Vocational Rehabilitation for Deaf Youth* (https://nationaldeafcenter.org/resource-items/plan-your-future-guide-vocational-rehabilitation-deaf-youth/) is an ASL-accessible resource for families and students that is designed to demystify the process of working with VR agencies.

Build Relationships With Agencies
Think about any agencies with which your students might need to work during the transition process and after high school. Some examples of agencies are transition programs, VR services, and employment agencies. As educators in the school system, it is beneficial to learn how your local agencies work and to learn more about the decision-making process they use to determine what kind and how much support they offer to individuals. Being familiar with this information makes it easier to address transition from a team-based and cross-agency approach. Depending on students' present or future needs, additional training may be needed in the areas of independent living, orientation and mobility, or job coaching, for example. To provide seamless transition support for your Deaf students, you should consider strategies to strengthen relationships with agencies that provide training in the specific areas students may need. Think about ways to develop collaborative partnerships with these agencies, such as identifying representatives and inviting them to your class to present to your students.

Many employment agencies have some counselors who are familiar with working with Deaf people; we recommend that you connect with these counselors to build relationships with your students early on. VR agencies are an important part of transition planning for Deaf youth; they provide important pre-employment training services and can support the next steps in career readiness. These resources help high school students prepare for jobs or continue their education. I (Kristin) introduce my students to VR when they are in ninth grade, and I have them apply for services when they start their junior year. The VR counselor is invited to their IEP meetings in their junior and senior year. Some schools and programs have established formal partnerships with their local VR agency, with designated VR counselors working more directly with the school to support students. Does your program do so? If not, consider ways you can work more closely with your local VR agency.

Stick It Into Action!

Connect Your Students With VR Counselors Early
Create opportunities for your students to connect with their VR counselor early in high school, and invite the VR counselor to IEP meetings during their junior and senior year.

By the time students leave high school, they should be connected with agencies that will continue to support them to ensure as seamless of a transition as possible. At the end of their program and their last IEP meeting (i.e., the "exit" meeting), you should confirm that a plan is in place and that the student has all the needed information about local resources, ideally as a part of their transition portfolio. As their teacher, be sure that you have supported the student throughout the process and that they, and their families, are connected to the resources they will need after leaving high school.

Additional Things to Consider

Supporting Transition Outside of the IEP Process

The goal of transition—to prepare students for life after high school—is foundational to everything that happens in educational settings. Although we have talked extensively about the formal transition planning process that involves IEP meetings, transition objectives, or formal transition class time, this process should not be limited to only those situations. Even though the IEP is a legal mandate and you are obligated to address all of the objectives and provide the accommodations outlined in the student's IEP, there are many things that you can address outside of the IEP process. The IEP should serve as a starting point that guides deeper thinking and building systems of support for each student. Just because something is not listed in the IEP does not mean it does not need to be addressed in the transition process.

Transition is a very broad topic that covers several grades and many topics. There are many transition curricula available that cover a variety of topics in transition. As with all curricula, there are pros and cons to each. Select from the curriculum that best suits your instruction, or create your own. For example, when out in the community on a field trip, allow students to take the lead in asking for directions or ordering their own food. They may not have objectives about asking for directions or ordering their own food, but it is still beneficial for them to practice these types of interactions. Across all educational activities, even in content area courses, teachers should be thinking constantly about equipping students with the tools they need to reach their goals after leaving high school. Transition teachers, specialists, and coordinators should not be the only people in high school settings who are supporting students through their transition process.

(ES) Transition Across Educational Setting

The transition process looks very different across a range of settings, and it is highly individualized for each Deaf student. Thus, all teachers of Deaf students should be familiar with the goals of transition and should be prepared to integrate some core concepts from transition planning in their content-level coursework and out-of-classroom activities. Each Deaf student has vastly different experiences and needs during the transition process. Their educational setting, and students' specific accommodation needs (and whether or not they receive services under the Individuals With Disabilities Education Act [IDEA] Amendments of 2004) significantly affects their experiences in the transition process. Students in public schools may not have specific transition objectives and goals on their IEP, and those on 504 plans do not even have an IEP. In these cases, it is typically left up to families to guide their high school students through the transition process with minimal support from guidance or career counselors. On the other hand, students receiving IDEA services and/or those attending Deaf programs and Deaf schools typically have transition objectives built into their IEP starting in ninth grade. You should carefully consider how you can support each of your student's transition needs whether or not an IEP is in place.

(MM) (DI) Teacher Tale

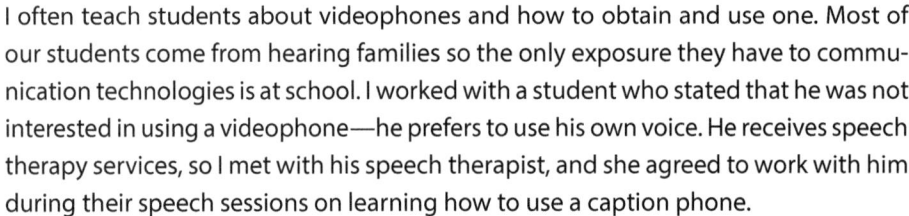

I often teach students about videophones and how to obtain and use one. Most of our students come from hearing families so the only exposure they have to communication technologies is at school. I worked with a student who stated that he was not interested in using a videophone—he prefers to use his own voice. He receives speech therapy services, so I met with his speech therapist, and she agreed to work with him during their speech sessions on learning how to use a caption phone.

—*Kristin Ryan*

(MM) (DI) Transition and Language Deprivation

Although transition is important for all youth, not only Deaf youth, the experiences of Deaf youth must be given extra consideration in this process. Deaf students vary widely, but the experience of language deprivation and reduced incidental learning are more common than we would like to see. In many cases, it is necessary to rely on explicit teaching and direct examples. It is important not to assume that your students are familiar with what you would consider to be the basics—internet safety, protecting passwords, or bank overdraft fees. Be authentic and transparent when working with Deaf youth, and use real-life examples whenever possible. Share examples of mortgage statements, car insurance fees, student loan payments, rental agreements, and more. Seek out stories from Deaf adults talking about their life experiences in an accessible way to support this process. Think about these strategies across all contexts within Deaf students' education as a way to increase the potential for their success after leaving the supportive space of high school. If you teach math, think about ways to integrate authentic financial literacy lessons in your teaching (see Chapter 10 for additional examples). If you teach health, think about ways to discuss healthy relationships with real-life examples that are applicable to their current experiences. Ultimately, you must truly prepare Deaf youth for life beyond high school, not just to meet their transition objectives.

(PI) (MM) (DI) (MT) Bringing It All Together

The core recommendations outlined in this chapter can be addressed through either a unit or a series of several lessons with your high school students. Because transition is tied directly to a student's unique needs, a good starting place would be the student's

IEP. Here, we provide a lesson plan on preparing students to be active participants in their IEP meetings. Although the lesson can be taught to any student with a transition IEP in high school or in a transition program, it should ideally be taught when the student is in ninth grade and then repeated every year. The purpose is for students to develop self-advocacy skills, learn about their IEP, and eventually lead their IEP meetings (see Table 14.2).

Lesson Objective

The students should become involved in their IEP meeting.

Materials and Resources

- Copy of students' IEPs
- IEP meeting template
  - This information may be shared by the student in multiple ways and with varying levels of support. They can use a worksheet or put together a slideshow. They may even want to prerecord a video to show at their IEP meeting.
  - Students often benefit from a sample. Consider developing one yourself to share with students.

 **Your Turn to Practice!**

Develop Teach and Reflect on a Transition Lesson

Now it's your turn! Develop, teach, and reflect on a lesson that integrates transition knowledge and skill learning objectives into a content area subject. You can modify a lesson you have developed previously or create a new lesson. If you are currently teaching, try it out with your own students. If you are a teacher candidate, you can practice with real or mock students. If you work with (or plan to work with) students in a younger age group, think about ideas for starting transition planning early. For example, if you work with students in elementary school, introduce Deaf students to Deaf role models who work in a variety of fields and occupations.

Here are the steps to follow.

Create a Lesson Plan
Develop or modify a lesson plan for a content area (e.g., science, math, Deaf studies, social studies, reading/writing, language arts, ASL).

Add a Transition Objective   Add a Deaf-specific objective related to transition (review Stick It Into Action, page 348)

Teach Your Lesson
Teach your lesson to your students or in a mock setting if you are a teacher candidate.

Table 14.2. IEP Lesson Plan

Day	Activity	Core Recommendation (CR)
1	Introduction to IEPs: • Lead a brief discussion about students' previous participation in their IEP meetings to date. • Use a KWL chart to see what students already know about IEPs and IEP meetings. Teach/Review target vocabulary: • IEP • IEP team • Discuss members and their roles and importance. • Transition planning • Present level of performance • Accommodations • Goals • Objectives • Services • Postsecondary goals • Vocational rehabilitation* • Age of majority	**CR 3: Rely on community resources.** Identify community resources that can provide the student with needed services and help them make better decisions about their postsecondary goals.
2	IEP review: • Have students review their own IEP and identify the various parts of their IEP.	**CR 1: Raise expectations.** Have students participate in their own IEP meeting and be involved in their future planning process.
3	IEP meeting agenda worksheet or slideshow: • Show the students your sample slideshow. • Have students prepare for their IEP meeting by filling out a worksheet or slideshow to share with their IEP team.	**CR 2: Set good goals.** By filling out the worksheet or slideshow, students are involved in setting new goals for their new IEP.
4	Practice: • Have students practice presenting. If needed, prerecord a video to show at the IEP meeting.	
5	Mock IEP meeting: • Have students participate in a mock IEP meeting. If possible, invite all of the IEP team members to the mock meeting.	**CR 4: Develop a strong collaborative team.** A vocational rehabilitation counselor should be invited to a student's IEP meeting when they are a junior.

Note. IEP = individualized education program; KWL = know–want to know–learn.

Reflect in Your Teaching

Reflect on your experience. Consider the following questions:

a. What went well?
b. What would you change/do differently if you taught this lesson again?
c. What benefits could you see for your students?
d. After assessing your students, how well did they learn your targeted objectives?
e. In what ways do the transition objectives include opportunities for the student to challenge themselves and learn new skills? (**Core Recommendation 1**)
f. Identify additional improvements to the transition objectives in the IEP.

Recommended Readings/Viewings

For Teachers/Teacher Candidates

- Download transition resources from national organizations that provide easy-to-read research summaries and highlight best practices for deaf students at Gallaudet's Clerc Center (https://gallaudet.edu/clerc-center) and the National Deaf Center on Postsecondary Outcomes (NDC; http://www.nationaldeafcenter.org/transition).
- Learn more about assessments that you can use as part of transition planning, like the Readiness Evaluation of Transition to Adulthood for Deafblind Youth (https://www.nationaldb.org/products/ready-tool/) at the National Center on Deaf-Blindness, or other assessments described in this article from NDC (https://nationaldeafcenter.org/news-items/transitionlife-skills-checklists-and-resources/).
- Visit this page for teachers at NTACT: The Collaborative (https://transitionta.org/educator-resources/) that covers topics such as work-based learning, IEP planning, and collaborating with VR.

For Using With Students

- Students can play Deafverse (https://deafverse.com/), a choose-your-own-adventure ASL-accessible online game to practice making their own choices in situations they might encounter in real life.
- Check whether your state has transition resources and roadmaps for Deaf students that can help them reach their goals. For example, see Minnesota Transition Roadmap (https://mn.gov/deaf-commission/assets/20MNDHS_DeafBlindBrochure_102620_tcm1063-457311.pdf) and Texas Transition and Employment Guide (https://www.texasdeafed.org/transition).

Conclusion

This chapter is unique in that even though it targets one age group, it also recognizes that transition needs to be a goal shared by teachers who work with Deaf youth of all ages. Although you may not be a transition teacher, all teachers should be familiar with the principles shared in this chapter. Even though transition is an important process and part of legal mandates for the education of Deaf students, don't forget to make the process fun for your students! The transition process is a fantastic opportunity to make learning more immediately relevant to their lives. Make connections between what students know and what they are learning. As much as possible, offer hands-on opportunities to learn, and to make learning "stick," with minimal lecture time. Students in high school are older, and they often prefer the opportunity to do things for themselves rather than being lectured to. Have fun with this process—this is the final stage of preschool through Grade 12 education, and it is a gift to be able to support Deaf teenagers as they figure out who they are, who they want to be, and how they plan to get there.

Sticking Points

- **Raise expectations** for Deaf students by checking your biases and identifying opportunities for students to advocate for themselves, lead IEP meetings, and take challenging courses.
- **Set good goals** as part of transition planning that are student-led, realistic, Deaf-specific, and data-driven.
- **Rely on community resources** to strengthen transition readiness—ensure that Deaf youth have multiple ways to engage with their communities, including Deaf role models.
- **Develop strong collaborations** while planning for transition that include families, VR agencies, local organizations, and employers.

Chapter 15

Conclusion and Next Steps

Marlon Kuntze
Debbie Golos
Kimberly Wolbers
Chris Kurz

Throughout *5S-IN-MIND: Multilingual Teaching Strategies for Diverse Deaf Students,* our goal has been to discuss teaching methods designed to increase equity in learning opportunities for Deaf students mainly by grounding them in multilingual, multicultural, multimodal, anti-bias, and antiracist (ABAR) principles. The field of Deaf education is large, and with the range of diversity of students being served, it is beyond the scope of the book to cover every need. We wanted to create a book that covers a variety of effective teaching methods for all subject areas and for all age groups from preschool through Grade 12. Each chapter has at least one Deaf coauthor, and it is because we value Deaf ways of knowing. We believe that the teaching and learning experiences of Deaf people contribute significantly to Deaf pedagogy as well as the field of Deaf education. This is also one reason we integrated Deaf studies into every chapter (see Chapter 1 for a broadened definition). This book is stocked with a lot of information, strategies, and examples. You know your students best, so ultimately, it will be you who will tailor ideas and information shared in the book to develop successful lessons and unit plans to meet the individual needs of the students you teach.

The intent of this book is not to provide you with all the answers but to get you started. At best, we strive to offer content that will help you reflect on yourself, your students, and how you teach or will teach in the future. Although we know you all have your own individual strengths, we also hope that this book will help you see your way toward an increased positive impact in your teaching—whether you are in a teacher training program and looking forward to the day when you set your foot in your first classroom, or you are a veteran teacher who seeks new ideas and perspectives to rejuvenate your teaching.

This conclusion chapter serves as a rearview mirror—a place for you to review and take stock of what you have learned as you move forward with innovations in your teaching. Here we revisit key concepts and points covered in the book so that they may serve as checkpoints as you navigate the route ahead of you—a route that will be of your making. The success with which you build the route will be driven by how you adhere to the principles laid out in the book and how you are able to use examples in each chapter as an inspiration for you to create ones that are more suitable for the particular grade and the particular students you are entrusted to teach. The depth with which we provide a description for the "effective" multilingual practices and learning activities discussed in each chapter was designed to provide you with a model you can use to modify or create new lessons that will best accomplish the learning objectives to meet the individual needs of each of your students.

Core Recommendations

The core recommendations represent the bulk of each chapter, and they are conceived mostly to address Deaf-specific needs. Although some of them do address the educational needs of students in general, they are highlighted in this book because they happen to be especially important for Deaf students. The lens through which the authors of each chapter discuss the core recommendations is the one of multilingual Deaf education. A limit was imposed on the number of core recommendations the authors could choose to identify. We wanted the authors to go into depth about the best practices for each recommendation and to show how they may be brought together as a learning unit. As such, this forced them to choose from a wide breadth of knowledge within their content area to two to three core recommendations to focus specifically on but with considerable depth.

One of the objectives of the book is to give you enough of a foundation within each chapter for you to develop, teach, and reflect on a lesson or unit plan related to the subject matter covered in the chapter. There are definitely more core recommendations derived from research and practice than we could cover. We hope the core recommendations discussed in the book will provide a set of multilingual, equity-driven practices to build on throughout your teaching career. The decision by the authors and the editors on the key core recommendations was not a small matter. Much of the editing process involved careful deliberation on what core recommendations to include in each chapter. This resulted in each chapter being designed to give you an idea of the best effective practices for each core recommendation and how they may be brought together in a lesson or unit plan. This book is also designed to help you combine content both within and across chapters to develop interdisciplinary units. The overall goal of the book is to lay a strong foundation based on equity principles for designing and carrying out teaching with Deaf students across content areas and the preschool through Grade 12 span.

> "There are situations I have had to address with colleagues regarding how their actions and narratives may be harmful to students. I appreciate the space that my teacher training program gave us to problem solve and walk through difficult conversations and situations. Going through a program that focuses on the whole child reminds us, as educators, that there is more to just working with and advocating for students who have varying Deaf identities and language needs. It equips us to become well-rounded as educators who can help make the school experience a more welcoming and inclusive place.
>
> —Autumn Moder,
> Deaf early childhood teacher

Intentional 8

In all chapters, the authors intentionally align with specific frameworks on which the book is based. All authors incorporated the following three of the "Intentional 8": multilingual and multimodal strategies, anti-bias/antiracist approaches or curricula, and differentiated instruction for diverse learners. Within each chapter, the authors specify where they try to articulate these three areas. Deaf students vary in language and cultural backgrounds and in modality strengths and needs for learning. They also vary in learning abilities; thus, differentiation in instruction helps make learning equitable. We hope that you keep these in mind in all aspects of teaching—from lesson planning to lesson delivery, across all subjects and levels.

The chapters also vary in the extent to which the remaining "Intentional 8" are incorporated. At a minimum, each chapter incorporates two of the five remaining areas. The appropriateness of each of those areas depends on factors such as students' ages, the grade level at which the content is taught, and the nature of the subject area. Some of them concern a student's overall development, such as the importance of fostering an individual student's positive sense of self or identity development. Another related area is social-emotional learning. Two other areas are related to classroom management and considerations for varying educational settings. Finally, it is also important to contemplate how you use educational media and technology.

We encourage you to keep in mind each area of the Intentional 8 every time you plan or modify a lesson. Also, the routine of reflecting on each lesson that you deliver is an important habit that will help you develop exemplary practice. Each area of the Intentional 8 will also help with the structure of your reflection. As a reminder, each area has an icon that helps direct you toward finding specific examples covered within each chapter. You can make use of those icons to quickly scan a given chapter to revisit how the specific part of the chapter conveys a given Intentional 8 area.

Next Steps

Now that you have finished reading, you may be wondering about next steps and how you may proceed in taking them. We recommend that you first go back to the chapters related to your area(s) of teaching or interest. We also strongly encourage you to read other chapters, even those that cover subject areas that you may not currently teach. There are ideas, strategies, and approaches in different subjects that may be modified or applied to your content. Also, these can help inspire you to create interdisciplinary units. Whichever chapter at whatever point in the future you may look into it, consider the following and stick it into action!

Final Stick It Into Action!

- Review all of the Stick It Into Action sections.
- Review the Bringing It All Together sections.
- If you haven't yet, try out one (or more!) of the Your Turn to Practice! sections.

Final Stick It Into Action! (*continued*)

- Modify as needed to match the abilities and learning objectives as well as the language and modality preferences of individual students.
- Also, be sure to modify as needed to match the educational settings (e.g., one-to-one, pair, small or large groups) in which you will be conducting the lesson.
- Read the recommended readings and viewings that are listed both for the teacher and for the students. Plan on how you want to include these resources in your classroom.

Final Sticking Points

- Get to know your students and learn about their families' cultures and home languages so you can best tap into them and incorporate them into your classroom.
- Use multilingual and multimodal strategies to connect American Sign Language (ASL), English, and additional languages and modalities.
- Provide opportunities for creative expression in the arts.
- Create and teach interdisciplinary units alone and/or in collaboration with others.
- Design lessons that involve and promote critical thinking.
- Teach ASL language arts and literature and reading and writing across the curriculum.
- Integrate ABAR and Deaf studies principles throughout your instruction.
- Teach about Deaf people from a variety of backgrounds, including race; gender; LGBTQIA+; cultures; abilities; and variations and dialects of ASL, including Black ASL.
- Provide access to Deaf role models from diverse backgrounds by inviting them into your classroom in person or virtually as well as through books and media.

Revisit 58-IN-MIND: *Multilingual Teaching Strategies for Diverse Deaf Students* any time! We welcome you to come back whenever you need a boost of inspiration for your teaching!

REFERENCES

Accessible Materials Project. (2020). *AASD Accessible Materials Project*. YouTube. https://www.youtube.com/channel/UClyngyD31Bj6fPGCDyobHYA

ACPA & NASPA. (2015). *Professional competency areas for student affairs educators*. Students Affairs Administrators in Higher Education. https://www.naspa.org/files/dmfile/ACPA_NASPA_Professional_Competencies_.pdf

Aikenhead, G. S. (1996). Science education: Border crossing into the subculture of science. *Studies in Science Education, 27*, 1–52. https://doi.org/10.1080/03057269608560077

Anderson, G. B., & Dunn, L. M. (2016). Assessing Black Deaf history: 1980s to the present. *Sign Language Studies, 17*(1), 71–77.

Andrews, J. F., & Rusher, M. (2010). Codeswitching techniques: Evidence-based instructional practices for the ASL/English bilingual classroom. *American Annals of the Deaf, 155*(4), 407–424. https://www.jstor.org/stable/26235081

Applebee, A. N., & Langer, J. A. (2011). A snapshot of writing instruction in middle schools and high schools. *The English Journal, 100*(6), 14–27.

Araceli Ruiz-Primo, M., & Furtak, E. M. (2006). Informal formative assessment and scientific inquiry: Exploring teachers' practices and student learning. *Educational Assessment, 11*(3–4), 237–263. https://doi.org/10.1002/tea.20163

Aristizábal, L. F., Cano, S., Collazos, C. A., Solano, A., & Slegers, K. (2017). Collaborative learning as educational strategy for deaf children: A systematic literature review. In *Interacción '17: Proceedings of the XVIII International Conference on Human Computer Interaction* (pp. 1–8). Association for Computing Machinery.

Athanases, S., & de Oliveira, L. (2014). Scaffolding versus routine support for Latina/o youth in an urban school: Tensions in building disciplinary literacy. *Journal of Literacy Research, 46*(2), 263–299. https://doi.org/10.1177/1086296X14535328

Bahan, B. (1994). *Bird of a different feather* [Videotext]. DawnSignPress.

Bahan, B., & Paul, F. A. (1988). *The American Sign Language handshape game cards*. Dawn Sign Press.

Bailes, C. N. (2001). Integrative ASL–English language arts: Bridging paths to literacy. *Sign Language Studies, 1*(2), 147–174.

Barnard, F. A. P. (1835). Existing state of the art of instructing the deaf and dumb. *Literary and Theological Review, 2*(7), 367–398.

Bauman, D., Rose, H., & Nelson, J. (Eds.). (2006). *Signing the body poetic: Essays on American Sign Language literature*. University of California Press.

Bayley, R., Lucas, C., Hill, J., & McCaskill, C. (2019). The sociolinguistic ramifications of social injustice: The case of Black ASL. In R. Blake & I. Buchstaller (Eds.), *The Routledge companion to the work of John R. Rickford* (pp. 133–141). Routledge.

Becker, H., & Phumiruk, D. (2018). *Counting on Katherine: How Katherine Johnson saved Apollo 13*. Henry Holt.

Bennett-Armistead, V. S., Duke, N. K., & Moses, A. M. (2005). *Literacy and the youngest learner: Best practices for educators of children from birth to 5*. Scholastic.

Berent, G. P., Kelly, R. R., Aldersley, S., Schmitz, K. L., Khalsa, B. K., Panara, J., & Keenan, S. (2007). Focus-on-form instructional methods promote deaf college students' improvement in English grammar. *Journal of Deaf Studies and Deaf Education, 12*(1), 824. https://doi.org/10.1093/deafed/enl009

Betts, W. (2010, May 15). *Deaf lens*. Presentation at TEDxIslay, Austin, Texas. https://www.youtube.com/watch?v=0cbyS9-3jjM

Bloom, C. L., Palmer, J. L., & Winninghoff, J. (2023). *Deaf postsecondary data from the American Community Survey* [Data visualization tool]. National Deaf Center on Postsecondary Outcomes, University of Texas at Austin. www.nationaldeafcenter.org/datadashboard

Boaler, J. (2022). *Mathematical mindsets: Unleashing students' potential through creative mathematics, inspiring messages and innovative teaching* (2nd ed.). Jossey-Bass.

Borron, R. (1978). Modifying science instruction to meet the needs of the hearing impaired. *Journal of Research in Science Teaching, 15*(4), 257–262. https://doi.org/10.1002/tea.3660150404

Bowers, L., Dostal, H., Wolbers, K., & Graham, S. C. (2018). The assessment of written phrasal constructs and grammar of deaf and hard of hearing students with varying expressive language abilities. *Education Research International, 2018*, 1–10. https://doi.org/10.1155/2018/2139626

Braidi, S. (2017, November). *The three read protocol with deaf learners*. Presentation at the DeafTec Math Conference, San Antonio, Texas.

Brett, J. (2009). *The mitten*. Penguin.

Briggs Martin, J., & Lee, J. J. (2017). *Chef Roy Choi and the street food remix*. Readers to Eaters.

Brisson, P., & Azarian, M. (2018). *Before we eat: From farm to table*. Tilbury House.

Bruce, S., DiNatale, P., & Ford, J. (2008). Meeting the needs of deaf and hard of hearing students with additional disabilities through professional teacher development. *American Annals of the Deaf, 153*(4), 368–375. https://doi.org/10.1353/aad.0.0058

Bruning, R., & Horn, C. (2000). Developing motivation to write. *Educational Psychologist, 35*(1), 25–37. https://doi.org/10.1207/S15326985EP3501_4

Bryne, A. P. J. (2013). *American Sign Language (ASL) literacy and ASL literature: A critical appraisal* [Unpublished doctoral dissertation]. York University, Toronto.

Burke, M. L. (2014). *Ableism in the Deaf community and the field of Deaf studies: Through the eyes of a DeafDisabled person* [Unpublished master's thesis]. Gallaudet University, Washington, DC.

California School for the Deaf, Fremont. (2021). *Early childhood education CSD channel*. YouTube. https://www.youtube.com/channel/UCOcOMtQDdFBXNovAefz2pTg

Cannon, J. E., Guardino, C., & Gallimore, E. (2016). A new kind of heterogeneity: What we can learn from d/Deaf and hard of hearing multilingual learners. *American Annals of the Deaf, 161*(1), 8–16.

Carle, E. (1993). *Today is Monday*. Putnam & Grosset.

Carle, E. (1994). *The very hungry caterpillar*. World of Eric Carle.

Carroll, L. (1871). Jabberwocky. In *Through the looking glass and what Alice found there*. T. Y. Crowell.

Cawthon, S. W. (2015). Issues of access and validity in standardized academic assessments for students who are Deaf or hard of hearing. In H. Knoors & M. Marschark (Eds.), *Educating Deaf learners: Global evidence*. Oxford University Press.

Cawthon, S. W., Garberoglio, C. L., Caemmerer, J. M., Bond, M., & Wendel, E. (2015). Effect of parent involvement and parent expectations on postsecondary outcomes for individuals who are d/Deaf or hard of hearing. *Exceptionality, 23*(2), 73–99. https://doi.org/10.1080/09362835.2013.865537

Cawthon, S. W., Johnson, P. M., Garberoglio, C. L., & Schoffstall, S. J. (2016). Role models as facilitators of social capital for deaf individuals: A research synthesis. *American Annals of the Deaf, 161*(2), 115–127. https://doi.org/10.1353/aad.2016.0021

Cawthon, S. W., & Leppo, R. (2013). Assessment accommodations on tests of academic achievement for students who are deaf or hard of hearing: A qualitative meta-analysis of the research literature. *American Annals of the Deaf, 158*(3), 363–376. https://doi.org/10.1353/aad.2013.0023

Center for ASL/English Bilingual Education and Research. (2004). *Signacy framework* [Manuscript]. New Mexico School for the Deaf.

Cheang, R., Gillions, A., & Sparkes, E. (2019). Do mindfulness-based interventions increase empathy and compassion in children and adolescents: A systematic review. *Journal of Child and Family Studies*, 1–15.

Christensen, K. (Ed.). (2017). *Educating Deaf students in a multicultural world*. DawnSignPress.

Churnin, N. (2022). *The William Hoy story: How a Deaf baseball player changed the game*. Albert Whitman.

Clark, A. (2022). *The cost of heaven*. Handtype Press.

Clark, J. L. (2008). *Suddenly slow: Poems*. Handtype Press.

Clark, J. L. (2014). *Where I stand: On the signing community and my DeafBlind experience*. Handtype Press.

Coates, G. D., & Thompson, V. (2003). *Family math II: Achieving success in mathematics*. Equals Publications.

Cole, H. (2012). *Unspoken: A story from the Underground Railroad*. Scholastic Press.

Collins, S. (2008). *The hunger games*. Scholastic.

Compton, S., & Compton, S. (2014). American Sign Language as a heritage language. In T. G. Wiley, J. K. Peyton, D. Christian, S. C. K. Moore, & N. Liu (Eds.), *Handbook of heritage, community, and Native American languages in the United States: Research, policy, and educational practice* (pp. 272–283). Routledge.

Cooley Peterson, M. (2019) *Amazing ants*. Pebbles.

Correia, M. P. (2011). Fiction vs. informational texts: Which will kindergartners choose? *Young Children, 66*, 100–104.

Crowe, K., McLeod, S., McKinnon, D., & Ching, T. (2015). Attitudes toward the capabilities of deaf and hard of hearing adults: Insights from the parents of deaf and hard of hearing children. *American Annals of the Deaf, 160*(1), 24–35. https://doi.org/10.1353/aad.2012.1602

Cue, K. R., Pudans-Smith, K. K., Wolsey, J. L. A., Wright, S. J., & Clark, M. D. (2019). The odyssey of Deaf epistemology. *American Annals of the Deaf, 164*(3), 395–422.

Culham, R. (2003). *6+ 1 traits of writing: The complete guide Grades 3 and up*. Scholastic.

Cummins, J. (2006). *The relationship between American Sign Language proficiency and English academic development: A review of the research*. http://www2.hihm.no/minoritet/KanfOkto6/ASL%20Lit%20Review%20Nov%202006.rtf

Cushman, K. (2005). *Fires in the bathroom: Advice for teachers from high school students*. The New Press.

Cutler, L., & Graham, S. (2008). Primary grade writing instruction: A national survey. *Journal of Educational Psychology, 100*(4), 907–919. https://doi.org/10.1037/a0012656

Davis, K., & McKenzie, R. (2017). *Children's working theories about identity, language, and culture (O faugamanatu a fanau e sa'ili ai o latou fa'asinomaga, gagana ma aganu'u)*. Teaching and Learning Research Initiative (New Zealand). https://eric.ed.gov/?id=ED593683

Daywalt, D. (2013). *The day the crayons quit*. Philomel Books.

Deedy, C. A. (2017). *The rooster who would not be quiet*. Scholastic.

De Meulder, M., Kusters, A., Moriarty, E., & Murray, J. J. (2019). Describe, don't prescribe: The practice and politics of translanguaging in the context of deaf signers. *Journal of Multilingual and Multicultural Development, 40*(10), 892–906.

Derman-Sparks, L., Olson Edwards, J., & Goins, C. M. (Eds.). (2020). *Anti-bias education for young children and ourselves* (2nd ed.). National Association for the Education of Young Children.

Dixon-Krauss, L. (Ed.). (1996). Spontaneous and scientific concepts in content-area instruction. In *Vygotsky in the classroom: Mediated literacy instruction and assessment* (pp. 43–58). Pearson.

Dostal, H., Bowers, L., Wolbers, K., & Gabriel, R. (2015). "We are authors": A qualitative analysis of deaf students' writing during one year of Strategic and Interactive Writing Instruction (SIWI). *Review of Disability Studies: An International Journal, 11*(2), 1–19. https://core.ac.uk/download/pdf/211326093.pdf

Dostal, H., & Gabriel, R. (2016). Literacy mash-up: Discipline-specific practices empower content-area teachers. *Journal of Staff Development: The Learning Forward Journal, 37*(2), 28–32.

Dostal, H., & Robinson, R. (2018). Doing mathematics with purpose: Mathematical text types. *The Clearing House: A Journal of Educational Strategies, Issues, and Ideas, 91*(1), 21–28. https://doi.org/10.1080/00098655.2017.1357409

Dostal, H., & Wolbers, K. (2014). Developing language and writing skills of deaf and hard of hearing students: A simultaneous approach. *Literacy Research and Instruction, 53*(3), 245–268. https://doi.org/10.1080/19388071.2014.907382

Dostal, H., & Wolbers, K. (2015). Video review and reflection for ongoing inservice teacher professional development. In E. Ortlieb, L. Shanahan, & M. McVee (Eds.), *Video research in disciplinary literacies: Literacy research, practice and evaluation* (Vol. 6, pp. 329–352). Emerald Group.

Dostal, H., Wolbers, K., & Kilpatrick, J. R. (2019). The language zone: Differentiating writing instruction for students who are deaf and hard of hearing. *Writing & Pedagogy, 11*(1), 1–22. https://eric.ed.gov/?id=ED603181

Dostal, H., Wolbers, K., Ward, S., & Saulsburry, R. (2018). A national survey of teachers of the Deaf on disciplinary writing. *Exceptionality, 29*(2), 95–113.

Duke, N. (2014). *Inside information: Developing powerful readers and writers of informational text through project based instruction, K–5*. Scholastic.

Duke, N., & Bennett-Armistead, S. (2003). *Reading & writing informational text in the primary grades: Research-based practices*. Scholastic.

Dunn, L. M. (1992). Intellectual oppression of the black deaf child. *Deafness, life, and culture: A Deaf American monograph, 42*, 75–79.

Dunn, L. M. (1998). The deaf community in the 21st century: A black deaf perspective. In *Deaf Studies V: Toward 2000—Unity and diversity. Conference proceedings* (pp. 122–128). College for Continuing Education, Gallaudet University.

Dunn, L. M. (2020). 2006 protest: From the black deaf side. *Deaf Studies Digital Journal, 5*, 1–10. https://quod.lib.umich.edu/d/dsdj/15499139.0005.003/—2006-protest-from-the-black-deaf-side?rgn=main;view=fulltext

Dunn, L. M., & Anderson, G. B. (2019). Examining the intersectionality of Deaf identity, race/ethnicity, and diversity through a Black Deaf lens. In I. W. Leigh & C. A. O'Brien (Eds.), *Deaf identities: Exploring new frontiers* (pp. 279–304). Oxford University Press.

Dweck, C. S., & Yeager, D. S. (2019). Mindsets: A view from two eras. *Perspectives on Psychological Science, 14*(3), 481–496.

Easterbrooks, S. R., & Dostal, H. (2021). *Oxford handbook on Deaf studies in literacy*. Oxford University Press.

Echevarria, J., Vogt, M., & Short, D. (2008). *Making content comprehensible for English learners: The SIOP model*. Pearson/Allyn & Bacon.

Englert, C. S., Mariage, T., & Dunsmore, K. (2006). Tenets of sociocultural theory in writing instruction research. In C. A. MacArthur, S. Graham, & J. Fitzgerald (Eds.), *Handbook of writing research* (pp. 208–221). Guilford Press.

English, D., Rendina, H. J., & Parsons, J. T. (2018). The effects of intersecting stigma: A longitudinal examination of minority stress, mental health, and substance use among Black, Latino, and multiracial gay and bisexual men. *Psychology of Violence, 8*(6), 669.

Enns, C., Henner, J., & McQuarrie, L. (Eds.). (2021). *Discussing bilingualism in deaf children: Essays in honor of Robert Hoffmeister*. Routledge.

Fellinger, J., Holzinger, D., Dobner, U., Gerich, J., Lehner, R., Lenz, G., & Goldberg, D. (2005). Mental distress and quality of life in a deaf population. *Social Psychiatry and Psychiatric Epidemiology, 40*(9), 737–742. https://doi.org/10.1007/s00127-005-0936-8

Ferjan Ramirez, N., Lieberman, A. M., & Mayberry, R. (2013). The initial stages of first-language acquisition begun in adolescence: When late looks early. *Journal of Child Language, 40*(2), 391–414. https://doi.org/10.1017/S0305000911000535

Fleischman, P. (2007). *Glass slipper, gold sandal: A worldwide Cinderella*. Henry Holt.

Flower, L., & Hayes, J. R. (1981). A cognitive process theory of writing. *College Composition and Communication, 32*(4), 365–387.

Foresman, S. (1989). *The little red hen*. Addison-Wesley.

Frayer, D., Frederick, W. C., & Klausmeier, H. J. (1969). *A scheme for testing the level of concept mastery* (Working Paper No. 16). University of Wisconsin Research and Development Center for Cognitive Learning.

Freeman, D. (1968). *Corduroy*. Viking Books for Young Readers.

Freeman, Y. S., Freeman, D. E., Soto, M., & Ebe, A. (2016). *ESL teaching: Principles for Success*. Heinemann.

French, M. M. (1999a). *Starting with assessment: A development approach to deaf children's literacy*. Gallaudet University Pre-College National Mission Programs.

French, M. M. (1999b). *The toolkit: Appendices for starting with assessment*. Gallaudet University Pre-College National Mission Programs.

Fung, P. C., Chow, B. W. Y., & McBride-Chang, C. (2005). The impact of a dialogic reading program on deaf and hard-of-hearing kindergarten and early primary school–aged students in Hong Kong. *Journal of Deaf Studies and Deaf Education, 10*(1), 82–95. https://doi.org/10.1093/deafed/eni005

Gallaudet Research Institute. (2013). *Regional and national summary report of data from the 2011–2012 annual survey of deaf and hard of hearing children and youth*. Gallaudet University.

Gannon, J. R. (1981/2011). *Deaf heritage: A narrative history of Deaf America*. National Association of the Deaf.

Gárate-Estes, M., Lawyer, G. L., & García-Fernández, C. (2021). The U.S. Latinx Deaf communities: Situating and envisioning the transformative potential of translanguaging. In M. T. Sánchez & O. García (Eds.), *Transformative translanguaging espacios in bilingual education: U.S. Latinx bilingual children rompiendo fronteras* (pp. 223–251). Multilingual Matters.

Garberoglio, C. L., & Cawthon, S. (Eds.). (2020). *Research in deaf education: Contexts, challenges, and considerations*. Oxford University Press.

Garberoglio, C. L., Palmer, J. L., & Cawthon, S. (2019a). *Undergraduate enrollment of Deaf students in the United States*. U.S. Department of Education, Office of Special Education Programs, National Deaf Center on Postsecondary Outcomes.

Garberoglio, C. L., Palmer, J. L., Cawthon, S. W., & Sales, A. (2019b). *Deaf people and educational attainment in the United States: 2019*. University of Texas at Austin, National Deaf Center on Postsecondary Outcomes. www.nationaldeafcenter.org/educationdata

Garberoglio, C. L., Palmer, J. L., Cawthon, S. W., & Sales, A. (2019c). *Deaf people and employment in the United States: 2019*. University of Texas at Austin, National Deaf Center on Postsecondary Outcomes. www.nationaldeafcenter.org/employmentdata

Garberoglio, C. L., Schoffstall, S., Cawthon, S., Bond, M., & Caemmerer, J. M. (2017). The antecedents and outcomes of autonomous behaviors: Modeling the role of autonomy in achieving sustainable employment for deaf young adults. *Journal of Developmental and Physical Disabilities, 29*(1), 107–129. https://doi.org/10.1007/s10882-016-9492-2

Garberoglio, C. L., Schoffstall, S., Cawthon, S., Bond, M., & Ge, J. (2014). The role of self-beliefs in predicting postschool outcomes for deaf young adults. *Journal of Developmental and Physical Disabilities, 26*(6), 667–688. https://doi.org/10.1007/s10882-014-9388-y

García, O. (Ed.). (2009). Bilingualism and translanguaging. In *Bilingual education in the 21st century: A global perspective* (pp. 42–72). Oxford.

García, O., & Lin, A. M. (2017). Translanguaging in bilingual education. In O. García, A. M. Y. Lin, & S. May (Eds.), *Bilingual and multilingual education* (pp. 117–130). Springer.

García-Fernández, C. (2020). Intersectionality and autoethnography: DeafBlind, DeafDisabled, Deaf and Hard of

Hearing-Latinx children are the future. *Journal Committed to Social Change on Race and Ethnicity, 6*(1), 41–67.

Gardeski, C. (2000). *Columbus day*. Children's Press.

Gibson, D. J., Gunderson, E. A., & Levine, S. C. (2020). Causal effects of parent number talk on preschoolers' number knowledge. *Child Development, 91*(6), e1162–e1177.

Girma, H. (2019). *Haben: The deafblind woman who conquered Harvard Law*. Hachette.

Glickman, N., & Hall, W. (2018). *Language deprivation and deaf mental health*. Routledge.

Goldenberg, C. (2008, Summer). Teaching English language learners: What the research does and does not say. *American Educator*, 13–44.

Golos, D. (2010). The representation of Deaf characters in educational television: A content analysis. *Journal of Children and Media, 4*(3), 248–264. https://doi.org/10.1080/17482798.2010.486130

Golos, D. & Moses, A. (2013a). The benefits of using educational videos in American Sign Language in early childhood settings. *Learning Landscapes 6*(2), 125.

Golos, D. B., & Moses, A. M. (2013b). Rethinking the portrayal of deaf characters in children's picture books. *Frontiers in Psychology, 4*, 889. https://doi.org/10.3389/fpsyg.2013.00889

Golos, D. & Moses, A. (2015). Supplementing an educational video series with video-related classroom activities and materials. *Sign Language Studies, 15*(2) 103–125. https://doi.org/10.1353/sls.2015.0005

Golos, D. B., Moses, A. M., & Wolbers, K. A. (2012). Culture or disability? Examining deaf characters in children's book illustrations. *Early Childhood Education Journal, 40*(4), 239–249. https://doi.org/10.1007/s10643-012-0506-0

Golos, D., Moses, A., Roemen, B., & Cregan, G. (2018). Cultural and linguistic role models: A survey of early childhood educators of the deaf. *Sign Language Studies, 19*(1), 40–74. https://www.jstor.org/stable/26638546

Golos, D., Moses, A., Gale, E., & Berke, M. (2021). Building allies and sharing best practices: Cultural perspectives of Deaf people and ASL can benefit all. *LEARNing Landscapes, 14*(1), 97–110.

Gothberg, J. E., Greene, G., & Kohler, P. D. (2019). District implementation of research-based practices for transition planning with culturally and linguistically diverse youth with disabilities and their families. *Career Development and Transition for Exceptional Individuals, 42*(2), 77–86. https://doi.org/10.1177/2165143418762794

Graham, S. (2006). Strategy instruction and the teaching of writing: A meta-analysis. In C. A. MacArthur, S. Graham, & J. Fitzgerald (Eds.), *Handbook of writing research* (pp. 187–207). Guilford Press.

Graham, S. C. (2012). *Deaf education pre-service teachers' perceptions of scientific inquiry and teaching science to Deaf and hard of hearing students* [Doctoral dissertation]. University of Tennessee, Knoxville.

Graham, S., Bollinger, A., Olson, C. B., D'Aoust, C., MacArthur, C., McCutchen, D., & Olinghouse, N. (2012). *Teaching elementary school students to be effective writers: A practice guide* (NCEE 2012-4058). What Works Clearinghouse. https://ies.ed.gov/ncee/wwc/practiceguide/17

Grosjean, F. (1989). The bilingual as a person. In R. Titone (Ed.), *On the bilingual person* (p. 35). Canadian Society for Italian Studies.

Gulati, S. (2018). Language deprivation syndrome. In N. S. Glickman & W. C. Hall (Eds.), *Language deprivation and deaf mental health* (pp. 24–53). Routledge.

Gunderson, E. A., & Levine, S. C. (2011). Some types of parent number talk count more than others: Relations between parents' input and children's cardinal-number knowledge. *Developmental Science, 14*(5), 1021–1032.

Haber, L. (1992). *Black pioneers of science and invention*. Clarion.

Hall, M., Hall, W., & Caselli, N. (2019). Deaf children need language (not just speech). *First Language, 39*(4), 367–395. https://doi.org/10.1177/0142723719834102

Hall, W. C. (2017). What you don't know can hurt you: The risk of language deprivation by impairing sign language development in deaf children. *Journal of Maternal Child Health, 21*(5), 961–965. https://doi.org/10.1007/s10995-017-2287-y

Hall, W. C., Levin, L. L., & Anderson, M. L. (2017). Language deprivation syndrome: A possible neurodevelopmental disorder with sociocultural origins. *Social Psychiatry and Psychiatric Epidemiology, 52*(6), 761–776.

Hartman, R., & Greene, J. M. (2022). *Signs of survival: A memoir of the Holocaust*. Scholastic.

Harvey, S., & Goudvis, A. (2007). *Strategies that work: Teaching comprehension for understanding and engagement*. Stenhouse Publishers.

Henning, M. B., Snow-Gerono, J. L., Reed, D., & Warner, A. (2006). Listening to children think critically about Christopher Columbus. *Social Studies and the Young Learner, 19*(2), 19.

Higgins, J. A., Famularo, L., Cawthon, S. W., Kurz, C. A., Reis, J. E., & Reis, L. M. (2016). Development of American Sign Language guidelines for K–12 academic assessments. *Journal of Deaf Studies and Deaf Education*. https://doi.org/10.1093/deafed/enw051

Hill, B. C., Noe, K. L. S., & Johnson, N. J. (2001). *Literature Circles resource guide: Teaching suggestions, forms, sample book lists and database* [with CD-ROM]. Christopher-Gordon Publishers.

Holcomb, L. (2020a). ASL rhyme, rhythm, and phonological awareness for deaf children. *Perspectives on Early Childhood Psychology and Education, 5*(2), 3.

Holcomb, L. (2020b, August 10). *Let's go for a walk* [Video]. YouTube. https://www.youtube.com/watch?v=m_ovqeVsEA8

Holcomb, L. (2020c, July 13). *Yummy cookies* [Video]. YouTube. https://www.youtube.com/watch?v=99p00sX8L3A

Holcomb, L. (2023). ASL rhyme, rhythm, and phonological awareness for deaf children. *Perspectives on Early Childhood Psychology and Education, 5*(2), art. 3. https://doi.org/10.58948/2834-8257.1058

Holcomb, L., & Wolbers, K. (2020). Effects of ASL rhyme and rhythm on deaf children's engagement behavior and accuracy recitation: Evidence from a single case design. *Children, 7*(12), 256–286. https://doi.org/10.3390/children7120256

Holcomb, L., Golos, D., Moses, A., & Broadrick, A. (2021). Enriching deaf children's American Sign Language phonological awareness: A quasi-experimental study. *Journal of Deaf Studies and Deaf Education, 27*(1), 26–36. https://doi.org/10.1093/deafed/enab028

Holcomb, T. K. (2010). Deaf epistemology: The deaf way of knowing. *American Annals of the Deaf, 154*(5), 471–478.

Holcomb, T. K. (2013). *Introduction to American deaf culture*. Oxford University Press.

Hoose, P., & Hoose, H. (1998). *Hey, little ant*. Tricycle Press.

Hoover, J., Giambatista, R. C., & Belkin, L. Y. (2012). Eyes on, hands on: Vicarious observational learning as an enhancement of direct experience. *Academy of Management Learning and Education, 11*, 591–608.

Horn-Marsh, K., & Horn-Marsh, P. (2010, November 10). *ASL specialist's palette*. Conference session]. ASL Round Table Conference.

Hughes, E. M., Witzel, B. S., Riccomini, P. J., Fries, K. M., & Kanyongo, G. Y. (2014). A meta-analysis of algebra interventions for learners with disabilities and struggling learners. *Journal of the International Association of Special Education, 15*(1), 36–47.

Humphries, T., & MacDougall, F. (1999). "Chaining" and other links: Making connections between American Sign Language and English in two types of school settings. *Visual Anthropology Review, 15*(2), 84–94.

Hyerle, D., & Yeager, C. (2007). *Thinking Maps: A language for learning*. Thinking Maps.

Isakson, S. K. (2018). The case for heritage ASL instruction for hearing heritage signers. *Sign Language Studies, 18*(3), 385–411.

Jewell, T. (2021). *This book is anti-racist—Journal*. Frances Lincoln Children's Books.

Johnson, R. E., Liddell, S. K., & Erting, C. J. (1989). *Unlocking the curriculum: Principles for achieving access in Deaf education* (Gallaudet Research Institute Working Paper 89-3). Gallaudet University.

Jones, R. C., & Lapham, S. (2004). Teaching reading skills in the elementary social studies classroom. *Social Studies and the Young Learner, 17*(2), 1–8.

Kamkwamba, W., & Mealer, B. (2010). *The boy who harnessed the wind: Creating currents of electricity and hope*. Dial Books.

Kilpatrick, J., & Wolbers, K. (2020). Beyond the red pen: A functional grammar approach to evaluating the written language of deaf students. *Psychology in the Schools, 57*(3), 459–474. https://doi.org/10.1002/pits.22289

Kritzer, K. L. (2009). Barely started and already left behind: A descriptive analysis of the mathematics ability demonstrated by young deaf children. *Journal of Deaf Studies and Deaf Education, 14*(4), 409–421. https://doi.org/10.1093/deafed/enp015

Kuhl, P. K. (2010). Brain mechanisms in early language acquisition. *Neuron, 67*(5), 713–727. https://doi.org/10.1016/j.neuron.2010.08.038

Kuntze, M. (1993). Developing students' literary skills in ASL. In B. Snider (Ed.), *Post Milan ASL & English literacy: Issues, trends, & research* (pp. 267–281). Gallaudet University, Continuing Education and Outreach.

Kuntze, M. (2008). Turning literacy inside out. In H. D. Bauman (Ed.), *Open your eyes: Deaf studies talking*. University of Minnesota Press.

Kuntze, M. (2023). Explicating the relationship between ASL and English in text comprehension. *American Annals of the Deaf, 167*(5), 700–726.

Kuntze, M., & Golos, D. (2021). Revisiting rethinking literacy. In C. Enns, J. Henner, & L. McQuarrie (Eds.), *Discussing bilingualism in deaf children: Essays in honor of Robert Hoffmeister* (pp. 99–112). Routledge.

Kuntze, M., Golos, D., & Enns, C. (2014). Rethinking literacy: Broadening opportunities for visual learners. *Sign Language Studies, 14*(2), 203–224. https://doi.org/10.1353/sls.2014.0002

Kurz, C. (2006). A historical analysis of mathematics education for the deaf during the nineteenth century [Unpublished doctoral dissertation]. University of Kansas.

Kurz, C. (2008). Two views on mathematics education for the deaf: Edward M. Gallaudet and Amos G. Draper. In B. H. Greenwald & J. V. Van Cleve (Eds.), *A fair chance in the race of life: The role of Gallaudet University in Deaf history* (pp. 50–64). Gallaudet University Press.

Kurz, C. (2009). Mental arithmetic and conceptual understanding: The pedagogical struggle for the deaf in the late nineteenth century. *International Journal for the History of Mathematics Education, 4*(1), 91–105.

Kurz, C., Golos, D., Kuntze, M., Henner, J., & Scott, J. A. (2021). *Guidelines for multilingual deaf education teacher preparation programs*. Gallaudet University Press. https://gallaudetupress.manifoldapp.org/projects/guidelines-for-multilingual-deaf-education-teacher-preparation-programs

Kurz, C., & Kurz, K. (2021). Debunking the myths of American Sign Language in academic settings. In E. Winston & S. Fitzmaurice (Eds.), *Advances in educational interpreting* (pp. 308–335). Gallaudet University Press.

Kurz, C., Kurz, K., & Harris, R. (2018). Effectively interpreting the content areas utilizing academic language strategies. In T. Holcomb & D. Smith (Eds.), *Deaf eyes on interpreting*, (pp. 253–268). Gallaudet University Press.

Kurz, C., & Pagliaro, C. M. (2019). Using L1 sign language to teach mathematics. In R. S. Rosen (Ed.), *The Routledge handbook of sign language pedagogy*. Routledge.

Kurz, C., Reis, J., & Spiecker, B. (2020). Ideologies and attitudes toward American Sign Language: Academic language and academic vocabulary coinage process. In A. Kusters, M. Green, E. Harrelson, & K. Snodden (Eds.), *Sign language ideologies in practice* (Vol. 12, pp. 287–308). Walter de Gruyter.

Kusters, A., Spotti, M., Swanwick, R., & Tapio, E. (2017). Beyond languages, beyond modalities: Transforming the study of semiotic repertoires. *International Journal of Multilingualism, 14*(3), 219–232.

Ladd, P. (2005). Deafhood: A concept stressing possibilities, not deficits. *Scandinavian Journal of Public Health, 33*(66, Suppl.), 12–17.

Ladd, P. (2007). Cochlear implantation, colonialism, and Deaf rights. In L. R. Komesaroff (Ed.), *Surgical consent: Bioethics and cochlear implantation* (pp. 1–29). Gallaudet University Press.

Ladd, P. (2008). Colonialism and resistance: A brief history of Deafhood. In D. Baumann (Ed.), *Open your eyes: Deaf studies talking* (pp. 42–59). University of Minnesota Press.

Ladd, P. (2022). *Seeing through new eyes: Deaf culture and deaf pedagogies—The unrecognized curriculum*. DawnSignPress.

Lamba, M., & Lamba, B. (2017). *Green green: A community gardening story*. Farrar, Straus and Giroux.

Landmark, L. J., Ju, S., & Zhang, D. (2010). Substantiated best practices in transition: Fifteen plus years later. *Career Development*

Lane-Outlaw, S. I. (2009). *A qualitative investigation of ASL/English bilingual instruction of Deaf students in secondary science classrooms* [Unpublished doctoral dissertation]. Gallaudet University.

Lang, H. (1994). *Silence of the spheres: The deaf experience in the history of science*. Praeger.

Lang, H. G., Kurz, K., & Kurz, C. (2006). Vital signs: Optimizing the teaching of science and mathematics through research. *NTID Research Bulletin, 11*(1–3), 1, 3–5.

Lang, H. G., & Lang-Meath, B. (1995). *Deaf persons in the arts and sciences: A biographical dictionary*. Greenwood.

Langdon, C., Kurz, C., & Coppola, M. (2021). The importance of early number concepts for learning mathematics in deaf and hard of hearing children. *Special Issue: Perspectives on Early Childhood Psychology and Education, 5*(2), 125–155.

Larsen, F. A., & Damen, S. (2014). Definitions of deafblindness and congenital deafblindness. *Research in Developmental Disabilities, 35*(10), 2568–2576.

Laurent Clerc National Deaf Education Center (2018). *K–12 ASL content standards*. Gallaudet University. https://aslstandards.org/wp-content/uploads/2021/05/K-12-ASL-Content-Standard.pdf

Lawson, M. J., Vosniadou, S., Van Deur, P. Wyra, M., & Jeffries, D. (2019). Teachers' and students' belief systems about the self-regulation of learning. *Educational Psychology Review, 31*, 223–251. https://doi.org/10.1007/s10648-018-9453-7

Leigh, I. W., Andrews, J. F., Harris, R. L., & Ávila, T. G. (2020). *Deaf culture: Exploring deaf communities in the United States* (2nd ed.). Plural Publishing.

Leigh, I. W., & O'Brien, C. A. (2020). *Deaf identities: Exploring new ideas*. Oxford University Press.

Levine, A. A. (2011). *Monday is one day*. Scholastic.

Levine, E. (2007). *Henry's freedom box*. Scholastic Press.

Levine, K. (2012). *The lions of Little Rock*. Putnam.

Lewis, J., Aydin, A., & Powell, N. (2013). *March: Book one*. Top Shelf Productions.

Lewis, W., Walpole, S., & McKenna, M. (2014). *Cracking the Common Core: Choosing and using texts in grades 6–12*. Guilford Press.

Lindquist, T. (2002). *Seeing the whole through social studies* (2nd ed.). Heinemann.

Lindstrom, C., & Goade, M. (2020). *We are water protectors*. Roaring Brook Press.

Loewen, J. W. (2018). *Lies my teacher told me: Everything your American history textbook got wrong*. The New Press.

Loman, S., Vatland, C., Strickland-Cohen, K., Horner, R., & Walker, H. (2010). *Promoting self-determination: A practice guide*. UCEDD Leadership Consortium.

Lonigan, C. J., & Whitehurst, G. J. (1998). Relative efficacy of parent and teacher involvement in a shared-reading intervention for preschool children from low-income backgrounds. *Early Childhood Research Quarterly, 13*, 263–290. https://doi.org/10.1016/S0885-2006(99)800386

Lowry, L. (1993). *The giver*. Delacorte Press.

Luczak, R. (2021). *Once upon a twin*. Gallaudet University Press.

Lupo, S. M., Strong, J. Z., Lewis, W., Walpole, S., & McKenna, M. C. (2018). Building background knowledge through reading: Rethinking text sets. *Journal of Adolescent & Adult Literacy, 61*(4), 433–444. https://doi.org/10.1002/jaal.701

Marbury, N. (2016). *Choir* [Videotext]. YouTube. https://www.youtube.com/watch?v=ET_cO7bpM3Y

Marbury, N. (2017). *Dream the impossible dream* [Videotext ASL poem]. YouTube. https://www.youtube.com/watch?v=NSDIqvgSRp4

Martin, J. E., Van Dycke, J. L., Christensen, W. R., Greene, B. A., Gardner, J. E., & Lovett, D. L. (2006). Increasing student participation in IEP meetings: Establishing the self-directed IEP as an evidenced-based practice. *Exceptional Children, 72*(3), 299–316. https://doi.org/10.1177/001440290607200303

Maslow, A. H. (1943). A theory of human motivation. *Psychological Review, 50*(4), 370–396. https://doi.org/10.1037/h0054346

Maze, S. (1999). *I want to be a veterinarian*. Harper Collins.

McCaskill, C., Lucas, C., Bayley, R., & Hill, J. (2011). *The hidden treasure of Black ASL: Its history and structure*. Gallaudet University Press.

McElhaney, K. W., Basu, S., Wetzel, T., & Boyce, J. (2019, March). *Three-dimensional assessment of NGSS upper elementary engineering design performance expectations* [Paper presentation]. NARST Annual International Conference.

Miller, H., Valentine, J. L., Fish, R., & Robinson, M. (2016). Is the feeling mutual? Examining parent–teacher relationships in low-income, predominantly Latino schools. *American Journal of Education, 123*, 37–67.

Miller, S. (2019). *Don't touch my hair*. Little, Brown.

Millman, I. (2004). *Moses sees a play*. Farrar, Straus and Giroux.

Mitchell, R. E., & Karchmer, M. A. (2004). Chasing the mythical ten percent: Parental hearing status of deaf and hard of hearing students in the United States. *Sign Language Studies, 5*, 83–96.

Mitchell, R. E., & Karchmer, M. A. (2005). Parental hearing status and signing among deaf and hard of hearing students. *Sign Language Studies, 5*(2), 231–244.

Moje, E. B. (2015). Doing and teaching disciplinary literacy with adolescents: A social and cultural enterprise. *Harvard Education Review, 85*(2), 254–278. https://doi.org/10.17763/0017-8055.85.2.254

Molander, B. O., Pedersen, S., & Norell, K. (2001). Deaf pupils' reasoning about scientific phenomena: School science as a framework for understanding or as fragments of factual knowledge. *Journal of Deaf Studies and Deaf Education, 6*(3), 200–211. https://doi.org/10.1093/deafed/6.3.200

Mosca, J., & Reilly, D. (2020). *The girl with a mind for math: The story of Raye Montague*. Innovation Press.

Moses, A. M., Golos, D. B., & Holcomb, L. (2018). Creating and using educational media with a cultural perspective of Deaf people. *Youth Culture(s) and Childhood, 96*(1), 67–71.

Moss, B. (2005). Making a case and a place for effective content area literacy instruction in the elementary grades. *The Reading Teacher, 49*(1), 46–55. https://doi.org/10.1598/RT.59.1.5

Muhammad, G. (2020) *Cultivating genius: An equity framework for culturally and historically responsive literacy*. Scholastic.

Musyoka, M. M., & Adeoye, S. O. (2020). Designing an inclusive culturally competent classroom for immigrant deaf students in the United States. In K. Sprott, J. R. O'Connor Jr., & C. Msengi (Eds.), *Designing culturally competent programming for PK–20 classrooms* (pp. 180–197). IGI Global.

Nagle, K., Newman, L. A., Shaver, D. M., & Marschark, M. (2016). College and career readiness: Course taking of deaf and hard of hearing secondary school students. *American Annals of the Deaf, 160*(5), 467–482.

National Association of State Directors of Special Education (NASDSE). (2018). *Optimizing outcomes for students who are Deaf or hard of hearing: Educational service guidelines* (3rd ed.). NASDSE. https://www.nasdse.org

National Council for the Social Studies (NCSS). (2013). *The College, Career, and Civic Life (C3) framework for social studies state standards: Guidance for enhancing the rigor of K–12 civics, economics, geography, and history*. NCSS. https://media.nationalgeographic.org/assets/file/C3-Framework-for-Social-Studies.pdf

National Deaf Center on Postsecondary Outcomes. (2017). *Root causes of gaps in postsecondary outcomes for Deaf individuals*. U.S. Department of Education. https://nationaldeafcenter.org/resource-items/root-causes-and-key-impact-areas/

National Governors Association Center for Best Practices & Council of Chief State School Officers. (2010). *Common core state standards*.

National Research Council. (2012). *A framework for K–12 science education: Practices, crosscutting concepts, and core ideas*. National Academies Press.

Neff, K. D., & Germer, C. K. (2013). A pilot study and randomized controlled trial of the Mindful Self-Compassion program. *Journal of Clinical Psychology, 69*(1), 28–44.

Nota, L., Ferrari, L., Soresi, S., & Wehmeyer, M. (2007). Self-determination, social abilities and the quality of life of people with intellectual disability. *Journal of Intellectual Disability Research, 51*(11), 850–865. https://doi.org/10.1111/j.1365-2788.2006.00939.x

Nota, L., Ginevra, M. C., & Santilli, S. (2015). Life design and prevention. In L. Nota & J. Rossier (Eds.), *Handbook of life design: From practice to theory and from theory to practice* (pp. 183–199). Hogrefe Publishing.

Nover, S. (2006). *Language planning in (Deaf) education*. https://www.michigan.gov/documents/Noverpdf_156992_7.pdf

Nunes, T., Bryant, P., & Pretzlik, U. (2006). *Using deaf children's visual skills to promote mathematics learning* [Poster presentation]. International Society for the Study of Behavioural Development 19th Biennial Meeting, Melbourne, Australia, pp. 1–5.

Nunes, T., & Moreno, C. (2002). An intervention program for promoting deaf pupils' achievement in mathematics. *Journal of Deaf Studies and Deaf Education, 7*(2), 120–133. https://doi.org/10.1093/deafed/7.2.120

Ortega, L. (2020). The study of heritage language development from a bilingualism and social justice perspective. *Language Learning, 70*, 15–53.

Padden, C., & Ramsey, C. (1998). Reading ability in signing Deaf children. *Topics in Language Disorders, 18*(4), 30–46. https://doi.org/10.1097/00011363-199818040-00005

Padron, A. P. (2010). *Brush, brush, brush*. Children's Press.

Pagliaro, C. M. (2010). Mathematics instruction and learning of deaf and hard-of-hearing students: What do we know? Where do we go? In M. Marschark & P. E. Spencer (Eds.), *The Oxford handbook of deaf studies, language, and education* (Vol. 2, pp. 156–171). Oxford University Press. http://doi.org/10.1093/oxfordhb/9780195390032.001.0001

Pagliaro, C., & Kurz, C. (2021). Using ASL to navigate the semantic circuit in the bilingual mathematics classroom. In C. Enns, J. Henner, & L. McQuarrie (Eds.), *Discussing bilingualism in deaf children: Essays in honor of Robert Hoffmeister* (pp. 187–196). Routledge.

Palmer, C. (2022). *The legend of Gravity: A tall basketball tale*. Farrar, Straus and Giroux.

Palmer, J. L., Cawthon, S. W., Garberoglio, C. L., & Ivanko, T. (2020). *ACCESS is more than accommodations: 2018–2019 deaf college student national accessibility report*. University of Texas at Austin, National Deaf Center on Postsecondary Outcomes. www.nationaldeafcenter.org/podreport

Parr, T. (2003). *The family book*. Little, Brown.

Paulsen, G. (2006). *Hatchet*. Simon & Schuster.

Petrone-Stratiy, A. (1998). *Pursuit of ASL: Interesting facts using classifiers* [DVD]. Interpreting Consolidated.

Petrová, Z. (2013). On the relevancy of using Vygotsky's theoretical framework to legitimize dialogic teaching/learning. *Journal of Pedagogy, 4*(2), 237–252. https://doi.org/10.2378/jped-2013-0013

Pichler, D. C., Reynolds, W., & Palmer, J. L. (2019). Multilingualism in signing communities. In S. Montanari & S. Quay (Eds.), *Multidisciplinary perspectives on multilingualism: The fundamentals* (Vol. 19, pp. 175–204). Walter De Gruyter.

Polacco, P. (2011). *The keeping quilt*. Simon & Schuster.

Raley, S. K., Shogren, K. A., Rifenbark, G. G., Lane, K. L., & Pace, J. R. (2021). The impact of the self-determined learning model of instruction on student self-determination in inclusive secondary classrooms. *Remedial and Special Education, 42*(6), 363–373. https://doi.org/10.1177/0741932520984842

RAND. (2003). *Reading for understanding: Toward an R&D program in reading comprehension*. RAND Reading Study Group.

Ray, D. (2006). *Singing hands*. Houghton Mifflin Harcourt.

Reagan, T., Matlins, P. E., & Pielick, C. D. (2021). Deaf epistemology, sign language and the education of d/Deaf children. *Educational Studies, 57*(1), 37–57.

Reynolds, J., & Kiely, B. (2017). *All American boys*. Simon & Schuster.

Reynolds Naylor, P. R. (2000). *Shiloh*. Atheneum Books.

Riggio, A. (2003). *Secret signs: An escape through the underground railroad*. Boyd Mills Press.

Roberts, B. (n.d.). *Ants, ants & more ants*. Reading A–Z. https://www.readinga-z.com/book.php?id=85

Roberts, J. C., & Roberts, K. A. (2008). Deep reading, cost/benefit, and the construction of meaning: Enhancing reading comprehension and deep learning in sociology courses. *Teaching Sociology, 36*(2), 125–140. http://www.jstor.org/stable/20058637

Robinson, K. (2005). Doing anti-homophobia and anti-heterosexism in early childhood education: Moving beyond the immobilizing impacts of "risks," "fears" and "silences." Can we afford not to? *Contemporary Issues in Early Childhood, 6*(2), 175–188.

Rockwell, T. (1973). *How to eat fried worms*. Dell.

Rocky Mountain Deaf School. (2021). *RMDS YouTube channel*. YouTube. https://www.youtube.com/channel/UC7clP2oTJIzKjNTba7APp2A

Roeser, R., Schonert-Reichl, K. A., Jha, A., Cullen, M., Wallace, L., Wilensky, R., Oberle, E., Thomson, K., Taylor, C., & Harrison, J. (2013). Mindfulness training and reductions in teacher stress and burnout: Results from two randomized, waitlist-control field trials. *Journal of Educational Psychology, 105*(3), 787–804.

Rolston, J., & Cox, E. (2015). *Engineering for the real world: Diversity, innovation and hands-on learning.* https://doi.org/10.1007/978-3-319-16169-3_13

Rosen, R. S. (Ed.). (2019). *The Routledge handbook of sign language pedagogy.* Routledge.

Ruurs, M. (2004). *When we go camping.* Turtleback.

Ryan, D. F., & Schuchman, J. S. (Eds.). (2002). *Deaf people in Hitler's Europe.* Gallaudet University Press and the United States Holocaust Memorial Museum.

Saeed, A. (2020). *Amal unbound.* Nancy Paulsen Books.

Saint-Exupéry, A. (2000). *The little prince.* Mariner Books.

San Francisco Unified School District. (2015). SFUSD signature strategy #2: The 3-read protocol. http://www.sfusdmath.org/signature-strategy-1-3-read-protocol.html

Sanborn, I. (2014, March 30). *Caterpillar* [Videotext]. https://www.youtube.com/watch?v=MTgGQnxX5Uw

Sanborn, I. (2014, April 23). *The squirrel story* [Videotext]. https://www.youtube.com/watch?v=lNha5u49igA

Sanders, D. M. (1986). Sign language in the production & appreciation of humor by deaf children. *Sign Language Studies, 50*(1), 59–72.

Saulsburry, R., Kilpatrick, J., Wolbers, K., & Dostal, H. (2015). Getting students excited about learning: Incorporating digital tools to support the writing process. *Odyssey, 16*, 30–34. http://files.eric.ed.gov/fulltext/EJ1064118.pdf

Schermer, T. (2016). Lexicon. In A. Baker, B. van den Bogaerde, R. Pfau, & T. Schermer (Eds.), *The linguistics of sign languages: An introduction* (pp. 173–195). John Benjamins.

Schleper, D. R. (1997). *Reading to deaf children: Learning from deaf adults.* Gallaudet University Press.

Schlick, N. K. L., & Johnson, N. J. (1999). *Getting started with literature circles.* Christopher.

Schoffstall, S., Cawthon, S. W., Dickson, D., Bond, M., Ocuto, O., & Ge, J. (2016). The impact of high school extracurricular involvement on the postsecondary outcomes of deaf and hard-of-hearing youth. *Journal of Postsecondary Education and Disability, 29*(2), 179–197.

Schonert-Reichl, K. A., Oberle, E., Lawlor, M. S., Abbott, D., Thomson, K., Oberlander, T. F., & Diamond, A. (2015). Enhancing cognitive and social-emotional development through a simple-to-administer mindfulness-based school program for elementary school children: A randomized controlled trial. *Developmental Psychology, 51*(1), 52–66.

School of Education, University of Wisconsin–Madison. (2021). *CCBC diversity statistics.* Cooperative Children's Book Center. https://ccbc.education.wisc.edu/

Scieszka, J. (1996). *The true story of the three little pigs* (2nd ed.). Puffin Books.

Scott, J. A., & Dostal, H. A. (2019). Language development and deaf/hard of hearing children. *Education Sciences, 9*, 135. https://doi.org/10.3390/educsci9020135

Scott, J. A., Dostal, H. A., Gabriel, R., & Graham, S. (2021). Developing the science writing of deaf developing bilinguals. *Journal of Adolescent and Adult Literacy, 65*(2), 149–161. https://doi.org/10.1002/jaal.1189

Scott, J. A., & Hansen, S. G. (2019). Comprehending science writing: The promise of dialogic reading for supporting upper-elementary deaf students. *Communication Disorders Quarterly, 41*(2), 100–109. https://doi.org/10.1177/1525740119838253

Seibert, P. (2001). *The three little pigs.* Brighter Child.

Selznick, B. (2011). *Wonderstruck: A novel in words and pictures.* Scholastic.

Seong, Y., Wehmeyer, M. L., Palmer, S. B., & Little, T. D. (2015). Effects of the self-directed individualized education program on self-determination and transition of adolescents with disabilities. *Career Development and Transition for Exceptional Individuals, 38*(3), 132–141. https://doi.org/10.1177/2165143414544359

Seriki, V. D., & Brown, C. T. (2019). Research on racism in teacher education in the United States. *Oxford Research Encyclopedia of Education.* https://doi.org/10.1093/acrefore/9780190264093.013.372

Serrano, J. (2010). *Bread around the world.* Newmark Learning.

Settlage, J. (2018). Equitable science outcomes and school organizational conditions. In J. Kay & R. Luckin (Eds., *Rethinking learning in the digital age: Making the learning sciences count. 13th International Conference of the Learning Sciences (ICLS) 2018* (Vol. 3). International Society of the Learning Sciences.

Settlage, J., Southerland, S. A., Semtana, L. K., & Lottero-Perdue, P. S. (2017). *Teaching science to every child: Using culture as a starting point* (3rd ed.). Routledge.

Shahaeian, A., Haynes, M., & Frick, P. J. (2023). The role of language in the association between theory of mind and executive functioning in early childhood: New longitudinal evidence. *Childhood Research Quarterly, 62*, 251–258.

Shanahan, T. (2016). Relationships between reading and writing development. In C. A. MacArthur, S. Graham, & J. Fitzgerald (Eds.), *Handbook of writing research* (Vol. 2, pp. 194–207). Guilford Press.

Shanahan, T., & Shanahan, C. (2008). Teaching disciplinary literacy to adolescents: Rethinking content-area literacy. *Harvard Educational Review, 78*(1), 40–59. https://doi.org/10.17763/haer.78.1.v62444321p602101

Shetterly, M. L. (2016). *Hidden figures: The American dream and the untold story of the Black women mathematicians who helped win the space race.* William Morrow Paperbacks.

Shogren, K. A., Wehmeyer, M. L., Palmer, S. B., Rifenbark, G. G., & Little, T. D. (2015). Relationships between self-determination and postschool outcomes for youth with disabilities. *The Journal of Special Education, 48*(4), 256–267. https://doi.org/10.1177/0022466913489733

Sign Media. (1994). *American freedom speeches* [Video]. Sign Media Press.

Simms, L., & Thumann, H. (2007). In search of a new, linguistically and culturally sensitive paradigm in deaf education. *American Annals of the Deaf, 152*(3), 302–311.

Slade, S., & Griffith, D. (2013). A whole child approach to student success. *KEDI Journal of Educational Policy, 10*(3), 21–35.

Slade, S., & Miller Jamison, V. (2019). *A computer called Katherine: How Katherine Johnson helped put America on the moon.* Little, Brown.

Slavin, R. E. (2015). Cooperative learning in elementary schools. *Education 3-13, 43*(1), 5–14. https://doi.org/10.1080/03004279.2015.963370

Smalls, I. (2012). *Pop Pop and me and a recipe.* Xist Publishing.

Smith, A. K., & Jacobowitz, E. L. (2006). *Have you ever seen . . . ? An American Sign Language handshape DVD/book.* ASL Rose.

Smith, D. H. (2013). Deaf adults: Retrospective narratives of school experiences and teacher expectations. *Disability & Society, 28*(5), 674–686. https://doi.org/10.1080/09687599.2012.732537

Sonnenstrahl, D. M. (2002). *Deaf artists in America: Colonial to contemporary.* Dawn Sign Press.

Southern Poverty Law Center. (n.d.). *Critical practices for antibias education.* SPLC Learning for Justice. https://www.learningforjustice.org/magazine/publications/critical-practices-for-antibias-education

Spinelli, J. (1999). *Maniac magee.* Little Brown Books.

Srinivasan, M. (2014). *Teach, breathe, learn: Mindfulness in and out of the classroom.* Parallax Press.

Stanovich, K. E., & Stanovich, P. J. (1995). How research might inform the debate about early reading acquisition. *Journal of Research in Reading, 18*(2), 87–105. https://doi.org/10.1111/j.1467-9817.1995.tb00075.x

Strassman, B. K., & Schirmer, B. (2012). Teaching writing to deaf students: Does research offer evidence for practice? *Remedial and Special Education, 34*(3), 166–179. https://doi.org/10.1177/0741932512452013

Sturley, N. (2007). *Milan.* Trafford.

Sulzby, E., & Teale, W. (1991). Emergent literacy. *Handbook of Reading Research, 2,* 727–757.

Supalla, T., Malzkuhn, M., & Limousin, F. (2014). Tracking our sign language heritage. *Deaf Studies Digital Journal, 1*(4).

Susperreguy, M. I., & Davis-Kean, P. E. (2016). Maternal math talk in the home and math skills in preschool children. *Early Education and Development, 27*(6), 841–857.

Swanwick, R. (2017). Translanguaging, learning and teaching in deaf education. *International Journal of Multilingualism, 14*(3), 233–249.

Tankersley, K. (2007). *Tests that teach: Using standardized tests to improve instruction.* ASCD.

Taylor, B. K. (2015). Content, process, and product: Modeling differentiated instruction. *Kappa Delta Pi Record, 51*(1), 13–17.

Taylor, S. G., Roberts, A. M., & Zarrett, N. (2021). A brief mindfulness-based intervention (bMBI) to reduce teacher stress and burnout. *Teaching and Teacher Education, 100,* 103284. https://doi.org/10.1016/j.tate.2021.103284

Teague, M. (2002). *Dear Mrs. LaRue: Letters from obedience school.* Scholastic Press.

Terry, C. E. (2016). *Unfolding the soul of Black Deaf expressions.* Blurb.

Test, D. W., Mazzotti, V. L., Mustian, A. L., Fowler, C. H., Kortering, L., & Kohler, P. (2009). Evidence-based secondary transition predictors for improving postschool outcomes for students with disabilities. *Career Development for Exceptional Individuals, 32*(3), 160–181. https://doi.org/10.1177/0885728809346960

Thierry, K. L., Bryant, H. L., Nobles, S. S., & Norris, K. S. (2016). Two-year impact of a mindfulness-based program on preschoolers' self-regulation and academic performance. *Early Education and Development, 27*(6), 805–821. https://doi.org/10.1080/10409289.2016.1141616

Thong, R., & Parra, J. (2015). *Round is a tortilla: A book of shapes.* Chronicle Books.

Thumann, H. R., & Simms, L. E. (2009). Who decides for us, deaf people? In W. Ayers, T. Quinn, & D. Stovall (Eds.), *Handbook of social justice in education* (pp. 209–226). Routledge.

Tracey, D. H., & Morrow, L. M. (2017). *Lenses on reading: An introduction to theories and models.* Guilford Press.

Trainor, A. A., Carter, E. W., Swedeen, B., & Pickett, K. (2012). Community conversations: An approach for expanding and connecting opportunities for employment for adolescents with disabilities. *Career Development and Transition for Exceptional Individuals, 35*(1), 50–60. https://doi.org/10.1177/0885728811419166

Traveling Morning Star/James Wooden Legs. (2019). *Native cultural stories* [Video]. https://www.youtube.com/watch?v=zKLmJ1E83Vs

Trussell, J. W., & Easterbrooks, S. R. (2015). Effects of morphographic instruction on the morphographic analysis skills of deaf and hard of hearing students. *Journal of Deaf Studies and Deaf Education, 20*(3), 229–241. https://doi.org/10.1093/deafed/env019

Uhlberg, M. (2005). *Dad, Jackie, and me.* Peachtree.

U.S. Bureau of Labor Statistics. (2020). *Labor force statistics from the current population survey: Employed persons by detailed occupation, sex, race, and Hispanic or Latino ethnicity.* https://www.bls.gov/cps/aa2020/cpsaat10.htm

U.S. Department of Education. (2018, January)., National Center for Education Statistics, *2015–16 National postsecondary student aid study (NPSAS:16).* National Center for Education Statistics. Regression data retrieved using PowerStats in June 2019.

Vacca, R. T., Vacca, J. A., & Mraz, M. (2016). *Content area reading: Literacy and learning across the curriculum* (12th ed.). Pearson.

Valdés, G., Poza, L., & Brooks, M. D. (2015). Language acquisition in bilingual education. In W. E. Wright, S. Boun, & O. García (Eds.), *The handbook of bilingual and multilingual education* (pp. 56–74). Wiley.

Valli, C., & Lucas, C. (2000). *Linguistics of American Sign Language: An introduction.* Gallaudet University Press.

Van de Walle, J., Karp, K., & Bay-Williams, J. (2018). *Elementary and middle school mathematics: Teaching developmentally* (10th ed.). Pearson.

Venn, J. (1881). *Symbolic logic.* Macmillan.

Vetter, A., & Hungerford-Kresser, H. (2014). "We gotta change first": Racial literacy in a high school English classroom. *Journal of Language and Literacy Education* [Online], *10*(1), 82–99. http://jolle.coe.uga.edu/wp-content/uploads/2014/04/We-gotta-change-first-Vetter.pdf

Visual Language and Visual Learning Science of Learning Center. (2010, July). *The importance of fingerspelling for reading.* (Research Brief No. 1). Sharon Baker.

Visual Language and Visual Learning. (2020). *VL2 storybook apps: Global digital library.* https://vl2storybookapps.com/digital-library

Visual Language/Visual Learning. (2020). *VL2 Storybook apps: Global digital library.* https://vl2storybookapps.com/digital-library

Von Bitter, M., & Turley, K. (2018). Deaf history, digital technology, and content-area literacy: Instructional strategies for secondary classrooms. *Sign Language Studies, 17*(1), 78–84.

Vygotsky, L. S. (1962). *Thought and language.* MIT Press.

Vygotsky, L. S. (1978). *Mind in society: The development of higher psychological processes.* Harvard University Press.

Wallace, C., Hand, B., & Prain, V. (2004). *Writing and learning in the science classroom.* Springer Netherlands.

Waxman, S. R. (2021). Racial awareness and bias begin early: Developmental entry points, challenges, and a call to action. *Perspectives on Psychological Science, 16*(5), 893–902. https://doi.org/10.1177/17456916211026968

Wehmeyer, M. L., Shogren, K. A., Palmer, S. B., Williams-Diehm, K. L., Little, T. D., & Boulton, A. (2012). The impact of the self-determined learning model of instruction on student self-determination. *Exceptional Children, 78*(2), 135–153. https://doi.org/10.1177/001440291207800201

Wellins, C. (2020). *Saturdays are for Stella*. Page Street Kids.

Willey, K. (2017). *Breathe like a bear*. Rodale Kids.

Williams, J. (2020). *Empowering educators: A guidebook on race & racism*. First Book.

Williams-Duncan, O. M. (2021). [Review of the book *Content area reading: Literacy and learning across the curriculum* (12th ed.), by R. T. Vacca, J. A. Vacca, & M. Mraz]. *Curriculum and Teaching Dialogue, 23*(1–2), 317–320.

Witzel, B. S., Riccomini, P. J., & Schneider, E. (2008). Implementing CRA with secondary students with learning disabilities in mathematics. *Intervention in School and Clinic, 43*(5), 270-276.

Wolbers, K., Bowers, L., Dostal, H., & Graham, S. C. (2013). Deaf writers' application of ASL knowledge to English. *International Journal of Bilingual Education and Bilingualism, 17*(4), 410–428. https://doi.org/10.1080/13670050.2013.816262

Wolbers, K., Dostal, H., Graham, S., Branum-Martin, L., & Holcomb, L. (2022). Specialized writing instruction for deaf students: A randomized controlled trial. *Exceptional Children, 88*(2), 185–204. https://doi.org/10.1177/00144029211050849

Wolbers, K., Dostal, H., Graham, S., Branum-Martin, L., Kilpatrick, J., & Saulsburry, R. (2018). Strategic and interactive writing instruction: An efficacy study in grades 3–5. *Journal of Educational and Developmental Psychology, 8*(1), 99–117. https://doi.org/10.5539/jedp.v8n1p99

Wolbers, K., Dostal, H. & Holcomb, L. (2023). Teacher reports of secondary writing instruction with deaf students. Advanced online publication. *Journal of Literacy Research*. https://doi.org/10.1177/1086296X231163124

Wolbers, K., Graham, S. C., Dostal, H. M., & Bowers, L. M. (2014). A description of ASL features in writing. *Ampersand, 1*, 19–27. https://doi.org/10.1016/j.amper.2014.11.001

Wolbers, K., Holcomb, L. & Hamman-Ortiz, L. (2023). Translanguaging framework in Deaf education. *Languages, 8*(1), 1–24. https://doi.org/10.3390/languages8010059

Wolfram, W., Hutcheson, N., Cullinan, D., & Blake, R. (Producers). (2020). *Signing Black in America* [Film]. North Carolina State University.

Wood, A. (1982). *Quick as a cricket*. Child's Play.

Wright, M. H. (1999). *Sounds like home: Growing up black and deaf in the South*. Gallaudet University Press.

Yellowhammer, A. L. R. (2016). *Letter to the Army Corps of Engineers*. https://americanindian.si.edu/nk360/plains-treaties/dapl

Yolen, J. (1992). *Encounter*. HMH Books for Young Children.

Zippert, E. L., & Rittle-Johnson, B. (2020). The home math environment: More than numeracy. *Early Childhood Research Quarterly, 50*, 4–15. https://doi.org/10.1016/j.ecresq.2018.07.009

INDEX

Tables are indicated by "t" and notes are indicated by "n" following page numbers. Illustrations are indicated by page numbers in italics.

AASD (Atlanta Area School for the Deaf), 125, *125*
ABAR. *See* anti-bias and antiracist education
ABC stories, 21, 53–54
ableism, 340
    anti-ableism within multicultural education, 10
    nurturing and supportive environment for those who have experienced, 175
accommodations
    arts and, 309
    in IEPs, 347
    transition planning and, 338–39, 343, 346–347, 354, 357–358
Achieve 3000, 133
action steps. *See* Stick It Into Action!
adjectives, modifying meaning in ASL, 45
advocacy, 11, 201, 205, 338, 346–347
affinity groups, 353–54
AI (artificial intelligence), 213–14
Akerman-Frank, Jessalyn, 33
All About Me projects, 178–80, *179*, 296–97
American Freedom Speeches (Sign Media), 217
American School for the Deaf, 44
American Sign Language (ASL). *See also* ASL immersion; ASL language arts; ASL literature; ASL translations; fingerspelling; vocabulary
    composition projects in, 76–77
    content area reading and, 151–52, *152*
    curricular learning and access to, 1
    designated time in daily schedule, 19–21
    glossaries for, 61
    integration across curriculum, 8–9, 56–63, *58*
    linguistic competence and, 83–84
    literacy in, 41, 98, 145
    mathematics vocabulary, 240–42, *240–41*
    mnemonics, ASL-centric, 60–61
    phonological awareness, 20
    publications, creation of, 51–52, 64, 302
    read-alouds, 121. *See also* storysigning
    science vocabulary, 275
    story problems, 249–51, 251t
    teaching strategies using, 263–65
    viewing areas for, 17–18
anti-bias and antiracist (ABAR) education
    for the arts, 287–94, *291*, 309–11, 311t
    for ASL immersion classes, 319–22, *320–21*
    for content area reading, 146–64, 166, 168
    for content area writing, 108–11, 109t
    for Deaf identities and social/cultural perspectives, 174–76, 178–83, 188–96, *189*, 195t
    for early childhood instruction, 17–34
    goals of, 5–6
    ground rules for, 176
    for language arts, 52–56
    for mathematics, 243–47, 252–54
    nurturing and supportive environment, 175
    for reading instruction, 130–34
    for science instruction, 259–61
    for social studies, 203–7, 212–19, 225–27
    for transition planning, 340, 349–51, 352–57
    for writing, 89–91, *91*, 92t
Anti-Bias Education for Young Children and Ourselves (Derman-Sparks), 174
archaeological mock excavations, 211, *212*
archives, 183–84, 213
arguments
    civil discourse, 207–8
    counterarguments in persuasive writing, 76. *See also* persuasive writing
    practicing for extended constructed response, 324–25
    scientific, 265–68
artifacts, 205
artificial intelligence (AI), 213–14
arts, incorporation across curriculum, 283–313
    content area reading, 162
    Deaf experiences and perspectives, 285–86, *286*
    differentiating instruction and the arts, 309
    effective practices, 287–308
    Deaf role models, 287–94, *291*
    opportunities for creative expression, 295–308
    example unit or lesson plan, 309–11, 311t
    exploring identities through creative expression, 304
    handstamps, 306–7, *306–7*, 308, *308*
    lesson development, 311–12
    recommended readings/viewings, 312–13
    Theater in Education, 295
artworks, displaying, 308, *308*
asides, 315
ASL. *See* American Sign Language
ASL Content Standards (Laurent Clerc National Deaf Education Center), 76–77, 111, 204, 221, 277
ASL immersion, 314–35
    Deaf experiences and perspectives, 315–17
    effective practices, 317–26
    broad range of topics, 322–26
    opportunities to learn about self and world, 318–19, *318–19*
    scaffolding topics from concrete to complex, 319–22, *320–21*
    entering and exiting class, 326–27
    example units/lesson plans, 327–30, *337–38*, 329–32t, *332*
    lesson development, 333

ASL immersion (continued)
    recommended readings/viewings, 334
ASL language arts, 41–68
    ASL immersion classes and, 327
    class environment, 64
    Deaf experiences and perspectives, 42–43
    differentiated instruction for, 64
    effective practices, 43–63
    ASL integration across curriculum, 56–63
    ASL literature, appreciation for, 52–56
    grammar mechanics and usage, 43–52
    example unit or lesson plan, 65, 66t
    field trips, technology for, 64
    lesson development, 67
    recommended readings/viewings, 67–68
ASL literature, 52–56
    defined, 52
    handshape-based stories, 53–54
    literary analysis, 55–56, 56
    mentor texts, 77–78
    rhyme and rhythm, 52–53
    storytelling genres, 54–55
ASL Poetry Slam (website), 54
ASL translations. *See also* storysigning
    for arts, 193–94
    for Deaf identities and social/cultural perspectives, 181
    for language arts, 54–55
    for mathematics, 244
    reading and demonstration of both languages, 22
    for reading instruction, 126
    for science instruction, 271–73, 272
    for social studies, 214–16, 215, 217
assessments
    ASL immersion and, 319, 326–27
    mathematics, 246, 247
    science, 271
    six traits of signing rubric, 51
    transition planning and, 344, 349–51
    writing, 76, 79
Atlanta Area School for the Deaf (AASD), 125, 125, 142
Atomic Hands (website), 274
audience for writing, 104, 113
audism, 6, 175–77. *See also* anti-bias and antiracist (ABAR) education; bias
authentic learning experiences, 208–12. *See also* purposeful learning activities
authentic writing, 84–86
author speaking events, 125, 125
autonomy, 338–39
Ayala, Kyra, 55

background knowledge
    arts and, 295
    asides for, 315
    content area reading and, 146–56
    equity issues and, 130–31
    funds of knowledge and, 131, 258
    incidental learning and, 201, 315
    mathematical concepts at home, 230, 243–44
    reading, making activities meaningful, 123–24
    scaffolding and, 122–23
    science concepts and, 257–60
Bahan, Ben, 55
baking bread unit in asl immersion class, 327, 337–38, 329–30t
balanced instruction, 86
Balard, Arnaud, 185
basic interpersonal communication skills, 319
Bauman, Ivelis, 319, 327–28
BCOOL strategy, 178
BCR (brief constructed response), 324–25
Beam, Fred Michael, 283–84
behavioral issues, 12, 31, 81
Benson, Camille, 83
bias. *See* anti-bias and antiracist education; discrimination and stereotypes
biculturalism. *See* multiculturalism
bilingual strategies. *See* multilingual and multimodal strategies
Bird of a Different Feather (Bahan), 55
Black, Indigenous, and People of Color (BIPOC). *See* diversity
Black Deaf theater, 291
Bloom, Carrie Lou, 336–37
book nooks. *See* reading areas
book reviews, 125
books. *See also* literature; reading; storysigning
    for ASL immersion, 318, 323–24
    for early childhood instruction, 18, 26, 28
    for mathematics concepts, 244
    for science instruction, 260
Bragg, Bernard, 54
Braidi, Samantha, 229, 230, 231, 245
brain development, 14, 15
bread baking unit in ASL immersion class, 327, 337–38, 329–30t
brief constructed response (BCR), 324–25

calendar time, 318–19, 318–19
California Association of Science Educators (CASE), 274
California School for the Deaf, Fremont (CSD), 142, 189, 217, 220
Call, Brenda, 229, 236
call and response as linguistic pattern, 19
Cannon, Annie Jump, 274
captioned video sources, 218
career goals. *See* transition planning
Carle, Eric, 53
Carroll, Lewis, 54–55
CASE (California Association of Science Educators), 274
cause and effect, 156
CCSS (Common Core State Standards), 111, 147
CER (claim–evidence–reasoning), 266–69, 267, 269
certification for Deaf educators, 2
chaining, 26, 58, 132, 133, 265, 275
ChatBox, 213–14
Chew on This!
    arts, 285, 287, 290
    ASL immersion classes, 315, 319
    ASL language arts, 42, 45
    content area reading, 146
    content area writing, 98, 111
    Deaf identities and social/cultural perspectives, 172, 184–85, 190
    early childhood instruction, 14, 23, 28

mathematics, 229, 230, 241, 243, 244, 246, 247
reading instruction, 119, 120
science instruction, 257, 270
transition planning, 337–39, 343, 346
writing, 70, 73
children of Deaf adults (Codas), 10
children's story classics unit in ASL immersion class, 328–30, 331–32t, 332
Choir (Marbury), 55
Choose Your Own Adventure Activity Kit, 351
Cifria, Erwan, 54
civil discourse, 207–8
claim-evidence-reasoning (CER), 266–69, 267, 269
Clark, Adrean, 186
Clark, Joh Lee, 186
classification of organisms mnemonic, 61, 61
classroom communities, 208–9
classroom dictionaries, 47, 61–62
classroom environment. *See* educational settings
classroom experiences. *See* Teacher Tales
classroom management (CM)
    for ASL immersion classes, 319–22, 320–21, 325–26, 333
    defined, 9
    for early childhood instruction, 30, 32
    for social studies, 208–12
classroom rules, 176
Clerc, Laurent, 44
cognitive apprenticeship in writing, 78–79
cognitive skills and development
    ASL immersion classes and, 316–17
    developmental readiness and, 207
    early childhood and, 14, 15
    reading instruction and, 121–23
Cohen, Scott, 256, 257, 261
collaborations among teachers, 164–65, 307
collaborative teams for transition planning, 354–57
College, Career, and Civic Life (C3) Framework for Social Studies State Standards (National Council for the Social Studies), 204
college completion rates, 337
Common Core State Standards (CCSS), 111, 147
communication breakdowns, 88–89
community helpers, 320–21, 320–21
community resources, 351–54
compare and contrast activities, 149, 321–22, 321
compassion, 176–77
comprehension
    for arts, 293–94
    for content area reading, 149
    in early childhood instruction, 24–25
    for language arts, 49–50, 49–50
    for reading, 119–20, 126–30
concepts of print, 23
Concrete-Representational-Abstract (CRA) Approach, 234–36, 235
concrete to complex language, 319–22, 320–21
constructed response, 324–25
content area reading, 144–70
    Deaf experiences and perspectives, 145–46
    effective practices, 146–64

critical thinking skills, development of, 156–59, 158t
interdisciplinary units and, 159–64
world knowledge, building, 146–56
example unit or lesson plan, 165–66, 167t
lesson development, 166, 168
recommended readings/viewings, 169
teacher collaborations for, 164–65
content area writing, 97–117
    Deaf experiences and perspectives, 98–99
    effective practices, 100–107
    model disciplinary discourse and thought process, 105–7, 107
    write to learn, 101–3
    write with purpose, 104–5
    example unit or lesson plan, 111–13, 112t
    lesson development, 114
    recommended readings/viewings, 115–16
    science instruction, 270–71, 270–71t
    text sets to support, 108–11
content knowledge, 99, 108, 114
context modeling outside world, 319
conversational proficiency levels, 326–27, 326nn1–2
Cook, Peter, 293
Cooperative Children's Book Center, 111
cooperative learning activities, 207–8, 210
CORE Learning Channel, 217
The Cost of Heaven (Clark), 186
course placement, 343–44
CRA (Concrete-Representational-Abstract) Approach, 234–36, 235
creative expression. *See* arts, incorporation across curriculum
critical thinking skills
    content area reading and, 149, 156–59, 158t
    linguistic competence in ASL and, 84
    mathematics and, 233–34
    reading and, 121–22
    social studies and, 201, 218, 219
CSD (California School for the Deaf, Fremont), 142, 189, 217, 220
cue cards for writing process, 75
culture. *See also* Deaf identities and social/cultural perspectives; multiculturalism; social studies
    cultural and social awareness, 12, 188–90, 189
    cultural heritage activities, 190, 217–18
    culturally relevant lessons, 259–60
    Deaf culture, 4, 9–10, 21, 207, 218
    transmission of, 42
Cummins, J., 319
curiosity, 190–91

daily activities. *See* time
The Daily Moth (news source), 217
data-driven goals, 349–50
David, James Michael, 245
DCMP (Described and Captioned Media Program), 218
Deaf and Hard of Hearing people, defined, 9
Deaf art, 289
Deaf artist-in-residence programs, 289–90, 289–90
#DeafAtWork videos, 353
Deaf beat, 52
DeafBlind students, 186, 309. *See also* differentiated instruction
Deaf culture, 4, 9–10, 21, 207, 218. *See also* Deaf identities and social/cultural perspectives

Deaf education licensure, 2
Deaf educators, certification for, 2
Deaf experiences and perspectives
    in arts, 285–86, *286*
    in ASL immersion, 315–17
    in ASL language arts, 42–43
    in content area reading, 145–46
    in content area writing, 98–99
    in Deaf identities and social/cultural perspectives, 172–73
    in early childhood instruction, 15–16
    in mathematics, 230–31
    in reading instruction, 119–20
    in science instruction, 257–58
    in social studies, 200–202
    in transition planning, 337–39, 358
    in writing, 70–73
Deaf geography, 218
Deaf Heritage (Gannon), 215
Deaf history, 183–84
Deaf History Month, 185
Deaf History That, 217
Deaf identities and social/cultural perspectives, 171–98
    content area reading and, 162
    Deaf experiences and perspectives, 172–73
    effective practices, 174–90
    cultural and social awareness, increase of, 188–90, *189*
    positive perceptions of self, 174–83
    teach about Deaf lives, 183–88
    example unit or lesson plan, 192–96, 195*t*
    integration across curriculum, 8–9
    lesson development, 196
    recommended readings/viewings, 197
    sensitive topics, engagement with, 190–92
Deaf lens, 52, 204, 206
Deaf literature, 185–88
Deaf-related mathematics, 245–46
Deaf RIT librarian, 184
Deaf role models
    in the arts, 285, 287–94, *291*
    in books and media, 40
    cultural transmission and, 42
    Deaf identities and social/cultural perspectives, 181–82
    early childhood education and, 28–29, 33
    field trips and, 147
    mathematicians, 245–46
    science instruction and, 259–60, 274
    social studies unit on, 220–24
    transition planning and, 339, 352–54, 358
    videos of, 353
Deaf-specific goal setting, 346–48, 347–48*t*
Deaf studies. *See* Deaf identities and social/cultural perspectives
#DeafSuccess videos, 353
Deafverse, 292
Deaf with disabilities. *See* differentiated instruction
debates, 211
Delta Explore, 133
Described and Captioned Media Program (DCMP), 218
DESMOS (graphing calculator app), 248

development. *See* brain development; cognitive skills and development
De'VIA (Deaf View/Image Art), *287*, 287–89
dialogic reading, 127, 128
dictionaries
    ASL, 152–53, *152–53*
    personal, 47, 61–62
differentiated instruction (DI)
    for the arts, 287–309, *291*, 311–12
    for ASL immersion classes, 315–28, *319–21*, 329–30*t*, 333
    for content area reading, 146–56, 160–61, 165–66, 168
    for content area writing, 112–13
    for Deaf identities and social/cultural perspectives, 187–88, 192–96, 195*t*
    defined, 9
    for early childhood instruction, 19–28, 32, 34
    for language arts, 46–52, 56–65
    for mathematics, 231–39
    for reading instruction, 123–25, *125*, 126–42
    for science instruction, 261–71
    for social studies, 201–2, 207–27
    for transition planning, 339–56, 347–48*t*, 358–59, 360*t*
    for writing, 87–89, 93–94
disabilities. *See* differentiated instruction
disciplinary literacy, 98, 145, 149, 207
discrimination and stereotypes, 12, 15, 174–75, 176–77, 181, 181, 246, 340. *See also* anti-bias and antiracist (ABAR) education
    literature detective's strategy to analyze, 157, 158*t*
    popular media reinforcing, 256
    reviewing books and materials for, 13, 181, 216
    social justice standards, 193
discursive practices, 104, 105–6
discussion groups or clubs, 187
Diverse Deaf artist, 290–92
diverse materials, 182–83
diversity
    in arts, 286, 290–92
    Deaf identities and social/cultural perspectives, 173, 182–86
    Deaf role models and, 29, 182, 286, 353
    in mathematics, 244–45
    reading in content areas and, 165
    in science instruction, 258
    in social studies, 201, 213, 216
    transition planning and, 337, 340, 347, 352–53
Dostal, Hannah, 81, 97, 98, 156
DPAN (news source), 217
dramatic play, 24, 25
drums, 19
dual-credit courses, 343
Dunn, L. M., 172
Dweck, Carol, 247

early childhood instruction, 14–40
    Deaf experiences and perspectives, 15–16, *16*
    effective practices, 16–34
    fostering a positive sense of self and identity development, 28–34
    language and emergent literacy activities, 19–28

language- and literacy-rich environment, 17–18
example unit or lesson plan, 36, 37–38t
lesson development, 38–39, 39t
numeracy and, 34–35
recommended readings/viewings, 39–40
ECR (extended constructed response), 324–25
educational media and technology (MT)
    for the arts, 292–311, 311t
    for ASL immersion classes, 315–17, 322–30, 327–28, 329–32t, 332
    for composition, 51–52
    for content area reading, 149–50, 152–53, 159–66, 168
    for content area writing, 108–11, 109t, 116
    for Deaf identities and social/cultural perspectives, 185–87, 192–96, 195t
    Deaf role models in, 29
    defined, 10
    for field trips, 64
    for language arts, 47–49, 61–62, 68
    for mathematics, 247–48
    for reading instruction, 123–25, 125
    for science instruction, 271–73, 276–79, 277–78t
    setting up classrooms for instruction, 86–87, 87
    for social studies, 212–20
    for transition planning, 347–49, 348t
educational settings (ES). *See also* visual representations and supports
    for the arts, 311–12
    for ASL immersion classes, 315–18, 326–27
    for Deaf identities and social/cultural perspectives, 175–76, 181, 191
    defined, 10
    for early childhood instruction, 17–18, 18
    guidelines for, 176
    for language arts, 47–49, 64
    for mathematics, 254
    for reading instruction, 134–42
    for science instruction, 276–79, 277–78t
    for social studies, 203–12, 220
    for transition planning, 352–53, 357–58, 359
    for writing, 82, 86–87, 87, 88–89
emergent literacy, 15, 16, 19–28
emotional learning. *See* social-emotional learning
emotion game, 31
empathy, 186
employment
    opportunities for, 352
    planning for. *See* transition planning
    rates of, 337, 339
empowerment
    classroom helper roles to learn, 209
    for community action, 202, 212
    mathematics using Deaf cultural information, 245
    social studies and history of oppression, 205
    for student leadership, 163
    of students to become independent language learners, 46, 47
end-of-unit activities, 211–12, 211

engagement. *See also* motivation to learn
    arts and, 293, 301, 303
    with books, 26
    content area reading and, 155, 159
    creativity and, 297–98
    Deaf identities and social/cultural perspectives, 177–78
    of families, 189
    reading instruction and, 121, 124–25, 125
    science instruction and, 257
    sensitive topics and, 190–91
    writing and, 84–86
English
    linguistic competence and, 84
    reading and, 120
environmental print, 16, 17, 17
equitable mathematics, 246
equity issues, 130–32, 134, 137, 200–201, 206
ESRU protocol, 262–63
essential questions, 204
evidence-based practice, 339, 342
example units or lesson plans
    for the arts, 309–11, 311t
    for ASL immersion classes, 327–30, 337–38, 329–32t, 332
    for content area reading, 165–66, 167t
    for content area writing, 111–13, 112t
    for Deaf identities and social/cultural perspectives, 192–96, 193–94, 195t
    for early childhood instruction, 36, 37–38t
    for language arts, 65, 66t
    for mathematics, 252–53
    for reading instruction, 134–38
    for science instruction, 276–79, 277–78t
    for social studies, 220–22, 223–24t
    for transition planning, 359, 360t
    for writing, 89–91, 91, 92t
expectations, raising, 338, 339–44
exploration centers, 18, 25–26
extended constructed response (ECR), 324–25
extracurricular activities, 353–54

facial expressions
    adjective intensity and, 45
    simultaneous meanings through, 81–82, 82
    storysigning and, 21
    visual vernacular storytelling, 54
fact-checking, 219
families and home life. *See also* home languages; language deprivation
    cultural awareness through relationships with, 188–89
    early childhood instruction and, 33–34
    funds of knowledge and, 258
    incidental learning and, 98–99
    mathematical concepts at home, 230, 243–44
    prior information and, 122–24, 131
    reading and, 119–21
    teacher–student relationships and, 182
    transition planning and, 356
farm animal unit for early learning, 36, 37–38t

Fields, Dynnelle, 71
field trips
    for arts, 292–94
    for content area reading, 146–47
    for early childhood instruction, 27, 28
    for language arts, 64
    for social studies, 210
    for transition planning, 340–41
58-IN-MIND, 3
filming. *See* video production
financial literacy, 248–49
finger counting, 241–42
fingerspelling
    content area reading and, 147–48
    early childhood instruction and, 23
    emergent literacy and, 16
    language arts and, 58
    reading and, 132
    writing and, 83
504 plans, 358
Flip (video prompt platform), 125, 276
folklore. *See* storytelling and folklore
Folse, Doralynn, 172
Foster-Mauro, Kiana, 108–11
framework for early literacy (Kuntze & Golos), 15–16
Franck, Anna Lim, 172
Frayer Model for vocabulary teaching, 132
Freeman, D., 207
funds of knowledge, 131, 258

Gabel, Sherry, 316, 324
Gallaudet University, 184, 204
    Archives, 213
    Gallaudet Center on Black Deaf Studies, 184
Gallucci, J. Piper, 111, 113
Gannon, Jack, 214–15
García-Fernández, Carla, 15
Garvey, Amy, 160–61
gender and diversity in mathematics, 244–45
Gentzke, Scott, 283, 284, 288, 290, 295, 297–98, 300, 307
geographical resources, 218, 219, 220
geometry, 63
girls and mathematics, 244–45
goal setting, 344–50
    data-driven, 349–50
    Deaf-specific, 346–48, 347–48t
    realistic, 350
    student-led, 344–45
    timeline and checklist for, 345–46
GOALS writing process, 73–76, 87
Golos, Debbie, 1, 2–3, 14, 15–16, 40, 144–45, 147, 154, 160, 171, 172, 178, 283, 284, 298, 299, 302, 303, 363
Grabelsky, Shira, 191
Graham, Shannon, 97–98, 104, 156
grammar mechanics and usage
    academic expression, struggles with, 315
    language arts and, 43–52
    metalinguistic awareness of ASL linguistic structure, 43–46

    translanguaging and, 70–72
    unbalanced instruction and focus on, 86
graphic novels, 214, 215–16
graphic organizers
    for ASL immersion classes, 316, 323–24
    for content area reading, 149, 157, 158t
    for reading comprehension, 129–30, *129–30*, 136–37
    for writing, 75–76, 87, 91
graphing calculators, 248
Grosso, Kenra, 78
group interactive writing, 79
growth mindset, 247
guided, interactive writing, 79–81, 88
Guidelines for Multilingual Deaf Education Teacher Preparation Programs (Kurz et al.), 4–5

Hall, W. C., 318
handshape stories, 21, 53, 60
Hands Land, 292
handstamp samples. *See* student sample work
Harris, Wendy, 159
health and nutrition, 161–62
Henderson, Elizabeth, 256–57, 263–64, 266–67, 274
heritage language/heritage language learner, 10. *See also* home languages
heroes like me unit for social studies, 220–22, 223–24t
Hidden Figures unit for arts, 310–11, 311t
higher order thinking skills, 121, 156–59, 158t. *See also* critical thinking skills; problem-solving skills
high school. *See also* transition planning
    completion rates for, 337
    content area reading, 150–51, 159
    content area writing, 111–13, 112t
    project-based learning in, 163–64
    reading instruction, 136–38
Hill, Brandon, 52
Hipskind, Courtney, 14, 27, 28, 29, 35–36
historical fiction, 216, 219
history, 183–84. *See also* social studies
Hocog, Courtney, 55
Holcomb, Leala, 14, 292, 303
home languages. *See also* multilingual and multimodal strategies
    cultural awareness and, 188–89
    culturally relevant lessons, 259–60
    early childhood experiences and, 15–16
    language arts and, 64
    recognized and used in classrooms, 1
    transition planning in, 355
    on word walls, 243
home life. *See* families and home life
Horn-Marsh, Kester, 314, 315
Horn-Marsh, Petra M., 314–15, 316
humorous storytelling, 54

IDEA (Individuals With Disabilities Education Act) Amendments (2004), 358
identity development. *See* positive sense of self and identity
IEPs (individualized education programs)

accommodations in, 347
exit meetings, 357
lesson plan for meetings, 359, 360t
preparation for meetings, 344–45
student-led meetings, 342
template for meetings, 342–43
timeline and checklist for meetings, 345–46
vocational rehabilitation counselors and, 356
immersion. See ASL immersion
incidental learning
asides for, 315
from ASL videos, 18
content area writing and, 98–99
defined, 315
lack of, 201
independent learning, 120, 127, 152
individualized education programs. See IEPs
Individuals With Disabilities Education Act (IDEA) Amendments (2004), 357–58
inferences, 121, 156
informal writing opportunities, 101
information texts, 148–49
inquiry-based learning, 203–7, 203, 221–25
interactive language skills, 322–23
interactive storysigning, 21–25, 22, 24
interdisciplinary units, 159–68, 186–87, 292–93
International Week of the Deaf (IWD), 185
investigative reports, 268–69
Isola, Katarina, 151–52
IXL Math, 248

"Jabberwocky" (Carroll), 54–55
Jackerson, Justin, 296, 298
jigsaw strategy for literature analysis, 56, 187
jokes, 54
Jones, C. J., 285, 292
Jones, Jennifer, 85, 87
Jordan, Ruthie, 54
journal prompts, 270–71, 270–71t
joy
arts instruction and, 297–98
reading instruction and, 121

Kendall Conversational Proficiency Level (P-Level) scale, 326–27
keyhole perspective, 183
key points. See Chew on This!
key strategies
for art education, 307
for ASL-centric mnemonics, 60
for ASL immersion classes, 324–25
for critical thinking, 157
for Deaf identities and social/cultural perspectives, 178, 186
for early childhood instruction, 26–27
for mathematics, 234, 237–38, 249
for reading, 128
for science instruction, 262–64, 266
for semantic memory, 48–49
for transition planning, 352

for writing, 76–77, 79
Kuntze, Marlon, 1, 3, 15–16, 118, 171, 172, 363
Kurz, Chris, 1, 3, 41, 42, 60, 171, 172, 229–30, 248–49, 256, 257, 259, 275, 283, 284–85, 296, 342, 363
Kusters, A., 11

Ladd, P., 172
language activities for early childhood instruction, 19–28
language arts. See ASL language arts
language delays
arts incorporation and, 286, 297–98
ASL immersion classes for, 315–16, 327
content area reading and, 149
Deaf identities and social/cultural perspectives, 179
language arts and, 64
literacy development and, 145
social studies and, 220–24
writing and, 87–88
language deprivation
ASL immersion classes and, 315, 327
behavioral issues and, 12, 31
critical thinking and, 201
defined, 5
developmental impacts of, 1
in early childhood, 15
as systemic deficiency, 337
transition planning and, 358
trauma and, 32
language functions and demands, 59, 316–17
language milestones, 15
language skill development. See ASL immersion
language zones, 82, 86–89
learned helplessness, 209
Learning for Justice frameworks of Southern Poverty Law Center, 174
Leith, Katie, 88
Leitson-Grabelsky, Shira, 172
lesson development
for the arts, 311–12
for ASL immersion classes, 333
for content area reading, 166, 169
for content area writing, 114
for Deaf identities and social/cultural perspectives, 196
for early childhood instruction, 38–39, 39t
for language arts, 67
for mathematics, 254
for reading instruction, 138–40, 141t
for science instruction, 279–80
for social studies, 225–26
for transition planning, 360t
for writing, 93–94
lesson plans. See example units or lesson plans
Let's Go for a Walk (Holcomb), 77
LGBTQIA+ people, 29, 183, 245, 259, 286, 290, 347, 353. See also diversity
Library of Congress archives, 184
Lima, Stephanie Alves de, 87
linguistic competence, 83–84

Lippy, Suzanne, 89
literacy. *See also* reading; writing
- emergent, 15, 16, 19–28
- skill development, 19, 41, 98, 145

literature. *See also* ASL literature; books; reading
- literary analysis, 55–56, *56*, 187
- literature circles, 128–29
- literature detectives strategy, 157, 158*t*

The Little Paper Family (newsletter), 183–84
lived experiences, 181, 187–88, 205, 259–60
Loom (video-recording program), 214
Luczak, Raymond, 187
Lutge, Autumn, 206

Malzkuhn, Eric, 55
many media, same message strategy, 301–2
maps, 218, 220
- relief maps, *219*, 220

Marbury, Nathie, 49, 55
marginalized populations, 185, 205, 246. *See also* diversity; LGBTQIA+ people
Marie Philip School for the Deaf, 152
Martin Luther King Jr. unit for writing, 90–91, *91*, 92*t*
mathematical lexicons, 239, *239*
mathematical practices, 231
mathematical talk, 230, 237
mathematics, 229–55
- arts incorporation, 300, *301*, 307
- ASL integration across curriculum, 59–60, 63
- content area reading and, 160–61
- content area writing and, 99–100
- Deaf experiences and perspectives, 230–31
- for early childhood instruction, 34–35, *35*
- effective practices, 231–47
- diversity in ideas and skills, 244–47
- family collaborations, 243–44
- multiple representations in instructions, 231–39
- optimize all languages for leaning, 239–43
- empowerment by using Deaf cultural information, 253
- example unit or lesson plan, 252–53
- financial literacy, 248–49
- growth mindsets for, 247
- lesson development, 254
- recommended readings/viewings, 254–55
- story problems, 249–51, 251*t*
- technology for, 247–48

Mbazima, Nenio, *82*
McAfee, Darcy, 82–83
McBee, Lisa, 54
McGaughey, Sarah Jerger, 69, 70, 144, 145
McGuigan, Judy Pratt, 297, 299–300
media and technology. *See* educational media and technology
media literacy, 219
mental health support, 354
mentor texts, 77–78, 99–100, 108
- unit for content area writing, 111–13, 112*t*

metalinguistic awareness
- of ASL linguistic structure, 43–44
- ASL phonological awareness, 20
- ASL time for, 19
- defined, 81
- word study and, 152
- writing and, 81–83, *82*

metamorphosis in animals unit for language arts, 65, 66*t*
Metro Deaf School, 51, 343
microaggressions, 181
Milan (Sturley), 187
milestones, language, 15
Miller, Bianca Hamilton, 221
mindfulness, 12, 32–33, 154–55, 176–78, 306
mindset, 247
mini metropolis for ASL immersion classes, 320–21, *320*
minority languages. *See* home languages
MLK unit for writing, 89–91, *91*, 92*t*
mnemonics, 60–61, 178
mobile phones, video production and, 64
mock trials and events
- arts instruction and, 298–99
- interdisciplinary unit, 144, 147, 154, 165–66, 167*t*
- social studies, 211–12, *211*

Mockus, Kathleen K., 199–200, 204, 210
modeling behavior. *See also* think aloud and expansion
- in ASL immersion classes, 320, 325
- content area writing, 105–7, *107*
- personal reflections, shared, 80
- reading instruction, 121

Moder, Autumn, 180, 364
monolingual bias, 15
Monroe, James, 44
Monroe, Victoria, 172
Monts-Tréviska, Ashanti, 172
morphemes, 44–45
morphological awareness, 44–45
motivation to learn. *See also* engagement
- arts and, 297, 301, 303
- basic needs fulfillment and, 120
- content area reading, 146, 159
- reading and, 125, 133
- writing and, 70, 86

Motylinski, Barbara, 41, 42, 48
MT. *See* educational media and technology
multiculturalism. *See also* diversity
- anti-bias learning and, 29–30
- defined, 10
- multilingual education and, 4–5
- science instruction and, 259

multilingual and multimodal strategies (MM). *See also* translanguaging
- for the arts, 287–312, *291*, 311*t*
- for ASL immersion classes, 315–30, *319–21*, *327–28*, 329–32*t*, *332*, *333*
- background knowledge and, 124
- for content area reading, 146–66, 168
- for content area writing, 99–107
- for Deaf identities and social/cultural perspectives, 178–79, 181, 188–90, *189*, 192–96, 195*t*
- defined, 10, 11
- for early childhood instruction, 15–16, 19–28, 33, 34, 36

for language arts, 43–48, 50–64
for mathematics, 231–44, 246–47, 249–54, 251t
metalinguistic awareness and, 81
for reading instruction, 121–23, 126–30, 133–42
for science instruction, 259–73, 276–80, 277–78t
for social studies, 201–7, 212–27
for transition planning, 344–61, 347–48t, 360t
for writing, 73–78, 81–84, 82
multiple meaning words, 132, 239–40
multiplication methods, 232–33, 233
music, 285

name letter stories, 54
name signs, 180
National Association of the Deaf, 201, 353
National Black Deaf Advocates (NBDA), 347, 353
National Core Arts Standards, 287, 295
National Council for the Social Studies, 204
National Deaf Center on Postsecondary Outcomes, 353
National Deaf Education Conference, 276
National Deaf History Month, 185
National Science Teaching Association (NSTA), 257
National Technical Institute for the Deaf, 213
nature, art instruction and, 306–7, 306–7
NBDA (National Black Deaf Advocates), 347, 353
negative labels, 11, 28–29
Newsela, 213
Newton's laws of motion workshop, 303–5, 305
Next Generation Science Standards (NGSS), 257, 274, 276
Nochese, Mary, 85–86
note-taking, 137, 270–71
NSTA (National Science Teaching Association), 257
NTID Sunshine 2.0 (Deaf educational theater troupe)
Newton's laws of motion workshop, 303–5, 305
order of operations rap song, 300, 301
role-play activities, 298, 299
number sense, 237
number stories, 21, 54, 60
number talk, 237
numeracy for early childhood instruction, 34–35, 35
nutrition and health, 161–62

Once Upon a Twin (Luczak), 187
open-ended questions
for ASL immersion, 324–25
for content area reading, 149
defined, 24
for early childhood instruction, 23–24
for mathematics, 237
for reading instruction, 121–22
for writing, 88
order of operations mnemonic, 60
order of operations rap song, 300, 301
OREO graphic organizers, 75–76
Outlaw, Susan, 144, 145

parallel talk for early childhood instruction, 26
Parsons, Amy, 172
PBL (project-based learning), 162–64

peers, language development and, 207–8, 316
pen-pal exchanges, 125
Perez, Justin, 54
personal boundaries, 181–82
personal dictionaries, 47, 61–62
personal reflections, shared, 80
perspective shifts, 54
persuasive writing, 76, 111
Peter's Picture series, 293
Phelps-Eliot, Krista, 76
phenomenon, 258, 261
phonemes, 44
phonological awareness, 44
picture cards, 319, 322
picture dictionaries, 152–53, *152–53*
Plan Your Future: A Guide to Vocational Rehabilitation for Deaf Youth, 356
poetry, 54, 186, 302–3
POINT (making a point), 266
Pop Art, 288
positive sense of self and identity (PI)
for the arts, 287–312, *291*, 311t
for ASL immersion classes, 315–17, 324, 327–30, 327–28, 329–32t, 332
for content area reading, 155, 159–66
for content area writing, 104, 113
for Deaf identities and social/cultural perspectives, 174–89, 192–96, 195t
defined, 11–12
for early childhood instruction, 17–18, 19–34
for mathematics, 244–47
for reading instruction, 121, 123–25, *125*
for science instruction, 274
for social studies, 208–12
for transition planning, 339–55, 347–48t, 358–60, 360t
for writing, 80, 84–86
preschool. *See* early childhood instruction
PRESIDENT, 44
primary source documents
for content area reading, 159
for Deaf identities and social/cultural perspectives, 183–84
defined, 203
for social studies, 203, 205–6, 212–13
print, concepts of, 23
prior knowledge
arts and, 295
asides for, 315
content area reading and, 146–56
equity issues and, 130–31
funds of knowledge and, 131, 258
incidental learning and, 201, 315
mathematical concepts at home, 230, 243–44
reading, making activities meaningful, 123–24
scaffolding and, 122–23
science concepts and, 257–60
privilege, 131, 174–75, 340
problem-solving skills
arts and, 284, 302
content area writing and, 106–7

problem-solving skills (*continued*)
    mathematics and, 249
    reading and, 121, 123
    social studies and, 207
    transition planning and, 338
    writing and, 78–79
professional development, 276, 292
project-based learning (PBL), 162–64
published signing opportunities, 84–86
purposeful learning activities
    for reading, 123–24
    for social studies, 208–12
    for writing, 84–86, 104–5, 113

QR codes to access videos, 181, 193–94, 271–73, *272*
questions. *See also* open-ended questions
    to check for comprehension, 24–25
    for reading comprehension, 121–22, 128
    for viewing and composition skills, 49–50, *49–50*, 293–94

race and ethnicity. *See* diversity
racism. *See* anti-bias and antiracist education
RAFT (Role, Audience, Format, and Topic/Tone/Theme) writing strategy, 186
reading, 118–43. *See also* content area reading
    appropriate materials for, 133–34
    Deaf experiences and perspectives, 119–20
    effective practices, 120–32
    ASL translations, 126
    cognition, boosting, 121–23
    comprehension skills, building, 127–30, *129–30*
    equity issues, 130–32
    meaningfulness, impact, and engagement, 123–25, *125*
    model joy, 121
    example unit or lesson plan, 134–38
    lesson development, 138–40, 141*t*
    multimodal strategies for, 133
    recommended readings/viewings, 140, 142
    vocabulary and, 132–33
reading aloud. *See* storysigning
reading areas
    for content area reading, 149–50, *150*
    for early childhood instruction, 17, *18*
reading levels
    content area reading and, 146, 154–55, 164
    reading instruction and, 129, 133–34
    social studies and, 213–15
recommended readings and viewings
    for the arts, 312–13
    for ASL immersion classes, 334
    for ASL language arts, 67–68
    for content area reading, 169
    for content area writing, 115–16
    for Deaf identities and social/cultural perspectives, 197
    for early childhood instruction, 39–40
    for mathematics, 254–55
    for reading instruction, 140, 142
    for science instruction, 281
    for social studies, 226–27

    for transition planning, 361
    for writing, 95
reenactments, 212
relief maps, *219*, 220
rhyme and rhythm, 19–20, 52–53, 54, 186, 302–3
Ridloff, Lauren, 285
Rivera, April, 14, 17, 25, 27, 36
Rochester School for the Deaf, 184, 290, *290*
Rocky Mountain Deaf School, 142, 244
role-play, 298–99, *299*
role-play dolls, 30
role shifts, 54
root words, 150–51
Rourke, Nancy, 287, *290*
Ryan, Kristin, 336, 337, 340, 341, 350–51, 358

St. Mary's School for the Deaf, *284*, *286*, *287*, 287, 289–90, *289*, 309
Sanborn, Ian, 54
sandwiching, 58, 132, 265, 275
scaffolding
    for ASL immersion classes, 319–22, *320–21*
    for reading instruction, 122–23, 124
    for social studies, 206, 213, 215–16
Schafer, Raye, 99, 100, 106–7
Schlinger, Glennise, *80*
science instruction, 256–82
    arts incorporation, 295, 303–5, *305*
    ASL immersion classes for, 326
    ASL integration across curriculum, 58–60, *58*
    content area reading for, 147–52, *152*, 156
    content area writing for, 101–2, 103*t*, 104–7, *107*
    Deaf experiences, incorporating into lessons, 274
    Deaf experiences and perspectives, 257–58
    effective practices, 259–73
    students' lived experiences and, 259–61
    talking about and doing science, 261–71
    technology and, 271–73
    example unit or lesson plan, 276–79, 277–78*t*
    lesson development, 279–80
    professional development and, 276
    recommended readings/viewings, 281
    rhythm and rhyme activity, 53
    vocabulary for, 275
scientific argument, 265–68
Scott, Charlotte Angas, 245–46
Scott, Jessica, 118
screencastify, 214
Seek the World, 217
SEL. *See* social-emotional learning
self-care, 12, 178. *See also* mindfulness
self-confidence
    arts and self-expression, 296–97
    content area writing and, 108
    reading and, 127, 131–32
    student-led IEP meetings and, 342
    transition planning and, 338
self-determination, 338–39. *See also* goal setting
Self-Determination Inventory: Student Report, 351
Self-Determined Learning Model of Instruction, 351

self-development. *See* positive sense of self and identity
self-expression, 285–87, 295, 301
semantic mapping, 48
semantic memory, 48–49, *48*
semantics, 45
semiotic representations, 232
sensitive topics, 190–92
sensory spaces, 32
sentence starters, 270–71, 270–71*t*
service-learning projects, 212
Shapiro, Stacey Katz, 118–19
Sidansky, Emily, 275
Sidansky, Michael, 215–16
Signing, Writing, Reading, and Listening (SWRL) teaching strategy, 263–65
signing process checklists and rubrics, 50–51
SignLens (Hill), 52
sign study bulletin boards, 151–52, *152*
Sign Union flag, 185
Simms, L., 172
Simos, Keila, 193, 196
SIWI (Strategic and Interactive Writing Instruction), 69, 73, 79, 83–84, 89, 93–94
6+1 trait writing assessment, 51
six traits of signing rubric, 51
Skahen, Christina, 293
Smith, David H., 199, 208
Smith, Elizabeth, 74
snack time, 27
social-emotional learning (SEL)
    for ASL immersion classes, 318–30, *319–21, 327–28,* 329–32*t, 332*
    for content area reading, 155
    for Deaf identities and social/cultural perspectives, 176–78, *177,* 181
    defined, 12
    for early childhood instruction, 30, 31–32, 33
    for mathematics, 247
    for reading instruction, 130–32, 134–38
    for transition planning, 354
social identities, 174
Social Identity Wheels, 179–80
social issues, 246–47
social justice, 193, 205, 246
Social Justice Quilt project unit, 192–96, *193–94,* 195*t*
social media, 125, 187, 219, 353
social skills, 339
social studies, 199–228
    arts incorporation, 291
    ASL immersion classes for, 326
    classroom setup and environment, 220
    content area reading and, 156–59, 158*t,* 162
    content area writing, 108–13
    Deaf experiences and perspectives, 200–202
    effective practices, 202–19
    authentic learning experiences, 208–12
    civil discourse practice, 207–8
    inquiry-based learning, 203–7
    text, media, and geographical sources, 212–19
    example unit or lesson plan, 220–22, 223–24*t*
    lesson development, 225–26
    recommended readings/viewings, 226–27
socioeconomic status, 201
Sounds Like Home: Growing Up Black and Deaf in the South (Wright), 187
Southern Poverty Law Center, 174
spelling, 23
Spencer, Casey, 89
Stai, Kristin, 150–51
standards
    for arts, 287, 295
    for mathematics, 252
    for reading, 147, 159
    for science, 147, 257, 274, 276, 277
    for social studies, 204, 221
    for writing, 76–77, 111
states of matter unit for science instruction, 276–79, 277–78*t*
stereotypes. *See* discrimination and stereotypes
Stewart, Julie, 41, 42
STICK, 3
Stick It Into Action!
    arts, 291, 293–95, 301–2, 304–5, *305,* 309
    ASL immersion classes, 320–24, 325–26
    ASL language arts, 44, 45–46, 49–50, 53, 55–59, 60–61, 63
    content area reading, 148–51, *150,* 155–57, 161–62
    content area writing, 105
    Deaf identities and social/cultural perspectives, 175, 177–90, 192
    early childhood instruction, 20, 23, 24–25, 26, 29, 30, 31, 32, 34, 40
    final, 365–66
    mathematics, 232–34, 238, *238,* 242, 243, 246, 249–50
    reading instruction, 122–23, 127
    science instruction, 260–62, 264, 266, 268, 270–73, 270–71*t,* 272, 275
    social studies, 202–3, 207–10, 216
    transition planning, 341–43, 345–48, 347–48*t,* 351–54, 356–57
    writing, 76, 77, 79
ST Math, 248
Stone, Nic, 125, *125*
story elements and structure, 323–24
story problems, 249–51, 251*t*
storysigning
    for ASL immersion classes, 323–24, 328–30, 330–31*t,* 332
    defined, 317
    for early childhood instruction, 21–25, *22, 24*
    for mathematics, 244
    for reading instruction, 121
    for social studies, 214, 216, *217*
storytelling and folklore
    ABC stories, 21, 53–54
    additional genres for, 54–55
    arts incorporation, 302–3, *304*
    defined, 317
    handshape stories, 21, 53, 60
    name letter stories, 54
    number stories, 21, 54, 60
    semantic memory and, 49

Strategic and Interactive Writing Instruction (SIWI), 69, 73, 79, 83–84, 89, 93–94
strategies. *See* key strategies
student interests, 187–88
student sample work
    arts, 287, *287*, 289, *289*, 306–7, *306–7*, 308, *308*
    content area writing, 102, 103*t*, 113
    Deaf identities and social/cultural perspectives, 193–94, *193–94*
    mathematics, 235–36, *235–36*
    reading instruction, 130, *130*
    science, 265, 267, *267*, 269, *269*, 273, 279, *279*
    social studies, 200, *200*, 222, *222*, 224, *224*
    transition planning, 355
    writing, 71, 72, 91–92, *92*
Sturley, Nick, 187
Suddenly Slow (Clark), 186
SWRL (Signing, Writing, Reading, and Listening) teaching strategy, 263–65

taboo topics, 190–92
target ASL words, 63
teacher collaborations, 164–65, 307
teacher creative expression, 300, *300*
teacher–student relationships, 182
Teacher Tales
    arts, 288, 290, *290*, 292, 293, 296–300, *296*, 302–3, 307
    ASL immersion classes, 316, 324
    content area reading, 147, 152–53, *152–53*, 154, 159–61
    content area writing, 100, 106–11, *107*, 109*t*
    Deaf identities and social/cultural perspectives, 180, 191, 193, 196
    early childhood education, 27, *27*, 35–36, *35–36*
    mathematics, 236, 248–49
    reading instruction, 122, 124, 134
    science instruction, 263, 266–67, 275
    social studies, 204, 206, 208, 210, 216, 217
    transition planning, 340–42, 350–51, 358
    writing, 74, 81, 83, 85–86, 88, 89
technological tools. *See* educational media and technology; video production
10-minute math talk, 237
Texas School for the Deaf, 343
textbooks, 213–14
theater, 291–92, 299–300
    Theater in Education (TiE), 295–96, *296*
think aloud and expansion
    for content area writing, 106–7
    for early childhood instruction, 26–27
    for reading instruction, 122
    for writing, 78–79
This Book Is Anti-Racist—Journal (Jewell), 174–75, 179–80, 185
3 acts talk for math, 238, *238*
3-Read Protocol, 249–51, 251*t*
    unit for mathematics, 252–53
Three-Dimensional (3-D) Learning, 257, 274, 276
Thumann, H., 172
time
    ASL immersion for concept of, 318–19, *318*
    ASL time in daily schedule, 19–21
    snack time, 27
    timelines for IEP meetings, 345–46
    timelines showing teaching units, 206, 220
    transition time in early childhood instruction, 25
token economies, 209–10
transition binders or portfolios, 352, 354, 357
transition evaluations, 349–50
transition planning, 336–62
    Deaf experiences and perspectives, 337–39
    effective practices, 339–57
    collaborative teams, 355–57
    community resources, 351–55
    goal setting, 344–51
    raise expectations, 339–44
    example unit or lesson plan, 359, 360*t*
    language deprivation and, 358
    lesson development, 359–62
    outside of IEP process, 357
    recommended readings/viewings, 361
transition time in early childhood instruction, 25
translanguaging
    for ASL immersion classes, 316
    chaining and, 26, 58, 132, 133, 265, 275
    defined, 12–13, 71
    in mathematics, 239
    reading and, 124
    science instruction and, 264–65, 273
    writing and, 70–72, 81
translations. *See* ASL translations; storysigning
trauma and trauma-informed approaches
    in ASL immersion classes, 320
    identity exploration and, 175, 185
    language deprivation and, 33
    sensory spaces and, 32
    slavery and racism as topics of, 157
    social-emotional learning and, 12
Tsiolkovsky, Konstantin, 245

Unlocking the Curriculum (Johnson), 1
Venn diagrams for compare and contrast, 321–22, *321*
verb semantics, 45
The Very Hungry Caterpillar (Carle), 53
videophones, 358
video production, 51–52, 64, 302
video relay, 349
viewing and composition skills, 49–52, *49–50*, 293–94
viewing areas for early childhood instruction, 17–18
viewing comprehension, 49
Virnig, Dack, 54
Visual Language/Visual Learning (VL2), 142
visual representations and supports
    for ASL immersion classes, 319, 320–22, *320–21*
    for content area reading, 152–53, *152–53*
    for language arts, 46, *46*
    for mathematics, 242–43
    for reading, 133
    for reading instruction, 123
    for science instruction, 271–73, *272*

for social studies, 217–18, 220
for writing process, 74–76, 87
visual textbooks, 214
visual vernacular storytelling, 54
VL2 (Visual Language/Visual Learning), 142
vocabulary. *See also* headings starting with "Word"
    academic expression and, 315
    ASL immersion classes and, 316, 318–19, *318*, 321
    complexity, progression of, 57–58, *57*
    dictionaries for, 47, 61–62, 152–53, *152–53*
    early childhood instruction and, 22–23
    field trips and, 293–94
    knowledge gaps and, 99
    mathematics terminology, 240–43, *240–41*
    metalinguistic awareness, 44
    reading instruction and, 124, 127, 132–33
    science instruction and, 275
    social studies and, 215–16, 219, 220
    strategies for broadening, 46–49, *46*
    target ASL word use, 63
vocational rehabilitation (VR) services, 347, 354–57
Vygotsky, L. S., 316

website credibility checklists, 219
WFD (World Federation of the Deaf), 185
Where I Stand: On the Signing Community and My DeafBlind Experience (Clark), 186
whole-child approach, 5
Wilson, Tori, 79, 87
Wolbers, Kimberly, 1, 3, 69–70, 363
word boxes, 46–47
word families, 48, 241
wordopoly in math, 243
word order variation, 46
word origins, 150–51
words with multiple meanings, 239–40
word walls, 46, *46*, 133, 220, 242–43
World Federation of the Deaf (WFD), 185
Wright, Mary Herring, 187
writing, 69–96. *See also* content area writing
    arts incorporation, 297–98, 303
    classroom environment and, 86–87, *87*
    Deaf experiences and perspectives, 70–73
    Deaf identities and social/cultural perspectives, 186
    delays in writing and language, 87–89
    effective practices, 73–86
    guided, interactive instruction, 78–81
    metalinguistic knowledge and linguistic competence, 81–84
    strategy instruction, integration of visual supports, 73–78
    writing and published signing opportunities, creation of, 84–86
    example unit or lesson plan, 90–91, *91*, 92*t*
    lesson development, 93–94
    recommended readings/viewings, 95
    strategy instruction in, 73–76
    text sets, 108
writing delays, 87–88
writing processes, 73

yoga for early childhood instruction, 32–33
YouTube, 54
Yummy Cookies (Holcomb), 78

zone of proximal development, 317
Zusti, Ellie, 290, *291*